ANCIENT NORTH AMERICA

Late Mississippian human effigy from Pecan Point,
Mississippi County, Arkansas.

BRIAN M. FAGAN

ANCIENT NORTH AMERICA

THE ARCHAEOLOGY OF A CONTINENT

Third Edition

With 375 Illustrations

Thames & Hudson

CONTENTS

To the memory of Jack Lobdell,
archaeologist extraordinary

© 1991, 1995 and 2000 Thames & Hudson Ltd, London

First published in the United States of America in 1991 by
Thames & Hudson Inc., 500 Fifth Avenue,
New York, New York 10110
Second edition 1995
Third edition 2000

Library of Congress Catalog Card Number 99-70860
ISBN 0-500-28148-3

Printed and bound in the United States of America

Preface

Ancient North America enters its third edition with the same goal as before: to provide a narrative account of what is known of the diverse ancient societies of North America, from first settlement before 12,000 BC up to European contact and beyond. The story is based on a complex archaeological record chronicled in print and, increasingly, in cyberspace, also on years of field and museum visits, attending conferences, and discussions with archaeologists working in every corner of North America. Increasingly, too, feedback from instructors, students, and the general public helps shape the volume in its evolving iterations. Some brief remarks about the nature of the book and the changes in the third edition are appropriate.

General Comments

I assume that the reader has some basic knowledge of the fundamental principles and terminology of archaeology, obtained in a college or university course, or through avocational or practical experience. Readers anxious to acquire knowledge of the basics of archaeological method and theory are referred to widely available textbooks on the subject. I have done all I can to write this book in such a way as to keep terminological labels and other technicalities to a minimum, but some intricacies are inevitable in a highly technical subject like this one.

The text is referenced, but only sufficiently so to allow the reader to delve more deeply into the technical literature when desired. Annotated "Further Reading" lists appear at the end of each chapter for initial guidance. Invariably, the sources in these lists contain comprehensive bibliographies. As a general principle, I have tended to cite key papers, reports, and syntheses that provide comprehensive citations for more detailed research.

Ancient North America covers over 15 millennia of the past, so it is an inescapable compromise between the harsh dictates of space and the need to be comprehensive. There are many places where I have had to compress local and regional data in the interests of brevity and clarity. Inevitably, I have overgeneralized and oversimplified in places, as I try to balance accuracy with economy. If you probe more specialized references, you will soon encounter the real complexities of what is, at times, a frustrating and complex literature.

North American archaeology is an increasingly specialized subject, the more so with the advent of multidisciplinary research and Cultural Resource Management. This reality has made it hard to keep one's eyes focused on the larger picture, which is, after all, the purview of this book. Archaeology, by its very nature, is a local subject with many narrow concerns and local culture-historical problems. However, I have omitted many local cultural terms, summarizing them occasionally for reference, but trying to keep them to a minimum in the narrative. The many detailed regional syntheses cited in these pages will fill in local detail.

Generations of North American archaeologists have grappled with the complex theoretical problems of both describing and explaining the past. The debates over theory continue unabated, which is healthy, but they confirm the wisdom of not encasing this book within a rigid theoretical doctrine. Part One gives a summary account of some of the major theoretical developments in North American archaeology. We also introduce many more specific controversies and theoretical insights at appropriate moments in later chapters. In this way, I balance narrative description with explanation, the broad sweep of the past with more descriptive concerns. I also strongly believe that ancient North America must be interpreted in terms not only of the global human past, but also in the context of later world history. For this reason, the closing chapter of the book examines the archaeology of post-contact North America and covers some of the devastating cultural changes that overtook native American societies after European exploration and settlement.

Sources

Anyone who writes a book like this faces an enormous and never-ending flood of articles, books, and reports. Just navigating the proliferating academic literature is hard enough, but the problem of sources has been compounded in recent years by the emergence of Cultural Resource Management (CRM) as the major factor in North American archaeology and also by the increasing use of the World Wide Web. To avoid complete intellectual indigestion, I have followed some rules in *Ancient North America*, which reflect the reality of archaeology in the public arena:

- *This book is written from published sources only*. No unpublished data appears in this book, unless I have the written permission of the researcher, in which case it is cited. Unpublished data is unverified in the scientific eye, so I have no option but to omit it here. The same rule applies to verbal reports and delivered, but not published, conference reports, regrettably often cited as if they are published references.

- *"Grey" literature contributes relatively little to this book*. CRM research has generated an enormous "grey" literature, commonly mimeographed or desk-top published for limited circulation. Some reports are even confidential and never distributed at all. Although significant progress in creating repositories for the "grey" literature has been made, much of it is effectively inaccessible to the more general researcher such as myself, even with all the facilities of a great university library system at hand. I have tried to minimize inaccuracies by consulting colleagues in all parts of North America, but some, inevitably, exist.

- *World Wide Web sources are used minimally.* The Web is a new reality of the archaeological world. Nearly every important site or project has its own Web site, making research a nightmare of transitory postings and constant updatings. Although some Web-based research has gone into this edition, I have avoided citing specific Web pages here, on the grounds that they change frequently. The reader is referred to Arch.net and other permanent sites, which provide links to every aspect of archaeology conceivable (for address, see Bibliography).

Changes in the Third Edition

The third edition of *Ancient North America* takes advantage of massive input from colleagues, students, and general readers, who took the trouble to write to me, also of a complex formal and informal review process. Almost all these many critics and reviewers urged minimal overall change to the book, which is now updated throughout. The third edition also coincides with the coming of age of Cultural Resource Management, and with new emphases on short-term climatic change and the archaeology of mind. The major changes in this edition include:

- Updates on theory and recent trends (Chapter 3),

- Incorporation of a new calibrated chronology based on ice cores, coral, and tree-rings for first settlement, including the Clovis tradition. This exciting, but provisional, development adds some 2,000 years to the chronology of Paleo-Indian settlement (Chapter 4),

- Inclusion of new, fine-grained data on short-term climatic change in western North America, which affects our interpretations of coastal populations and emerging hunter-gatherer complexity in major ways (Chapter 11),

- New research on Southwestern pueblo cultures and developments after the Anasazi dispersal (Chapter 15),

- Major revisions of Archaic archaeology in the Southeast (Chapters 17, 18),

- New insights into Hopewellian settlement patterns (Chapter 19),

- A major revision of the Mississippian chapter (Chapter 20), to reflect a new generation of research which focuses on ideology and socio-political change.

Despite all these revisions, the story in these pages is still very incomplete, at a time when North America's past is under siege from collectors, looters, tourism, and the ravages of industrial civilization. All of us, whether professional archaeologist, avocational enthusiast, or lay person, have a responsibility to be stewards of the past for future generations. If we are not faithful stewards, there is a real danger that our grandchildren will curse us roundly for letting the finite archaeological record vanish.

I urge any reader with comments, criticisms, or suggestions for the next edition to contact me at brian@brianfagan.com. Your insights are much appreciated.

Acknowledgments

My debt to dozens of colleagues is enormous, in the field, in museums, libraries, and university departments, even on the shores of the Arctic Ocean, in the quiet peace of a prairie valley near Saskatoon, and 20 miles off the southern California coast. I cannot possibly thank all of them individually, and hope they will take this book as a measure of my appreciation. I am humbled by their dedication to the past, often under very difficult circumstances.

I am indebted, too, to the many friends and correspondents, who took the time to send me their (often trenchant) comments on the draft manuscript and the second edition. They were generous with opinion, insights, also encouragement (and sometimes, even, gossip!). My special thanks to David Anderson, Kenneth Ames, Rob Besell, Bruce Bourque, Gary Crawford, Ted Goebel, Jack Lobdell, Mark Lynott, Allan McCartney, Robert McGhee, Herbert Maschner, George Michaels, Tim Pauketat, Stephen Plog, Mark Raab, Ken Sassaman, Dean Snow, Tom Thiessen, Nicholas Tripcevich, and William Turnbaugh, who provided critical insights and patiently answered question after question. I only hope they approve of the final revision. Thank you, everyone!

Lastly, my thanks and appreciation to my colleagues at Santa Barbara, who have been a constant source of intellectual stimulation and ideas for more than 30 years. I value our long association more than I can say.

BRIAN FAGAN
Santa Barbara, California

A Note on Radiocarbon Dates

Until very recently, few North American archaeologists quoted radiocarbon dates calibrated with tree-rings. Now C14 calibration is becoming increasingly sophisticated, as its range extends into the Early Holocene and corals, varves, and other independent dating approaches are added to dendrochronology. These new calibrations are giving us cause to treat radiocarbon dates earlier than about 9500 BC with great caution, as there is evidence to suggest there is a "plateau" affecting radiocarbon ages in the 11,000 to 14,000-year range. For example, there is now good reason to believe that the Clovis culture of early North America is 2,000 years earlier than thought until very recently (see Chapter 4). Despite these advances in calibration methods, most North American archaeologists still use radiocarbon ages.

I have adopted the following conventions for the purposes of this book:

- Dates earlier than 10,000 BC are quoted in years before present.

- The AD/BC convention is used, not CE/BCE.

- Unless otherwise stated, all dates derived from radiocarbon in this book are radiocarbon ages. Calibrated dates (notably in Chapter 4) are quoted as [cal].

- Calibrated dates are given in a special column in each of the chronological tables.

Radiocarbon Calibration Table

The following table gives calibrated readings for the past 10,000 years, and earlier:

Tree-ring calibrations	Radiocarbon Age		Calibrated Age in Years using Tree-rings	
	AD	1760	AD	1945
		1505		1435
		1000		1105
		500		635
		1		15
		505 BC		767 BC
		1007		1267
		1507		1867
		2007		2477
		3005		3795
		4005		4935
		5005		5876
		6050		7056
		7001		8247
		8007		9368
		9062		9968

AMS Carbon 14 (Barbados) and Uranium/Thorium calibrations	AMS Radiocarbon Dates	Calibrated Age in Years using Uranium/Thorium
	7760 BC	9140 BC
	8270	10,310
	9320	11,150
	10,250	12,285
	13,220	16,300
	14,410	17,050
	15,280	18,660
	23,920	28,280

(increasing differences after 25,000 BC [calibrated])

Calibrations based on tables in *Radiocarbon* 40 (3), 1998. It should be stressed that these calibrations are provisional, statistically based, and subject to modification, especially before 7000 BC.

PART ONE

BACKGROUND

"None of the dead can rise up and answer our questions. But from all that they have left behind, their imperishable or slowly dissolving gear, we may perhaps hear voices, 'which are now only able to whisper, when everything else has become silent,' to quote Linnaeus."

BJÖRN KURTEN
How to Deep-Freeze a Mammoth (1984)

CHAPTER 1

EUROPEAN DISCOVERY

In about the year AD 982 (the exact date is disputed), Norseman Eirik Thorvaldsson the Red sailed west from Iceland to explore the mysterious lands that sometimes appeared distantly on the far horizon when the winds blew from the north. Three years later, he and his men returned with glowing tales of a fertile, uninhabited land where fish were plentiful and the grazing grass lush and green. Eirik named it the Green Land, a name retained to this day.

Eirik persuaded 25 shiploads of settlers to sail for Greenland in 986. They founded tiny, remote Brattahlid in the southwest, and the so-called Western Settlement at Godthaab some 400 miles (644 km) to the north. For centuries, these tiny hamlets were bases for Norse wanderings far to the north, among icebound fjords and islands on the fringes of the Arctic Ocean, and west 186 miles (300 km) across the Davis Strait to Baffin Island, Labrador, and beyond.

The restless and adventurous Greenlanders farmed, kept cattle and sheep, fished, and were skilled hunters who took game on land and sea. Above all, they were seamen, who explored every nook and cranny of southwestern Greenland. Very early on, it seems, bold young men ventured far north toward the arctic ice, and across the Davis Strait to the *Ubygdir*, "the unpeopled tracts," new lands beyond the western horizon.

Only the faintest records of these western voyages have come down through the centuries. They survive in two fragmentary Icelandic documents, often called the Vinland Sagas, written at least 200 years later. *The Saga of the Greenlanders* and *The Saga of Eirik the Red* are tantalizingly vague and contradictory accounts of extraordinary voyages. Unfortunately, it is almost impossible to separate historical fact from fantasy, geographical information from vague description written and copied several times over (Wahlgren, 1986).

The Saga of the Greenlanders tells how a young merchant named Bjarni Herjolfsson comes home to Iceland from Norway with a full cargo. He finds that his father has moved to Greenland with Eirik the Red, sets out to visit him, but the voyagers become lost in a wilderness of North Atlantic fog. Days or weeks later, they encounter a low, forested coast, which faces east. Bjarni realizes that this cannot be Greenland, so he turns north, sights more forested land a few days later, then an island with mountains and glaciers. Herjolfsson turns east, sails across Davis Strait, and reaches Greenland safely.

(Opposite) Routes of the early European explorers in and around North America.

Perhaps some 15 years later, in the 990s, Leif Eiriksson, son of Eirik the Red, sets out on a journey of exploration to the west. He sails across to the icy island that was Bjarni's last landfall, then voyages southward until he is well below the latitude of southern Greenland. Eiriksson and his 35 followers winter in a sheltered location where they are amazed and delighted to find wild grapes and grapevines growing. They survive an unusually mild winter, explore the countryside, load up with timber and return home to Greenland. Leif Eiriksson names the new lands: *Helluland*, "Slabrock Land," perhaps Baffin Island and northern Labrador, *Markland*, "Forest Land," probably central Labrador and Newfoundland, and *Vinland*, "Wineland," to the south, whose location is a matter of vigorous controversy. In a meticulous analysis of the sagas, Erik Wahlgren (1986) has argued persuasively that Eiriksson wintered over somewhere near Passamaquoddy Bay, close to the border between Maine and New Brunswick. The grapes that so enraptured his men were wild grapevines that are common in New England. Others believe, on the basis of a 16th-century Icelandic chart, that Vinland was Newfoundland, and that Eiriksson simply embellished his account with wild grapes to encourage prospective settlement (McGhee, 1984a).

Leif Eiriksson never returned to Vinland. His brother Thorvald followed in his footsteps, mounting an expedition that lasted two years. He appears to have explored the Bay of Fundy, was killed in a clash with local people, and buried there. A visiting Icelandic merchant named Thorfinn Karlsefni was next in Vinland. He took a 60-person expedition back to Leif's winter settlement and traded with some visiting Indians. There was fighting and men perished on both sides. After two winters, Karlsefni sailed back to Greenland, probably sometime around 1012. More sporadic and unrecorded Norse voyages to Labrador probably ensued in the following three centuries, ventures in search of timber, which was in short supply in Greenland (McGhee, 1984a).

Norse Settlement in North America

Archaeologists have searched diligently for traces of Viking settlement in North America. There have been the usual archaeological fantasies – stones inscribed with Norse runic script and mysterious towers in New England and the celebrated Kensington Stone discovered in Minnesota in 1898. None stand up to scholarly scrutiny (Wahlgren, 1986).

The logical place for such sites would be Labrador or Newfoundland, and it is at L'Anse aux Meadows in northern Newfoundland that the only known trace of Norse settlement has come to light. Helge Ingstad and Anne Stine discovered the remains of eight sod-walled structures on a terrace overlooking a shallow bay (Ingstad, 1977; 1985). These turf houses contained Norse artifacts such as a spindle whorl and a needle hone. One of the houses was too long to have been covered by a single roof. It consisted of several dwellings built together, perhaps forming a kind of sleeping hall. The settlement had a work shed, a smithy situated well away from the houses, and a possible bath house, also four turf boat sheds, perhaps once roofed with sod-covered rafters or branches. There are signs of both earlier and later native American settlement on the site.

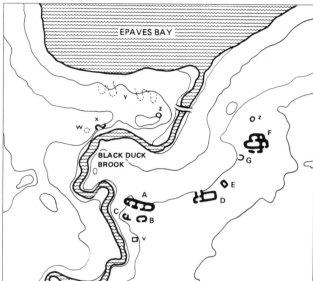

L'Anse aux Meadows, in northern Newfoundland. (Above left) Aerial photograph of the marine terrace at Epaves Bay, showing partially excavated house-sites. (Above right) Layout of the site: A–D, houses; E, work shed; F, large house; v, natural deposit of iron ore; w, charcoal kiln; x, forge; y, boat sheds; z. cooking pits. (Right) Three sod houses reconstructed by Parks Canada. One is a longhouse, others a small dwelling and a workshop. The reconstructions are based on archaeological data and information from other Viking sites.

L'Anse aux Meadows is a shallow bay, but a site with one major advantage – ample grazing for cattle. It lies at a strategic point, surrounded by water on three sides, an excellent base for exploring the St Lawrence Valley, if such a Norse enterprise was ever contemplated. Radiocarbon dates from the dwellings date the settlement to about AD 1000, but the precise identity of the builders is unknown.

No other indisputable traces of Norse settlement have come to light in North America. A Norwegian penny dating to between AD 1065 and 1080 was found at the Goddard site on the coast of Maine's Penobscot Bay. As far as can be established, this penny reached the site during the 12th or 13th centuries, probably as a result of indirect trading contacts with Inuit people far to the north (McGhee, 1984a)[1]. Some disputed longhouse foundations on Ungava Bay, across Davis Strait from Brattahlid, are almost certainly of Inuit manufacture, and not the work of Norsemen.

As early as the 12th century, Norsemen had sporadic contacts with Inuit groups living in the Canadian Archipelago and along the western Greenland

[1] For the purposes of this book, the term Eskimo is used to refer to Alaskan maritime peoples, while Inuit is used for their Canadian Arctic relatives.

Clues to a Norse presence in the High Arctic. (Above) Wooden figurine of a Norseman found in a Thule (Inuit) house at Okivilialuk. (Above right) Fragment of Norse woollen cloth from Skraeling Island.

coast, in the Nordrsetur (the central west coast), the area around Disko Bay, and probably much farther north (McGhee, 1984a). A scatter of Norse artifacts has come from Inuit settlements in the High Arctic – especially from the Ellesmere Island area. These include non-lnuit copper and iron fragments, pieces of woollen cloth, chain mail, and carpenters' tools, also boat nails and rivets, even carvings that give impressions of Norsemen. There are Norse stone cairns, some reworked bottom sections of casks, and a single runic inscription from Kingiqtorsoaq high on Greenland's western coast, probably dating to 24 April 1333.

The Norsemen called the Inuit Skraelings. "They possess no iron, but use walrus tusk for missiles and sharpened stones instead of knives," we learn from the *History of Greenland*, a work based on a 13th-century manuscript (McGhee, 1984a). Contacts between Norse and Inuit were probably sporadic, the result of summer bear- and walrus-hunting expeditions far to the north. Walrus ivory was the medium in which Greenlanders paid their annual tithe to the church in distant Norway, on some occasions at least 400 tusks annually, far more than could be obtained around the Greenland settlements.

As far as we can tell, the contacts between Inuit and Norse were sometimes friendly, occasionally violent, apparently rarely prolonged. In all probability, the Norse came in touch with both Inuit and American Indians, the latter Beothuk, Algonquian-speakers who were summer visitors to the Labrador coast and Newfoundland (McGhee, 1984a; for archaeology, see Chapter 21). Norse artifacts have come from as far afield as the western shores of Hudson Bay and latitude 79°N, 500 miles (819 km) north of the Kingiqtorsoaq rune stone. That is not to say that the Norse themselves actually traveled this widely, for many prized exotica may have passed along Inuit barter networks.

However, the Norse did not colonize North America. In AD 1000, Europe was not ready to, or capable of, settling the lands to the west. The tough and resourceful Norsemen could survive on Greenland coasts. However, they lacked the sheer numbers and the resources to expand and maintain pioneer settlements, to confront and compete with much larger indigenous populations. Nor were there strong motives for colonization – no religious persecution at home, no promise of great wealth to attract the greedy adventurer. Eventually, even Greenland proved beyond their capabilities. Norse civilization survived there until around 1500, progressively debilitated by increasing arctic cold that brought Inuit hunters farther south, by economic deprivation and competition for game resources, and perhaps by declining birth rates and sheer cultural isolation from the homeland. There were occasional hostile visitors, too, perhaps even some piracy, for Basque whalers from northern Spain had been sailing in Greenland waters since at least 1372.

Eventually, the Norsemen quietly withdrew, leaving two geographical legacies behind them for later explorers – the term "Skraeling" and two place names: Markland, a land of forests, and Promontorium Winlandiae, a land of vines – actually northern Newfoundland. Their epic journeys survived in European consciousness as hints of exotic peoples living at the very edge of the known world. "There are animals of such enormous size that the inhabitants of the inner islands use their bones and vertebrae in place of wood in constructing houses. They also use them for making clubs, darts, lances, knives, seats, ladders, and, in general, all things which elsewhere are made from wood ..." Thus did the great Arab geographer al-Idrisi describe the North Atlantic and its rich fisheries in his *Nuzhet al-Mushtaq*, written in about AD 1150 (McGhee, 1984a). Like the medieval geographers, al-Idrisi relied not only on first-hand experience, but travelers' accounts from every corner of the world. Perhaps, among these accounts, he heard vague stories of northern whale hunters from the far north. Were these "inhabitants of the inner islands" Inuit hunters, native Americans from the Canadian Arctic, living at the extreme edge of the known medieval world? If al-Idrisi was indeed writing of Inuit peoples from North America, the tales of their whalebone houses had probably reached him through many hands from Norse sources in Greenland and Iceland.

The first, fleeting contacts between Inuits, native Americans, and Western voyagers did nothing to alter hunter-gatherer cultures that had been evolving in a vast, isolated continent for more than 13,000 years. Centuries were to pass before Westerners again voyaged along North American shores.

The Search for a Strait

On 12 October 1492, Christopher Columbus, Admiral of the Ocean Sea, sailing under the Spanish flag, set foot on San Salvador in the Bahamas. There he found naked people, "very well made, of very handsome bodies and very good faces." Columbus himself believed he had found the outlying islands of east Asia, and called the inhabitants of the new lands "Indios," Indians. The Admiral's explorations brought a torrent of settlers to the Caribbean, settlers who came to "serve God and get rich." They soon encountered an astounding diversity of different peoples – simple hunters, village farmers, and magnificent civilizations like that of the Aztecs of highland Mexico. When Hernan Cortés and his soldiers gazed down on the great Aztec capital at Tenochtitlán in the Valley of Mexico in 1519, they marveled at a gold-laden civilization that rivaled those of Christendom in its magnificence.

Only seven years after Columbus' death in 1506, conquistador Vasco Nuñez de Balboa trekked across Central America and gazed on the Pacific. The Indies were not part of China at all, but what "we may rightly call a New World more densely peopled and abounding in animals than Europe, or Asia, or Africa." For years afterward, Europeans had but two ambitions in the New World – to find another gold-rich civilization, and a navigable strait to China.

Just as the last Norse colonists vanished in southern Greenland, Genoese-born John Cabot sailed west from Bristol, England, in search of a short, northern route to the Indies (Morison, 1971). The *Mathew* sailed in 1497, made landfall on Newfoundland, coasted down the west coast, and discovered the rich cod fisheries of the Grand Banks. Cabot encountered no human beings, but observed snares and nets, presumably belonging to Beothuk groups.

Two years later, Portuguese explorer Gaspar Corte Real sailed northwest from the Azores and made landfall on "a land that was very cool and with big trees," almost certainly Newfoundland. He returned the following year. His men kidnapped 57 Beothuk Indians, who "live together by fishing and hunting animals, in which the land abounds, the skins of which they use for garments and also make houses and boats thereof." The people lived in "rocky caves and thatched huts." After their first experience with Europeans, the Beothuk retreated to the interior and were very hostile to later visitors.

The next quarter-century saw the icebound and foggy north with its forested, rocky shores fade into relative oblivion. Only cod fishermen penetrated northern waters, people with little interest in exploration or the local inhabitants. Everything else was eclipsed by the brilliant discoveries that followed on Columbus far to the south. Then, in September 1522, Juan Sebastian del Caño in the ship *Vittoria* anchored at Seville in Spain, carrying just 18 of the 239 men who had set out on Ferdinand Magellan's epic circumnavigation of the globe. He had sailed into the Pacific through the stormy Magellan Strait at the southern tip of South America. Spanish and Portuguese explorers had now covered the entire east coast of the Americas from Florida to Patagonia, but had been unable to find any other strait north of Magellan's. On most maps of the time, Newfoundland floated in the North Atlantic, without any seeming link to the lands farther south. Thirteen degrees of latitude from Maine to Georgia remained unexplored. Here, surely, lay either a strait to the west, or, even better, open sea that would carry European mariners to the "happy shores of Cathay."

In January 1524, the French gentleman explorer Giovanni da Verrazzano sailed west from Madeira (Morison, 1971). Instead of dropping down to the West Indies, he sailed well north of Columbus' track just over 30 years before. About 1 March, he made landfall at Cape Fear, North Carolina, then sailed up the east coast as far as Newfoundland. He encountered many friendly Indian groups along the way, mostly simple farmers and fishermen, wearing leaves or skins. The people of Casco Bay, Maine, apparently more familiar with foreigners, were less welcoming. "They used all signs of discourtesy and disdain, as was possible for any brute creature to invent, such as exhibiting their bare behinds and laughing immodestly." Verrazzano named this coast *Terra Onde di Mala Gente*, the "Land of Bad People," in revenge.

The prospect of a northern route to China brought Jacques Cartier, French Master Mariner of Saint-Malo in Brittany, to Newfoundland in April 1534. He returned to France five months later, having sailed completely around the Gulf of St Lawrence, where his men lived off great auk meat, salmon, and other fresh fish, goose eggs and wild strawberries. He was accompanied by two Huron Indian teenagers, a chief's sons, who were to act as guides on his second voyage. Cartier returned a year later to penetrate deeper into the Gulf. His Huron guests knew the great river well, all the way upstream to modern Quebec. It was, Cartier realized, a highway to the interior. "No man has been to the end, so far as they had say," he wrote.

Cartier made contact with Huron people living near modern Quebec, and arrived at Hochelaga, the site of present-day Montreal, on 2 October 1535. There, more than 1000 Indians greeted him, bringing gifts of corn bread and performing welcoming ceremonies. They lived in a fortified village surrounded by corn fields, partly situated on the grounds of today's McGill University. The fortifications consisted of palisades with two redoubts "garnished with rocks and stones, for defense and protection." There were 50 bark and wood houses inside, each with several rooms and a central fireplace, grouped around a central plaza. The people were in a constant state of readiness, for their home was close to the militant Five Nations of the Iroquois, notorious for their sudden raids. Cartier was impressed by his friendly reception in what were the golden days of race relations along the St Lawrence. They were not to last. When Cartier returned in an abortive attempt to found a colony, the Huron were hostile, attacked his settlement and killed at least 35 people. For more than a half-century, the Huron were left alone, as exploration and settlement faltered.

Raleigh's Virginia

On 27 April 1584, two ships slipped out of Plymouth, England, on a voyage of reconnaissance along the more southern coasts explored by Verrazzano 60 years earlier. Philip Amadas and Arthur Barlow sailed at the behest of Walter Raleigh, who held letters patent from Queen Elizabeth granting him permission to colonize an unspecified area of North America. Four months later, the two vessels anchored close to Nag's Head in present-day North Carolina. They soon came in contact with the local Powhatan Indians, Algonquian-speakers, "very handsome, and goodly people," who entertained them royally (Morison, 1971). "The soil," Barlow wrote enthusiastically if mendaciously, "is the most plentifull, sweete, fruitfull and wholesome of all the world." All this was good publicity for prospective colonists and for royal ears. Queen Elizabeth I knighted Walter Raleigh and allowed him to name his prospective colony Virginia.

In April of the following year, Sir Richard Grenville led an expedition of five ships and about 500 men, including 108 prospective colonists, to Virginia. This time, Raleigh sent along a scientist, Thomas Hariot, an Oxford mathematician, and an artist, John White. The settlement was a complete failure, but Hariot and White had ample opportunity to visit several Indian settlements. White sketched the people and their villages with astounding, if romantic detail. Hariot's *Briefe and True Report of the New Found Land of Virginia* appeared in 1588. Illustrated with White's sketches, it became a basic source of information on American Indians for more than a century (Rountree, 1989) (illus. p. 24).

Despite later efforts, no permanent colony was established in Virginia until that at Jamestown on the James River, about 35 miles (56 km) from Chesapeake Bay in 1607. That effort succeeded both because of sustained economic support from England, and because the colonists exported tobacco home. A year later, Samuel de Champlain established a colony at Quebec on the St Lawrence, 12 years before the Pilgrim Fathers landed at Plimoth in

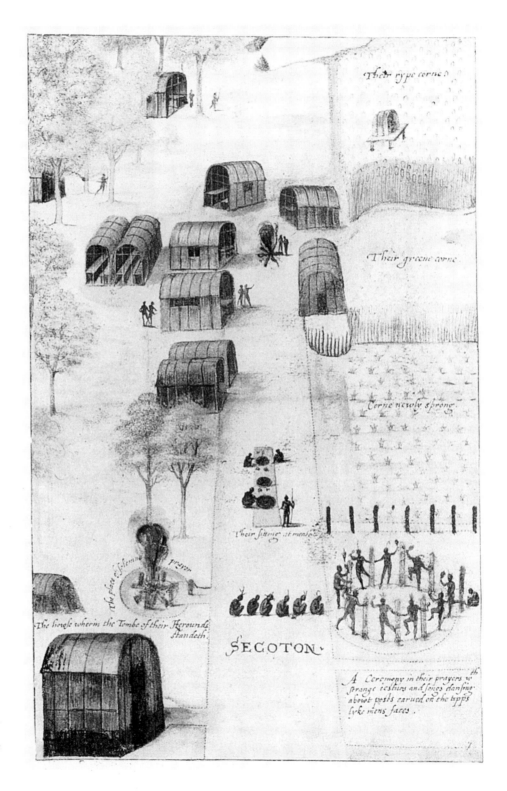

Their rype corne

Their greene corne

Corne newly sprong

Their sitting at meate

The place of solemne prayer

The house wherin the Tombe of their Herounds standeth

SECOTON

A Ceremony in their prayers w strange geftures and fones dansing about pofts carued on the topps lyke mens faces.

The Algonquian village of Secotan in Virginia, sketched by John White in about 1585. A romanticized view of the American Indians that shows many details of daily life.

New England. The first two decades of the 17th century saw the era of permanent European colonization in North America finally begin – with catastrophic effects on the native peoples that lay in the white settlers' path.

Spanish Explorations in the Southeast

A century earlier, however, the Spanish had tentatively explored North America from the south – from New Spain (Mexico) and the Caribbean. Not that this exploration had followed immediately upon the conquest of Mexico, for it took 10 years and innumerable military campaigns to subdue the Indian population of Central America. The lust for gold intensified as more and more territory was opened up to European exploitation. Vast land masses lay to the north of wealthy Mexico. Did these also contain fabulous riches? Applicants willing to lead expeditions into the unknown importuned the Spanish Crown for permission to find out (Fagan, 1977).

The first man to sail north from the Indies was a soldier named Ponce de Leon, who landed near present-day Palm Beach, Florida, in 1513 (Milanich and Hudson, 1993). He was searching for the mythical "Fountain of Youth" that chroniclers insisted was to be found on an island north of Cuba. His search was fruitless, the country sandy and low-lying, the local inhabitants fierce and unfriendly. Six years later, Alonso Alvarez de Piñeda entered the Mississippi River estuary, where he spent six weeks. The area was quite densely populated, but devoid of gold.

The sinister and red-bearded Panfilo de Narvaez followed Piñeda north, but landed to the east, in what is now Tampa Bay. There his men obtained some gold objects that fired their greedy imaginations. Sending his vessels to find a better harbor, Narvaez set out to march west along the coast with 260 men, promptly losing touch with his ships. The soldiers constructed temporary boats, but these foundered off the mouth of the Mississippi. The last vessel was cast ashore off modern Galveston, Texas. Only a junior officer named Alvar Nuñez Cabeza de Vaca, two soldiers, and a black slave survived. The five men withstood incredible hardships, and walked all the way from Texas to New Spain. Their report gives little information on the country and its inhabitants, except for an impression of people with few material possessions living in a dry environment. Again, there were no signs of gold or great treasure.

In 1537, the wealthy conquistador Hernando de Soto came home to Spain after making a small fortune under Francisco Pizarro in Peru (Garcilaso de la Vega, 1951; Milanich and Hudson, 1993). He was restless for farther adventure, and lobbied for the governorship of Cuba and Florida, which he obtained. By 1539 this remarkable adventurer had raised a force of 622 men and had landed in Tampa Bay. De Soto hoped to find a kingdom as wealthy as that of the Aztecs or Inca. His only objectives were gold, the acquisition of wealth, and colonization (for archaeology, see Chapter 22).

Tampa was unpromising. The local people lived in "a town of seven or eight houses, built of timber and covered with palm-leaves. The chief's house stood near the beach on a very high mount made by hand for defence; at the other end of the town was a temple, on top of which perched a wooden fowl with gilded eyes." The surrounding countryside was flat and swampy, and no metals were to be found.

De Soto set off through marshy terrain until he reached higher ground. His soldiers treated the local people brutally, burning villages, then seizing food stocks and adults as slaves. Eventually, the conquistadors reached the large settlement of Cofachiqui, where an important female chieftain greeted them in a shaded canoe. Apparently terrified of the Spaniards, she ordered that all yellow and white metals in her domains were to be laid before the foreigners. Large quantities of copper were forthcoming, also sheets of mica, which local artisans fashioned into fine ornaments. The Spaniards asked for freshwater pearls, but were told they were imported from far away. In desperation, the chieftain directed them to the "upper part of the town," where a temple covered the burial place of long dead chiefs and their relatives. The soldiers looted the burials. Some 350 lbs (158 kg) of discolored freshwater pearls were divided between them.

During their journey to Cofachiqui, the conquistadors had passed many abandoned villages, as if the local people had lived there for a long time. Three miles (4.8 km) from Cofachiqui lay Talomeco, a larger settlement with the usual artificial earthen mounds upon which a temple and the chief's house formerly stood. The temple was still standing, a structure over 100 ft (30 m) long and 40 ft (12 m) wide, with a steep roof of reeds and split cane adorned with sea shells. The Spaniards forced their way in and wondered at wooden statues mantled with pearls, at enormous bundles of skins and dyed cloth. There were caches of copper-bladed ceremonial weapons, battle axes and clubs, delicately inlaid bows and arrows, wooden and woven cane shields, all of the finest workmanship – but no gold.

The taciturn and inflexible De Soto was so obsessed with the yellow metal that he ordered his men westward over the Blue Ridge Mountains into what is today Tennessee. Hardships multiplied. Choctaw raiders attacked the

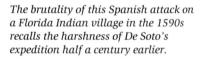

The brutality of this Spanish attack on a Florida Indian village in the 1590s recalls the harshness of De Soto's expedition half a century earlier.

The French in Florida. (Above right) Chief Athore in 1564 showing French explorer René de Laudonnière a stone pillar erected by a previous French expedition two years before. The pillar (labeled "F" in the sketch map above left) bore the coat-of-arms of the King of France. The scene of friendship and harmony by artist Jacques le Moyne de Morgues may have been used to recruit emigrants to the New World.

party. More than 150 men perished in a counterattack to recover lost baggage. The conquistadors wintered near the Yazoo River in Mississippi, where they encountered "fine looking" Indians in a fleet of canoes that "appeared like a famous armada of galleys." Next spring, De Soto led his men through the Ozarks into eastern Oklahoma. There they heard stories of "many cattle," whose skins the local Indians gave them in abundance as bed covers. But they never set eyes on the bison themselves.

Finally, De Soto realized that the gold-laden kingdoms over the horizon were a fiction. He headed southeast toward the Gulf of Mexico. The journey was a harsh one, through unfriendly territory occupied by suspicious Indians. De Soto himself perished of fever, but half of the 622 men who had set out with him managed to reach Cuba.

De Soto's expedition put paid to any dreams of fabulous, golden kingdoms in the north. Apart from two abortive French expeditions to Florida in the 1560s, the Mississippi Valley and the Southeast with their elaborate chiefdoms were left in peace for over a century. By the time the 16th-century Spaniards encountered them, many large Indian settlements had been abandoned, as if the population had declined sharply. Some archaeologists believe this may have been the result of epidemics of exotic diseases like smallpox that spread across the interior long before the Indians had direct contact with Europeans (Crosby, 1986). (This is a controversial subject, see Chapter 22.) The large earthworks built by some of these people were to puzzle white settlers and scholars for generations.

The Seven Lost Cities of Cibola

When Alvar Nuñez Cabeza de Vaca reached Mexico City overland from Texas in 1536, his tales of a harsh and arid land to the north astounded the gold-hungry colonial government of New Spain. So greedy were they that they shrugged aside Vaca's tales of suffering. Ever since Cortés and Pizarro had plundered Mexico and Peru, there had been talk of the fabled Seven Cities of a mythical land named Cibola, cities founded as long ago as the 8th century by a legendary bishop from Lisbon (Fagan, 1977). Where, then, were these cities, if they were not to be found in Mexico or Peru? When

Hawikuh pueblo, Zuñi settlement in New Mexico, photographed in the late 19th century.

Vaca returned with vague rumors of large towns to the north, towns crowded with Indians and rich in gold and silver, the authorities were goaded into action. The Viceroy of Mexico sent Franciscan friar Fray Marcos de Niza in search of the cities, a man said to have "great experience in the affairs of the Indians." He was accompanied by Esteban, the black slave who had traveled with Cabeza de Vaca as a guide. They were a curious pair: the sober priest and the jaunty, freed slave who journeyed in great style, dressed in ribbons and feathers, for he had acquired somewhat of a reputation as a sorcerer among the Indians.

The expedition was a disaster. Esteban explored far ahead of the main caravan, sending back optimistic messages along the way. After a 15-day desert crossing, his party arrived at a Zuñi pueblo in what is now New Mexico, only to be massacred by the inhabitants. Marcos claimed that he heard of the killings from a survivor, then traveled secretly within sight of the pueblo, where he gazed undetected at "a faire citie," with many houses "builded in order . . . all made of stone with divers stories, and flatte roofs, as farre as I could discerne." The people were light skinned, possessed "emeralds and other jewels," and used "vessels of gold and silver, for they have no other metal, whereof there is greater use and more abundance than in Peru."

As can be imagined, Marcos' report fueled the flames of gold lust when he returned to Mexico City with "more feare than visuals." The friar was a good storyteller, and embellished his report at every opportunity. In fact, historians are almost certain that he turned and ran, never penetrating much farther north than the Gila River in southern Arizona, a long way from Zuñi country. Marcos' stories fell on fertile ground. In February 1540, Francisco Vasquez de Coronado, a competent young nobleman and royal courtier, led a much larger expedition in Marcos' footsteps: 225 horsemen, 60 foot soldiers, and a motley crowd of slaves and Indian allies marched north, with Fray Marcos as their guide (Fagan, 1977).

Coronado and his men found themselves traveling along Indian trails through harsh, dry country. Horses and men suffered greatly in the shimmering heat, but emerged from the desert within reach of six Zuñi pueblos. These were the "Seven Lost Cities," a disappointing sight to the conquistadors. "It is a small, crowded village," wrote Pedro de Castaneda, Coronado's chronicler, of Hawikuh pueblo, "looking as if it had been all crumpled up together. There are haciendas in New Spain which make a better appearance at a distance." Marcos' celebrated city was little more than a glorified village. Coronado routed the defenders in less than an hour. The hungry soldiers made a beeline for the storehouses, where they found "much corn and beans, and fowl." Of gold and precious stones there were no signs.

In the months that followed, Coronado explored much of the Southwest – without finding any gold. His men entered Hopi country, penetrated as far as the Grand Canyon, and visited Pecos pueblo close to modern Santa Fe, a settlement so large it could field 500 warriors. The town "is square, situated on a rock, with a large court or yard in the middle, containing the steam rooms," reported Pedro de Castaneda. "The houses are all alike, four stories high. One can go over the top of the village without there being a street to hinder." The houses could be entered only by means of ladders from the roofs, with doors that led into the passages.

Conquistador Hernando de Alvarado was sent onto the plains that lay east of Pecos to investigate stories about strange animals like cows with hairy skins. Alvarado and his men were soon surrounded with enormous herds of bison, "the most monstrous thing in the way of animals that has ever been seen or read about." Later, Coronado himself ventured onto the plains and deep into Kansas, where he encountered Plains Indians who relied on bison for food, hunting them in game drives or at water holes.

Barely a hundred men marched into Mexico City in the fall of 1542 when the dispirited expedition returned home. There were only a handful of Indian blankets and turquoises, and a wealth of new geographical knowledge, to show for more than two years' arduous traveling. It was half a century before attempts were made to settle the arid, goddless Southwest. Even then, the Spanish hold on these remote lands was tenuous at best, although Catholic missionaries and explorers had traveled widely through the region by the late 18th century.

"A Young People, Younger a Thousand Years..."

Columbus and his successors revealed a vast continent teeming with new forms of animal and plant life, and with a bewildering diversity of human societies both simple and complex (Fagan, 1987). Who were these "Indians," exotic, feathered people that Columbus paraded before the Spanish court, people according to Pope Alexander VI "well disposed to embrace the Christian faith?" Where had these strange humans come from and why were they so diverse? Soon, Europeans back home could see a surprisingly wide variety of native Americans, shipped back by explorers, missionaries, and slavers. The Aztec nobles and acrobats from Mexico who spellbound the Spanish Court in the 1520s, were a far cry from North Americans "clothid in beastys skinnys" who ate raw meat and had the manners of "brut bestis." In contrast, John White's Virginia Indians were depicted as friendly, noble-minded people, who did not abuse nature. The Inuit of the far north were apparently hardier. Martin Frobisher brought back a man and woman from Baffin Island in 1576. The hunter obligingly paddled his skin kayak on the River Avon near Bristol and shot ducks with his bow and arrow.

The 16th century saw a torrent of speculation about the origins of the American Indians, speculations about ancient Carthaginian migrations, about the Ten Lost Tribes of Israel exiled by Assyrian King Shalmaneser in 721 BC (Wauchope, 1972). There were more serious observers, too, like the celebrated Dominican Friar Bartolomé de las Casas, a champion of the Indians, who wrote that "there is not a great argument that the people of these islands and continent are very ancient." But he, and other historically minded religious scholars, turned to the only historical sources available to them – the Scriptures. They believed that all American Indians were related to familiar ancient societies in the Scriptures, like the Tartars, Scythians, and biblical Hebrews.

The Elizabethan philosopher Francis Bacon, on the other hand, marveled "at the thin population of America, for you must accept your inhabitants of America as a young people: younger a thousand years, at least, than the rest of the world."

An Inuit man captured by explorer Martin Frobisher in 1576.

Whatever their antiquity, everyone agreed that the Indians had come from the Garden of Eden. How, then, had they reached the Americas? Had they sailed across a vast ocean, or had they walked? Siberia was still a geographical blank in the 16th century, the Bering Strait between Asia and Alaska unknown. In 1589, Jesuit missionary José de Acosta published a remarkable work, his famous *Historia Natural y Moral de las Indias* (Fagan, 1987; Willey and Sabloff, 1993). It was entirely possible, he wrote, that "men came to the Indies driven unwittingly by the wind." However, he believed that most of the Indians had reached the New World in the same manner as the unfamiliar beasts that abounded in the Americas – by land. He theorized that small groups of "savage hunters driven from their home-lands by starvation or some other hardship" had taken an overland route through Asia to their present home. There were, he argued, "only short stretches of navigation" involved. At first, Acosta wrote, only a few Indians settled in the Americas. But they were successful. Their descendants developed not only agriculture, but elaborate states like those of the Aztecs and Inca. Acosta calculated that first settlement had taken place as much as 2000 years before the Conquest of Mexico.

It was to be a century and a half before Russian explorer Vitus Bering sailed through the Bering Strait in 1728, and seven decades after that before North American archaeology was born. By that time, Western explorers had penetrated all the oceans, and encountered a myriad unfamiliar human societies on remote shores. The Age of Enlightenment had made science fashionable in the intellectual circles of 18th-century Europe. Captain James Cook had mapped much of the Pacific, and the Russian scientist Pfefferkorn was able to state in 1794 that "it is almost certain that the first inhabitants of America really came by way of the strait." Not that such sober observations quenched the wild fire of speculations about the ancient Americans. They were the background to the first archaeological researches in North America.

Further Reading

Fagan, Brian M. 1977. *Elusive Treasure*. Charles Scribners, New York.
A popular account of early archaeological research in North and Central America. Copiously illustrated.

Milanich, J. T. and Hudson, Charles. 1993. *Hernando de Soto and the Indians of Florida*. University Press of Florida, Gainesville.
A fascinating account of De Soto's landing.

Morison, Samuel Eliot. 1971. *The Discovery of America. Volume 1: The Northern Voyages*. Oxford University Press, New York.
This is the definitive account of early explorations of the North American shoreline by a master of historical analysis and narrative.

Sabloff, Jeremy A. and Willey, Gordon R. 1993. *A History of American Archaeology*. 3rd ed. W.H. Freeman, New York.
The standard work on the history of American archaeology for the serious student. Lavish illustrations and comprehensive bibliography.

Wahlgren, Erik. 1986. *The Vikings and America*. Thames and Hudson, London and New York.
An authoritative, closely argued essay on the Viking exploration of North America.

CHAPTER 2

CULTURE HISTORY AND NORTH AMERICAN ARCHAEOLOGY

When Thomas Jefferson withdrew temporarily from public life to his Virginia estate in 1781, he settled down to complete a long questionnaire from the French Government, seeking information on his home state. What plants and animals flourished in Virginia? What minerals, products, and industries were to be found? What was known of the native inhabitants? His famous *Notes on the State of Virginia* (published first in France in 1784) was the result, a lengthy treatise that discussed, among other things, the "aborigines," and the first archaeological investigation in the United States (Jefferson, 1797).

The First Excavation
1782

Jefferson was an influential member of Philadelphia's coffee house society, one of many intellectuals who speculated about American Indian life, about abandoned towns and earthworks said to exist out west. He was a friend of the celebrated botanist William Bartram, who traveled widely through the Southeast in the 1770s, through country still densely inhabited by Indian tribes. The Cherokee, Bartram noted, built their meeting houses on large artificial mounds, as high as 20 ft (6 m). They did not build these earthworks, for they found them "in the same condition as they now appear." Bartram thought the mounds were the work of biblical peoples (Fagan, 1977).

Bartram was by no means the only person theorizing about the mounds. Many travelers believed that the Indians were incapable of building such elaborate earthworks. Rather, they hypothesized, Toltec Indians from Mexico had erected them before migrating southward. Others argued for Welshmen, or for some lost race that had occupied North America long before the Indians had arrived.

Jefferson listened to these hypotheses and resolved quietly to test them by digging into a small mound by the Rivanna River. His trenches revealed layers of burials and artifacts of Indian origin, separated by levels of stones and earth. Jefferson observed the strata with care, and remarked: "That they were repositories of the dead, has been obvious to all; but on what occasion constructed, was a matter of doubt." This was one of the first stratigraphic excavations anywhere, and was unique not only for its time but for generations afterward (Willey and Sabloff, 1993).

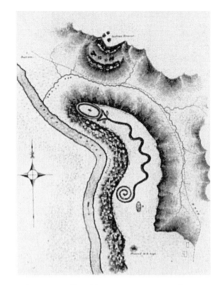

The Moundbuilder controversy. The Great Serpent Mound, Adams County, Ohio (above), attributed to the Fort Ancient culture, was one of the many mounds accurately mapped for the first time by Ephraim Squier (below) and his colleague Edwin Davis in the 1840s. But they continued to believe in a mythical race of moundbuilders.

The Myth of the Moundbuilders
1770s to 1894

After 1815, a flood of settlers poured over the Alleghenies, clearing farmland and exposing mounds, enclosures, and other exotic earthworks. The land itself was largely depopulated, the result, probably, of catastrophic 16th- and 17th-century epidemics of exotic European diseases. The newcomers were convinced that golden treasure lay in the mounds, and dug for their fortunes. They found no gold, but dozens of skeletons and exotic artifacts such as carved soapstone pipes, mica silhouettes of birds and animals, and fine copper ornaments and artifacts. The finds caused an intellectual furor, a wave of sentiment for theories of a "lost race" of white Moundbuilders, who had once settled and conquered the fertile lands of the Midwest. Such wild theories appealed to the romantically inclined, to people who believed that American Indians were incapable of building anything as elaborate as a burial mound (Silverberg, 1968).

Meanwhile, a few scholars and antiquarians set out to acquire more information about the earthworks and their builders. Caleb Atwater, the postmaster of Circleville, Ohio, spent his ample leisure time exploring the mounds near his home town and described them in a two-part paper published in 1820 that separated observation from pure speculation. Atwater's descriptions were accurate enough, but his theories a product of his time: migrating Hindus from India had built the mounds, then moved on to Mexico (Atwater, 1820). Only a few observers, like Dr James McCulloh, an armchair antiquarian, argued that the Indians were the Moundbuilders. By and large, their findings were ignored.

In 1839, a pioneer physical anthropologist, Samuel Morton, published his famous *Crania Americana*, in which he analyzed eight Moundbuilder skulls and compared them with modern Indian crania. He stated that they represented but a single race, even if he distinguished between "Toltecs" and the "Barbarous" on purely cultural grounds (Morton, 1839).

Just under a quarter-century after Caleb Atwater's report appeared, two Ohio antiquarians, E.G. Squier and E.H. Davis, completed one of the first scientific monographs published by the newly founded Smithsonian Institution. *Ancient Monuments of the Mississippi Valley* was a comprehensive, descriptive work, with plans so accurate that they are still used today (Squier and Davis, 1848). Squier and Davis' descriptive research was remarkable for the time, but they still referred to the "great race of Moundbuilders," and believed that the American Indians and their ancestors were incapable of building the earthworks.

Although most antiquarians believed in exotic Moundbuilders, a growing minority of influential scientists thought otherwise. Foremost among them was Samuel Haven, the Librarian of the American Antiquarian Society. In 1856, Haven published a remarkable essay, *Archaeology of the United States*, in which he surveyed everything that was known about ancient North America, and the origins of the American Indian. A judicious and dispassionate observer, Haven set the tone for all future scholarly enquiry into the native Americans. His conclusions were admirably cautious. "We desire to stop where evidence ceases," he stated at the outset. The Indians were of high antiquity, he believed. "All their characteristic affinities are found in the early conditions of Asiatic races," he wrote. Haven set the stage

The Moundbuilder controversy. Three scientists, Samuel Haven (below left), John Wesley Powell (below center), and Cyrus Thomas (below right), were among those instrumental in proving beyond doubt that the American Indians themselves had built mounds such as those at Marietta, Ohio (left, a sketch by Squier and Davis).

Frederick W. Putnam (far right) and other archaeologists photographed on a mound near Fair Grounds, Chillicothe, Ohio, in 1883. Putnam has been called the "professionalizer of American archaeology" for his work as an excavator, and as an administrator or founding father of several North American museums and departments of anthropology.

for a new era of systematic, much more scientific, research into the North American past.

The Moundbuilder controversy dragged on from the 1850s into the late 1890s, kept alive by continual amateur diggings and by the publication of often bizarre tomes that added new, and ever more offbeat, chapters to the ancient saga (Silverberg, 1968). Meanwhile, however, professional science grew hand in hand with the establishment of new universities and colleges, and thanks to the increasing influence of government agencies such as the US Geological Survey. Both the Survey and Harvard University's Peabody Museum played an important role in the controversies surrounding Stone Age settlement in North America (Meltzer, 1983).

The Smithsonian Institution's Bureau of Ethnology was founded in 1879, thanks to the lobbying of John Wesley Powell, the first man to traverse the Grand Canyon by boat. The Bureau was founded specifically to recover rapidly vanishing information about American Indian peoples in the far west. Under Powell's Directorship, it also embarked on ambitious archaeological programs on a broad geographical scale.

Powell moved into Moundbuilder studies because Congress insisted in 1881 that he spend the then large sum of $5000 annually on mound investigation. Forced to sponsor archaeological research, he appointed Cyrus Thomas, an entomologist from Illinois, to head a Division of Mound Exploration in 1882. At first Thomas believed in a "separate Moundbuilder race," but fortunately, he realized that he would have to embark on an extensive campaign of survey and excavation, both to support his hypothesis, and to save hundreds of earthworks from imminent destruction. He and his assistants fanned out over the Midwest, surveying, digging, studying artifacts, and making plans of sites large and small. The steady flow of data from the excavations soon convinced Thomas that the mounds were the work not of a "separate race," but of ancient Indians, the ancestors of modern populations. His monumental report appeared in the 12th *Annual Report* of the Bureau of Ethnology in 1894, a description of hundreds of sites, thousands of artifacts, and a pioneering effort at studying the remote past by working back from known modern sites and artifacts as a basis for comparison with earlier cultures.

With the publication of Thomas' great work, every serious scholar of North American archaeology accepted that the Moundbuilders were native Americans. All modern research into these peoples is based on this fact.

First Descriptive Efforts
1874 to 1914

The 40 years between 1874 and 1914 saw the first systematic descriptions of ancient pottery styles in eastern North America, early attempts to define the criteria for establishing the date of the first Americans (Chapter 4), and stratigraphic excavations in shell middens on the East Coast and by the German-trained archaeologist Max Uhle along the California coast. As early as 1880, Canadian geologist John Dawson of McGill University in Montreal attempted to link ancient artifacts with the Huron village of Hochelaga, visited and described by Jacques Cartier in 1535 (Willey and Sabloff, 1993).

Such research stemmed from the logical subdivision of anthropology into three subdisciplines – ethnography (today part of cultural anthropology), which dealt with living peoples, physical anthropology, which studied their biology, and archaeology, the study of the ancient native Americans. Close links between archaeology and cultural anthropology were forged by John Wesley Powell at the Smithsonian from the very beginning. Cyrus Thomas' work on the eastern mounds with its rich finds of artifacts and human remains confirmed the importance of a joint anthropological and archaeological approach to the study of the American Indian. This perspective, soon taught at Harvard, Pennsylvania, and Berkeley, was in sharp contrast to European approaches, where the three disciplines of anthropology developed separately and archaeology was thought of as an extension of history. At the time, there was some scholarly logic in this, for American archaeologists were investigating ancient non-European peoples, not the Romans and indigenous Europeans who formed a historical continuity with the modern inhabitants of that region of the Old World (Kehoe, A., 1998; Willey and Sabloff, 1993).

This close association with cultural anthropology has been a powerful catalyst for North American archaeology, providing a rich reservoir of modern analogies for interpreting the archaeological record, and offering chances to work back from the known present into the unknown past. It has also offered theoretical perspectives on ancient times that are of great benefit to a discipline that is an unrivaled way of examining and interpreting human cultural change over very long periods of time indeed.

For most of the late 19th century, the doctrines of biological and social evolution were extremely fashionable in anthropological circles. In an era when human progress was a watchword, anthropologists theorized that human societies everywhere had passed through successive stages of universal evolution. These theories culminated in the brilliant researches of lawyer-turned-anthropologist Lewis Henry Morgan. Morgan (1877) proposed no fewer than nine stages of linear social evolution, beginning with simple Savagery, and progressing from there through successive stages of Barbarism, culminating in Civilization. Morgan's unilinear evolutionary scheme proved popular, but was soon abandoned, as it was far too simplistic to explain the great diversity of American Indian groups.

Cushing, Bandelier, and the Southwestern Pueblos

The earliest archaeological investigations in the west were at the hands of government scientists or members of private expeditions, often surveyors who came across abandoned pueblos and dry caves where surprisingly well-preserved artifacts were to be found. Serious research began with two remarkable pioneers, Smithsonian anthropologist Frank Cushing, and Adolph Bandelier, a Swiss-born mine engineer who became an anthropologist.

Frank Cushing arrived at Zuñi pueblo in 1879, intending to stay for three weeks. He stayed for four-and-a-half years, learned to speak the Zuñi dialect fluently, and, through participant observation, recorded an extraordinary wealth of information about pueblo life. Cushing was not an archaeologist, but he made a rich collection of Zuñi oral traditions about earlier times that helped him realize that the best way to study ancient times was by working back from the present into the past (Cushing, 1882–83).

Adolph Bandelier arrived in the Southwest in 1880. A mine administrator and amateur anthropologist, Bandelier had come under the influence of Lewis Henry Morgan, who obtained a grant for him to work in the west. For 12 years, he wandered from pueblo to pueblo on a mule, carrying all his worldly possessions in a saddle bag. At pueblos like Pecos, he recorded centuries of Southwestern history, oral traditions and local histories that reached back into the remote past. He soon realized that the way to study early pueblo history was to work back in time, "from the known to the unknown, step by step" (Bandelier, 1884).

(Above) Frank Cushing: Zuñi war chief and US Government ethnographer. Cushing was a pioneer of participant observation in anthropology and became famous for his descriptions of Zuñi life.

(Right) A scene of Zuñi life: decorating pottery, from Cushing's My Adventures in Zuñi. *During this process "no laughing, music, whistling, or other unnecessary noises were indulged in," he wrote. The potters believed the sound would enter the clay and cause the vessel to shatter when fired.*

William Henry Holmes in an ocean of "paleoliths," c. 1890. This carpet of flaked stone was, Holmes discovered, a recent Indian quarry, like many of the supposed ancient chipping sites uncovered in the late 19th century.

Ales Hrdlička investigates an ancient skull.

Franz Boas and "Historical Particularism"

By the 1890s, evolutionism was in considerable disrepute among many anthropologists, partly because of slavish insistence on Morgan-like universal stages, and also because of extravagant claims by its proponents. The result was a strong reaction against any form of evolutionary theory, especially simplistic, linear schemes of human progress. A new generation of anthropologists led by the great fieldworker Franz Boas insisted on factual evidence, data on cultural traits collected from systematic field investigation (Lyman and Dunnell, 1997). Boas and his many students devoted years to the meticulous collection of cultural data throughout North America, founding a school of American anthropology known as "Historical Particularism." The result was a stifling intellectual climate, where any form of search for cultural change was a low priority. The effects on North American archaeology were serious.

On the face of it, one might have expected archaeologists to resist this current of anti-evolutionism. However, there were compelling reasons not to do so. In the first place, everyone was convinced that the American Indians had settled in their homeland only a relatively short time ago. Under the guidance of the strong-willed, indeed authoritarian, personalities of archaeologist William Henry Holmes and physical anthropologist Ales Hrdlička at the Smithsonian, almost every prehistorian accepted that the earliest human settlement of the New World had taken place no more than about 4000 years ago (Meltzer, 1983). Thus, there had been little time for significant cultural change.

Stratigraphic observation was also in its infancy, for few North American sites were thought to have multiple layers. Nor had North American scholars developed the excavation or analytical techniques to observe cumulative, small changes in human culture over even short periods of time. In brief, archaeologists were hardly in a position to rebut the historical particularists. And when they started to use stratigraphic techniques and the Direct Historical Method, they began to develop their own conceptual frameworks quite separately from cultural anthropology.

The Birth of Culture History
1914 to 1940

Culture history, the reconstruction of the remote past, is based on two fundamental principles that were enumerated in the early years of this century (Lyman and Dunnell, 1997; key papers collected in Lyman, O'Brien, and Dunnell, 1997). The first was inductive research methods, the development of generalizations about a research problem that are based on numerous specific observations. The second was what is called a "normative" view of culture. This is the notion that abstract rules govern what cultures consider to be normal behavior. The normative view is a descriptive approach to culture, which discusses it during one long time period or throughout time. Archaeologists base all culture history on the assumption that surviving artifacts, such as potsherds, display stylistic and other changes that represent the changing norms of human behavior throughout time. Culture history resulted from careful stratigraphic observation, meticulous artifact classifications and orderings, and accurate chronologies. The culture-historical approach resulted in a descriptive outline of ancient North America in time and space that took generations to assemble.

Stratigraphic Observation was introduced to North American archaeology in about 1914 and came into universal use during the next two decades. This was the time when the principles not only of stratigraphic observation, but also of seriation (artifact ordering in a time sequence) became allied with artifact typology and classification. The result were the first culture-historical syntheses of major culture areas of North America.

Nels Nelson was a large, earthy Scandinavian archaeologist who was trained by the great anthropologist Alfred Kroeber at Berkeley. As a young man, he had visited French cave excavations and worked with eminent scholars like Hugo Obermaier and Henri Breuil, experiences that convinced him of the importance of stratigraphic excavation. Working for the American Museum of Natural History in 1914–16, young Nelson excavated in the Galisteo Basin area of New Mexico, an area where Bandelier and another pioneer, Edgar Hewett, were convinced that there had been "cultural transformations in prehistoric times." A series of excavations at San Marcos and other pueblos provided stratigraphic proof of different pottery styles, but Nelson's sequence was incomplete until he excavated the 10-ft (3-m) deep middens at San Cristobal. There he described a sequence of changing pottery styles, from black-and-white painted that was common in earlier levels to glazed, then painted-and-glazed forms (Nelson, 1916).

The Direct Historical Method. Nelson's Galisteo research was a major breakthrough, and a foundation of what became known as the Direct Historical Method, working from the present into the past. The first large-scale application of stratigraphic methods came with Alfred V. Kidder's classic excavations at Pecos pueblo (Kidder, 1924). Kidder had been trained at Harvard and had taken a course in field methods with Egyptologist G.A. Reisner, a leading excavator of the day. He had also traveled in the Near East and observed modern European excavation methods at first hand. These he now applied at Pecos after 1916, in the largest excavation so far conducted in North America, dissecting refuse middens over 20 ft (6 m)

Labels in cross-section drawing:

Wall Stones and Humus
Modern Rubbish
Modern Floor
Glaze 6 Rubbish
Fallen Wall Stones
Gl. 5 Floor
Glaze 5 Wall
Modern Wall
Wall Stones and Humus
Modern Rubbish
Modern Terrace
Fill
Glaze 5 Floor
Gl. 5 Wall
Glaze 5 Rubbish
Glaze 4 Grave
Glaze 3
Glaze 1, 3, and 4 Walls evidently lie in this direction
Glaze 3 Grave
6 and
Glaze 4 Rubbish
Glaze 1 Rubbish
B on W Wall
Black-on-White Rubbish
Glaze 1 Grave
B on W Rub and Floor

Pecos excavations in 1916 with (inset) A.V. Kidder at the site, and his cross-section drawing of Pecos refuse stratigraphy with building walls and floors. Different ceramic styles found in the different layers are indicated by "Glaze 5," "Black-on-white," etc.

deep at both the Fork Lightning and Pecos sites. Kidder excavated with careful controls, assembling selected potsherd samples at first, then digging further trenches with meticulous care. After several seasons of work, he constructed a stratigraphic sequence of pottery styles for each pueblo, confirming the general sequence from the Galisteo Basin, and ultimately creating a regional sequence for the ancient Southwest (Kidder, 1927).

Thus was born a careful sequence of research strategies for developing culture histories that were to be applied by dozens of North American archaeologists in coming years – preliminary site survey, selection of criteria for ranking these sites in chronological order, then comparative study of these criteria, followed by a search for, and excavation of, stratified sites. Finally, more survey and additional excavations to confirm the results and refine cultural and stratigraphic findings.

The Direct Historical Method became even more formalized by important researches elsewhere in North America during the 1920s and 1930s. It was used in New York State as early as 1916 to relate ancient settlements to historic Iroquois villages. However, the greatest impetus came from excavations by W.D. Strong and Waldo Wedel in Nebraska (Strong, 1935, 1940; Wedel, 1938). These two archaeologists started with a rich lode of historical information collected by anthropologists and amateur historians. They excavated historic Pawnee sites, then went on to dig settlements from the contact period and from remoter times. The results were extraordinary, for the application of the Direct Historical Method revealed dramatic cultural changes on the Plains, shifts from bison hunting on foot to horticulture in river valleys, then back to bison hunting again, this time on horseback. Strong's *Introduction to Nebraska Archaeology* (1935) became a model for such research in many areas of North America.

Classification. Typology and artifact classification were fundamental to the emerging culture history of North America. The first systematic attempts to classify ancient pottery were at the hands of William Holmes of the Bureau of Ethnology in the 1890s (Holmes, W., 1903). He worked on potsherds from mounds and other eastern sites, while early Southwestern archaeologists like Hewett and Nelson wrestled with different pottery types from their excavations in the Galisteo Basin and elsewhere. These early attempts at classification were basically descriptive taxonomy. As excavations in the Southwest introduced at least a degree of chronology into stratigraphic sequences, archaeologists were forced to refine their typologies to take account of change through time. Inevitably, since it was the most common artifact, the humble potsherd became the yardstick of classification, a kind of changing marker that was used to subdivide ancient times into ever more minute subdivisions (Gladwin and Gladwin, 1931; Sayles, 1936).

The Pecos Classification. Kidder's Pecos excavations added much new data to Southwestern archaeology, and Kidder himself called a conference at the pueblo in 1927, where the leading archaeologists working in the area came together to develop a standardized classificatory scheme and chronology for the Southwest (Kidder, 1927). From this, the first Pecos Conference – they are held annually to this day – emerged a chronological classification of Southwestern cultures that has survived, albeit in modified form, until today.

The earliest peoples identified in the Pecos classification were the "Basketmakers" of the Four Corners area, people who lived in pithouses and surface pueblos and were incipient farmers and hunters. There were two stages of Basketmaker culture, followed by five Pueblo periods, each distinguished by changes in architecture, community arrangement, pottery styles, and other artifacts. Pueblo IV and V straddled the first centuries of European contact and the transition from historical to modern Pueblo culture.

The Pecos classification was developed at a time when Southwestern chronology was still relatively imprecise. When more precise dates were forthcoming, it became apparent that the Pecos periods were better thought of as stages, which developed at different times in different local areas. Furthermore, the classification was better suited to the northern Southwest than to areas further south.

The Gladwin Classification. In 1934, Harold and Winifred Gladwin proposed another kind of culture classification, this time, a framework based on three broad "roots," the major cultural regional subdivisions of the Southwest: Basketmaker (later to be called Anasazi), Mogollon, and Caddoan (later named Hohokam). Each root was divided into "stems" which were major geographical areas. For example, the Basketmaker root contained "San Juan" and "Playas." Stems were split into even smaller units known as "branches." Each branch delineated a culture area within a stem such as "Chaco" or "Kayenta." These branches were divided into "phases," and generally named after local geographic features. Phases were units, defined by comparing individual culture traits from different sealed levels at different archaeological sites. The Gladwin classification grouped archaeological cultures by using culture traits, linked in space and time by a branching scheme that was almost genetic in nature – the assumption was that everything had started from a single root, then branched outward in a gradual evolution of Southwestern culture.

Gordon Willey and Jeremy Sabloff (1993) refer to the Pecos classification as "Chronologic" and the Gladwin scheme as "Chronologic-Genetic," a fairly apt description. The two systems were by no means incompatible, for the Gladwin hierarchy was a regional and local one, and the Pecos classification a useful way of generalizing over the entire area.

The Midwestern Taxonomic System. While Gladwin was wrestling with roots and stems in the Southwest, a group of Midwestern archaeologists under the leadership of W.C. McKern was developing a classificatory scheme for eastern North America. This was the famous Midwestern Taxonomic System, sometimes called the McKern Classification (McKern, 1939).

Midwestern archaeologists grappled with very different problems from those in the Southwest, notably an apparent lack of stratified sites and much poorer conditions of preservation. However, they had access to enormous numbers of artifacts from every millennium of the past, most of them without provenance, collected by private individuals and professional excavators alike.

The McKern scheme dealt not with time and space, but entirely with artifact classifications. Its architects assumed that formal similarities between artifact forms signified both cultural origins and cultural history. They proposed a taxonomic hierarchy that began with *components*, a unit of a culture complex that could be a site, or a distinct layer in a site. Several components were then grouped into a focus, components that shared high frequencies of similar culture traits. Foci were classified into *aspects*, broader groupings where there were still many culture traits in common. The highest levels in the McKern Classification were the *phase*, the *pattern*, and the *base*, all of them founded on increasingly more generalized cultural traits.

The Midwest Taxonomic System started off as just that – a taxonomic scheme, with no explicit chronological or spatial contexts at all. It was much criticized by Southeastern archaeologists, who had acquired a great deal of valuable time-and-space data during the great River Basin Surveys carried out during the Depression (Fagette, 1997). These ambitious surveys involved large quantities of data that were described minutely by James A. Ford and others (Ford and Willey, 1941). In time, however, the Midwestern system was found so effective that its rapidly multiplying taxonomic categories began to acquire chronological and spatial dimensions.

Seriation. The Midwestern system required, and still requires, precise methods for ordering artifacts through time – seriation. Seriation is based on two assumptions: that cultural change is gradual, and usually from the simple to the more complex, and that similarity between artifacts is a measure of their cultural relationship. The first American scholar to demonstrate the effectiveness of seriation was anthropologist Alfred Kroeber, who wrote a classic paper on potsherds he had collected from eighteen sites in the desert near Zuñi pueblo (Kroeber, 1916). He seriated these into six sub-periods by style and frequency of occurrence, arguing that his seriation showed that the cultural history of the Zuñi region resulted from "a steady and continuous development on the soil."

Leslie Spier (1917) refined Kroeber's work the following year and was the first person to use the term "seriation." His researches caused seriation to become standard archaeological practice in North American archaeology, not only for classifying potsherds, but also for pueblo architecture, stone

James A. Ford's stylized seriations of pottery-type frequencies. The table illustrates different types and tries to correlate pottery sequences from northeast Texas, Louisiana, and Florida.

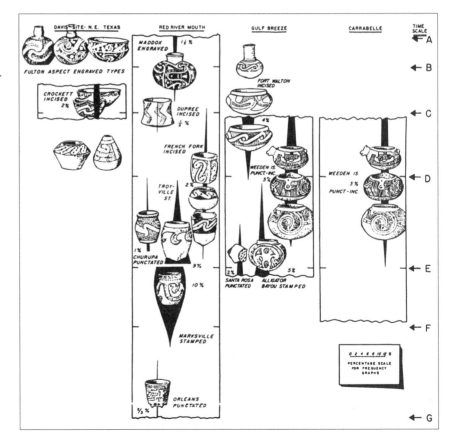

tools, and other artifact forms. The arctic archaeologist Henry Collins used both stratigraphic observation and the associations of ancient Eskimo settlements with ancient beach lines as a chronological framework to seriate bone and ivory tool forms over many centuries (Collins, 1937). One of the young fieldworkers with him was James A. Ford, who took seriation back with him to the Southeastern United States, where he developed elaborate artifact-based chronological schemes between the 1930s and 1960s.

As time went on, many important area syntheses appeared, each of them adding to the emerging, and increasingly bewildering, diversity of ancient North American cultures (for examples, see Deuel, 1935; Ford and Willey, 1941; Kidder, 1924; McGregor, 1941; Strong, 1935; and many others). From these pioneer syntheses emerged the fundamental principles of culture history and nomenclature that are in use today, among them chronological schemes like the familiar Archaic-Woodland-Mississippian terminology of the Eastern Woodlands (Griffin, 1946).

The 1920s through the early 1950s saw North American archaeologists focusing on sites, artifacts, and chronologies, with any form of speculation or theoretical discussion considered not only unnecessary, but intellectually unsound. Archaeology was basically a descriptive, historical methodology that paid lip service to anthropology. Many anthropologists considered it peripheral to their research. "Archaeology ... is always limited in the results it can produce. It is doomed always to be the lesser part of anthropology," wrote anthropologist E. Adamson Hoebel in a revealing and devastating comment of the day (Lyman and Dunnell, 1997).

Dating Ancient North America
1901 to 1960

We should not be surprised that the archaeologists of a half-century ago were preoccupied with chronology. Their preoccupation was similar to that of colleagues in every part of the world, simply because there were no reliable ways of dating the remote past. Until the 1920s, all absolute chronologies for ancient North America were based on intelligent extrapolation from historical records, and on guesswork, instinct, and an assumption that the first human inhabitants of the Americas were of relatively recent date (Meltzer, 1983). Artifact typology and seriation merely ordered cultural material in a relative chronological sequence, without being anchored to "true" dates.

The bastions of the short chronology crumbled in 1924, with the well-known discoveries at Folsom, New Mexico, that proved that early native Americans had hunted extinct forms of Plains bison. Soon estimates of 10,000 years for Folsom were considered not unreasonable, but there was still no accurate method of dating even recent archaeological sites. Even such comprehensive syntheses as those of Ford and Willey (1941) in the Southeast were based on very short time scales indeed, in the order of 2000 to 3000 years. It was the development of two accurate, easily applicable chronological methods that was to prove to be the catalyst for new approaches to North American archaeology. In both cases, these methods came to archaeology from the hard sciences.

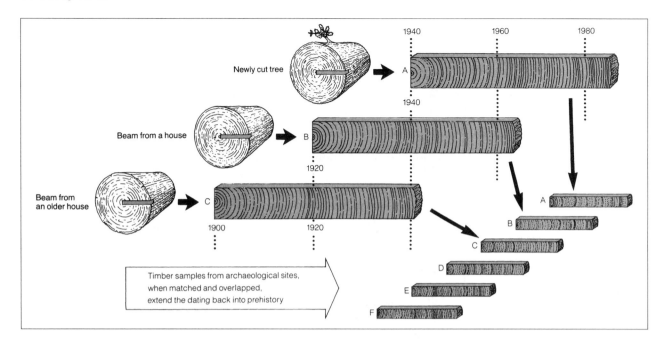

Timber samples from archaeological sites, when matched and overlapped, extend the dating back into prehistory

Dendrochronology: using tree-ring sequences to date North American archaeology.

Dendrochronology. Astronomer A.E. Douglass of the University of Arizona, Tucson, was interested in tree-rings as a means of dating sunspot activity. He began his research in 1901 with live trees, then searched for wooden beams preserved in ancient pueblos. By 1929 he had two tree-ring sequences, the one extending back from the present through Spanish contact into late Pueblo times, the other a chronology that was not anchored to historic trees, which covered a long period of earlier times. Douglass searched hard for the beams that would link his two tree-ring sequences, and eventually found a charred log of AD 1237 in a pueblo at Show Low, Arizona. Once he had secured his master tree-ring chronology, Douglass could apply dendrochronology (tree-ring dating) to ancient sites simply by comparing the ring sequences from their beams with the master sequence.

By the mid-1930s, later Southwestern cultures had an accurate chronology. Basketmaker II dated to before AD 500, Basketmaker III between AD 500 and 700, and the four Pueblo stages from AD 700 to 1600.

Dendrochronology was an important advance, albeit a local one, for the chronology it produced could not be expanded far beyond the Southwest and contiguous arid areas. It is only in recent years that more sophisticated methods have enabled the development of tree-ring chronologies based on oak trees and other temperate species in the Midwest and elsewhere, chronologies that act as a useful check on radiocarbon dates. The new tree-ring dates showed Southwestern scholars that the various periods of the Pecos classification were more stages of cultural development than precise time periods. For the first time, the archaeologist could study not just rigid cultural sequences, but such phenomena as rates of cultural spread and change, also minute changes in rainfall over long periods of time.

Radiocarbon Dating. Other than for the Southwest, dating the remote past was more-or-less a matter of intelligent guesswork and careful extrapolation backward from sites of known age. Then, in 1949, University of Chicago chemist Willard Libby published the new and revolutionary radiocarbon dating method (Marlowe, 1999). This operates on the principle that the radioactive carbon in the atmosphere is, and was, absorbed by all living organisms. This absorption ceases when they die, and a steady, and measurable decay of carbon then begins. Libby tested his new method with objects of known age like ancient Egyptian boats, then extended his tests to charcoal and other organic materials excavated in association with artifacts of unknown age. He found that he could date sites up to 40,000 or more years old. By the mid-1960s, radiocarbon dating was a routine procedure in every corner of the world.

It is no exaggeration to say that radiocarbon dating revolutionized North American archaeology. Within a few years of Libby's announcement, radiocarbon dates had shown that human beings had lived in the Americas for at least 11,000 years. Other samples filled in the chronological vacuum between Paleo-Indian and much later sedentary cultures such as the Mississippian of the Eastern Woodlands. The radiocarbon revolution was far more profound than merely an opportunity to date cultural sequences from all corners of the continent. It enabled the archaeologist to look at the rate of cultural evolution with far greater precision. It was a chance to compare rates of change in different places and in different environments, and an opportunity to compare cultural developments in widely separated areas. For the first time, one could move beyond simple cultural sequences and study the complex processes that triggered cultural change. Libby's discovery laid the foundations for the dramatic theoretical and methodological advances of the 1960s. The radiocarbon revolution took hold at a time when the sciences began to have an increasing impact on North American archaeology. Tree-ring dating was further refined, and is now used as a method of studying very fine-grained climate change in the Southwest. New, but still somewhat experimental, dating methods have been developed, among them paleo-magnetism, obsidian hydration, and thermoluminescence (for details of dating methods, see Fagan, 1999; Renfrew and Bahn, 2000).

Science and Archaeology
1950 onward

By the 1950s, many North American archaeologists had realized that the sciences had much to offer archaeology. Fossil pollens offered opportunities to study ancient environments, animal bones a chance to examine ancient subsistence activities. Closer collaboration with geologists, biologists, botanists, and other scientists led to numerous interdisciplinary research projects, which studied the evolution of human cultures against a backdrop of major climatic changes over the past 15,000 years (summary: Willey and Sabloff, 1993). This collaborative research yielded detailed results, especially when geomorphologists, pollen experts, paleontologists, and archaeologists cooperated in the field, as was, and still is, the case with the study of the Bering Land Bridge (see Chapter 4).

The development of quantitative approaches to artifact analysis, increasing use of computers, aerial photography, and remote sensing from space – these are but a few of the scientific methods that have had a profound effect on North American archaeology since the 1960s.

Method and Theory in American Archaeology

These experiments coincided with an explosion of archaeological research after World War II, partly as a result of massive federal flood control projects that had started before the war and continued into the 1950s. These works led to a great deal of salvage archaeological work carried out in advance of dam building, projects such as the Glen Canyon project in Utah (Jennings, 1966). Much more basic culture-historical data flowed from these projects, and also from important, purely academic researches of the 1940s and 1950s.

All these researches led to a proliferation of historical and developmental syntheses of ancient North America, the most famous of which was Gordon Willey and Philip Phillips' *Method and Theory in American Archaeology*, published in 1958. This classic work drew on years of gradually evolving area syntheses from the Southwest, the eastern United States, and on ideas developed in Mesoamerica and Peru. In it, Willey and Phillips referred to five broad developmental, or culture, stages, based not only on technology, but on economic data, settlement patterns, art traditions, and social factors, too. Chronology was less significant. These stages were:
— The Lithic (Paleo-lndian and other early cultural manifestations in the New World),
— Archaic (post-lce Age hunter-gatherers),
— Formative (village agriculture and/or sedentary life). There were two additional stages that did not exist in North America:
— Classic (urban development),
— Postclassic (imperialistic states such as the Aztec and Inca).

The Willey and Phillips scheme created a ferment of discussion, and was rejected by some archaeologists out of hand, and modified by others (Willey and Sabloff, 1993). Many scholars were unhappy with the strong evolutionary undertones of the work, an approach that had long lain dormant in American archaeology. The book was a sign of the times, for archaeology was on the move. Now the stage was set for new approaches that did not merely describe the past, but attempted to explain why ancient American cultures had changed, and how they had adapted to their very diverse environmental settings.

A Study of Archaeology

In 1948, W.W. Taylor published *A Study of Archaeology*, a detailed critique of archaeological approaches of earlier years. Taylor singled out Kidder's Southwestern research for attack, describing it trenchantly as a "comparative chronicle." Kidder never reconstructed life in the past, nor did he use his data to discuss functional matters, Taylor alleged. Not that Kidder alone was singled out for criticism. Taylor swept a broad brush across North

TABLE 2.1

Commonly Used General Subdivisions of Ancient North America

North American archaeologists commonly subdivide ancient times into broad cultural stages that are a terminological relic from earlier attempts at culture-historical reconstruction. Like the Three Age System in the Old World, the terms have little more than very general theoretical application in our data-rich scientific environment. Since they are still commonly used, and occur frequently in the pages of this book, we should define them in general terms here.

Two terms used throughout North America:

Paleo-Indian. Human cultures ancestral to later, Archaic developments. This very generalized term subsumes the first Americans, the Clovis people, and other pre-Archaic groups.
In strictly chronological terms, the boundary between Paleo-Indian and later cultures is usually about 10,000 years ago.

Archaic. Archaic cultures evolved from Paleo-Indian ones, to the point that the boundary between the two is often impossible to draw. Archaic peoples hunted smaller, more varied animals, placed greater emphasis on plant foods, and developed a toolkit for processing same. They also created increasingly diverse, and often specialized, adaptations to local environments. Archaic cultures survived in some parts of the western United States until modern times.

Two other terms are commonly used in the Eastern Woodlands culture area:

Woodland. Woodland subsumes many local adaptations. Generally, the label Woodland implies hunter-gatherer societies augmented with some cultivation, manufacture of some pottery, also more elaborate tools and art traditions, and cemetery burials, often associated with earthen mounds and more elaborate ritual and trade activities.
The Woodland continued in many areas of the east until European contact, but by AD 800 the **Mississippian** tradition replaces it in the Midsouth, between the Mississippi River and the Appalachians (see Chapter 20).

American archaeology, accusing its practitioners of being more concerned with artifact classification and chronology than with culture change or social behavior in the past. He proposed a new, "conjunctive" approach that used all possible lines of research to work on specific archaeological problems, problems with far wider focuses than merely pottery classification and chronological sequences, everything from settlement patterns to food remains.

Predictably, *A Study of Archaeology* raised many academic hackles, for many archaeologists sincerely believed that archaeological data were too limited for anything much more than classification and description. On the other hand, a significant number of scholars chafed under the narrow

TABLE 2.2

Culture–Historical Terminology

Major North American language groups (below right). The early 20th-century photographer Edward Curtis made a priceless record of American Indians (below, Yellow Owl [Mandan]; bottom, Sitting Bear [Arikara]).

There is no agreed-upon terminology for North American culture history. However, the following hierarchy of terms is in wide use, and is employed in this book:

Component. A culturally homogeneous stratigraphic unit within a site. A settlement occupied but once will consist of a single component, but one occupied four times will have four. Components occur at one location. To produce a regional chronology, one must synthesize components from different sites, using the next analytical step.

Phase. Similar components from more than one site. They are limited to a locality or region and span a relatively limited amount of time. Distinctive culture traits distinguish one phase from another. Phases enable one to establish regional contemporaneity, but, as time goes on and more discoveries are made, may be broken down into more and more precise sub-phases.

Archaeological Regions. Normally defined by natural geographic boundaries, archaeological regions usually display some cultural homogeneity. They are often defined by natural geographic features as well – for example, the Santa Barbara Channel region.

Culture Area. These define much larger tracts of land, and often coincide with broad ethnographic culture areas identified by early anthropologists. The Southwestern United States is one such area, in turn subdivided into distinctive sub-areas (see Chapter 13).

North American archaeologists also use two units that synthesize archaeological data over wide areas:

Horizon. Horizons link a number of phases in neighboring areas that

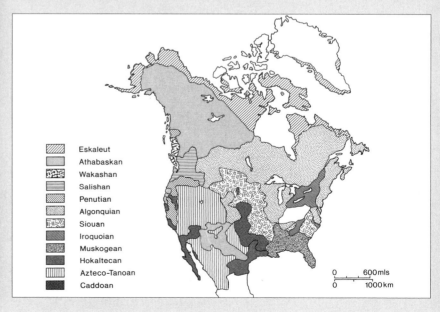

Eskaleut
Athabaskan
Wakashan
Salishan
Penutian
Algonquian
Siouan
Iroquoian
Muskogean
Hokaltecan
Azteco-Tanoan
Caddoan

0   600 mls
0   1000 km

Names of major groups and the main culture areas of North America: 1a Arctic, 1b Subarctic, 2 Great Plains, 3 Eastern Woodlands, 4 Southeast, 5 California, 6 Great Basin, 7 Southwest, 8 Northwest Coast, 9 Plateau. For the purposes of this book, 1a and 1b have been grouped as the Far North, 3 and 4 as the Eastern Woodlands, and 5, 8, and 9 as the Far West.

contain rather general cultural patterns in common. In some parts of the world, all-embracing religious cults may transcend cultural boundaries and spread over an enormous area. Their distinctive artifacts, like those of the famous Chavín art style of Peru (900–200 BC), can be identified in phases hundreds of miles apart.

Tradition. A widespread term in North American archaeology. It is used to describe a lasting artifact type, assemblages of tools, architectural styles, economic practices, or art styles that last much longer than one phase or even the duration of a horizon. Tradition implies a degree of cultural continuity, even if shifts in cultural adaptation have taken place in the meantime. A good example is the so-called Arctic Small Tool tradition of Alaska, dating to as early as 2000 BC (see Chapter 8). The small tools made by these hunters were so effective that they remained in use until relatively recent times.

restrictions of culture history (Ford, J., 1952; Spaulding, 1953). In 1958, Gordon Willey and Philip Phillips wrote that archaeologists had used such explanatory terms as "acculturation" (the assimilation of one culture by another) and "diffusion" (the spread of culture traits and ideas from one culture to another), but only in very local contexts. Few people had attempted generalizations, indeed "so little work has been done in American archaeology on the explanatory level that it is difficult to find a name for it." They proposed the term "processual interpretation" for such attempted explanations.

The publication of *Method and Theory in American Archaeology*, and of *A Study of Archaeology* marks an important watershed in North American archaeology, the end of a period of transition from arid culture-historical studies to a new era that focused not only on questions of "how," but on questions of "why" as well. With their insistence on multi-dimensional, problem-oriented research, more imaginative hypotheses, and their cautious flirtation with the then unrespectable notion of cultural evolution, these landmark essays paved the way for the theoretical debates and scientific approaches that now dominate North American archaeology.

Further Reading

Fagan, Brian M. 1977. *Elusive Treasure*. Charles Scribners, New York.
    A popular introduction to the history of American archaeology, which focuses on the Moundbuilders and Southwestern archaeology in the context of this book.
Lyman, R. Lee, and Dunnell, Robert C. 1997. *The Rise and Fall of Culture History*. New York: Plenum.
    A definitive assessment of the role of culture history in American archaeology.
Lyman, R. Lee, O'Brien, Michael, and Dunnell, Robert C. (eds.). 1997. *Americanist Culture History*. Plenum Press, New York.
    A useful anthology of key writings on culture history. Invaluable for serious students.
Meltzer, David J. 1983. "The Antiquity of Man and the Development of American Archaeology," *Advances in Archaeological Method and Theory*, 6:1-51.
    A detailed essay on the controversies surrounding the antiquity of humankind in North America, which contains an invaluable account of the emergence of government archaeology in North America.
Sabloff, Jeremy A. and Willey, Gordon R. 1993. *A History of American Archaeology*. 3rd ed. W.H. Freeman, New York.
    The best comprehensive source on the early history of North American archaeology. Especially strong on the development of culture history and classification.
Silverberg, Robert. 1968. *Moundbuilders of Ancient America: The Archaeology of a Myth*. New York Graphic Society, Greenwich, Connecticut.
    A well-researched and vividly written account of the Moundbuilder controversy for the general reader.
Willey, Gordon R. and Phillips, P. 1958. *Method and Theory in American Archaeology*. University of Chicago Press, Chicago.
    The classic essay on culture history in American archaeology. Essential reading for any serious student of the subject.

CHAPTER 3

NORTH AMERICAN ARCHAEOLOGY SINCE THE 1960s

The theoretical and methodological revolution that overtook archaeology in the 1960s began with three major developments that took hold in the preceding decade – cultural ecology, settlement archaeology, and environmental reconstruction.

Evolution, Cultural Ecology, and the Environment

During the 1940s and early 1950s, anthropologist Julian Steward searched for ways of identifying common cultural features in societies distributed in many parts of the world. In so doing, he assumed that certain basic types of culture would develop in similar ways under similar conditions. Steward was by no means the first anthropologist to think in terms of multilinear cultural evolution, but he added a new dimension to the discussions of cultural change – that of the natural environment. He looked to it for causes of cultural change, and spent much time studying the relationships between environment and culture, calling his new approach "cultural ecology."

Cultural ecology is based on three fundamental assumptions. First, similar adaptations may be found in different cultures when their environments are similar. Second, no culture has ever achieved an adaptation to its environment which has remained unchanged over any length of time. Third, differences and changes during periods of cultural development in any area can either add to societal complexity, or result in completely new cultural patterns (Steward, 1955).

Steward applied cultural ecology to the study of a fundamental question: why does the adjustment of human societies to different environments result in certain distinctive types of behavior? Thus, to diffusion, the spread of culture traits and ideas, and evolution, he added a new concept – changing adaptations to the natural environment. In other words, the study of culture change involved not only human cultures, but their changing environmental conditions as well. This entailed not only studying ancient environmental change and cultural adaptations, but shifts in human settlements on the natural landscape over long periods of time.

Steward himself was one of the first anthropologists to study human settlement patterns, in his case the distribution and annual ranges of Shoshone hunter-gatherers in the Great Basin. It was he who encouraged

TABLE 3.1

Stages of Socio-Cultural Evolution

All theories of cultural evolution are based on the premise that human societies have changed over long periods of time, and that the general trend throughout the past has been toward a greater complexity of human culture and social institutions. How, then, does one classify North American societies before European contact? The most widely accepted classification divides human societies into four broad categories – bands, tribes, chiefdoms, and states. This classification has won wide acceptance, but is much criticized for its arbitrary rigidity. Many archaeologists prefer a broader grouping:

Pre-State Societies. Societies on a small scale, based on the community, band, or village, which vary greatly in their degree of political integration. These societies lack the highly stratified class structure and other characteristic features of …

State-Organized Societies. Societies on a large scale with centralized social and political organizations, class stratification, and intensive agriculture. States have complex political structures and many permanent government institutions, with social inequality a reality. The Maya and Aztec civilizations of Mexico were state-organized societies.

Although the issue is much debated, it is safe to say that all ancient North American societies fell in the pre-state category. Only the Mississippian of the American Bottomlands was close to the critical economic, political, and social thresholds of an emerging state. Pre-state societies can be divided arbitrarily into three broad categories. *It should be stressed, however, that these categories are far too rigid to reflect anything more than the most general reality, and are little more than labels of convenience.*

Bands. Autonomous and self-sufficient groups that consist of fairly small numbers of people, usually a few families. This form of organization is highly adaptive for hunter-gatherers, people constantly on the move with

Harvard archaeologist Gordon Willey to carry out a large-scale survey of changing settlement patterns in the Virú Valley on the Peruvian coast in 1946, generally agreed to be the study that launched similar research all over the Americas (Willey, 1953). Since the 1960s, important settlement surveys have been carried out in the Southwest and other areas, many of them as a result of Cultural Resource Management projects.[1]

Environmental reconstruction was even slower to come to North American archaeology. This may be because there were no known spectacular waterlogged sites in North America at the time, sites that spurred pollen studies and other ecological approaches long used on

[1] Cultural Resource Management, the investigation of North American archaeology as part of the inventorying, salvage, and management of the archaeological record, is now the dominant context for archaeological research north of the Rio Grande. We cannot cover this complex topic here. For discussion, see Green and Doershuk, 1998.

band size varying constantly. Band societies are egalitarian, leadership coming from experience and personal qualities rather than political power.

In general terms, more complex pre-state societies are a form of transitional society between simple bands and elaborate, state-organized societies in their social and political complexity:

Tribes. Egalitarian societies, like bands, but ones that have achieved a greater level of social and cultural complexity, also mechanisms to accommodate more sedentary living, the need to redistribute food, and to organize some communal services. While some complex hunter-gatherer societies can be classified as tribal, most tribes were associated with village farming. Political, religious, and social authority is basically egalitarian, communal decisions being based on public opinion. The basic social and economic unit is the household, the nuclear family, and close kin that produce and store food. These kin links provide effective mechanisms for social control.

Chiefdoms. Societies headed by important individuals with unusual ritual, political, or entrepreneurial skills. In many cases, it is hard to distinguish them from tribes. Society is still kin-based, but is more hierarchical, with power concentrated in the hands of powerful kin leaders, who are responsible for redistribution of resources. Chiefdoms tend to have higher population densities, to display the first signs of social ranking, often reflected in more prestigious material possessions. Chiefdoms vary widely in their elaboration, the degree elaboration depending on many complex factors, including the distribution of the population over the landscape. Judging from their elaborate ritual artifacts and the large public works under their control, the major Mississippian chiefdoms were extremely elaborate societies, with complex social, religious, and political hierarchies.

Waldo R. Wedel, right, with George S. Metcalf at an archaeological site in Rice County, Kansas.

(Below left) Emil Haury, left, with Vance Haynes at the Paleo-Indian Lehner site, Arizona.

Scandinavian sites, and in the 1950s at Star Carr in northeast England (Clark, J.G.D., 1954). Waldo Wedel, a Plains archaeologist, was one of the first North Americanists to attempt environmental reconstructions, interpreting Plains subsistence patterns against a backdrop of changing environmental patterns on the grasslands (Wedel, 1953). Emil Haury at Ventana Cave in the Southwest, Jesse Jennings in Utah, and Robert Heizer in California were some of the other scholars who attempted descriptive rather than interpretive analyses of ancient environmental conditions, even of ancient diets (Willey and Sabloff, 1993).

Steward's cultural ecological approach was, perhaps, the most important theoretical development in North American archaeology in a century, even if his work could be faulted on several grounds, not least because he lacked a holistic, truly ecological view of ancient cultures. Modern schools of evolutionary ecology in North American archaeology have a direct ancestry in Steward's work.

Processual Archaeology

As younger scholars started examining the delicate and ever changing relationships between human societies and their natural environments, they cast around for theoretical models, borrowing models from biologists, ecologists, even sociologists. The impact of philosophers of science like Thomas Kuhn and Carl Hempel, and of general systems theory, began to be felt in archaeology during the 1960s. Systems theory was particularly attractive as a conceptual model, for it allowed an archaeologist to think of human cultures as complicated systems of interacting elements, such as technology and social organization, which interacted in turn with the ecological systems of which they were a part.

During the 1960s, Lewis Binford (1983) published a series of papers in which he argued for more rigorous scientific testing, for the development of independent methods for testing propositions about the past. He argued for the use of formal research designs, for scientific approaches that provided interaction among old data, new ideas, and fresh data that would enable archaeologists to pose research hypotheses. Working hypotheses were nothing new in archaeology, but Binford's approach was different because he advocated that these hypotheses be tested explicitly against archaeological data collected in the field, and against other hypotheses that had been rejected. Once a hypothesis was tested against raw data, it could join the body of reliable knowledge upon which further, more precise, hypotheses could be erected.

Binford and his many disciples also challenged the assumption that because the archaeological record is incomplete, reliable interpretation of the non-material and perishable components of ancient society and culture was impossible. Their argument was that all artifacts found in an archaeological culture occur in meaningful patterns that are systematically related to the economies, kinship systems, and other contexts within which they were used. Artifacts are far more than material items. Rather, they reflect many of the often intangible variables that went into determining the actual form of the objects preserved.

The debates over what came to be known as "processual archaeology" raged fast and furious in the 1960s and 1970s. Some scholars argued that archaeology was a science, whose objective was to study basic laws of human behavior. Other archaeologists viewed archaeology as examining the activities of past human beings, as a discipline that was less a science than a historical discipline with its own limitations, resources, and explanatory methods (Flannery, 1973a; Spaulding, 1973). Everyone agreed, however, that mathematical models, statistical approaches, and rigorous scientific methods would become ever more important.

Processual archaeology, with its strongly materialist and ecological approach, has become a mainstream framework for much North American archaeology. Research designs are far more sophisticated than those of a generation ago. Highly technical scientific techniques like isotope analysis and remote sensing are commonplace. But frustration remains, for many of the rich theoretical expectations of the 1960s remain unfulfilled (Dunnell, 1982). Archaeology, like the other social sciences, is undergoing the same kind of change that biology went through a generation ago – a serious attempt to assemble a body of theory for archaeology as distinctive as that for physics and other established sciences (Trigger, 1989).

Part of the current theoretical debate in archaeology revolves around the relationship between the archaeological record of the present, and the human behavior of the past. Archaeology is unique among the sciences in that it relies on inference for interpreting the past. We can study that past only by means of material evidence that has been changed by centuries, even millennia, underground. How, then, can we explain the archaeological record? Ethnographic analogy and ethnoarchaeology play a vitally important role in this process.

Ethnographic Analogy and Ethnoarchaeology

North American archaeologists use analogy on many levels. In a simple one, someone infers that carefully pressure-flaked Paleo-Indian points are spearheads, because there are ethnographic records of peoples making

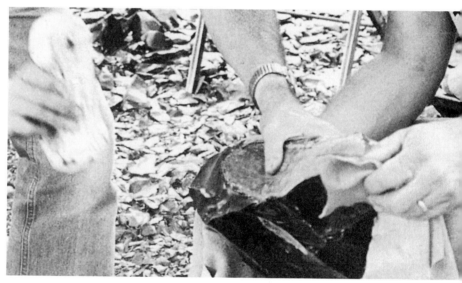

Experimental archaeology is one way in which archaeologists study the relationship between the archaeological record of the present and the human behavior of the past. Lithic expert Jeffrey Flenniken demonstrates the making of a Folsom point replica. A hammerstone (above) reduces the large obsidian cobble to a series of flakes suitable for point manufacture. Using careful percussion and pressure flaking (left), the projectile blank is shaped until the final channel flake can be removed using a punch, resulting in the finished artifact (right).

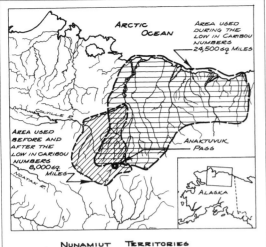

Ethnoarchaeology: Lewis Binford's research among the Nunamiut of Alaska. (Above) Binford's map of Nunamiut hunting territories before and after the 1910 crash of the local caribou population. The people's response to food stress was to triple the territory they covered to obtain food. Note the location of Anaktuvuk Pass, where Binford carried out detailed research. (Right) Map of the Anaktuvuk Pass area showing, among other sites, the three locations illustrated on these two pages: Tulugak Lake, Hunting Stand R&B (no. 6 in the key), and the Mask site. (Above right) Hunting Stand R&B revealed a caribou skin-bed where a man slept while his partner watched for game.

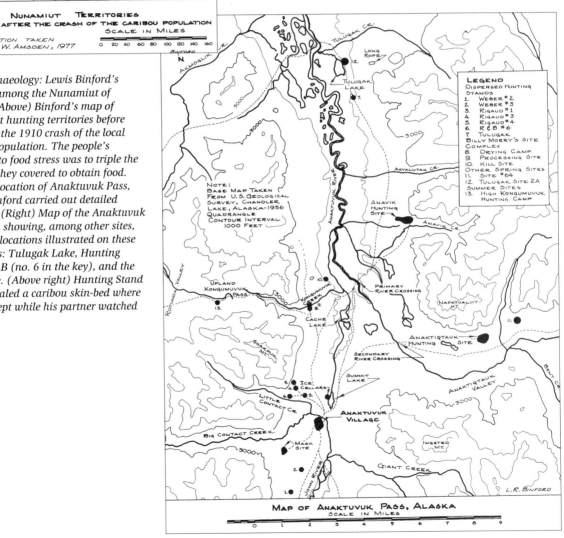

LEGEND
DISPERSED HUNTING STANDS
1. WEBER #2
2. WEBER #3
3. RIGAUD #1
4. RIGAUD #3
5. RIGAUD #4
6. R&B #6
7. TULUGAK
BILLY MORRY'S SITE COMPLEX
8. DRYING CAMP
9. PROCESSING SITE
10. KILL SITE
OTHER SPRING SITES
11. SITE #64
12. TULUGAK SITE 2A
SUMMER SITES
13. HIGH KONGUMUVUK HUNTING CAMP

NOTE:
BASE MAP TAKEN FROM U.S. GEOLOGICAL SURVEY, CHANDLER LAKE, ALASKA-1956 QUADRANGLE CONTOUR INTERVAL 1000 FEET

AK-MOGLIK R.
TULUGAK CR.
LONG ROPE
TULUGAK LAKE
AKVALUTAK CR.
ANAVIK HUNTING SITE
ANAVIK CR.
ANAKTUVUK RIVER
ROTUNDO VALLEY
UPLAND KONGUMUVUK PASS
KONGUMUVUK CREEK
CACHE LAKE
PRIMARY RIVER CROSSING
NAPKTUALUIT MT.
SOAKPUK MT.
SECONDARY RIVER CROSSING
ANAKTIQTAUK HUNTING SITE
ANAKTIQTAUK VALLEY
BENT CR.
ICE CELLARS
LITTLE CONTACT CR.
SUMMIT LAKE
ANAKTUVUK VILLAGE
BIG CONTACT CREEK
MASK SITE
JOHN RIVER
INGSTED MT.
GIANT CREEK

L.R. BINFORD

MAP OF ANAKTUVUK PASS, ALASKA
SCALE IN MILES
0 1 2 3 4 5 6 7 8 9

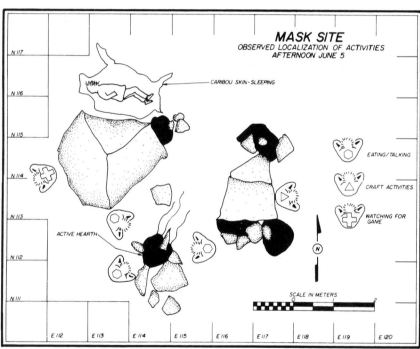

Nunamiut ethnoarchaeology (continued). (Above) "Soldier rocks" were used by the Nunamiut to form a caribou drive line running up the mountainside east of Tulugak Lake in Anaktuvuk Pass. (Right) Binford's drawing of various Nunamiut activities observed by him at the Mask site, Anaktuvuk Pass, on a spring afternoon. Studies such as this have helped ethnoarchaeologists assemble a mass of empirical data to aid in the interpretation of archaeological sites.

MASK SITE
OBSERVED LOCALIZATION OF ACTIVITIES
AFTERNOON JUNE 5

CARIBOU SKIN-SLEEPING

EATING/TALKING

CRAFT ACTIVITIES

WATCHING FOR GAME

ACTIVE HEARTH

SCALE IN METERS

broadly similar points for the tips of lances. This form of simple, and commonly used, analogy is a far cry from claiming analogies between the ways in which an ancient culture used the spearpoint and the ways in which a living society uses it. To do the latter is to assume that the relationship between the form and the function of the artifact has remained static over the centuries. If you explain the past simply by analogy with the present, then you are assuming that nothing new has been learned.

Analogy is based, ultimately, on the Direct Historical Method, the notion of working back from the present into the remote past (Wylie, 1985). Direct historical analogies are highly effective with historic sites, such as, for example, the Colonial village at Martin's Hundred, Virginia, where textual sources provided valuable analogies about house ownership and other details of the archaeological record (Nöel-Hume, 1982). Such analogies lose much of their effectiveness as one moves back further in time.

The selection of appropriate analogies from the ethnographic literature is only one step in the quest for interpretation. Ethnoarchaeology, and to some degree controlled experimentation, have added important new dimensions to analogy as it is practiced today.

Ethnoarchaeology, sometimes called "living archaeology," is the study of contemporary societies to aid in the understanding and interpretation of the archaeological record. In a way, it is a logical extension of the Direct Historical Method in that it uses the present to throw light on the past. By living in, say, an Eskimo hunting camp and observing the activities of its occupants, the archaeologist hopes to record archaeologically observable patterns, knowing what activities brought them into existence. Lewis Binford lived among the Nunamiut people of Alaska, hunters who gain over 80 percent of their subsistence from caribou hunting. He wanted to find out as much as he could about "all aspects of the procurement, processing, and consumption strategies of the Nunamiut Eskimo and relate these behaviors directly to their faunal consequences" (Binford, 1978). Binford chose to concentrate on animal bones rather than artifacts, because, although the bones were not humanly manufactured, their use patterns were the result of cultural activity.

Thanks to studies of actual Nunamiut hunting, of their intimate knowledge of caribou anatomy, and of existing and "archaeological" camps and caches, Binford assembled an enormous mass of empirical data on human exploitation of animals that was applicable not only to the Nunamiut and other caribou hunters, but to the interpretation of archaeological sites elsewhere. He showed how local cultural adaptations could be, how the Nunamiut depended on interacting topographic, climatic, logistical, and other realities. He showed how changes in stone tool frequencies or pottery forms may reflect no significant change in adaptation at all. It is impossible to tell without understanding the strategies behind the local adaptation through time. And such understandings can be obtained only from sites where food remains and other such data are available.

Controlled experiments include replications of stone tool reduction strategies, such as those used to make Paleo-lndian projectile points, experiments with maize cultivation in the Southwest, and with the construction and then controlled burning of Mississippian houses in the Midwest. All of these controlled experiments are designed to give archaeologists the kind of objective data that will be needed to understand the static archaeological record, as studied in the dynamic present.

Post-Processual Archaeology

We are currently in a period of sometimes intense debate about a new generation of archaeological theory to amplify the processual approach of the 1960s and 1970s (anthologies of key writings: Preucel and Hodder, 1997; Whitley, 1998). A diverse school of "post-processual" archaeologists argues that we can no longer interpret the past purely in terms of ecological, technological, and other material considerations. Culture is interactive, created by people as actors, who create, manipulate, and remake the world they live in. We are doing this ourselves in the rapidly changing industrial societies of today, where ethnic identity, gender roles, and social inequality are constant issues in daily life. Surely, post-processualists point out, the same kinds of behavior marked the diverse societies of the past and played a major role in the creation of civilizations and myriad societies large and small, simple and complex.

Processual archaeology uses multilinear cultural evolution on the widely held assumption that all human societies progress, in the long term, from the simple to the more complex. Post-processual schools of thought are more "horizontal" in their thinking. The thinking shifts constantly, but in general post-processualists are more concerned with the *meaning* of ancient cultures and the diversity within them than with general, more "vertical" models of increasing cultural complexity, which emphasize individual power and social ranking.

Post-processual archaeology contributes three important elements to our study of ancient North America:

- Culture is interactive, the result of people's actions, whether individuals, groups, or entire societies.
- We cannot interpret culture change without examining the hitherto neglected perspectives of what have been called "the people without history," including women, ethnic minorities, and anonymous, illiterate commoners.
- Archaeologists, whatever their cultural or political affiliation, bring their own cultural biases to their interpretations of the past. In other words, there is no such thing as a totally dispassionate take on ancient societies. Many Westerners believe that science offers the broadest perspective on human history. Others consider the Old Testament the literal historical truth. Native Americans often discount scientific archaeology and prefer their own world view. All archaeologists can do is act as active mediators of the past.

Every post-processual archaeologist grapples with a fundamental question: can one study the development of human consciousness, religious beliefs, and the whole spectrum of human behavior – what has been called "the archaeology of mind" – from the material remains of the past? How does one bring together the best of scientific, processual approaches with the more all-embracing, sometimes instinctual, methods of post-processualists? The archaeology of mind includes all those aspects of ancient culture that are the product of the ancient mind. This includes cosmology, religion, ideology, iconography, and all forms of human intellectual and symbolic behavior.

The archaeology of mind will never be an easy undertaking. Pursuing the people of the past and their intangible behavior requires large data sets, excellent preservation, and sophisticated theoretical models. The pursuit is often frustrating and relies on a broad array of scientific methods from dozens of scientific disciplines, among them botany, nuclear physics, and zoology. The processual approach with its cultural systems may give one a better understanding of what archaeologists know, but this is useless without a better comprehension of what human behavior produced the archaeological record. For example, there may have been far greater variation in human behavior than processual archaeologists allow for. Human behavior is far from orderly, is not always trending in a direction of more complexity, and yet is not entirely random. The debate, and research, continues.

Cultural Resource Management

North American archaeology is at an important turning point at the beginning of the 21st century. We are entering an era of sadly diminished archaeological resources, when our primary responsibility is to act as stewards of the past for future generations. Almost all archaeology in North America is now conducted as part of Cultural Resource Management projects. We have become aware that native Americans have strong views about the interpretation of their past, that we do not have a monopoly in ancient North America. At the same time, the destruction of the archaeological record in North America has been of epidemic proportions for generations, in the face of rapid urban development, large-scale agricultural and mining activity, and also widespread pot-hunting. In many areas of the continent, few undisturbed archaeological sites remain for future archaeologists, as the archive of native American history erodes daily.

(Below) A wide variety of excavations in North America are undertaken as Cultural Resource Management projects. At this site in Charleston, South Carolina, a backhoe is used to reveal the mid-18th-century brick foundations of a sugar house. Project conducted by New South Associates for the City of Charleston.

Wanuskewin Heritage Park. (Above) On-site excavation undertaken by the University of Saskatchewan archaeology laboratory. Nineteen pre-Contact sites have been discovered at Wanuskewin. (Top) View of Wanuskewin Heritage Park visitors' center which houses exhibits exploring the archaeology and history of the Northern Plains Indians.

In the face of widespread destruction, fieldwork has become more selective, as stewardship of the archaeological record, and of stored finds, becomes of paramount importance. Future years will see an upsurge in collection-based research, which draws not only on artifacts, but on the archives of field notes which document their excavation. At the same time, both the federal government and states are becoming increasingly aggressive in their prosecution of looters and pot-hunters, who still ravage many parts of North America virtually unchecked. Not even Civil War battlefields or 19th-century factory sites are exempt from collectors of spent cartridges, military buttons, and bottles. There are no short-term solutions to the looting problem. What is needed is a massive effort to change social attitudes toward archaeology and the collecting of artifacts. And that requires the fundamental reordering of both professional and educational priorities.

Cultural tourism is becoming a major factor in North American archaeology, especially in Canada, where Parks Canada and provincial authorities are well aware of the economic potential of interpretative centers, museums, and archaeological exhibits. The famous Head-Smashed-In Buffalo Jump in southern Alberta (Chapter 6) shows thousands of tourists a year how Blackfoot and earlier Plains groups engaged in cooperative hunting. Wanuskewin near Saskatoon, Saskatchewan, is another cultural center sited on the edge of a small valley, where the visitor can experience the many facets of the environment exploited by ancient and recent groups. Local native Americans played a leading role in developing Wanuskewin. While Canada leads the world in its sensitive depictions of native peoples, the United States lags behind, partly because federal and state government has chosen not to invest heavily in archaeological tourism. Increasingly, however, archaeologists are becoming involved in this area of public archaeology, on the grounds that it will help preserve the archaeological record.

A generation ago, North American archaeology was largely an academic discipline. Now it is rapidly becoming a profession. Without question, the greatest change in recent years has resulted from a dramatic shift from academic research to fieldwork conducted under the general rubric of Cultural Resource Management (CRM). The earliest "rescue" or "salvage" projects dated from the river basin surveys of the 1930s, and from pioneer projects like the Glen Canyon survey in Utah in the 1950s (Jennings, 1966). Since the National Historic Preservation Act of 1968 and the promulgation of Executive Order 11593 in the early 1970s, CRM has become the dominant enterprise in North American archaeology, to the point that more archaeologists work in non-academic settings than in colleges or universities (Zeder, 1997). CRM in its implementation is very different from academic archaeology, with its closely drawn contract requirements and deadlines (the latter often very tight), need for legal compliances and mitigation measures (King, T., 1998). CRM has raised important practical and theoretical questions that are only now beginning to be addressed.

CRM projects take many forms, from small one-day investigations covering a single city lot to multiyear projects covering entire river drainages in the Southwest. On the face of it, there are potentially serious conflicts between the academic objectives of archaeology and those of any CRM project which is born, after all, from legal requirements. Furthermore, many of the reports generated by CRM fieldwork are of limited circulation, or even, in extreme cases, not circulated at all. Thus, large quantities of new information about North America's past are inaccessible to the wider audience. Fortunately, efforts have been made in recent years to address this situation, while some major CRM projects have produced notable publications with strong theoretical underpinnings, like, for example, the remarkable Lower Verde Project in Arizona (Whittlesey and others, 1997) and many CRM archaeologists contribute to important academic projects (Jones and others, 1999).

Apart from emerging shifts in theory and training, CRM has had a notable impact on field methods, especially in the use of such advanced technologies as subsurface radar and Geographic Information Systems. It has also opened up entirely new, and important, research topics, including urban archaeology in such cities as New York and Annapolis, Maryland, and African-American archaeology. CRM is the new face of archaeology, increasingly conducted in the private sector, and a healthy development, for it has taken the study of America's remote past out of the ivory tower (see Green and Doershuk, 1998).

Archaeology and Native Americans

All societies have an interest in the past. It is always around them, haunting, mystifying, tantalizing, sometimes offering potential lessons for the present and future. The past is important because social life unfolds through time, embedded within a framework of cultural expectations and values. In the high Arctic, Inuit preserve their traditional attitudes, skills, and coping mechanisms in some of the harshest environments on earth. They do this by incorporating the lessons of the past into the present. In many societies, the ancestors are the guardians of the land, which symbolizes present, past, and future. Westerners have an intense scientific interest in the past, partly borne of curiosity, but also out of a need for historical identity. There are many reasons to attempt to preserve an accurate record of the past, and no one, least of all an archaeologist, should assume that they are uniquely privileged in their interest in the remains of that past.

We have no monopoly on history. Native American views of archaeology cover the whole spectrum, from violent revulsion to profound interest in the objectives and findings of the science (Swidler and others, 1997). Many American Indians resent the cavalier attitudes of excavators in the past and regard "scientific" accounts of ancient North America (such as that outlined in this book) as a formulation of Western science and irrelevant to their culture and to their lives. They believe their view of the world, based as it is in cyclical time and on a close relationship between the living and spiritual worlds, offers them an adequate explanation of human existence. They also point out that many archaeologists have chosen to ignore oral traditions, a major source of native American history and legend. Many native Americans have a deep suspicion of archaeologists, calling the identification of different ancient societies from pottery styles "mere white man speculation and fiction" (Deloria, 1992). They resent being treated like scientific specimens, and, one must admit, they have a point. At the same time, they are deeply concerned at the invasion of sacred sites by New Agers and other folk on bizarre spiritual quests. In rare instances, Indian spiritual leaders are contacting archaeologists whom they trust to assist in the recording of such sites before they are destroyed or dispersed.

Most human societies of the past were non-literate, which meant that they transmitted knowledge and history orally, by word of mouth. Many oral histories are mixtures of factual data and parables which communicate moral and political values. But to those who hear them, they are publicly sanctioned history, performed before a critical group, and subject to the critical evaluation of an audience who may have heard the same stories before. (A valuable anthology of native American literature: Swann, 1994.)

All too often, the archaeologist and a local community have different interests in the past. To the archaeologist, the past is scientific data to be studied with all the rigor of modern science. To local people, the past is often highly personalized and the property of the ancestors. Such histories are valid alternative versions of history, which deserve respect and understanding, for they play a vital role in the creation and reaffirmation of cultural identity. And they raise a fundamental question, which lies behind many native American objections to archaeological research. What do archaeologists, usually outsiders, have to offer to a cultural group which already has a valid version of their history? Why should they be permitted to dig up the burials of the ancestors or other settlements and sacred places under the guise of studying what is, to the people, a known history? It is a question that archaeologists have barely begun to address. We should never forget that alternative, and often compelling, accounts of ancient times exist, which play an important role in helping minority groups and others to maintain their traditional heritage as it existed before the arrival of the Westerner. Certainly, anthropological perspectives of past cultures need to be integrated into archaeological theory in collaboration with native Americans, so that we interpret the past in a useful manner, of interest to more than just archaeologists (Dongoske and others, 1997).

Reburial and Repatriation. For generations, many native American communities have been incensed by the excavation of ancient burials and the desecration of sacred places by archaeologists, with scant concern for American Indian culture (McGuire, 1992). They have pushed for laws forbidding grave excavation and compelling reburial or repatriation of excavated skeletons. The result was the Native American Grave Protection and Repatriation Act of 1990 (NAGPRA) (Powell and others, 1993). Under this Act, all federal agencies and museums receiving federal funds are required to inventory their holdings of native American human remains and associated grave goods, and all "objects of cultural patrimony". The inventory process will attempt to establish the cultural affiliations of their holdings, and, in the case of skeletons, direct lineal connections with living native American groups. If such relationships are established, then the organization is required to notify the relevant native American organization and offer them the opportunity to repatriate the material. A second requirement protects all native American graves and other cultural objects found within archaeological sites on federal and tribal land. The Act also requires consultation with native American authorities over the disposal and treatment of any finds, whether made during scientific investigations or by accident.

NAGPRA is having a profound effect on North American archaeology. The Native American Rights Fund estimates there may be as many as 600,000 native American human skeletons in private and public collections. Archaeologists and anthropologists worry that much of their scientific database for studying such topics as ancient diseases and diet will be lost for ever with systematic reburial of ancient populations. They argue that reburial would deprive future generations of vital scientific information. Others, including many archaeologists, believe that reburial and repatriation are ethical issues and should outweigh any scientific gain. (The recent controversy over the Kenniwick skeleton in Washington State is a good example.[2]) While there are points to be made on both sides, native Americans feel strongly about repatriation for many reasons, not least because they wish to preserve traditions and values as a way of addressing current social ills. Many of the issues concern basic questions about the morality of archaeological research. Certainly, no archaeologist in North America will be able to excavate a site or a historic burial on federal or state land without close consultation with native Americans and working with them in ways that archaeologists had not imagined until recently. While, in some instances, such consultation may prevent some research and some excavations, there is no question that nothing but good will come of a close working relationship between native Americans and those who excavate their sites.

The sometimes angry polarization of archaeologists and native Americans is slowly giving way to a new era in which both groups cooperate, albeit sometimes cautiously. But once trust is built, the results can be rewarding. The Hopi, Navajo, and Zuñi Nations of the Southwest have their own Cultural Resource Management programs, and other groups are following suit. The future of North American archaeology lies in collaborative research, in which

---

[2] An 11,000-year-old burial found by accident in river deposits on federal land was examined hastily by scientists and said to display unusual "Caucasian" features. Local Indian groups protested at the removal of the bones, a confrontation with archaeologists and government officials resulted, and the matter ended up in court. At the time of writing, the bones are being studied under close scientific and native American supervision, but the ultimate fate of the bones is undecided.

native Americans play a leading role. And, to a considerable degree, research policies and access to archaeological sites and finds will be under their direction.

Intellectual Trends

A number of important intellectual trends have emerged in recent years and are resulting in new perspectives on ancient North America. We can only mention them briefly here.

Gender. The issue of gender and engendering archaeology has assumed growing importance in recent years. Archaeologists have long studied people and households, but only recently have turned their attention to the complex issue of gender and gender relations, a promising avenue of new research. Gender is not the same as sex, which refers to the biological male or female. Gender is socially and culturally constructed. Gender roles and relations acquire meaning in culturally and historically meaningful ways. This means that gender is a vital part of human social relations and a central issue in the study of ancient human societies.

The expression of gender varies from society to society and through time. Some archaeologists, like Joan Gero and Margaret Conkey (1991), write of "engendering archaeology," an attempt to reclaim men and women in non-sexist ways in the past. This goes much further than merely demonstrating that pots were made by women, stone projectile points by men, or trying to identify women's activities in the archaeological record. The archaeology of gender deals with the ideology of gender, with roles and gender relations – the ways in which gender intersects with all aspects of human social life. How are roles and social relationships constructed? How did men and women contribute to ancient societies? An engendered archaeology uses a wide diversity of archaeological methods and approaches to find how out gender "works" in ancient societies, to unravel its cultural meanings. Such research is still in its infancy in North American archaeology and is limited mainly to local studies (see bibliography and analysis in Nelson, S., 1997).

Short-term Climate Change. Paleoclimatology has taken giant strides in recent years. Ice and deep-sea cores, tree-rings, and pollen analysis now provide us with increasingly fine-grained portraits of long- and short-term climate change over the past 15,000 years. For the first time, archaeologists can study such developments as cultural complexity among West Coast foragers, the Anasazi dispersals, Southeastern chiefdoms in the context of such events as the Medieval Warm Period of about 1000 years ago and the Little Ice Age (*c.* AD 1400 to 1850), and even major El Niño events.

Calibrated Radiocarbon Dates. Willard Libby revolutionized archaeology with radiocarbon dating in 1949. A half-century later, radiocarbon dating has become a more precise tool, thanks to the advent of accelerator mass spectrometer (AMS) dates, which allow the dating of even tiny seeds. At the same time, calibration tables for radiocarbon dates, using tree-rings, tropical corals, and ice cores extend back earlier than 15,000 years, even if calibrations before about 8000 BC are still somewhat imprecise. One immediate effect of this has been to extend some Paleo-Indian cultures like Clovis 2000 years further back into the past (Chapter 4). New calibration tables released in 1998 (see Preface) will make for a more accurate chronology of ancient North America.

Evolutionary Ecology. More accurate chronologies and new paleoclimatic data go hand-in-hand with an array of emerging theoretical approaches based on evolutionary ecology (for discussion, see Broughton and O'Connell, 1999). This kind of research focuses on the interactions between evolutionary forces and evolutionary variables as specific human adaptations develop over time. The archaeologists using this approach are concerned with explaining behavioral variability – behavioral ecology – in the past. They ask specific questions about ancient human behavior and use a series of hypotheses revolving around benefits and costs of such behavior in a model of an optimal behavior pattern (discussion: Chapter 11). Evolutionary ecology is proving especially productive in the western states.

Ideology and Religious Beliefs. The accelerated CRM research of recent years has yielded enormous quantities of new archaeological data, much of it from regional surveys. As a result, archaeologists can now focus on major explanatory questions such as the sudden emergence of chiefdoms or the meaning of ancient mortuary customs in ways that were inconceivable even a decade ago. A new generation of research into the Mississippian tradition of the Mid-South and Southeast uses cosmology and ethnographic data to offer completely new interpretations of Cahokia, the most spectacular archaeological site in North America (Chapter 20). Post-processual theory plays an important role in such research.

Tragically, North American archaeology is realizing its full potential at a time when the finite archaeological record is vanishing almost uncontrollably before our eyes. All of us, whether professional, avocational archaeologist, or lay person, have a responsibility to ensure the survival of ancient North America for as yet unborn generations.

Further Reading

King, Thomas F. 1998. *Cultural Resource Laws and Practice: An Introductory Guide.* Altamira Press, Walnut Creek, CA.
   A basic guide to legislation surrounding antiquities in the United States. An invaluable volume.
Swann, Brian. (ed.). 1994. *Coming to Light.* W.W. Norton, New York.
   Swann's anthology of native American literature is the best yet.
Swidler, Nora, and others. (eds.). 1997. *Native Americans and Archaeologists: Stepping Stones to Common Ground.* Altamira Press, Walnut Creek, CA.
   Essays on archaeology and native Americans by archaeologists and others.
Trigger, Bruce G. 1989. *A History of Archaeological Thought.* Cambridge University Press, Cambridge.
   A definitive history of archaeological theory placed in a wider scientific context.
Whitley, David S. (ed.). 1998. *Reader in Archaeological Theory: Post-Processual and Cognitive Approaches.* Routledge, London and New York.
   A useful anthology of basic writings on recent archaeological theory.

PART TWO

THE PALEO-INDIANS

"In this isolated land [the past] has been a hoary hermit, to the verge of the newest creations of nature and the latest institutions of man. The flint utensils of the Age of Stone lie upon the surface of the ground … The peoples that made and used them have not yet entirely disappeared."

SAMUEL HAVEN
(1864)

CALIBRATED YEARS	RADIO-CARBON YEARS AGO	NORTHEAST ASIA	NORTH AMERICA			
			ALASKA	WEST	PLAINS	EASTERN WOODLANDS
9368 —	8000 —			WESTERN EARLY ARCHAIC	EARLY PLAINS ARCHAIC	EARLY ARCHAIC
9968 —	9000 —	SUMNAGIN CULTURE	PALEO-ARCTIC TRADITION			
12,285 —	10,000 —			REGIONAL PALEO-INDIAN STYLES		DALTON
			NENANA COMPLEX			
c. 13,500 —	11,000 —			CLOVIS	CLOVIS	CLOVIS
						?Meadowcroft
c. 14,000 —	12,000 —			Manis	Monte Verde (Chile)	
		D'UKTAI CULTURE				
16,800 —	13,000 —		?? FIRST SETTLEMENT			
17,000 —	14,000 —					

These tables are intended as a general guide only. Not all sites, phases or cultural terms used in the text appear in these tables. The following key is used throughout the tables:

——————— Well-established chronology. Time span may continue beyond the line.

———————| Limit of the chronology is generally agreed.

- - - - - - - - - Chronology doubtful.

CLOVIS   A name in capital letters is an archaeological culture, horizon, or tradition.

Meadowcroft   A name not in capital letters is an archaeological site.

CHAPTER 4

FIRST SETTLEMENT

After five years' research on the problem of the first Americans, this author was moved to write (1987) that "Anyone studying the first Americans sets sail in hazardous academic seas, beset on every side by passionate emotions and contradictory scientific information." This most fundamental of issues in North American archaeology is among the most controversial, and we summarize the main areas of agreement and disagreement in this chapter (for a detailed analysis, see Dillehay, 2000; Dillehay and Meltzer, 1991; Meltzer, 1989).

Stone Age Foragers in Asia
30,000 to 14,000 years ago

Despite some unsubstantiated claims to the contrary, only anatomically modern humans, *Homo sapiens sapiens*, settled in the Americas. Their arrival was the end result of cultural developments in northeast Asia and much further afield (Fagan, 1990).

There is general agreement that modern humans spread widely over the Old World and into the Americas as part of a general expansion of Stone Age hunter-gatherers into arctic latitudes after about 40,000 years ago, during the last cold snap of the Würm glaciation.[1] No one knows exactly when Stone Age groups adapted to the vast, treeless arctic plains that stretched northeast from eastern Europe and the Ukraine during the late Würm, but it was at least 35,000 years ago. These plains extended into arid central Asia and Siberia, places of limited glaciation, nine-month winters, and endless steppe-tundra, a distinctive, open landscape with sparse, arid grass and cottonwood scrub cover. Small, local river valleys and drainages may have supported stands of willowbrush, with deltas and coastal flats near large lakes and some sea coasts. This arctic landscape supported a sparse diversity of game animals – mammoth, woolly rhinoceros, musk ox, steppe bison, reindeer, and wild horse, animals that were the staple of Stone Age hunters for millennia.

It was *Homo sapiens sapiens* who developed the technology and the social institutions that enabled widely scattered hunting bands to live permanently in this extremely cold environment with its widely dispersed

[1] The last glaciation is known as the Würm in the Old World, and the Wisconsin in North America. This terminology is used here.

In order to survive the bitter winters of the west Eurasian plains at the height of the last Ice Age, modern humans cooperated in the construction of substantial base camps. The 18,000-year-old Mezhirich site, on the Dnepr River in the Ukraine, has yielded the remarkable complete remains of oval dwellings built out of mammoth bone. Partially dug into the ground for insulation, these structures would have had a final roof covering of hides and sod.

game herds. Each group covered very large distances, resulting in a rapid expansion of Stone Age hunters over the steppe-tundra from the west. The concentrations of game animals changed constantly through the year, so human populations would gather and disperse according to the season, and the need for cooperative hunting. The result was remarkably standardized Stone Age culture over enormous areas.

Mal'ta and D'uktai (Dyukhtai). Two major clusters of Stone Age sites provide our best clues to Stone Age settlement in Siberia. One lies near Lake Baikal in the Trans-Baikal, typified by the Mal'ta settlement, occupied between about 21,000 and 20,000 years ago. The Mal'ta people were mammoth hunters, whose dwellings and lifeway were strongly reminiscent of big-game hunters in the Ukraine far to the west (Gerasimov, 1935).

The second cluster comes from the Middle Aldan Valley in extreme northeast Asia. Here, there is said to be evidence of human occupation from as early as 35,000 years ago, perhaps even earlier, but there is some controversy over the dates (Mochanov and Fedoseeva, 1996). Yuri Mochanov (1977) has excavated D'uktai Cave on the Middle Aldan, where mammoth and musk-ox hunters lived between about 14,000 and 12,000 radiocarbon years ago. Unfortunately, Mochanov's early dates come from much churned-over river terrace deposits and may be unreliable, but some authorities accept them (West, 1996).

Many American and Russian archaeologists believe that the D'uktai culture is no older than about 25,000 to 18,000 radiocarbon years ago, and

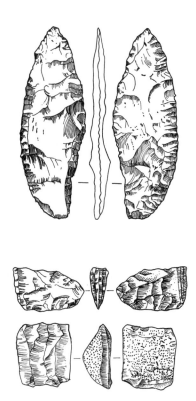

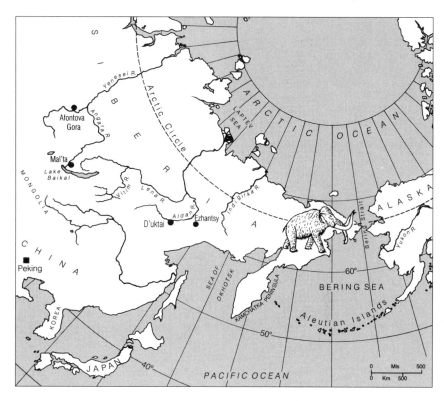

Northeast Asia: map of relevant sites (above right), and D'uktai tools (above) from Verkhene-Troitskaya, Siberia (a biface, top, and two wedge-shaped microblades; length of biface 14 cm).

that it was widespread over northeast Asia about 14,000 radiocarbon years ago. The D'uktai toolkit includes well-made bifacial (bifacial: flaked on both sides) projectile heads and knives, large stone choppers that probably served as butchery tools, and numerous wedge-shaped and disc-shaped cores used to produce small "microblades," used as stone inserts for hunting weapons (Hoffecker and others, 1993).

Most D'uktai sites date to the closing millennia of the Würm glaciation. They lie between the Angara River in the west, as far south as the Amur Valley on the Manchurian border, on the coastal plain of the Sea of Okhotsk, even in the Kamchatka Peninsula, and perhaps in Japan. There are also late Stone Age sites with microblades in northern China that date between 30,000 and 15,000 radiocarbon years ago, reaching an even higher level of technological sophistication between 15,000 and 10,000 radiocarbon years ago (Chung and Pei, 1986). In short, D'uktai-like microblade technology was widespread in northeast Asia during the late Würm, even if there was widespread local variation on a common technological tradition. Some D'uktai-like artifacts, including microblades and the wedge-shaped cores used to produce them, also occur in Alaska, across the Bering Strait, but they appear to be of later date than in Siberia. There were also biface traditions in maritime northeast Asia and Japan, but it is still not clear how these relate to early biface assemblages in Alaska. Does this mean, then, that the first Americans originated, ultimately, among late Stone Age hunting traditions in northern China and inner Asia? We can evaluate this hypothesis from two directions, one biological, the other archaeological.

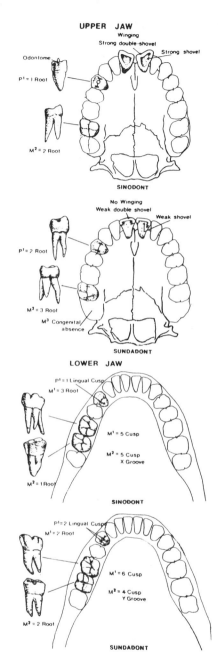

Dentochronology: Sinodonty and Sundadonty. Sinodonts display strong incisor shoveling (scooping out on one or both surfaces of the tooth), single-rooted upper first premolars, and triple-rooted lower first molars.

Sinodonts and Amerinds

Physical anthropologist Christy Turner (1984, 1986) has examined the teeth of thousands of ancient and modern individuals from Old World and New, specimens going back as far as 25,000 years ago and to Paleo-Indian times. He points out that ancient Americans display fewer variations in dental morphology than do eastern Asians, and their crown- and root-trait frequencies are similar to those of northern Asians. The three "Sinodont" (Chinese-like teeth) groups share incisor shoveling, double-shoveling, single-rooted upper first pre-molars, and triple-rooted lower first molars, among other features.

Sinodonty only occurs in northern Asia and the Americas, not among the Mal'ta people of Lake Baikal, or in the Stone Age Ukraine. Turner argues that the northern Chinese may have evolved from a southeast Asian population, people they resemble more closely than the eastern Siberians and native Americans who evolved in turn from the northern Chinese. He used statistical calculations based on dental morphology to date the approximate moments at which Sinodont populations split off from the ancestral Chinese groups. The first of these divergences, Turner believes, led to the migration of Sinodonts into Mongolia about 20,000 years ago, and across the Bering Strait about 14,000 years ago.

Turner's dental work gains support from both genetic and linguistic researches. Mitochondrial DNA has proved a useful tool for calibrating mutation rates and studying human genealogies, because it is inherited through the female line and accumulates mutation rates much faster than nuclear DNA. Mitochondria trace modern human ancestry back to tropical Africa at least 150,000 years ago, while no fewer than five mitochondrial DNA lineages are shared by ancient and modern native American populations in North and South America. The molecular biologists believe that all native Americans are descended ultimately from a single, somewhat diverse group of Asians, who were most closely related to modern Mongolians (Merriwether and others, 1994; Stone and Stoneking, 1998). But the date for this genetic migration is not established accurately, because different researchers have assumed different mutation rates. Estimates range from 40,000 to 20,000 years, with expert Mark Stoneking preferring a fast mutation rate formula that gives a date between 19,000 and 11,000 years ago. This agrees fairly well with Turner's dentition estimate.

Back in 1956, the Stanford linguist Joseph Greenberg proposed that most North American and all South American languages were part of a single, large "Amerind" family. Aleut-Eskimo and Na-Dene were quite separate linguistic groups, making a total of three for the whole of the Americas. Greenberg then spent years compiling a vast database on the vocabulary and grammar of the 140 families of American Indian languages, which confirmed his belief that there were three linguistic groups that corresponded to migrations into the Americas. Greenberg estimates that his Amerind group arrived before 9000 BC, Na-Denes around 7000 BC, and that Aleuts and Eskimos diverged about 2000 BC (Greenberg and others, 1986; Greenberg, 1987). Greenberg's research has been severely criticized by other linguists, but is widely accepted. It does not seem to contradict either the dental or genetic evidence (Goddard and Campbell, 1994).

There is substantial, if superficial, agreement between the biological and linguistic evidence. What, then, of the archaeological data? At present, though Stone Age groups were in southern Siberia around Lake Baikal as early as 40,000 years ago and perhaps earlier, there is no solid evidence for northern Siberian sites dating to earlier than 18,000 radiocarbon years ago, and sophisticated microblade sites appear to be later than that. There are suspected technological links between northern Chinese and Siberian microblade sites, but these are still ill-defined. The only possible link may be a very general, adaptive one. Paleontologist Dale Guthrie believes (1982) that D'uktai microblades were inset into antler shafts as slotted points. He links the distribution of microblade production to that of reindeer hunting. Could it be that this inset-weapons system emerged in China and other parts of eastern Asia, in Siberia, and northwestern America, as a widespread adaptation to tundra conditions, where migratory reindeer herds roamed? Perhaps, he argues, the widespread microblade tradition reflects a widely shared and successful material culture that emerged at the very end of the last glaciation and flourished well into Holocene times.

The most likely ancestors for the first Americans were Sinodont late Stone Age hunter-gatherers with a dental and genetic morphology remarkably like that of the modern American Indians. They subsisted off big-game, smaller animals, perhaps fish and sea mammals, and some wild vegetable foods. At some point, a few of these people, perhaps no more than a few families, walked or paddled eastward across the Bering Strait into North America. David Meltzer has argued persuasively (1989) for migratory "dribbles" of early settlers, for many tiny population movements, some of which failed. On these general points, there is little disagreement. The date of first settlement is another matter, for archaeologists divide sharply into two schools of thought – those who believe settlement took place well before the end of the Ice Age some 15,000 years ago, and those who argue for first occupation at about that time.

Beringia

Some 18,000 years ago, when world sea levels were more than 300 ft (91 m) lower than today, a vast, low-lying landmass known to geologists as Beringia linked Siberia and Alaska. Central Beringia was an exposed coastal plain, denuded and dissected by many rivers, that covered the floors of the Chukchi Sea and the northeast Bering Sea. This was the famous Bering Land Bridge, commonly believed to be the land route by which human beings first reached the Americas (Hopkins and others, 1982; Schweger, 1990; West, 1996).

The Bering Land Bridge has a complicated geological history, known both from land-based studies and deep-sea cores. These cores show that the last glaciation began about 100,000 years ago, with a gradual cooling trend that exposed the land bridge from about 75,000 to 45,000 years ago. A lengthy period of less cold climate ensued from about 40,000 to 25,000 years ago, when the land bridge was no more than a narrow, periodically flooded isthmus. Bitter cold returned as sea levels fell about 25,000 years ago. This time, parts of the land bridge lasted until around 11,000 years ago. During this last period of intense cold, the windy land bridge stretched

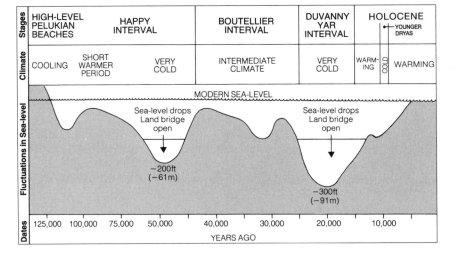

Climate and sea-level fluctuations over the past 125,000 years in the Bering Strait areas.

from Asia to Alaska, and covered much of the Chukchi Sea. Its southern coastline extended from the Gulf of Anadyr in Siberia to the Alaskan Peninsula in North America.

As sea levels rose at the end of the Ice Age, the geography of the land bridge changed dramatically. The Bering Strait and Gulf of Anadyr were submerged when the sea level rose to −157 ft (−48 m). Much of the Siberian coastline assumed its modern appearance about 10,000 years ago, but the North American coastline was still up to 63 miles (100 km) offshore at the very threshold of modern times.

The low-lying land bridge was no landscape of gently waving grass, where half-naked hunters pursued big-game from Asia into a new continent. Beringia was a treeless, arctic land, covered with a patchwork of very different types of vegetation. Palynologists are sharply divided on the nature of this plant life. Paul Colinvaux (1980) thinks the land bridge was sparse tundra, "a dusty plain, stretching to the horizon, vegetated between the bare patches with a low mat of sedges and grasses looking like a drier version of arctic plain." An arctic tundra fauna lived on the plains, a fauna somewhat similar to the rodents of the modern tundra. Such large mammals as existed were outliers of much larger populations that lived in more hospitable terrain in neighboring Asia and Alaska.

Palynologist Steven Young (1982) and Dale Guthrie (1990) take a less pessimistic view. They think that the land bridge was part of a now vanished ecosystem where many different animal species lived in productive harmony, just as they do on the African savanna today. Young and Guthrie argue that the land bridge was a mosaic of steppe rather than tundra, with shallow ponds and swamps in the center and south, where grass-dominated wetlands might have attracted large herbivores in summer. Several large rivers, among them the Anadyr and the Yukon, once crossed the land bridge. They would carry huge amounts of spring and summer glacial meltwater, creating great flood plains, where abundant fodder would have grown. The land-bridge environment was somewhat drier and more steppe-like than modern-day Alaska, an environment capable of supporting large mammals (Matthews, 1982).

Recently, a 400-square-mile (1,000-sq.-km) patch of the Beringian landscape of 17,000 years ago has come to light under a thick volcanic ash. The

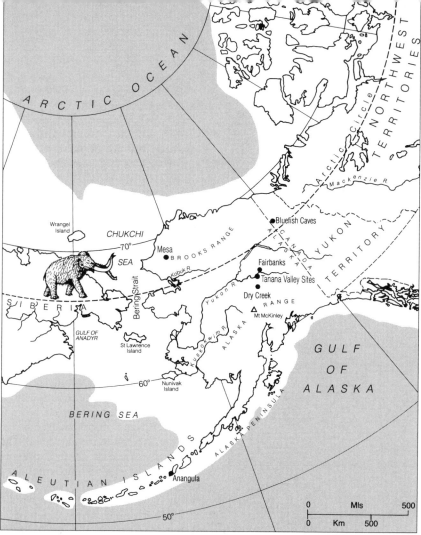

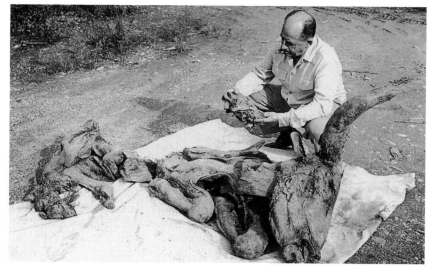

Beringia (untinted area of map, above right) and its bestiary. The Ice Age bestiary is known from fossil discoveries, frozen animal carcasses and Eurasian cave paintings and engravings. (Above) Ice Age deposits all the way from Europe to Siberia and Alaska yield the remains of – from top to bottom – woolly mammoth, steppe bison, wild horse, and reindeer/caribou, all seen here as depicted by Upper Paleolithic artists in southwest France. (Right) Paleontologist O.W. Geist examines a hide fragment and bones from the partial carcass of an extinct bison (Bison crassicornis) found during gold mining operations on Dome Creek, near Fairbanks, Alaska, in 1951. The hide was subsequently radiocarbon-dated to around 31,400 years ago.

plant samples include grasses, sedges, mosses, and many other varieties in a nearly continuous ground cover, just as Guthrie predicted. But the root mat was thin with no soil formation, meaning that the plant cover enjoyed little long-term stability, as Colinvaux had suggested (Geotcheus and others, 1994). Whatever the precise environment, it was certainly a region of violent climatic extremes and strong winter winds, which may have kept animal and human population densities low. James Hoffecker and others (1993) have gone so far as to argue that a shortage of firewood during the late Ice Age would have inhibited human settlement until warmer temperatures saw trees becoming established in Beringia.

Whether or not all the animals in this fauna existed together in Beringia at one time is highly uncertain. Matthews points out (1982) that bison, caribou, mammoth, and horse, also two forms of musk ox, a wild sheep, and arctic predators made up a mammalian community with twice as many species as that of the modern tundra. The land bridge could have supported a diversity of herbivores, provided it had sufficient variety, and quantity, of plant communities to do so. It never teemed with game animals, for they were probably scattered through the landscape, concentrated at dozens of special sites, in lowland meadows and near rivers. They would have succeeded one another, utilizing patches of the bare, treeless environment in an endless succession of grazing patterns that persisted as long as the continental ecosystem of the land bridge remained intact.

Hardly surprisingly, no archaeological remains have yet come from the floor of the Bering Strait, so we can only assume that there was once a sparse human population dwelling on the land bridge, preying on the great herbivores that lived there. There may have been coastal settlements on the southern shores, too, settlements now flooded by rising sea levels, where people might have taken fish and sea mammals. However, without effective canoe technology, they would have been severely limited in their ability to take maritime resources. In all likelihood, the first Beringians were big-game and, perhaps, sea-mammal hunters, practicing a lifeway that had flourished for thousands of years on the steppe-tundra. When human beings first set foot on the land bridge remains a complete mystery, but, given the present dates for D'uktai sites in Siberia, it may have been after 18,000 radiocarbon years ago. And, at some point afterwards, some of these people hunted their way across to higher ground in the east and ultimately into the Americas. At present, it is not possible to give an even slightly precise date for this crossing. Alternatively, it may have been a response to the rapid flooding of the land bridge after 14,000 years ago, although it was at least partially in existence until around 11,000 years ago.

The Younger Dryas

Recent years have seen a revolution in our knowledge of short-term climatic change at the end of the Ice Age, derived from ice cores, pollen analysis, coral studies, and the now-accurate calibration of early radiocarbon dates (Fiedel, 1999). In the light of newly precise dates, and additional evidence of unusually high ratios of radiocarbon in the early

Holocene, there have been major revisions of the dates for the Clovis culture and other early archaeological sites in the 14,000- to 10,000-year range.[2]

When the last cold episode of the Ice Age ended about 14,700 years ago [cal], widespread global warming ensued, followed by an abrupt cold snap. Paleoclimatologists divide the earliest part of the Holocene (Greek: *holos,* "recent") into two phases:

***Bølling-Allerød Interstadial** (c. 14,700 to c. 12,500 years ago [cal]).* This 2000-year-period saw dramatic global warming, massive ice-sheet retreats, sea-level rises, and much higher temperatures. It conventionally marks the end of the Würm/Wisconsin glaciation.

***Younger Dryas Interval** (c. 13,000 to 11,650 years ago [cal]).* The Younger Dryas witnessed a dramatic fall in temperatures, back to near-glacial conditions in a mere decade or so. This 1100-year-long cold snap ended as abruptly as it began with the onset of warmer conditions.

The short Younger Dryas cold snap may have had an effect on early settlement (Fiedel, 1999).

First Settlement of Alaska and the Yukon Territory

About 20,000 years ago, glaciers covered the Alaska Range and the Alaska Peninsula, as well as the Brooks Range, but much of the land immediately east of the Bering Strait was dry and ice-free. Some archaeologists believe these ice-free areas of Alaska were uninhabitable during late Wisconsin. Others have considered Alaska little more than a passageway, a "natural highway" to more temperate latitudes. In fact, a sparse population spread over this vast arctic landscape, adapted to it in many ways, and evolved distinctive cultures over very long periods of time indeed. Unfortunately, the archaeological potential of Alaska and the Yukon has hardly been tapped. The level of speculation about first settlement vastly exceeds the amount of archaeological data. Only a handful of sites give us clues (summary in Rainier, 1995).

Broken Mammoth, Mead, and Swan Point are three locations in the Tanana Valley, 60 miles (97 km) southeast of Fairbanks. Charles Holmes and David Yesner have investigated these sites, which were temporary encampments on well-drained ridges overlooking marshy lowlands where

---

[2] Recent advances in radiocarbon-date calibration and climatic research are producing new dates for the Clovis culture and other early societies, in the order of 2,000 years earlier than generally accepted even a year ago (Fiedel, 1999). In this chapter, I have used the new chronology where available and appropriate, labeling calibrated dates in brackets as such [cal]. Unless otherwise designated, dates in years in this chapter should be assumed to be in radiocarbon years, with the possible (and variable) 2000-year inaccuracy this may imply. This is an interim measure, until a new calibrated chronology is widely available and accepted. The general arguments in this chapter are little affected by the new time scale. It should also be mentioned that the calibration scale for radiocarbon dates based on tree-rings has, until very recently, extended back little more than 8000 years. As a general, and I stress general, rule, adding 2000 years to a radiocarbon date in this chapter will approximate the new calibrated chronology (see "Note on Radiocarbon Dates" at the beginning of the book for the general conventions for calibrated dates used in this work).

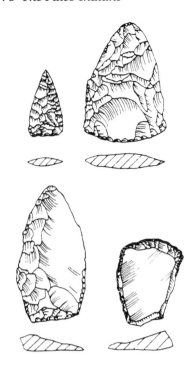

Nenana Complex tools from Dry Creek, Alaska. Clockwise, from top left: small triangular point, large triangular point, end scraper on a blade, and lanceolate point (length of end scraper 5 cm).

game would have grazed in summer (Holmes, C., 1996; Holmes, C., VanderHoek, and Dilley, 1996). Each site contains stratified occupation layers containing stone tools and animal bones. The Tanana sites contain not only stratified levels, but bone, ivory, and even a bone needle. AMS dates from the three locations place the earliest occupation to between 11,700 and 11,000 years ago, with the most likely date being about 11,700 years ago (about 13,700 years ago [cal]). The Swan Point levels contain unmistakable microblades as well as swan bones, which means that some form of terrestrial flyway between the heart of North America and Alaska existed at this time – an argument for the existence of some form of ice-free corridor with ample water and marshes at the time.

Dry Creek on the Nenana River Valley in the northern foothills of the Alaska Range contains two radiocarbon-dated levels. The earliest, Dry Creek I, dates to about 11,200 radiocarbon years ago, and contains some cobble and flake tools, also broken blades, thin bifacial knives, and points. Roger Powers compares the artifacts to tools from the Kukhtyi III site in eastern Siberia, a site belonging within the D'uktai tradition (Powers and Hamilton, 1978). Dry Creek II above dates to about 10,700 years ago, and contains microblades and other artifacts associated with such technology. The Moose Creek site in the same general area contains bifacial projectile points and dates to about 11,200 years ago (about 13,200 years ago [cal]), contemporary with Clovis peoples far to the south.

Walker Road, about 10 miles (16 km) north of Dry Creek in the Nenana River Valley has been AMS-dated to between 13,400 and 13,100 years ago [cal]. Walker Creek's cultural occupation, stratigraphic position, and age is similar to that of Dry Creek I. Two concentrations of stone tools, including small bifacial points and scrapers, but no microblades, cluster around small hearths and represent a single Nenana occupation (Goebel and others, 1996).

There are other possible early sites, including the Mesa location in the Brooks Range (Kunz and Rainier, 1995), but their dating is still uncertain.

Broken Mammoth, Dry Creek, and Walker Road belong within a generalized, and as yet poorly defined, "Northern Paleo-Indian Tradition," which is thought of as a northern equivalent of the Paleo-Indian traditions to the south. Roger Powers and John Hoffecker (1989) place Dry Creek I in the so-called Nenana Complex, assemblages with bifaces dating in the Nenana Valley to between 11,800 and 10,500 years ago. The new calibrated chronology for the Nenana Complex is in the 13,950 to 13,450-year range, making it near-contemporary with Clovis far to the south. In all probability, Nenana is a local variant of the Northern Paleo-Indian Tradition but both are distinct from the Paleo-Arctic Tradition, which subsumes the many microblade traditions widespread in Alaska after and perhaps before 13,000 years ago [cal].

At present, there is no evidence for the human settlement of Alaska and the Yukon before 15,000 years ago [cal]. This raises the possibility that eastern Beringia was settled only when Stone Age people retreated to higher ground as the land bridge was progressively submerged after 14,000 years ago [cal]. If the paucity of sites is any guide, the initial human population was tiny. Only after about 13,000 years ago [cal] do a variety of Paleo-Arctic occupations appear throughout Alaska. In contrast, the Siberian interior was dominated by the microblade tradition of the D'uktai culture from at least 18,000 radiocarbon years ago. Whatever the actual direction of migration, however, what is known from the archaeological evidence meshes well with what we know of the human biology and linguistic history of the first Americans.

If one was to use a global terminology, the earliest Alaskan archaeological sites would belong within the Upper Paleolithic, a term used to describe late Ice Age cultures and technology over a broad area of Europe and Eurasia. Under this argument, the Clovis Paleo-Indian tradition of North America, with its links to projectile-point-using groups in Alaska 13,500 years ago [cal], also belongs in the Upper Paleolithic, thereby confirming the Siberian origin of the earliest native Americans (West, 1996).

Ice-Free Corridors and Continental Shelves

During the late Wisconsin, when the Bering land bridge was exposed for the last time, northern North America was mantled by the vast Cordilleran and Laurentide ice sheets. The Laurentide was centered on Labrador and the Keewatin areas of Canada, a complex glacial mass fused into a single icebound wilderness with an ever-changing margin that extended from the Atlantic coast, along the southern shores of the Great Lakes, into southeastern Alberta. The mountain ranges of Alaska and British Columbia were also heavily glaciated, forming the Cordilleran glacial complex in the west that extended to about 30 miles (48 km) south of Seattle by about 14,500 years ago. For at least 10,000 years after 25,000 years ago, these icy barriers would have inhibited travel between Beringia and the ice-free zones to the south.

In the 1950s, Canadian geologists reported that Cordilleran ice did not fuse with the western margins of the Laurentide, creating an "ice-free corridor" (sometimes called the Mackenzie Corridor) between them. This corridor was absorbed by the popular imagination, and became, in the minds of some, a kind of Paleo-Indian superhighway to the south, where mammoths and people traveled. This appealing picture is a geological myth, for the boundaries of the ice sheets are slowly being mapped, revealing only a partial corridor, and one that was very inhospitable indeed (Bobrowsky and Rutter, 1990; Burns, 1996). Rugged terrain, mazes of meltwater lakes, crumbling rocks, and only the scantiest of vegetation and few game animals – there was little incentive to travel through this ice-free zone at the height of the late Wisconsin. If human beings did travel south, the most likely times for them to do so would have been either before the last glacial maximum beginning 25,000 years ago, or soon after 15,000 years ago, as the ice sheets began to retreat. Recent research has suggested that the corridor may have been quite wide by 14,000 years ago (Holmes, C., 1996).

If the ice-free corridor was an inhospitable and late migration route to the south, what about other paths? Recent evidence suggests that long stretches of northern coastline from the Kuril Islands off Japan to Beringia and south through the Aleutians were more extensive 13,000 years ago than was once

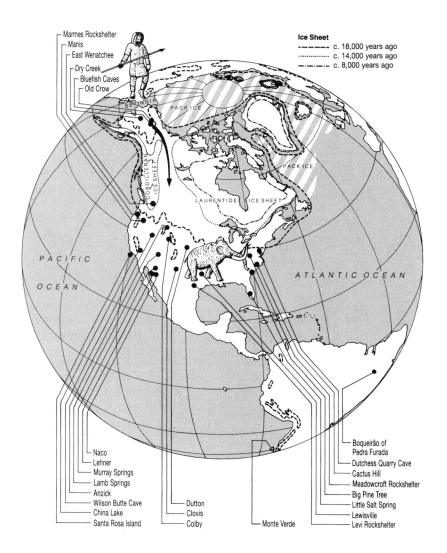

Major early archaeological sites and other locations in the Americas during the last stages of the Ice Age, when human colonization took place. The routes that humans used to move south are still uncertain. One much discussed and controversial route is shown here: the widening corridor between the Cordilleran and Laurentide ice sheets.

suspected. Some of these might have sustained biologically rich and diverse coastal environments that might have sustained Ice Age travelers. Furthermore, much of southeastern Alaska and British Columbia was deglaciated by 12,000 years ago. Canadian archaeologist Knut Fladmark has uncovered traces of human occupation on the Queen Charlotte Islands of British Columbia, and suspects that human occupation of this region may date to as early as 10,000 to 12,000 years ago. He points out (1983) that the Pacific coast of North America was relatively warmer and more productive than other shores. Perhaps, he speculates, the ice-free Pacific coast could have sustained human life, especially societies that used skin boats and other technological innovations adapted to the pursuit of marine mammals. Unfortunately, there is no evidence that such societies existed in late Wisconsin Beringia, although, of course, their settlements may have been submerged by rising sea levels.

The case for early coastal settlement is still unproven, for many of the most promising locations lie under modern sea levels.

The Case for Human Settlement Before 15,000 Years Ago

Those who believe that the human settlement of the Americas took place before 15,000 years ago, either during the late Wisconsin, or even earlier, are faced with the problem of documenting such activity in stratified, properly dated archaeological contexts. It is only fair to say that no archaeological site dating to earlier than 15,000 years ago in any part of the New World has received complete scientific acceptance – for a variety of highly complex reasons (for discussion, see Dillehay, 2000; Fagan, 1987; Meltzer, 1993).

The most widely discussed claims for early settlement come not from North America, but far to the south, from northeast Brazil and northern Chile. Among the numerous rockshelters from the Piaui area of northeastern Brazil is Toca do Boqueirão da Pedra Furada, a large rockshelter with a stream channel cutting through it. There is abundant evidence for later occupation in the shelter, artifacts such as knives and scrapers made on exotic chert or flint. The putative earlier occupation consists of "crude" artifacts made on local rocks such as quartz and quartzite that are extremely hard to identify as being of human manufacture. Charcoal from the stream-deposited lower levels has been dated to as early as 40,000 years ago, and is claimed to come from hearths (Guidon and Delibrias, 1986). Boqueirão da Pedra Furada bristles with unanswered questions – what were the forces that fashioned the artifacts from the stream-deposited lower levels? Is the charcoal from these levels naturally formed, or the result of human activity? Why did the earlier inhabitants of the shelter prefer coarse quartz and quartzite when much finer-grained rocks were available a short distance away? North American experts on the first Americans, who have visited the site and studied the excavations argue that the earliest human "occupation" is the result of local geological forces and not the result of human activities at all (Meltzer and others, 1994). Neither Pedra Furada nor any of the other Central and South American sites claimed as evidence for pre-15,000-year-old settlement stand up to rigorous scientific scrutiny. There is even debate as to what constitutes valid criteria for establishing such occupation (Dillehay and Meltzer, 1991).

In recent years, there has been a widespread, if tacit, acceptance of a date for first settlement at around 15,000 years ago, but it is only fair to say that there is little firm evidence for any date earlier than about 14,500 years ago.

A Scenario for First Settlement after 15,000 Years Ago

Until recently, the earliest firm evidence for first settlement coincided with the Clovis tradition, long radiocarbon-dated to between 11,200 and 10,900 years ago. But new discoveries and a dramatic redating of the end of the Ice Age with recalibrated dates has placed the entire timescale of first settlement back about 2000 years (Fiedel, 1999). The scenario laid out here is based on this new, tentative chronology.

While Clovis is widely accepted as the first widespread Paleo-Indian culture, there are a series of earlier sites which provide some evidence for somewhat earlier settlement.

Monte Verde, Chile. Tom Dillehay of the University of Kentucky investigated the Monte Verde site in Chile, which lies alongside a low-lying creek that was occupied by people living off game animals and vegetable foods between 14,050 and 13,600 years ago [cal] (12,000 to 11,800 years ago radiocarbon readings) (Dillehay, 1997). The occupation includes wooden huts, hearths, and a wishbone-shaped structure, associated with bone and stone artifacts. The artifacts are very simple, some little modified from their natural state and it is by no means certain that all of them are humanly manufactured. None of the Monte Verde toolkit bears any resemblance to later Clovis artifacts elsewhere. Monte Verde is widely accepted as an early human site (Meltzer and others, 1997).

Calibrated radiocarbon dates associated with fishtail-like projectile points, which derive from Clovis prototypes at caves like Cueva de Medio in Patagonia, are in a somewhat later 13,000-to-12,300-year range (Fiedel, 1999).

North America: Meadowcroft Rockshelter in southwestern Pennsylvania was occupied from at least 12,000 until nearly 700 radiocarbon years ago, and perhaps from much earlier. James Adovasio (1982, 1984) excavated this large shelter meticulously between 1973 and 1977, revealing no fewer than 11 strata, dated by more than 70 radiocarbon samples. The lowest level containing traces of human occupation is known as Stratum IIa. Adovasio and his colleagues divide this into three subunits. The uppermost dates to between about 10,950 and 7950 radiocarbon years ago. It is separated from Middle Stratum IIa by a layer of rock spalls from the roof and walls of the shelter. This middle zone accumulated between about 12,950 and 10,950 radiocarbon years ago, while the lowermost subunit, again sealed by rock spalls, has yielded seven radiocarbon dates ranging from 19,600 to 13,230 radiocarbon years ago.

The geologist and archaeologist Vance Haynes (1980) and other critics questioned the dates from the earlier strata, arguing there was a danger they contained large percentages of soluble humic acids, or "dead" carbon in the form of coal particles. The reason the humates were earlier is because acids in groundwater were permeating, or had in the past permeated, Stratum IIa. Other critics suggested that there might have been stratigraphic mixing in the lower levels. Adovasio and his colleagues (1990), in a line-by-line rejection of these criticisms, published not only accelerator dates from the lowest (pre-human) level and from later strata that are consistent with other readings, but also produced a conservative averaging of the radiocarbon chronology. This gave a minimum age for the presence of humans in the 12,000-to-10,600 radiocarbon years ago range. An averaging of the six deepest radiocarbon dates associated with cultural materials suggests, controversially, that humans were at Meadowcroft between about 14,555 and 13,955 radiocarbon years ago.

Some critics of Meadowcroft believe that the small samples of flora and fauna from the early levels are types that flourished in the area after the ice sheets retreated. Adovasio counters by pointing out that the site lies in a

Meadowcroft Rockshelter, Pennsylvania. (Top) Miller lanceolate (unfluted, lance-shaped) projectile point, length 4.4 cm. (Middle and bottom) Small prismatic blades from Paleo-Indian occupation levels, length of each c. 4 cm.

Meadowcroft Rockshelter, Pennsylvania.
(Above) Overhead view of excavations
near the beginning of the seven-year
project in 1973. The large rock at left
was once part of the shelter's roof.
(Right) Portion of the stratified layers
of Meadowcroft Rockshelter, with layer
11a at the base.

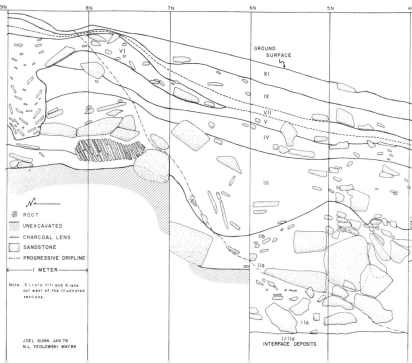

sheltered region that could have fostered a more temperate ecology. Meadowcroft remains an enigma, and may, ultimately, prove to be a sparsely occupied very early Clovis site.

Other Early North American Sites. A scatter of 12,000-radiocarbon year or older sites are found elsewhere in North America. The most coherent western US evidence comes from Washington, Oregon, and Idaho, at sites dating back to 12,000, perhaps 14,000 radiocarbon years ago. These locations include the Manis mastodon kill of some 12,000 radiocarbon years ago from near Sequim, Washington.

Claims of earlier human settlement from California, New Mexico, and Texas have either been based on conflicting field evidence or have not withstood close scientific scrutiny (for a summary, see Dincauze, 1984). Far away in the Southeast, a small association of stone tools, including small bladelets and cores, lies under a Clovis occupation at Cactus Hill in southern Virginia, and is said to date to as early as about 15,000 years ago (dates from dispersed charcoal, which may not be reliable). Similar bladelets are also reported in an early scatter from the Big Pine Tree site near Allendale, South Carolina (Fiedel, 1999). A wooden stake thrust by a hunter through a tortoise shell in the Little Salt Spring sinkhole in Florida is radiocarbon-dated to about 12,000 years ago (Clausen and others, 1979).

The evidence is still a matter of shreds and archaeological patches, but there are enough hints to lay out a possible scenario for first settlement, as follows (Fiedel, 1999):

Few human beings lived in frigid Beringia during the height of the last glaciation. So far, there is no evidence that there were many people living in extreme northeast Siberia before 18,000 years ago, if then. Somewhere around 14,700 years ago [cal], temperatures rose rapidly in the far north with the beginning of the Bølling/Allerød period. The vast Laurentide ice sheet melted rapidly, releasing enormous amounts of freshwater into northern oceans. This may have been the moment at which the first human groups crossed the vanishing Bering Land Bridge and settled in Alaska. By this time, too, the ice-free corridor was already passable, even if it was not an attractive place to live. The rapidly warming climate may have drawn tiny numbers of Paleo-Indians southward into the heart of an uninhabited continent after 14,700 years ago [cal].

These initial forays into new lands must have involved a diversity of groups. Judging from Monte Verde and some other locations, they ranged widely and far to the south. We know almost nothing of these people, beyond knowing that they were not purely big-game hunters and that they adapted to a broad range of local environments. Their toolkits may have included tiny stone bladelets.

After 13,000 years ago [cal], the world entered another near-glacial cold snap, the Younger Dryas. In most parts of the New World, especially North America, the climate was probably relatively cold and arid. But a change in the jet stream path may have brought dry conditions to the Northwest, but wetter, more favorable circumstances to the Plains and Southwest, where the Clovis culture (see below) developed significant technological and adaptive advantages. People using Clovis technology now rapidly expanded through North America, accounting for the widespread distribution of their distinctive fluted points over a period of several centuries. Not that human populations were large or densely packed anywhere in the Americas. Every group was isolated, with relatively few contacts with neighbors. As a result, they adapted to a wide variety of local environments, as their projectile points and other tools developed new forms as a result of what is called stylistic drift. (The fish-tail points of extreme South America are a good example. So is the Dalton tradition of Arkansas (see Chapter 17)).

All this is, of course, still little more than a theoretical scenario. There is only one certainty: about 13,400 years ago [cal], the Clovis culture appears, marked by a veritable explosion in the number of archaeological sites throughout North America, from the California deserts to the Eastern Woodlands.

Clovis Culture
c. 13,500/13,350 years ago [cal] to 12,900 years ago [cal]

The Clovis began perhaps as early as 13,500 to 13,350 years ago [cal], with this distinctive culture expanding over a wide area of North America by about 13,000 years ago. Everything points to their having been successful, efficient foragers (recent summaries in Fiedel, 1999; Hofman and Graham, 1998).

At the end of the Wisconsin and during the millennia that followed, the areas in the rain shadow of the western mountains of North America were dominated throughout the year by the dry mid-Pacific air mass. The Plains were an area of seasonal extremes during the Late Wisconsin, a place where big-game species like the mammoth and large Ice Age bison adapted to conditions where growing seasons were short and intense. The grasslands provided high-quality nutrients in the dry fall and into the winter, sustaining large herbivores during the lean months. These grasslands were apparently reasonably well watered during the Younger Dryas, at the time they were home to scattered bands of Clovis people, who ranged over enormous territories. Within a few centuries, small groups of Clovis people had spread throughout North America. They camped on low terraces along rivers and streams, in places where big-game came to feed, to obtain water. Some Plains groups favored perennial springs and waterholes, while others visited caves and rockshelters, some probably winter encampments.

The Clovis people were far more than merely big-game hunters, even if the bones of larger animals are normally those that are preserved. Undoubtedly they took not only big Ice Age species, but medium-sized animals like deer, and small rabbits and other mammals as well. They must also have exploited wild plant foods in spring, summer, and fall, as well perhaps as fish and other aquatic resources when the occasion arose. While the hunting of large mammals was important, and the people wandered far and wide in search of them, we can be sure that there were many distinctive adaptations to locally plentiful and predictable resources, which are not yet reflected in the archaeological record. Many bands may have lived on coastal plains, on now sunken continental shelves, where, conceivably, they relied heavily on marine resources.

Judging from Plains sites, the Clovis people were especially fond of mammoth and bison. Mammoth bones occur at almost every kill site known. These lumbering beasts were attractive quarry for many reasons. A single animal could provide meat for weeks on end and, if dried, for much of the winter, too. Hides, tusks, bones, and pelts were used to make household possessions and weapons, for shelter, even clothing. Precious fat from the internal organs could be melted down and used for cooking and burning in lamps – just as it had thousands of years before on the steppe-tundra of Eurasia.

We do not know whether the hunters attacked mammoth individually or in groups. Most Clovis mammoth kills lie on low ground, near creeks, springs, or ponds. The hunters could have ambushed the animals at watering places, spots where the soft ground impeded movement. Our only analogies come from modern elephant populations in the tropics. There, herds are highly mobile and respond quickly to fluctuations in food availability. Their matriarchal social organization means that they wander in family units, a pattern that allows the development of traditions of resource-oriented movements. Generation after generation, the elephants would return to the same salt licks, waterholes, trails, and favored patches of vegetation. It is hardly surprising to find hunting sites close to permanent water supplies in an arid landscape.

Clovis hunters were obviously shrewd observers of mammoth behavior. Vance Haynes believes (1966) they followed matriarchal groups for weeks

Excavations at the Murray Springs Clovis site, Arizona.

Clovis points found with the mammoth skeleton at Naco, Arizona, four times the number discovered with any other such kill. This suggests the animal may have got away from its hunters only to die somewhat later.

on end, observing the behavior of individual elephants with great care. They would then catch individuals off guard and cull the herd one by one at the same location over the years, perhaps in a place like Lehner, where 13 mammoth carcasses were found. George Frison has experimented with stone-tipped Clovis spears on dead African elephants in Zimbabwe, Central Africa. He found that Clovis weapons could indeed inflict lethal wounds, especially if the hunter stood still and took careful aim. He argues that the hunters worked in pairs, the one attracting the beast's attention, while the other loosed off a spear. Such an approach means concentrating on individual beasts, and positioning oneself carefully for the kill. Most probably, the Clovis people took individual animals.

Eleven bison and a mammoth died at Murray Springs, Arizona, yielding enough meat to support as many as 50 to 100 people, perhaps many fewer. A single mammoth, from Naco in Arizona, had no fewer than eight Clovis points in its carcass, four times more than any other known kill. Perhaps it escaped wounded, only to die later. If each point belonged to an individual hunter, then at least eight men attacked the beast or four if each fired off two spears. Vance Haynes believes that the hunters may have represented about a fifth of a band of about 20 to 40 men, women, and children. Not that the Clovis people used all the meat they butchered. Whenever they killed a mammoth, they only partly dismembered the carcass, taking away some choice parts with them. At Clovis itself, Murray Springs, and the Colby site in Wyoming, they created piles of disarticulated bones, perhaps left as winter meat caches. Bison carcasses were more heavily utilized and less was left at the site.

Clovis Technology. Clovis toolkits were highly effective, lightweight, and portable, as befits people who were constantly on the move. Their stone technology was based on precious, fine-grained rock that came from widely separated rocky outcrops, outcrops that were exploited for thousands of years afterwards by later peoples. Some of the stone came from sources more than 186 miles (299 km) away. These included alibates, a form of banded, agatized dolomite from the Canadian River area of Texas. Translucent dark brown chalcedony came from the Knife River Valley of North Dakota and Manitoba. There was chalcedony from Ohio, volcanic obsidian from the Yellowstone Park region. The hunters traveled long distances to obtain rock, and, judging from Eastern Woodlands sites (Chapter 5), exchanged it over considerable distances. Sharp-edged stone was vital, for effective procurement of other raw materials such as bone, hide, sinews, even wood, depended on an adequate supply of fine-grained rock to kill and process big-game and cut down trees.

Clovis stone workers used a careful reduction process that started with large bifaces and branched out into smaller artifacts with maximum economy and logical efficiency. The bifaces themselves were not only a "bank account" of potential artifact blanks, but served as heavy butchery knives and choppers into the bargain. These were constantly flaked as butchery proceeded. At Murray Springs, Bruce Huckell of the Arizona State Museum pieced together clusters of thin bifacial trimming flakes to reconstruct the bifaces that produced them. At the same site, a few projectile points and other tools, and thousands of thinning and sharpening flakes, lay among the dismembered carcasses. Only 36 finished tools came from

Experimental archaeology plays an important role in Paleo-Indian archaeology. Here Bruce Huckell of the Arizona State Museum makes the initial skinning cut with a biface into the hide of a deceased circus elephant.

the entire site, presumably because the hunters conserved their best artifacts and took them away for reuse. The ratio of finished tools to waste flakes was 6:10,000, a startling demonstration of the high value Clovis people put on fine-grained rock.

The fluted projectile point is the most celebrated, distinctive part of the Clovis toolkit. A cache of some of the finest known specimens came from the East Wenatchee site in Washington State, deposited soon after an eruption of nearby Glacier Peak about 11,250 years ago [radiocarbon date] (Mehringer and Foit, 1990). Judging from modern experiments, Clovis points were time-consuming to prepare, so the hunters resharpened them again and again when they were damaged in the chase. Exactly how the points were hafted is unknown, but the men probably carried a series of them mounted in wooden or bone foreshafts that worked loose from the spear shaft once the head was buried in its quarry. Besides projectile points, the Clovis people used bifacially trimmed points and other woodworking and butchering artifacts, as well as flakes used simply as sharp-edged, convenient tools in their struck-off form.

Clovis Origins. As we have seen, there are isolated hints of human settlement south of the ice sheets earlier than 13,500 calendar years ago, at places like Meadowcroft Rockshelter, but none of these sites prove that there were indigenous ancestors for Clovis. The evidence is simply too sparse and the range of tools too inadequate to suggest a local origin for the highly developed Clovis technology. Vance Haynes (1982; 1987) was one of the first to argue that the Clovis people came originally from north of the ice sheets and migrated south at the very end of the Wisconsin glaciation, as the glaciers melted and the ice retreated (see also Tankersley, 1994).

Are there, then, archaeological links between Clovis artifacts and Stone Age tools made in the far north at the same time, or earlier? Distinctive Clovis points with or without fluted bases are found in all the Canadian provinces and throughout North America. In Alaska, the new discoveries at Broken Mammoth, Dry Creek, and Mesa include bifaces and other artifacts, which are reminiscent of early Paleo-Indian points and tools from temperate North America. There are still too few artifacts from any Alaskan site to make detailed, meaningful comparisons, but it seems increasingly likely that Clovis origins, and those of its immediate, and putative, ancestors, lie among very early cultural traditions in Alaska. The Clovis point itself may have been an indigenous development, first fabricated south of the ice sheets and not in the Arctic at all (Hoffecker and others, 1993).

The microblade and wedge-shaped core traditions of Alaska are really no earlier than Clovis itself, and at many sites perhaps a millennium or so later. Only Dry Creek I offers hints of an ancestral occupation in the far north, and there are too few artifacts from this location to make meaningful comparisons. However, Vance Haynes and German archaeologist Hansjurgen Müller-Beck argue (both 1982) that the mammoth was to the late Stone Age hunter what the reindeer is to the Lapplander or the caribou to the inland Eskimo. They both believe that general similarities between Clovis stone and bone tools and those from classic mammoth hunting sites in eastern Europe and the Ukraine mean that the first settlement of the New World was part of a big-game hunting tradition that spread across Russia into northeast Asia.

Clovis points from the Lehner site, Arizona (left), and Blackwater Draw (right). Length of Lehner point c. 9 cm.

This line of thinking agrees well with Turner's dental calculations for the land bridge crossing. However, modern native Americans display Sinodonty, a feature found not at Mal'ta and other late Stone Age sites in the west, but in northern China and Asia generally. Did, then, the ancestral populations come from the south in Asia? The inconsistency between the two points of view may not be important, for northeast Asia was environmentally highly diverse, a region that may have supported a far more varied population than just big-game hunters, peoples with distant cultural roots in the far east as well as in the west. It is not illogical to argue that Clovis derived ultimately from late Stone Age cultural roots, even if details of their technological ancestry remain enigmatic. This ancestry may always remain somewhat of a mystery, for the archaeological signature is but transitory, indeed, the earliest Americans may have used artifacts that bore no resemblance to those that ultimately came into use south of the ice sheets.

Unfortunately, our knowledge of the Clovis people comes from kill sites rather than habitations, so our picture of these primeval hunters may be somewhat skewed. However, everything we know about their culture is strongly reminiscent of late Stone Age hunters in the Old World. The people lived in small bands, ranged over enormous distances, and relied significantly on big-game hunting. They shared the same basic cultural traditions and toolkits over vast areas, giving at least a superficial impression of cultural standardization, even if recent discoveries in the Southeast and elsewhere point to far more diverse lifeways than merely big-game hunting (Anderson and Sassaman, 1996).

Clovis and Megafaunal Extinctions

The Clovis people hunted in all corners of North America until about 12,900 years ago [cal], when they abruptly vanish from the archaeological record, to be replaced by myriad local hunter-gatherer cultures. By an intriguing coincidence – if coincidence it be – the disappearance of Clovis coincides with one of the great mysteries of vertebrate paleontology, too – the mass extinction of Ice Age big-game animals, the megafauna. Inevitably, this has led to speculation that Clovis people overhunted these mammals and drove them into extinction. Therein lies a major controversy in Paleo-Indian studies (Grayson, 1991; Martin and Klein, 1984).

Everywhere in the world, the end of the Ice Age saw massive, even catastrophic, extinctions of big-game species, including the mammoth, the mastodon, giant sloth, and many camel species, to mention only a few. During the 1960s, Paul Martin of the University of Arizona developed a provocative hypothesis. He argued that an exploding population of big-game hunters, fanning out over a virgin continent, rapidly drove the megafauna into extinction through wasteful hunting methods and before the fauna learned defensive behaviors. The result was a human population crash following the big-game extinctions (Martin, 1967).

Martin's theory provoked opposition from those who believe that drier climatic conditions at the end of the Ice Age led to mass starvations in game populations and to eventual extinction. Others argue that as the climate dried up, so water tables fell and reliable water supplies were hard to come by. Mammoth were still to be found, but the hunters had to cover far

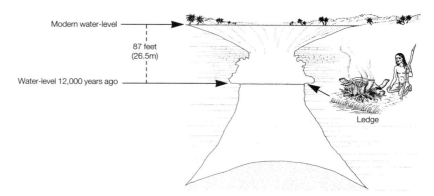

Little Salt Spring in southern Florida yielded a turtle killed with a wooden spear by a man who apparently fell into the sink hole, butchered and ate the turtle, then died of starvation 12,000 years ago. Larger mammals like the turtle became extinct soon afterward, as part of the mass extinction of American megafauna.

Modern water-level

87 feet (26.5m)

Water-level 12,000 years ago

Ledge

greater distances to take them. There may always have been low human population densities, so there was no population crash when extinction took place, but, instead, a steady, slow growth, one that brought neighboring bands together in cooperative hunts, this, and other developments, leading to far greater cultural diversity in later centuries.

Most likely, a complicated set of factors spelled the extinction of the American megafauna, and probably Clovis hunters were one of the factors involved (for full discussion, see Grayson, 1991).

Whatever the cause of megafaunal extinction, the later Paleo-indians adopted far more diverse adaptations to their new homeland, a process that was to continue for the rest of ancient times and long after European contact.

Further Reading

Dillehay, Tom. 2000. *First Settlement of the Americas*. Basic Books, New York.
A summary of what we know about first settlement by a leading authority in the field. (Not available in time for this revision.)

Dillehay, Tom, and Meltzer, David (eds.). 1991. *The First Americans: Search and Research*. CRC Press, Boca Raton, FL.
Specialist essays on every aspect of first settlement, which represent state-of-the-art thinking on the subject. Some articles look at the problem from a welcome, and unusual, global perspective.

Fagan, Brian M. 1987. *The Great Journey*. Thames and Hudson, London and New York.
An evaluation of the evidence for first settlement. Aimed at both the specialist and general reader. Now somewhat outdated.

Fiedel, Stuart. 1999. "Older Than We Thought: Implications of Corrected Dates for Paleoindians." *American Antiquity* 64(1): 95–115.
A highly technical, but important, analysis of the new dates for first settlement in the light of new radiocarbon calibrations and climatic data.

Hopkins, David M. and others (eds.). 1982. *The Paleocology of Beringia*. Academic Press, New York.
Essays that seek to reconstruct the environment and ecology of Beringia and the Bering Land Bridge, also its fauna and inhabitants. Authoritative, but technical.

Meltzer, David. 1993. *Search for the First Americans*. Smithsonian Institution Press, Washington DC.
A lavishly illustrated popular account of early American archaeology and first settlement. Quite up-to-date and well argued.

West, Frederick Hadley (ed.). 1996. *American Beginnings*. University of Chicago Press, Chicago.
West has brought together summary essays on every aspect for first settlement. A technical volume.

CHAPTER 5

LATER PALEO-INDIAN CULTURES[1]

When the Ice Age megafauna vanished about 9000 BC, Paleo-Indian groups throughout most of North America diversified away from big-game hunting. Some bands adapted to increasingly arid conditions in the west and placed major emphasis on plant foods. The sparse Paleo-Indian population of the Eastern Woodlands pursued deer and other forest game, also relying on seasonal vegetable foods. Only on the Great Plains did big-game hunting remain a viable lifeway, a lifeway that was to survive into historic times (Stanford and Day, 1992). Paleo-Indian cultures flourished during a period of dramatic biogeographical change throughout North America, as global warming after the Ice Age continued and vegetational distributions changed dramatically. Thus, it would be a mistake to project modern-day hunter-gatherer adaptations back more than 11 millennia and assume that Paleo-Indians followed the same hunting and gathering practices.

Unfortunately, our knowledge of these later Paleo-Indian cultures is still incomplete. Throughout North America, their archaeological signature is usually little more than a confusing multiplicity of projectile points and small scatters of scrapers and other generalized artifacts. Much of the most complete information comes from bison kill sites on the Plains that may give a skewed idea of Paleo-Indian life. One has an impression, however, of a relatively generalized hunter-gatherer lifeway, with considerable standardization of material culture over thousands of square miles of sparsely populated, but varied terrain. It was only later, in Archaic times, that more specialized, often highly local adaptations arose.

After Clovis on the Plains
c. 11, 000 [cal] to 6000 BC

A scatter of Paleo-Indian sites in Canada document occupation to the south of retreating ice sheets. The Vermillion Lakes site in Alberta's Banff National Park was discovered during road widening for the Trans-Canada Highway in 1983–85 and investigated by Parks Canada archaeologists (Fedje and others, 1995). During its earliest phases of Paleo-Indian occupation, the site lay at the head of a sheltered bay of a then much larger Lake Vermillion. Excavations revealed a series of transitory occupations

---

[1] Dates in this, and subsequent, chapters are radiocarbon ages unless otherwise stated.

*Later Paleo-Indian sites of
North America.*

dating from *c.* 8800 to 7000 BC, some probably lasting no more than a few days, others for longer periods, when some form of dwellings lay between the scatters of stone tool debris. The inhabitants preyed on mountain sheep during the Younger Dryas cold snap (between 11,000 and 9,650 BC [cal]), a worldwide cold interval, when local conditions were considerably colder than today, with a lowered tree line and an expanded range for both sheep and caribou. The Vermillion Lakes artifacts include projectile points of forms known from elsewhere in Alberta, British Columbia, and Manitoba.

By this time, the landscape of North America had changed drastically from late Ice Age times. In 9000 BC, a vast tract of arid grassland extended from the frontiers of Alaska to the shores of the Gulf of Mexico. This was the "Great Bison Belt," which lay in the rain shadow to the east of the Rocky Mountains. It was dominated throughout the year by the dry mid-Pacific air mass. Spring and early summer rains supported, and still support, short grasses that keep much of their biomass beneath the soil. Such grass retains moisture at the roots, so grazing animals like bison can find high-quality nutrients in the dry autumn. Bison succeeded where other Ice Age animals failed because they diversified to become short-grass feeders as this type of grassland expanded in postglacial times (McDonald, 1981). By 8500 BC, the Plains Paleo-Indians, once broad-spectrum big-game hunters, had turned to bison hunting instead.

The bison hunters moved around in small family groups most of the year. They tended to return to the same springs and other favored locations on higher ground year after year. There they would camp for a few days, dig a fire pit, perhaps erect a temporary shelter depending on the weather

Excavations at the Lindenmeier site, Colorado, by Frank Roberts, c. 1936.

conditions, make some stone tools or process some meat, then move on (Bamforth, 1988; Frison, 1992). Nevertheless, some locations like Lindenmeier, Colorado (illus. p. 93), were exploited for communal drives on a regular basis, thereby anchoring the people to specific points on the landscape. Communal kills were concentrated from fall to spring. Apparently, many hunts did not involve large-scale processing of meat for later use, as if there was sufficient food to support large groups of people during the summer months. Thus, one can argue for a lifeway that involved at least some seasonal aggregation and dispersal of Plains populations.

Almost certainly, Paleo-Indian population densities were considerably lower than those of later times. In most areas, groups had to remain widely dispersed and constantly mobile in their quest for game. Some of their mass kills appear to have produced more meat than the groups could use, for their high degree of mobility may have had another adaptive feature as well. The hunters needed to maintain social contacts with a considerable number of other widely separated social groups, if for nothing else but to provide mates (Wobst, 1974; Bamforth, 1988).

Most excavated later Paleo-Indian locations are kill sites that tell us much of the drama of hunting bison on foot. They may also give us a misleading impression of bison hunting as a kind of macabre orgy of mass game drives, of people herding dozens, if not hundreds, of beasts to their death. In fact, conducting bison drives is a difficult art, especially on foot. Most likely, a combination of solo and cooperative hunting ensured a regular supply of bison flesh, strategies that survived far beyond Paleo-Indian times (Chapter 6) (Frison, 1992).

When left alone, bison soon become less fearful of humans. Subjected continuously to pursuit, however, they become unpredictable and far harder to drive. If Paleo-Indian hunters were anything like historic bison hunters, they watched their prey constantly. They were probably careful to pursue the herds intermittently, driving them small distances, giving them time to calm down. Modern bison can be moved a mile or so without trouble; then they start to break and run, when it is almost impossible to stop them. Thus, large-scale game drives probably required careful orchestration and organized cooperation.

A mass bison drive demanded intimate knowledge of the surrounding countryside. The topography of the approach to the selected trap or jump had to stampede the animals in a predictable direction. Judging from 18th- and 19th-century accounts, the hunters were careful to "arrange" the layout of the approach in such a way that the drive direction was controlled. A skilled group of hunters could subject their quarry herd to gentle influences over periods of days, moving them a little way in the right direction when conditions were favorable. They would line the approach with decoys, with shouting men, while hunters dressed in bison hides would approach the unsuspecting animals. Once the drive began, the hunters would run and shout, even wave skins at the thundering herd. Clouds of dust rose from the plain as the sheer mass and weight of the herd forced the leaders over a precipice to their deaths, or into a corral lying under a low cliff or at the mouth of a narrow defile.

Many hunts may have taken place in favored locations, places used more than once, intermittently over the millennia. The Folsom type site in New Mexico was a place where several bison were killed, probably in late fall or

Bison jump on the northern Plains. A diorama commissioned by the Montana Historical Society.

The Casper site, Wyoming. (Above) Looking into the northeast and leeward end of part of the trough of the old parabolic sand dune containing the Casper site bison. (Above right) Close-up of butchered bison skeletons.

early winter. At Lindenmeier, 46 miles (74 km) north of Fort Collins, Colorado, generations of bison hunters of about 8800 BC camped in a small, well-watered valley near the Plains grasslands. On the basis of careful analyses of bone and stone artifact scatters, Ed Wilmsen believes Lindenmeier was visited by at least two semi-autonomous groups, who cooperated in bison hunts and regular social transactions (Wilmsen and Roberts, 1978).

The Casper site in Wyoming of about 6000 BC showed how the hunters used a parabolic sand dune with steep, loose sides to trap a herd of about 100 bison during a late autumn hunt (Frison, 1974). They drove the animals into the curve of the steep-sided dune, animals that may have been grazing near a natural pond nearby. The bisons' hooves sank into the loose sand. As the beasts panicked, the hunters moved in to kill them as fast as they could. Each hunter, or group of hunters, would select a single animal, and aim deliberately to thrust their spears through the rib cage into the heart.

George Frison took a typical Hell Gap projectile point (see below) that had been found on the surface and mounted it with a sinew binding in a slotted pine shaft, bonding the heft with pine pitch without using a foreshaft. He thrust and threw the 11-ft (3.3-m) long spear into the carcass of a domesticated ox. Frison found that an extremely hard thrust would penetrate the rib cage and hide, sometimes even reaching the heart, causing a lethal wound. Occasionally, the point would break, but it was easily sharpened for re-use later. The heft was strong enough not to break, even after the hardest thrust. A skilled hunter with a long spear that gave him some distance from his quarry could deliver very lethal blows in short order without endangering himself unduly.

The Jones-Miller site in extreme eastern Colorado contains the remains of several hundred animals, which may have been killed over a period of some months, perhaps a single winter. Dennis Stanford (1978) believes the bison may have been driven into a specially constructed corral, where they were dispatched under the watchful eye of a waiting shaman. He found

The Olsen-Chubbock site, Colorado: a reconstruction of Paleo-Indian butchery methods. The hunters skinned the bison down the back to get at the layer of tender meat (hatched area) just beneath the surface. When this was removed, the bison's forelegs and shoulder blades could be cut free (1), exposing the much-prized hump meat (2) as well as the rib meat and inner organs (3). The next step was to sever the spine and take off the pelvis (4) and hind legs (5). Finally the neck and skull were cut away as a single unit (6), their tough meat being dried and converted into pemmican.

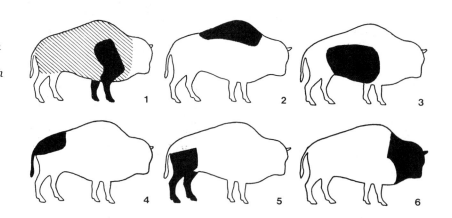

traces of a stout wooden pole near the corral. An antler flute and a miniature projectile point lay nearby. Stanford believes the wooden upright may have served as a shaman pole, and the nearby artifacts as part of the priest's paraphernalia.

The Olsen-Chubbock site 16 miles (25.7 km) southeast of Kit Carson, Colorado, on the central Plains offered a unique chance to record a Paleo-Indian bison hunt of about 6500 BC (Wheat, 1972). The hunters had located a large bison herd and stampeded them into a dry gully. The leading bison arrived at the steep edge and were swept on by the animals behind them. About 157 beasts were immobilized and trampled to death in the dry defile. Ten animals were pinned with their heads down and their rumps up. Two lay on their backs. Most of the skeletons lay where they had perished, facing south. Given the excavator Joe Ben Wheat's reasonable assumption that the hunters approached the herd from downwind, the wind would have been blowing from the south on the day of the hunt.

Once the stampede was over, the hunters faced many hours of arduous work. First, they maneuvered the carcasses into a position where they could be cut up at the edge of the arroyo. The bison wedged at the bottom were butchered where they lay. The butchers worked in teams and cut up several animals at once. They rolled the animals on their bellies, slit the hide down the back, and pulled it down the flanks to form a carpet for the meat. Then they removed the blanket of prime flesh on the back, the forelimbs, shoulder blades, hump meat, and rib cage. They probably ate the tongues and some internal organs as they went along, piling the bones in the arroyo.

The Olsen-Chubbock hunters butchered 75 percent of the animals they killed, acquiring about 54,640 lbs (24,752 kg) of meat in the process. They also obtained 5400 lbs (2449 kg) of fat and 4000 lbs (1812 kg) of edible internal organs as well. The meat from this ancient hunt may have sustained over 100 people for a month or more.

As George Frison argues (1992), the Paleo-Indians knew their prey so well that they did not necessarily require natural arroyos, sand dunes, or low cliffs for their game drives. Rather, they relied on their stalking skills and on infinite patience to maneuver the bison on their own terms. Perhaps this is why large kill sites such as Olsen-Chubbock are rare phenomena (see also Frison and Todd, 1987).

Post-Clovis Material Culture on the Plains

For thousands of years, Paleo-Indians all over North America, and not just on the Plains, relied on a very simple, highly portable material culture that changed very slowly over a 3000-year period, from before 9000 until at least 6000 BC. Projectile points of different type usually constituted between 10 and 20 percent of the toolkit. At least seven forms of later Paleo-Indian Plains projectile point alone are known after 9000 BC, all apparently descended from the fluted Clovis point. To what extent these represent actual cultural differences is a matter for discussion (Knudsen, 1983). Side and end scrapers (20 to 54 percent) were invariably the most common tools. Knives were another characteristic Paleo-Indian artifact, tools that are easily confused with projectile-point blanks or even finished points. The most famous on the Plains is the so-called Cody Knife, an asymmetrical implement up to 3.9 in (10 cm) long with a transverse cutting edge, usually with a shoulder on one side. Some of these artifacts were made from broken projectile points (Irwin and Wormington, 1970).

Folsom (11,000 [cal] to between 8500 and 8000 BC). The Folsom tradition with its distinctive fluted point follows Clovis on the Plains. Folsom projectile points have been found over an enormous area of the Plains, in the Southwest and the far west. Everyone assumes that the Folsom tradition originated in Clovis, but no intermediate projectile-point forms have been radiocarbon dated or found in a stratified context. One possible candidate is the so-called Goshen Complex at the Hell Gap site in southeastern Wyoming, dated at another site to *c.* 8500 BC (Frison, 1996).

Undisturbed sites like Lindenmeier or the Folsom type site itself are rare. Most locations were kill sites where small or large numbers of bison were

Some of the major Plains Paleo-Indian projectile forms.

	APPROXIMATE CHRONOLOGY OF MAJOR PLAINS PROJECTILE POINTS						
Years AD/BC [cal]	11,400 BC	10,300 BC	10,000 BC	8500 BC	8250 BC	7500 BC	7000 BC
Point Type	Clovis	Folsom	Midland Firstview, San Jon Agate Basin	Hell Gap	Alberta	Fredrick-Firstview Cody Knife Scottsbluff Eden	Jimmy Allen Cascade

Clovis · Folsom · Midland · Agate Basin · Hell Gap · Fredrick · Scottsbluff · Eden

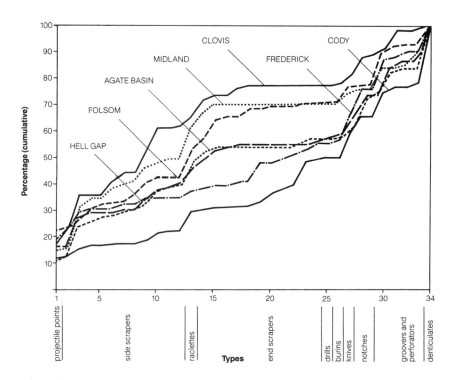

Cumulative curves of the percentages of different Plains Paleo-Indian artifact types, constructed by Irwin and Wormington.

taken, often within a relatively short period of time. For example, the Lipscomb site on the Southern Plains contained the remains of 55 bison killed in late summer or early fall (Todd and others, 1992). Perhaps the best-known Folsom site is the Hanson settlement near chert and quartzite outcrops in the northern Bighorn Basin of central Wyoming (Frison and Bradley, 1981). Three hard-packed areas may have been the remains of circular lodge structures, that have been radiocarbon dated to at least 8000 BC. The animals eaten at Hanson included bison, mountain sheep, deer, marmot, and cottontail rabbit, ample proof that the Paleo-Indians took many more animal species than just bison. Important new sites include the Certasin location in Oklahoma, an arroyo filled with bison bones from a mass drive, including a centrally placed skull, its forehead adorned with a red lightning bolt. Folsom may, in fact, include other traditions, such as the Midland, which is thought to date to between 8700 and 8400 BC (Amick, 1995; Wendorf and Kreiger, 1959).

After Folsom. The late Plains Paleo-Indian traditions that follow on Folsom are defined very largely by stratified, unfluted projectile-point forms, sequences that appear to apply to quite broad areas of the Plains. There were several contemporary Paleo-Indian occupations on the Plains after Folsom times, some of them oriented toward open plains bison hunting, others adapted to hunting and foraging in foothill and mountain areas at the edge of the Plains. Projectile-point forms include Alberta, Cody, Frederick, Eden, Scottsbluff, and many others, sometimes linked together under the general label of Planó cultures. The reader is referred to more specialist works for details (Frison, 1992; Knecht, 1997; Wheat, 1972).

Irwin and Wormington (1970) constructed a series of cumulative curves of the percentages of different artifact types, to compare the various toolkits in their samples. The cumulative graphs for Clovis, Folsom, and Midland were very similar, with Folsom and Midland being the closest, especially in scraper inventories. Hell Gap and Agate Basin form a second, very closely similar, group, both containing more specialized tools than the first one. Frederick and Cody are the latest of the samples, and they form a third group, marked by even more specialized tools.

Joe Ben Wheat (1972) argued that different projectile forms were in use on the northern, central, and southern Plains. He proposed grouping post-Folsom assemblages from the central and southern Plains into a single First View Complex. However, more recent analyses argue for a more complex sequence of forms that include intermediate groups such as the Plainsview and Fairview forms (Johnson and Halliday, 1980; discussion in Hofman and Graham, 1998).

Culture Change on the Plains

Given that we have mainly stone artifacts to work with, it is hard to study Paleo-Indian cultural change on the Plains. Douglas Bamforth (1988) has shown that Early Holocene climatic change reduced the overall abundance of large animals over much of the Plains. At the same time, the size and mobility of the herds increased. The primeval Clovis population was widely dispersed, with relatively rare mass hunts. In contrast, with increased numbers of game, Folsom groups came together for communal hunts more regularly, especially at preferred locations. As conditions became drier after Folsom times, herd distributions became less predictable, so the hunters used many more locations, engaging in communal hunts as and when the opportunity arose, on a far less predictable basis. Thus, argues Bamforth, social complexity should have increased from Clovis to Folsom times, and decreased thereafter.

Clovis and Folsom points are harder to manufacture than later Paleo-Indian points, which boast of no fluting. Folsom points are thin, well-flaked, and fluted with a single channel flake along most of their length (Knecht, 1997), apparently requiring more skill on the part of the stone worker than the Clovis point. If this is so, then Folsom groups may have relied more heavily on elaborate tools, perhaps another sign of greater social complexity and of a degree of specialized production (Bamforth, 1988). High-quality stoneworking declined noticeably at the end of the Paleo-Indian period (Hayden, 1982). This may reflect circumstances where essentially modern climatic conditions forced most members of society to make their own tools, under circumstances where it was difficult to maintain a more complex social structure.

One can theorize that as a patchwork of more predictable food resources developed over the Plains during Folsom times, it tended to favor larger and more regular concentrations of human populations (Bamforth, 1988). In turn, these human societies became more complex. Whether this provocative theory and the models derived from it hold up in the future depends on more sophisticated analyses of stone technology and of animal bone fragments than have hitherto been undertaken on the Plains.

Paleo-Indian Occupation in the West

Everything points to an extremely sparse human population in western North America before about 9000 BC. Most recorded Paleo-Indian sites are little more than surface scatters of stone artifacts, including Clovis fluted points. One of the earliest may be Borax Lake near Clear Lake in northern California, a site which may date to as early as 10,000 BC (Meighan and Haynes, 1970). There is evidence of human occupation on southern California's Channel Islands as early as 9000 BC. Fluted points are widespread in the west and many Paleo-Indian sites lie on gravel bars or higher ground, and are often close to former marshy deltas or to streams that once fed large lakes.

Some of the best Paleo-Indian evidence comes from the Southwest, where higher rainfall filled some low-lying basins with large lakes. Vegetation patterns were very different, with widespread boreal forests and little temperature variation between winter and summer. There was apparently plentiful water and grazing grass for large herbivores to range widely over the Southwestern landscape. With such environmental diversity, it is hardly surprising to find considerable variation in Paleo-Indian projectile forms, some of which resemble those of the Plains to the east (for a full discussion of different traditions, see Cordell, 1998).

Some Southwestern locations were visited for many centuries. Blackwater Draw is a shallow valley in the Llano Estacado that extends from eastern New Mexico into west Texas. Today, dry playas of the Llano only carry water after heavy rains and sand dunes line either side of the valley. This is grassland country, with occasional trees and shrubs, as it was in 10,000 BC. There were shallow ponds in the valley between 9000 and 8000 BC, which became marshes in later millennia (Wendorf and Hester, 1975). Clovis people hunted in Blackwater Draw between 9500 and 9200 BC, leaving some of their artifacts by a spring. The small mammals of the time suggest a climate with mild winters and cool summers.

Folsom and Midland points are stratified above Clovis artifacts in the Draw, with Folsom implements occurring in a diatomaceous earth (chalk-like earth filled with freshwater diatoms) deposit laid down between about 8500 and 8300 BC, at a time of greater rainfall. Later Paleo-Indian implements lie in silts that were laid down at a time when conditions became drier at the end of Paleo-Indian times (Haynes, 1975).

If conditions were somewhat wetter and there was more standing water in Clovis times, it would have been possible for the sparse human population to range far and wide, and to achieve a similarly highly mobile lifeway. At Blackwater Draw, for example, the hunters obtained fine-grained rock from up to 186 miles (300 km) away, either through exchange, or by actually traveling to the source across all manner of landscapes. The Folsom inhabitants may have enjoyed a high degree of mobility, a mobility that followed from pursuing widely dispersed bison populations, as well as other animals and plant foods. No less than 78 percent of the Folsom points found in the valley were made from Edwards Plateau chert, only obtainable some 186 miles (300 km) away. Perhaps the hunters were obtaining their large cores of raw material from one location as they followed bison and other animals moving along the valley.

The San Dieguito Complex hunter-gatherer culture, which extended from Arizona into southern California, was broadly contemporary with the

Students working in a Cody level (c. 4800 BC) at Blackwater Draw, New Mexico.

occupation of Blackwater Draw (Warren, 1967). The culture dates to as early as 9000 BC and flourished until after 8000 BC. San Dieguito may represent a once broadly distributed hunting culture that flourished over much of southern California as far north as the Death and Owens Valleys and perhaps originated in the Great Basin (Wallace, 1978; Warren and True, 1961). It emerged in an area where drowned river valleys were commonplace along the coast, so the exploitation of marshlands and lakeside resources was probably important. For example, various forms of leaf-shaped and shouldered projectile points have come from the dried up shores of Lake Mojave in the Mojave Desert. This was an ideal location for Early Holocene hunters, for the shores must have teemed with game and plentiful vegetable foods.

Along the southern California coast, people were exploiting fish and marine mammals, as well as shellfish, perhaps as early as 8000 BC. At that time the Pacific coastline was some miles further offshore, and is now submerged under higher sea levels. One has a strong sense of cultural continuity from late Paleo-Indian into Archaic times throughout the west. As western environments became drier and resources more localized, the Paleo-Indians developed ever more diverse local adaptations and much greater cultural diversity, as well as highly varied population densities. In much of southern California, for example, drowned river valleys persisted until as late as 3500 BC, accounting for a continued human presence in these regions, while population densities apparently fell further north.

Paleo-Indians in the Eastern Woodlands

Around 8600 BC, only a thin scatter of human beings lived in eastern North America, the descendants of a few early Paleo-Indian families who had hunted their way eastward perhaps 1500 years earlier. They are sometimes classified under the general label "Eastern Fluted Point Tradition" (Meltzer, 1988). These Paleo-Indians hunted and foraged over thousands of square miles of tundra, coniferous forest, and deciduous woodland, mostly in river valleys, near lakes, swamps, and perhaps sea coasts where game and other food resources were most abundant. One or two families would form a small band, occasionally encountering neighboring groups during the brief summer months, times when wives were exchanged, initiation ceremonies held, fine-grained rock and finished projectile points exchanged.

Like their distant western relatives, eastern Paleo-Indians were constantly on the move. They left thousands of fluted points (many of them, in fact, probably hefted knives) behind them, all the way from Nova Scotia to Florida. In fact, fluted projectile points are much more common east of the Mississippi than in the west. They also display far more variation in size, shape, and technique of manufacture. The Paleo-Indian archaeology of the Eastern Woodlands, like that of the Archaic, is largely based on these artifacts (see Anderson, D.G. and Sassaman, 1996).

As we have seen, there were at least two major environments in eastern North America during the Early Holocene – a northern tundra and spruce parkland and a more southern complex of boreal and deciduous forests. The Paleo-Indians who lived in the more northern regions, at sites like Gainey in central Michigan, would necessarily have exploited caribou, the only significant Holocene game species capable of providing sufficient food for long-term human occupation (Shott, 1990). More southern groups living in forest areas must have been both hunters and gatherers, people who exploited both forest game and wild plant food. It is hardly surprising that Eastern Fluted Point Tradition sites and artifacts show great variation.

At least seven distinctive Paleo-Indian fluted point styles are known from the Northeast alone, the earliest of which is somewhat similar to the western Clovis form. There are fluted points with constricted edges, some with pentagonal shapes, others are long, and almost triangular. Generations of archaeologists have classified and labeled eastern Paleo-Indian points, naming them after the sites or areas where they were found – Debert, Bull Brook, and so on. As on the Plains, the problem is to decide what these stylistic variations mean in cultural and functional terms. In general, however, eastern fluted points are so basically similar to Clovis and Folsom points from the west that they are assumed to be of approximately the same age.

As the Ice Age megafauna vanished, the easterners turned to more diverse subsistence strategies. The Early Holocene environment of the Eastern Woodlands was far more diverse than that of the west. In some areas, especially large river valleys, there may have been plentiful seasonal supplies of nuts and fish that allowed people to live for the summer and fall in larger base camps, but such bounty was highly localized. Tens of thousands of square miles of Early Holocene woodland were but sparsely endowed with vegetable and aquatic resources. The only viable adaptation was one based on the pursuit of game of all sizes, often solitary species like deer that had to be hunted and trapped over very large hunting territories indeed. In archaeological terms, the result is a superficial uniformity of basic hunting toolkits over an enormous area, with, however, significant local variation (Anderson, D.G. and Sassaman, 1996; Tankersley and Isaac, 1990; Tankersley, 1998).

The close similarities between fluted points throughout the east argues for a rapid expansion of Paleo-Indian hunters over the centuries. Despite very low population densities and constant mobility, neighboring bands kept in touch with one another over long distances, probably through marriage and kin connections. We know this because of finds of exotic, fine-grained rocks in artifact scatters in many parts of the east. Some rocks were highly prized: Knife River flint from North Dakota, Upper Mercer cherts from Ohio, Peoria and Burlington flints from Illinois. We know from many excavations that fine-grained rock was passed from hand to hand, from one band to another over hundreds of miles, perhaps as gifts. So constant was the exchange of fine-grained rocks that it was to be thousands of years before an equivalent level of interaction was ever reached again, perhaps not until Hopewell times, some 8000 years later.

The rapid spread of early Paleo-Indian culture is hardly surprising, for the carrying capacity of the woodlands was very low. There were few, if any, earlier inhabitants to resist the arrival of newcomers. At first there was plenty of hunting territory for everyone, even with the sparse populations concentrated in more favorable hunting and foraging areas. When population pressure on local resources became too intense, a son or daughter's family could simply branch off into new country nearby. In time, of course, the prime territories would be filled to the limits of their sparse capacities, so people no longer had the luxury of moving into new, unexploited terrain. By this time, in some areas perhaps as early as 8800 BC, environmental constraints came into full play, so more focused adaptations based on local game and vegetable resources emerged, reflected in the archaeological record by regional variations in projectile points and, after 8000 BC, by Dalton and side-notched points everywhere. Many later Paleo-Indian groups were initially generalized foragers, who developed into regional cultures in late Paleo-Indian and Early Archaic times throughout the east (Anderson, D.G. and Sassaman, 1996) (Chapter 16).

Northeastern Sites. Unfortunately, only a handful of dated sites chronicle Paleo-Indian occupation in the Eastern Woodlands, several of them close to the northern frontiers of the Early Holocene landscape. About 8600 BC, the Debert site on the Nova Scotian tundra was occupied again and again by a small band of between 15 and 50 people, who hunted caribou and perhaps exploited sea mammals (MacDonald, 1968). They probably dwelt in simple wood and skin structures like recent sub-arctic hunting peoples. Debert may have been an important base camp, for the diverse artifacts suggest a wide variety of activities – everything from butchery to hide processing and wood-working. The contemporary Bull Brook site near Ipswich, Massachusetts, is another large fluted-point site with artifacts, animal bones, and floral remains apparently concentrated in at least 45 circular areas, perhaps distributed in a large semi-circle about 295 ft (90 m) across (Byers, 1954). Many of the Bull Brook artifacts are made from chert from the west, from the Hudson Valley or Pennsylvania, as if the inhabitants were involved in gift exchanges with people further inland.

Most Paleo-Indian sites were much smaller, like Vail in northwest Maine, where a group made a kill and camped on the bank of the Magalloway River. The stone workers made fluted points and other tools from raw material found between 15 and 18 miles (24 and 28.9 km) away.

Kenneth Tankersley (1998) has drawn attention to two clusters of base camps, food procurement and processing sites, and stone tool making locations, one in the Erie-Ontario Plain of upstate New York, the other more than 600 miles (1000 km) away within a 22-mile (35-km) radius of the confluence of the Mississippi, Missouri, and Illinois rivers in the western

Paleo-Indians in the Northeast: indented-base fluted points from the Debert site, Nova Scotia (length of left specimen 11.3 cm).

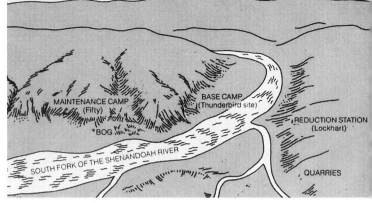

Paleo-Indians in the Mid-South: Thunderbird site and Fifty site, Virginia. (Above) South Fork of the Shenandoah River. The Thunderbird site is located on the floodplain on the river's right bank. (Above right) Locations and functions of the various sites. (Below) Excavators using a mapping frame to map Clovis level activity areas at the Thunderbird site.

Midwest. He believes that in both areas, the Paleo-Indians obtained fine-grained rock for stone tool making at specific locations visited each year during the warmer months, with most, but of course not all, hunting taking place in the winter. Sources for tool-making stone were vital to each group, dependent as they were on such sources and animal behavior for their survival, as opposed to the more regional focuses of later hunter-gatherer cultures. Tankersley believes that similar settlement/resource systems were in use over large areas.

Middle Atlantic. Further south, many Paleo-Indian camps were probably little more than temporary hilltop hunting locations, places visited for short times at regular seasons, as much part of the people's large territorial range as the quarries where they obtained their chert. The hilltop Shoop site in the Susquehanna drainage near Harrisburg, Pennsylvania, may be one such camp (Witthoft, 1952; Cox, 1986). In Paleo-Indian times, the hill probably overlooked the open tundra and thin forest of the river valley, offering a commanding view of the surrounding country. Most of the artifacts and waste flakes from Shoop were of Onondaga chert, quarried more than 186 miles (300 km) up the Susquehanna Valley to the north. John Witthoft identified 11 artifact concentrations, each about 32 ft (10 m) across, located on separate hilltops about 328 ft (100 m) apart. The site is estimated to date to about 9000 BC.

River valleys were favored locations, too. The Shawnee-Minisink camp on a terrace of the Delaware River near Stroudsburg, Pennsylvania, was occupied by Paleo-Indians some time between 8700 and 8500 BC (McNett, 1985). The Paleo-Indian level lies below approximately 9.8 ft (3 m) of soil and is isolated from later Archaic and Woodland occupations by over 5 ft (1.5 m) of sterile overburden. Shawnee-Minisink is one of the few Paleo-Indian sites to yield evidence for fishing and foraging. The excavators used flotation techniques to recover hackberry, wild plum, grape, blackberry, ground cherry and goosefoot, as well as some tiny fish bones, from the abandoned hearths. These vegetable foods are abundant in late summer and early fall. The Shawnee-Minisink group may also have harvested salmon that spawned in the Delaware and its tributaries in fall.

William Gardner's excavations of a series of interrelated northern Virginia Paleo-Indian sites known as the Flint Run complex are especially important, for they document human occupation in this area from about 9500 to 6500 BC (Gardner, 1974; 1977). The major sites – the Flint Run Quarry, Thunderbird, and Fifty – lie within a three-quarter-square-mile

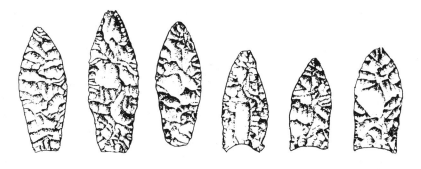

(Far right) Three lanceolate points from the Sawmill site, Erie County. (Right) Fluted and unfluted lanceolate points from the Mathewson site, Hardin County. Length of specimen far left 7 cm.

area on the Shenandoah River's South Fork. The Thunderbird site lies on the Early Holocene bank of the Shenandoah, a series of floodplain encampments scattered over an area almost 500 ft (152 m) long by 250 ft (76.2 m) wide. The location is thought to have been a base camp with many uses, a place where the local jasper was fashioned into finished artifacts and tool blanks. Gardner plotted the distributions of stone artifacts and identified different activity areas – places where hunting tools were fabricated, living areas often situated with reference to wind and sunlight and availability of food resources.

Thunderbird and the stratified Fifty site chronicle 3000 years of the Flint Run complex, a long sequence of seven phases of intermittent occupation that began with Clovis people after 9500 BC, with the only apparent cultural change the appearance of edge-notched projectile points about 8000 BC, perhaps the moment when atlatls (throwing sticks used to extend the range of a spear) came into use. The sites also document a cultural continuum from Paleo-Indian into Archaic life.

Gardner believes that Thunderbird was a central base for a mobile Paleo-Indian population hunting within a broadly prescribed territory, then returning regularly to the same location, where fine-grained jasper was abundant at nearby quarry sites. The people used their floodplain base camp again and again, perhaps in the summers when they gathered with other bands to quarry and trade jasper and socialize. The same form of territorial mobility based on a quarry- and game-rich area may have occurred elsewhere at places like the Williamson and Dismal Swamp locations in southeast Virginia, where considerable densities of projectile points lie near outcrops of fine-grained rocks.

The same phenomenon marks the flint outcrops of Tennessee and Ohio, where points are also abundant. Away from these favored locations with their quarry sites and hunting base camps, the density of points, and presumably of Paleo-Indian population, drops sharply. This "centrally-based wandering" model may not apply in the Northeast. Debert, Bull Brook, and other sites in this region are far from quarry locations. They may have been large hunting camps where the people hunted caribou that ranged over large distances.

Midwest. Paleo-Indian fluted points and other artifacts have been found near the Great Lakes, sometimes lying on Early Holocene shorelines. These include the Potts site inland of the southeastern corner of Lake Ontario, located on a promontory overlooking what were marshy lowlands after about 9500 BC. The Barnes site in central Michigan to the west may have been a hunting camp, perhaps used no earlier than about 9200 BC – the date is disputed.

In Ontario, William Roosa, Peter Storck, and others have found a series of undated fluted-point sites on the ancient Lake Algonquin shoreline in Ontario, perhaps temporary camps left by generations of a single band ranging along ancient beaches on the eastern side of the Huron basin (Storck, 1984, 1997). Parkhill, near London, Ontario, was once a lakeside camp that Roosa estimates to have housed between 45 and 74 people grouped in small families, perhaps caribou hunters (Roosa, 1977). The excavators could isolate separate debris concentrations, perhaps the remains of individual tents. Roosa analyzed the artifacts and debris so thoroughly that he claimed to be able to identify the individual work of different stone workers. Parkhill is undated, but pollen from the site compares closely with radiocarbon-dated pollen samples found in a 8900–7900 BC context elsewhere.

The greatest concentrations of fluted points in Ohio and Indiana are to be found in the southern parts of each state. They are also widespread in southern Illinois and southern Wisconsin, but few locations have been dated. The Kimmswick kill site in eastern Missouri has yielded mastodon remains associated with Clovis points (Graham and others, 1981).

Southeast. Clovis points are found all over the Southeast, with the greatest concentrations in the lower Cumberland, central Tennessee, and central Ohio river valleys (regional summaries in Anderson, D.G. and Sassaman, 1996). These fertile areas may have been the places of initial colonization, perhaps from the Mississippi Valley. Initially, the tiny Paleo-Indian population was probably concentrated in resource-rich areas, at a time when the climate was cooler and drier, quite different from the lush environment of today. Many Southeastern Paleo-Indian settlements of 10,000 BC are probably submerged below modern sea levels. The interior populations were sparse and concentrated near rivers and sink holes, where game would also feed. At a time of lowered sea level, present-day southeastern Florida rivers left large sink holes that could be exploited by animals and humans. Carl Clausen, Wilburn Cockrell, and other archaeologists have recovered a wealth of paleoenvironmental information from them (Clausen and others, 1979).

At Warm Mineral Springs in Sarasota County, Wilburn Cockrell discovered a human burial on a ledge in a sink hole. The skeleton was 42.6 ft (13 m) below the modern water level. The dead man had been deposited in an earthen grave that had subsequently been submerged. A shell spearthrower hook lay with the skeleton. This burial was radiocarbon dated to about 8300 BC. Some further human remains have come to light beneath a 9.8 ft (3 m) ledge at the Springs, in the same clay layer as the bones of a ground sloth, a saber-toothed tiger, and other extinct species. These people were exploiting not only large game, but animals as small as the raccoon and the frog, also plant foods. Some of the Warm Mineral Springs occupation may date to before 9000 BC.

Later Paleo-Indian settlement probably originated in the core river valley areas, with groups spreading out over the Eastern Woodlands over many centuries, forming discrete groupings, perhaps about 150 to 250 miles apart

(250 to 400 km). The proliferation of local point forms which characterizes the later Paleo-Indian in this large region may reflect this emerging local diversity (for discussion, see Anderson, D.G., 1996).

Social Organization and Settlement Patterns

We still know virtually nothing about Paleo-Indian social organization anywhere in North America, of the kin and marriage ties that linked one isolated band to its neighbors. Sharing, social flexibility, egalitarian status – these were probably vital necessities in Paleo-Indian life. The realities of Early Holocene woodland environments would have led to a constant state of social flux within bands consisting of only a few adults and children. A single hunting accident could have wiped out all the hunters in a single band in a day, leaving the survivors with only one recourse – joining a neighboring band. Perhaps, then, we can speculate that many highly mobile Paleo-Indian bands were patrilocal and exogamous. This meant that the men remained with the same band into which they were born, while the women married into neighboring groups. The intricate kin relationships between neighboring bands also facilitated the exchange of vital commodities like the fine-grained rock that made the best projectile points.

The archaeological evidence for Paleo-Indian settlement is so incomplete that it is well-nigh impossible to reconstruct a detailed model of subsistence and settlement patterns anywhere in North America. It has even been argued that their lifeway was quite unlike any modern hunter-gatherers, on the grounds that population densities were so low that no one could rely on the specialized environmental knowledge of their neighbors (Kelly and Todd, 1988). Did, for example, the Paleo-Indians wander from camp to camp without any major base, or did they hunt within large territories on a seasonal basis, "anchoring" their annual round on one much-visited location, which served as the focus of a "centrally based wandering system?" Judging from the Flint Run Complex sites in the Eastern Woodlands, raw materials like jasper may have indeed served as "anchors" for centrally based wandering systems, but perhaps only in a few, relatively rich resource areas. Or is David Anderson (1996) correct when he writes of initial settlement in major river valleys and other resource-rich "staging areas", then a gradual dispersal of small groups into much wider areas? The debate continues.

The Paleo-Indians must have depended on a highly flexible social organization, adaptive because of far-reaching kin ties and marriage alliances that allowed each band access to fine cherts and other resources hundreds of miles away through gift exchange. As the Early Holocene climate continued to warm up, the megafauna vanished, and many hunting territories filled up, their successors had to adapt to new environmental circumstances that challenged their hunting and foraging abilities to the full.

If there is one overall trend in Paleo-Indian adaptations, it was toward increasing cultural diversity. At the end of Paleo-Indian times, western hunter-gatherers were already pursuing very diverse subsistence strategies, relying heavily on plants and non-migratory small game. Plains bands still depended heavily on big-game, on regular bison kills. Eastern groups relied on deer and small game as staples, also on seasonal plant foods as supplements. In all areas, one can reasonably and generally assume that subsistence strategies were based on the notion of maximizing a range of food resources that were mentally ranked by the Paleo-Indians in terms of energy return. One can assume that the availability of these staple ranked foods had a considerable effect on the rate of population growth and on the population density levels that developed. Thus, conditions existed for very different population growth rates in east and west.

On the Plains, population growth and expansion must have depended on fluctuations in bison populations dictated by constantly varying, and often abrupt, expansions and contractions of local range land. Thus, overall population growth would be slow, but with constant, often sudden, movements into bison-rich areas. In the west, the people were dependent on much more diverse game and plant resources. Again, slow population growth would result, but population growth that would soon reach an equilibrium point at a relatively low density, except, perhaps, in the most resource-abundant areas. Eastern Paleo-Indians lived in locally very diverse environments with generally low population densities in vast areas where the carrying capacity was very low. Only in local areas where food resources were predictable and seasonally more abundant than usual did populations rise to higher levels. As we shall see, in both east and west, these local concentrations of hunter-gatherer populations were to develop complex adaptations during the Archaic.

Further Reading

In addition to the sources cited for Chapter 4:

Anderson, David G., and Sassaman, Kenneth E. (eds.) 1996. *The Paleoindian and Early Archaic Southeast.* University of Alabama Press, Tuscaloosa.
A comprehensive, technical survey of the problem with important syntheses and regional essays.

Frison, George. 1992. *Prehistoric Hunters of the High Plains.* 2nd ed. Academic Press, New York.
Frison's thorough analysis is the standard work on northern Plains Paleo-Indian cultures.

Knecht, Heidi. (ed.) 1997. *Projectile Technology.* Plenum Press, New York.
An informative collection of technical papers on every aspect of projectiles and projectile points. Strongly recommended for serious readers.

Meltzer, David J. 1988. "Late Pleistocene Human Adaptations in Eastern North America," *Journal of World Prehistory* 2, 1:1-52.
A technical synthesis of the evidence for Paleo-Indian settlement in the Eastern Woodlands. Good on the Eastern Fluted Point Tradition.

PART THREE

THE GREAT PLAINS

"The new people asked Inktomi what they should eat. Inktomi did not want people to eat his friends, so he created buffalo... He taught the men how to kill the buffalo, and how to skin the animals. He showed them how to make knives to remove the skin, and he taught the women how to make scrapers and how to scrape the skin so it was soft and pliable. He showed the people how to butcher the buffalo and what parts could be eaten."

Assiniboine Creation Legend

CALI-BRATED DATES	RADIO CARBON AGES	THE PLAINS			CLIMATIC CHANGES
		HUNTER GATHERERS	FARMERS	DEVELOPMENTS	
Modern Times	Modern Times		Hidatsa, Mandan, Arikara, Pawnee	Horses introduced to Plains (after 1640)	
AD 1541 —	AD 1541 —	PROTOHISTORIC PERIOD LATE PREHISTORIC PERIOD	PLAINS VILLAGE (Central Plains & Middle Missouri)	Onate expedition (1598) Coronado expedition (1541)	LATE HOLOCENE
				Communal bison hunting reaches greatest intensity after AD 550	
AD 15 —	AD 1 —	LATE PLAINS ARCHAIC	PLAINS WOODLAND	Bow and arrow introduced to the Plains Pottery appears (*c.* AD 500) Maize appears (*c.* AD 300)	
1267 BC —	1000 BC —				
2477 BC —	2000 BC —	MIDDLE PLAINS ARCHAIC			- - - - - - - - -
3795 BC —	3000 BC —			McKean Complex on Northwestern Plains Head-Smashed-In site first in use	
4935 BC —	4000 BC —	EARLY PLAINS ARCHAIC			MIDDLE HOLOCENE
5876 BC —	5000 BC —				
7056 BC —	6000 BC —			Olsen-Chubbock site Bison hunting assumes predominant importance	- - - - - - - - -
8247 BC —	7000 BC —	PALEO-INDIANS			EARLY HOLOCENE
9368 BC —	8000 BC —			Extinction of Ice Age megafauna	
11,400 BC —	9000 BC —				

CHAPTER 6

BISON HUNTERS ON THE PLAINS

During the early 19th century 27 tribes of horse-mounted Indians dominated the Great Plains. All of them were either nomadic buffalo (bison) hunters subsisting almost entirely off Plains game herds, or semi-nomadic farmers, who relied on crops for a substantial part of their diet. These groups were of diverse biological and linguistic origin, but they shared a common culture based on the horse, a culture that valued bravery in war and ardent militarism.

Such colorful cultures were the stuff of which legends were made. Years of spectacular raids and battles against encroaching white settlers gave the Plains Indians a villainous and warlike reputation. Reports of these many skirmishes by traveling correspondents and small town reports gave the "feathered brave" an air of romantic invincibility that was grist to the mill for dime-store novelists. Without conscious effort, thousands of 19th-century Americans absorbed inaccurate and misleading stereotypes of Indians in the far west, images of fierce, colorfully dressed and mounted Indian braves and their romantic squaws.

The stereotypes persisted in the circus ring and later in the movies. William F. (Buffalo Bill) Cody employed a large troop of Plains Indians and a band of cowboys to tour eastern cities in his famous Wild West Show (illus. p. 113). Bands of gaily painted warriors in bright robes dashed around the arena on their "Indian ponies." They wore glamorous regalia and showy war bonnets with twin tails, attire that was, in fact, never worn to war but only on ceremonial occasions. The warriors attacked covered wagons and stage coaches, only to be gunned down by gallant cowboys who arrived at just the right moment to dispatch the pesky redskins. To add authenticity to his shows, Cody engaged veteran warriors such as the Dakota leader Sitting Bull, men who had recently featured in well-publicized skirmishes on the Plains.

The Wild West show gradually gave way to the circus and the western movie. Many western stories that appeared in that bastion of Middle Class America, the *Saturday Evening Post*, became Hollywood films, and later television shows. The Indians that formed the backdrop to the story were almost invariably dressed in Plains costumes, even if the plot unfolded at a location thousands of miles away from the open grasslands.

Generations of western tales and movies led not only to persistent stereotypes of Indian society, but also to the widespread assumption that Plains Indian culture was static over long periods of time. The Plains peoples were

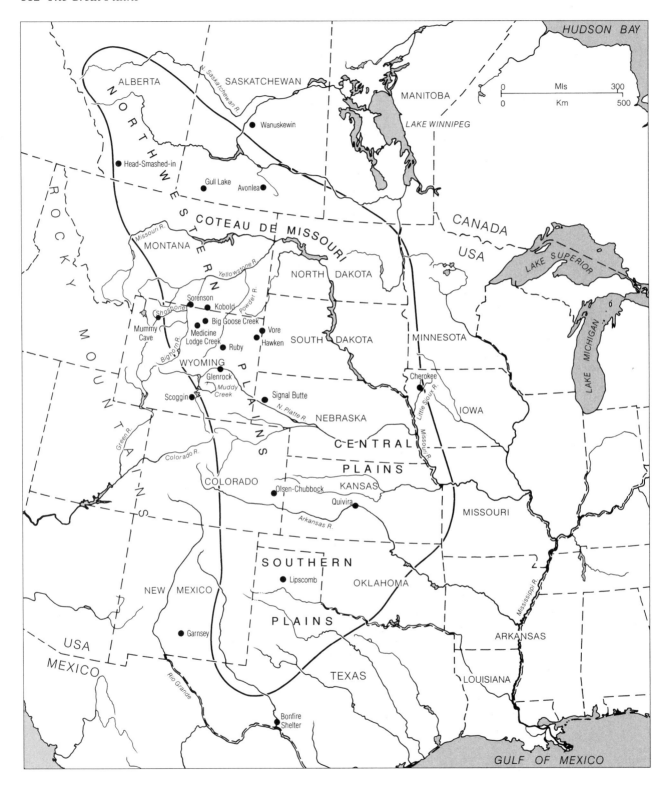

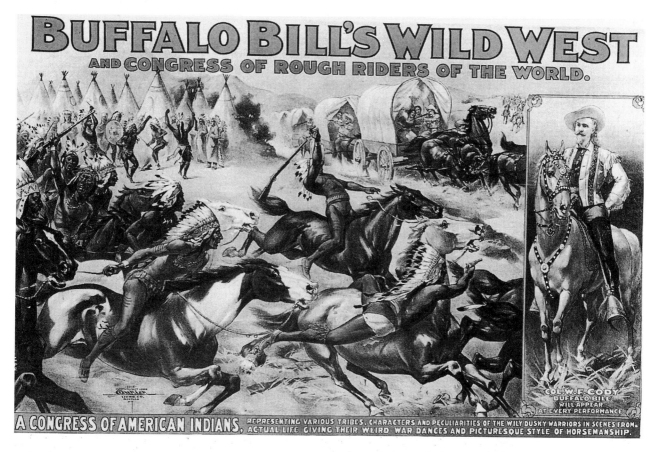

A stereotyped image of Plains life. In the late 19th century Buffalo Bill's Wild West Show promised "wily dusky warriors giving their weird war dances."

(Opposite) Archaeological sites of the Great Plains referred to in the text.

frozen, as it were, in the form in which they flourished during the stirring years between 1830 and 1880, the decades of white expansion into the far west.

Spanish adventurers first encountered the Great Plains in the mid-16th century. They reached the grasslands after hundreds of miles of scrub-covered countryside and marveled at the prodigious numbers of "wild cows" that roamed the Plains. Fur traders from eastern Canada explored the northern reaches of the treeless country. It was late 18th-century British fur traders who first called the treeless grasslands the Great Plains. American explorers of the 1800s were less sanguine, considering the central plains unfit for human habitation, calling it "The Great American Desert."

Most 19th-century authorities were content to accept the judgment of the great anthropologist Lewis Henry Morgan – that American Indians only settled the harsh Plains when they acquired the horse and the rifle. He claimed the grasslands had been uninhabited by human beings until about 1000 BC. Then a few groups had moved to the edge of the Plains and remained there until the Spaniards brought horses to the Southwest. The Indians had embraced these strange beasts with enthusiasm, then settled rapidly in buffalo country where they flourished until European contact.

The Folsom discoveries of the 1920s and other archaeological finds proved that the Plains had been continuously occupied by hunter-gatherer peoples for at least 10,000 years. Chapter 5 described Paleo-Indian settlement on the Plains; we must now examine later adaptations to this diverse and challenging environment.

The Plains Environment and Climate Change

The Great Plains cover an enormous area of North America's heartland from the Rockies in the west to the Eastern Woodlands near the Mississippi. They are a grass sea that extends across about a half-billion acres from Canada in the north to Mexico's Rio Grande in the south. The Plains are a vast area of low-to-moderate relief with relatively low rainfall. They were, and still are, a harsh place to live, with often brutally hot summers and long, bitterly cold winters. The original native vegetation was perennial grasses, with trees limited to stream valleys and occasional higher ground (Kay, 1998a).

The actual boundaries between the Plains and neighboring environments are often blurred. Sometimes one can literally draw a line between the Rocky Mountain foothills and the Plains. In other places, long mountain ridges finger into the open country, forming intermontane basins that obscure the boundary. The eastern frontiers of the Plains pass imperceptibly into the Eastern Woodlands as annual rainfall rises and short grass prairie gives way to tall, lusher grasses, then woodland.

Flying over the Plains at 40,000 feet gives a misleading impression of environmental homogeneity over hundreds, if not thousands, of miles. One can drive for hours across gently rolling landscape, over seemingly drab, unchanging plains. Then one encounters an unexpected stream, a local spring, or a deep gully that alters the entire landscape. It is then one realizes that the Plains are a very diverse environment, where complicated changes in climatic conditions produce major variations in local rainfall and climate.

Waldo Wedel (1961) aptly described the Plains as a grassland triangle, with the irregular base resting on the foot of the Rocky Mountains in the west, the apex meeting in the deciduous forests of the Mississippi Valley in the east. The natural vegetation consists mainly of grasses, with sparse tree coverage along many watercourses. The grass coverage itself varies with rainfall. In the drier west, from the South Saskatchewan Valley into Montana and western North Dakota, then far southward into Texas, are the short-grass plains. The low-growing, shallow-rooted grasses grow rapidly in the spring, then enter a period of dormancy when they cure to a highly nutritious winter forage, which was an ideal food for bison and antelope. Between the 98th and 100th meridians, between southern Manitoba and Oklahoma, the short-grass plains with their steppe-like vegetation, become a transition zone of mixed grasses, followed by the tall-grass cover of the true prairie. In Texas, both the short-grass and mixed-grass plains become mesquite and desert-grass savanna.

The Plains are windy, subject to dramatic temperature changes, and very harsh winters. Long, hot summers can bring scorching winds from the south, which shrivel vegetation, dry out the soil, and cause catastrophic crop failures. The western regions are drier than the east, but evaporation rates are all-important, being far higher in the south than on the Canadian plains, where about 15 in (38 cm) of rain is equivalent to 22 in (56 cm) in

Texas. Summer rainfall was crucial to Plains farmers. As much as 75 percent of the annual precipitation fell in spring and summer, for the exiguous winter rains leave very little stored moisture in the soil for growing crops (see Chapter 7). Unfortunately, rainfall varied greatly from year to year, coming mainly in highly localized thunderstorms, which leave one area soaked, another a few miles away baking in the hot sun. Agriculture was a high risk proposition at the best of times. Of even greater importance than rainfall to the indigenous population was the length of the growing season, for crops like maize and beans are very sensitive to frost. In the Central and Southern Plains, about as far north as the Platte River, the season was about 140 to 200 days. Unpredictable frosts to the north shortened the season drastically, to as little as 100 to 120 days in four years out of five. Constantly fluctuating rainfall and persistent aridity made farming difficult west of the 98th meridian, the arbitrary frontier between the nomadic bison-hunting groups of the west and the settled village peoples of the eastern Plains.

The Plains cover such an enormous area that archaeologists have divided them into five regions. The Northwestern Plains extend deep into Alberta and Saskatchewan and along the eastern flanks of the Rocky Mountains. They encompass the Upper Missouri River drainage, the interconnected depressions of the Wyoming Basin, and some of the driest land on the Great Plains. At the time of European contact, the Blackfeet hunted bison north of the Missouri River in western Montana and ranged deep into Alberta. To the east were the Plains Cree in southern Saskatchewan, who were in constant conflict with the Blackfeet. Numerous other groups hunted over the High Plains, especially after the arrival of the horse in the 18th century, but there is evidence of bison hunting going back to at least 10,000 years ago across the High Plains. The middle Missouri Valley forms another distinct segment of the Plains. Eight hundred miles (1288 km) long, the middle Missouri extends from the confluence of the Yellowstone in western North Dakota to the Fort Randall Dam area of South Dakota. The middle Missouri has a rich archaeological record, as well as being a major travel route for early European explorers and fur traders, who documented the historic peoples of the region (Lehmer, 1971; Zimmerman, 1985). The latter include the Arikara in South Dakota, the Mandan upstream of the Grand River, and the Hidatsa of the Knife River region.

The Northeastern Periphery extends north and east from the middle Missouri, passing into a prairie landscape dotted with marshes, lakes, and patches of deciduous woodland. It ends deep in Saskatchewan and near Winnipeg, merging into northern woodland well north of the 49th parallel. At European contact, various Sioux groups dominated this region, but the earlier history of the Northeastern Periphery was very complicated.

Considerable topographic diversity marks the Central Plains, which extend from the semi-arid short-grass High Plains steppe of eastern Colorado across Nebraska and Kansas and the southeastern corner of Wyoming. During the 19th century, the Dakota, Cheyenne, Arapaho, Comanche, Kiowa, and Apache ranged over the arid High Plains of the west. The fertile and well-watered alluvial plains and terraces of the rivers to the east of the 100th meridian provided opportunities for semi-sedentary settlement by corn-growing Village tribes, among them the Poncas and Omahas of northeastern Nebraska, and the Pawnees of eastern central

Nebraska, and other groups like the Kansas and Wichita to the south. Much Central Plains archaeology has focused on the Republican River Basin, which extends nearly 400 miles (644 km) from east to west, from Colorado to central Kansas (Wedel, 1986). Here, the archaeological record chronicles the changing, long-term relationships between humans and the Central Plains environment over more than 10,000 years. The Southern Plains lie south of the 37th parallel, in Oklahoma, Texas, and eastern New Mexico. In Oklahoma, they end on the Ozark Plateau, and at Cross Timbers in eastern Texas. Their southern boundary lies in central Texas. They include the High Plains of the Llano Estacado, ending in the Pecos Valley to the west (Wedel, 1961). The Southern Plains were home to the Apache, Comanche, and Kiowa in the west, to the semi-horticultural Caddoan in the east.

The archaeological record of the Great Plains is so diverse that I cannot do it justice within the narrow confines of these pages. In the interests of clarity, I have divided my account into two chapters. The present chapter focuses mainly on the bison hunters of the west, while Chapter 7 discusses the village farmers east of the 98th meridian. It should be noted, however, that the discussion of bison hunters covers Paleo-Indian and Archaic peoples throughout the Plains, narrowing to the arid west for later times.

Holocene Environmental Change

The Great Plains lie in the rain shadow of the Rocky Mountains, their climate dominated by three major air masses that usually move across North America from west to east. Mild Pacific air from the west has lost most of its moisture by the time it crosses the Great Basin and Rockies. On the Plains, it meets moist, warm subtropical air from the Gulf of Mexico and cold, dry arctic air moving southward from Canada. A strong westerly air flow over the Plains enhances arid conditions over the western Plains. But there are constant local changes caused by ever-altering air-mass circulation patterns that weaken prevailing westerlies and allow moist tropical air over the grasslands. The result is constant variations in plant and animal distributions throughout the Plains, an environmental characteristic that has persisted through thousands of years of prehistory, and, indeed, much earlier into geological time.

During the Early Holocene, after forest developed on newly deglaciated land, continued climatic warming led to major vegetational changes, with spruce forests giving way to prairie grasslands as early as 9000 BC (Wright, H.E., 1983). Further east, a brief interlude of deciduous woodland in a parkland landscape also gave way to open prairie about 7500 BC. In some places in the extreme east of the Plains, deciduous woodland survived until about 5000 BC.

This boundary between prairie and woodland is especially important, for pollen samples provide strong evidence for a progressive decrease in moisture as the dry Pacific air masses shifted position when the Laurentide ice sheet retreated across central and eastern Canada. This meant that dry, cold arctic air flowed less frequently over the Plains. During the Early Holocene, the deciduous forest was dominated by elm and other cooler weather trees, with warmer-loving oak much less widely distributed than in later times.

Vegetation is the most important factor in controlling the distribution of animals, and it is noteworthy that most large Ice Age animals became extinct before 8000 BC, just as these major vegetational changes were taking place. Some paleoecologists believe that the increased seasonality at the end of the Ice Age may have led to shorter, warmer winters with cooler summers than today. This would have allowed temperate trees like ash and oak to mingle with spruce and other colder-loving trees, creating a greater range of habitats for a more diversified mammalian fauna. The warming climate set in motion a series of progressive environmental changes that resulted in a form of dynamic equilibrium during the Middle Holocene, although much climatic change was highly localized.

The increasingly dry conditions peaked during the Middle Holocene, when the prairie/deciduous forest border was more than 62 miles (100 km) east of its present position. This so-called Prairie Peninsula reached its maximum extent between 6000 and about 3000 BC, but changed its position somewhat, probably in response to fluctuations in the lingering Lauren-tide ice sheet on the Labrador Plateau far to the north. The Peninsula is a mosaic of prairie and forest, its shift to the east during the Middle Holocene signaling the more frequent occurrence of warm, dry westerly air flow across the Plains.

The eastward expansion of the Prairie Peninsula in the Middle Holocene coincided with Ernst Antevs' so-called Altithermal episode of 6000 to 2500 BC. This was when temperatures and dry conditions reached their maximum on the Plains, to the point that some scholars have argued that the grasslands were completely devoid of human habitation because of the dry conditions (Reeves, 1973). This seems unlikely, for there is evidence of Altithermal occupation at several major bison kill sites including Hawkens and Head-Smashed-In (see below). Bison population densities may at times have been much reduced, but we can be certain that the animals were a constant resource on the Plains, although arid conditions impacting on grazing range may have reduced herd populations considerably or affected vital seasonal migration patterns.

Some idea of the localized conditions that affected bison hunting can be gained from Vaughn Bryant's palynological researches in southwest Texan caves (Bryant and Holloway, 1985). Bonfire Shelter is located hundreds of miles south of the Great Plains, and is the southernmost site in North America where mass bison hunts took place. There are two discrete zones of bison bones in the shelter, each apparently representing repeated bison jumps over relatively short periods, perhaps no more than 50 to 100 years. The earliest bone deposit resulted from Paleo-Indian hunts, the later one from another episode of repeated game drives in about 500 BC. What happened during the 7500 years that separated the two bone beds? Bryant's pollen samples revealed that the Bonfire Shelter region enjoyed good grass cover only twice since 10,000 BC. Each of these periods coincided with a layer of bison bones, each time when it was possible for the area to support large herds of grazing animals. At other times, such as during the Altithermal, the grass cover was much reduced, suggesting that opportunistic hunters followed the bison into the Bonfire Shelter area, and chose that ideal location for their hunts. Throughout ancient times, survival depended on careful observation of changing grazing conditions, and of bison movements.

Ancient Plains people appear to have responded to dry conditions by diversifying their subsistence strategies. The Cherokee Sewer Site in northwest Iowa consists of three stratified cultural horizons in an alluvial fan at the edge of the Little Sioux River. Each horizon is associated with bison butchery, dating to about 6400, 5300, and 4350 BC respectively (Shutler and others, 1974). The small animal bones, gastropods, and pollen samples from the Cherokee site show that the local climate was drier than today in about 4400 BC, with slightly higher mean winter temperatures. There may also have been some diversification of hunting economies. The Coffey site in northeast Kansas dates to about 3100 BC, and was a place where people not only exploited bison, but hunted deer, shot waterfowl, and foraged for many species of wild vegetable foods. Sites like Mummy Cave in northern Wyoming (Wedel and others, 1968) (occupied as early as 7000 BC) and Medicine Lodge Creek, 99 miles (160 km) to the east (Frison and Wilson, 1975), also reflect a more diverse subsistence strategy at the edge of the Plains during the Altithermal. Other locations, like the Hawken site in Wyoming, were the scene of communal kills, another strategy for maximizing the hunt when food resources were scarce (Frison, 1992).

Bison and Humans

For most of the past, the Great Plains were a favorable habitat for large, gregarious herbivores. At the time of first European contact, a north–south belt of short grasses such as *Bouteloua* and *Bucloe* flourished in the west beyond the 100th meridian. This grass was well adapted to dry soils and a short growing season in an environment under the rain shadow of the Rockies where as little as 14.7 in (37.5 cm), or less, precipitation fell every year. The average annual rainfall rises gradually as one travels eastward, reaching 24.6 in (62.5 cm), to as high as 39 in (100 cm) on the tall bluegrass prairie, sometimes called the *needlegrass-pronghorn-grama grass* biome. This was the heart of the bison's range, the animal that was the staple of human diet on the Plains. Not that the staple was a reliable one. The amount and distribution of annual rainfall was especially important to bison, for grass production was not uniform over the Plains. So the grazing animals shifted location from one year to the next, following fresh, green spring grass. The condition of the graze was vital, for successions of dry years with short grass could force the bison to grub close to the ground, wearing out and breaking their teeth on the soil and grass stems. As the teeth wear down, the grinding surfaces become less efficient, until the animal finally can no longer feed itself and dies. Thus, human populations were constantly on the move, following bison herds on their annual range.

Bison colonized North America long before the Wisconsin glaciation. Primeval forms often reached enormous sizes, with great horns measuring 6 ft or more (2 m) from tip to tip. The smaller Wisconsin long-horned form, *Bison antiquus*, was distributed between Alberta and Texas, but also as far afield as California and Florida. After the Ice Age, bison became more abundant, but also decreased in size. A postglacial type, *Bison occidentalis*, invaded the Plains and came into contact with the much larger *antiquus* form. From their genetic mixing evolved the Plains bison, *Bison bison*.

American buffalo, named Black Diamond, from the National Zoological Park: this animal served as the model for the $10 bill of 1901. He also appeared on a US postage stamp of the same period.

Ice Age steppe bison had a very short spring calving period, for their young had to be reared before the next harsh winter. In contrast, *Bison bison* has a longer rutting season that covers more than a month. As post-Ice Age bison adapted to the short grasslands of the "Great Bison Belt," their winter mortality declined, the breeding season lengthened, and they became much less selective eaters. *Bison bison* flourished while other large Pleistocene mammals came under increasing stress. The arid, western Plains had always been inhabited by hunter-gatherers, who were concentrated along stream valleys and near springs. They supplemented bison meat with other food resources, among them pronghorns, deer, elk, bears, and other, small animals such as marmots. Fish and shellfish were occasionally important, as were seasonal wild vegetable foods such as the prairie turnip (*Psoralea*), groundnuts (*Apios*), ground beans (*Amphicarpa*), sunflowers, and Jerusalem artichokes, as well as seasonal fruits.

The mixed and tall-grass prairies of the eastern Plains supported soils that were more suitable for horticulture. Fertile, easily cultivable river bottoms enabled many eastern Plains groups to grow substantial food surpluses that were used in trade with non-farmers to the west (for a full discussion of the rise of agriculture, see Chapter 14). Agriculture took hold in these regions about 500 years before European contact, with farming being combined with seasonal bison hunting. The agricultural traditions of the eastern Plains have close ties to contemporary cultures in the Mississippi Valley and further afield. But the basic cultural roots of many of these groups lay in big-game hunting traditions that flourished for thousands of years on the Plains.

Plains Archaic Traditions
c. 5600 BC to c. AD 500

Plains Indians moved around in small bands in a highly mobile lifeway, where relatively few locations were exploited on a regular basis (Chapter 5). As Douglas Bamforth has argued (1988), there was probably some seasonal aggregation and dispersal of Plains Paleo-Indian populations. To some degree, too, population movements depended as well on the availability of fine-grained rock for the making of large bifaces that were the sources, in turn, of the flakes used to make fluted and other projectile points (Wobst, 1974).

Population densities were lower than in later times, too, the hunters relying heavily on their stalking skills and on patient observation during the chase. During earlier periods, Paleo-Indians were less selective in their killing, whereas later groups took mainly cow and calf herds. Perhaps mass bison kills were much rarer than they were to become in later times, when both technology and hunting methods became more efficient and apparently more standardized. In addition, there is some reason to believe that Paleo-Indian groups lacked the manpower to butcher all the animals they took in occasional mass drives, even when hunting cooperatively with others. In some cases, the hunt may have taken place in winter, so the hunters let the carcasses freeze, then lived alongside their kill for some time (Reher and Frison, 1980; Kelly and Todd, 1988).

There were probably substantial differences in bison adaptations and game densities in different areas of the Great Plains. Recent and historical records show, for example, that bison herds in the drier southwestern Plains would have been smaller, fewer, and more mobile and less predictable in their movements than those to the northeast. Using ethnographic records and a sophisticated climatic index, Douglas Bamforth has argued (1988) that the more complex Plains societies were indeed in those areas where favorable climatic conditions should have supported larger, less mobile, and thus more predictable bison herds.

The Paleo-Indians gave way to much more varied Archaic hunting traditions on the Plains after 8000 BC, traditions associated with gradually more sophisticated bison procurement methods. With the onset of the warmer and drier climate of the Middle Holocene in about 6000 BC, the human population of the Plains may have declined considerably, although earlier hypotheses of complete abandonment, based on lack of sites, seem too extreme.

The Plains Archaic is still little known, with the most thoroughly researched sites occurring on the Northwest Plains. I have used Northwestern Plains as a framework for the discussion of the Archaic which follows, adding further details from other areas where appropriate (Frison, 1992).

Early Plains Archaic
c. 5600 to 3000 BC or later

The onset of the Plains Archaic is marked by an abrupt change in projectile-point forms from lanceolate Paleo-Indian types to characteristic side-notched Archaic points. The side notch was an important innovation, for the notches presumably allowed a much tighter and stronger binding of the head to foreshaft or spear handle. The effectiveness of the improved design is shown by the rapid spread of the innovation over the Plains.

The point changeover is well documented at Mummy Cave close to the Shoshone River near Yellowstone National Park in Wyoming, in an occupation level dating to about 5600 BC. Similar side-notched points have been recovered from other sites such as the Medicine Lodge Creek location and the stratified Sorenson site in Bighorn Canyon (Husted, 1969).

Though still little known, several local variations of Early Archaic projectile points are found throughout the Plains, which are fundamentally

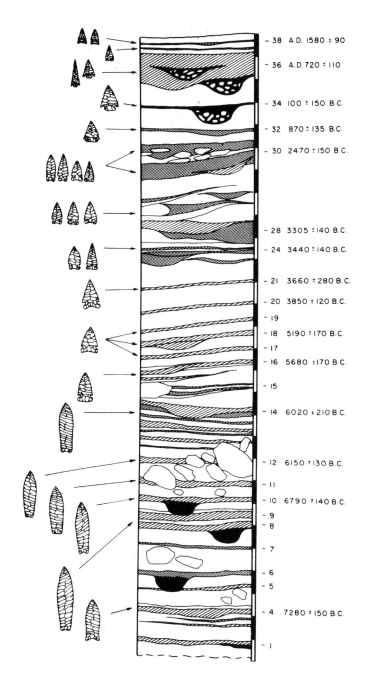

- 38   A.D. 1580 ± 90
- 36   A.D. 720 ± 110
- 34   100 ± 150 B.C.
- 32   870 ± 135 B.C.
- 30   2470 ± 150 B.C.
- 28   3305 ± 140 B.C.
- 24   3440 ± 140 B.C.
- 21   3660 ± 280 B.C.
- 20   3850 ± 120 B.C.
- 19
- 18   5190 ± 170 B.C.
- 17
- 16   5680 ± 170 B.C.
- 15
- 14   6020 ± 210 B.C.
- 12   6150 ± 130 B.C.
- 11
- 10   6790 ± 140 B.C.
- 9
- 8
- 7
- 6
- 5
- 4   7280 ± 150 B.C.
- 1

Mummy Cave, northwestern Wyoming: stratigraphic profile showing periods of human occupation separated by layers of silt. Projectile-point forms illustrated at left show the change from Paleo-Indian lanceolate forms to side-notched and then stemmed forms, starting about 5600 BC.

Well field on Middle Holocene surface, Mustang Springs, Texas.

of local interest (Frison, 1998; Kay, 1998b). There seems to have been a proliferation of different forms toward the end of the Early Archaic. By all indications, Early Archaic hunter-gatherers lived in much the same way as their predecessors, even if they relied on a wider variety of game and vegetable foods. The famous Head-Smashed-In Buffalo Jump in Alberta was in use in about 3500 BC. Levels of this approximate age contain Mummy Cave-style Early Archaic projectile points.

The Hawken site in Wyoming of about 4400 BC records an Early Archaic hunt where bison were driven up a narrow arroyo until they reached the knickpoint barrier, a perpendicular cliff band that impeded further progress up the gully. Hawken was used at least three times, and, judging from the bison jaws, the hunts occurred in early or mid-winter. The hunters were taking both mature beasts and driving nursery herds, but the killing was tough work. At least 300 projectile points were found among the bones, many of them broken by the brutal impact against struggling animals. Many of the Hawken points had been reworked again and again, with carefully ground bases and needle sharp tips that penetrated hides and muscles very effectively.

The Plains Archaic flourished during the Mid-Holocene climatic optimum, which had varied effects on local Plains environments (McKinnon and Stuart, 1987). That the warmer and drier conditions affected bison populations seems certain, but we know nothing of the effects of drier, warmer conditions on the distributions of Archaic human populations and their hunting practices.

The warmer and drier conditions may have diminished grass cover throughout the Central Plains, allowing short-grass steppe to expand at the expense of tall-grass prairie, which may have resulted in significant reduction of the large herbivore population. Archaic groups could have responded by focusing more intensively on plant foods. Such occupation is marked by surface finds of projectile points, but few sites have received detailed attention. At the Spring Creek site in the Republican River Valley, Nebraska, Archaic hearths have been exposed over 17 acres (7 ha), associated with bison bones and radiocarbon dated to about 3700 BC. In about 3250 BC, another group of Archaic people occupied the Coffey site on the edge of an oxbow lake of the Big Blue River, north of Manhattan, Kansas. Coffey represents a series of seasonal occupations, when people took not only bison and other game, but also pursued waterfowl and collected goosefoot and other plants. They also caught large numbers of catfish, as if the site was occupied during the late summer, when fish crowded into small shallow pools at the edge of the drying oxbow (Schmidts, 1978). Wedel (1986) believes that both Spring Creek and Coffey show that Archaic people supplemented a perhaps depleted game supply with plant foods and aquatic resources taken during seasonal visits to areas with permanent water supplies. The effects of the Altithermal's drier conditions would have been felt most on the uplands, where game populations were much diminished by near-desert conditions. Similarly diminished human groups would have tended to stay anchored to major river courses, where there were at least some predictable food resources. Further north, the Signal Butte sites in the North Platte Valley of western Nebraska chronicle bison hunting in about 3500 to 3000 BC (Strong, 1935).

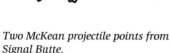

Two McKean projectile points from Signal Butte.

Middle Plains Archaic
c. 2900 to c. 1000 BC

The Middle Archaic saw the progressive refinement of both hunting toolkits and bison-hunting methods. We know most about Northwest Plains groups, who appear to have moved onto the open plains and into the interiors of intermontane basins, also increasing their emphasis on plant foods. These moves are associated with the sudden appearance of the so-called McKean Complex as early as 2900 BC (Kornfeld and Todd, 1989). In the Bighorn Basin, for example, the people now commonly used sandstone grinders to process wild vegetable foods, as well as roasting pits that were often used again and again for centuries. This is not to say that the Plains people of this region gave up hunting bison all together. Rather, they developed a hunter-gatherer adaptation that relied on carefully planned scheduling of economic activities throughout the year, activities closely tied to seasons of wild plants and the annual movements of game herds. Each band may well have ranged over a wide area annually.

The label McKean is somewhat controversial, on the grounds that it may disguise greater cultural elaboration. McKean at present subsumes not only the lanceolate McKean point with indented base and convex blade edges, but numerous variations on this artifact theme as well. Judging from the highly localized and distinctive points found with several Middle Archaic bison kills, it may be that some almost-McKean forms may, in fact, have been used for highly specialized activities.

On the Northwestern Plains, the Middle Archaic also saw the appearance of large numbers of stone rings, circles between 11 and 24 ft (3.3–7.3 m) in diameter that could been the bases for circular lodges or tipis. However, they may have served many other purposes as well (Kehoe, 1960; Hoffman, 1953). Many of them were used for very short periods of time, perhaps only a few days or weeks, sometimes single circles. At other locations, concentrations of hundreds lie on higher ground or along stream terraces. Unfortunately, nearly all of the circles are devoid of artifacts, except for the occasional flake or broken projectile point.

Middle Archaic sites in the Northwest include not only bison kills but seasonal camps where mule deer and some mountain sheep were taken. About 2500 BC, bison remains become more common in many Northwestern Plains sites. There were major shifts in bison procurement throughout the Plains, for the people now mainly hunted them in the fall. These hunts were often concentrated at favored locations that were used again and again. The resulting carcasses were processed very thoroughly, and much of the meat made into pemmican (a mixture of pounded flesh and fat), as if the emphasis was on long-term storage, apparently less important in earlier times. The hunters still used tried and tested methods employed by their remote ancestors, especially the arroyo trap system. Bison jumps were also used, witness the Kobold site in southern Montana that remained in use right into later times. Kobold is a 25-ft (7.6-m) high sandstone bluff close to well-watered grazing land. The arroyo below the cliff is wide and spacious, which was ideal for butchering large numbers of animals. The terrain is favorable for game drives, allowing but one approach to the bluff, an approach, which was narrowed even more closely by rows of stone piles, at least in later times. Judging from the many broken bones among the bison

The jump-off point at the Kobold site, southern Montana.

remains, many of the animals were killed by the precipitous fall, and fewer projectile points were present than at Hawken, for example. There are four Middle Archaic kill sites in this general Powder River area. Frison (1992) believes that the people of the area conducted communal bison hunts during fall and winter, and perhaps in early spring, collaborating to kill large numbers of beasts, not only for fresh meat but also for dried flesh that was stored for use during cold periods when hunting was impossible.

Middle Archaic hunters are also known to have made use of artificial corrals, like the enclosure dating to about 2500 BC found at the Scoggin site north of Rawlins, Wyoming. Scoggin lies at the end of a natural gap in a long ridge astride a route that bison took when going to water. The site was ideal, for the stampeding beasts could be driven over a short steep slope into a specially constructed stone and wood corral. The walls were probably covered with hides preventing the animals from seeing out and trying to force an exit.

Late Plains Archaic on the Northwestern Plains
c. 1000 BC to AD 500

Once again, the changeover from Middle to Late Archaic is marked by projectile-point innovations rather than by any significant alteration in lifeway. The distinctive Pelican Lake point appears, a corner-notched point with wide, open notches that form sharp points as they intersect both the edges and base. Pelican Lake sites occur in southern Saskatchewan, and bison kills by these people are dated to between about 1000 and 700 BC at Head-Smashed-In, Alberta.

In the 3rd century BC, a highly sophisticated Late Archaic bison hunting culture emerged on the Northwestern Plains, a culture known by

Besant projectile point from the Muddy Creek site, length c. *9 cm.*

characteristic, long-sided and dart-like Besant projectile points (Wettlaufer, 1955; Frison, 1971). These people used much more complicated bison corrals built of logs set in deep post holes known from two Wyoming locations. The Ruby site lies on a dry tributary of the Powder River, while Muddy Creek is on a small side stream of the North Platte River.

The Ruby corral was placed on the low-lying stream bed in such a way that the stampeding animals did not see the enclosure until the last minute. The hunters also used natural features like ridges and arroyo banks to "funnel" their quarry toward the pen. Significantly, it is just at the moment when the bison would have sighted the corral that projectile points first appear, as if the hunters were goading the animals on toward the entrance. The Ruby hunters were real experts at handling stampeding animals, for to steer them into the corral required pursuing and prodding the fast-reacting bison at just the right moments.

The corral bears a surprising resemblance to modern cattle corrals. Almost certainly the hunters erected pairs of stout posts separated by the diameter of the horizontal timbers wedged between them. The result was a strong structure that could withstand the onslaught of penned animals, even if they could see out. The Ruby corral was built on a slope, and the lowest wall was subjected to the most stress. Frison observed that it had been rebuilt several times, strengthened perhaps, as this was the place where the animals could be crowded for slaughter purposes. The excavators found bison ribs and jaws that were used for digging the post holes into the soft, sandy soil. The builders used juniper wood, perhaps burning off suitable poles rather than cutting them down, and they used dead timber as well. Frison estimates 20 hunters would have taken between 10 and 14 days to build the Ruby corral, final drive lane, and wing walls. He believes that this substantial investment of time and labor was made with the intention of using the corral over a long period of time.

The downslope side of the corral was filled with bison bones to a depth of over a foot (0.3 m), so many animals were killed there. A so-far unexcavated processing area covering at least 10,000 sq. ft (929 sq. m) lies about 1000 ft (304.8 m) up the arroyo. Nearby, also, lies what appears to have been a ceremonial structure formed by the intersection of two arcs of circles each about 33.5 ft (10.2 m) in radius. The outline of the 39-ft (11.8-m) long structure was delineated by post holes, with the ends oriented on a north–south axis. Five post holes across the 15-ft (4.5-m) widest axis separated the structure into two enclosures, at least one of which was roofed. Eight male bison skulls lay at the southern end. Frison believes the stout building was a form of shaman's structure, where the priest who supervised corral construction sang and smoked to invoke his spirit helpers (Frison, 1971). Judging from both historical accounts and archaeological observations at other sites, ritual observances played an important part in communal bison hunting.

The Muddy Creek site corral was also built on sloping ground, a structure about 40 ft (12.2 m) in diameter. It lay upslope from extensive, fertile grazing tracts, and was hidden from view by a low ridge until the very last moments of a drive. Both this, and the Ruby corral, were designed to handle relatively small numbers of bison, perhaps a nursery herd of about 25 beasts. The teeth from both sites suggest they were used in fall and early winter, when calves were 5 to 8 months old (Frison, 1992).

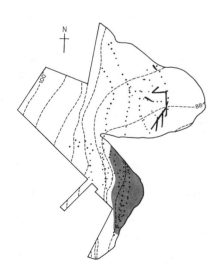

Plan of the Ruby site.

These sites chronicle much more sophisticated bison hunting methods that were introduced to the Plains during the Late Archaic. Now the hunters were less dependent on the arroyo trap and the jump. Instead, they constructed skillfully contrived artificial corrals that could be set up in a much wider variety of optimum locations, corrals that were erected with the aid of the powerful supernatural forces that governed human life on the Plains, forces that were still invoked 1800 years later, when Europeans spilled onto the grasslands.

Southern Plains bison populations rose sharply during the Late Archaic (Dillehay, 1974), reflected in dense accumulations of bison bones at Bonfire Shelter, Texas, and in the Texas Panhandle (Hester and others, 1989). While bison appears to have assumed greater importance during the Late Archaic, each group probably relied heavily on plant foods and other resources for much of their diet.

Bison Jumps

Communal bison hunting on foot reached its greatest intensity after AD 550, during a period that saw the bow and arrow reach the Plains, perhaps from the northwest. George Frison (1992) argues that the bow and arrow was not that much more effective than stone-tipped spears unless it penetrated the animal through the ribs. However, the stone points could be made from more easily obtainable rocks, and arrow shafts were easier to make than long, well-balanced spears to be launched with the atlatl. The bow had a longer range, and many arrows could be carried in a convenient quiver without the need to mount new foreshafts all the time. Furthermore, the bow was easier to handle, for the hunter could adopt any stance, take his time aiming, and do so from a slightly greater range. The bow was adopted quite quickly, but still did not solve the problem of driving and controlling the movement of the quarry. As time went on, the hunters made increasing use of bison jumps, high bluffs approached by long lines of stone piles, over which they could stampede large herds. These drive lines served as markers for the stalkers moving the herd into position.

Bison jumps were situated at strategic locations, such as convenient bluffs, precipitous cliffs, sink holes, and other natural features that, combined with one another, made for a suitable killing site. Unlike a corral, a successful jump hunt depended on a large number of animals, so that the pursuers could stampede them, by moving them close together at a high rate of speed. With a large group, the leaders would be prevented from turning aside, as would happen with a small herd. Frison, with his extensive experience of cattle ranching and herding, points out that 10 mounted and well-trained cowboys should be able to maneuver 100 head of buffalo into the proper place and stand a better than even chance of stampeding them over a cliff, if conditions are favorable.

The classic bison jump sites of the northwest Plains document bison jumps, and the drive lines of stone piles associated with them, in great detail. Locations such as Glenrock, Big Goose Creek, and Vore, Wyoming, document how the hunters moved herds over distances of several miles to their deaths. At Vore (Reher, 1974), the excavators used layered pond sediments in the sink hole "jump" to estimate that five bison hunts took

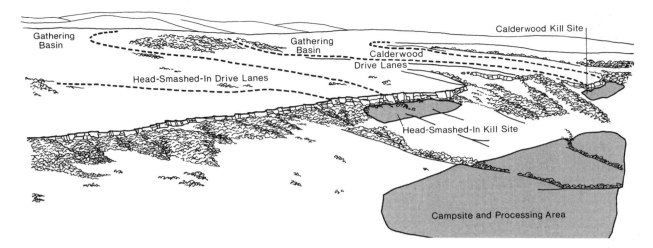

Gathering Basin
Gathering Basin
Calderwood Kill Site
Calderwood Drive Lanes
Head-Smashed-In Drive Lanes
Head-Smashed-In Kill Site
Campsite and Processing Area

Head-Smashed-In, Alberta, is among the oldest, largest, and best preserved of the western Plains buffalo jump sites. (Top) Major features of the site and the neighboring Calderwood site, including gathering areas where the hunters maneuvered the herds into position, drive lanes, and kill and processing areas. (Above) Reconstruction of a bison jump at the Head-Smashed-In kill site.

place, each after a period of higher rainfall, spaced at about quarter-century intervals over a 140-year period after about AD 1550. Frison wonders whether these higher rainfall cycles improved the grazing grass, which led to better breeding conditions, a better calf crop, and ultimately a minor population explosion. This created optimum conditions for communal bison kills.

The famous Head-Smashed-In buffalo jump in western Alberta was used for more than 7000 years. Six streams feed into a shallow basin in the plains surrounded by higher ground. A large creek forms the only entrance. More than 500 stone cairns up to a foot (0.3 m) high mark drive lines as much as 5 miles (8 km) long leading to the sandstone cliff that formed the jump. Deep deposits of bison bones lie below the cliff, dating back to as early as about 5400 BC (Brink, 1989; Reeves, 1978).

This type of bison drive was still in use when Hudson Bay Company trader Peter Fidler spent six weeks among the Piegan Indians in 1797. He witnessed many bison drives as he camped among them at one of their drive pounds. At one drive, the hunters killed more than 250 beasts and would have taken more. But "when the wind happened to blow from the pound in the direction of the tents, there was an intolerable stench of the large numbers of petrified [sic] carcasses, etc. on which account the reason of our leaving it."

Mass kill sites like Olsen-Chubbock and Head-Smashed-In represent relatively unusual events in Plains life. For such mass hunting strategies to be successful, the bison density would have had to reach a critical level, a density only reached at certain times of the year, when patterns of animal migration permitted it. Many communal hunts may have been annual affairs, or conducted after periods of higher rainfall as we have seen, when the bison population increased.

John Speth's excavations at Garnsey, New Mexico, reveal that ancient Plains hunters were expert observers of their prey. About AD 1550, a group of hunters visited a small gully where they knew bison would congregate in late March or early April. Instead of just killing every animal on sight, they tended to concentrate on the male beasts. Speth (1983) believes this was because males are in better condition in the spring, and their bone marrow has a higher fat content. Hunters everywhere prefer fatter meat, for it is an important source of energy and essential fatty acids. In spring, such flesh was hard to come by, for the herds were still recovering from the lean winter months. So the hunters selected male beasts at Garnsey, only consuming the choicest parts with higher fat content from the few cows they killed.

The Northeastern Plains Periphery
500 BC to historic times

The Northeastern Periphery forms the northeastern margin of the Plains culture area, as the steppe and short-grass plains give way to marshy and often wooded prairie. In historic times, Dakota Sioux groups dominated much of this area, which never supported dense ancient populations. Evidence for human occupation is usually sparse before the 1st millennium BC, with a dearth of stratified sites. This large region was one where cultural influences and peoples from the east and south mingled with Plains traditions, manifested in the appearance of exotic artifacts from the Eastern Woodlands and in unusually elaborate mortuary customs (Epp and Dyck, 1983).

The most complete archaeological record covers the last 3000 years, the time when bison hunting intensified and became more efficient, perhaps as a result of the introduction of the bow and arrow in the 1st millennium BC. A long tradition of such hunting comes from such locations as Wanuskewin on the outskirts of Saskatoon, Saskatchewan, where a small tributary valley of the South Saskatchewan River provided ideal locations for bison jumps, as well as abundant plant foods and winter shelter. The location was visited by bison-hunting groups as early as AD 400.

The Gull Lake site in southwestern Saskatchewan lies in the Northwest Plains culture area, but is close to the Northeast Periphery. It lies across from the glacial hills of the Missouri Coteau, which divides the plains from the dry northeast prairie. In historic times, the western Saskatchewan uplands were the boundary between the Blackfeet and Atsina of the High Plains and the Cree and Assiniboine of the prairies (Kehoe, 1973). At Gull Lake, the hunters lured the bison along the uplands from the south until they could be driven down a deep ravine. The stampeding beasts would tumble over a landslide, which formed a convenient drop, falling into a natural depression that served as a corral. Both tipi rings and evidence of camp occupations lie nearby. Tom Kehoe excavated 20 ft (6 m) below the modern land surface in the kill area, recovering dense concentrations of bison bones. The Gull Lake area was visited as early as the 1st century BC, with the first well-documented jump episodes associated with Avonlea projectile points. Six bone layers document the Avonlea occupation, ending in the 7th century AD. Gull Lake continued in use in subsequent Prairie and Plains occupations between the 8th and 14th centuries. Kehoe believes Avonlea points (named after a site of that name in Saskatchewan) were the first to be used with bows and arrows – tiny, needlesharp, but broad enough to penetrate deeply into tough bison hide and cause loss of blood when shot from close range. He argues that complex, highly ritualized bison hunting began with the introduction of the bow and arrow by Athabaskans to the Plains.

As we shall see in Chapter 7, the Avonlea and Besant complexes of southern Canada and the Northeastern Periphery were contemporary with Plains Woodland traditions further south on the eastern Plains.

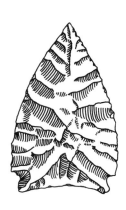

Avonlea point from Gull Lake bison drive site.

Later Bison Hunters
c. AD 500 to the 16th century

The appearance of the bow and arrow ushers in the Late Period, reflected in Avonlea and other side-notched points. Avonlea, like Gull Lake, was a highly organized bison kill site, one where the hunters were killing large numbers of bison not only to satisfy their own needs, but, perhaps, to produce surplus meat and by-products for exchange with new horticultural societies at the eastern edges of the Plains (Chapter 7). These new exchange patterns persisted into historic times.

Several pottery traditions appear on the Plains during this period, a useful chronological marker, most of them introduced from outside. Such wares include Shoshonean and Crow pottery, as well as Woodland vessels in the east. Predictably, Fremont and Pueblo wares are found in areas contiguous to the Great Basin and Southwest respectively (Chapters 12 and 15).

The great efficiency of Late Period bison hunting can be seen at the Wardell site and other locations. Wardell, in Wyoming's Green River Basin, was a bison corral from about AD 350 to 1050 (Frison, 1973). Over the centuries, local hunters used it to intercept bison moving between nearby grazing and water supplies. The corral lay at the foot of a steep cliff at the confluence of two arroyos, strengthened by slopes on three sides. At least 1000 bison were killed here over five centuries, many of them processed at a butchery camp nearby. The killing took place in fall, using bows and arrows. Much of the meat was dried or made into pemmican on-site, for stone heating and cooking pits abound. Everything points to economical butchery, with little going to waste. Frison believes the hunters lived off antelope, rabbit, and other game as well as fresh bison meat while processing their kills.

Without horses, ancient bison hunters were dependent on ever-changing herd densities for successful communal hunts. Individual or small group hunting would be far more adaptive with lower densities, for bison drives have a high failure rate and a herd could move out of foot range if allowed to escape unless herd densities were unusually high. In the final analysis, everything depended on the hunters' knowledge of bison habits and of their natural behavior. Larger hunts were surrounded by complex dance rituals. These prepared both humans and bison for the hunt, and controlled the direction and conduct of the drive. Such controls were an essential part of the organization of game drives, for success depended on the animals being kept together in tight formation, pushed along at top speed, and headed in exactly the right direction. Judging from Dennis Stanford's discovery of shamans' artifacts at a Paleo-Indian kill site, the same basic rituals sustained bison hunts for thousands of years. It was only when Europeans introduced the horse and the rifle to the Plains that the age-old hunting patterns changed and the bison virtually disappeared.

While the most spectacular finds come from the Northwestern Plains, there is abundant evidence for widespread, specialized bison hunting in later times, from the northern limit of the Plains at Wanuskewin near Saskatoon, Saskatchewan, to the Southern Plains. Space precludes a description here, and the reader is referred to Marvin Kay's recent summary (1998b). The so-called Toyah phase of central Texas and the south Texas coast provides good evidence for intensive bison hunting in the

Dance-drama: detail of a Mandan okipa (or buffalo dance) in the 1830s, depicted by the Swiss artist Karl Bodmer.

south during later times (Ricklis, 1992). The Toyah phase dates to between AD 1400 and 1600, and involved bison hunting with bows and arrows. The small Perdiz stemmed points are characteristic of this phase. As Tom Hester and his colleagues point out (1989), specialized bison hunting was a widespread phenomenon on the Southern Plains in later times, and was an activity which cut across numerous local, broad-spectrum hunter-gatherer adaptations.

Protohistoric Period
16th century AD to modern times

In AD 1541, at about the same time as a small band of hunters was killing bison at Garnsey, New Mexico, Spanish conquistador Francisco de Coronado ventured eastward from Pueblo Indian country in the Southwest from Pecos onto the Plains, in search of rumored Indian gold. One of his captains had traveled east the year before, emerging onto vast grasslands where his men were surrounded by enormous buffalo herds. Coronado's chronicler Pedro de Castañeda remarked on their "extremely large bodies and long wool." The conquistadors had some difficulty killing the large beasts, until they discovered that it was safer for their horses if they used their pikes from a distance.

Coronado journeyed east for 37 days, over featureless plains without landmarks except occasional lakes and buffalo wallows. The huge herds of domesticated animals that traveled with them obliterated their tracks, so the soldiers erected bones and cow dung to mark their route for the rear guard. The Spaniards soon encountered Plains Indian groups who depended entirely on the buffalo for their livelihood. At one point in northwestern Texas the soldiers came across a huge pile of buffalo bones by a salt lick that was a "crossbow shot long," about 12 ft (3.6 m) high and 18 ft (5.4 m) across, eloquent testimony to the hunters' expertise. After 48 days of exhausting riding across what is now the northern Texas Panhandle and into Oklahoma and Kansas, the Spaniards reached a place they named Quivira, actually a location somewhere near Great Bend, Kansas. There they found Wichita Indians living in grass lodges, in country "with mesas, plains, and charming rivers with fine waters," also plenty of wild fruit and buffalo. Coronado returned without gold, but left one momentous legacy behind him – the horse.

The Spaniards encountered nomadic hunting bands who used large numbers of dogs to transport their tents and supplies (Vehik, 1986). Some of these groups may have acted as commercial hunters and middlemen between the pueblos of New Mexico and the settled maize farming villages of the Central and Southern Plains (Spielmann, 1992) (Chapter 7). They may have been Apache speakers, who arrived in the region not long before Coronado. A century after the Spanish *entrada*, they were occupying an enormous area of the Plains east of the Rio Grande, and north of the Arkansas River, where rainfall was uncertain and maize agriculture very risky. In archaeological terms, the sites of these people belong in the Dismal River culture (*c.* AD 1675 to 1725), known from sites extending from the Black Hills of South Dakota to the Rockies, and as far south as northern New Mexico. The Dismal River people were mainly hunters, with agriculture a secondary consideration, dwelling in semi-permanent oval structures quite unlike the substantial earth lodges used by Plains farmers (Wedel, 1986).

Just over half a century after Coronado, on 15 September 1598, Juan de Oñate, the first Spanish colonizer of New Mexico, sent an expedition of 60 officers and men to explore the plains that lay to the east. They found enormous herds of "cattle" roaming over "some extremely level mesas that extend for many leagues." They were hairy animals with black horns "similar to those of the *bufalo*" (the Asiatic buffalo or wild ox).

Occasional Indian settlements dotted the Plains. One was "A rancheria of 50 tents made of tanned skins which were very bright red and white in color. They were round like pavilions, with flaps and openings, and made as neatly as those from Italy. They are so large that in the most common ones there is ample room for four individual mattresses and beds." The buffalo hide was soft and pliable, so well tanned that not even the heaviest rain passed through. "To carry these tents ... the Indians use medium sized, shaggy dogs, which they harness like mules. They have large droves of them, each girt around the breast and haunches, carrying a load of at least one hundred pounds. They travel at the same pace as their masters. It is both interesting and amusing to see them traveling along, one after the other, dragging the ends of their poles...."

A few days later the Spaniards tried to drive buffalo for themselves. They built a corral of large cottonwood logs, a task that took three days. The wings leading to it were so large that they blithely assumed they would trap hundreds of beasts. Next day they set out to drive an enormous herd toward the corral. The herd moved toward the corral at first, but suddenly stampeded straight for the horsemen. Confusion reigned as the horsemen frantically dodged the charging animals. There was no way the Spaniards could take the buffalo alive. Despite the confusion, they shot a large number, though they lost three horses. Many of their steeds were slashed by razor sharp horns.

The Spaniards soon developed a healthy respect for Plains bison. "There is no one so melancholy who if he were to see them a hundred times would not laugh heartily just as soon or marvel at the sight of such fierce beasts." They admired the way the Indians killed drinking bison with a single shot with bow and stone-tipped arrow, hiding in brush shelters near their favorite water holes. They saw some arrows with "large bone tips, although only a few, as the flint is better for killing the cattle than the spear."

In the late 1600s, Apachean groups were living over a wide area of the western Plains, some of them part-time horticulturalists. To the north, the Blackfeet and Assiniboine inhabited the Canadian Plains, Arapahoe and Gros Ventre in what is now North Dakota, with Kootenai and Salish (Flathead) close to the Rocky Mountains, venturing rarely onto the Plains. The Kiowa controlled the eastern Black Hills along the Little Missouri River. Their Crow neighbors had originally been part of the horticultural Hidatsa along the Missouri River. They had split from them at an unknown date, perhaps *c.* AD 1400, and now occupied the Bighorn Mountains in northeastern Wyoming, and areas of Montana and the Dakotas.

The Shoshone were Numic speakers, who had moved out of the Great Basin through the mountains of Utah and Wyoming onto the Plains at some time after the 15th century. They may have occupied most of the

French traders bartered firearms for furs in the northeastern Plains: a well-armed Cree Indian with his family, depicted by Peter Rindisbacher in 1821.

Indians hunting bison by Karl Bodmer (1843).

northwestern Plains from Wyoming to the Canadian border before the introduction of the horse. Two other groups of Numic speakers lived on the High Plains in the 16th century – the Ute and Comanche. The latter split off from the Shoshone after their migration onto the Plains. The Ute expanded out of the Rockies at about the same time as the Shoshone did.

All these groups hunted on foot. The causes of tribal movements before European contact are poorly understood. Those since 1650 are closely connected to the introduction of the horse to the Plains, to European expansion, and to the ability of different tribes to obtain firearms.

It took about a century for horses, "mystery dogs," as the Indians called them, to reach the northern Plains. Horses were commonplace long before firearms, a reflection of strict Spanish policies that forbade the trading of muskets to the Indians. The Plains people obtained horses through barter and through theft. In contrast, the French fur traders in Canada and along the Mississippi had few horses but plenty of firearms and ammunition that they traded for furs. As a result, there tended to be more horses on the southwestern Plains, and more firearms to the northeast.

The Plains Apache obtained large numbers of horses after 1650, soon developing a form of mounted warfare that gave them marked military superiority over their neighbors. Horses reached Caddoan groups to the east by 1700, the Comanche and Ute at about the same time. The Shoshone of Montana and Wyoming were raiding the Blackfeet and Crow on horseback by 1730. They expanded to the south at the expense of the Apache, settling by the banks of the Arkansas River by about 1725. Constant tribal wars, raids, and stealing had the Blackfeet mounted by 1740.

The Assiniboine and Cree were armed by English Hudson's Bay traders after 1670. By the mid-18th century, firearms were relatively commonplace throughout the Plains. Tribal movements were now dependent on the military capabilities of each group, with the stronger triumphing at the expense of the weaker. The Shoshone, for example, were driven from the Plains in the late 18th century.

One major effect of the introduction of the horse was an enhanced ability on the part of the mounted hunter to locate bison (Osborn, 1983). In other words, areas of the Plains that supported dispersed bison populations that could not be exploited effectively by hunters on foot were now suited for mounted, more complex hunting societies to exploit. The horse extended the range of the hunter as well as his ability to carry large quantities of meat. Plains groups were now less dependent on the year-by-year, season-by-season fluctuations of bison herds, for they could cover enormous distances in search of their quarry.

The horse put the nomadic groups of the Plains in a strong position. They could either live off their farming neighbors, or could trade bison meat and hides for grain when it suited them (for discussion, see Chapter 7). The nomadic population of the Plains grew as the bison dwindled. Some formerly sedentary groups like the Dakota and Cheyenne became nomads, joining others like the Blackfeet and Comanche, who had been hunting for centuries. The Bison Belt became an economic battleground, as war parties raided each others' camps, to seize horses and loot food stores.

Douglas Bamforth believes (1988) that there was an ecological context for the changing balance of power on the Plains. Military advantage was obviously important, for warfare was constant, and the ability to defend oneself the key to survival. This ability depended on numerical strength – concentrating large numbers of people in the largest camps possible, even if many raids were on a small scale. To do this, one had to have the ability to support oneself in the Plains environment. The communal hunt was a time when large numbers of people came together at one location, providing not only more food, labor and hunting skills, but also information on the whereabouts of bison herds. The hunters could even work several corrals or jumps at the same time. Larger concentrations of population meant more marriage partners, also access to trade goods obtained from a wide geographical area. The number of a leader's followers depended on his skills in war and in the chase. Ambitious individuals could manipulate the communal hunt to their benefit, to obtain power and prestige, more followers, and, eventually their groups would obtain long-term military advantage.

Bamforth argues that the mechanisms for social control that could flow from increased aggregation may have given some societies the longer-term military edge. This is reflected in the uniformly northeast–southwest pattern of recent tribal migration on the Plains, and in the absence of expansion from the east onto the southern Plains. It is no coincidence that the more complex groups who moved onto the Plains were those who lived adjacent to areas where larger populations could support themselves. The most complex of these groups lived in the Black Hills area of the north. In contrast, the peoples living on the margins of the less productive southern Plains did not expand far onto the grassland steppe, perhaps because they could not subsist there, or preserve their existing social order.

The changeover to horses, and to a certain extent the rifle – a weapon that made people dependent on European traders – led to a chronically imbalanced and unstable way of life. In archaeological terms, the increasing value of European imports is reflected in occasional finds of glass trade beads, metal arrow points, and some locally made iron spear heads. In social and cultural terms, the changes were far more radical. The millennia-old communal values that stressed cooperation for survival gave way to highly individualistic doctrines that pitted biological family against biological family, with little concern for the common welfare. Individual fortunes could change almost overnight as a result of a successful raid. The wealth obtained in battle could be used to promote family status. The ranks of individuals changed constantly, as hunter vied with hunter for the allegiance of followers and fellow warriors. A flamboyant, almost frenzied era of Plains life dawned, one where most nomadic groups believed old age was evil, that it was better for a man to die in battle.

The combination of horses and firearms was a volatile mixture in the hands of bold warriors. The Blackfeet of the northern Plains were among the last hunters to receive the horse, in about 1740. They acquired guns from the Cree to the east at about the same time. Living as they did in a strategic position where they could control the spread of horses and firearms, the Blackfeet took to the warpath. They became masters of the lightning raid. A war party would swoop down, drive away horses, slaughter people without mercy and vanish over the horizon. By 1850, Blackfeet territory extended from the North Saskatchewan River to what is now Yellowstone National Park.

Plains Indians at a rendezvous, their tipis stretching away into the distance – detail of a 19th-century painting by A.J. Miller.

The Blackfeet rose to prominence as European fur traders and settlers pressed onto the age-old Plains hunting grounds. Fur traders were among the first to sow the seeds of wholesale bison slaughter, for they gladly exchanged firearms for beaver pelts. Now white hunters with their repeating rifles joined the fray, leaving thousands of wasted carcasses rotting on the Plains. Like the beaver, the bison began to dwindle, affected, also, by exotic cattle diseases. Then the railroads spread over the prairies. During the 1860s and 1870s, special excursion trains took hunters into a sea of bison. The great herds of thundering animals, with their seemingly inexhaustible supplies of meat and hides disappeared almost overnight. And, at the same time, the last vestiges of the primeval North American hunting life vanished in an orgy of 19th-century musketry. Only a handful of buffalo survived, to form the nucleus of the managed herds that graze on the Plains today.

A few European travelers were fortunate enough to witness Plains bison hunts before horses became commonplace. Fur trader Alexander Henry watched expert Assiniboine hunters set out on foot in 1776. "They were dressed in ox-skins, with the hair and horns. Their faces were covered, and their gestures so closely resembled those of the animals themselves, that had I not been in the secret, I would have been as much deceived as the oxen," Henry wrote.

The decoys slowly lured the herd toward the corral. Dogs were muzzled, men and women surrounded the corral. The decoyers bellowed like buffalo as the herd paused to feed about a half-mile away. As the bison approached, the decoys fell back until the leaders were inside the jaws of the pound. Then the hunters pounced as the leaders scrambled to safety. The slaughter continued until evening, ensuring ample meat supplies for the winter months ahead. But the Assiniboine hunt was the end of a big-game hunting era that extended back to the very beginnings of the North American past, to the time when a handful of hunting families set foot in a virgin continent. The same basic cultural traditions might have continued for millennia, had not Europeans intervened.

Further Reading

Bamforth, Douglas. 1988. *Ecology and Human Organization on the Great Plains.* Plenum Press, New York.
An innovative study of cultural diversity on the Plains based on a multidisciplinary perspective.
Frison, George. 1992. *Prehistoric Hunters of the High Plains.* 2nd ed. Academic Press, New York.
The definitive work on the archaeology of the northwest Plains that has wide applicability elsewhere. Comprehensive references to many fine excavations.
Speth, John. 1983. *Bison Kills and Bone Counts.* University of Chicago Press, Chicago.
This remarkable study gives invaluable perspectives on bison hunting.
Wheat, Joe Ben. 1972. "The Olsen-Chubbock Site: A Paleo-Indian Bison Kill," *Memoirs of the Society for American Archaeology,* 26.
An exemplary monograph on a famous mass bison kill of 6500 BC.
Wood, W. Raymond. (ed.) 1998. *Archaeology on the Great Plains.* University Press of Kansas, Lawrence.
Wood's edited volume offers an up-to-date summary of all aspects of Plains archaeology from Paleo-Indian to historic. Strongly recommended. Comprehensive bibliographies.

CHAPTER 7

VILLAGE FARMERS OF THE PLAINS

Chapter 6 covered the hunter-gatherer societies of the Plains from the earliest times up to the advent of the horse and the first European explorations of the great grasslands. The Spaniards traveled for days over short-grass plains, encountering nomadic bison hunters who traded with people living far to the east. And in 1541, Francisco de Coronado's conquistadors reached a place he named Quivira, somewhere near Great Bend, Kansas. There they visited Wichita Indian encampments in lush, well-watered river valleys, inhabited by people with quite different lifeways from the hunters and gatherers of the plains to the west. As we have seen, the Spaniards introduced the horse to the Plains, thereby revolutionizing bison hunting, hitherto conducted on foot. Two centuries were to pass before horses were common among Plains peoples, ushering in a brief efflorescence of the warrior cultures immortalized in 19th-century literature.

To many people, the Plains mean nothing more than vast herds of bison pursued by small bands of nomadic hunters. Such a portrait is thoroughly misleading, for semi-sedentary farming groups flourished on the eastern Plains. For the most part, agriculture was confined to major river valleys and their tributaries, such as the middle Missouri Valley, the Republican River Valley, and the Arkansas and Red rivers to the south. Here perennial rivers meandered over fertile floodplains overlooked by low terraces where villages were somewhat sheltered from the constant winds. It was in these valleys that some of North America's most remarkable farming societies flourished for many centuries (Wood, 1988).

The challenges of this farming environment are epitomized by the middle Missouri Valley, intensively studied by archaeologists of the River Basin Surveys after World War II. Unfortunately, the massive flood control efforts of the Corps of Engineers mean that well over 80 percent of the once-fertile river valley is now under water along with the priceless archaeological sites which lie on the inundated terraces and floodplain (Lehmer, 1971).

Before the Corps moved in, the middle Missouri was a world of its own, a deep incised trench which flowed through North and South Dakota. The Missouri cut deeply into the surrounding plains as it flowed toward much lower and distant seas. In places the valley drops 200 to 400 ft (60 to 120 m) below the adjoining higher ground. The so-called "breaks," which delineate the edge of the valley, are steep and heavily eroded, the trench itself being between a half-mile and 4 miles (0.8 and 6.4 km) wide. Long, grass-covered

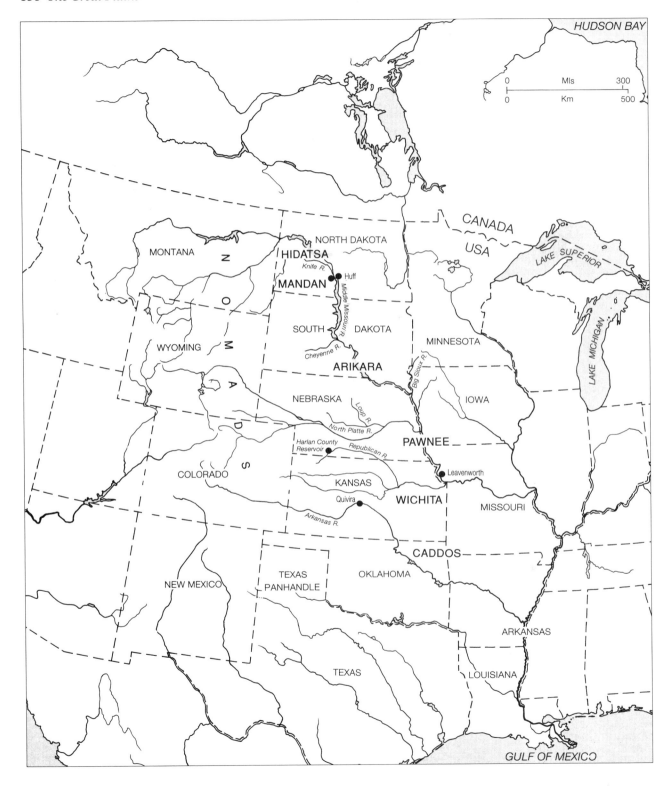

HUDSON BAY

0 — Mls — 300
0 — Km — 500

CANADA
USA

LAKE SUPERIOR

MONTANA
NORTH DAKOTA
HIDATSA
Knife R.
Huff
MANDAN
Middle Missouri R.
SOUTH   DAKOTA
MINNESOTA
WYOMING
Cheyenne R.
ARIKARA
Big Sioux R.
LAKE MICHIGAN
NEBRASKA
Loup R.
IOWA
North Platte R.
PAWNEE
Harlan County
Reservoir
Republican R.
COLORADO
Leavenworth
KANSAS
MISSOURI
Quivira
WICHITA
Arkansas R.
CADDOS
NEW MEXICO
TEXAS
PANHANDLE
OKLAHOMA
ARKANSAS
TEXAS
LOUISIANA

N O M A D S

GULF OF MEXICO

terraces line much of the valley, dropping sharply onto the river floodplain itself. Here the Missouri once meandered across a tree-covered, and often flooded alluvium. Most human settlement was on the terraces, as it was elsewhere on the eastern Plains, escaping even the highest spring and summer floods.

To the east and north, the Missouri Plateau is typical glacial terrain – a scarred and dissected landscape of rolling hills, which merges into the central lowlands of the Eastern Woodlands. Today's cities, like Bismarck, lie, for the most part, immediately east of the Missouri, where modern cereal farming flourishes. West and south of the valley lie open, drier plains, where bison once roamed in large numbers. The west bank has easy access to the nearby open country, now sparsely populated cattle-ranching country. These plains were a vital part of village life along the river, which depended not only on maize and bean agriculture, but on large-scale bison hunting. The middle Missouri Valley and other such sheltered locales, were places where two worlds met, the world of the nomadic Plains bison hunter, at first on foot, much later on horseback, and the settled world of the village farmer. The people of the middle Missouri Valley and other eastern Plains river valleys had a foot in both worlds, that of the settled farmer to the east, and that of the hunter to the west.

The middle Missouri experiences a harsh climate, with weeks of bitter, sub-zero weather in winter and great heat in summer. The winds are constant, bringing intense wind-chill factors in winter, withering crops in summer. The rains are unpredictable, falling mostly in spring and early summer. Two realities affected agriculture in the valley. The first was irregular and often highly localized rainfall, the second the constant risk of early or late frosts. Anyone farming maize in the Missouri trench was planting a tropical crop at the northern limits of its range, with a growing season which averaged about 160 days in the southern portions of the valley to a mere 130 days in the Knife-Heart rivers area of North Dakota. This frost-free growing season was considerably longer in the valley than on the surrounding plains. Rainfall was slightly higher in the north, which compensated somewhat for the short farming season. Only the hardiest maize varieties flourished in this harsh environment. It is of interest to note that the modern Great Northern bean was originally a native American form developed along the river.

For all its harsh conditions, the middle Missouri Valley was a remarkably diverse environment, especially for people who relied on a combination of agriculture, hunting, and foraging. The valley itself provided not only winter game and many edible plant foods, but fish in abundance. The Missouri Valley was a major flyway for migrating waterfowl in spring and fall. Those who lived on the western (right) bank enjoyed ready access not only to the bison-hunting grounds on the plains, but to ancient trade routes which crossed open country to the Rocky Mountains and far to the north and west. The Plains hunters interacted regularly with the settled valley farmers, for each group produced commodities the other lacked. The hunters brought hides and blankets, pemmican, and tool-making stone. The farmers bartered grain and other agricultural products. For centuries, two ways of life, one very ancient, the other more recent, interacted across the eastern boundaries of the Plains.

(Opposite) Map showing the archaeological sites and Plains Village Indian groups referred to in the text.

Before the Farmers

Paleo-Indian and Archaic settlements in larger river valleys like the middle Missouri or Republican are few and far between, for many of them were either swept away by later flooding or are buried under feet of more recent alluvial settlement. Paleo-Indian projectile points along the middle Missouri make it clear, however, that such peoples exploited the river valley. Paleo-Indians quarried and made tools from a creamy brown chalcedony known as Knife River Flint, dug from several locations just west of the Missouri River in North Dakota. Near Vermillion, South Dakota, recent finds of seasonal camp sites from Clovis times through the Early Archaic should fill out many details of their lifestyles. McKean and Duncan points have come from Archaic sites in the Big Bend area, also in South Dakota, dating to as early as 2500 BC. On the Central and Southern Plains, Paleo-Indian and Archaic projectile points are common surface finds, but stratified sites are much rarer. As David Meltzer and others have shown (Chapter 6), the drought conditions of the Middle Holocene and other local climatic changes affected not only the distribution and population density of bison herds, but also human settlement across much of the Plains. Throughout the middle Missouri and Central and Southern Plains, farming societies date to the past 1000 years, with constant experimentation in earlier centuries.

The Plains Woodland Tradition
1st millennium AD

About the beginning of the Christian era, Central Plains lifeways changed significantly. Many more burial and habitation sites appear in the archaeological record, yielding artifacts which have many parallels with contemporary toolkits from the Eastern Woodlands. The Central Plains and middle Missouri Valley were open to cultural influences from the east, which passed up rivers and along inter-village trails. It comes as no surprise to find Woodland settlements and burial mounds in the valley, marked by the appearance of characteristic plain, or cord-roughened pottery similar to that found over a wide area of the Eastern Woodlands (Benn, 1990). This "Plains Woodland Tradition" is remarkable for four major innovations (Johnson and Johnson, 1998). First, the bow and arrow came into use. Second, maize and beans were cultivated for the first time, even if infrequently. Third, many groups manufactured pottery. And fourth, they buried their dead in burial mounds. No one knows whether these innovations were brought by immigrant newcomers, or whether the descendants of Archaic hunter-gatherers adopted new ideas and mortuary customs. Nor do we know if maize agriculture and pottery-making arrived simultaneously.

We can be sure there were Hopewell people living at the eastern margins of the Central Plains, and it may be from them that agriculture and pot-making first diffused to the north and west. According to Wedel (1959, 1961), the earliest Hopewell-like settlements lie along the Missouri River near Kansas City, where the thick deposits suggest at least some degree of permanent settlement. They date to the first half of the 1st millennium AD, broadly contemporary with later Hopewell in the Eastern Woodlands. Small burial mounds with rectangular chambers lie on the bluffs near the villages. Wedel calls the Hopewell of the Missouri Valley and Kansas River Valley a "watered-down version" of the classic Hopewell, the first evidence of at least part-time farmers on the margins of the Plains. Hopewell-like artifacts in this region include platform pipes and stone gorgets, also clay vessels with pointed bases and pots modeled in animal and bird forms.

The Avonlea and Besant complexes of the bison hunters of southern Canada (Chapter 6) are contemporary with the Plains Woodland Tradition of the Middle Missouri and Central Plains, which brought both technological innovations and new ideas from the Eastern Woodlands. They coincide in part, also, with the appearance of distinctive burial mounds and earthworks over much of the Northeastern Periphery. Such sites abound north and east of the Missouri Coteau, throughout the eastern Dakotas and southern Manitoba. The majority occur in the eastern portions of this region, with some along the Red River south of Winnipeg. These earthworks date to between 500 BC and AD 1000, and are usually built on bluffs overlooking river valleys, lakes, or creeks, with few signs of camp sites in their vicinities. Most often, circular mounds cluster in groups of as many as 40. Linear earthworks are much rarer and consist of simple platforms or low embankments running in straight lines for hundreds of feet, occasionally connecting one mound with others. One or more circular to oblong burial pits, containing a single or several skeletons, lie under many of the mounds which have been excavated. Most were roofed with poles or logs, while bison carcasses and skulls were sometimes placed with the dead, testimony to the importance of bison hunting to the builders of the burial mounds. The cultural associations of these mounds is a matter of some controversy but there are clear influences from Woodland practices further south and east (Vehik, 1983). Conceivably, some of the dead in these sepulchers represent populations which were ancestral to the Assiniboine, Cheyenne, Dakota, and other historic bison-hunting groups.

But the powerful Hopewell ideology of individual power and prestige did not necessarily diffuse to the north. David Benn argues (1990) that the artifacts found in Plains mounds are personal ornaments, which symbolize an individual's subordinate status in nature: the ability to kill large animals like bison but powerlessness in the face of drought and other natural phenomena. Humans reconciled themselves with the forces of nature by subordinating themselves to the animals they killed, an ideology which Benn believes to have originated among Archaic societies and to have persisted into Woodland times. The family band was still the focus of most subsistence activity, in contrast with many contemporary Eastern Woodland societies, where individual status and prestige were coming to the fore. But, as exploitation of game and plant foods intensified in Late Woodland times and semi-sedentary communities became more common, so rankings of different families and kin groups emerged, to reach a high degree of development in later village communities.

The Plains Woodland Tradition also occurs further southeast along the Missouri River in eastern Nebraska and southern Iowa, also in other parts of Nebraska, South Dakota, Iowa, and Kansas (A. Johnson, 1992; Kivett, 1953). The earliest sites date to before the Christian era, the latest to the late 1st millennium AD, by which time maize agriculture was well established on the Central Plains. Plains Woodland sites are mostly small and inconspicuous, often lying on river terraces, where many are buried under alluvial deposits. Corn and squash remains occur at several late sites, while often small differences in pottery styles and other artifacts have been used to distinguish local variants such as the Valley focus in Nebraska and Kansas, and the Keith focus in central and western Nebraska. Some middle Missouri Woodland sites have yielded an artifact that was to come into widespread use in later centuries, a simple hoe made from the shoulder blade of a bison. Plains Woodland pottery is coarse and heavily built, many vessels being large, wide-mouthed jars with pointed bottoms and simple bossed or cord decoration. We know little of Plains Woodland settlements, but some Nebraska sites contain shallow basins up to 18 ft (5.5 m) in diameter, which may have been the foundations of pole-and-brush dwellings set low into the ground. Other villages have yielded post holes, even lumps of reed and bark, as if people lived in small thatched structures, like those used in the Eastern Woodlands at the time.

The highly elaborate mortuary customs practiced by contemporary Eastern Woodland societies are absent on the Central Plains, although small burial mounds abound. Along the lower Republican River, for example, burial mounds lay on bluffs and headlands overlooking the river valley. They were between 20 and 50 ft (6 and 15 m) across and up to 6 ft (2 m) high. Some of these burial mounds covered a basin cut into the prairie sod. Others consisted of earth and stones with occasional burials, or lay over pits containing disarticulated human remains. The Hopewell people of the Kansas City area erected more elaborate dry-masonry-chambered mounds. Some tumuli have yielded clear evidence that the dead were sometimes dismembered before burial, while cremation was not uncommon (Wedel, 1986). Nebraska Woodland groups occasionally buried their dead in ossuaries, shallow basins or pits used for communal sepulchers instead of burial mounds. Middle Missouri Woodland burial mounds are dome shaped, as much as 100 ft (30 m) across and only a few feet high, much smaller than their contemporaries to the east (Neuman, 1975). Each mound covers a subterranean burial pit roofed with logs containing a primary interment and numerous secondary burials. Some linear mounds near the Knife River may represent effigy mounds, but are possibly of relatively modern, Hidatsa origin.

Donald Lehmer remarks (1971) that he has the impression Woodland people along the middle Missouri hunted bison more regularly than Central Plains groups, who subsisted off deer and smaller game in wooded river valleys, but this is nothing more than an impression. We can be sure that bison hunting was deeply ingrained in Plains Woodland culture, for efficient pursuit of these animals by semi-sedentary farmers continued long after European contact. But traditions of village existence were also an ancient component in valley life, among peoples who lived along a frontier between the settled farmers of the east and the hunter-gatherers of the Plains. Their culture in its many local forms was a synthesis of different traditions, a unique hybrid of settled and nomadic lifeways.

Plains Village Indians
c. AD 1000 to 1500

By the 10th century AD, perhaps one or two centuries earlier, the Woodland cultures of the eastern Plains had changed into more sedentary societies dependent on a sophisticated mix of maize and bean agriculture in fertile valley bottoms and hunting and gathering (Wedel, 1983). Maize and beans appear to have become important staples in the Central Plains between AD 700 and 1100, during four centuries of warmer, moister conditions, which fostered western expansion of the tall-grass prairie. Good climatic conditions sometimes allowed the spread of cultivation well into the High Plains, even to the foothills of the Rockies, along drainages such as the Arkansas River. These new agricultural societies, often called "Plains Village Indians," developed a way of life which dominated the eastern Plains from the Dakotas to Texas for nearly 1000 years. Over most of the arid west, nomadic Plains groups continued to hunt and gather, using ancient subsistence strategies developed over more than 8000 years.

The many Plains Village Indian cultures all share five general characteristics. Every society used lodge houses that were much more substantial than earlier Woodland dwellings. All developed permanent settlements, sometimes fortified with ditches and stockades and containing underground storage pits, which were of vital importance to farming societies like these, living in environments with short growing seasons and unpredictable rains. Every group used bone hoes, manufactured from bison scapulae (shoulder blades) set at an acute or right angle to a wooden handle. Everyone's toolkit included small triangular stone arrowheads with or without side notches, readily distinguished from earlier, and often larger, projectile points. All made and used round-bottomed or globular pottery.

Central Plains Tradition. Central Plains archaeologists subsume Plains Village Indian cultures in their region under the Central Plains Tradition (Steinacher and Carlson, 1998; Wedel, 1986). They sometimes divide the Central Plains Tradition into Early Village and Late Village periods.

The Central Plains Tradition began about AD 1000 and is found in the major river valleys of the region as far south as the northern side of the Arkansas drainage. The Upper Republican Culture of the Republican River Basin is the best known Early Village Tradition on the Central Plains, studied intensively in surveys and excavations of the Medicine Creek and Harlan County Reservoirs of southeastern Nebraska (Kivett and Metcalf, 1997; Wedel, 1986). These people lived along smaller tributaries of the Republican River, where soils were firmer and more suitable for agriculture and tree growth more plentiful than along the sandy main river. There was less danger of flooding on the tributaries, with easy access to well-watered travel routes to the west and south. Both areas had rich hinterlands where game and edible plant foods abounded. Each settlement was a loose aggregation of small houses spaced out in such a way that defense cannot have been a consideration.

Upper Republican dwellings were square or sub-rectangular, the sides between 26 and 28 ft (8 and 8.5 m), sometimes longer, with rounded corners and long, covered entrance passages facing away from the prevailing northwesterly winds. A simple hearth burned in the center. Four or more wooden posts placed midway between the central hearth and the corners supported a roof of poles, grass and sod, held up at the outer edges by closely spaced posts around the house perimeter. Several subfloor storage pits lie under the floors of most houses, and there was often a trash heap just outside the door. Wedel believes most Upper Republican houses were single-family dwellings, grouped together in hamlets of about 50 to 75 people, occupied for a relatively short time, perhaps 7 to 10 years, before the community moved on. Each village was an unfortified string of houses, sometimes built along ridges, on bluffs, or on creek terraces. Each buried their dead in graves within the village, or, more commonly, exposed the bodies of the deceased, then interred their bones in large communal pits on bluffs overlooking the community (Kivett, 1953). Each hamlet grew maize, beans, and other crops on alluvial soils. But the people always combined agriculture with hunting and plant gathering.

Upper Republican villages yield round-bottomed jars with constricted necks and mouths and collared or braced rims. The potters left the exterior surface plain, or roughened it with a cord-wrapped paddle. Their products were thinner walled and better made than Woodland vessels, often tempered with sand or fine gravel, presumably used for cooking, water carrying and storage. Upper Republican people enjoyed contacts with neighbors to east and west. They obtained most tool-making stone from local sources, but sometimes from quarries as far afield as Sterling, Colorado, 175 miles (280 km) north-northwest, Wyoming, and the Texas Panhandle. Some settlements have yielded artifacts made of Gulf conch shell, and freshwater snail shell common in the Ohio and Wabash Rivers (Strong, 1935).

A greater emphasis on maize and bean agriculture had some obvious advantages in terms of efficient exploitation of the local environment, and in terms of sedentary living. But Central Plains Tradition communities like the Upper Republicans were more closely tied to their land than nomadic hunters and gatherers. If they moved away to hunt or gather plant foods, their crops were at risk from animals, pests, and, indeed, neighboring human predators. Unpredictable rainfall could play havoc with growing maize plants, for corn is a tropical grass which requires ample moisture and high temperatures in the range of 60 to 90°F (16 to 32°C) day and night to achieve maximum growth and yield. Nevertheless, selective breeding by native American farmers in harsh environments like the Plains produced extremely hardy maize forms, among them Northern Flint, which is represented in Central Plains Tradition settlements. Wedel (1986) argues each family cultivated only about 1.5 to 3 acres (0.6 to 1.21 ha) of easily turned bottomland soil each spring, preferably in locations protected from the hot, dry winds of high summer. Yields may have been as modest as 10 to 20 bushels (350 to 700 liters) an acre, compared with about 26 bushels (900 liters) an acre from early 20th-century fields enjoying about 10 in (255 mm) of summer rainfall. At the same time, the people probably engaged in short- to medium-range bison-hunting trips. Broad-spectrum hunting, like plant gathering, was a seasonal activity, based on immediate need and opportunity, hunts which yielded enough meat to feed a small village rather than a large population of several bands. Plant gathering was seasonally important, and certainly, and unusually, in the Republican River Valley, fishing and shell-fish collecting also.

The Upper Republicans and their contemporaries were small-scale farmers, who lived in dispersed communities very different from the large densely populated settlements encountered by European explorers in later centuries. As far as we know, these were egalitarian groups, without strongly centralized social or political organization. In all probability, they engaged in regular exchange with neighbors as a means of mitigating food shortages caused by irregular, and highly localized summer rainfall.

The Upper Republican culture was but one of several regional groups identified on the Central Plains between AD 1000 and 1450. Others include the Itskari phase of the Loup River, the Nebraska culture along the Missouri River in the eastern part of that state, the St Helena phase of northeastern Nebraska, and the Smoky Hill phase of northeastern Kansas (for the archaeology of Kansas, see Wedel, 1959). All these cultures flourished in a region with eastward-draining streams and good access to the Missouri River Valley, making it easy for eastern and southeastern artifacts, beliefs, and ideas to spread westward. One could easily move from south to north too. Waldo Wedel writes of visualizing the "central plains streams ... as the rungs of a ladder up which human populations could travel from south to north with comparative ease" (Wedel, 1986). While some roots of the Central Plains Tradition lie in the local Woodland, new groups, or at least fresh ideas, may have moved gradually into the region from Mississippian societies to the east and south, creating a meld of indigenous and outside culture in a distinctive Plains setting.

Plan of an earth-lodge village along the Missouri River.

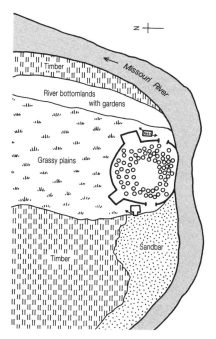

Middle Missouri and Coalescent Traditions. The numerous local cultures of the middle Missouri Valley region have for some time been grouped into two major units, but the classification is being modified as a result of more recent research (C. Johnson, 1998; Lehmer, 1971; Winham and Calabrese, 1998). The "Middle Missouri Tradition" was contemporary with the Central Plains Tradition to the south. Its origins are more eastern, probably resulting from contact with the Mississippian traditions of Cahokia (Chapter 20). These cultures are ancestral to the Siouan-speaking villagers of the historic period, the Mandan. The "Coalescent Tradition" developed slightly later, around AD 1150, when Central Plains Tradition farmers moved into the middle Missouri region. These groups displaced some of the Middle Missouri Tradition groups and acquired some cultural traits from them. They developed new ones, too, the most important being the circular earthlodge. Coalescent peoples originated in the south and are ancestral to the historic northern Caddoan speakers such as the Arikara and Pawnee. The Middle Missouri and Coalescent peoples had cultures that were remarkably similar in subsistence activities and material culture, though they had very different social structures.

The first Plains village sites along the middle Missouri River date to the 9th or 10th century and lie in southeastern South Dakota, from the valley of the Big Sioux River near Sioux Falls to the east and, in the west, up the main river from Chamberlain to the Cheyenne River confluence (Toom, 1992; Winham and Calabrese, 1998). These earliest Middle Missouri Tradition settlements appear to be confined to larger river valleys, whereas later settlements lie further upstream, near the North and South Dakota border and the Knife River confluence. The two traditions overlap near the Cheyenne River. Like the Central Plains Tradition, early Middle Missouri Tradition sites are remarkable for their large rectangular houses. The dwellings were built in and over a straight-walled pit up to 5 ft (1.5 m) deep and between 30 and 65 ft (9 and 19.8 m) long. The axis of the dwellings was north–south, with a long, sloping passage entrance at the south end. Rows of posts in the center and at the sides of the pit supported a pole framework covered with willow branches, saplings, and earth, with closely set rows of posts at each end. A large central hearth and several storage pits lay inside the house. Each village consisted of between half a dozen and 20 houses, each housing between 7 and 15 people. The largest communities held between 200 and 300 people. Sometimes, a ditch and palisade protected the village, while hamlets on terrace promontories sometimes dug a ditch with a fence across the neck of the point. The village potters made coarse, but easily identifiable ceramics, decorated with varied motifs using stamping and comb decoration. Villages of this period contain many bison-bone artifacts, including not only bison shoulder-blade hoes, but picks, fleshers, hide-dressing tools, and fish hooks.

The Huff site, on the right bank of the Missouri River 20 miles (32 km) south of Bismarck, North Dakota, was occupied between AD 1450 and 1550. This large village, built by ancestors of the historic Mandan, has rows of over a hundred rectangular houses with wattle and daub walls, up to 33 ft (10 m) long (Wood, 1967). A massive earthen embankment with a wooden palisade protected the village, with ten projecting bastions spaced along the sides and at the corners.

The origins of both these initial village farming traditions, the Central Plains and the Middle Missouri, are controversial, but they almost certainly had strong indigenous roots. Donald Lehmer theorizes (1971) that some cultural influences, and perhaps agriculture, came to the Middle Missouri tradition from farming groups living in northwestern Iowa and southwestern Minnesota. *Busycon* shells from the Gulf of Mexico and potsherds bearing "weeping eye" motifs with Mississippian associations testify to at least sporadic contacts with people to the south and east (Zimmerman, 1985). At the same time, both Pacific *Dentalium* shells and some possible Avonlea points from the Northwest Plains hint at contacts with groups living to the north and west. Apparently, maize agriculture first spread widely in the Central Plains and along the middle Missouri at a time of warmer and wetter climate after AD 900, which brought moister Pacific air to the Plains and was marked by major cultural developments in the Southwest. Significantly, too, the initial period of Plains village culture ended when climatic conditions became drier and colder in about AD 1250, making agriculture more risky, especially in more exposed locations.

In the Central Plains, deteriorating horticultural conditions forced populations northward and into contact with the first Middle Missouri villages. Many of these communities in turn moved northward to preserve their culture. The Central Plains immigrants often located their new villages in places occupied by Middle Missouri communities. They adopted some cultural patterns of the Middle Missouri peoples, such as fortifications around settlements, but developed new traits such as the round earthlodge. This dwelling later became the "classic" earthlodge painted by 19th-century artists like Karl Bodmer and George Catlin.

(Opposite above) The interior of an earthlodge of a Mandan chief by Karl Bodmer. (Opposite below) Plan of Crow Creek, site of the massacre of 500 Plains Indian villagers.

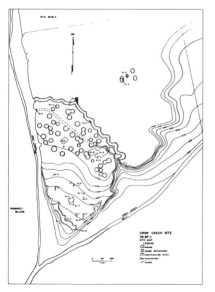

New villages were rapidly founded along the river as populations expanded.

Drought cycles and unstable climatic conditions brought major disruptions and constant competition for farming land after the early 14th century. Village fought village over territorial boundaries, as warfare caused people to disperse into small, less permanent villages along smaller drainages (Zimmerman, 1985).

Large villages were only reestablished along the Missouri Valley in the late 15th century. These eventually became the focus of the groups visited by the first European explorers in the 16th century.

Southern Plains. Early village cultures on the Southern Plains share common rectangular or square house forms, the making of cord-decorated pottery, and other features with equivalent cultures in the Central Plains and middle Missouri Valley (summary in Drass, 1998). The Custer and Washita focuses of western Oklahoma date to between AD 800 and 1375, archaeological representations of cultures which developed out of a Woodland base and paid more attention to horticulture (Wedel, 1983). Perhaps Village Indian groups were attracted to the western grasslands of Oklahoma by the abundant bison during the favorable centuries after AD 1000. The

Washita focus disappears during the 14th century, perhaps because of drought, or because of hostile newcomers like ancestral Apache (Chapter 6). All these early village cultures were highly flexible adaptations, functioning within an arid environment with unpredictable rainfall. Thus, in drought cycles, people would tend to rely more heavily on bison hunting and plant foods rather than agriculture, adapting their settlement patterns and toolkits accordingly, while placing a greater emphasis on agriculture during wetter years.

The Antelope Creek focus appeared in AD 1200 and flourished along major drainage systems of the Southern Plains in the Texas and Oklahoma panhandles (Lintz, 1984). Antelope Creek villages are remarkable for their houses with stone-slab wall foundations, which often supported adobe and masonry walls. House designs varied considerably, the most elaborate having a rectangular, semi-subterranean room with a vestibule, benches. and bins. Like all Plains Village societies, the Antelope Creek people subsisted off hunting, gathering, and maize agriculture, but they controlled important sources of Alibates, agatized dolomite, used for making stone projectile points and traded widely since Paleo-Indian times. Antelope Creek communities mined the outcrops in the middle of the Texas Panhandle intensively. They traded both finished tools and quarry blanks over a wide area. At least some of this exchange was with the Rio Grande and Upper Pecos areas of the Southwest, for sea-shell ornaments, Pueblo pots, and obsidian are found in Antelope Creek sites (for interactions between the Southwest and Southern Plains, see Spielmann, 1991). There was also some sporadic trade with other Plains groups and with Caddoan communities to the east. Between AD 1450 and 1500, Antelope Creek communities vanish, probably as a result of Apache intrusions into the Southern Plains and because drought turned sedentary farmers into full-time nomadic hunters (Huebner, 1991).

By the time of European contact, Plains Village cultures were centered on major river valleys. Their settlements clustered on river terraces and on bluffs overlooking fertile valleys. The clusters may represent different extended families working the adjacent bottomlands and sharing in the harvest.

Bundles, Chiefs, and Villages

As Preston Holder points out (1970) in his classic study of Plains farmers, based largely on the Caddoan-speaking Arikara of the middle Missouri River Valley, there are striking analogies between this Central Plains settlement pattern and that of the Caddos of eastern Texas in the late 17th century. French explorers describe small villages of 6 to 15 houses scattered along rivers and streams, but widely separated from one another. Eight to 10 families occupied each circular house, which was about 60 ft (18 m) in diameter. Occasionally, the French came across a larger chief's house and ceremonial center, perhaps like the larger houses sometimes found in Upper Republican settlements, associated with occasional caches of ceremonial-looking artifacts like pipes. Holder argues that the Central Plains Tradition may be ancestral to the historic Caddoan cultures of later centuries, the Wichita, Pawnee, and Arikara, which were organized in volatile chiefdoms, but firmly based on the oldest of eastern Plains farming institutions: the village.

Over centuries of rapid, sometimes fundamental, cultural change, which saw some farming groups abandon their fields to adopt the life of horse-riding nomads, the riverine village remained a distinct, resilient unit. Preston Holder believes that the village institutions described by 18th- and 19th-century observers mirrored those which had operated for centuries. The members of each village community shared common traditions and customs. They had their own social hierarchy, their own ways of organizing communal labor, of distributing wealth and measuring prestige. Their relationships with other communities were based on territorial proximity, on common language, and sometimes ties of kin or religion. Caddoan and other riverine villages were nominally permanent, but in practice the villagers abandoned their settlement for much of the year, moving out onto the plains for spring and summer bison hunts to acquire meat surpluses for the winter and for the harvest ceremonies which lay ahead. Come winter, they shifted to smaller encampments on sheltered terraces where game could be found and firewood was abundant. But the agricultural months were at the very center of village life, and farming was the enterprise that integrated all other activities in the community.

Holder points out that a well-defined social hierarchy was fundamental to village farming life: there were men of rank – the leaders – and commoners. These in turn represented families with rank, and those without. At the very pinnacle of village life were people belonging to a small core of leading families, whose rank came from spiritual powers and monopoly over wealth, and was virtually hereditary. For most high-ranking families, rank had to be validated by lavish gifts and by personal achievement, but no commoner could perform such acts and achieve high rank. These rankings were far from the stratified classes so characteristic of pre-industrial civilizations. Rather, they were what Holder calls "stable ranked groups," consisting of leaders and commoners. Such stable ranked groups existed in historic Natchez society on the Mississippi River (Le Page du Pratz, 1758), and probably in much earlier Eastern Woodlands societies, too. The Caddoan villages of the eastern Plains preserved traditional cultural patterns which they probably acquired from societies far to the east, right into historic times.

Holder describes how the organizational and spiritual rationale of Caddoan farming villages was centered around the sacred village bundle, "a physical device which contains, and reminds the owner, and outsiders, of the supernatural powers controlled by its individual possessor." The bundle also had group affiliations, to the point that Holder describes it as a "sort of portable ceremonial center." He draws attention to descriptions of mound temples from Natchez, Caddo, and other historical groups which contained baskets and bundles filled with ritual objects. Among the Arikara and the Pawnee, the village bundle was a skin envelope which contained objects that symbolized complex ideologies and rituals. They were devices which showed how the keeper of the bundle was said to be descended from the original owner. He kept it in his house, where it was cared for by his wife. But the knowledge associated with the bundle and the actual manipulation of the contents fell not to the owner but to a priest, who had spent many years learning its secrets. The priest received gifts for his work and slowly passed his knowledge to a younger assistant, usually a close relative, who assumed his powers when he died. The powers contained within the bundle assured the continuity of the village, powers which can be described loosely as the powers of the universe. A bundle was also the basis for controlling all production and social relations within the village. Hereditary chiefs considered themselves stars living on earth, the "earthly reservoirs," as Holder puts it, of a power which made them protectors of their people. They were the life forces of the village through the power given them by the bundle. If the bundle was lost or destroyed, then the people would die. Village bundles were symbols of a political and religious order which maintained the chief and ensured the loyalty of his people. The priests were the designated custodians of religious lore and ritual, a role which was acquired through long apprenticeship and lavish gifts.

Chiefs and priests were quiet men, secure in their power. They never doubted their authority or engaged in violence or war. They were men of knowledge, patience, and complete understanding, individuals of serenity with a reputation for generosity and largesse. It was they who presided over the great seasonal ceremonies: the winter bison hunt when meat was obtained for planting ceremonies, spring gatherings which focused on the bundle – their contents handled by priests, their magical forces renewed by the spring sun so the world would be born again for the harvest. There were ceremonies which accompanied the summer bison hunt and the Twenty Day ceremony which celebrated the harvest with sorcery duels and theatrical performances. These were occasions when individuals and the people as a whole came in contact with the powers of the world through private mystic experiences and communal feasts. Maturity came late to men in these societies, and they were allowed much leeway in their behavior while serving as warriors. Men under 40 years of age belonged to an age-group often called "Boys," famous for their striking costumes and cosmetic adornments. They were the warriors, responsible for defending the village, for raiding others. Much of their time was spent gambling, dancing, and hunting.

Plains farmers lived in relatively self-sufficient villages, with close ties to the earth and their corn fields. Each community had its own web of social and economic relationships, which, like its fertile gardens, acted as a form of insurance for survival in a harsh, unpredictable environment. These were highly conservative communities, with social mechanisms that organized every aspect of human activity and limited innovation. Had not Europeans arrived with their infectious diseases, horses, and insatiable appetite for furs, the same river valley adaptation could have continued indefinitely. In historic times, these conservative qualities were to preserve village farming life in the face of extraordinary pressures from the outside, not only from European traders, but from nomads on the nearby open plains.

Origins of Historic Groups: Caddoans and Siouans

We can only summarize the complex origins of recent Plains groups (see Hanson, 1998). At European contact, three village farming groups lived along the middle Missouri Valley. The Arikara, a Caddoan-speaking culture, were dominant along the Missouri, living in 30 or 40 earthlodge villages along the lower portions of the river. Upstream were the Siouan-speaking Mandan in as many as 13 communities, while a small number of Hidatsa flourished further north, near the confluence of the Heart, and later the Knife Rivers. The first pre-cursors of earthlodges appear in the Central Plains Tradition, which blended with the Middle Missouri Tradition in the Coalescent to produce the elaborate village cultures of the 17th to early 19th centuries. No one knows how many village farmers lived along the river valleys of the eastern Plains at European contact. Conservative estimates allow for at least 45,000, but these calculations are affected by the devastating losses from smallpox and other exotic diseases after contact. Whatever their numbers, the origins of historic groups lie deep in the remote past.

All Plains farmers belong, in general terms, within two language groups. The Caddoan-speaking peoples were relatively homogeneous and included the Arikara, Pawnee, and the Wichita. They lived along the middle stretches of the Plains rivers from South Dakota to eastern Texas. The Caddos were in the south, people whose cultural affiliations lay closer to the Mississippi Valley and the Eastern Woodlands than the Pawnee, Wichita, and other groups to the north. Caddoan farming culture achieved considerable complexity as maize agriculture took hold in the fertile river bottomlands from eastern Texas and Oklahoma into Kansas and to the north. Over the centuries, the Caddoan-speakers showed a tendency to coalesce into larger political units than merely single villages, often into ephemeral chiefdoms which linked larger regions into more complex polities. In the south, such developments culminated in the Mississippian traditions centered in Spiro, Oklahoma and other major ceremonial centers (Chapter 19) (Brown, 1984). In the north, they resulted in the earthlodge villages and elaborate ceremonial lives of the Arikara and Pawnee.

The Siouan-speaking Hidatsa and Mandan of the middle Missouri Valley were part of a much more varied linguistic group, with linguistically, but not culturally, related peoples living in such diverse areas as the Carolinas and along the Gulf Coast. For example, the northernmost Middle Missouri groups have cultural links with the central Mississippi Valley and the western Great Lakes, while the Crow and Assiniboine to the north and west were historic nomadic Plains peoples.

Caddoan Speakers: Wichita and Pawnee
AD 1500 to modern times

In the Kansas, Oklahoma, Texas area, the Caddoan-speaking Wichita people can be traced back to the 1st millennium AD, their cultural roots lying among the earlier Washita people and other Plains Village groups. In the 16th century, the Wichita were living in the Great Bend region of the Arkansas River Valley, and dominated the southern prairie-plains. The Great Bend communities were visited by Spanish explorers in the 16th century. The Taovaya group moved southward into Oklahoma, where they settled in large, concentrated villages located on rivers which provided access to French outposts at New Orleans. The Wichita traded furs, horses, hides, and other products for firearms, household goods, and ornaments. As the French trade intensified, so Wichita dependence on imports increased, some settlements moving to the Red River in southern Oklahoma to take advantage of changing trading patterns and to avoid the

Osage, who were harassing their territory. Wichita communities still live in central Oklahoma and Kansas today.

In the 19th century, the Caddoan-speaking Pawnee comprised a loose confederacy of 7000 to 10,000 people, living in four bands centered around the confluence of the Platte and Loup Rivers in east central Nebraska (O'Shea, 1989). The four bands lived in permanent earthlodge villages. At first European contact in the mid-16th century, the most important Pawnee settlements lay in what is sometimes called the Pawnee Crescent, between Schuyler and Genoa close to the Platte/Loup confluence itself. Early travelers describe how each village was ruled by head chiefs and a council of lesser chiefs and important men, "braves." This combination of hereditary chiefs, elected leaders, priests, and braves formed a privileged Pawnee upper class. The Pawnee priesthood exercised great power, based on their control of medicine bundles, astronomical knowledge, and ceremonial roles.

Archaeologically, the earliest Pawnee village sites belong within the Coalescent Tradition's Lower Loup phase (*c*. AD 1550 to 1750), marked by grit-tempered pottery, often with handles, and corrugated and incised decoration. Such motifs are commonplace on contemporary vessels from the Missouri Valley in South Dakota, which may hint at possible Central Plains Tradition and Coalescent origins, and very indirect cultural links to groups along the Mississippi and Ohio River Valleys (this is a controversial and unresolved issue). Lower Loup sites lie mostly on elevated terraces or on bluffs overlooking small valleys. In dramatic contrast to earlier Central Plains Tradition settlements, they cover 15 to more than 100 acres (6 to 40 ha). The people lived in substantial, circular earthlodges from 25 to 50 ft (7.6 to 15.2 m) in diameter, the floor sunk slightly below ground level. Four substantial posts supported the rafters, which also rested on a circle of shorter, outer posts. A long, covered passage led to the outside, invariably placed away from the prevailing winds. Judging from historical accounts, each of these houses, with a central hearth, storage, "cache," pits and often a small altar platform, was home to between 10 and 20 people. Most Pawnee settlements covered a large area, for fortifications were usually deemed unnecessary with so many warriors close to hand.

Pawnee subsistence was based on maize agriculture and bison hunting. The women planted at least 13 varieties of corn with bison scapula hoes and digging sticks, probably with a higher success rate than earlier Central Plains people like the Upper Republicans, for they lived about 100 miles (160 km) further east in an area of higher, more predictable rainfall. Crop yields could be substantial and were adequate enough in good years to provide a considerable stored surplus. The Pawnee claimed maize was their most important food, but they still relied heavily on wild roots and grasses, as well as bison meat. For at least half the year, each village traveled on the chase. Between late June and August or September, when the maize was ripe, men, women, and children led their horses in single file west to the bison plains. Scouts would locate the herds, which were then hunted on horseback with bows and arrows. Such hunts yielded large quantities of meat, much of which was dried for use on the march. The Pawnee camped out on the hunt from late October through March, traveling hundreds of miles from their home villages. Such a balance between sedentary agriculture and hunting was essential to people living in large, permanent villages with populations in the hundreds, far larger than could be supported by farming alone, or by local hunting and gathering.

The Pawnee came in contact with Spanish traders as early as the 17th century, but the volume of trade was never large on account of the 850 miles (1350 km) which separated their homeland from Santa Fe. The French traded furs from the Pawnee in the early 18th century, especially after the establishment of a trading post on the Missouri River in Kansa country near present-day Fort Leavenworth. By 1806, Americans, French, and Spaniards were competing for Pawnee furs. In exchange, the Pawnee received iron tools, beads, and a wide range of trade goods, even government-issued medals, which are found in graves and settlements dating from after European contact. At the same time, native pottery and other indigenous artifacts declined in quality. European encroachment on Pawnee territory accelerated after Colonel William Becknell pioneered the first wagon route from the Missouri River and Santa Fe in 1821. And in the 1830s, the Oregon Trail to Oregon and California branched off, causing further disruption, as Europeans with their repeating rifles decimated bison herds and wagon trains felled precious trees for firewood. Beset both by encroaching Europeans and roaming Cheyenne and Sioux war parties, the Pawnee ceded some of their lands to the United States in 1833. By 1875, they were unable to maintain their traditional lifeways and joined the Wichita and other Caddoan-speaking groups in a reservation to the south.

Middle Missouri Valley: Arikara, Mandan, Hidatsa
AD 1500 to modern times

A Mandan chief in State dress, painting by J. Hürlimann after Karl Bodmer 1840.

The ancestry of these Middle Missouri Valley groups is fraught with controversy, since they only appear in historical documents as late as the 18th century. There are claims of movements upstream, or from farming communities to the east, but Arikara, Mandan, and Hidatsa roots lie ultimately in the Missouri Valley itself. As we have seen, the late 15th-century Huff site, near Bismarck, North Dakota, with its rectangular houses and palisades, is thought to be an ancestral Mandan settlement.

Some time before European contact, but after AD 1500, the long rectangular houses were replaced by circular dwellings. The new Coalescent Tradition, already mentioned, resulted from the mingling of Central Plains and Middle Missouri groups, especially in the Big Bend area of South Dakota (Zimmerman, 1985). This blending of two related cultures was one of many major population movements over the next six centuries which brought different groups into constant contact and hybridized cultures. The Coalescent Tradition led eventually to the emergence of the historic Arikara nation. The Arikara were living in numerous villages in the Big Bend area of South Dakota when they first came in contact with French traders in the early 18th century. Fifty years later, they had congregated in a few densely occupied, fortified communities. Frequently, the new settlements overlie older, rectangular houses, as if the same spots were used many times, but with a lower density of houses than earlier villages. The earliest circular-house communities were rambling settlements, with dwellings scattered over many acres and marked by lodge rings or shallow depressions. All the Middle Missouri circular houses have a saucer-like basin dug up to 3 ft (0.9 m) into the ground and were covered with poles, willows, grass, and earth or sod, leaving only a small smoke vent at the roof apex.

North from Pierre, South Dakota, other village settlements were probably the ancestors of the Mandan, whose oral traditions speak of at least two population movements up the river. The French traveler Pierre Gaultier de Varennes de la Verendrye first contacted the Mandan in December 1738 (Wood, 1980). Four years later, two of his sons lived among them and found the people living in six or seven well-fortified villages, said to contain between 100 and 200 houses each. These populous communities were the climax of Plains Village Indian culture on the middle Missouri. The extensive middens and varied artifact inventory found in these settlements make it clear that the maize, beans, and squash agriculture of the Middle Missouri villages was now highly productive, yielding dependable food supplies, easily supplemented by hunting bison on horseback. One reason for their prosperity was constant exchanges with their nomadic neighbors, who traded grain for hides and other commodities. The farmers had always been middlemen. Now their role became even more crucial in an emerging, and ever more complex trading environment. The villages acquired horses and firearms from the south and west and soon became important trading centers, which attracted English, French, and Spanish traders. As Waldo Wedel wrote many years ago: "They participated deeply in the main currents of Plains cultural development; and like other middlemen before and since, rose to pre-eminence and prosperity. There was a price on this pre-eminence, however, and part of it is reflected in the defensive works with which the communities found it necessary to surround themselves" (Wedel, 1961).

These large, circular or oblong 18th-century village sites have as many as 50 house sites, closely packed together, often with only narrow walkways between them. A deep ditch, as much as 10 ft (3 m) deep when freshly dug, surrounded each settlement, backed on the inner side with a massive log-and-brush palisade. The circular houses maintain the same general design, but are now much larger, earthlodges between 30 and 50 ft (9 and 51 m) in diameter, the outer walls closely set circles of poles covered with earth, grass, and willow saplings. So crowded were fortified Mandan villages that refuse was piled up against the palisades or thrown in the surrounding ditches, a bounty for the archaeologist, but malodorous at the time. The middens have yielded stamped and incised clay vessels, and a wide variety of bone artifacts, including bison-bone hoe blades, scoops, fish hooks, leather-working tools and hunting weapons.

Historic Mandan villages were located on terraces above the river. Several nuclear families, all members of the same matrilineal kin group, occupied several dozen earthlodges in each settlement, all clustered around a central open space for games and public ceremonies. Early European visitors wrote vivid descriptions of the comfortable, if odiferous, lodges, with their four massive uprights and open smoke hole at the peak of the earth-covered roof. A short, timber entrance way led into the house, the central hearth placed in the square formed by the four roof posts. Curtained beds lined the walls, while deep storage pits in the floor contained corn and other food supplies. A favorite horse might be corralled near the entrance, while a small shrine lay behind the fire opposite the entrance. These permanent settlements were almost deserted during the summer bison hunts, and also for much of the winter, when the people camped in sheltered woodlands in the valley, where game and firewood were plentiful.

The trend toward compact, fortified villages was common to the entire middle Missouri Valley, but is difficult to explain. By the mid-18th century, most settlements lay on the west bank of the river, perhaps withdrawing from the threat of the nomadic Dakota, who were an increasingly powerful force to the east. At the same time, smallpox epidemics may have depopulated the valley long before the historically recorded infection of 1780–81, which swept through the Upper Missouri and far to the north and west, with devastating effects. Whatever the causes, by 1804, when the celebrated explorers Meriwhether Lewis and William Clark traveled by the Missouri, the Hidatsa, Mandan, and Arikara were a shadow of their former selves, with many villages abandoned and survivors clustered in poorly fortified settlements (Lehmer and Jones, 1968; Deetz, 1965). By 1800, the Sioux were a constant threat, so the surviving populations congregated in large villages. The Arikara Leavenworth site south of the Grand River housed as many as 1800 people living in two groups of 60 to 80 lodges each (Krause, 1972). Artifacts of European origin are now common, but the Missouri people were still trading steatite from Wyoming with groups west of the Rocky Mountains, as they had in earlier centuries. They also bartered catlinite from the pipestone quarries in southwestern Minnesota.

During the 19th century, the Arikara, Hidatsa, and Mandan were decimated by further epidemics and by increasing encroachment by Europeans. The survivors of all three groups joined together at the last earthlodge village, Like-a-Fishhook, north of the Knife River confluence, in 1862 (Smith, G.H., 1972). Their Three Affiliated Tribes descendants still live in the same area today and maintain distinct cultural identities.

Big Hidatsa village site, at the confluence of the Knife and Missouri Rivers, North Dakota. The aerial view shows circular earthlodge depressions and trails emanating from the village. The settlement was occupied by Hidatsas between AD 1600 and 1845, after which they moved upstream to found a new village where they were joined by Mandans and Arikaras. Today the three groups are known as the Three Affiliated Tribes.

A skin lodge of an Assiniboine chief, depicted by Karl Bodmer.

Nomads and Plains Farmers

By the 18th century, the Plains west of the farmers were home to linguistically diverse equestrian nomads (Chapter 6). The history of these groups is extremely complicated, for different groups coalesced, split up then coalesced again. The Cheyenne, for example, who had withdrawn from country around Lake Superior under pressure from the Assiniboine, once lived in earthlodge villages along the Sheyenne River in the Red River drainage. By the end of the 18th century, some of them were among the Arikara on the middle Missouri, forsaking farming permanently to move to North Dakota's Black Hills for a while, some then shifting further west into Colorado and Wyoming. For the most part, the Cheyenne now lived in small, self-sufficient bands, constantly on the move in search of bison. They did not cut themselves off completely from the sedentary life, for some of their social institutions, especially the important role of women in influencing public opinion and camp life, survived from farming days. The Cheyenne were famous as traders, meeting Arikara, Mandan, and other friendly horticulturalists at regular trade fairs in Missouri villages or on the edge of the Black Hills. Here, large numbers of people assembled to exchange horses and animal produce for grain and European trade goods. The relationship between nomads and farmer was friendly, and based on mutual need.

While the Cheyenne enjoyed mainly friendly relations with the farmers, the Dakota were the main enemies. The Dakota came to the Plains from country north and east of the Missouri River, from the westerly grasslands and woodlands near the Mississippi and toward the Great Lakes. While the related Sioux of the woodlands continued to farm until the 19th century, those of the prairies were hunters living in skin tents, forced ever westward by the ripple effect of pressure from the Iroquois far to the east (Holder, 1970). They acquired the horse during the 18th century, making the changeover from hunting on foot within a remarkably short time, perhaps two generations.

Sioux groups drifted west across the Missouri. They were constantly at war with the Mandan by 1790 and were soon alienated completely from their ancient way of life. By this time, they ranged over an enormous area of the Plains from Alberta and Saskatchewan in Canada to the Rockies and far west of the 100th meridian. All Sioux groups spoke the same language, but formed many divisions and bands. The Teton Division of the north comprised about 8000 people, clustered in at least seven bands, among them the Blackfoot and Oglala. During the summer months, bands of their warriors raided for horses as far south as the Platte and the Arkansas. Their way of life contrasted sharply with that of horticulturalists like the Pawnee. Glamorous although their nomadic life has been depicted, they were often close to starvation, dependent not only on the movements of bison, but on the surplus food of farming villages, especially when herds were reduced by greater hunting pressure from higher nomadic populations. The nomads depended on food surpluses from farmers, acquired either by bartering or gift, or by raiding parties. Nowhere was the contrast more marked than in the spiritual realm. Sioux society was based on individual competition, in an environment where chiefs had little authority and feuding and factionalism were endemic. The personal vision quest, where a person acquired power for themselves by fasting and personal propitiation, was the foundation of Dakota and Sioux beliefs. In contrast, the farmers lived in stable villages, where authority was well defined and carefully organized to ensure long-term stability and clear lines of power. The farmer's life unfolded within a deeply embedded religious framework.

The ever more complex economic relationship between nomads and farmers developed at a time when the horticulturalists were living dangerously close to the edge. Agriculture depended on the women, but as the volume of trade with Europeans increased, many of them spent most of their time processing furs and hides, producing commodities for the trade. A crop failure, a sudden raid, or other unusual demands on their precious food surpluses would once have thrown them back on bison meat. But now

Detail from a Dakota Indian painting on muslin c. 1890.

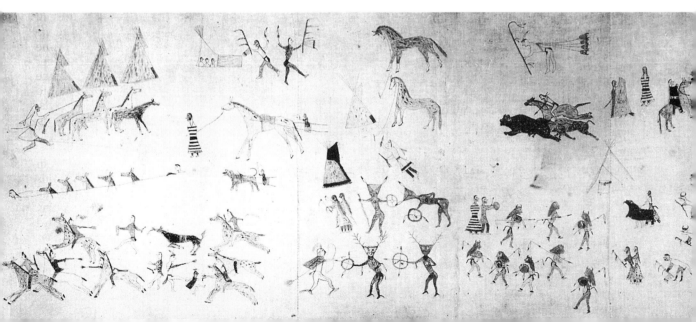

meat supplies were diminished, predatory warriors hovered on the fringes, and their ecological situation was badly out of balance. The effects were somewhat reduced by extensive trade between groups like the Mandan and the Cheyenne, who bartered turkey feathers and food and European goods. But any advantages gained from this summer bartering were often lost when Dakota raiding parties attacked laden trading parties and emptied precious storage caches. The villagers had become successful middlemen, but overextended and decimated by smallpox epidemics, they paid a terrible price for their success. Racked by internal stresses, depopulated, and facing frequent food shortages and warfare, villages from different groups coalesced for survival, moves which diminished the power and authority of many chiefly families. At the same time, young commoners, especially warriors, could find new opportunities to climb the ladder of social success, creating dissent within hitherto stable societies. But the conservative culture of the farmers managed to hold on, making it impossible for these communities to make the transition to equestrian nomadism despite enormous pressure to do so. It was only when the chiefs became the economic equals of their followers in the face of European settlement that the structure of village life collapsed.

Further Reading

Ahler, S., Thiessen, T., and Trimble, M. 1991. *People of the Willows: The Prehistory and Early History of the Hidatsa Indians.* University of North Dakota Press, Grand Forks.
A popularly written volume on the Hidatsa with numerous photographs and maps.
Holder, Preston. 1970. *The Hoe and the Horse on the Plains.* University of Nebraska Press, Lincoln.
A classic account of Plains farmers and their relationships with equestrian nomads. Ideal for the general reader and of vital importance to me when writing this chapter.
Lehmer, Donald J. 1971. *Introduction to Middle Missouri Archaeology.* Anthropological Papers of the National Park Service no. 1, Washington DC.
A synthesis of the River Basin Surveys, which is a basic source. A technical description, but still intelligible to non-specialists.
Nebraskaland Magazine 1994. *The Cellars of Time.* Nebraska Game and Parks Commission, Lincoln 72(1).
Beautifully illustrated essays on ancient Nebraska, which touch on many of the cultures described here.
Wedel, Waldo R. 1986. *Central Plains Prehistory: Holocene Environments and Culture Change in the Republican River Basin.* University of Nebraska Press, Lincoln.
Describes excavations and surveys along the Republican River, while ranging widely over the Central Plains. Definitive, but a specialist publication.
Wood, W. Raymond. (ed.) 1998. *Archaeology on the Great Plains.* University of Kansas Press, Lawrence.
An up-to-date volume of essays on Plains archaeology for the serious reader.
Zimmerman, L. 1985. *Peoples of Prehistoric South Dakota.* University of Nebraska Press, Lincoln.
A good account of northern Plains prehistory, which helps update Lehmer and other earlier accounts.

PART FOUR

THE FAR NORTH

"The lakes melted, and the hunter wondered, 'What did the Snow Man mean when he said he was going to help me?' He began to hunt, and he saved all the fat from the animals he caught and stored it in bladders. He also cut lots of wood, which he arranged in deep piles. And he went on all summer and into the fall storing grease and piling up wood. He did not know why he did these things. Something seemed to impel him..."

Northern Athabaskan legend

CALIBRATED DATES	RADIOCARBON AGES	ALASKA			EASTERN ARCTIC	SUB ARCTIC
		ALEUTIANS	KODIAK AREA	BERING STRAIT AREA		
Modern Times	Modern Times	MODERN ALEUTS	MODERN ESKIMO GROUPS		MOD. INUIT	MODERN ATHABASKAN-SPEAKING GROUPS
			KONIAG	PUNUK BIRNIRK	T H U L E POST-CLASSIC CLASSIC THULE EXPANDS	
AD 1105 —	AD 1000 —	Chaluka A L E U T I A N T R A D I T I O N	K A C H E M A K K O D I A K T R A D I T I O N	N O R T O N N O R T O N I P I U T A K T H U L E OLD BERING SEA	D O R S E T	N O R T H E R N A R C H A I C S H I E L D A R C H A I C M A R I T I M E A R C H A I C
AD 15 —	AD 1 —					
1267 BC —	1000 BC —	Chaluka		CHORIS ARCTIC SMALL TOOL TRADITION	ARCTIC SMALL TOOL TRAD. S A R Q A Q PRE-DORSET INDEP. I	
2477 BC —	2000 BC —					
3795 BC —	3000 BC —		OCEAN BAY TRADITION	?		
4935 BC —	4000 BC —			?		
5876 BC —	5000 BC —				No human settlement	
7056 BC —	6000 BC —	Anangula		PALEO-ARCTIC TRADITION	No human settlement	
8247 BC —	7000 BC —					

CHAPTER 8

EARLY ARCTIC CULTURES

For at least four centuries, the far northern reaches of North America have been a focus of intense interest, a challenge that has exercised a powerful spell on the Western imagination. The Europeans who first explored the Arctic had been raised in lands with fertile soils and long summers, where the enemies were late frosts and early winters. To these explorers, the geographical and social environments of the people of the north were a startling reversal of the human condition (McGhee, 1996).

The distance that an English ship could penetrate into the Arctic during the ice-free summer months usually left her crew frozen into the territory of the Central Canadian Arctic, where the Inuit used dog sleds and dwelt in snow houses. Their "igloos" and hunts became the "Eskimos" of popular imagination. The people of the north were seen as happy, optimistic hunters dressed in cozy furs, despite a harsh life of never-ending work and fatalism in an environment of impossible terrain and intolerable weather. This abiding stereotype was epitomized by Robert Flaherty's celebrated movie *Nanook of the North*, which appeared in 1922. This documentary told the story of a man pitted against the ferocious and unrelenting environmental odds of the frozen north. The film was an international hit in a naive, romantic era. When the hunter who had played Nanook starved to death on the tundra a few years later, movie-goers as far afield as China mourned his passing. (For another perspective, see Kind and Lidchi, 1998.)

The haunting stereotypes perpetuated by Europeans disguise a great diversity of thriving human cultures that extend back to the very earliest generations of ancient settlement in the Americas. Today, after more than 10,000 years of human settlement in the Far North, the mosaic of environments and societies in the North are much more elaborate than any scientific investigations have so far revealed. The northern peoples express differences between themselves in a myriad ways – by the patterning of impressions left by sealskin boots, by pronunciations of words, by preferences for different hunting methods and camp sites. The archaeological record represents an inevitable blurring of cultural differences that persisted over many centuries.

At the time of European contact, arctic peoples were strung across the Far North from Attu Island at the extreme western end of the Aleutian Islands to the eastern shores of Greenland, more than 6800 miles (11,000 km) by reasonably direct boat and sled routes. There was considerable physical variation between them. The Eskimos and Aleuts display some anatomical

One of the scenes from the movie, Nanook of the North *(1922).*

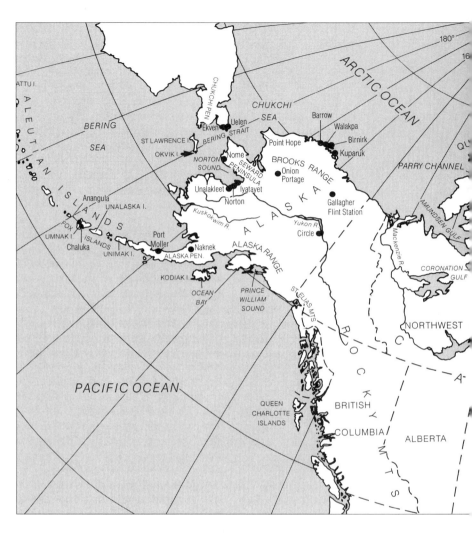

(Right) Major sites and regions of the Far North referred to in Chapters 9–10.

differences, but are generally considered to be the most Asian of all native Americans. They have been classified as "Arctic Mongoloids," as have the peoples of northern Siberia. This type is distinct from that of most American Indians to the south.

Linguistically, all Eskimos and Aleuts belong within a single Eskimo-Aleut language stock (for a summary, see Dumond, 1987). However, there are differences between the Eskimoan and Aleutian branches, which have been likened to those between Russian and English in the Indo-European language group. When the first Russian explorers arrived, Aleutian dialects were spoken along the entire island chain and onto the Alaska Peninsula as far east as 159˚W. Eskimoan flourished from there eastward to Kodiak Island and around the Alaskan coast and across Canada to Greenland. There are two distinct segments of Eskimoan. Western Eskimo includes at least five different languages and is centered in an area between the Chukchi Peninsula, Norton Sound, and Prince William Sound. Eastern Eskimoan is spoken from St Michael and Unalaklete northward and

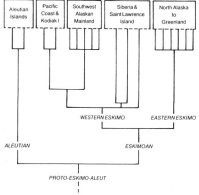

(Below) A generalized family tree
of the Eskimo-Aleut languages, after
Dumond (1987). The highest order
of branches, shown on all but the
three Siberian languages, indicates
the presence of dialects.

eastward all the way to Greenland. Linguists generally agree that Eskimo-Aleut languages are related to Siberian speech stocks, either to that of the Chukchi, close Siberian neighbors, or to the more widely distributed Ural-Altaic group found throughout much of Siberia.

Throughout the vast regions of the Far North, from Greenland across arctic Canada to Alaska, and along the Alaskan coast to the Alaska Peninsula, human societies at European contact practiced a highly varied hunter-gatherer economy based on the bounty of land and water. Sea mammals large and small, lake and river fish, caribou, musk ox, and small game supplemented by wild vegetable foods – most were available over wide areas and were taken with basically similar techniques. However, the emphasis of the hunting and gathering economy varied greatly from locale to locale depending on local environmental conditions. The exact dates at which maritime exploitation began are the subject of much debate, complicated by constant tectonic activity along Alaskan coasts, which has submerged many important sites (Mann and others,

1998). As David Yesner (1998) has pointed out, the ever-changing climatic conditions of the Early Holocene may have pulled people to and from the coast depending on short-term changes, with maritime adaptations becoming widespread with the onset of the warmer, more stable Middle Holocene.

The Arctic Environment

Alaska was joined to Siberia for much of the Wisconsin glaciation, part of the sunken continent of Beringia that formed a natural highway for human settlement of the New World (Chapter 4) (West, 1996). The Arctic Slope runs across the northern portion of the modern state of Alaska, separated from the interior by the Brooks Range that reaches an altitude of 9842 ft (3000 m) in a few places (Dumond, 1987). The Alaska Range, which includes Mount McKinley, forms another ridge across the south, merging into the Aleutian Range. These mountains extend southwestward along the Alaska Peninsula and become the 1000-mile (1600-km) Aleutian Island chain that stretches far into the Pacific. Two major rivers, the Yukon and the Kuskokwim, drain through the broken country and swampy lowlands of central Alaska into the Bering Sea from headwaters far in the interior. Vast numbers of salmon run up these rivers, a vital subsistence resource for the ancient (and modern) inhabitants.

Canada's Yukon Territory lies to the east, rugged country where the Rocky Mountains, the Coast Mountains, and the St Elias Range come together to form a massive backbone that extends south into what is now British Columbia. During the Ice Age, the mountain glaciers of northern and southern Alaska nearly joined in the Yukon, leaving the Alaskan interior nearly unglaciated during the Wisconsin.

East from the Yukon extends a vast tract of low-lying, undulating territory that was covered with the massive Laurentide ice sheet during the Wisconsin glaciation. The Canadian mainland surrounding Hudson Bay is fundamentally a shallow basin, with several large rivers flowing into the depression, among them the Churchill and Nelson from the west, the Great Whale and Eastmain from the east (Harp, 1976; Maxwell, 1985). The western rivers flow through an undulating plain covered in many places with glacial tills or marine deposits. To the east of Hudson Bay lies a rocky, glaciated plateau which lies at an altitude of about 984 ft (300 m) above sea level. The glacier-scoured and polished rocks of this area coincide with the Canadian Shield, made up of ancient pre-Cambrian rocks and devoid of most vegetation.

North of the mainland lies the Canadian arctic Archipelago, covering an enormous area of the Arctic Ocean, and extending as far as Greenland. A small portion of the islands is covered with permanent ice and mountain glaciers. The barren terrain is characterized by various land forms, but stands in contrast to the mountain chain along the fjord-indented eastern edge of the Queen Elizabeth Islands that reaches altitudes of nearly 10,000 ft (3048 m) in places.

Greenland lies to the east of the Canadian Archipelago, the northernmost landmass in the world, reaching to within 435 miles (700 km) of the North Pole and mantled with an enormous ice cap. This reaches the sea in places, but there is a fringe of ice-free territory along much of Greenland's deeply indented coasts.

The border between arctic and sub-arctic North America coincides approximately with the northern limits of the treeline, well south of the Arctic Circle. It is really a misnomer to call this a line, for in reality it is a broad transitional zone between the tundra and boreal forest. Archaeologist Elmer Harp puts it well (1983): "Approaching it [the treeline] from the north, one first encounters outlying isolated clumps of stunted conifers in sheltered valleys; these increase in size and density toward the south, until at last the closed boreal forest appears." Large-scale forest growth is impossible where the average temperature of the warmest month of the year, usually July, is below 50°F (10°C), and the arctic treeline coincides in general terms with the 50°F (10°C) isotherm for that month. This is, of course, an average temperature. Depending on location, actual summer readings can be much higher.

The northern climate is savage, with long, dark, and severely cold winters and brief summers with no more than about three frost-free months a year. Temperatures are never warm enough to allow total thawing of the ground, so permafrost occurs close to the surface, resulting in widespread summer bogs and swamps that make travel inland extremely difficult – to say nothing of the hordes of mosquitoes that torture both man and beast. Even at the southern edge of Labrador and Hudson Bay, sea ice rings coasts and islands for at least seven months every year. Mid-winter temperatures average below –25°F (–32°C) for weeks at a time, with winter storms with harsh northwesterly winds dropping them as low as –100°F (–73°C).

With such temperatures and only short summers, vegetational cover is sparse tundra at best, with occasional stands of dwarf willow, alder, and birch in sheltered locales. The early summer growth season is short and intense, as mosses, lichens, and other ground-hugging species grow rapidly in the long hours of welcome sunlight. In the Canadian Archipelago the protection is minimal and the sparse vegetation gives way to barren, rocky terrain.

Only a few species of land mammal flourish in the Arctic. The most common is the caribou, a gregarious species that occurs throughout the Far North, in several large herds west of Hudson Bay, and in smaller aggregations elsewhere. Musk ox thrive in Greenland, over much of the northern Archipelago and in remoter parts of the mainland. Other animals include hares, lemmings, arctic fox, wolves, and bears. Bird life is abundant, especially migratory waterfowl, which breed and nest in the Arctic during the summer.

Aquatic resources abound in northern waters, not only arctic char, salmon, and whitefish, but many species of sea mammals, including whales. For thousands of years, ancient peoples subsisted off a bounty of seal and walrus, developing specialized toolkits for sea-mammal hunting throughout the Far North.

South of the treeline, the boreal forest, often called taiga, is virtually impenetrable, meaning that the traveler must traverse it along natural drainage systems (Harp, 1983). Spruce is dominant in the northern taiga, giving way to more hemlock, tamarack, and pine further south. Winters are just as severe as they are on the tundra, but there are more frost-free days and greater variety of land animals. Woodland caribou, moose, and migratory waterfowl were important food sources in ancient times. Fur-bearing animals such as the beaver and mink assumed great economic importance after European contact.

The biology of the Far North is far richer and more dependent on the cold than might appear. The open tundra is a perfect habitat for the lichens, grasses, and sedges that are the staple diet of caribou. The permafrost guarantees vast areas of shallow lake and swamp that never seep away, rich habitats not only for mosquitoes but many other insect species. They provide nourishment for many birds and fish. Throughout the Arctic and Sub-Arctic, the sunlight of spring and summer ensures that grasses and insects are turned into the protein upon which northern hunters depend.

Every year, millions of small seawater plankton, krill, shrimp, and tiny fish move into arctic waters. There they take advantage of the microorganisms that have been growing at the base of the sea ice, organisms that are released into the ocean as the ice melts in spring and summer. Much larger creatures such as dolphins and beluga whales feed on the small fry, while baleen whales like the arctic bowhead eat krill. The same food chain provides enough nutrients for a vast seal population year round.

Ironically, while southerners tend to think of the summer as the only bearable time in the Arctic, the warm months can be the most hazardous ones for the northern hunter. The tundra is awash in standing water, making walking and boat travel the only viable means of transport. Unpredictable summer storms can make canoe and boat travel slightly hazardous, and mosquitoes plague life ashore. The boreal forests are tangled with undergrowth, making tracking and snaring both hazardous and uncomfortable. Many interior groups tended to find more open camp sites in summer, which was a time for important social gatherings and relative inactivity.

The Paleo-Arctic Tradition
c. 8000 to c. 5000 BC

In 8000 BC, Alaska was still a cultural province of Siberia, as it had been in earlier times, occupied by peoples whose ultimate cultural roots lay to the west, in the D'uktai tradition of Siberia. Their microblades and other artifacts were part of a Stone Age cultural tradition that extended east from the Lena Basin in Siberia throughout most of the unglaciated area of Alaska and the Yukon, south and east along the Pacific coast, and perhaps as far south as British Columbia. After about 8000 BC, D'uktai gave way to the Sumnagin culture in Siberia, seasonal hunters and fisher folk who pursued both forest moose and tundra animals like the reindeer with a somewhat different technology from their predecessors (Dumond, 1987). A greater diversity of hunter-gatherer cultures also flourished in Alaska after 8000 BC. These cultures are subsumed under the Paleo-Arctic tradition. There was on-going interaction between Siberia and Alaska from before 10,000 BC until about 9000 BC, when rising sea levels in the Bering Strait interrupted regular communication (See essays in *Arctic Anthropology* 35(1), 1998).

The Paleo-Arctic tradition is still a shadowy entity, a patchwork of local Early Holocene cultural traditions that flourished over an enormous area of extreme northwestern North America for at least 4000 years, and longer in

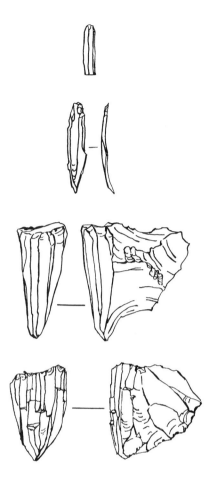

Paleo-Arctic tradition. (Top two rows) Two microblades from Ugashik Narrows, Alaska Peninsula. (Third and fourth rows) Two microblade cores from Onion Portage, Alaska. (Height of largest core 4.3 cm.)

many places. Other terms such as the Northwest Microblade tradition, Denali Complex, and Beringian tradition have been used to describe these same general adaptations, but "Paleo-Arctic" is the most appropriate because it is the kind of general label that reflects a great variety of different human adaptations during a period of increasing environmental diversity and change (discussion in West, 1996).

Undoubtedly, many Paleo-Arctic sites were buried by rising Holocene sea levels, perhaps a significant number of them in places where people exploited marine resources and lived in more permanent base camps. The settlements that survive are, for the most part, temporary land hunting camps where only stone tools remain. However, it is interesting to note that coastal sites with microblades occur as early as 7000 BC along ice-free coasts south of the Alaskan Peninsula.

Hardly surprisingly, the Paleo-Arctic is known mainly from stone artifacts – microblades, small wedge-shaped cores for making them, some leaf-shaped bifaces, also scrapers and graving tools. Perhaps the most distinctive stone objects are the wedge-shaped microcores. Their elliptical striking platforms were fashioned by removing a transverse flake. The stone worker then pressed off microblades at one end in such a manner that he made economic use of the precious raw material, ending up with a keel-shaped core. The tiny microblades were usually less than 2.5 in (6.5 cm) long, far smaller than classic Upper Paleolithic blades from Eurasia. Many microblades were used as sharp-edged barbs for hunting weapons, mounted in wood, antler, or bone points with slotted sides. Many microblades were snapped across, as if the mid-sections were used for this purpose. Paleo-Arctic stone workers also fashioned bifaces that were used both as tools and as cores for the production of larger artifact blanks. There is great variation in stone tool inventories from one Paleo-Arctic site to another. Some sites contain well-made stone projectile points, others no bifaces but many microblades, others a large inventory of scrapers. Rare fluted projectile points were also part of the Paleo-Arctic tradition.

The Paleo-Arctic tradition occurs throughout Alaska, and as far east as the west and southwest Yukon Territory. Wedge-shaped cores and microblades are known from the Icy Strait region of southeast Alaska where they date to between 6000 and 2000 BC. They date to as early as 8000 BC a short distance further south, and also occur inland. The Queen Charlotte Islands off northern British Columbia were occupied by about 5000 BC, by people who manufactured microblades by striking them off much cruder cores. These bear little resemblance to the fine blades found further north, while microblades and crude cores have come from Namu on the British Columbia coast dating to as early as 7000 BC. Owing to rising sea levels, we do not know to what extent human settlement was focused on the coast, as it was in later millennia (Chapter 10) (Fladmark, 1986).

There are a number of early Alaskan sites that can be described as variations on the Paleo-Arctic tradition. These include Gallagher Flint Station in the north-central Brooks Range, the Groundhog Bay site from southeastern Alaska, and the Kagati and Ugashik Narrows locations in the southwest (West, 1996), also the famous Anangula site from the Aleutian chain.

Anangula is unusual in that it was occupied for a long period of time. The site lies on an islet off the coast of Umnak Island in the eastern

Paleo-Arctic tradition from Anangula Island, Aleutians. (Right) Microcore and two microblades (height of core 3.7 cm). (Below) A core together with the refitted blanks struck from it.

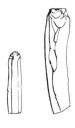

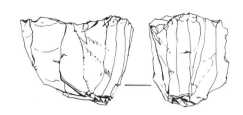

Aleutians, about a third of the way along the Aleutian chain (Aigner, 1970), atop a 65-ft (19.8-m) bluff. The many radiocarbon dates range between 6100 and 5900 BC. The inhabitants made blade tools of various sizes and many microblades. There are signs of elliptically shaped houses that were partially dug into the ground and perhaps entered through the roof. Anangula was probably occupied when the sea level was at about its modern height and was only accessible by boat. This argues strongly for a marine adaptation at the site, an economy that relied on sea mammals and fish. However, none of the rather generalized stone artifacts from the site appear to have had specialized uses for sea-mammal hunting. Judging from later sites, many such artifacts were probably manufactured of perishable bone and ivory.

Coastal Adaptations on the Pacific Coast
5000 BC to c. AD 1000

By 4000 BC, the Pacific Ocean had stabilized at more-or-less its modern level, with ice-free coasts extending at least 15° further north on the Alaskan coast than to the west in Siberia. This led to the widespread distribution of maritime cultures along the full length of the Aleutian Islands by at least 1000 BC.

As was the case elsewhere in North America, we find an increasing emphasis on coastal adaptations after 4000 BC, but there are good reasons to suspect that such lifeways were commonplace before then (McCartney and others, 1998). Judging from sites such as Anangula, the exploitation of ocean fish and marine mammals was almost certainly practiced along the

Eskimo two-person kayak, Nunivak Island, Alaska.

Aleutian chain and on Kodiak Island by at least 3000 BC. Here, the climate is oceanic, with cool summers and relatively warm winters, where the mean temperature rarely falls below 20°F (–6°C). In this damp, often foggy environment, coastal waters teemed with sea otters, hair seal, and sea lion, with regular fur seal and whale migrations. The greatest population densities over the millennia concentrated near Kodiak Island and westward to Unimak Island, where whales were especially abundant. One would expect cultural uniformity over this entire area, but in spite of the relatively uniform ecosystem the ancient and modern populations fall into two major linguistic groups – Aleutian and Eskimoan. And therein lies a major controversy in arctic archaeology: when did Aleutians diverge from the Eskimoan stock of the mainland?

From the strictly archaeological point of view, it makes good sense to link the Aleuts and Pacific Eskimos into a single cultural unit, ignoring their linguistic differences and some major differences in material culture. Both Aleuts and Eskimos shared a relatively uniform ecological zone and many subsistence techniques and basic artifacts. The single-person skin kayak for open-water hunting, multi-barbed harpoons for taking large sea mammals, and many other bone and antler artifacts show close similarities, similarities that distinguish them from coastal peoples to the north. For instance, later northern peoples used toggling harpoons. However, the stone implements fabricated by Aleuts and Eskimos show major differences, and provide one way of approaching the problem of distinguishing between the two groups in remoter ancient times.

Three major cultural entities have been identified over this large region after 5000 BC.

Kodiak Island has yielded over 7000 years of human occupation, beginning with the marine-mammal-hunting Ocean Bay tradition, which flourished for about 3000 years. These people used thrusting spears with large stone blades against large sea mammals, including whales, spears that were most likely coated with aconite poison from the Monkshood plant, a practice that was commonplace in historic times.

The Kachemak Tradition developed in about 1800 BC and flourished to about AD 1000 (Clark, D.W., 1997; 1998). This sea-mammal-hunting, salmon-fishing, and caribou-hunting culture appears to have originated in Ocean Bay, with the addition of techniques for working slate by grinding and sawing. Later Kachemak sites contain a wider variety of slate artifacts, many of them shaped by chipping before grinding and polishing. Perhaps the most characteristic is the transverse-edged knife known as the *ulu*, not found on earlier sites. Bone artifacts including barbed harpoon heads testify to the importance of sea-mammal hunting.

The greater variety of bone and slate artifacts that appears during the Kachemak stage is part of a general trend along much of the southeast Alaskan and Northwest Coast beginning in the early 2nd millennium BC. During the thousand years after Christ, Kachemak material culture became ever more elaborate, greater site density and increased midden accumulation indicating higher population densities. Common artifacts include notched net weights, also heavy, pecked stone lamps with human and animal figures carved emerging from the bowl. The Kachemak people were constantly at war and practiced elaborate mortuary rituals, dismembering

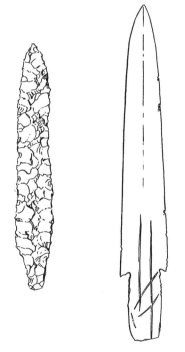

(Above left) Ocean Bay tradition: large chipped-stone projectile point from Takli Island, length 15 cm. (Above right) Kodiak tradition: polished-slate dart or lance blade from the Takli stage, Alaska Peninsula, length 21 cm.

Pecked and polished oval stone lamp with upper part of human figure inside, from Knik River, Cooks Inlet, Alaska. Drapery-like design on the outside in relief. Length 32 cm.

some of the dead, retaining some skulls as trophies, burying other people intact.

After about AD 500, cultural influences from both the Bering Sea area and from coastal regions to the southeast appear in Kachemak settlements. The Kachemak tradition evolved into the historical Eskimo-speaking Koniag culture of the region after AD 1000. This may have been an amalgam of Kachemak, Prince William Sound, and Thule cultural traits from the north.

The Aleutian Tradition
c. 2500 BC to AD 1800

The second widespread cultural entity occurs in the Aleutian Islands. The earliest-known human occupation in the Aleutians comes from the Anangula site. Anangula plays a critical role in the Aleutian past, and is the subject of three competing hypotheses (McCartney, 1984a). First, does this important site, with its emphasis on sea-mammal hunting and long occupation dating back to about 6000 BC, represent ancestral Aleutian occupation in the islands? Some scholars, notably William Laughlin, one of the investigators of Anangula, believe that it does. This would imply an 8000-year linguistic, racial, and cultural continuum. Others argue that recent Aleut culture is a blend of later Eskimoid influences from the Alaska Peninsula and the older Anangula tradition. A third hypothesis contends that the Anangula people died out, to be replaced by a second occupation of the island chain by at least 2500 BC.

The first and second hypotheses both call, essentially, for cultural continuity, but one can argue with some justification that there is at present no archaeological evidence for cultural continuity between Anangula and much better-documented later occupations, except for a maritime site with microblades at Margaret Bay site on Unalaska Island, said to date to about 3500 BC. The later occupations form the Aleutian tradition, which began before 2000 BC and lasted until modern times. The third theory, the

Historic Aleut winter house. This form of large, semi-subterranean house was occupied by many related families, each with its own lamp and living space. Space was allocated on the basis of rank, the highest-ranked occupant living on the eastern side of the house. The inhabitants used notched logs as ladders to enter and leave through the roof.

Aleutian tradition, Umnak, western Fox islands. (Left) Barbed harpoon head, length c. 10 cm. (Right) Ivory figurine, length 6 cm.

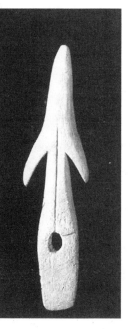

so-called Dual Tradition Model, argues that the basic stone technology of Anangula is very different from that of later Aleutian tradition industries, manufactured some 3500 years later. These two technologies, separated by many centuries, reflect quite different cultural traditions.

The Aleutian tradition is dominated by chipped-stone artifacts rather than the slate so common in the Kodiak area, especially Ocean Bay-like stemmed points and knives. This is a core-and-flake tradition, with bifacially trimmed projectile points and tanged and untanged knives, that also contains adze blades. The bone industry is elaborate (McCartney, 1984a). The absence of such Anangula tools as prismatic cores, gravers, and other artifacts is a powerful argument for a lack of cultural continuity, for such implements have never been found in contexts as late as 2500 BC. Allen McCartney and other scholars believe that Anangula is the isolated remnant of a much older Asiatic tradition that is very rare in northern North America, a tradition that predates the much later Aleutian. The controversy is still unresolved.

Everywhere the emphasis is on marine mammals and sea fish such as cod and halibut, also sea urchins and migratory animals like whales, especially in the eastern islands. Some settlements, like the Hot Springs site at Port Moller on the Alaska Peninsula, were occupied; off and on for thousands of years, from as early as 2000 BC to about AD 1000. Here the houses were elliptical to rectangular, dug about 18 in (0.5 m) into the ground, roofed with driftwood and sod, and were probably entered through the roof.

In the western Fox islands, the Chaluka site on Umnak Island was occupied over a long period beginning in about 2000 BC. The early and middle periods of occupation lasted from about 2000 to 1000 BC, a settlement of semi-subterranean dwellings lined with stone slabs and whale bones with fire pits and some stone paving. The inhabitants made numerous chipped-stone projectile points and apparently subsisted off sea mammals. Sometime between AD 1000 and 1500, slate implements came into use at Chaluka. What is striking, however, is that the basic lifeway remained very similar, with the same fundamental bone harpoon heads, spear points, chisels, awls, and ornaments in use throughout.

Sea-mammal hunting and fishing communities also flourished further west on Amchitka and among the Rat Islands. Here, the people took large numbers of sea otters and harbor seal, some migratory whales and fur seals, sea fish, ducks, geese, swan, and sea birds, also sea urchins and limpets. One excavated house was semi-subterranean, a sub-rectangular dwelling about 16.4 by 19.6 ft (5 by 6 m), radiocarbon dated to about AD 1500. A storage bench and depressed sleeping area surrounded a center section where a fire pit lay. As early as 600 BC, sea-mammal hunters of the Aleutian tradition were living on the Near Islands, the extreme western Aleutians.

The Aleutian tradition continued to flourish into historic times, a tradition reflected by considerable stylistic variation in artifacts between one island and the next. These variations have been little studied (McCartney, 1984a; Veltre, 1998).

Arctic Small Tool Tradition
c. 2750 to 800 BC

The third broad cultural entity was terrestrial: the Arctic Small Tool tradition. As early as Paleo-Arctic times, tiny groups of hunter-gatherers settled along the Alaska Peninsula and round Bristol Bay in the south, also on the eastern shores of the Bering Strait. By 2500 BC, a new and highly distinctive stone toolkit appears along these coasts, the Arctic Small Tool tradition. The new artifacts were indeed small, often diminutive blades or microblades, pointed at both ends, used as end or side barbs in antler or bone arrows or spear heads. The stone workers also made scrapers, graving tools and adze blades with polished working edges. Unfortunately, we know little of the organic components of the tradition, especially in the west.

The Arctic Small Tool tradition may have developed from Paleo-Arctic roots in Alaska. More likely, however, it was an intrusive culture, for equivalents of nearly all common Arctic Small Tool artifacts can be found in contemporary Chuktotkan reindeer hunting and river fishing cultures across the Bering Strait. In about 3000 BC, sea-level rises slowed, forming beaches around the Bering and Chukchi Seas. This may have been the time when summer boat trips across the Strait assumed importance in local life, bringing new contacts between Siberia and Alaska, even if fishing and sea-mammal hunting were apparently still unimportant.

For many years, researchers have assumed that the bow and arrow were introduced from Asia in about 2000 BC by Arctic Small Tool people. They assumed that this weaponry was highly effective against caribou and waterfowl. Arctic Small Tool people may indeed have introduced the bow and arrow to the Arctic, but it is uncertain just how far the new technology spread. Some investigators working in more southern regions have argued that the earliest bows and arrows were used during the Archaic and as early as 2000 BC, with unifacial flakes used as the arrow tips that preceded the small, standardized hafted bifaces that first appear in the Late Archaic (Bradley, 1997). A long period of experimentation and refinement followed. Bow-and-arrow weaponry did not become well established until as late as AD 700, when standardized arrow-tip technology came into widespread use, including the small triangular and corner-notched points that are commonly associated with the widespread adoption of the bow in the late

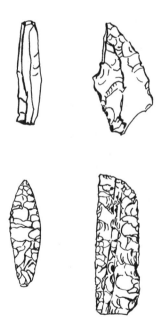

Arctic Small Tool tradition, upper Naknek Drainage, southwestern Alaska. (Top row) Microblade and burin. (Second row) Projectile point and side blade. (Length of side blade c. 3.3 cm.)

Coronation Gulf Inuit using composite bows in the chase, photographed in 1913. The introduction of the bow and arrow allowed the hunter to shoot accurately 30 to 40 m, although an arrow could fly as far as 120 m. The men are clothed for winter conditions, the hair side of their paneled coats outwards.

1st millennium AD (Nassaney and Pyle, 1999). Perhaps this development was associated with intensified hunting and more frequent warfare – we do not know. Nassaney and Pyle (1999) believe that the bow may have been invented independently in North America by many groups during the Archaic.

The Alaskan manifestation of the Arctic Small Tool tradition is sometimes called the "Denbigh Flint Complex," after the stratified finds at a temporary caribou hunting camp on Iyatayet Creek by Cape Denbigh on Norton Sound (Giddings and Anderson, 1986), but the term has been loosely used in recent years and really only applies to the Denbigh region itself. Iyatayet yielded mainly microblades and small burins. The site is remarkable for its numerous finely worked blades, many of them carefully pointed at both ends, often with delicate workmanship.

Arctic Small Tool-style implements occur in the Brooks Range and as far south as the Alaska Peninsula and Kachemak Bay. Some of these sites are little more than stone scatters, perhaps traces of hunting camps where a single tent was pitched. On the Peninsula, Small Tool camps lie along rich salmon streams, presumably to take advantage of summer runs. The people may also have hunted seal on the coasts. Several locations have yielded evidence of more permanent structures, among them the Chugachik Island site in Kachemak Bay, and also Onion Portage and the Brooks River site

Arctic Small Tool tradition, southwestern Alaska. Excavated remains of a semi-subterranean house at Brooks River, upper Naknek Drainage, radiocarbon-dated to about 1450 BC. A pile of fire-cracked pebbles lie beside the central hearth. Four holes may mark the locations of structural posts around the fireplace.

on the upper Naknek Drainage, where 14 sod-roofed houses have been excavated (illus. p. 171). There, the inhabitants had dug roughly square pits into the subsoil, about 13 ft (4 m) on each side, with a sloped entryway on one side and a central hearth (Dumond, 1987).

The western Arctic Small Tool tradition represents a cultural break from earlier Paleo-Arctic and interior Northern Archaic occupation. Its precise relationships with Ocean Bay and later traditions are still little understood, despite their close geographic relationship in some places (Workman, 1998). Apparently, the small indigenous population withdrew into the inland forests as Small Tool groups moved in. Both populations lived alongside one another for a long period of time.

First Settlement of the Eastern Arctic
c. 2000 BC

At approximately the same time as their first appearance along the shores of the Bering Strait, Arctic Small Tool-using groups appear along the shores of the Arctic Ocean, among the islands of the Canadian Archipelago, and in western Greenland (Maxwell, 1985). The tiny numbers of people who brought this technology eastward were the first human settlers of the Eastern Arctic. What caused this remarkable, and still largely undocumented, migration remains a complete mystery. The archaeology is confused by the changes in artifact forms that apparently took hold soon after the movement east. In general terms, however, the Arctic Small Tool tradition of the Eastern Arctic is divided into two variants: Independence in the High Arctic and Pre-Dorset in the Low Arctic.

Independence I Stage (2500 to 500 BC). Independence Fjord forms part of Pearyland, an enormous arctic desert in northeast Greenland. Small tent rings marked by circles of large boulders lie along the shores of this, and neighboring, fjords, associated with scatters of stone tools, including the spalled burins that were used by Arctic Small Tool people for splitting and grooving bone and antler. These artifacts are quite similar to those from Cape Denbigh in the far west, but Independence tools are larger, with many minor variations on smaller implements (Maxwell, 1985). There are bone needles, evidence for sewn clothing, pieces of bone arrowheads, and two harpoon heads with drilled holes for the line and slotted to receive a stone barb. These were not toggling harpoons, harpoons designed to detach from the head and twist in the wound, a later innovation. It was the barb that held the harpoon in the animal.

Danish archaeologist Eigil Knuth (1967) has recorded 43 settlements with 157 dwellings, all lying on old beach strands between 33 and 69 ft (10 to 21 m) above modern sea level. The highest density of settlements is around Independence Fjord, but elsewhere they average 8.6 miles (14 km) apart. Radiocarbon dates range between 1930 and 1730 BC. As many as 20 tents occurred at some locations, but most sites were no more than isolated dwellings. The tents themselves were probably fashioned of musk-ox hide. Covered with snow and equipped with a hearth and a passage-like storage area made of flagstones, they sufficed as winter homes.

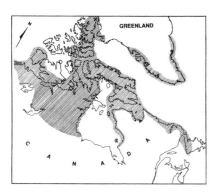

Probable distribution of the Arctic Small Tool tradition in the Eastern Arctic.

Knuth believes the Independence people were constantly on the move, mainly subsisting off musk ox, animals which wander in extensive, but restricted ranges, unlike caribou, which migrate along predictable routes every year. Occasionally, the hunters took sea birds, ring seal, arctic char, and other aquatic resources. Everyone lived in tiny hunting bands, perhaps no more than four to six people, existing without stone lamps. Their fuel was driftwood, occasional stunted willow branches, and the fat from musk-ox bones. With such heating sources and a food supply that was constantly on the move, the Independence people had to be nomads, perhaps coming together in slightly larger groups during the two-and-a-half months of darkness in mid-winter. Moreau Maxwell (1985) gives a vivid description of their existence in the dark of winter. The houses may have been unbearably smoky when fires were lit, so perhaps they were only kindled to cook or thaw ice for water. "The bitter winter months might have been spent in a semi-somnolent state, the people lying under thick, warm musk-ox skins, their bodies close together, and with food and fuel within easy reach." Trips to the outside were kept to a minimum.

Spring and summer were the critical months, when the hunters had to accumulate large surpluses of dried fish, seal, and game meat for the winter. Knuth found one winter house with an impressive meat cache nearby – three fully grown musk ox, two calves, several hares, foxes, and fish, enough to provide about 6.6 lbs (2 kg) of meat a day for all the members of a family over a three-month winter. Perhaps about 200 people lived in this area of northeastern Greenland, a reasonable population density of about 1 person per 112 sq. miles (130 sq. km).

These Arctic Small Tool people lived nearly 750 miles (1200 km) further north than their distant relatives on the Bering Strait far to the west. Some of the sites are only about 434 miles (700 km) from the North Pole. The distribution of Independence I stage settlements extends south from Pearyland to Devon Island in the Canadian Archipelago. Knuth traced Independence sites 559 miles (900 km) south along Greenland's east coast as far as Dove Bugt, the easternmost ancient settlement in the Americas. There is, however, considerable debate as to whether Independence is a discrete culture in its own right.

Much of the Low Arctic seems to have been populated by Arctic Small Tool groups in later movements by descendants of the first settlers. Conceivably, settlement further southward may have been triggered by harsher climatic cycles in the high arctic that took people into the Barrenlands and the adjacent boreal forests.

Pre-Dorset (2500 to as late as 500 BC). Another Danish archaeologist, Jorgen Meldgaard, worked in the Melville Peninsula area west of Baffin Island. There he discovered more sites with Arctic Small Tool-like artifacts, that are often grouped with the so-called Pre-Dorset culture, with technological links to the Arctic Small Tool tradition. Equivalent artifacts have been found at other sites scattered throughout the southern portions of the Eastern Arctic, with at least one Melville Peninsula site being contemporaneous with the Independence variant. There are many minor artifact differences between Pre-Dorset and Independence, although both appear to have common roots in the Arctic Small Tool tradition far to

Remains of a Pre-Dorset house at Port Refuge. The circular depression in the ground marks the place where a tent or perhaps a snowhouse once stood. The vegetation inside the circle is feeding off nutrients in the refuse left inside the house more than 3500 years ago.

the west. Many arctic archaeologists believe they are both an integral part of the tradition, not even separate cultures.

The relationship between Independence and Pre-Dorset is much debated, mainly on the basis of a series of beach-side settlements in Port Refuge on Devon Island's Grinnell Peninsula in the Canadian Archipelago. Here, seal-hunters' tent sites lie on raised beaches, the earliest yielding microblades and other artifacts that resemble roughly contemporary Independence forms from Pearyland, more than 497 miles (800 km) to the north. Some 300 years later, some other seal hunters camped on lower raised beaches, using Pre-Dorset-like harpoons.

Robert McGhee (1979) uses his Port Refuge excavations to argue for two early migrations into the Eastern Arctic. The first was represented by the Independence stage of the far northeast, the second by Pre-Dorset further south, a quite separate population that occurred some 300 years later. Moreau Maxwell (1985) believes that Independence settlements may, in fact, exist in the south, but that they are obscured by later occupations in the rare places where people could pitch tents, places used again and again in later centuries. He argues for a single Arctic Small Tool migration that split into northern and southern waves. As time went on, different cultural traditions developed: Independence in the High Arctic, northern Labrador, and perhaps in the Disko Bay area of Greenland, Pre-Dorset in the Foxe Basin and Hudson Strait region. Then, some centuries later, some Pre-Dorset groups moved north into places like Port Refuge.

The relationship remains unresolved, but some research in the central Canadian Archipelago has focused on differences between coastal and inland sites, also on seasonality (Bielawski, 1988). These excavations and surveys strongly suggest that seasonality may explain much of the variation in artifacts and dwellings between one region and another. Much earlier work is based on variations in artifact styles and dwellings, mainly from coastal sites. Small, dispersed Arctic Small Tool groups were capable of exploiting both coastal and inland resources, and did so in an apparently efficient and economical manner, covering large and harsh territories. Thus, the differences between Independence and Pre-Dorset may be some-what illusory, with all three forming not two or more separate cultures, but variations on the Arctic Small Tool tradition.

The Independence occupation of the High Arctic ended about 500 BC, perhaps at a time of increasing cold after the Altithermal, the Holocene climatic optimum, that made these regions untenable for human settlement. In the south, the Pre-Dorset tradition flourished until about the same time.

One focus of early Pre-Dorset culture was an area centered on the islands in northern Hudson Bay, the northern and southern shores of Baffin Island, northern Labrador, and the west coast of the Foxe Basin. This has been called a "core" of Pre-Dorset occupation, but this concept is much debated (Bielawski, 1988). Further to the west, no early Arctic Small Tool sites have yet been reported between the Canadian/Alaskan border and Pelly Bay, some 1099 miles (1770 km) to the east.

This area is a region where no one food animal is dominant. Rather the number of these available species and the number of individuals within each species are sufficient to allow a diverse food supply throughout the year. These conditions are found through much of the Eastern Arctic, but are especially favorable in the northern Hudson Bay and surrounding regions (Maxwell, 1976a, b). It is in this well-circumscribed area that archaeologists have been able to trace centuries of more-or-less continuous human occupation, from early Pre-Dorset up to modern Inuit occupation.

This region supported caribou migrations northward from the mainland along Melville Peninsula and across the ice to Bylot Island. There were resident caribou herds on Baffin Island, too, herds with their own migration patterns. Small musk ox populations may have flourished in the region, as did five species of seal. Walrus and large bearded seal were common, as were migrating waterfowl, and smaller mammals. Harp seal migrations and whales passed through the Hudson Strait. This was an area where more permanent settlement was possible. The lgloolik site and other settlements literally followed descending sea levels down gravel beaches, from 203 ft (62 m) to 13 ft (4 m) above modern sea level. Over the centuries, local environmental conditions changed. Resources expanded and contracted, often with disastrous consequences for those who moved out into favored areas, where people starved when climatic conditions became more severe. Throughout the area, there was constant interaction between neighboring and more distant settlements, to the point that artistic styles and technological changes emerge almost simultaneously everywhere.

Inuit hunting seals at a breathing hole in the ice.

Subsistence. The Pre-Dorset people relied heavily on seals for their subsistence, hunting them from the ice-edge and at their winter breathing holes. This latter requires great patience and keen powers of observation. The hunter waits for hours for the moment when the seal comes up to breathe. A quick harpoon thrust snares the prey. Then the hunter rapidly widens the breathing hole with the chisel-like butt of his harpoon so he can drag the seal onto the ice before it carries the harpoon, and perhaps the hunter, into the water. This hunting method is most effective when there are enough hunters to keep watch on a number of breathing holes within a short distance. The thrusting harpoon used for ice-hole hunting is also useful for taking bearded and ring seals at the edge of ice floes, and for stalking walrus and seals basking on the ice. Pre-Dorset people also hunted sea mammals from light boats. Perhaps as a result, harpoon designs became increasingly sophisticated through time, and form a useful typological yardstick for rough dating of Pre-Dorset and Dorset sites (Maxwell, 1985).

Musk ox, caribou, polar bear, and small animals were taken with spears, and bows and arrows. The hunters probably made bows from fragments of driftwood, antler, and musk-ox horn carefully joined and bent to form small bows that were bound and backed with sinew. These weapons probably required expert stalking, for they may have been effective only at a distance of about 65 ft (20 m) or so. The hunters apparently used large dogs in the chase, for their bones have been found in Pre-Dorset middens.

The arctic char was an important food source, an anadromous species (fish that swim up rivers to spawn) that was taken in weirs and traps, then dried for use in the lean fall months before the ocean froze over. The people used leisters, barbed fish spears with trident heads that speared and held

Trapping fish in weirs and dams was a technique used as early as Pre-Dorset times. Here Copper Inuit dressed in summer garb spear fish at a dam.

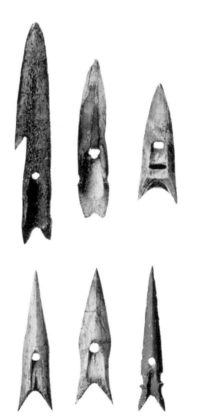

Pre-Dorset and Dorset harpoon heads. Their stylistic changes through time are useful chronological markers. The harpoon head top left dates to about 1700 BC, the specimen above right to about AD 1000.

the wriggling fish, and could be sprung apart to release it on shore. (For details of the Pre-Dorset toolkit, see Maxwell, 1985: 90ff.)

Western Pre-Dorset. West of Hudson Bay, sizeable populations appear not to have developed until after the late 14th century BC, and they were predominantly caribou hunters. The western region of Coronation and Amundsen gulfs may have been a dispersal area for hunting bands that pursued migrating caribou deep into the mainland interior. They were land hunters and fisher folk, only occasionally sealing on the coast. Some of these bands are thought to have followed caribou herds far south during a period of increasing cold between 1200 and 900 BC and may have penetrated far below the treeline, perhaps as far south as Lake Athabasca by 900 BC (Wright, 1972). Sparse Pre-Dorset populations occur across the interior of the Barren Grounds, as far as the modern settlement of Churchill on the western shore of Hudson Bay. Judging from the major shifts in the treeline in response to colder and warmer temperatures, these peoples' hunting territories fluctuated constantly.

Eastern Pre-Dorset. To the east, and in the core area, sea-mammal hunting was more important. Pre-Dorset occupation has been identified along the Labrador coast as far as the Strait of Belle Isle and western Newfoundland, the population concentrated in favored areas (Fitzhugh, 1980; Maxwell, 1985). The first settlement was almost as early as Independence I and Foxe Basin, about 1880 BC, with a peak settlement about 1500 BC, thereafter declining, with only very sparse occupation, if any, until the mid-8th century BC. Perhaps, argues Maxwell (1985), this was due to encroaching Indian populations.

Saqqaq Complex (c. 2500 to c. 300 BC). Across the Davis Strait from Baffin Island, Arctic Small Tool (Pre-Dorset) people occupied the Disko Bay area of eastern Greenland. The earliest Saqqaq sites date to around 2500 BC, to about the time when Independence occupation began. Some have argued that Saqqaq resulted from southern migrations from the bitterly cold Independence area.

The Qeqertasussuk site on an island in Disko Bay was occupied between 1950 and 1150 BC and reveals the great complexity of Saqqaq and Arctic Small Tool culture. The permanently frozen occupation deposits have yielded a wealth of organic finds, including wooden artifacts and human bones (Grønnow, 1994). The excavations uncovered a complex and perishable toolkit based on hafted stone artifacts, baleen, ivory, and bone, as well as wood. The Qeqertasussuk people used very light, toggle-headed harpoons that were thrown long distances with atlatls. They also carried light lances and bird spears as well as bows and arrows. All their artifacts were skillfully and precisely manufactured, used with great effectiveness against harp and ringed seals and other sea mammals, also waterfowl. The Saqqaq technology at this site changed but little over many centuries, with slate microblades, heavy bifaces, and end scrapers being skillfully hafted for domestic and hunting use. Qeqertasussuk was predominantly a summer camp, used during the harp seal migration season in June and July. Ring seals were the dominant winter prey. The meticulous Danish excavations confirmed that Arctic Small Tool culture was far more complex than one might expect from merely perusing its stone artifacts.

The Saqqaq Complex is also known from the Itivnera site, some 93 miles (150 km) inland from the coast. Itivnera, occupied between about 1250 and 340 BC, lies astride a migration route for caribou, the staple diet at the site.

Saqqaq was an Arctic Small Tool enclave for over 1000 years, marked in archaeological terms by high percentages of ground and polished tools, artifacts as small as arrow barbs manufactured mainly on silicified slate. The relationship between Saqqaq, Pre-Dorset, and Arctic Small Tool is still somewhat uncertain, but they all form part of the same general arctic cultural tradition.

Archaic Foragers in the Sub-Arctic
c. 5000 BC to European contact

The Laurentide ice sheet was centered east of Hudson Bay and covered most of Sub-Arctic North America 15,000 years ago, then melted rapidly but not uniformly. The area southeast of Great Bear Lake was ice-free by about 8000 BC, the central Keewatin District some 2000 years later. The Great Lakes were ice-free by 9000 BC, south-central Quebec by 5000 BC, and the last traces of Laurentide ice vanished from the Labrador mountains by about 3800 BC. Only some scattered remnants linger in the Canadian Archipelago and Greenland today (Campbell, 1962).

The spread of hunter-gatherer groups into this vast region was, in effect, a centripetal movement along the radii of progressively shrinking ice sheets (Harp, 1978). Newly deglaciated land would emerge from its icy mantle. Tundra vegetation and animals would migrate into the barren landscape. As the ice retreated north, so did taiga replace tundra in more southern areas. Human beings followed the game and the vegetation, often arriving somewhat later, for the bands had to surmount natural obstacles such as ice-dammed lakes or flooded lowlands. During the Early and Middle Holocene, two sparse, but important, population movements penetrated

An Inuit hunter with caribou carcasses, Coppermine region, Northwest Territories, 1949. Some Sub-Arctic groups lived off the same migrating herds for generations.

the Sub-Arctic. The first was from the west of Hudson Bay, the later one developed around the Great Lakes and spread along the St Lawrence Valley into the Quebec-Labrador Peninsula (see Chapter 16).

***Northern Archaic** (before 4000 BC to modern times).* Some sparse Paleo-Indian settlement is recorded from the Canadian Shield area of the Sub-Arctic west of Hudson Bay, people who used projectile points reminiscent of Great Plains forms. As the taiga belt widened and separated the Arctic from temperate latitudes, new adaptations were necessary. It was during this period that the Northern Archaic developed, a cultural tradition thought to be associated with Athabaskans.

The Northern Archaic, which appears to be quite distinct from the Paleo-Arctic tradition of the Far North, has been identified as far northwest as the Arctic Ocean coastal plain north of the Brooks Range at Kuparuk Pingo (Lobdell, 1986) and dated to just after 4000 BC. Here the people took caribou and waterfowl, probably retaining cultural ties further inland.

Northern Archaic: Palisades complex projectile point, Onion Portage, Alaska, length 4.8 cm.

Keewatin lanceolate point, Shield Archaic, Barren Grounds region.

Northern Archaic hunters lived at Onion Portage, Alaska, by 4000 BC, with an artifact assemblage that included side-notched, often asymmetrical, projectile points, unifacial knives, and end scrapers (Anderson, D.D., 1988). The projectile points evolved into smaller forms over time and stemmed heads appeared. Northern Archaic hunting camps are widely scattered through the Brooks Range north to the Arctic Ocean coast, along the Yukon River downstream of the modern town of Circle, and into the central Alaskan Range, also close to the southwest Alaskan coast (for a fascinating ethnohistoric account, see Burch and Mishler, 1995). Such settlements with side-notched projectile points also occur in the southwestern Yukon Territory and in the southwestern Northwest Territories of Canada, dating perhaps to as early as 3000 BC (Noble, W.C., 1971).

Shield Archaic (c. 5000 BC to European contact). Caribou hunting was the primary activity on the northern fringes of the taiga to the west of Hudson Bay (Harp, 1961; 1962). Some Archaic bands were living on the shores of Great Slave Lake by 5000 BC. Further south and west elk, moose, and deer were staple prey. These adaptations changed little over many centuries, as Archaic populations rose slowly and more sedentary settlements developed in resource-rich areas where fishing or shellfish collecting were important (Dumond, 1987). This basic forest culture has been named the Shield Archaic by James Wright (1972, see Chapter 16). Such is the cultural continuity between ancient and modern culture over the entire Canadian Shield that he has argued on very slender grounds that these people spoke an Algonquian language and that they were ancestral to the central and eastern Algonquian peoples of historic times.

Immediately west of Hudson Bay, caribou hunting was always the staple, in the transitional country between the taiga and tundra, a landscape of plentiful lichens, marshes, and shallow lakes. Archaic bands could live on the edge of the forest, drawing on woodland resources and following migrating caribou herds into the more open barren lands in summer. This caribou adaptation survived into historic times, albeit with occasional incursions by Arctic Small Tool groups from the north. It was also the means by which human settlers first exploited the Barren Grounds during a period of warmer temperatures before 3500 years ago. Archaic groups settled in the Central Keewatin region, where they camped along rivers and lakes on caribou migration routes, ambushing their prey at crossings and other strategic spots. At least four major caribou herds are distributed across the Barren Lands today, each moving north and south along regular migration routes. The lives of the Archaic groups who preyed on these long-established caribou herds must have been governed by the movements of individual herds, in a long-lasting relationship between humans and caribou that endured for thousands of years – as it does today.

The Archaic peoples of the western Sub-Arctic shared a basic stone toolkit that varied but little throughout the region. The hunters used flaked-stone lanceolate projectile points, discoidal biface knives, and various scrapers, also stone adze blades, basic artifacts for hunting and processing game. Here, as elsewhere in North America, stone projectile points provide some typological signposts. The Paleo-Indians used "Keewatin" lanceolate points with ground edges. These developed into various stemmed forms, as projectile heads became smaller.

Maritime Archaic (?7000 BC to modern times). The so-called Maritime Archaic is best known from Port aux Choix, Newfoundland (see also Chapter 16). Here, a community of Archaic sea-mammal hunters flourished in the 2nd and 3rd millennia BC (Harp and Hughes, 1968; Tuck, 1970). More than 100 red ocher-adorned graves contained elaborate barbed bone points, open socketed toggling harpoons, and bone foreshafts. Many of the deceased had worn skin clothing adorned with shell-bead ornamentation, also antler, bone, and ivory daggers. The Maritime Archaic occurs at many contemporary sites up and down the Atlantic coast from Maine to Labrador. Some settlements included longhouses and their inhabitants engaged in long-distance exchange. A number of these Maritime Archaic groups may have achieved some level of social complexity (for a review, see Fitzhugh, 1978, 1984). Coastal occupations were probably seasonal. During the winters, the people exploited elk, moose, caribou, and other land resources, as always the staple of Archaic life in the Sub-Arctic. The Maritime Archaic reached its apogee during the warmer centuries after about 4000 BC, and then waned when Pre-Dorset and Dorset groups moved southward along the Labrador coast in the 1st millennium BC and during the early Christian era.

The Archaic cultures of the Sub-Arctic slowly evolved into the native American groups that occupied the region at European contact. These include the Beothucks of Newfoundland, the Innu of Quebec and Labrador, the Cree and Ojibwa of the Hudson Bay lowlands, the Chipewyan west of the Bay, and other Athabaskan-speaking peoples to the northwest.

Further Reading

Damas, David (ed.). 1984. "Arctic," *Handbook of North American Indians,* vol.5. Smithsonian Institution Press, Washington DC.
The authoritative compendium on the native peoples of the Arctic. An invaluable source book.

Dumond, Don. 1987. *The Eskimos and Aleuts.* Thames and Hudson, London and New York. 2nd ed.
A brief summary of Arctic and Sub-Arctic archaeology.

Fitzhugh, William (ed.). 1988. *Crossroads of Continents.* Smithsonian Institution Press, Washington DC.
A joint Soviet-US exhibition of Siberian and Alaskan artifacts prompted this magnificently illustrated account of arctic peoples. Strongly recommended for the general reader.

McGhee, Robert. 1996. *Ancient People of the Arctic.* University of British Columbia Press, Vancouver, and the Canadian Museum of Civilization.
McGhee's popular account of arctic archaeology is aimed at a broad audience. Superb illustrations.

Maxwell, Moreau. 1985. *The Prehistory of the Eastern Arctic.* Academic Press, New York.
Another authoritative synthesis, which focuses on both culture history and basic issues.

Schledermann, Peter. 1990. *Crossroads to Greenland.* Arctic Institute of North America, Calgary.
An exemplary monograph describing excavations and surveys on Ellesmere Island in the Canadian Archipelago. Extensive and valuable bibliography.

CHAPTER 9

NORTON, DORSET, AND THULE

Some time between 600 and 500 BC, the Pre-Dorset culture of the Eastern Arctic merged into the fully fledged Dorset culture, with its magnificent and distinctive art style. In the west, Arctic Small Tool people vanished in every part of Alaska, a process that may have taken several centuries. There was an apparent hiatus, still little understood, before new cultural traditions flourished along the shores of the Bering Strait (for a general summary, see McGhee, 1996).

The Norton Tradition of the Western Arctic
c.1000 BC to c. AD 800

Conservative Archaic cultural traditions survived for millennia in the Sub-Arctic interior, isolated cultures that persisted up to European contact and beyond. In the Western Arctic, however, major, almost revolutionary innovations in subsistence strategies radically transformed the ways in which ancient peoples exploited the maritime environment of the Far North. These innovations first appeared in the Bering Strait region, and, around AD 1000, spread into the Eastern Arctic.

The Arctic Small Tool tradition gradually disappeared along the Bering and Chukchi Sea coasts about 1500 BC, as late as 1000 BC in the south. There appears to have been somewhat of a cultural vacuum, for few sites along these shores date to the next few centuries. Then the more maritime Norton tradition appears, named after the bay of that name where it was first identified (Giddings, 1960). Norton is still poorly defined, and sometimes referred to as an "interaction sphere" not a tradition, on the grounds that considerable cultural interaction was involved over a large area (Dumond, 1982; Shaw and Holmes, 1982). Norton people used flake-stone tools reminiscent of the Arctic Small Tool tradition, but introduced technologies such as lamps for burning oil and clay vessels.

Origins. The Norton tradition is best known from the Alaskan shore of the Bering Strait, but there were strong cultural links with Siberia. Cord-impressed pottery occurs widely in northeast Asia and occurs in Norton sites, persisting right into the Christian era. Furthermore, contemporary Siberian chipped-stone tools have strong ties with Arctic Small Tool forms, and included asymmetrical knives like Norton artifacts of the same general type.

Norton stage. Ivory-handled slate ulu or woman's knife, c. 500 BC length c. 10 cm.

Closer to the Bering Strait, a maritime, Norton-like tradition with pottery, polished adzes, and projectile heads flourished on the Anadyr River during the 2nd millennium BC, a culture adapted to fishing, sealing, and caribou hunting. In addition, isolated finds of Norton-like pottery have been reported from the Chukchi Peninsula. Further south, sea-mammal hunters had settled along the shores of the Sea of Okhotsk by the end of the 1st millennium BC, peoples with Norton-like stone artifacts and some pottery. Under this argument, the Norton tradition developed over a wide area of the Bering and Chukchi Sea coasts during the 1st millennium BC. This was a period of cultural and technological innovation that witnessed sporadic long-distance trading contacts across the open waters of the Strait, and some connections with ancient cultures in Siberia.

These developments coincided with a period of warmer Arctic temperatures and with great cultural diversity. About 700 BC, the climate had deteriorated considerably, a cold cycle that lasted for about five centuries. Now the Norton people moved south of the Bering Strait and settled throughout coastal Alaska north of Pacific waters. About the time of Christ, Norton sea-mammal hunters migrated over the base of the Alaska Peninsula and exploited the rich waters of the northern Pacific from Takli Island and other locations, overwhelming the indigenous Kodiak tradition. These developments can be traced through at least three still ill-defined cultural stages – Choris, Norton, and Ipiutak (detailed essays in Shaw and Holmes, 1982).

Subsistence. Everything points to the Norton having been a culture that was oriented toward both land hunting and marine resources. Caribou and smaller mammals were still an important source of meat and antler for artifact manufacture, but marine resources were increasingly important. Norton groups settled near fish-rich Arctic Ocean river estuaries, and in the south up the banks of major salmon streams, where migrating fish could be trapped and speared. There can be no doubt that open-water sea-mammal hunting was a significant activity. Toggling-head harpoons of various sizes have come from Bering Strait sites, including some large enough for whaling purposes, artifacts that were essential for such activity.

Settlements. Hardly surprisingly, many Bering Sea Norton sites were occupied more-or-less permanently, great concentrations of substantial year-round dwellings. The Norton stage Safety Sound site near Cape Nome has yielded almost 400 house depressions, Unalakleet on Norton Sound itself almost 200. Not all the houses were occupied at once, of course, but they reflect dense, long-term occupation. At both these locations, people lived in square, permanent dwellings excavated about 20 in (50 cm) into the ground, with short, sloping entryways, central hearths, and pole-and-sod roofs. During the summer months, many groups used temporary hunting and fishing camps. The Ipiutak stage houses at Point Hope and elsewhere testify to the richness and elaboration of late Norton culture in the Bering Strait region. Certainly, later, Norton was based on year-round sea-mammal hunting both in open waters and through the winter ice.

TABLE 9.1

Norton Tradition Stages

(Below) Choris stage linear-stamped potsherd from Iyatayet, Cape Denbigh, height 14 cm; Choris stage projectile points, from a cache of about 60 points found at Cape Krusenstern, length of longest specimen 17.5 cm. (Bottom) Ipiutak stage ivory object, perhaps a comb, c. AD 500, length c. 26 cm. (Below right) Ipiutak stage engraved ivory "mask," found in a burial at Point Hope, probably once with a wooden backing.

Choris Stage (*c.* 1000 to 500 BC). Coastal sites north of the Bering Strait, found in Kotzebue Sound, on old beach levels at Cape Krusenstern, on the Seward Peninsula, perhaps in the Brooks Range, and at Onion Portage. Characterized by fiber-tempered pottery adorned with linear stamping all over the exterior surface, Choris sites show considerable local cultural variation as if most communities were isolated ones. The exact relationship between Norton and Choris is still ill-defined.

Norton Stage (*c.* 500 BC to AD 800). Probably derived from Choris, and subsumes several local cultures in the Bering Strait area, the Ugashik and Naknek River drainages, and the Alaska Peninsula. Also occurs along the Arctic Ocean coast to extreme northwestern Canada. Caribou and small-mammal hunting were important, but open-water sea-mammal hunting and fishing were of vital importance. More refined pottery with both Choris-type stamping and check stamps applied with ivory paddles. Stone seal-oil lamps, cruder stone work, asymmetrical knives, slate projectile points, and many local artifact forms (Dumond, 1987; Giddings, 1964).

Ipiutak Stage (*c.* AD 1 to 800). A distinctive, highly developed form of Norton culture around Cape Krustenstern, Point Hope, and Point Barrow on the shores of the Chukchi Sea. Interior Ipiutak known from Brooks Range. No pottery, oil lamps, or ground-slate artifacts. Far more sophisticated harpoon heads with elaborate decoration. Summer and winter sea-mammal hunting important and much permanent settlement. The Ipiutak art tradition was lavished on ivory artifacts – carvings of animals, human figures, some of which may recall Scythian and Siberian art motifs (Larsen and Rainey, 1948).

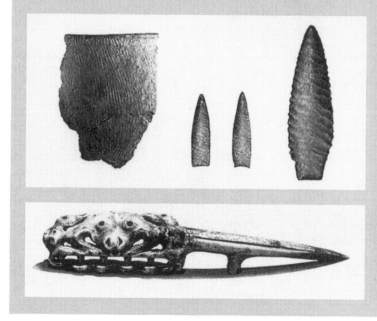

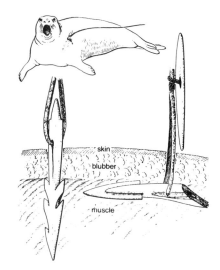

The Thule Tradition
c. 700 BC to modern times

In about 700 BC, the Norton inhabitants of St Lawrence and other Bering Strait islands developed an even more specialized culture, based entirely on the ocean. This resulted in part from their geographical location, with narrows that determined the direction of summer sea-mammal migrations and natural current upwellings, which maintained areas of open water even in mid-winter. Like the Ipiutak people, these hunters were expert artists, who adorned their toggling harpoons and other weapons with elaborate and intricate motifs. The new sea-mammal hunting technology with its efficient toggling harpoons and other ingenious devices was to revolutionize coastal life throughout the Arctic. This technology was the foundation of the Thule tradition (pronounced the Danish way – Tuleh).

No one knows whether such Thule innovations as working polished slate or the sophisticated toggling harpoon originated in the Bering Strait area or further south along either Asian or Alaskan coasts (Dumond, 1968). Whatever the origins of the new maritime culture with its new emphasis on whale hunting, it was the catalyst for a new chapter in the Arctic past.

Old Bering Sea Stage (*c. 200 BC to AD 800*). The earliest Thule sites, subsumed under the Old Bering Sea stage, come from St Lawrence and Okvik islands, also from the Chukotka coast of the Bering Strait (Collins, 1937; Rudenko, 1961). Occasional Old Bering Sea artifacts have been found on both shores of the Bering Strait, presumably as a result of sporadic trading with the mainland. Both kayaks, and *umiaks*, large skin boats, appear in the archaeological record for the first time.

Old Bering Sea toolkits are dominated by polished-slate rather than flaked-stone artifacts, including lanceolate knives, projectile heads, and the *ulu* transverse-bladed knife. Pottery is cruder, often gravel tempered, and decorated with broad corrugations. Bone and antler dominated local technology, including ivory harpoon heads and other harpoon parts, bird darts and fish spears, snow goggles, blubber scrapers, needles, awls, and mattocks, also walrus shoulder-blade snow shovels. The hunting artifacts also include important innovations that made for far more efficient hunting. The hunters

(Above) Harpoon technology. The non-toggling or "male" harpoon point holds an animal by its barbs (left). The toggling harpoon, a more complex design, was developed later for sea-mammal hunting. The head toggles beneath the skin and blubber where it cannot be dislodged by ice, and is effective with heavier prey like walrus and whales.

(Below) Old Bering Sea stage toggling harpoon components and reconstructed assembly. The weight of the ivory harpoon head (left), foreshaft, and socketpiece (center) were counterbalanced by an ivory winged object (right) fixed to the butt of the harpoon.

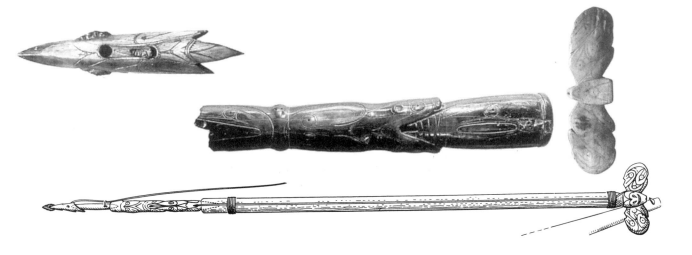

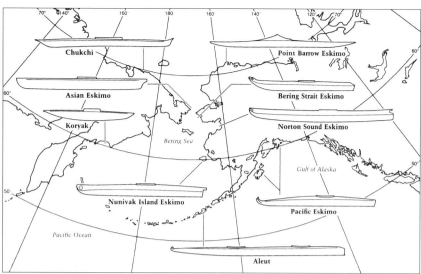

Kayak hunting. (Above right) Regional kayak styles in historical times, reflecting a 2000-year-old tradition of kayak technology. (Above) Handlining and clubbing a halibut from kayaks, a painting by H. Elliott, 1872. (Right) Use of floats enabled hunters to recover sea mammals such as these belugas, line and inflated float sill attached, photographed with a harpoon-wielding Eskimo in 1865.

now used harpoon-mounted ice picks for winter seal hunting, also ivory plugs and mouthpieces for inflated harpoon-line floats, floats that enabled them to recover larger sea mammals when dispatched. These were people who relied heavily on the ocean for subsistence, especially on seal and walrus, as the modern inhabitants of the Bering Strait islands do to this day.

Old Bering Sea artists lavished their skill on their socketed toggling harpoon heads, which is fortunate for the archaeologist, for the forms of these weapons changed but little through the centuries. However, the curvilinear dots, circles, and shorter lines of the Old Bering style are so distinctive that the style can be distinguished from later forms (illus. p. 186). The art style from Okvik Island, one of the Punuk Islands, is often distinguished from the Old Bering style from St Lawrence Island and other locations (Rainey, 1941). Some believe Okvik is an earlier style that evolved into Old Bering Sea, but radiocarbon dates suggest the two were contemporary phenomena, local variants of the same brilliant tradition.

Okvik

Old Bering Sea II

Old Bering Sea III

Old Bering Sea art styles. Stratified house floors at St Lawrence Island, Alaska, revealed stylistic changes in Eskimo art. The Okvik flat, angular style dates to about 500 BC. Contemporaneous and later Old Bering Sea II and III styles were increasingly more ornate, more plastic, and curvilinear. After AD 500, Old Bering Sea art gave way to the simpler designs of the Punuk phase.

Evolution of Punuk art, as exemplified by winged objects (harpoon butts) from St Lawrence Island. (Left) Early Punuk stage winged object in "butterfly" shape, width 16 cm. (Center) Middle Punuk trident-like winged object, width 10 cm. (Right) Late Punuk winged object with hardly any wings, resembling a coronet, width 7 cm.

Across the Strait, at Uelen and Ekven, Russian investigators have uncovered some richly decorated Old Bering Sea graves adorned with fine ivory artifacts, including harpoon parts, mattocks, and pots. Some graves were partially lined with whale bones, sometimes floored with wood. Conceivably, these were the sepulchers of important individuals, perhaps whaleboat captains, men of prestige who were owners of whale-hunting *umiaks*. Such social distinctions are known to have been important in later centuries, and these may be the first signs of social differentiation in the north (Mason, O., 1998).

***Punuk and Birnirk Stages** (c. AD 800 to 1400 and later).* Harpoon styles and art motifs serve to distinguish two later Thule variants in the Bering Strait area, but variants that have a wider distribution than their Old Bering Sea predecessor (Collins, 1937; Geist and Rainey, 1936).

The Punuk stage is a development of Old Bering Sea, with a distribution that coincides closely with it, on the major Strait islands and along the shores of much of the Chukchi Peninsula. Artifact forms remain much the same, albeit with some elaboration of hunting weapons. Punuk art strongly recalls Okvik motifs, but became more geometric and eventually simpler as time went on.

Punuk settlements were larger and more common than earlier villages, settlements of houses that soon assumed the familiar 19th-century St Lawrence form. These were semi-subterranean, square or rectangular dwellings with wooden floors, sleeping platforms along the walls, and drift-wood or whale-jaw sides, the sod roofs held up with whale-bone rafters.

Whale hunting was of great importance in Punuk life. Hunters in *umiaks* killed them in narrow ice leads during spring and in the open sea in fall, an enterprise that required skilled leadership, teams of expert boatmen and hunters, and usually the cooperation of several boats. The whaleboat captain, the *umialik*, is still prominent in Arctic communities today. He played an important role in 19th-century village life, and probably in Punuk times as well. He was wealthy and an influential leader, often competing with his fellow captains in neighboring communities. It may be no coincidence that slatted bone armor now appears in Punuk villages, also a superior bow-and-arrow technology, based on sinew-backed bows of Asian form. Inter-village raiding was a frequent occurrence and became the basis for the so-called "bow-and-arrow wars" of late pre-contact times.

The Birnirk variant on the Old Bering Sea tradition developed between AD 500 and 600, along the shores of the Chukchi Sea from Cape Nome northward, also on the Siberian coast west from East Cape to at least as far as the mouth of the Kolyma River. Although the Birnirk people used much the same hunting weapons as Punuk and Old Bering Sea, they were no artists.

Only rarely did they adorn their antler harpoons or other artifacts with any form of decoration, confining their artistic talents to concentric and spiral motifs executed on clay pots with bone paddles. They did, however, use sledges, of the same basic designs as were later used with dog teams. However, no traces of bone harness parts occur at Birnirk and other settlements, so they may have relied on man-hauling. As far as is known, the Birnirk people were sea-mammal hunters who also engaged in fishing and whaling. Some of their sites, like those near Barrow and Point Hope, are situated close to whale-rich locales.

Owen Mason (1998) believes that the intensification of long-distance trade, warfare and whaling in the Bering Strait region between AD 600 to 1000 led to intense competition between the Ipiutak, Old Bering Sea, and Birnirk polities. The main center of political power lay at East Cape in Siberia, at the twin sites of Uelen and Ekven. Ekven was contemporary with kingdoms on St Lawrence Island and at Point Hope on the Alaskan side. Mason argues that the East Cape people were the powerbrokers in the region, while Ipiutak, ruled by powerful shamans, with its elaborate art tradition and burials, was a place where spiritual capital was more highly valued. But the similarities in artifacts to East Cape sites may hint at some form of political alliance with the western side of the Strait. There were connections with caribou-hunting groups in the Siberian and Alaskan interiors as well.

Whale hunting generated enormous food surpluses, but seal oil was probably the mainstay of the Strait economy. Old Bering Sea held sway over most of the southern Bering Strait coast on the Siberian side, while Ipiutak with its powerful shamans controlled much of the Alaskan shore. The Birnirk peoples were less influential, settled as they were on the northwest Chukotkan coast, but may have fought with both more powerful polities when food shortages caused stress at home. The overall political situation seems straightforward, but Mason is probably right when he describes the reality as "a welter of small villages with divided and shifting loyalties, multiple origins, and limited spans of occupation." There was some fighting, but the threat of war may have been more prevalent than war itself.

Mason argues for still-undocumented links with climatic conditions as well. The success of the Bering Strait/Chukchi Sea polities depended on the persistence of southerly wind conditions that prevailed during the stormy months of fall. Such conditions may have endured through the late 1st millennium, at the time of the so-called Medieval Warm Period.

Thule Expansion in the West
AD 900 to 1100

Thule settlements were flourishing at Cape Denbigh on Norton Sound by AD 900, on Nunivak Island even further south a century later, and in the Naknek Drainage of the Alaska Peninsula by AD 1100. This spread was not necessarily a population movement, but more likely a diffusion of new artifact styles, more efficient house designs, and hunting methods to southern coastlines and river estuaries, much of it connected with seasonal sea-mammal migrations. Some people may have moved into new areas, but everywhere the Thule tradition amalgamated with the older Norton.

Thule artifacts were in use close to the end of the Alaska Peninsula in about AD 1000, although the use of polished-slate tools, a characteristic Thule trait, spread slowly throughout the Aleutian Islands thereafter. Thule gravel-tempered pottery, polished-slate tools, and sunken dwellings replaced earlier Norton styles on the southern side of the Alaska Peninsula, too, resulting in a culture much closer to the Kodiak tradition of earlier times (Dumond, 1987). Here, as elsewhere, there were strong local preferences in harpoon styles and other artifact forms. Not all artifacts moved as a group. Pottery, for instance, never moved into the Aleutian Islands, possible for lack of suitable clays.

Throughout the Bering Strait and along the Alaskan coast from Barrow to the Alaska Peninsula, and far offshore to the islands and Siberian coast, communities of Thule sea-mammal hunters were in constant, and regular, contact for many centuries. This led, inevitably, to a degree of linguistic and cultural standardization, and, perhaps, to the spread of Eskimo dialects to the Kodiak Island area, dialects spoken by modern Koniag people.

The Eskimo peoples of what is now Alaska, who came into contact with Europeans during the 18th century, all formed part of this powerful and long-lived cultural tradition.

The Dorset Tradition of the Eastern Arctic
500 BC to AD 1200

The Pre-Dorset culture of the Eastern Arctic developed into the Dorset tradition in about 500 BC, at a time when climatic conditions became colder after some centuries of warmer temperatures (Maxwell, 1985). Preservation conditions were poor in warmer, Pre-Dorset times, but permafrost has refrigerated many organic objects from Dorset sites, resulting in a far more complete knowledge of this remarkable Arctic culture.

The actual archaeological evidence for the transition from Pre-Dorset to Dorset is limited to some isolated locations like the Killilugak site on Baffin Island, where Pre-Dorset and Dorset artifacts are found in an occupation level dated to about 600 BC (Maxwell, 1973). There are signs of continuous Pre-Dorset to Dorset occupation in northern Labrador, in sites where Pre-Dorset occupation passes into what is called the Groswater Dorset in about 850 BC, a culture centered around Hamilton Inlet (Fitzhugh, 1980).

In the High Arctic, some small groups reoccupied the area of northern Greenland and the Canadian Archipelago abandoned by the Independence people in about 1600 BC. Some 600 to 1000 years later, Independence groups reoccupied the region in another warmer period, living in scattered dwellings lined along the same beaches as their predecessors, but at lower levels on the shore. Some of their stone artifacts, especially notched blades, recall Groswater Dorset in Labrador and southern Newfoundland (Knuth, 1967).

The Pre-Dorset/Dorset transition can be explained in many ways. Was it the result of a population decline of Arctic Small Tool people in the Eastern Arctic about 3000 years ago, a decline that was followed by an expansion of Dorset peoples? Or was it a time when dwindling caribou herds in Quebec caused major adjustments in both population distribution and hunting methods (Fitzhugh, 1976)? Or was it, as Moreau Maxwell argues, a period

Probable distribution of the Dorset tradition.

Dorset culture. (Left) Dorset artifacts. From upper left, clockwise: two styles of harpoon head, perhaps for different hunting tasks; a bone lance; a microblade knife in a bone-and-wood handle; a ground flint, burin-like tool in a similar handle; two styles of projectile point, and a ground-slate point; an ivory fish spearhead; a bone needle; and an ivory "ice-creeper," lashed on the foot to prevent slipping on smooth ice. (Right) Remains of a Dorset house on western Victoria Island, central Arctic, dating to c. AD 1000.

of interregnum between two relatively stable lifeways that lasted some centuries?

Maxwell has created a possible scenario for the transition as follows: The impression is that the Pre-Dorset people were predominantly caribou hunters, while their Dorset successors were, above all, sealers. Maxwell notes that the bow and arrow vanished during the transition period, a hunting weapon that was useful for hunting caribou by stalking. Perhaps, he speculates, the Dorset people turned to new caribou hunting methods, driving them into shallow lakes and spearing them with stone-tipped spears. Perhaps, in time, the caribou herds were much reduced by the new methods or migration patterns changed. The new hunting methods were now inadequate, so the only solution was to turn to the coasts. The climate was becoming colder, so the people developed new, ice-hunting techniques that were successful in intensely cold winters, leading to the emergence of the Dorset tradition (for a full discussion, see Maxwell, 1985).

As for the Dorset tradition itself, Maxwell and others define it by a series of distinctive culture traits. These include rectangular, semi-subterranean buildings, many more triangular projectile points used for sealing, the appearance of a ground-slate industry that manufactured notched knives and other utilitarian artifacts, distinctive harpoon-head forms, and a rich artistic tradition with strong symbolic and magical undertones (Plumet, 1985).

The Dorset Lifeway. Dorset people possessed no dog sleds, so their land-travel range was restricted to the limits of human pulling and walking ability. They had no bows and arrows, or throwing boards, just simple lances and harpoons. The hunters did not possess sophisticated whale-hunting gear, harpoon floats for pursuing sea mammals from kayaks, and, incredible although it may seem, even tiny stone drills for boring through bone and antler. The Dorset people had only small oil lamps and far-from-sophisticated winter houses. One marvels at their adaptive ability under such harsh environmental conditions, yet they managed to flourish for many centuries. In some ways they were even less prepared for arctic conditions than their predecessors (Meldgaard, 1962).

Like all Eastern Arctic peoples, the Dorset people were predominantly hunters, although they undoubtedly consumed berries and other plant foods in season (Maxwell, 1985). They pursued caribou, musk ox, smaller land mammals, and some nesting birds, perhaps snared with nets on long poles. Seals were an important staple, and the hunters were not afraid to tackle such formidable animals as the walrus, narwhal, and even the occasional whale or polar bear – using a spear-based technology that put the hunter at very close range with his quarry, and in constant peril of his life. Such hunting requires not only remarkable skill but an intimate knowledge of animal habits during all seasons of the year.

A great deal depended on the design of Dorset harpoons. Later hunters used toggling designs, where the head slips off the foreshaft inside the wound, leaving only the head and line attached to the animal. Dorset harpoons were thrusting weapons, the heads bound to the foreshaft so that the shaft slid backward and the head came off attached to the line wedged in a split in the harpoon shaft. This design works much better at close quarters, when the hunter thrusts the head into the animal. Such weapons were probably effective for ice hunting, and had some limited use against basking seals pursued from kayaks.

Caribou hunting was probably a group effort involving carefully controlled game drives through rows of stone cairns or into shallow water where waiting spearsmen or kayaks dispatched the confused beasts. The staple fish was the arctic char, a species that is easily filleted and speared during seasonal runs. The Dorset fish spear was usually tipped with delicate ivory barbed heads that were used like harpoons, perhaps thrown rather than thrusted, unlike the elegant trident-like fish spears (leisters) used by later Thule and Inuit peoples. These weapons required considerable skill and accuracy against fast-running fish that would be swimming over a rocky bottom.

Dorset Art. The Dorset art tradition is justly famous, especially for its life-like portraits of what were once living individuals (Taylor and Swinton, 1967). Dorset carvers worked with antler, bone, ivory, soapstone, and wood to make tiny figures, depicting almost every arctic animal. More than half their carvings were of human beings or polar bears, sometimes highly naturalistic, sometimes merely stylistic impressions. The attention to minute detail is astonishing – complete polar-bear skulls, tiny seals modeled complete with whiskers and miniature eyes. Unlike later Thule and Inuit artists, Dorset carvers and engravers usually ignored utilitarian objects and created work that had a strong ideological undertone. Masks, figurines, and plaques probably played important roles in funeral rites, and in shamanistic and magical ceremonies.

Dorset art. (Left) Ivory bear with skeleton depicted, length 15.2 cm. (Right) Joined pair of ivory swans, the one at left 6 cm long.

Human beings sometimes appear in distinctive portraits, in carvings that display rectangular or round eyes, outward facing nostrils, and a pug nose. This portrait may represent a living person, perhaps a famous shaman, who suffered from an infantile skull condition that made him stand out from his fellow priests. The Late Dorset site at Button Point on Bylot Island yielded wooden masks, one with simulated tattooing and at one time pegged-in hair and a moustache. There are smaller masks, too, no more than 2.3 in (6 cm) long, many with X incisions across the face, even dolls with detachable arms and legs. Small animal amulets to provide good fortune during the chase are common, often suspended on thongs or sewn to clothing. The carvers also made small ivory teeth plaques with ridges on the back, plaques that may have been worn over the mouth during shamanistic rituals.

The Dorset art tradition was a unique efflorescence over an enormous area of the Eastern Arctic, a reflection of basic ideologies that were to survive for many centuries. Without question, some of the fundamental spiritual beliefs of modern Inuit groups have their roots in the complex spiritual life of the Dorset people.

Evolution of the Dorset Tradition

The Dorset tradition is conventionally subdivided into Early, Middle, Late, and Terminal stages (for a full description of sites and artifacts, see Maxwell, 1985). Early Dorset culture may have developed in one core area and then spread rapidly over a much wider region. The most logical place is the northern Foxe Basin, where earlier traditions flourished. There was such regular communication with other communities in the general area that cultural change must have been more-or-less simultaneous over a wide area.

The same basic lifeway flourished throughout Dorset times, but with constant adjustments in response to everchanging cold and warm cycles. During Middle Dorset times, the climate was becoming progressively colder, so parts of the High Arctic and northern Labrador may have been abandoned. In some places, people may have chosen to live in more sheltered locations and in larger dwellings. Perhaps some groups of 2000 years ago moved out onto the ice, living in snow dwellings near favored sealing grounds.

By AD 100, the settlement pattern was changing. Many of the favorite locations in the core area around Foxe Basin were abandoned as populations along the south coast of Hudson Strait, and on Southampton and Victoria Islands, apparently declined. The surviving population adopted some minor technological changes – fresh needle designs came into use, soapstone lamps became oval rather than rectangular, and slate artifacts were less commonplace.

The populations of Newfoundland and the Labrador coast increased as people retreated from the north (Fitzhugh, 1980; Tuck, 1984). Many Middle Dorset settlements in these areas were small villages, some of them, like Port aux Choix, Newfoundland, semi-permanent locations where people fished and hunted throughout most of the year (Harp, 1976). Port aux Choix was also a base for hunting pupping harp seals in late winter, a

Dorset wooden doll body from Button Point, Bylot Island.

place favored earlier by Maritime Archaic groups. One house midden from this site yielded a sample of 25,000 bone fragments, 98 percent of them from harp seals. Up to between 30 and 35 people lived at Port aux Choix, using a toolkit that has clear ties to northern Dorset, but with a strongly local flavor. The site was finally abandoned at about the time when temperatures warmed up again at the onset of Late Dorset times, *c.* AD 500.

The five or six centuries that followed saw a population increase, with an explosion in artistic skills, resulting in an art tradition that ranks among the best in ancient North America. The Late Dorset saw an expansion of relatively standardized arctic culture not only over the Foxe Basin area and into northern Labrador north of Nain, but into the High Arctic again. Meteoric iron from Cape York, northwestern Greenland, was widely traded (McCartney, 1988). Many widespread communities appear to have participated in a vast cultural network, in which shamans may have played a leading role. Some sites, like Button Point on Bylot Island, may have been ceremonial centers. As we have seen, Button Point is rich in carved wooden figures, including life-sized ceremonial masks and wooden dolls of humans and stylized animals. There are fragments of drums, too. "It is easy to imagine nighttime ceremonies where rhythmic chants and drumbeats restored the sacred balance of nature," writes Moreau Maxwell (1985). "In the dimly lit houses, shamans, frighteningly masked, would manipulate little figures for magical protection from the only predators dangerous to humans – the giant polar bear and humans who were not part of the kinship web."

Late Dorset groups moved north in some numbers, establishing at least three significant village concentrations in the High Arctic (McGhee, 1976). They occupied many islands of the Canadian Archipelago, and hunted as far north as land permitted. Many Late Dorset settlements at favored locations were reoccupied by later Thule and Inuit groups.

Terminal Dorset. The Dorset tradition reached its climax by AD 1000. A century later, it had all but vanished except in some isolated areas. The conventional explanation is that Thule newcomers moved in from the west. With their superior hunting technology, more elaborate social organization, and vastly enhanced mobility by sled and boat, they took over Dorset hunting territories, assimilating the original inhabitants or driving them out to starve in marginal areas.

What actually happened? There is no archaeological evidence for sustained contact between Dorset and Thule, even if some artifacts like ivory sled shoes, snow knives for building snow houses, and the use of iron and soapstone, were culture traits borrowed by the newcomers from Dorset groups. Maxwell (1985) believes the explanation may lie in the radically different subsistence strategies employed by the two traditions. The Dorset people tended to hunt prey that was within walking distance of home, concentrating on the more easily taken, most abundant animals. Thule hunters ranged over much larger territories in their boats and with sleds. They exploited a wider range of food resources, were better organized, and had the ability to move in and take over, say, a seal migration route through a narrow defile miles from their base, thereby depriving the local people of the resource at a critical time of year. Over a few generations, the cumulative effects of such opportunism would have been felt in reduced reproduction and lower survival rates among Dorset populations. Exotic diseases from Asia may have played a role, too, diseases introduced by the Thule newcomers from distant Asian populations that spread like wildfire among Dorset groups, decimating communities in short order.

Nevertheless, deeply conservative Dorset and innovative Thule groups existed alongside one another in the Arctic for two or three centuries, the former virtually without change alongside the newcomers (Harp, 1976).

The Thule Expansion into the Eastern Arctic
c. AD 1000

Sometime around the beginning of the 2nd millennium AD, Thule people, perhaps speaking an archaic form of Inupiat language, began migrating to the east. By the 13th century, they had settled throughout the coasts of the Canadian Arctic and Greenland. Especially in the central and eastern Arctic, many scholars make a useful distinction between Paleoeskimos (Pre-Dorset and Dorset) and Neoeskimos (Thule/recent).

As we have seen, the Thule tradition had strong Norton undertones, with technology and subsistence strategies that resemble those of late Norton developments to the south of the Bering Strait – with one significant difference. Like their predecessors, Thule people subsisted off caribou and fishing, but they combined these activities with much more efficient exploitation of sea mammals, including whales. This expertise is reflected in great elaboration of specialized artifacts for such hunting. Thule men and women lavished great care and much time on their harpoons and domestic artifacts, making them highly efficient, very functional, and ingenious tools indeed. Thule art was impoverished, however, and decorated artifacts were much rarer than in Dorset contexts. Even their semi-subterranean dwellings were relatively energy efficient, with deep entrance tunnels below floor level. Cooking areas were usually close to the doorway, where the entry tunnel met the interior of the house. This elaborate cultural tradition flourished for several centuries after about AD 600 around the Bering Strait and along Chukchi Sea coasts, then spread very widely indeed, far eastward across the High Arctic.

The Thule culture of the Eastern Arctic was first identified during the highly productive interdisciplinary researches of Danish scholars between 1921 and 1924. A team of anthropologists, archaeologists, and natural scientists compiled a massive description of the Canadian Arctic which they published promptly in the ten seminal volumes of the Fifth Thule Expedition (Birket-Smith, 1929; Mathiassen, 1927; Rasmussen, 1931, and others). All subsequent researches have built on these pioneer investigations. Therkel Mathiassen identified more than 100 Thule culture traits, a distinctive and highly effective toolkit for hunting on land, ice, and open water. Mathiassen argued that the tradition originated in northern Alaska or Siberia. Mathiassen claimed Thule hunting efficiency was based on three major innovations: the dog sled, the large skin boat, and the kayak. All of these enabled people to range over much larger hunting territories, to participate in widespread trade, and to transport heavier loads. Over many years of arduous fieldwork, this remarkable scholar not only hypothesized correctly about Thule origins, but traced almost the entire extent of the

Probable distribution of the Thule culture in the Eastern Arctic.

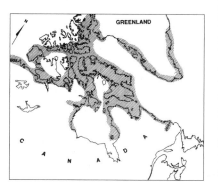

A Thule innovation, according to Therkel Mathiassen: the dog sled.

Thule migration, even interaction between Greenland Thule and newly arrived Norsemen from the east.

The Thule adaptation was infinitely more efficient and effective. Quite apart from their prowess at baleen whale hunting, an activity where one kill could feed several families for an entire winter, the leadership, craft specialization, and team organization needed to hunt whales spilled over into the entire spectrum of daily life. Thule communities were better equipped to cooperate, to take concerted action, compared with more loosely knit, smaller Dorset groups. Their technology was far more effective, with dog sleds and large boats to carry even large groups to new hunting grounds and new settlement sites at short notice. Above all, Thule hunters were ingenious, well-equipped predators, capable of harvesting Arctic seas and coasts in almost any weather conditions.

By Thule times, hunters in the Eastern Arctic were equipped with kayaks, like this man with his gear for open-water sea-mammal hunting.

Migration Theories. Many investigators have argued that the Birnirk stage of Thule culture on the shores of the Chukchi Sea was the base for the Thule migration (McGhee, 1970). The exact cause of the Thule migrations remains a mystery. Robert McGhee used Thule radiocarbon dates clustering around AD 1000 to trace the migrations from Birnirk roots at the very end of that stage. There were no signs of population pressure in the Birnirk homeland. However, he pointed out that the migrations occurred during a period of warmer temperatures throughout the Northern Hemisphere known as the Medieval Warm Period, which lasted from about AD 900 to 1350. This was a time when the southern boundary of arctic pack ice retreated northward in the Atlantic, allowing Norse seamen to expand to Iceland, onward to Greenland, and as far south as Newfoundland. The warming was never sufficient to melt the ice block between the Amundsen Gulf and Lancaster Sound, a distance of about 600 miles (1000 km), but some reduction of ice may have allowed bowhead and Greenland whale populations to mingle, distributing abundant populations of these great mammals right across the north.

Whales migrate east along the Alaskan coast in spring, and west in fall, keeping to narrow ice leads close to shore. For centuries, ancient hunters watched these spring and fall leads and preyed on migrating pods with great efficiency. Some Thule Eskimo lived close to the ice edge – the demarcation between permanently frozen ocean and the boundary where the ice melted in summer. They hunted whales from this location, and were well placed to take early summer whales as the ice broke up. Since whales migrate close to the ice, the pods followed the pack, making conventional hunting methods far too dangerous. At the same time, reduced ice between the Canadian Arctic islands may have opened up the normal summering grounds of the bowhead whale to open-water hunting. So people could pursue whales for many months, and not just for short periods in spring and fall.

Open-water whaling required substantial modifications in hunting technique (McCartney, 1984b). The hunters had to sight the whales from ice-edge, land, or boat, then chase them with teams of kayaks and larger skin boats, dispatch their prey offshore, then tow the carcass to land. Open-water whaling became the hallmark of the Eastern Thule, a less productive hunting technique than the traditional ice-lead and ice-edge method, but one where the long season compensated for the lower productivity of the chase.

The whale hunters spread far and wide over the Canadian Arctic, founding widely separated settlements that were smaller (only a few as large as 25 to 35 houses) than those in the far west, for kayak and *umiak* teams from five or six families were far more effective than the teams of *umiaks* used close to land in the west. In the east, Thule hunters used kayaks to chase and locate whales (McCartney and Savelle, 1985). In both east and west, the *umiak* was the stable platform used for harpooning the whale.

Thule whale hunting was highly efficient, witness the consistent size of their prey: 26 to 28 ft (8–8.5 m) long (McCartney and Savelle, 1985). The successful hunters would tow their prey ashore, then butcher them, storing enormous quantities of meat and blubber for the winter. They would winter over in permanent peat-block houses that were occupied regularly for many years. Throughout the summer, they could move large amounts of meat and blubber from outlying areas to winter villages by boat or sled.

The winter bases themselves were often built near coastal ponds, where abundant supplies of peat-blocks for house construction could be found.

Eastern dwellings tended to be less subterranean, often round. The sleeping platforms were stone-paved, with stone and whale bone forming walls and entrance tunnels, everything roofed with whale bone and sod. In some areas, ivory snow knives may be a sign that domed snow-block houses were in use.

There were other cultural differences, too. Pottery was used as far east as Greenland, but east of the Mackenzie Delta it was soon replaced by more durable and more easily obtainable soapstone. In many areas, soapstone vessels replaced ceramics, with large, crescent-shaped soapstone lamps favored over pottery versions. Most important of all, dogs tethered with rawhide and ivory or bone harnesses now pulled ladder-like sleds with narrow runners, making for rapid winter travel on land.

The ease with which Thule people moved across the north is very striking, and may also be connected with other ecological changes related to warmer temperatures. As McGhee points out (1970), less pack ice may have fostered walrus and bearded-seal populations, but it reduced the number of denning sites that were attractive to ring seals, the sea mammal that Dorset people depended upon most heavily. This may have helped the Thule people take over vacated Dorset hunting territories.

By no means everyone accepts McGhee's closely argued whaling model. Dennis Stanford (1976) excavated the Walakpa site west of Point Barrow, where he traced an evolving coastal culture from early Birnirk through a late Thule occupation of AD 1400. There was little evidence of whaling activity at Walakpa, where ring sealing was all important. Stanford observed a progressive reduction in seal-bone size in the later levels, as if ring seals were being overhunted. He argues that a quest for new sealing grounds rather than whales sent Thule groups eastward.

Another hypothesis involves not only the Birnirk culture, but Punuk as well. Some Eastern Thule artifacts from Cornwallis and Ellesmere Islands in the High Arctic show striking connections with Punuk toggling harpoon heads from the Bering Sea (Schledermann and McCullogh, 1980; Yamaura, 1979). This whale and walrus hunting culture was in full swing by about AD 800 and may have been a major force in the Thule migrations. Perhaps population pressure in the west and warring factions in northeastern Siberia caused some Punuk groups to move eastward, bringing their whale hunting expertise with them. Under this argument, the Thule migrations into the Canadian Arctic were an amalgam of Birnirk and Punuk traits, brought about not only by warmer temperatures, but by population pressure and increased emphasis on whale hunting.

Finally, McGhee (1984a) has also speculated whether the Thule moved eastward in search of iron, both meteoric iron which had been exploited by Dorset groups for centuries, and iron traded into the Archipelago settlements by visiting Norse.

Despite general, and somewhat uncritical, agreement that Thule migrations took place about AD 1000, the dating is insecure. Radiocarbon dates are unreliable (Schell, 1983), so many workers have relied on seriations of harpoon-head forms (Maxwell, 1985). Using the distributions of five early harpoon types, a possible early migration route follows a somewhat more southerly path than McGhee's hypothetical migrations. The "harpoon route" follows the northern Alaskan shore into Amundsen

Gulf and Victoria Strait, then north and east through Barrow Strait and Lancaster Sound. Emerging from the islands, the hunters turned north, along the east coast of Ellesmere Island and across Kane Basin into northwestern Greenland.

One could argue that the eastern sites with the most western traits are the earliest, sites like Nugdlit and Ruin Island in northwestern Greenland and on Skraeling Island, and others on eastern Ellesmere Island (Schledermann and McCullogh, 1980). These have been grouped into the so-called Nugdlit-Ruin Island phase (Holtved, 1954). House forms, harpoon heads, and other decorated items are said to recall western Thule. Many of the excavated houses also contain some Norse artifacts in wood, iron, copper, and cloth. Unfortunately, the radiocarbon dates from these fascinating sites are confusing. Some are too early for the Norse artifacts found with them, a few cluster in the 11th century, the widely accepted date for this phase, but the most reliable dates appear to belong in the 12th and 13th centuries. One could argue Nugdlit-Ruin three ways. First, all the radiocarbon dates are unreliable. Second, Thule people did not expand into the east until as late as AD 1200. Third, southerly regions of the eastern Arctic were colonized as early as the 11th century. Then, in the early 13th century, hunters with strong Punuk ties moved further north. There are some grounds for suspecting that the third hypothesis may be the most reliable one (for discussion, see Maxwell, 1985).

To summarize: most early Thule sites were probably occupied by groups whose ancestry lay in Birnirk communities along the northern Alaskan coast near Barrow. These communities had been influenced by new whale-hunting techniques and innovative technologies developed by Punuk people, some of whom had moved into the Barrow area as a result of population pressure before AD 900. Perhaps, hypothesizes Maxwell (1985), it was a small number of Punuk groups who first followed whales along the summer pack to the east as far as the eastern parts of the High Arctic. Later in the same century, many more people, this time with Punuk and Birnirk artifacts, followed in their footsteps, settling along the southern shores of the Canadian Arctic. This was a much larger migration that resulted in the emergence of the true Eastern Thule tradition.

Classic Thule
AD 1100 to 1400

During the 12th and 13th centuries, Eastern Thule people increased their settlement of the High Arctic, but also expanded in the south. By the end of the 13th century, Thule people were living along Hudson Strait coasts, in the Hudson Bay region, on the shores of the Foxe Basin, along the mainland from the Mackenzie Delta to Melville Peninsula. Thule villages flourished across northern and eastern Greenland shores.

Alan McCartney (1977) described "Classic Thule" winter settlements that depended on bowhead whaling, not only for food, but for building materials and artifacts as well. Many of these Thule groups lived in large semi-subterranean winter houses constructed of stone, sod, and whale bones. Some of these winter settlements were of considerable size and occupied for many generations, others little more than one or two winter dwellings. Four to six houses holding some 20 to 25 people appears to have been a widespread norm, an adaptive size for efficient hunting of available resources in many areas (McCartney, 1979a). In summer, Thule groups moved into skin tents, the edges held down by circles of stones, the most ubiquitous archaeological sites in the Eastern Arctic today. Sometimes they would move only a short distance, perhaps to get away from the stench of rotting sea-mammal carcasses that had been deep-frozen through the winter.

This sophisticated Arctic society maintained constant contact between dozens of scattered communities, and there may have been a continual drift eastward of more Alaskan groups, perhaps encouraged by reports of the favorable hunting conditions in the Canadian Arctic. Exotic materials were passed from community to community over enormous distances, among them copper and iron.

Northern peoples used iron long before European contact both along western Alaskan and Siberian coasts, and in the east. In the west, Okvik and Old Bering Sea peoples used iron in small quantities for carving knives and for engraving other tools (Collins, 1937). Iron implements are also known from Birnirk and Punuk sites. All these occurrences date to the 1st millennium AD. The bone, antler, or ivory handles for iron blades are more common, suggesting that iron was a well-known, if scarce, commodity throughout the region. Most of this terrestrial iron probably came from the Amur River-Okhotsk Sea region, where it was being exploited as early as the 1st millennium BC. However, it was not until around AD 1000 that trade between the western and central Arctic picked up, resulting in the movement of some Siberian iron eastward.

Both native copper and meteoritic and terrestrial iron were used in the central and eastern Arctic before European contact. Native copper came from southern Victoria Island and Coronation Gulf. Meteoritic iron from a large shower in the region, near Cape York, was used by Dorset people as early as the 11th century AD as substitutes for slate burins. Many Thule communities also used meteoritic iron. Non-meteoritic iron occurs in 13th- and 14th-century Thule sites, iron that is assumed to be of Norse origin (McCartney and Mack, 1973; McGhee, 1984a). The trading distribution of metals was widespread, reaching the limits of Classic Thule population expansion during the 10th to 13th centuries. This trade coincided with the Norse expansion, and the iron, never common, was used in the Thule area not for engraving, but for projectile points and knife blades for butchery and sea-mammal hunting. McCartney argues that metal was not only more widely distributed than appears from the archaeological record, but that it made possible the large whale-bone artifacts that Thule peoples used long before there was direct European contact with Inuit groups. A form of what McCartney (1988) calls "epi-metallurgy" arose among late Thule communities, a technology where metal was not smelted but used and reused Norse or meteoritic iron or native copper as knife blades, engraving tips, and similar tools. These were more effective than slate counterparts. Metal was part of the Thule adaptation to the Canadian Arctic, and the trade in this precious commodity was a unique aspect of their culture. As McCartney (1991) argues, metal was a solution to the basic problem of reducing large bones, antlers, and wood fragments to finished tools, boat frames, and other artifacts. A steady stream of metal was needed. McCartney believes the trade was controlled by *umialiks*,

Classic Thule seal-hunting equipment: a whale harpoon head, two sealing harpoon heads, an arrowhead, and a fish-spear prong.

(Above) Three scenes from Thule life incised on an ivory bow-drill from near Arctic Bay. Top, summer tents with men hunting with bow and arrow. Center, kayakers meet a swimming caribou. Bottom, whalers harpoon a spouting whale as bear skins dry in front of a tent camp.

family heads and captains of skin whaling boats, who controlled, managed, and distributed resources like metal obtained down land and maritime trade routes extending over large distances.

Classic Thule culture is remarkable not only for its hunting skills, but for the extraordinary range of ingenious gadgets that the hunters developed for the chase. The Thule people were ardent technologists, as clever with their low-tech life as we are with computers today. Thus, any report on a Classic Thule site is a weighty listing of myriad artifact traits, of whale and seal hunting gear, of specialized lances and harpoons used for pursuing game on land and sea. Like Birnirk in the west, however, Thule artistic endeavors were relatively modest, confined in the main to simple engravings on utilitarian artifacts such as combs, often Y motifs and straight lines. Sometimes, the engraver depicted humans and animals, even scenes of the chase. Three-dimensional figures in wood and ivory often depict women without arms or legs, often with topknot hairstyles. Tiny floating ivory carvings of loons and other birds are relatively commonplace, perhaps game pieces, or important ideological symbols, links between the people and the supernatural world (Sproull-Thomson, 1979).

Thule Subsistence. Thule whale hunters concentrated on bowhead whales, *Balaena mysticetus*, relatively placid creatures which swim near the surface (McCartney, 1980; 1984b; Savelle and McCartney, 1988). Their thick blubber means that the carcass floats even when dead, a major advantage for hunters with skin boats. The average baleen whale from Thule sites is between 13,225 and 26,450 lbs (6,000 to 12,000 kg). As little as 18,840 lbs (9000 kg) of blubber would have provided heating, lighting, and cooking oil for months. The bones were invaluable for rafters and house walls.

The whalers used slate-tipped toggling harpoons attached to large foreshafts and wooden shafts. Entire sealskins formed the floats attached to the harpoon line that helped tire the harpooned whale. Judging from

Classic Thule technology made use of many materials. Artifacts illustrated here include, clockwise from the left: an antler adze handle; a whale-bone adze head with polished stone blade; a flensing knife with ground-slate blade; an ulu with iron blade; a whale-bone snow knife, used to cut blocks for snowhouses; a bone scraper for preparing hides; an ivory engraving tool with a small iron point; and a drill bit with a groundstone point.

Umiak and crew, Cape Prince of Wales, Northwest Territories, 1927.

contemporary engravings, the sealskin and driftwood *umiaks* were manned by between four and seven or more people. The helmsman would approach the whale from the rear as it came up to breathe (Nelson, 1969). The harpooner in the bow would cast at a vital spot, the man behind him throwing out the floats. Several casts and a long fight might ensue, until the dead whale could be towed tail-first to a convenient beach or into shallow water, where butchering could proceed.

Bowheads were undoubtedly staples in coastal communities in whaling areas (Savelle and McCartney, 1988). While some other foods were consumed, the sheer mass of whale meat and blubber probably overshadowed other supplies. Outside the whaling zones, the other classic arctic resources formed the diet – caribou, walrus, seals, and fish (Stenton, 1991). Thule hunters with their more efficient technology and transportation took a wider range of prey than their Dorset predecessors, not only musk ox and smaller mammals like fox, but birds, clams, even bird eggs. However, predictable caribou migrations and seal harvests, especially of ring seal, often helped determine where winter settlements were located. The hunters took seals in open water from their kayaks, waited for hours at the ice edge or by breathing holes in winter. They would drive caribou into shallow lakes where waiting hunters in kayaks would kill the frightened animals. On land, they drove small herds through converging lines of stones piled up to resemble human beings, killing the stampeding beasts with recurved bows and arrows at a range of about 32 ft (10 m). Birds were taken with multibarbed spears or small whale-bone bolasses, snared with gorges and hooks embedded in blubber.

Postclassic Thule
AD 1400 to European contact

During the 12th and 13th centuries, Thule sites appear south of Parry Channel and along mainland coasts near Hudson Bay, in northern Labrador, and on Baffin Island, areas where whales were scarcer. The caribou, seal, and fish bones from these settlements argue for a more gradual settlement of less whale-rich areas, using the familiar subsistence strategies of the west. Thule settlements are also found far to the north, into the Independence Sound area of Pearyland in far northern Greenland. Eigil Knudsen made a dramatic discovery during the 1960s in Independence

Sound in the very far north – an abandoned camp site of about AD 1450 with the remains of a wrecked Thule *umiak* nearby. Before walking away from their camp, and presumably perishing, for there is no settlement nearby, the hunters killed a whale, a narwhal, and bearded seal, in open water. Today, the area is ice-bound and never navigable by boat. Some time after that date, some Thule groups spread south along the Labrador coast as far as Hamilton Inlet.

This redistribution of population may reflect growing population pressure in the classic areas, but climatic change may have been a more important factor. The onset of the little Ice Age brought cooler conditions after 1400 and very cold temperatures between 1600 and 1850, a time when glaciers advanced on Greenland and Baffin Island. Summer pack ice may have been so heavy that boat work was severely restricted, shortening the seasons for open-water whale hunting. The number of whales may have been smaller, too, for pods require open water to breath every five minutes or so. Many Thule sites show that baleen whale hunting declined after AD 1400 in many areas (Schledermann, 1979). By the late 16th century, *umiak* and kayak whaling had ceased in the High Arctic. The people probably turned to fishing, musk-ox hunting, and fox trapping for much of their sustenance.

These may have been hard times. Moreau Maxwell (1960) excavated an isolated postclassic dwelling at Ruggles Outlet, on Lake Hazen in the interior of Ellesmere Island. A hunter took several foxes and a musk ox before he died. His widow buried him under some rocks outside the house. She was left alone and ate three sled dogs, then died on the sleeping platform inside the house. Climatic conditions became so severe that by AD 1600 much of the High Arctic was abandoned.

Further south, some whaling continued where open-water conditions permitted. Ringed seal, caribou, and fish continued to be staples, with more regional variation than in earlier times. This may have been the time when local groups such as the Copper Inuit, Netsilingmuit, and Inglulingmuit emerged, the Inuit groups encountered by white explorers after the 16th century.

Eastern Arctic: open-water whalers in skin kayaks and an umiak, *1905.*

European Contact
AD 1000 onward

European contact began with the Norsemen, who settled in southern Green-land by AD 1000 and traded with the Inuit for furs, walrus ivory, and gyr-falcons (Chapter 1). The Norsemen may not have had much direct contact with Thule people, but their iron tools, smelted copper, cloth, and other trade goods were diffused far and wide through Eastern Thule territory down long-established exchange networks (McCartney and Mack 1973; McCartney, 1991; McGhee, 1978; Maxwell, 1985). Iron soon became a critical factor in Thule technology, for both imported European and natural meteoritic iron were employed to fashion iron-bladed knives, harpoon tips and other artifacts.

Norse trade with the Thule collapsed by about 1480, and it was a century, in remoter areas much longer, before there were new contacts with Europeans. English voyager Martin Frobisher was the first to search for the elusive Northwest Passage between 1576 and 1578. He made three voyages to the Baffin Island region, thought he had found gold but it was merely black rock. Frobisher was followed by John Davis, Hendrick Hudson, and other explorers. Some of them had men killed in violent disputes with the Inuit. Others traded with friendly groups. These occasional contacts with Europeans had little effect on Inuit culture, except for the importation of rare foreign goods, especially iron tools. It was not until European ships managed to winter over successfully in the mid-19th century that significant populations of whalers, fur traders, even miners, arrived in the Far North. Within a few generations, many Inuit bands became heavily dependent on European trading stations for goods purchased with furs. In some areas, however, Inuit groups perpetuated ancient hunter-gatherer lifeways into the 1950s, when superpower rivalries led to the development of strategic defense networks in the Canadian Arctic.

Further Reading

In addition to the references at the end of Chapter 8.

Bandi, Hans-Georg. 1969. *Eskimo Prehistory*. University of Alaska Press, Fairbanks.
    A classic account of the subject.
Harp, Elmer, Jr. 1978. "Pioneer Cultures of the Subarctic and the Arctic," in Jesse D. Jennings (ed.). *Ancient Native Americans*. W. H. Freeman, New York, pp.303-371.
    An excellent synthesis of what little is known of Sub-Arctic archaeology.
McGhee, Robert. 1996. *Ancient People of the Arctic*. University of British Columbia Press, Vancouver and Canadian Museum of Civilization.
    An admirable general summary for a lay audience.
McCartney, Allen. (ed.) 1979b. *Thule Eskimo Culture: An Anthropological Retrospective*. Mercury Series. Archaeological Survey of Canada Paper 88.
    Invaluable papers on Thule archaeology aimed at a specialist audience.
Schledermann, Peter. 1996. *Voices in Stone*. Arctic Institute of North America, Calgary.
    Another excellent general account.
Shaw, R. D. and Holmes, C. E. (eds.) 1982. "The Norton Interaction Sphere," *Arctic Anthropology*, 19(2) 1-149.
    Important papers on the Norton tradition that describe relatively recent research.
Tuck, James A. 1976. *Newfoundland and Labrador Prehistory*. National Museums of Canada, Ottawa.
    A useful handbook on the archaeology of extreme northeastern Canada, one of a series covering Canadian prehistory, province by province.

PART FIVE

THE WEST

*"In the beginning, the earth was
square and flat, and below its
surface were four layers. All
people, birds, and beasts lived in
the bottom layer or world.
Everything was in darkness.
There was no sun, no moon. It
was dark and it was crowded.
But the people did not know
how to get out. At last two boys
pierced the roof of the lowest
layer, making an opening ... "*

Keresan Origin Myth

| CALIBRATED DATES | RADIOCARBON AGES | WEST COAST | | GREAT BASIN | SOUTHWEST | CLIMATIC STAGES |
		NORTHWEST	CALIFORNIA			
Modern Times	Modern Times	MODERN GROUPS		MODERN GROUPS	MODERN GROUPS	
AD 1105 —	AD 1000 —	L A T E P E R I O D — M I D D L E P E R I O D	A U G U S T I N E — LATE — B E R K E L E Y — W I N D M I L L E R — MIDDLE PERIOD — Many other variants	L A T E A R C H A I C — M I D D L E A R C H A I C	H O H O K A M — M O G O L L O N — A N A S A Z I	LATE HOLOCENE
AD 15 —	AD 1 —					
1267 BC —	1000 BC —				S O U T H W E S T E R N A R C H A I C	
2477 BC —	2000 BC —	E A R L Y P E R I O D	E A R L Y P E R I O D	E A R L Y D E S E R T A R C H A I C		- - - - - - - -
3795 BC —	3000 BC —		?			MIDDLE HOLOCENE
4935 BC —	4000 BC —					
5876 BC —	5000 BC —					
7056 BC —	6000 BC —		? NORTH SOUTH			
8247 BC —	7000 BC —			PALEO-INDIAN		- - - - - - - - EARLY HOLOCENE

EARLY FORAGERS ON THE WEST COAST

The Russian, Spanish, and English explorers who first sailed the western coasts of North America between the 16th and 18th centuries found themselves in one of the richest marine environments on earth. Here they encountered a great diversity of native American populations, not only small bands of hunter-gatherers, but elaborate, highly sophisticated societies, where people lived in large, permanent communities under powerful leaders. Ocean fishing and sea-mammal hunting were important all along the West Coast, especially after about 4000 BC, but assumed particular importance along the Northwest Coast, and in central and southern California. Here, people developed highly specialized fishing and sea-mammal hunting cultures that evolved into some of the most complex and elaborate hunter-gatherer societies in the world. The study of this remarkable cultural complexity has engaged archaeologists for generations, as have the origins of the simpler societies that preceded them.

Environmental Diversity

During the Early and Middle Holocene, the Northwest Coast became a strip of green, forested landscape that stretched from the mouth of the Copper River in Alaska to the Klamath River in northern California. Here the great mountain ranges of the interior were covered with vast stands of spruce, cedar, hemlock, and Douglas fir, trees that occurred in abundance throughout the coast. The Pacific and the rivers that flowed into it provided whales, porpoises, seals, sea lions, and dozens of fish species. Among these were halibut, some of which weighed up to a quarter of a ton. Herring, smelt, and candle fish swarmed in coastal waters. No fewer than five salmon species appeared in inshore waters each year, jamming rivers as they crowded upstream to spawn. Shellfish, waterfowl, some game like deer and fox, and wild plant foods were important elements in human diet throughout the coast. The rich and diverse coastal environment provided over 300 important edible animal species alone. The ancient inhabitants of the coast had an abundant cushion of natural resources to fall back on, in addition to the thousands of fish they could smoke dry and store in times of plenty (Ames and Maschner, 1999; Matson and Coupland, 1995).

At European contact, most human settlement along the Northwest Coast was concentrated on river banks or on the islands and shores of the coast,

Archaeological sites and regions of the Far West.

Haida village photographed in the 19th century, with totem poles, large plank houses, and canoes.

(Below) John Webber, artist on Captain Cook's voyage, drew the inside of a Northwest Coast Indian house on Nootka Sound in the 1770s. Elaborately carved supporting posts can be seen at the rear of the house. Dried salmon and other fish were staples during the winter months.

especially north of the Columbia River, where an abundance of fish and sea mammals allowed relatively sedentary settlement. The damp, oceanic Northwest Coast climate provided abundant natural resources to create an elaborate material culture with only the simplest of tools. The dense forests of the coastal zone were rich in easily split, straight-grained softer woods like red and yellow cedar, fir, and spruce. The local carpenters used tough, polished rocks, shell, or antler blades in their adzes and chisels, taking advantage of the straight-grained wood to build large plank houses at winter villages and other important locations. They reserved some of their finest wood-working artistry for their canoes, large and small. Skilled canoe builders fashioned war and heavy load-carrying canoes from specially felled tree trunks and then carved and smoothed them carefully. The carpenters made a magnificent array of wooden artifacts, adorning many of

(Right) Engraved and painted Haida storage box.

(Below) Portal pole, a carved entrance to a Haida house.

them with a heraldic art style that is among the most celebrated of American Indian art forms. Renowned ancestors, mythical birds, and humans appear on many boxes and small objects. Commemorative posts, portal poles, and great totem poles recounted family genealogies and celebrated the deceased. By the time Europeans arrived on the Coast in the 18th century, these flamboyant cultures had been flourishing for many centuries.

South of the Klamath River stretches more than 1242 miles (2000 km) of Pacific coastline, backed by the rugged Klamath Mountains in the north, and by many separate and lesser coastal ranges from Oregon to central California. The Transverse Ranges abut the coastal mountains at the border of central and southern California, the only ones to run east–west in the state. These ranges rise from the Mojave Desert in the east. The western outliers jut from the Pacific, forming the offshore islands of the Santa Barbara Channel. To the south, the Peninsula Ranges form the spine of Baja California and extend north into the United States as far as the Los Angeles Basin. Three-quarters of inland California comprises the Great Central Valley, with flat lowlands drained by the Sacramento and San Joaquin rivers that merge into a great delta, pass through a gap in the coastal ranges, and ultimately flow into San Francisco Bay. The Lower Sacramento Valley region supported some of the highest population densities in ancient California. Relatively high concentrations also flourished in the Lower San Joaquin Valley, the San Francisco Bay area, and in the Santa Barbara Channel area.

This vast coastal region of great environmental diversity enjoys the highest rainfall in the north and northwest, with some 15 in (38 cm) a year falling in the southern coastal regions, much less inland. In central and southern California, there are generally two seasons, a warm, wet winter and a warm, dry summer with ocean-moderated temperatures along the coast. Many local climates affect the indigenous vegetational cover, and the distribution of animals.

California alone supports more than 30 natural vegetation types, which provided its ancient inhabitants with a variety of staple foods. Oak grassland covers the foothills of the Sierra Nevada, the Transverse ranges, and coastal mountains. It was a vital resource for ancient populations, for the oaks provided acorns and the grasslands edible seeds. The same vegetation also supported populations of deer, rabbits, coyote, bear, and many bird species. Thick chaparral flourishes on steep, rocky slopes between the oak grassland and conifers at higher elevations. Unsuitable for human occupation, the chaparral did support deer and provided a variety of berries and wild plants.

From Monterey to the Oregon border and further north, redwoods grow in a narrow belt from sea level up to about 2000 ft (660 m) or more, nurtured by the moist air and fogs from the nearby Pacific. This highly varied zone supports a very diverse fauna, everything from Canadian elk to beaver, bear, deer, and many smaller mammals.

The diverse coastal environment could provide a wide range of food resources in good years, but drought cycles and changing ocean temperatures were among the factors that made such resources highly unpredictable. The risk of food shortages was always present.

Ancient Food Staples

The peoples of coast and interior lived by hunting and gathering, subsisting in a patchwork of environments that provided local food resources of every kind. Only a handful of later groups in interior southern California ever engaged in agriculture, growing maize, beans, and gourds – subsistence strategies derived from the neighboring Southwest. However, the sheer unpredictability of food resources of all kinds along the Pacific coast and in the Central Valley caused some groups to burn off dry grass to foster new growth, and occasionally to sow wild seeds and irrigate favored food plants.

Three staple food categories comprised the diet of ancient peoples along the West Coast and immediately inland – large and small game animals, edible plants, and sea foods.

Ancient hunters stalked feeding deer and sometimes ambushed them, killing them with spear, and, after AD 500, with the bow and arrow. Pronghorn antelope (*Antilocapra americana*) grazed in large numbers in the Central Valley, as did tule elk. Every human group preyed on smaller game like coyotes, rabbits, and many species of rodents.

Acorns became an important food in the far west after mortars and pestles made their appearance between 4000 and 3000 BC. Even in areas like southern Oregon where fish were abundant, acorns served as an important supplement. California peoples knew of many different oak species, some of which yielded more desirable acorns than others (Baumhoff, 1963). In many places, the foragers would travel a considerable distance to collect acorns from a preferred species, while ignoring large groves of less desirable oaks closer to home (Baumhoff, 1978).

The acorn was by no means the only wild plant staple eaten in ancient times, for many other plant foods served as secondary staples or supplements, especially in acorn-lean years. In southern California, for example, Buckeye (*Aesculus californica*) is a nourishing seed that, like the acorn, is poisonous unless the poison is leached out by pouring water over the seeds. Since animals did not eat it, human beings never had to compete for seed with them, so it was a valuable food in lean years. Chia, sage seed (*Salvia* sp.),

Acorns (drawing below) were a staple food of California and southern Oregon groups. They had to be carefully processed: (bottom) a Hupa woman leaches acorn meal in a basin of sand. A burden basket lies at the left, a basketry bowl in her hand, tightly twined to make it waterproof, and a cooking basket at the right.

was especially plentiful along the southern California coast from Point Conception to San Diego. Harvest yields were small, so the seeds were combined with other famine foods in times of scarcity. People collected the seeds of many species of bunch grasses, also seasonal fruits and tubers, like, for example, the epos root, or yampa (*Perideridia* sp.). This edible root, widely eaten in northern California, had an aromatic, nutty taste when raw, and a flavor somewhat like that of a carrot when boiled.

The ancient Californians had a considerable impact on the natural landscape by their use of fire (Timbrook and Johnson, 1982). They were well aware of the fire danger to valuable acorn crops posed by natural fires, spreading through dense brush from natural lightning strikes in the mountains. So they burned off the growth to prevent such accidents, and to foster deer populations. For example, modern experiments have shown that regular fires in chaparral increase the production of shrubs and herbaceous plants, with accompanying rises in deer populations. In one experiment, the summer deer density was 30 per square mile in an unburned area and up to 131 in a burned one (Biswell, 1967). By burning open areas in chaparral in spring and fall, hunter-gatherers could maximize the amount of edible vegetation along the edges of chaparral. New sprouts appear within three or four weeks of a spring burning, making excellent feed for deer, while fall burning ensures edible sprouts for humans the following spring.

Important staple foods came from the Pacific and the rivers that flowed into the ocean. Vast fish shoals and annual salmon runs contributed to dense populations along parts of the West Coast. King and Coho salmon, also steelhead trout, provided a bounty of fish along the Northwest Coast, and the Klamath, Smith, and Eel rivers in northern California. Annual runs occurred as far south as the Santa Barbara Channel and what is now the Los Angeles area. Many other fish species abounded off the coast, both in dense kelp beds and in deeper water. Bonito, tuna, yellowtail, and halibut were commonly taken from canoes close offshore. Sea mammals could be killed on rocky outcrops and near kelp beds, also on the offshore islands. Harbor seals and sea lions were often clubbed on shore. Sea otters were another favorite prey. Inland river species provided abundant food sources along the Sacramento and San Joaquin rivers.

Vast shell middens line many parts of the West Coast, large whitish-grey mounds densely packed with shell. Abalone, clams, oysters, and sea mussels were collected where abundant. Northern groups also took Washington clams and bent-nosed macomas, while more southern shellfish included the abalone, Pismo clam, scallop, and California Venus clam.

The successful exploitation of sea foods depended to a considerable degree on the presence of good perennial streams, and on ready access to the shoreline. The sheltered, heavily forested, tidal waters of the Pacific Northwest were perfect for intensive sea-mammal hunting and fishing. Along California shores, north of San Francisco and south of Point Conception, for example, the coastline is relatively low-lying, with many streams and natural indentations to attract marine life and to provide shelter for those who live off them. The famous Big Sur coast of central California has steep cliffs that fall directly into the Pacific. Even here, shell middens are commonplace. The densest ancient coastal populations flourished in areas of easy access to the ocean, and, above all, in regions like the Santa Barbara Channel, where offshore islands protect the coastline from surf. Major

Fishing for salmon with a plunge net on the Klamath River, California, before 1898.

riverine areas like the Lower Sacramento and Delta regions were also favored locations.

The great environmental diversity of the far west confronted ancient peoples with a patchwork of locally abundant food resources, resources that varied greatly in their availability. These patterns of resource availability had a strong influence on population density, settlement size, food-getting strategies, and on the degree to which local groups depended on one another. In the long term, this environmental diversity helped shape societies that were interdependent, passing both essential foods and exotic goods and materials through complex barter networks that linked Vancouver Island to the northern mainland, and extended from the offshore islands far into the Southwest, and from the northern coast to the Sierra Nevada and beyond. These trade networks carried acorns, salt, fish, shell artifacts, clothing, baskets, even dogs, over a network of trails that joined a myriad small bands and larger societies with tenuous links. The obsidian trade was a vital element in these networks, as, in later times, was the use of beads made of clam shells or *olivella* as a form of simple "money."

First Settlement of the West Coast
before 10,000 BC to c. 3500 BC

Archaeological knowledge of the Northwest Coast is spotty, with some areas, like the Gulf of Georgia on the southern coast being fairly well known, while others, like the west coast of Vancouver Island, are still little explored. As elsewhere in North America, the evidence for first settlement

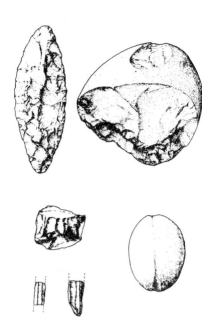

Stone tools from the Namu site.
Clockwise from top left: bifacial point,
chopper, grooved bola or sinker,
microblades, and a microcore.
Length of biface c. 9.3 cm.

is sparse, mainly taking the form of scattered stone tools. The earliest settlement of the Northwest Coast was probably a complex process, involving both coastal groups from the north taking advantage of lower Early Holocene sea levels and other populations from the south, as people moved into formerly glaciated areas (Ames and Maschner, 1999). This complexity of early settlement is reflected in some authorities seeing at least four early cultural traditions, identified by stone tools, along the coast and in the interior (Carlson, 1983). To what extent these represent actual cultural diversity is unknown.

The earliest human occupations on the northern Northwest Coast date to about 8000 BC, documented by bifaces and scrapers in the lowest level of the Ground Hog Bay site on Icy Strait in southeast Alaska (Ackerman and others, 1985). The so-called Paleomarine Period is estimated to last from about 10,000 to 3000 BC. Ground Hog Bay's later levels and other Paleomarine occupations contain many small Alaskan-style microblades, with clear evidence of fish and sea mammals from the Chuck Lake site on Heceta Island, also in southeast Alaska (Ackerman and others, 1985). Southeast Alaska's On-Your-Knees Cave dates to about 7300 BC and contains human remains that have an isotopic ratio strongly suggestive of an entirely marine diet. Paleomarine sites also occur on the Queen Charlotte Islands and date to between 6500 and 3300 BC, yielding microblades, but no bifaces. Earlier settlement is entirely possible. Sites as early as 6000 BC may exist underwater in Prince Rupert Harbor on the northern British Columbia mainland.

The Namu site on the central British Columbia coast documents fishing economies along the mainland shore. The earliest of the two components at the site dates to 10,000 to 5000 BC, with microblades appearing in about 7000 BC as well as numerous sea-mammal bones. By 5000 BC the inhabitants were relying heavily on salmon runs and herring fisheries, to the point where semi-sedentary winter occupation of the site was the likely norm (Cannon, 1991). Then, in about 3000 BC, the Namu people turned their attention to shellfish as well as salmon. Knut Fladmark (1975) argues that favorable environmental conditions enhanced salmon productivity, making a combination of seasonal salmon-run exploitation and intensive shellfish consumption a highly viable lifeway, which persisted for 2000 years.

Some Paleo-Indian groups hunted and foraged in the interior, while there are clear signs of maritime adaptations on the Queen Charlotte Islands and at places like Namu along the British Columbia mainland as early as 5000 BC. Some of these groups may have been ancestral to the Tlingit, Haida, and other Athabaskan-speaking peoples in the Northwest (Carlson, 1983). Carlson argues that as Northwest river waters warmed and lost their icy mantles, their up-river habitats became suitable for salmon spawning grounds. As lake-spawning salmon began spreading up-river, the ancient peoples who preyed on them also moved inland, into areas where they may have met expanding groups from the interior. From these complex movements emerged such historically known groups as the Salishan and Wakashan-speaking peoples of coast and interior today.

Further south, in what is now Oregon and California, initial Paleo-Indian settlement inland is chronicled by isolated fluted point finds. These groups were probably big-game hunters, who may have exploited wild vegetable foods, smaller animals, and marine resources as well. Grinding implements are rare on Paleo-Indian sites, as if intensive exploitation of wild vegetable foods was relatively unimportant. Undoubtedly, foraging assumed greater

Seed-gathering technology: California Pomo Indian woman collects seeds with a beater and basket.

importance after 9000 BC, with the vanishing of the Pleistocene megafauna, but the major shifts in subsistence strategies that occurred about this time are poorly documented anywhere in the far west (for discussion, see Ames and Maschner, 1999). This is because many of the key artifacts used for plant or shellfish gathering are perishable items like baskets, skin bags, or wooden digging sticks. Only stone artifacts used for breaking up shells, and durable *manos* and *metates* survive. The latter grinding and milling implements become more common in western sites after 6000 BC, by which time shellfish collectors, fish and sea-mammal hunting groups were flourishing along the California coast.

The changeover is best documented along the southern California coast where foraging sites occur from San Luis Obispo in the north to the Mexican border. The people still hunted some game and used stone projectile points, but judging from the abundant milling stones, much of their diet came from seeds and edible plants. The material culture from these sites tends to be somewhat monotonous, consisting of heavy, deep seed mills and heavy handstones. But settlement sites are much larger than in earlier times, associated with middens of considerable size. Here, as in the Pacific Northwest, the basic patterns of coastal adaptation that were to persist for millennia were already established by 5000 BC. These patterns depended to a considerable degree on the diversity of food resources available close offshore, in the coastal hinterland and along rivers or lakes, and in the interior.

Northwest Coast Early and Middle Periods
c. 3500 BC to c. AD 500

While shellfish had been exploited sporadically along the Northwest Coast since at least 6000 BC, their intensive use exploded after 3000 BC, not only in southeast Alaska and in the Namu area of central British Columbia, but throughout the entire region. Increasingly, Northwest archaeologists see 3000 BC as the beginning of what can loosely be termed "later times" along the Northwest Coast. (Ames and Maschner, 1999 refer to the period c. 4400 BC to AD 1775 as the "Pacific Period.") Roy Carlson divides the last 5000 years into a Middle and Late Period, with the transition between Middle and Late coming in about AD 500. Local subdivisions deviate somewhat from the Carlson sequence. For example, the later culture history of the northern coast is divided into three, not two stages (Ames, 1994; Maschner 1991; Ames and Maschner, 1999). An Early Period (c. 3500 to 1800 BC) is marked by an abundance of shell middens. This was a time when ground-stone artifacts replaced chipped-stone tools, and when organic materials came into use on a much larger scale for tools of all kinds. In central British Columbia, the Namu settlement enjoyed excellent salmon runs and a peak of economic productivity, which ended about 2000 BC, when estuary development and increasing river sedimentation caused salmon productivity to decline.

The north coast's Middle Period lasted from 1800 BC to AD 500. If artifacts known from modern analogies to be associated with prestigious individuals are to be believed, then, by 1000 BC, northern Northwest Coast society displayed at least some signs of social ranking in the Prince Rupert region of the mainland (MacDonald, 1983). Emerging social ranking and complexity seems to have resulted from what Ken Ames (1994) calls "a mosaic of local and regional

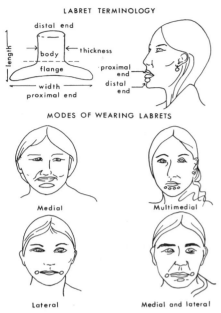

LABRET TERMINOLOGY

MODES OF WEARING LABRETS

Medial

Multimedial

Lateral

Medial and lateral

The variety of ways in which labrets could be worn.

events and dynamics at differing temporal and social scales." Stone labrets (lip ornaments), worn as a sign of social ranking, left distinctive facets on the wearer's teeth, even if the artifact is absent, so burial data is of value. Labret wear occurs on the teeth of a few individuals between about 3000 and 2500 BC, while, on the south coast, cranial deformation replaced labrets as a social marker after about 500 BC, a custom that persisted along the north coast until modern times. But labrets have problems as social markers, since they were worn by all women, even if higher-status individuals wore large ones (Moss, quoted by Ames, 1994; Ames and Maschner, 1999).

Mortuary patterns were complex long before 500 BC, but graves with costly and exotic goods only become common along the entire coast after that date. Ames and others believe this elaboration reflects the appearance of a social elite along the entire coast by 500 BC, but others believe that labrets signal this development at least 1000 years earlier.

Biological anthropologist Jerome Cybulski examined skeletons from the coast dating to between 1500 and 200 BC and found clear evidence for decapitation, depressed skull fractures, and the kinds of injuries inflicted on forearms by parrying vicious blows, all clear signs of combat, and, presumably, competition between neighboring groups. He believes that a high ratio of male burials relative to females in the Prince Rupert Harbor site population may be a sign of slavery, for slaves were rarely buried, but this is still speculative (Cybulski, 1993). By this time, northern coastal peoples were fishing on a large scale, employing specialized technology including fish weirs (Moss, Erlandson, and Stuckenrath, 1990), while harvesting herring and cod in favored areas like Tebenkof Bay in southeast Alaska (Maschner, 1991). A rapid increase in shell-midden size along the coast may reflect a decline in salmon stocks or a significant population increase.

Just how important were salmon along the Northwest Coast? In parts of the central and southern coast, local groups lived for long periods of time at the same location while not placing a great emphasis on salmon (Croes, 1989; Mitchell, 1988). As Cannon (1991) has pointed out, local salmon stocks varied dramatically over short and long periods of time and from one area to another, making it well-nigh impossible to assess salmon's importance in cultural change along the coast. Monks (1987) has drawn attention to the virtual fixation of many Northwest archaeologists on salmon (as stored food) as a key element in the development of sedentism and social complexity. He calls this "salmonopia," "the inability to see all the food resources because of salmon," drawing attention to the dozens of other, often easily storable, food resources available in the Northwest. As Ames (1991b) argues, the course of intensification varied considerably from one area to the next, sometimes resulting in extreme specialization in one or two food resources, in others in broad-spectrum foraging. In general terms, we can say that increasing food production was widespread between southeast Alaska and southern Oregon by 1500 BC, and that adequate storage technology, perhaps coinciding with the appearance of plank houses along the coast, was of vital importance. And it was between 3000 and 2000 BC that coastal groups began an increasingly intensive manipulation of their diverse environment to meet not only subsistence and other economic requirements, but to satisfy social and ideological needs. This progressively more efficient exploitation of marine and land resources was a key factor in the appearance of social complexity along the Northwest Coast and in the hinterland.

Even as early as 3500 BC, it is possible to recognize a nascent Northwest Coast cultural tradition that evolved continuously until European contact. Many sites of this period have been grouped together into the Charles Phase, centered on the Strait of Georgia area but representative of generalized cultural developments over a much wider area (Borden, 1975), even as far north as the Alaska Peninsula. By the Middle Period, the cultural diversity of earlier millennia gave way to greater homogeneity throughout the Northwest Coast except in basketry styles (Croes, 1989). The reasons for this are little understood, but may be connected with shifts in adaptations and rising population densities, with the stabilization of sea levels and environmental conditions during the Middle Holocene. There are signs of a higher level of interaction between neighboring groups, too, reflected in widespread trade in fine-grained, tool-making obsidian. Judging from X-ray fluorescence studies, much of the obsidian came from sources in eastern Oregon, reaching the Puget Sound region, Vancouver Island and the Gulf Islands, and the mainland as far north as Namu (Carlson, 1994). Mount Edziza in northwestern British Columbia, as well as local sources, provided supplies for ancient communities at the headwaters of the Yukon, near Juneau, Alaska, and throughout much of coastal northern British Columbia. These exchange networks, and others handling different commodities, may have contributed to the spread of ideas and culture traits throughout the coastal regions (Croes, 1989).

This was the time when the basic characteristics of historic Northwest Coast culture appeared – an emphasis on status and wealth, and on elaborate ceremonial, reflected in new art traditions (Ames and Maschner, 1999). Specialized woodworking tools became more common during the Middle Period, and finely made polished chisels and adze blades appeared by about 1500 BC, heavier woodworking tools such as mauls and pile drivers after AD 500. By this time, too, cedar bark was being fabricated into cloaks and other garments, basketry had reached a high level of sophistication, and planked houses were probably in use. Hunting and fishing technology now reached new levels of elaboration. Some 400 bent wood and composite fish hooks came from the Hoko River site on the Olympia Peninsula (Croes, 1995), arguing for more emphasis on offshore fishing, while many forms of stone, bone, and wooden projectile points were in use. Hunting of such animals as the elk, deer, bear, and beaver was important in many areas. Ocean and estuarine fishing certainly assumed greater significance during the Middle Period.

The Middle Period may have seen the accumulation of large food surpluses, surpluses that led to complex mechanisms for redistributing food and other goods throughout society. A few wealthy and powerful individuals may have controlled such redistribution as a way of acquiring personal prestige. One mechanism for doing this may have been ceremonial feasts, the ancestors of the elaborate *potlatches* of historic times. It is hard to identify such personages in the archaeological record. Some Middle Period burials from Namu, Prince Rupert, and elsewhere dating to about 500 BC have more elaborate grave furniture, and might be the graves of more important people, but poor preservation makes the evidence tantalizingly uncertain. Some status artifacts such as labrets, lip ornaments, and gorgets worn at the throat, occur at many later sites, as do superbly flaked stone knives of a form that were used by important people in historic times. Middle Period art with its animal motifs carved on spoons and bowls recalls the prestigious crests that were commonplace in later times.

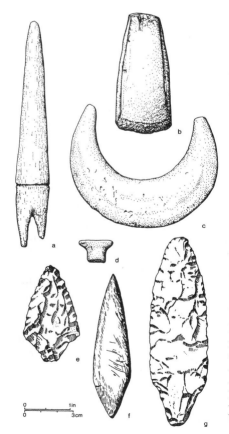

Middle Period artifacts: (a) harpoon foreshaft, (b) stone adze or chisel blade, (c) scallop-shell gorget, (d) labret or lip ornament, (e) chipped-stone point, (f) ground-slate point, and (g) chipped-stone knife.

For all the relative homogeneity of Middle Period culture, there were important clusters of more elaborate culture in such areas as the Lower Fraser River Valley and the Gulf of Georgia, on the west coast of Vancouver Island, and along the central British Columbia coast. These are reflected in differences in toolkits, harpoon forms (Carlson, 1983), and in basketry and cordage (Croes, 1989). There are other artifacts such as stemmed projectile heads, tobacco pipes, and slate projectile points, that entered the narrow confines of the Northwest Coast during the Middle Period, with cultural influences percolating in both from Alaska and from the south.

Northern California Early Archaic
6000 to 1500 BC

Further south, the rocky and mountainous habitat of the northern California coast supported Archaic populations for thousands of years, populations that survived comfortably with little contact with neighboring culture areas. The people subsisted off wild vegetable foods, moving seasonally from one concentration of edible foods to another. They probably changed their highly flexible adaptations to accommodate plant distribution changes resulting from minor climatic fluctuations. The size of local bands seems to have varied considerably, with little of the elaboration found in later coastal and Sacramento Delta cultures.

In the San Francisco Bay area, early sites were located not only on bay and ocean shores but in hill country, and considerable distances inland. Some groups collected shellfish, but nothing like on the scale of later coastal societies.

Southern California Early Period
before 6000 to 1000 BC

The early culture history of the southern California coast is best known from the offshore Channel Islands and the Santa Barbara Channel coast. Unfortunately, many early sites lie beneath the higher sea levels of the Middle and Late Holocene. During the Early Holocene, many coastal groups may have exploited highly productive estuaries at the mouths of now-submerged coastal canyons (Erlandson and Colten, 1991; Erlandson, 1994; Glassow, 1996). But there is good reason to believe some of the earliest maritime occupations in the Americas flourished in southern California. San Miguel Island, at the western end of the Santa Barbara Channel to the north, was settled as early as 8500 BC. There is good reason to believe there was a widespread Early Holocene maritime adaptation throughout the coast and offshore islands, which flourished for many millennia, to as late as 1000 BC (Raab, Bradford, and Yatsko, 1994).

This Early Period has been broken down into three divisions, known locally as Ex, Ey, and Ez (Glassow, Wilcoxon, and Erlandson, 1987). Ex passed into Ey in about 4450 BC, with the final phase assigned to between 2350 and 1350 BC, but the chronology is little refined.

Early Period groups flourished at a time of steady sea-level rise, so many important sites may be buried under the Pacific, or have been eroded away by rising sea levels. Some settlements were built on higher ground away from

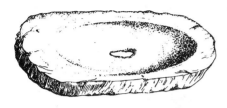

Southern California mano *and milling stone, Topanga Complex. Length of* mano *9 cm.*

the ocean. On the offshore islands, people built semi-subterranean pithouses, leaving numerous seed-processing *metates* and *manos* behind them. Some houses of this type on San Clemente Island had whale-bone roof structures and dated to 3000 BC (Raab, Bradford, and Yatsko, 1994). The inhabitants sometimes buried their dead in red ocher-sprinkled graves. Other sites occur near coastal wetlands and on lower ground.

Early investigators believed that plant foods were more important than hunting or fishing during the Early Period. While it is true that basin *metates* and *manos* are common on sites of this period, shellfish were an important resource throughout these millennia. Judging from modern analogies, basin *metates* and *manos* were mainly used to process small nuts and seeds. Mortars and pestles appear in Ey and Ez sites, artifacts that may be associated with the introduction of acorns and other pulpy nuts and seeds into the diet.

Land and sea-mammal hunting may have assumed greater importance as time went on. Deer and sea-mammal bones are more common in later Early Period sites, coinciding with a change from crude, percussion-flaked lanceolate projectile points to abundant side-notched and stemmed heads. The people used bone gorges and barbed, multi-part fish hooks to catch both shallow- and deep-water fish. Chester King (1984) believes that gorges and nets served to obtain inshore fish, while the larger, compound fish hooks, and perhaps harpoons, took deeper-water fish like sharks, and dolphins, species more common in later times. Mainland beaches were convenient places to net smaller species.

The Early Period settlement pattern was probably a balance between seasonal hunting and foraging, especially at the time of fall nut and seed harvests. However, shellfish, sea mammals, and fish of all kinds played an increasingly greater role, perhaps allowing the people to occupy base camps for long periods of time, despite unpredictable short-term climatic change.

The origins of this early coastal tradition are still little understood. Glassow points out that the earliest solidly documented traces of Archaic occupation, dating to about 7000 BC, come from north of the Santa Barbara Channel, from the cool, foggy environment of Point Conception and further north, where the coast is rocky and conditions are slightly wetter. This region may resemble primordial Ice Age environments more closely than drier areas further south, but the field information is very sketchy (Glassow, Wilcoxon, and Erlandson, 1987).

This entire (Archaic) tradition owes much to earlier Paleo-Indian cultures, with new artifacts for seed processing grafted onto an existing material culture. Several authorities have pointed out that the earliest Early Period dates, and readings from equivalent sites near La Jolla, coincide with the early Altithermal, when inland lakes dried up and there was a major warming trend. Some inland foraging populations may have moved to the coast in response to increasing aridity in the interior.

Judging from a rise in site numbers, admittedly a somewhat tenuous yardstick to use, and the frequencies of radiocarbon dates through time, Santa Barbara Channel populations may have first reached significant levels about 6000 BC, with a drop in coastal populations in the Middle Holocene between about 5000 and 3500 BC, the lowest density occurring between 4000 and 3500 BC, perhaps during the dry and warmer Altithermal (Glassow, 1996). Coastal populations rose relatively rapidly after 3500 BC, at a time coinciding with the first use of mortars and pestles, perhaps with more intensive acorn

TABLE 10.1

Holocene Climate Change in the West

Early Holocene (*c.* 14,700 years ago to 6500 BC). Between 14,700 and 13,000 years ago, western glaciers receded and montane ice caps were reduced, woodlands and basin lakes diminished, and the Ice Age big-game vanished. This universal warming was interrupted for about 1100 years by the Younger Dryas cold interval (Chapter 4). Basically modern environmental conditions were reached just after the Early Holocene, between 6000 and 5000 BC. The first human settlers of the west and their immediate successors lived in a constantly changing, indeed transitional, environment. Over more than five millennia, the distribution of water supplies changed radically, major ecosystems like piñon-juniper woodland were on the move. Sea levels rose rapidly, flooding estuaries and coastal plains. Paleo-Indian and Early Archaic societies lived in transitional environments very different from those of today.

Middle Holocene (6500 to 2000 BC). The Middle Holocene (sometimes called the Altithermal in older literature (Antevs, 1948)) brought a general rise in temperatures, sometimes to higher levels than today. Many of the large interior lakes dried up, making surviving freshwater marshes and lakes of the greatest importance to hunter-gatherer populations. Piñon woodlands vanished in the southern Great Basin and expanded in more northerly areas. But the highly diverse environment of the west makes it virtually impossible to generalize about the effects of warmer Middle Holocene conditions. While some areas may have been abandoned during the Middle Holocene when water supplies dried up, others were still occupied, sometimes even more intensively than before.

Late Holocene (2000 BC to the present). The Late Holocene may have seen three colder episodes, some expansion of freshwater lakes, and a slight lowering of tree lines in some areas of the west. Again, the effects of environmental diversity are hard to measure. In some areas, upland resources may have been enhanced, while some lakeside areas were flooded by rising water, thereby reducing marsh areas available for human exploitation. The basic animal and plant communities of today were firmly established during the Late Holocene, ushering in a period not of climatic transition, but of fundamental stability.

Deep-sea cores from the Santa Barbara Channel, California, pollen sequences, and tree-rings from interior locations reveal dramatic shifts in rainfall patterns over the past 2,000 years, including prolonged drought cycles during the Medieval Warm Period (AD 800 to 1400). Tree-ring researches in the Southwest document two major drought cycles between AD 1130 to 1180 and the "Great Drought" of AD 1275 to 1299 (Dean, 1988, 1996), which had widespread effects across the west.

exploitation, certainly with a greater emphasis on fishing and sea-mammal hunting. Similar patterns are thought to occur elsewhere in southern California.

About 4000 BC, sea temperatures cooled considerably, but the land vegetation was still that of a warm, arid climate. Sea levels were rising, drowning the seed-rich coastal plain. The gradual reduction of these seed communities between 5800 and 4000 BC may have contributed to the shift to acorn harvesting as a major element in human subsistence in an environment of unpredictable rainfall and ocean temperatures, oaks having become more frequent than in the Early Holocene.

Did these changes in subsistence and settlement pattern result from major environmental change? There is a more specific question: did new subsistence strategies result from changes in availability and abundance of food resources (Erlandson and Glassow, 1995)? The Early Period begins just as the pine and fern tree cover of the cooler and damper Early Holocene climate gives way to more open vegetation. The changeover took place about 5800 BC. As the early Ex phase ended, warm and dry conditions prevailed, with higher sea temperatures and a shift to oak forest and much more open vegetation. During Ex times, sea levels were up to 49 ft (15 m) lower than today, with dry land extending more than half a mile (1 km) from the present mainland. The coastal plain would have been much larger than today, and may have supported grasslands and sage brush, which themselves would have produced productive harvests of small seeds processed with basin *metates* and *manos*.

The period between about 5800 and 4000 BC coincides with warmer ocean temperatures, a time when peak temperatures would have inhibited the growth of the coastal kelp so typical of the California coast today. Kelp forests support large inshore fish populations, important prey for sea mammals. A reduction in kelp beds may have diminished near-shore fish populations, also the sea mammals that preyed on them, removing part of the local resource base. Perhaps this was responsible for low population densities during part of the Altithermal. By the same token, the population growth after 4000 BC may coincide with an increase in the productivity of the inshore marine habitat as kelp beds reappeared, even if climate conditions were as unpredictable as they are today.

Why did the people of the coast take advantage of this enhanced productivity? Why was similar increased productivity not taken advantage of much earlier, during the Ex phase? These issues are much debated. Glassow and his colleagues argue that while the timing of subsistence changes may have resulted from short-term environmental shifts, additional factors may have played an important role. One was a relatively rapid population increase during the Ey and Ez phases of the Early Period. As populations grew, the overall energy cost of providing food for everyone would also increase, especially in drought cycles. More effort would have been needed to obtain food, perhaps triggering a shift to new food sources that may have required a greater time and energy investment to catch or process (Basgall, 1987; Raab, 1996).

There are some obvious signs of change. Both large sea mammals and deer were favored resources as long as they were fairly easy to obtain. As population densities rose, these same resources probably became scarcer, requiring more energy to collect. For example, seals and sea lions that frequented convenient beaches are an easily hunted resource. But once the hunters had to mount special expeditions to remoter outcrops frequented by the animals, the hunting cost rose rapidly.

Acorn storage: the Nisenan village of Yupu near Yuba City, showing acorn granaries and large, dome-shaped, earth-covered dwellings. Illustration from Gleason's Pictorial Drawing Room Companion *(1882).*

Fishing, too, has varied costs. Catching inshore fish by hook and line in tide pools or from outlying rocks is a cheap way of catching food, but the yield is usually low. Canoes would be needed to exploit the rich kelp beds close of shore, but the yields would be much higher. However, building and maintaining boats requires considerable, and constant effort, as does sewing and repairing seine nets to be used from shore or canoe. Sea craft more substantial than a reed raft would have been adaptive for the catching of larger fish like halibut or sharks as well, species with a high meat yield per specimen landed.

Acorns are the most obvious example of a higher-cost food resource, for the elaborate processing procedure has been documented from ethnographic observations. Both seeds and acorns have a major advantage: they are easily stored for long-term use, as foods that can be drawn upon in lean winter months. Both require considerable collecting and processing effort, but acorns probably came into widespread use when population growth as well as rising sea levels reduced seed harvests, making harder-to-process plant foods a competitive, easily stored resource for feeding more people.

During the Early, and especially the Middle, Holocene, coastal peoples expanded the breadth of their diet, a diet that probably included small amounts of most food resources from the very beginning. It was only when populations grew and traditional staples became scarcer that people turned to alternative, more costly sources. The Middle Holocene also saw an increase in long-distance exchange, especially of exotic materials and ceremonial objects such as pipes. Interestingly, a rare, but distinctive shell bead known as "Olivella Grooved Rectangles" appears at many sites on the southern Channel Islands, in coastal and inland California, Nevada and central Oregon dating to about 2500 to 4000 BC, evidence for a large cultural interaction sphere that extended over an enormous area of the west (but not offshore to the northern Channel Islands off southern California (Jenkins and Erlandson, 1997; Raab, 1997).

This broadly distributed Archaic lifeway survived into later millennia, adapting to changing climatic conditions, and devising far more diverse subsistence strategies. Notable among these was a much greater focus on acorn harvesting, fishing, sea-mammal hunting, and shellfish collecting, which coincided with the more complex California foraging societies described in Chapter 11.

Further Reading

Ames, Kenneth, and Maschner, Herbert. 1999. *Peoples of the Northwest Coast.* Thames and Hudson, London and New York.
An authoritative and up-to-date account of Northwest Coast archaeology for the general reader.
Carlson, Roy (ed.). 1983. *Indian Art Traditions of the Northwest Coast.* Archaeology Press, Simon Fraser University, Burnaby, British Columbia.
Essays on the ancient background to Northwest Coast art, which range widely over archaeological and historical issues.
Heizer, R. F. and Whipple, M. A. 1971. *The California Indians: A Source Book.* 2nd ed. University of California Press, Berkeley.
A carefully selected series of essays on California Indian societies of great use to the general reader.
Moratto, Michael J. 1984. *California Archaeology.* Academic Press, New York.
The definitive account of California culture history, which is widely used as a teaching text. Technical, at times demanding, but authoritative.

CHAPTER 11

THE MYTH OF THE GARDEN OF EDEN: LATER SOCIETIES OF THE WEST COAST

Anthropological writers since the pioneer scholar Alfred Kroeber have waxed lyrical about the assured food supplies that existed for the taking along the ancient Pacific coast. From there, it was a short step to generations of theories that linked abundant food supplies with the development of sedentary, complex forager societies in the Northwest and parts of California. The Northwest and California coasts have long been considered a natural laboratory for studying the origins of complexity in hunter-gatherer societies, partly because of this long-cherished illusion of a veritable "Garden of Eden."

Over the past decade, this popular stereotype has crumbled in the face of an enormous body of new information and fresh models and theoretical approaches. Today, a growing body of theorists argue that neither area was a natural paradise, that ancient culture change was far more rapid and irregular than once suspected. Furthermore, cultural adaptations such as social complexity were not unqualified examples of adaptive success. Rather, they were a product, at least in part, of stressful cultural and environmental conditions. In recent years, researchers have played close attention to short-term climate change and such phenomena as warfare as major sources of stress.

In Chapter 10, we surveyed what is known of the earliest coastal societies. Now we must examine the theories that now account for cultural complexity in later times.

Complex Hunter-Gatherers

Complex forager societies differed from simpler hunter-gatherers in a number of important respects (Ames and Maschner, 1999). The former enjoyed semi- to fully sedentary lifeways, living in one place for most of the year, often for several generations, or settling at one location for long periods of the years, such as the winter. Sedentism changed relationship to the environment, to ownership of land and food resources such as nut groves or salmon runs. Sedentary foragers inherited property rights and had more complex social organization which reflected such inheritance, the need for reciprocity, and to resolve disputes, which festered at close quarters. They often built substantial, permanent houses, such as the planked dwellings of the Northwest Coast, and owned many more

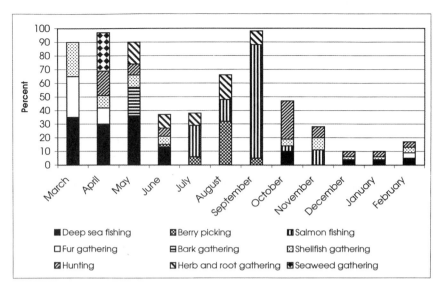

Graph of food-gathering yields over time. The relative amount spent on gathering resources among the northern Tinglit, a coastal group living mainly in southeastern Alaska. While patterns varied locally, all Northwest groups had complex annual shedules.

possessions, possible because they did not have to carry everything with them everywhere.

The same societies were invariably household-based, even if the extended household consisted of as many as 100 people living in the same permanent dwelling. These households developed elaborate storage technologies, which allowed them to accumulate large quantities of food, such as dried salmon or acorns, exploited intensively at certain seasons of the year. At the same time, they maintained access to surplus food stuffs by kin ties and reciprocal relationships with households living in nearby environments.

Almost all complex hunter-gatherer societies, like Northwestern Coastal peoples or Woodland groups in the Midwest, exploited very productive food resources like edible nuts or fish intensively, but, by the same token, worked a wide range of them, in the case of Northwestern peoples, everything from salmon to sea mammals. In other words, they never put themselves unduly at risk by only focusing on, say, acorns or salmon, to the exclusion of secondary foods. Not only did they have a cushion in scarce years, but they could deploy many families to work a salmon run, so that large numbers of fish could be caught and processed in a short time before they rotted. This intense exploitation of the environment meant that they could have a major impact on their surroundings, by burning grass cover to foster new growth for feeding game to overfishing a lake.

Technologically, complex hunter-gatherer societies developed elaborate toolkits for fishing, sea-mammal hunting, watercraft, and nut processing. Such elaboration is a logical extension both of intense resource exploitation and of sedentary living, where portability is not a factor. A much greater complexity extended into society itself, where larger communities sheltered from several hundred to as many as 2000 people. This more densely packed society produced large enough food surpluses to support full- and part-time male and female specialists – canoe makers, woodworkers, shamans, and basketmakers, to mention only a few. Sometimes even entire communities specialized in a particular craft, such as stone tool manufacture.

Sedentism and higher populations led to more elaborate social hierarchies, where leadership fell to shamans, kin leaders, and others with exceptional abilities. Most complex hunter-gatherer societies had a degree of social stratification, with a chiefly elite, some individuals with more-than-average wealth and influence, and commoners. Sometimes such leadership roles were hereditary, carrying status, power, and wealth with them. In many societies, they were achieved by sheer ability. The word "power" has a sophisticated meaning here, for these individuals were not despots with dictatorial powers. Their positions came from their perceived supernatural abilities, their skills at attracting followers, and, above all, from their ability to read and act upon the trends of public opinion. Wealth derived from one's household was an important basis of power, for what one did with that wealth was all-important in terms of social obligations and participating in long-distance exchange networks. Another key was marriage ties, for a well-placed marriage preserved social links that maintained high social status for both men and women. Slaves, usually war captives, played an important role in many more complex societies. Such individuals had no rights.

It should be emphasized that the achievement of social complexity was not necessarily a permanent condition, witness the complex histories of forager societies in both the Pacific Northwest and southern California.

We examine the evidence from the Northwest Coast and California separately.

Emerging Cultural and Social Complexity on the Northwest Coast
c. 1000 BC to modern times

The Late Period on the Northwest Coast begins in about AD 500, the culmination of thousands of years of sometimes tumultuous cultural change along the coast. The staples behind this long process of change were fishing, shellfish collecting, sea- and land-mammal hunting, and some plant gathering. These varied food sources provided the resource base for a great elaboration of Northwest culture, reflected in intensive economic specialization, relatively high population densities, and considerable sophistication of social and political organization (Ames and Maschner, 1999; Matson and Coupland, 1995; Moss, 1993).

Controversy surrounds the emergence of cultural and social complexity along the Northwest Coast (summary of major theories in Ames and Maschner, 1999). Many authorities speculate that it was connected to a combination of a greater focus on anadromous and offshore fish, population growth, and local resource depletion. Efficient exploitation of resources required centralized authority in the form of socially prominent people who managed territories they owned, coordinated their work forces of extended families and associates, and redistributed the resulting food resources (Yesner, 1987).

A second group of theories argues that populations increased and local groups responded to higher densities by developing more efficient ways of exploiting rich maritime food sources. Social elites came into being to organize sea-mammal hunts, salmon harvesting, food storage, and redistribution (Johnson and Earle, 1987). A third school of thought believes social and political factors led to competition for resources, to warfare and conflict, to trade and exchange, and to the emergence of powerful chiefs who vied with one another for power and prestige

(Coupland, 1988). None of these theories does justice to recent archaeological data from along the coast, partly because they have all tried to explain prehistoric culture change by working back from the rich ethnographic record. Many researchers have fallen into the fatal intellectual trap of thinking the "ethnographic present" of first European contact in the 18th century AD was a static phenomenon. In fact, the complex societies on the Northwest Coast lived through a long and turbulent history of constant cultural change.

One foundation of theorizing about cultural complexity in the Pacific Northwest has been an assumption that the climate changed relatively little over the past 5000 years. In fact, deep-sea cores and pollen samples show major temperature fluctuations, which had a major effect on glacial activity, rainfall, and such resources as salmon (Grove, 1988). For example, the climate was relatively warm and wet at first, then became colder between 1250 and 850 BC. Thereafter temperatures rose to a peak during an optimal period between AD 900 and 1350 (the Medieval Warm Period), which ended with colder conditions that climaxed in 1700 during the so-called Little Ice Age. The hunter-gatherer populations of the Northwest Coast had to adapt not only to changing climatic conditions, but to sea-level fluctuations caused by geological uplift and other phenomena. Any explanation for the complexity of Northwest Coast society must take climatic factors into account.

Unfortunately, few archaeological sites along the coast provide stratigraphic or organic information, let alone climatic data, to document emerging complexity during the Late Period. We know that in AD 500 the Northwest Coast cultural pattern was well established everywhere, marked by an increasing emphasis on salmon in the diet and the appearance of both artifacts and art styles which reflect historically known cultures. Although large houses are known from sites in the Prince Rupert region, there are no architectural clues as to emerging cultural complexity.

Along the northern coast, from southeast Alaska to northern and central British Columbia, the Late Period saw the development of large, sedentary villages inhabited by people living in sizeable houses, in groups of 20 to 60 individuals. At the same time, many settlements became fortified redoubts on bluffs and cliff tops. Herbert Maschner's researches in Tebenkof Bay, southeast Alaska (1991), have identified major settlements, made up of congregations of formerly independent villages, which lay not near the best food resources, but along straight coastlines, at easily defended locations where one could see for long distances. Maschner argues that the bow and arrow was a strategic weapon, which forced people to live in fortified villages, where they could protect themselves against enemies, living cheek-by-jowl with families from other kin groups. On the basis of his Tebenkof data, Maschner theorizes that from being small, independent kin-group-based hamlets, northern Northwest Coast settlements became large, multi-kin-group villages, circumscribed by the realities of locally dense populations, regular conflict, and the need to redistribute food resources many of which came from some distance away.

Ames and Maschner (1999) argue that the development of political complexity along the northern Northwest Coast resulted from several closely linked circumstances. To begin with, they assume population density reached a critical size in an environment where food resources were distributed unevenly or within well-defined areas. Such realities caused individual groups to organize their lives around the areas where food was most abundant, and to take advantage of periods when they were most plentiful. Under such circumstances, social complexity is likely to develop. At some moment, they argue, the coastal population rose to the point where groups in competition or conflict could not simply move away to another area with plentiful food supplies. Under such circumstances, the natural striving among humans to achieve status and political advantage came into play, as a few individuals assumed control over the redistribution of food supplies and over political relationships between neighbors. The result was politically and socially more complex societies, which reflected volatile and rapidly changing circumstances. Ames and Maschner's provocative hypothesis relies less on environmental factors than some other theories.

Status artifacts known from modern analogies to be associated with high-ranking people, differences in house sizes, and evidence for warfare, an activity said to have been associated with historical, ranked Northwest Coast societies, are the three lines of evidence to suggest emerging cultural complexity before AD 500. Thereafter, argue many experts, the northern Northwest Coast was culturally stable until European contact (MacDonald and Inglis, 1981). In fact, as Ames and Maschner (1999) point out, there is evidence from excavations and settlement studies in southeast Alaska that some Northwest Coast populations may have been greater during the climatic optimum, between AD 750 and 1400, than three centuries later when conditions were colder and more severe.

The southern Northwest Coast, from northern Vancouver Island to Cape Mendocino, witnessed a similar trend toward more complex societies, with locally high population densities, heavy reliance on storage, and intense manipulation of the environment. Here, also, local populations rose rapidly after 1000 BC, then fluctuated considerably in the centuries of climatic change after AD 500 (Ames, 1991a). Ames measures social change through changing architectural trends, both on the coast and in the interior, arguing that changes in house design reflect increasing sedentism, stable social networks, and altered domestic organization. Semi-subterranean dwellings

House styles typical of the Northwest Coast. Type 1 are northern-style houses; type 2 houses are found on the southern coast.

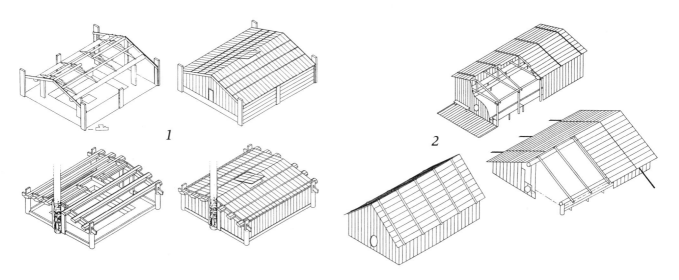

are the earliest domestic structures on the coast and in the interior, with rectangular plank-built houses appearing by 1100 BC. These structures, occupied for several centuries, required enormous communal effort to build. Such plank houses represent long-term investments in permanent village sites, and, presumably, some major changes in the prevailing social order.

Coastal plank houses (and long houses built of thatch and matting in the interior) now increased in size, housing large domestic groups. Ames believes they reflect not only dense village populations, but societies where domestic tasks such as harvesting salmon runs or catching and drying herring were highly organized and closely supervised, as part of a strategy for intense manipulation of the environment and for creating large stocks of food. This manipulation was locally focused, but had much broader regional implications. We can be certain that large-scale social networks, reflected in different art styles, tattooing, and ornaments, connected widely separated parts of the Northwest Coast. The relations between these different, still little-known, networks changed considerably over the last 3500 years. Affiliation with one of these regional networks, which exchanged foodstuffs, obsidian, and exotic objects, was part of everyone's personal identity in society. But, for all these long-distance links, intensification of food production along the coast was closely tied to ever-changing local conditions. As Ames (1991a) remarks, "homogeneous evolutionary processes across a broad region [produced] locally heterogeneous effects." We now know enough to be able to say that social complexity did not appear once and for all by about AD 500, then remain constant until European contact. Rather, complexity developed in many forms along the Northwest Coast, probably in different places at different times, and on more than one occasion. Such complexity did not necessarily involve social stratification, even if it was reflected in sophisticated division of labor, specialized production, and very intricate patterns of regional exchange (Ames and Maschner, 1999).

The Hoko River Site complex near the northwest tip of the Olympia Peninsula offers a perspective on local manipulations of the environment, and on the social complexities which could result (Croes, 1989, 1995). There are two sites close to the ocean. The first is an up-river waterlogged and dry camp-site area dating to between 1000 and 200 BC, the second a river-mouth site within a large rockshelter, occupied from about AD 1000 to 1850, after European contact. The former belongs to the Middle Period, which is thought to reflect a more specific adaptation to the coastal environment than earlier cultures. The artifact inventory from this settlement includes over 400 cod and halibut offshore fishing hooks, complete with floats and cordage leaders, indicating an early specialization in such fisheries. The fish bones include 52 percent flat fishes, 20 percent

(Opposite) Hoko River sites, Washington. (Top left) Map showing the two site locations, an earlier upriver camp and a later rockshelter site. (Top right) Halibut hook as it was found at the wet site. Note the bone barb, the Indian plumb wood shanks, and two-strand spruce root leader attached. (Center right) Makah fisherman displays a modern replica of the Hoko halibut hook, used to catch a fish close offshore. (Center left) Hoko rockshelter excavations in progress. (Bottom) Reconstructed Makah canoe used for the halibut fishing experiment at Hoko River.

(Below) Zoomorphic carving on (?) whale bone, probably representing a bird figure, found near the base of the Hoko River rockshelter trench excavation. Makah elders believe it may be a hair pin, pushed through the hair bun typically worn on the back of the head by fishermen.

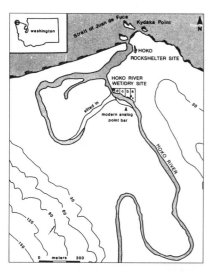

cod, and 16 percent salmon, all of them caught offshore. Traces of fires and wooden racks on shore are convincing evidence for the drying of catches.

The bone tools from the nearby Late Period Hoko River rockshelter are very different from the artifacts found at the earlier site up-river. Bone is now the dominant technology for making artifacts, as it was elsewhere along the nearby Gulf of Georgia. Over 800 years of occupation, the inhabitants took an average of 10 percent cod, 59 percent salmon, and only 5 percent halibut, probably consumed in dried form. The rockshelter was probably used in fall and early winter when salmon could be taken. Shellfish and mussels were also a significant part of the diet.

Dale Croes and Steven Hackenberger (1988) use the Hoko sites to argue for the importance of spring and summer bottom fisheries to sedentary populations. Offshore flatfish and halibut are of predictable occurrence and are relatively easy to catch and process in large numbers. At Hoko, there is great elaboration of offshore, jigging (hook-and-line), and trolling (used with a towed line) fish hooks, as if the inhabitants were venturing close offshore to catch large numbers of fish before they entered rivers in summer and fall. Croes and Hackenberger feel that the need to intensify the use of bottom fish and anadromous species did not in itself require the development of ranked societies to manage people and food supplies. Rather they predict that food resource depletion combined with a rapid growth of extended families led to the ownership of well-defined territories.

Technically, many Late Period Northwest Coast societies can be defined as chiefdoms, chiefdoms that were dominated by powerful clan leaders, very often individuals with exceptional entrepreneurial and leadership powers. (Another classification terms them "Big Men" polities (Johnson and Earle, 1987).) Their authority and power depended on their ability to attract followers and to retain their loyalty, through their control, acquisition, and redistribution of resources. It may be that the emergence of complex hunter-gatherer societies on the Northwest Coast depended to a considerable degree not only on the careful management of fluctuating food resources, but on the proper training of the elite individuals who inherited the rights to control particular territories. Unfortunately, it is almost impossible to trace the emergence of social ranking in the archaeological record of the Northwest Coast, but there are some hints of its existence as early as 1000 BC at the Hoko "wet/dry" settlement. There, Croes (1995) found remains of conical basketry hats with both distinctive knob-shaped and flat tops. At the Ozette site and in historical Makah Indian society, commoners wore flat-topped hats, while the higher-ranking owners of family territory had knob-topped forms. He believes that similar hat styles and rank differentiation were in use 2500 to 3000 years earlier, in the Middle Period.

Late Period: Links to Historic Peoples

There is strong evidence of cultural continuity throughout the entire Northwest Coast from Alaska to extreme northern California over a long period of time. Nineteenth-century ethnographies and historical accounts tell of the great diversity of Northwest Coast culture at European contact and beyond (Boas, 1905-1909, among others), but it is a great mistake to assume that the same cultural patterns remained unchanged in earlier centuries and millennia. The first appearance of historic cultures and groups in the archaeological record is hard to document, largely because of poor preservation conditions at many sites.

At European contact in the late 18th century, the northern Northwest Coast supported some of the most socially complex hunter-gatherers along the Pacific coast (Ames and Maschner, 1999). At least 43,500 Tlingit, Tsimshian, and Haida lived along this indented coastline of deep inlets and offshore islands, from southeast Alaska to the Queen Charlotte Islands and the Prince Rupert area of the British Columbia mainland. Many Late Period fishing and sea-mammal hunting sites are known from these shores (Maschner, 1991; Moss, Erlandson, and Stuckenrath, 1989). There is abundant evidence for volatile cultural change and elaboration over the past 3000 years, processes at first accelerated, then drastically interrupted, by European contact – by Russians in 1741, by Spaniards in 1774, and by Captain James Cook four years later.

Some archaeological sites along the central and southern Northwest Coast document historic cultures during earlier times. For example, the Middle Period Marpole culture of southern Vancouver Island, also the San Juan and Gulf Islands, developed from earlier, Locarno Beach roots about 400 BC and flourished until about AD 400 (Matson and Coupland, 1995). By this time there are clear signs of differing social status, both in the value and amount of grave goods and in the presence of skull deformation, a characteristic of socially prominent birth on the Northwest Coast. Marpole art traditions and antler and bone artifacts are quite distinct from those of the Coast Salish, the people living in the area at European contact. Salish culture can be traced back to at least AD 1200, a culture that relied heavily on bone artifacts, and used side-notched arrowheads, probably introduced from the interior plateau to the east. Despite the major differences between Marpole and Salish, most authorities believe that the one developed into the other during the 1st millennium AD.

Nootka-speaking peoples flourished along the shores of the Strait of Juan de Fuca, and on the west coast of Vancouver Island. Basketry styles from Hoko River reflect 3000 years of Nootkan style (Croes, 1995). The Yuquot site at Friendly Cove on Vancouver island documents a basic continuity of Nootka sea-mammal and fishing culture from historic times right back into the Middle Period (Dewhirst, 1980).

Whaling became more important during the Late Period, as it was at the famous Ozette site on the Pacific coast south of Cape Flattery, perhaps the most important sea-mammal hunting site for thousands of miles along the West Coast. Ozette lay at the back of a protected beach on the Pacific, an ideal place to hunt whales, fur seals, dolphins, and other deep-water fish, with plant foods, shellfish, and shallow fishing grounds close by. One late spring night about AD 1750, a massive mud slide cascaded over the village, smashing and burying at least four houses (Kirk, 1975). Preservation conditions under the mud are such that even fragile organic finds such as barkcloth, hide, and netting were preserved, giving a remarkably complete picture of Late Period culture at Ozette before European contact. Hundreds of fish hooks for cod and halibut, pieces of harpoons and whaling kit come from the Ozette houses, one of the most important archaeological sites in North America, and one where ancient Northwest life is being reconstructed in great detail (Samuels, 1991).

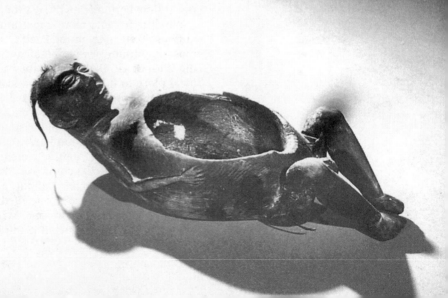

(Opposite) Ozette, Washington. (Top right) Carved panel depicting Thunderbird and Wolf found in a broken state on the floor of a house. (Top left) Carved detail of a whale-bone club. (Bottom right) Oil dish in the shape of a human figure. (Bottom left) This club was probably used for killing seals after harpooning.

(Right) Ozette, Washington. Carved cedar representation of a portion of a whale's back, including the closed fin. One surface is decorated with more than 700 sea otter teeth. This object was probably used in whale-hunting ceremonies, and is unique in the archaeological record, although Cook recorded one on his voyage. Length c. 1 m long.

Ozette art and artifacts show connections with that of other Nootka-speaking peoples, and with people living to the south, with Salish culture on Puget Sound. The decorated objects include wooden boxes, clubs, whale harpoons, bows, and a magnificent whale fin adorned with a mythical thunderbird outlined in sea otter teeth. The motifs are lively, mainly zoomorphic and anthropomorphic, with many complex geometric patterns that were reproduced on materials as diverse as bone and basketry.

The Interior Plateau
8500 BC to modern times

Before traveling south along the California coast, we must describe the hunter-gatherer societies of the northwestern interior, which interacted intensively with coastal communities in later prehistory, and probably in earlier times as well. The roots of these interior societies lie back in Paleo-Indian times.

The interior Plateau lies between the Pacific coast and the Great Basin and is bisected by two major rivers: the Columbia in the sagebrush grasslands of the southern Plateau and the Fraser in the more wooded north. In historic times, the northern Plateau was occupied by Salish-speaking peoples, whose languages were related to those of the southern Northwest Coast. Penutian-speakers dwelt along the middle and upper Columbia River, long-term residents with linguistic relatives living along the coast south of the Columbia.

The earliest traces of human occupation on the Columbia Plateau come from riverine or lakeside environments, where people once camped in rockshelters on river terraces. A few fluted Clovis points have come from the Snake River plain, and the Puget Sound lowlands in undated contexts. The Charlie Lake Cave near Fort St John, British Columbia, contains an occupation deposit with a fluted point dating to about 8500 BC, associated with an extinct form of bison (Fladmark, 1986). The well-known Clovis site at Wenatchee, Washington, is the best evidence in the interior.

A "Windust" phase is known from the Marmes Rockshelter and Windust Caves on the Lower Snake River, from the Hatenai site on the Clearwater River. Windust sites were occupied by small-scale, highly mobile foragers and the phase dates to between about 10,600 and 7100 BC. Leaf-shaped projectile points and knives come from levels dating to between 8500 and 5500 BC at Lind Coulee in east-central Washington (Aikens, 1983; Ames, 1988). These people hunted a variety of game including deer and elk, also subsisting off fish and plant foods, and traded sea shells from the Pacific coast. Here, as elsewhere, changes in hunting tackle are marked by variations in projectile-point forms (Ames and Maschner, 1999). Judging from the large numbers of milling stones, gathering was of vital importance to Windust groups. The Paulina Lake site in central Oregon has yielded a small oval Windust structure dating to *c.* 7600 to 7100 BC, the earliest known dwelling in the Northwest (Connelly, 1998).

During Paleo-Indian times, the climate was cooler and moister than today, with the Altithermal bringing warmer and drier conditions after 6000 BC. The effect of warmer temperatures was to reduce pine forest cover, as grassland and shrub-steppe covered much of the semi-arid landscape. The Cascade phase along the Snake River lasted from about *c.* 7100 to *c.* 4300 BC, perhaps a millennium later, marked by a toolkit little changed from Windust times. Pithouses appear in about 4300 BC, at which times Ames argues for a greater concentration on plant foods (Ames, 1991b). Most people appear to have lived in small, nomadic groups, foraging over large territories based on major rivers. In historic times, salmon and plant foods were the staples of Plateau diet. For a long time, it was assumed fishing was a late development, for there were few signs of large winter villages along major rivers. In fact, such evidence, in the form of pithouses, may have been destroyed by the floods which periodically swept down the major rivers. So Cascade groups may have harvested salmon runs in summer and fall. Along the Lower Snake, we know fishing increased after 3000 BC, and winter villages of substantial, semi-subterranean pithouses appear along the Snake River. Salmon runs assumed great importance after 1500 BC and during the "Harder" phase (500 BC to *c.* AD 1000), when people lived in earthlodge villages which can be linked to the historic Nez Perce peoples of the region.

Fishing has a long history elsewhere on the Plateau. The Dalles of the Columbia River are long, rapids-choked narrows at a natural boundary between the Plateau and the coast, an extremely productive salmon fishery in historic times and for many thousands of years before that. Clovis points have been found at Wenatchee to the north (Chapter 4), while sites at Five-Mile Rapids on the Oregon side of the river document human occupation since 8000 BC (Cressman and others, 1960). Judging from the number of salmon bones, local groups were exploiting salmon runs up the narrows

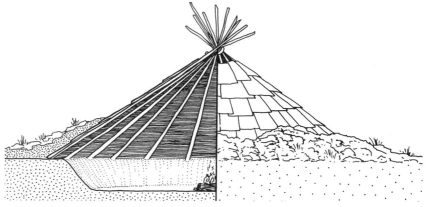

(Above left) Reconstruction of a Thompson Indian pithouse from British Columbia. (Above right) Reconstruction of a Harder phase (500 BC to c. AD 1000) pithouse.

with great efficiency as early as 5800 BC. Pithouse settlements flourished near the mouth of the John Day River by 3000 BC. Along both the Columbia and the Snake rivers, the frequency and size of pithouse settlements increased over the centuries.

Along the Fraser River in British Columbia, hunter-gatherer groups were catching salmon as part of a generalized foraging pattern at the Drynoch site as early as 5100 BC. The Milliken site, lower down the river, lies near rapids and was occupied by salmon fishermen as early as 7000 BC. By 3500 to 2500 BC, fishing assumed greater importance, as it did during the Middle Period on the British Columbia coast (Fladmark, 1985). As the Late Period dawned in about 2500 BC, the pithouse appeared, used as a winter dwelling. These were substantial, well-insulated circular houses dug about 5 ft (1.5 m) into the ground, with a diameter of 30 ft (9 m). Four sloping rafters supported a roof of logs, poles, and bark, covered with earth and sod, with a smoke hole at the top which also served as the entrance. Knut Fladmark believes such pithouses spread northward from the Columbia Plateau and

Reconstruction of a typical Columbia Plateau village.

northern California, where they date to as early as 3000 BC. As in the south, the number of pithouses and pithouse settlements increased dramatically in late times, some of them reaching a considerable size, as much as 60 ft (20 m) across. Some of the larger structures may have been dwellings for higher-status families.

The best British Columbia fisheries lay along short stretches of narrows, near rapids, and in canyons, where the people took thousands of salmon in summer and fall. As the men speared and netted salmon, the women gutted and dried the catch, storing dried fish in bark-lined pits as much as 6 ft (2 m) deep. Salmon stored in such pits could be eaten up to a year later. As fishing increased in importance, the fishermen developed more specialized barbed fish spears and composite toggling harpoons, as well as a wide variety of ingenious nets and weirs. Other foods were not neglected. Many interior groups used pits to roast enormous quantities of wild onions, balsam roots, and other tubers. Bows and arrows came into use by 500 BC.

During the Late Period, the coast and interior were linked by complex trade networks, which brought sea shells far inland, even Great Basin and Southwestern turquoise from the south. Eulachon (fish) grease was exchanged for hides, slaves for exotic raw materials. Art objects like wooden masks used to proclaim rank and status moved from the coast to the interior, as some individuals and families acquired greater wealth and political power (Hayden and Schulting, 1997). As in other parts of North America, strategic locations like the Dalles on the Lower Columbia or the mouth of the Nass River on British Columbia's North Coast were the sites of regular trade fairs in historic times, which brought widely separated groups together to trade and exchange information. We can assume such gatherings began much earlier, contributing to the distribution of new ideas over wide areas.

Further inland, salmon runs are less bountiful. Far upstream on the Snake River in southern Idaho, salmon were not the dietary staple they were much lower downstream. The local people had to rely on more meager, widely scattered food resources in an increasingly arid environment with strong ecological resemblances to the northern Great Basin. The archaeological record includes not only plant-processing equipment, but angular side-notched, corner-notched, and stemmed projectile points, all forms found throughout the Great Basin. These are not necessarily a sign of migration between the Great Basin and the Plateau, for similar point forms occur not only in these regions, but throughout the northern Rocky Mountains and on the northern Great Plains. As Melvin Aikens points out (1983), they are evidence of highly mobile hunter-gatherer populations, which were in regular contact with others living long distances away. As a result, artifacts, ideas, and geographical information were shared over an enormous area of the ancient west.

The California Coast: Diversification and Regional Specialization

The 1250 miles (2000 km) of the California coast encompassed extraordinary biophysical and cultural diversity during the Late Holocene – rugged, stormy coasts, placid, sandy beaches protected by kelp beds, offshore islands and deep bays and marshes. Natural upwelling off the southern California coast brought rich plankton supplies to the surface. Spanish explorers who first sailed these waters in the 16th century found themselves in one of the richest maritime environments on earth. Great schools of tuna and other deep-sea fish, myriad shoals of sardines and lesser species, regular whale migrations, and enormous herds of sea mammals frequented coastal waters. The Spaniards also encountered a great diversity of indigenous populations living along the Pacific coast, among the coastal mountains, and further inland. As late as 1769, when actual Spanish colonization began, some 300,000 Indians lived in what is now California, perhaps a greater number than in any area of comparable size anywhere in North America. But population densities varied greatly, from less than 0.5 person/sq. mile (0.20/sq. km) in inland desert areas to more than 10.4 people/sq. mile (3.85/sq. km) in the biologically rich Santa Barbara Channel region of southern California (Cook, 1976).

California's later cultures were remarkable for their intensive and often highly specialized hunting, gathering, and fishing activities. After 3000 to 2000 BC, the climate was essentially the same as today. The implements used on land and sea were basically the same all along what is now the Oregon and California coasts, with, however, major elaborations and local variations, depending on specific environmental challenges and needs. Acorn crops were important everywhere, on the coast and in the interior. Shellfish played a major role in the San Francisco Bay area, while the peoples of the Santa Barbara Channel region and further south exploited not only mollusks but sea mammals and shallow-water sea fish. The intensive exploitation of acorns and marine resources coincided with a great elaboration of technology, art, and social organization in some areas, especially in the Santa Barbara Channel and the San Francisco Bay–Sacramento–San Joaquin Delta regions. The people also developed complex social mechanisms to regulate long-distance exchange and the redistribution of resources – political alliances, kin ties and ritual obligations, and formal banking of resources among them. Intricate coastal and riverine adaptations gave rise to societies that reached the effective limits of social complexity without adopting agriculture. They were still flourishing in constantly changing forms along the Pacific coast at the time of European contact.

How, then, can we explain this increasing complexity in coastal foraging societies? Most modern research is based on increasingly complete data on ancient climatic change, which paints a picture of a coastline affected by constant and often severe drought cycles, with dramatic short-term fluctuations in rainfall and sea-water temperatures over the past 5000 years. Some of these changes are linked with the celebrated El Niño condition, which regularly brings warmer sea temperatures and violent storms to the California coast. Others represent the kinds of short- and long-term drought cycles which affect the California climate to this day. The California coast was a high-risk environment, where rainfall and ocean temperature changes caused major fluctuations in food supplies from one year to the next. Thus, current explanations of complexity revolve not around bounty, but around responses to environmental and cultural stress.

In a landmark study, William Hillebrandt and Terry Jones (1992) argued that earlier human societies along the California and Oregon coast encountered easily accessible abundant sea-lion and fur-seal rookeries. These breeding colonies vanished rapidly, leaving everywhere except offshore islands devoid of resident sea-mammal populations. As a result, the coastal people of most of northern and central California and the extreme south near San Diego lived off terrestrial resources and never developed sedentary settlements. In contrast, the groups residing near off-shore rocks or islands in northwestern California and the Santa Barbara Channel region developed watercraft between AD 700 and 900 and intensified their exploitation of offshore marine mammal populations. Such were the communication difficulties that they never eliminated entire colonies. Sedentary villages developed in these areas, where dried fish and acorn stores became vitally important. The cost of building canoes was so high, Hillebrandt and Jones argue, that wealthy headmen were the only individuals who could pay for boats, and thus controlled the resources obtained from the canoes, a development that led to greater social complexity. It is also known that sea otter-hunting and fishing increased dramatically during the later Holocene in many coastal locations. To what extent this trend affected culture change is debated (Colten and Arnold, 1998), but striking similar shifts in subsistence patterns occur in late sites in the San Francisco Bay and Sacramento Delta, where large mammals and anadromous fish give way to small species and, increasingly, mollusks, at a time when the human population was still rising (Broughton, 1994a, b, 1997). He sees people responding to stress by widening the kinds of foods they foraged and obtaining them with reduced efficiency as rising populations depleted edible resources of all kinds over many generations.

Generations of scholars have known that fishing intensified greatly after the Middle Holocene. Until now, they have tended to assume this was because of "rich" fisheries. In fact, the shift to more intensive fishing came about because this was the only major subsistence activity that could be intensified with greater labor investment (Raab and others, 1995). However much effort went into the foraging, large sea mammals and shellfish could produce no more.

Mark Basgall (1987) conducted a study on acorn use in the southern Coast Ranges, which bears on the reduced efficiency hypothesis. Acorns, he notes, were an important food because they were highly productive and nutritious, with good storage qualities for the winter months. But they required milling and leaching, both processes that require long hours of preparation. In many western societies, acorns were a low-priority food, because of the high energy costs involved in preparing them. Thus, argues Basgall, people exploited them intensively only when a significant imbalance between food demand and food supply arose. Acorn consumption rose dramatically in California after about 2000 years ago, prompting Basgall to attribute this sudden interest in a hard-to-process food to shortages in other resources caused by rising populations. By focusing on acorns, people exploited smaller territories, moved around less, and claimed specific territories, all behaviors which could lead to greater organizational complexity in local societies. In the same vein, Terry Jones (1996) has drawn attention to the marked division of labor in historic California societies. He believes this resulted from the increased labor demands imposed by widening dietary breadth caused by intensification of the food quest.

Much recent research no longer supports the classic notion that California coastal societies evolved slowly and progressively over long periods of time. In other words, the greater complexity and sedentism of some coastal societies may be the result of unpredictable climatic shifts and resource depletion.

Evolutionary Ecology and Optimal Foraging

The latest generation of California hunter-gatherer research is making constructive use of evolutionary ecology and optimal foraging strategy. The unified, uniformitarian theoretical perspective of evolutionary ecology is based on the proposition that variation in the behavior of individual organisms is shaped by natural selection (Broughton and O'Connell, 1998). Thus, it identifies a single goal, the maximization of potential reproductive success, toward which all behavior is directed and in terms of which it can be predicted.

Evolutionary ecology does not require rational choice on the part of its subjects, nor does it deny the existence of intentional behavior. All it assumes is that natural selection has designed organisms (including people) to behave in ways that tend to enhance fitness. In other words, the process of selection will tend to favor the best strategy among various alternatives available at the time. Evolutionary ecology has the advantage of being comprehensive, so that it can generate predictions about any aspect of fitness-related behavior. At the same time, it allows integration and provides a basis for predicting linkages between variation in one aspect of behavior with that in others. Above all, evolutionary ecology's predictions are testable.

Most evolutionary ecology in archaeology has been applied to settlement and subsistence, using optimal foraging models. Optimal foraging strategy is a theoretical model that argues that the most efficient foraging strategies that will be adopted by human groups are those that produce the greatest return in energy relative to time and effort expended (Bettinger, 1991; Kelly, 1995). From the archaeological perspective, optimal foraging theory assumes that, under certain well-defined circumstances, human decisions are made to maximize the net rate of energy gain. These decisions can revolve around diet or breadth of diet, around where to forage, the amount of time spent on different activities, or on settlement location or group size. The hunter-gatherer would logically not choose to pass over a higher ranked resource to exploit one with fewer benefits – there is no benefit in doing so. Therein lies the nub of optimal foraging theory – the implication that the hunter-gatherer uses all higher-ranked resources when available.

This is fine in a world where everything is infinitely abundant. In practice, resources vary greatly in distribution and abundance, and, thus, in the time needed to search for them. A new twist to optimal foraging theory now enters the picture. When a hunter in the Sacramento region hunted, say, a deer, a highly valued prey, he might have encountered a rabbit warren on the way, rabbits being the second- or third-highest ranked food resource on his mental list. He stopped and took six rabbits, and forgot about deer, deciding on a new course of action based on anticipated energy consumption and immediate food needs at the time he encountered the warren. In this case, exploitation of the food resource is independent of its abundance, what optimal foraging theorists call a "contingency model" (Bettinger, 1991). Such models are important, for they imply a basic reality that repeats itself again and again in North American archaeology: as food resources decline in abundance, the time required to search for them increases, and the breadth of the hunter-gatherer diet widens to compensate for this reality. Conversely, as resources become more abundant, so does selectivity increase.

In the case of California archaeology, a Prey Model has come into wide use, which assumes that foragers will try and maximize the net rate of energy capture. The model predicts that foragers will exploit the highest-ranked prey should they encounter it, whereas lower-ranked items move in and out of the diet as rates of foraging return rise and fall within an area.

As Mark Basgall's study has shown (1987), acorns offer a classic example of a resource that was extremely expensive to process relative to its caloric return, yet they assumed increasing importance to California foragers over the millennia and especially in late pre-Columbian times. This suggests that overall foraging return rates declined during the late Holocene as populations rose and food resources became harder to find, reflected by an increase in acorn exploitation. In many areas such as the Bay area, central and southern California, smaller terrestrial animals and acorns assume ever greater importance through time. It is probably no coincidence that the technology used for processing such foods as acorns and small animals became more sophisticated as time went on, reflecting a far greater energy expenditure on such activities, in environments where high-yielding prey were rare.

Climatic Change: The Medieval Warm Period

New, increasingly accurate paleotemperature curves for California over the past 8000 years show clearly that the coast was no paradise on earth. The curves draw on both deep-sea cores and on tree-rings, for the sediments of the Santa Barbara Channel provide exceptionally accurate information, with a resolution of less than a decade in many cases. An emerging marine paleotemperature model hypothesizes that sea temperatures were a major factor in the development of coastal societies, since water temperature exerts a powerful influence on the availability of fish, sea mammals, and other marine resources (Raab and others, 1995). For example, many miles of the California coast are edged by giant kelp beds, in which many species of fish, crustaceans, and sea mammals can be taken close inshore. Kelp forests are sensitive to warmer-than-average sea temperatures above 68° F (20° C) and can vanish or thin out during major El Niño events. Such thinning could have had a severe effect on nearby coastal populations (Arnold and Tissot, 1992), whereas cooler conditions would enhance marine productivity. Kelp beds may have responded to short-term temperature changes, but the sea-bed cores also suggest that ocean temperatures were warmer than today for more than 50 percent of the past 8000 years. In recent centuries, El Niño events with their warm water temperatures had the potential to disrupt vital coastal fisheries at a time of frequent droughts inland.

Sea-temperature variations in the Pacific stem from three causes: the short-term effects of winter and summer changes, periodic El Niño events of varying severity, and longer-term fluctuations measured in centuries. Clearly, the long-term temperature cycles had a pervasive influence on coastal human life – to measure these in our present state of knowledge is near-impossible. But the enhanced precision of sea-temperature and rainfall observations over the past 2000 years makes it easier to look at the effects of short-term change.

An important pollen sequence from San Joaquin Marsh at the head of Newport Bay in southern California records major rainfall shifts over the past 7000 years and long periods of aridity that settled over the west coast during the past 2,000 years. The driest and most prolonged dry cycle was between AD 200 and 1300, with extreme drought conditions between AD 1120 and 1300 also recorded from another location in the Transverse Ranges of Santa Barbara County. The later droughts coincide with the well-documented, global Medieval Warm Period, or climatic anomaly, which lasted from about AD 900 to 1350, a time of decreased rainfall, warm summer temperatures, and frequent natural brush fires over the west (Jones and others, 1999). Conditions were by no means uniform, but marked in some areas by prolonged droughts, in others by brief, intense dry spells, and even by years of unusually high rainfall. The main impact appears to have been on land, where terrestrial resources were decimated by long drought cycles – with inevitable effects on human populations.

The archaeological record of both the California and the interior as far east as the Great Basin and Colorado Plateau chronicles declining environmental productivity during the Medieval Warm Period, while human populations continued to rise (Jones and others, 1999). Throughout this enormous region, people responded to demographic stress and drought by moving to new areas and abandoning long-occupied homelands, changing ways of obtaining food and patterns of long-distance exchange, and by fighting with one another for territory and control of food resources. The stresses wrought by the drought conditions of the Medieval Warm Period and later unpredictable climatic shifts are clearly documented in California coastal populations of the day. The evidence leaves one in no doubt that frequent food shortages rather than plenty were the lot of recent coastal groups, however complex.

Culture History: Northern California

Any understanding of the later societies of northern California must take into account the linguistic history of the area. Not that this is an easy task, for California Indians spoke about 20 percent of the nearly 500 separate languages spoken in North America in the 15th century AD. There were 23 language families and isolated languages, making a total of some 90 languages that themselves formed innumerable dialects (Moratto, 1984). For our purposes, it is sufficient to assume that the Hokan and Penutian language stocks incorporate about 67 of the 90. Another, Uto-Aztecan, probably originated within California. Two others – Algic and Athabaskan – belong to stocks that are mostly distributed outside California. The Yukian stock is a mystery, unrelated as it is to any other group (Shipley, 1978).

Reconstructing culture history from language distributions is always a high-risk proposition. It is possible to draw some general conclusions. Hokan-speaking groups are commonly thought to be among the first settlers, partly because their languages show the greatest diversity and possible time depth. Before 4000 BC, the population of what is now California may have been almost entirely Hokan-speaking, except for the North Coast Ranges, where Yukian speakers lived (Moratto, 1984). There were considerable language shifts between 4000 and 2000 BC, especially among Uto-Aztecan groups in eastern California. In northern California Penutian speakers may have moved into the marshy lower Sacramento Valley from the Columbia Plateau or Great Basin in about 2500 BC, a movement often associated with the so-called Windmiller Pattern (see below). Utian-speaking peoples spread and diversified in later centuries, expanding westward into the Bay area with its swamps and marshes soon after 2000 BC, where they came into contact with earlier Hokan people. In time, two traditions emerged and intermingled, the one a primeval one associated with Hokan, the other associated with the Penutians. They were to survive for 4000 years (Gerow, 1968).

The later linguistic history of California is very complex, and beyond the scope of this book. The maps (below) summarize major language changes about 2000 BC–AD 1 and immediately before European contact. The reader is referred to Moratto's summary (1984) for an analysis.

The archaeology of northern California coastal areas is known mainly from shell middens, and from dense settlements in the Bay area and in the Sacramento Delta region. The outline sequence that follows is based on

Probable distributions of language groups in California:
(left) about 2000 BC to AD 1;
(right) about AD 1000 to 1769.

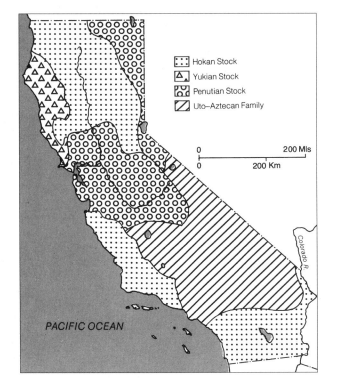

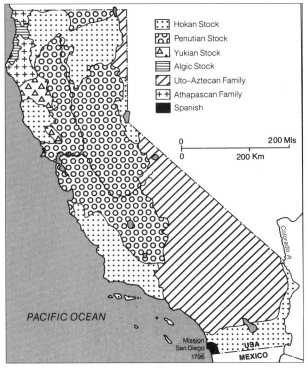

excavations at dozens of sites large and small. The North Coast is isolated and relatively mountainous, but it still came under influence from neighboring areas. The Yurok of the extreme northwest came under strong influence from the Northwest Coast peoples in Oregon and Washington, while groups living to the south were open to ideas and contacts from their California neighbors.

However, each local group had its own distinctive adaptation, with most of them forming what the great anthropologist Alfred Kroeber called "tribelets," small groups presided over by a local chief or headman, each with their own territory, often a local river drainage area. Each tribelet usually had a principal settlement, a ceremonial center, and several outlying camps used at different seasons of the year.

Each group followed its own subsistence strategy, exploiting rugged terrain that was deceptively rich in both predictable marine resources and more dispersed game and plant foods. Michael Moratto and other California archaeologists talk in terms of "searchers" for dispersed resources, and "pursuers" of more predictable resources like anadromous fish. The people would shift from searcher to pursuer mode depending on the season, a shift that could mean major changes in social organization as isolated tribelets came together, usually in the fall, and cooperated with others in catching, cleaning, smoking, and storing salmon, or when netting enormous numbers of smelt on the fringes of sandy beaches each fall. Come winter, most groups resided in winter villages, relying heavily on foods stored during the bountiful summer months. This general form of lifeway was followed throughout the North Coast region, albeit with considerable local variation, depending on the distribution of resources and environmental circumstances.

The Gunther Pattern (?150 BC to recent times) of the Humboldt Bay area and of the lower reaches of the Eel and Mad rivers was first identified from excavations at Gunther Island in Humboldt Bay. The artifacts from these excavations show strong influences from the Northwest Coast culture area to the north (Heizer and Elsasser, 1964). The Gunther Pattern is a specialized riverside and coastal adaptation that was brought into the area by ancestors of the Wiyot and Yurok peoples who lived there at European contact. Gunther sites with their distinctive barbed projectile points are concentrated along rivers like the Klamath and Trinity, also at strategic lagoons. The inhabitants relied heavily on seasonal salmon runs and other predictable marine resources, using mountainous areas for hunting and seasonal acorn harvesting. There are clear signs of long-distance trade in obsidian from sources at least 248 miles (400 km) away, and evidence for social ranking in Gunther cemeteries.

Further south, the Eel River region and the Russian River area are less mountainous, with some major rivers and large coastal lagoons, especially to the south. Here anadromous fish were less important and the people fanned out over the neighboring country in search of wild vegetable foods during the summers. With offshore marine-mammal rookeries, seasonal fishing, some mollusk collecting, and inland foraging, the different bands adjusted their annual rounds and settlement patterns to ever-changing distributions and availabilities of animals and plants. This was the area into which the Augustine Pattern spread about 1700

Gunther-Pattern barbed projectile point, length c. 3 cm.

years ago, a widespread culture in central California (see below) characterized by intensified hunting, fishing, and foraging, especially for acorns. A migration of Penutian-speaking Wintun peoples from the Sacramento Valley may have been a stimulus to the development of this Pattern (Fredrickson, 1973).

Culture History: San Francisco Bay and the Central Coast

Widespread, but scattered, populations of hunter-gatherers lived in this large region before 2000 BC. These sparse populations lived on the coast and in the mountainous interior, with both hunting and plant gathering being important elements in the diet. In contrast, coastal resources seem to have been less important.

Windmiller Pattern (before 2500 BC to 2000 BC and later). About 2500 BC, people well adapted to riverine and marshland environments settled in the Sacramento Delta region. It is thought that these Penutian speakers may have originated in the Columbia Plateau or western Great Basin, settling in a bountiful, low-lying region where their successors were to flourish for more than 4000 years.

The Windmiller economy was focused on hunting deer, pronghorn, and rabbits, also waterfowl. The people fished for sturgeon, salmon, and other fish with spears and nets and lines, as well as gathering storable plant foods such as the fall acorn harvest. Almost certainly many groups hunted in the nearby Sierras during the summer months. Delta groups acquired obsidian from Coast Range sources, and also from the eastern side of the Sierra. They traded coastal shells and ornaments from the Pacific, and obtained other exotic materials such as quartz crystals. Windmiller burials and cemeteries show evidence of considerable ceremonial, including the use of red ocher, with many bodies oriented toward the west (Fredrickson, 1973; Ragir, 1972).

The Windmiller Pattern spread widely in the Central Valley, also westward into the Bay area, forming the foundations of a cultural tradition that was to survive into recent times.

Windmiller Pattern of Sacramento Delta region. Left to right: large stone projectile point; charmstone of blue amphibolite schist; ground-slate pin.

Berkeley Pattern (c. 2000 BC to AD 300). Soon after 4000 years ago, new peoples moved into the Bay area, Utian-speaking peoples with a basically Windmiller culture. These were people adapted to estuaries, bays, and marshes with their diverse resources. This spread may have coincided with a great expansion of bayside and coastal marshlands, local environments that supported a fish and shellfish, large waterfowl populations, also game and many edible plant species (Bickel, 1978). By AD 1, numerous Berkeley Pattern villages flourished throughout the San Francisco Bay area, along the Central Coast, and in the Monterey Bay area, associated with exploitation of acorn and some shellfish collecting.

Judging from the larger site size, local populations were denser than in earlier millennia, but still egalitarian. Most people were buried with but a few utilitarian objects, except for occasional individuals associated with what are known from ethnographic records to be shamans' kits – bone whistles, quartz crystals, and charmstones (Fredrickson, 1973).

According to Tom King, the Bay region of 2000 BC to the Christian era offered a wide diversity of environments, everything from oak woodland to grassland and marshland. Many Berkeley Pattern settlements were sited to take full advantage of this diversity, often lying near freshwater streams and marshlands. By settling in such ecotones, the people could exploit both inland and bayshore locations. Tom King (1970) argues that the earliest settlements were located in these prime locations, places where there were few gaps in the annual "harvest" of different resources. Later, smaller camps were established in the interior, the result, he argues, of dense populations splitting off to form satellite communities in more marginal lands. Eventually, each major community was surrounded by peripheral settlements, to the point that its territory was circumscribed, redefining the relationships between them. They may have shared resources, exchanged them, or even competed in war. Whatever the vehicles of interaction, the result would have been more formal social and political relationships, with the emergence of important kin leaders and non-egalitarian political systems (King, 1974).

Augustine Pattern (c. AD 300 to recent times). Between AD 300 and 500, the Berkeley Pattern gradually evolved into the Augustine Pattern, a pattern associated not with major population movements but with technological innovations such as the bow and arrow, harpoons, tubular tobacco pipes and an unusual custom, that of burning artifacts in a grave before the body was interred (Fredrickson, 1973). These developments coincide with the Medieval Warm Period with its accompanying drought cycles. There were complex population movements from the interior toward the coast, perhaps as a result of people moving into more temperate zones where food could still be found (Jones and others, 1999).

Jack Broughton's studies of fish and other food resources in Bay area and Sacramento sites and shell middens chronicles a widening of the foraging quest and sharp declines in large mammals and anadromous fish, as people relied on ever-smaller prey. One factor may have been intensified human harvesting of acorns off oak trees. Deer forage for acorns once they have fallen to the ground, so deer populations may have suffered as a result of human competition for this resource. Under circumstances where environmental barriers and similarly high population densities nearby prevented groups from moving onto unexploited territories, their best option was to exploit intensively foods like acorns which were expensive to process on a large scale, through careful organization of the work. Such organization could have made for more complex societies in central, and, indeed, southern California in late times (Beaton,1991).

After AD 1400, the number of Augustine settlements proliferated dramatically, settlements fostered by kin leaders who maintained constant ties with neighboring communities. An elaborate ceremonial involving secret societies and cults came into being. Inter-community exchange assumed such importance that clam shell disk "money" came into widespread use. This increasingly more complex cultural system survived until European contact and beyond, to disintegrate in the face of inexorable Spanish missionary activity.

Culture History: Southern California Coast

"The natives are well appearing, of good disposition ... As to their government, it is by captaincies over villages ... They have cemeteries set apart for the burial of their dead. The god whom they adore, and to whom they offer their seeds, fruits, and all that they possess, is the sun ... Their houses, shaped like half-globes, are neatly built; each is capable of sheltering four or five families..." (Fages, 1972 [1775]).

The Santa Barbara Channel and other parts of the southern California coast supported exceptionally sophisticated hunter-gatherer societies at European contact (Erlandson and Colten, 1991). These groups maintained long-distance exchange networks that carried sea shells, soapstone, and other exotica as far into the interior as the Southwest (Erlandson, 1994). They faced stressful environmental conditions, including food shortages caused by intense human predation of individual fish species (Raab, 1996).

Chester King (1990) used distinctive shell bead forms found in dated graves in the Santa Barbara Channel area to reconstruct a cultural sequence for the mainland and offshore islands (illus. p. 246). He argued on the basis of changing bead styles that local culture evolved steadily over more than 7000 years. He recognized three periods, each with different phases and further subdivisions, which provide a widely used cultural framework (for a slightly different formulation, see Chartkoff and Chartkoff, 1984).

Early Period (before 6000 BC to c. 1000 BC). It was during the Early Period (already described) that the distinctive maritime adaptation in the Santa Barbara Channel area evolved. The direction of cultural change was toward increasing complexity.

Middle Period (c. 1000 BC to c. AD 1300). The trends of the Early Period toward more maritime exploitation accelerate over these two millennia. Changes in beads and ornaments reflect a new role for such artifacts in local society. Originally they served an ornamental function. Now they may have been used as status markers in society, often exchanged or as a form of storable wealth. Seals, porpoises, dolphins, whales, swordfish, and shark bones now occur in coastal middens as well as thousands of shellfish remains. Bones of deep-water fish show that much more sophisticated watercraft, including plank canoes, were used for offshore fishing.

A reconstruction by Travis Hudson and Peter Howorth of a plank canoe (tomol), used by both the Chumash and Gabrieleño groups for fishing, sea-mammal hunting, and transportation.

Late Period (c. AD 1300 to 1804). The society of the Hokan-speaking Chumash people of the Santa Barbara Channel region reflects a long history of constant environmental, cultural, and social change. Thanks to the remarkable anthropologist John Harrington, we know a great deal about the Chumash (Harrington, 1942; Hudson, T. and others, 1979; Landberg, 1965; Glassow, 1996). They exploited the marine environment intensively, as well as acorn groves inland. Spanish observers of the 18th and early 19th centuries reported that the Chumash peoples of the mainland and offshore islands were skilled navigators and expert fishermen, capable of navigating long distances over open water in their frameless, planked canoes about 25 ft (7.6 m) long paddled by three or four men (or more) with double-ended paddles (Hudson and others, 1978).

The mainland Chumash were described by one early Spanish missionary as "well formed and of good body, although not very corpulent." Neither men nor women wore many clothes. The men normally went naked except for a deerskin, bird feather, or fur cape in cold weather. The women wore knee-length, two-piece aprons of mule deerskin, or sea otter pelts. The Chumash made much use of body paint, the various designs serving to distinguish one group from another. They pierced their ears and wore necklaces of shell and stone.

Chumash villages consisted of well-built, dome-shaped dwellings made on a pole frame, settlements housing extended families of several dozen people. The occupants slept on sleeping platforms arranged in tiers along the walls, behind mats hung to give some privacy. Each village had one or two sweat houses and a nearby cemetery protected with a stockade, the graves marked with painted poles. Some Chumash settlements in the resource-rich Santa Barbara area housed as many as 1000 people and were centers for important ceremonies and trading activities. They served as

Chronological chart of shell bead types in southern California compiled by Chester King.

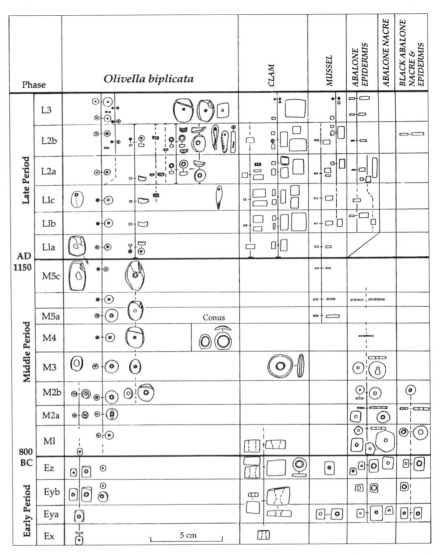

political "capitals" over several lesser villages, even small "provinces," loose political confederations of communities large and small (Hudson and Blackburn, 1983).

Each Chumash village was ruled by a hereditary chief (*wot*) and his assistant. *Wots* served as war leaders and patrons of ceremonial village feasts. Once during the fall and at the winter solstice, outlying communities near and far flocked to major settlements for rich ceremonies that honored the earth and the sun. Chumash villages and provinces were constantly quarreling with one another over food supplies and territory, often over resources at the edge of one another's territory. Disputes over wives, social insults to chiefs (such as not attending a feast), and blood feuds were commonplace.

The Chumash were artists, too, their petroglyphs and pictographs the most spectacular north of the Mexican border (Grant, 1965). Chumash

(Opposite above) Chumash rock art at the San Emigdio pictograph site and (right) Chumash baskets.

(Opposite below) Reconstruction of Chumash village life: Santa Barbara Museum of Natural History diorama.

shamans and specialists served as the artists, painting the walls of remote inland caves and rockshelters with abstract representations of the sun, stars, human beings, birds, fish, and reptiles. The meaning of the art is unknown, but at least some of it is connected with astronomical observances, and to a calendrical system. Some painted sites may have served as solstice observatories (Hudson, T. and Underhay, 1978; Hudson, T. and others, 1979).

Despite unpredictable droughts and El Niños, the Santa Barbara Channel coast with its diverse resources supported a relatively dense mainland and island population at European contact in the 16th century. Early Spanish records are vague on population estimates, but scholarly calculations place some 15,000 Chumash in the Santa Barbara-Ventura area, with the densest populations in the Santa Barbara region. The offshore islands were reached by a 17-mile (27.3-km) canoe ride and supported perhaps as many as 3000 people living in small fishing villages. The islanders traded shells and fish for plant foods and raw materials from the mainland.

Chumash groups maintained exchange contacts with other coastal communities to the south, also with peoples living far in the interior. The Gabrieleño occupied the Pacific coast areas now under the urban sprawl of Los Angeles and Orange County. They controlled valuable steatite outcrops on Catalina Island offshore, a soft stone ideal for making stone griddles and pots, which they traded widely. Further south, the Luiseño and nomadic bands of Diegueño peoples moved seasonally between coast and interior harvesting acorns, seeds, also shellfish and marine mammals, as well as fishing. The former's political organization was somewhat similar to that of the Chumash.

Complexity and Stress

King (1990) believed that cultural complexity resulted from powerful social processes, fueled by population growth and enhanced competition between neighboring groups living in a rich environment. He hypothesized that the Chumash lived in such a varied environment that shell money came into its own, creating what he calls a "monetized" economy, which was more efficient in evening out regional differences in food supplies from one year to the next. Thus, shell ornaments played a significant role in the growth of more complex societies along the coast. King downplayed the importance of climate change in the gradual evolution of Chumash culture.

King's hypothesis is challenged strongly by more recent workers, who believe that the Medieval Warm Period and major, and often short-term, climatic shifts such as El Niños played a vital role in triggering periods of rapid cultural change and more elaborate social institutions such as chiefdoms (Raab and Larson, 1997). Foragers' responses to environmental stress have been little studied, but those who rely heavily on the extensive exploitation of relatively few foods like nuts or acorns and store their harvests are highly vulnerable to longer-term drought cycles, such as those that descended on the west during the Medieval Warm Period. The well-documented response along the coast was to exploit a much wider range of marine habitats, to elaborate fishing and sea-mammal hunting technology, and to invest much greater amounts of labor in such activities. At the same time, coastal populations, like those elsewhere, were rising, with larger settlements, anchored to permanent water supplies and places where coastal fisheries produced relatively predictable food supplies. Meanwhile, territorial boundaries probably solidified, as more densely packed village populations resulted in higher incidences of disease and malnutrition. The increasing complexity of coastal populations may have resulted not from bounty, but from severe drought, movements of inland groups nearer more reliable food supplies at the coast, and from the necessity to maintain territorial boundaries and regulate food supplies and exchange. While some island settlements were abandoned in the face of drought, marine resources became increasingly important on the mainland. Jeanne Arnold argues (1992) that as food became scarce on the Channel Islands, the inhabitants relied on shell-bead manufacture and trade, controlled by a small elite as a way of alleviating food shortages. Changing burial patterns on the mainland suggest that religious leaders gave way to a new, hereditary nobility based on kin groups.

Dramatic evidence for demographic stress comes from human skeletons of the period. Biological anthropologist Phillip Walker (1986) has studied Channel Island skeletons during the drought period and believes that chronic anemia, manifested by a condition called cribra orbitalia, was caused by high nutrient losses resulting from food shortages. Thus, severe drought, chronic illness, and, above all, water shortages, may have caused widespread distress, the abandonment of many island settlements, and violence stemming from competition for scarce and dwindling water supplies.

Patricia Lambert and Walker (1991) have expanded this study to evaluate the skeletal evidence from ancient populations on a wider canvas. They drew on stable isotope analyses on human bone collagen in their studies of offshore island, coastal, and inland populations. They found the islanders relied heavily on marine foods, while the people living inland had isotopic values like those of deer, with the coastal people having readings intermediate between the two. At the same time, women on Santa Rosa Island offshore suffered from more severe dental caries than the men, presumably because they collected plant foods. But, as time passed the incidence of caries diminished, as if marine resources became all-important. The same shift to sea foods brought an increase in arthritis in both men and women, but a decrease in stress to womens' backs and knees as a result of less time spent on plant processing. As these changes took place, so the incidence of malnutrition, reflected in dental hypoplasia, increased in large, late mainland villages.

At the same time, especially after AD 500, when the bow and arrow arrived in California, wounds caused by projectile points increased dramatically until about 1150, when they declined again, for reasons which are not clear. Lambert and Walker believe that environmental change was an important cause of cultural adjustment, with major transitions in local culture coinciding with extended periods of warm sea-water temperatures when near-shore marine resources were much reduced. Tree-rings tell us that the last of these incidents, in about 1150, coincided with a severe drought. Cemeteries dating to such transition periods suggest they were times of cultural change, poor health, and violent conflict. Thus, periods of resource stress may have been powerful stimuli for social and political change, and perhaps for greater complexity.

A complex interplay between ocean temperatures, rainfall, and other environmental conditions, whether natural or humanly induced, was but one factor in an intricate equation that affected and changed the complexity of hunter-gatherer societies along the coast over more than 3000 years.

Further Reading

In addition to the sources at the end of the previous chapter:

Glassow, Michael A. 1996. *Purisimeño Chumash Prehistory*. Harcourt Brace, New York.
  A case study which includes much valuable background information on the Chumash and coastal adaptations.

Hudson, Travis, and Blackburn, Thomas. 1983. *The Material Culture of the Chumash Interaction Sphere*. Ballena Press, Socorro, California.
  The definitive account of Chumash material culture based on Harrington's notes and ethnographic collections.

King, Chester. 1990. *Evolution of the Chumash*. Garland, New York.
  A general account of the development of Chumash culture. Somewhat outdated.

Kirk, Ruth. 1975. *Hunters of the Whale*. Morrow, New York.
  A popular account of the Ozette site, which gives a wealth of information about this important Makah settlement.

Kroeber, Theodora. 1965. *Ishi in Two Worlds*. University of California Press, Berkeley.
  This classic tale of the last "wild" California Indian is a must for every student of California archaeology.

CHAPTER 12

THE GREAT BASIN AND WESTERN INTERIOR

The European immigrants of the 1850s and 1860s who penetrated the mountain fastnesses of the Rockies and moved beyond Utah's Wasatch Mountains into the Great Basin encountered only scattered bands of Indians west of the mountains. Here, small groups of Western Shoshone, Paiute, and Washoe roamed the land on foot. They lived by hunting small animals and foraging for desert roots and seeds, in a land of dramatic contrasts – high mountains and arid plains, deep canyons and occasional bountiful lakes, territory completely different from the Great Plains to the east (D'Azevado, 1986; Grayson, 1993). Mobility, flexibility, and detailed ecological knowledge – these were always the secrets of survival in the Great Basin from the earliest human settlement of this varied region before 10,000 BC.

The Great Basin Environment

The Great Basin comprises about 400,000 sq. miles (1,036,001 sq. km) of the west between the Rocky Mountains and the Sierra Nevada. A definition on hydrologic grounds commonly used by archaeologists includes nearly all of Nevada and parts of California, Oregon, Utah, and Idaho. This is a region of great environmental diversity, of high mountains and intervening valleys, with the loftiest peaks and deepest valleys in the south and west. Climate, vegetation, animals, and human populations display great variations with topography, the lower temperatures and higher rainfall totals occurring at high elevations. The lowest rainfall and severest evaporation is in the arid southwestern portions of the Basin, which support the sparsest vegetation. The mountains have somewhat wetter and more complex climatic regimens, with many ranges supporting relatively dense vegetation and lakes or ponds. Despite these variations, most of the Great Basin receives little rainfall, and, as in other areas of low precipitation, the amount varies dramatically from year to year. This means that the potential plant food supply can be as much as six times more plentiful in a wet year than in a dry (Hutchings and Stewart, 1953). As a result, the ancient and historic peoples of the Great Basin have always subsisted on a very broad range of food resources. To specialize in one particular resource is to invite disaster (Jennings, 1978). Throughout the past, there have been great variations in group size, group stability, and degree of sedentary

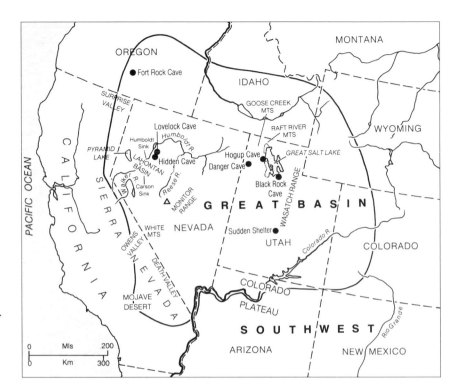

(Right) *The Great Basin showing sites and regions mentioned in the text.*

(Below) *Southwestern Great Basin, looking northwest from the Greenwater Range, Inyo County, California: a landscape of mesas and basins. The distant Funeral Mountains are tilted blocks of Paleozoic rocks.*

settlement, variations depending on the availability of food resources and the subsistence adaptations that developed to exploit them (Madsen, 1982).

None of the Great Basin drains to the sea, so over 150 more-or-less closed basins have developed over millions of years. During the Wisconsin glaciation, many of the basins were filled to overflowing by cool snow meltwater, joined by fish-rich rivers, and linked by green belts of vegetation (Mehringer, 1986). Woodlands grew where there is now treeless, arid steppe. Camels, wild horses, and mammoth grazed on open plains and on the fringes of great marshes. Between about 10,500 and 8600 BC, Early Holocene lakes shrank, many rivers dried up, and the lusher vegetation retreated northward and to high elevations. Most subsequent climatic shifts have been relatively minor.

The Great Basin became increasingly arid during the Middle Holocene, a time of rapid climatic fluctuations. Temperatures rose until about 4000 to 3000 BC, and drier conditions persisted until modern times. Not that climatic conditions were stable, for dramatic changes in local environments were possible even within the confines of a single year. The diverse environments of the Great Basin were dynamic and ever-changing, affecting human populations in many dramatic, cumulative ways. Everywhere, resource distribution was patchy, with highly productive areas separated from sparser environments. The environmental realities of the Basin resulted in constant population movements, basically conservative hunter-gatherer adaptations, and a broad, if varied, cultural continuum over wide areas. Some groups lived in exceptionally rich lake-side or marshy environments. They dwelt in larger, more sedentary camps for most of the year, perhaps enjoying more complex social organization. At the other end of the continuum were tiny family groups, constantly on the move, living off seasonal foods at widely separated locations. For all this variation, the same basic hunter-gatherer material culture remained in use throughout the Basin for thousands of years.

A viable, but generalized, model of Great Basin subsistence and settlement assumes such a continuum of human settlement, with differences in subsistence and settlement patterns being due to different optimal extraction strategies in areas of highly varied resource availability. David Madsen (1982) used this model to hypothesize that the earliest sites in the Basin were found in areas with the greatest concentration and productivity of resources, such as lake and riverine marshes. Relatively permanent settlements were primarily associated with such rich habitats. Following initial settlement, he believed there was population growth in productive environments, resulting in expansion into less productive environments.

Tree-ring studies from timber 2000 years or more old show that changing lake levels, beeline shifts, dune activity, and both earthquakes and volcanic eruptions could affect human populations in important ways. Game distributions would change, trade routes be cut off by deteriorating climate, vegetational cover be decimated by a sudden volcanic eruption. All of these, and many other local phenomena, made highly flexible and mobile adaptive strategies essential in all but the most favored of Great Basin environments.

Wherever ancient peoples lived in this vast area, they utilized a wide array of food resources. The utilization varied from region to region, and from millennium to millennium, as a result of local and more widespread climatic changes. For instance, the distribution of piñon pines changed drastically during the Holocene, and peoples' exploitation of these vital nuts fluctuated dramatically through time. Human groups settled in every kind of high and low altitude imaginable. Regional surveys have identified many complex settlement patterns. For instance, detailed archaeological surveys of the Raft River Mountains of northwestern Utah and the Goose Creek Mountains of northeastern Nevada investigated all manner of sites, everything from large caves to tiny open air camps (Wylie, 1971-72, quoted from Harper, 1986). Wylie found that no less than 82 percent of the sites investigated lay between 5000 and 7000 ft (1524 to 2133 m) above sea level, a diverse environment that supported sagebrush, juniper-piñon, and mountain brush. People seem to have avoided the hot and inhospitable deserts, where only 11 percent of their settlements were found. A further 7 percent lay above 7000 ft (2133 m), in high-altitude environments that were inaccessible much of the year. Most of the medicinal plants known to have been used by Indians and found in these sites came from the favored zone. Rigorous environments above and below the foothill zones of the Great Basin tended to concentrate much of the ancient population and game animals in areas where most forage was to be found, and where winters were relatively benign.

The foothill zones supported not only deer and other game, but the plant foods upon which the Great Basin people depended (Jennings, 1978). For thousands of years, the inhabitants used a variety of technologies for obtaining and processing plant foods of many kinds (Fowler, C., 1986). The seeds of nut pines, especially piñons, were much prized, especially in the central core areas of the Basin. During the early fall, the people used long poles to gather green cones by the thousand, carrying them to central processing stations in large baskets. They pit-roasted the cones until they opened and the seeds were partially released. Next, the foragers beat the pile of cones with sticks, or tapped individual cones against a flat anvil with a hammerstone. The extracted seeds were then given a preliminary parching in an open, fan-shaped tray, shelled with a flat grinding stone, and ground before being eaten in gruel form, mixed with hot or cold water.

Abundant piñon harvests were the rule in three-to-seven-year cycles, so the people stored thousands of cones in open pits under piles of stones, grass- or bark-lined pits, or skin bags. Stored in this way, cones could last four or five years. By the same token, piñon groves were so important a resource that many groups considered different groves family property. Acorns were gathered on the western, southern, and eastern fringes of the Basin, and were less important than piñons. Mesquite (*Prosopis juliflora*) and screwbean (*Prosopis pubescens*) are desert plants found in the Mojave and Sonoran deserts. Their fresh pods were taken in the spring and eaten raw as snacks. In late summer and fall the people gathered dried-up pods, placed them in large tree-stump mortars and ground them to a fine powder. The bean meal was dried thoroughly in baskets, where it formed large cones that could be stored in pits for long periods of time. Like piñons, mesquite bean meal was a staple for many Great Basin people.

Great Basin plant staples. (Top) Colorado piñon. (Center) Honey mesquite, Prosopis juliflora, *with fruit. (Bottom) Mature pods of the screwbean,* Prosopis pubescens.

Agave (*Agave utahensis*) are natives of the hot southern deserts of the southern Great Basin and the Southwest. The plants were harvested in spring just before they flowered and the leaves baked in a communal pit for 24 hours. The sweet, dark mass of agave was then pounded into large, flat cakes that were used to flavor meat and vegetable stews.

Perhaps the most vital artifacts in the Great Basin were the wooden digging stick, the flat *metate* or grinding stone and the small stone muller. These simple artifacts enabled people to process an enormous range of seeds, plants, and tubers with the simplest of technologies. The people would harvest stands of grasses by knocking the seeds into baskets or gathering them by hand. Hardwood digging sticks assumed great importance when harvesting root crops, especially in the northern Basin, where biscuit roots (*Lomatium* spp), yampa (*Perideridia*), and other tubers were abundant in spring. Berries and other fruit were important crops wherever they were found, sometimes gathered by the women with special chest-mounted baskets. Most berries were sun dried and stored in pits and bags. Many plants had not only food value but important medicinal uses as well.

Below the foothill zones, river banks, marshes, and lakes acted as magnets for human settlement, offering a great diversity of food resources. People camped near the water for much of the year, except, perhaps, during summer when mosquitoes and other insects are a plague. Such areas were highly localized, but were always of the greatest importance to communities residing in their vicinity. Marshes were especially productive, not only because of their plant foods, but for their diverse game populations.

Hopi man from the Southwest using a digging stick, c. 1915. Similar forms of artifact were used for excavating wild tubers for thousands of years in the Great Basin.

Elsewhere in the Great Basin game is rarely seen, for the animal species of the deserts and mountains tend to be solitary and secretive, and invisible to anyone but an expert tracker. But the marshes abound in wildlife. In spring, a visit to any large Great Basin marsh means a "sky likely to be full of raucous birds representing as many as 40 species with each individual intent on intimidating and expelling the intruder from the nesting ground" (Harper, 1986). Areas like the Humboldt-Carson Sink in Nevada have been major breeding and nesting grounds for waterfowl for thousands of years. It is no coincidence that some of the Great Basin's major archaeological sites are found near such marshes.

Bird hunting was most common in marshy areas where major north–south flyways for migrating waterfowl passed. Both land and water birds were taken with nets suspended on sticks, or driven into netting tunnels. The hunters often used blinds to shoot birds, luring waterfowl with finely made tule reed decoys. Some expert fowlers swam up to their prey wearing a duckskin helmet or a mound of reeds. They would then grab the unsuspecting bird by the legs. Not only waterfowl, but a diverse mammal fauna lived in the same marshes. Muskrats, rabbits, and many other rodents abounded. Grasses, wild vegetables and many rhizomes were harvested at the marsh margins in spring and fall, while tule reeds (*Scirpus acutus*) made fine mats, and other plants such as dogbane and milkweed provided ideal fibers for cords and basketry.

The forests and meadows at higher elevations were attractive hunting grounds with deer, pronghorns, and bighorn sheep in summer, as well as yielding harvests of gooseberries, strawberries, and other plant foods. The hunters used many techniques, sometimes stalking their prey in skin disguises, using snares and traps, and with cooperative game drives.

Throughout the Great Basin, ancient people fished in lakes and rivers, large and small. Along the Snake and Truckee rivers, for example, the fishermen built platforms out from the bank to fish with dip nets or spear their catch. Large gill nets harvested trout, chub, and other species in shallow waters, while basket traps and rock or brush dams were effective in many situations. Sometimes, women would even scoop fish from still water with shallow baskets.

With such a diversity of environments and altitudes, it is difficult to generalize about Great Basin hunter-gatherer diet in ancient times. The lake- and river-side peoples of Pyramid Lake and Walker River in Nevada may have obtained as much as 50 percent of their diet from fish, and a further 20 percent from large and small game, with the balance coming from wild plant sources. In contrast, the inhabitants of the Owens Valley region of the Sierra Nevada relied on wild plants for over half their food, the rest being game meat, with fishing accounting for but 10 percent. Whatever the Great Basin environment, wild plant foods provided a significant, and often the dominant, part of the diet. These were foods that tended to be low in protein, elements that had to be obtained from meat or fish. Such a diet makes the carbohydrates from plant foods of much greater importance than usual. Perhaps it is significant that pine nuts were a staple over so much of the Basin, for they are a valuable protein source, also exceptionally high in both fats and carbohydrates.

In such a diverse series of environments, where food resources are both patchy, and subject to cycles of plenty and scarcity, it is hardly surprising that the historic Great Basin peoples deliberately "managed" parts of their environment to increase its productivity and to conserve precious resources. Many groups burned the natural vegetation to increase natural yields of such plants as tobacco and a variety of seed-bearing grasses. Burning also served to increase available fodder for deer and other game, as well as helping drive prey toward waiting hunters. In historic times, several Great Basin groups such as the Shoshone not only burned the natural vegetation but scattered wild seeds as well.

Throughout most of the Great Basin the native Americans remained hunter-gatherers throughout ancient times, essentially preserving the Archaic lifeway right up to European contact in the 17th century AD. This general hunter-gatherer adaptation lasted for at least 10,000 years, from Early Archaic times onward. Even where agricultural economies did take hold, people still relied heavily on game and wild vegetable foods. However, as David Madsen (1982) and other authors have pointed out, it is a mistake to use the historic inhabitants of the Great Basin as ethnographic blueprints for interpreting earlier cultures. Their adaptations were another example of the highly flexible, opportunistic way in which humans adapted to one of the most diverse environments in North America.

Conceptual Frameworks

For years, the Great Basin was regarded as peripheral to adjacent areas like California and the Southwest (Condie and Fowler, 1986; Fowler, D. and Jennings, 1982). Since there were some Southwestern traits to be found in the Great Basin, the area was considered tangential to mainstream cultural developments elsewhere. The advent of radiocarbon dating showed conclusively that many Southwestern traditions were derived from much earlier cultures, some of which occurred in the Great Basin, a quite independent culture area in its own right.

Jesse Jennings excavated the deep deposits of Danger Cave in Utah and used the long sequence of human occupation there to offer a new interpretation of the Great Basin past based on anthropologist Julian Steward's theory that ecological factors regulated population densities, local subsistence economies, and patterns of social organization in the region. Jennings formulated the concept of a Desert Culture that persisted for thousands of years, a culture whose behavior could be interpreted by using the general patterns of pre-European behavior proposed by Steward's pioneer work on Numic speakers in the Basin (Jennings and Norbeck, 1955; Jennings, 1957; Steward, 1938).

The Desert Culture was a valuable idea, for it triggered a great deal of detailed local research, but the concept came under attack from several directions. Some people argued that the Danger Cave sequence was too incomplete for such generalizations, that Jennings had ignored local variations. Furthermore, the Jennings model assumed that climatic change had been relatively uniform over large distances and over long periods of times, something that many archaeologists found it hard to accept (Fowler, D. and Jennings, 1982). Eventually, the concept was abandoned, even by Jennings himself, being transformed into the Desert (or Western) Archaic.

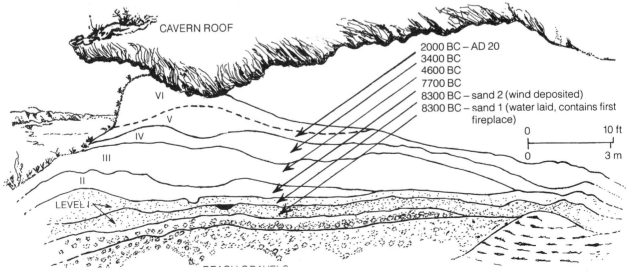

CAVERN ROOF

2000 BC – AD 20
3400 BC
4600 BC
7700 BC
8300 BC – sand 2 (wind deposited)
8300 BC – sand 1 (water laid, contains first
fireplace)

0   10 ft
0   3 m

VI
V
IV
III
II
LEVEL I

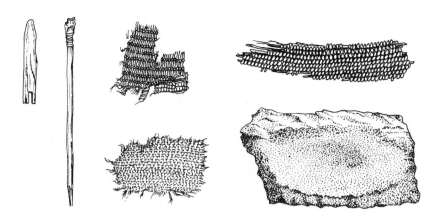

Danger Cave, Utah. (Opposite) General view and stratigraphic profile of the cave with estimated dates of layers extrapolated from radiocarbon from three laboratories. (Right) Clockwise from top left: wooden knife handle; arrowshaft with broken projectile in place; twined matting; coiled basketry; milling stone; coarse cloth. (Below) Gaming sticks, the longest 27 cm in length.

In recent years, research has shifted away from single sites to an approach focused on overall settlement-subsistence systems within individual valleys, watersheds, or sub-areas. A large site like Danger Cave or Hogup Cave in Utah (illus. pp. 260–261), or Lovelock Cave in Nevada, may contain long sequences of ancient occupation, but the archaeological record in their deposits only represents a single stop in a complicated annual round of hunting and foraging. This approach has been highly productive in such areas as the Reese River Valley, Nevada (Thomas and Bettinger, 1976), in the Monitor Valley (Thomas, 1983), and in the Surprise Valley, California (O'Connell, 1975). It has led to models that stress the basic continuum among ancient Great Basin societies, from small, family-based hunter-gatherer groups to much larger, more sedentary societies, perhaps with more complex social organization, that flourished in resource-rich areas (Madsen, 1982).

A new generation of hunter-gatherer research has turned to evolutionary ecology for models of changing Great Basin settlement and subsistence (Broughton and O'Connell, 1998). Such approaches, discussed in Chapter 11, combine behavioral ecology with optimal foraging models and have proved illuminating both in California and in the Great Basin (Janetski, 1999; O'Connell, 1995). For example, seeds were added to Great Basin diet after 6500 BC, a dietary change that is widely agreed to be connected with Early Holocene climatic change. The mechanisms of the change-over are poorly understood. The optimal foraging model argues that resources can be ranked according to the ratio of gains made from consuming them (in calories) relative to the cost of collecting and processing them (measured in time). The proportions of resources exploited vary according to the abundance of the highest-ranked ones. In the Great Basin, the extinction of Ice Age big-game, a high-ranked resource, may have led to the addition of more seeds to the diet, probably lower-ranked food than game meat.

Research using evolutionary ecology is in its early stages, but such an approach may be peculiarly suitable for Great Basin conditions, where arid environments often preserve a wide range of ancient food remains. With such complete preservation, optimal foraging strategy models may offer a way of making specific predictions about continuity and change

Hogup Cave, Utah. (Above)
Excavations in progress. (Right)
Incised stones; the significance of the
incised patterns is unknown.

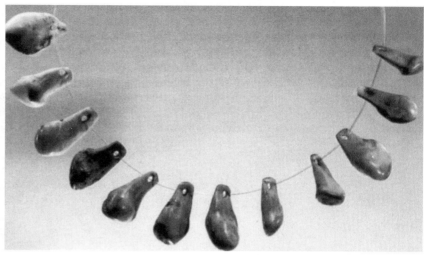

*Hogup Cave, Utah. (Above)
Anthropomorphic figurines. (Above
right) Elk-tooth necklace.*

in Great Basin subsistence economies, integrating population densities, resource abundance, and technology. The same models may enable the archaeologist to identify precise information to test them in the field, information on resource ranking obtained from ethnographic information, historical records, or from experimentation with traditional tools and techniques. Once these rankings are developed, one can then try and trace their relative importance over long periods of time.

The description of the Great Basin past that follows reflects not only these new approaches, but the broad culture-historical framework that has been developed over generations of field research. As is the case in other parts of North America, this framework is based on stone artifact typologies, often projectile points (Table 12.1; Thomas, 1981; Beck, 1995).

Unfortunately, there is such diversity of ancient populations in the Great Basin that it is impossible to construct a chronological framework that brings together neatly cultural connections across the desert west. Some scholars even argue that local adaptations are so diverse that it is pointless even to try. In the interests of convenience and clarity, we have superimposed four general periods across the Great Basin (Jennings, 1986, 1987). (For more detailed regional descriptions, see Madsen and O'Connell, 1982.)

Paleo-Indian
before 11,500 to 7000 BC

The first human settlement of the Great Basin dates to about 11,500 BC [cal], but the exact date is uncertain (Chapters 4 and 5) (summary in Beck and Jones, 1997). Population densities remained extremely sparse for thousands of years, with most Paleo-Indian settlement centered around lakes and along river banks where game was more abundant. Judging from fossil finds in caves and rockshelters, wild horses, camels, bison, mammoth, and other species flourished in the Basin. As elsewhere, they became extinct by about 10,000 BC [cal] (Grayson, 1993).

TABLE 12.1

Projectile–Point Typology in the Great Basin

Projectile-point typology in the Great Basin is complicated by considerable geographical variation, and substantial disagreements between local archaeologists. The so-called Berkeley Typological System was in widespread use until the 1970s (Hester; 1973, Heizer and Hester, 1978), but this has been revised in recent years. The scheme that follows relies heavily on David Hurst Thomas' researches in Monitor Valley, Nevada, and elsewhere in the western Basin (Thomas, 1981). His excavations and analyses quantified the original definitions so anyone could replicate them, and confirmed the original chronology proposed by earlier workers.

Corner-Notched Projectile Points

Gatecliff Series (*c*. 3000 to 1300 BC). Medium-to-large contracting stem projectile points, further subdivided into: Split-stem points with contracting stems and concave bases, commonly referred to as Pinto points and a contracting stem type with straight, pointed, or convex base. Some Gatecliff Series points may also predate 3000 BC.

Elko Series (1300 BC to AD 700). Large, corner-notched points with concave, straight, or slightly concave bases. Two widely recognized forms, one with corner notches, the other with ears on the base (O'Connell, 1967).

Rosegate Series (AD 700 to 1300). Small, corner-notched points, once known as Rose Spring and East Gate types. The two types grade into one another, the stem expanding slightly.

Early Desert Archaic in the Eastern and Northern Great Basin
c. 7500 to 2000 BC

The major adaptive shift in Great Basin life came around 7500 BC with the beginning of the Early Archaic. The inhabitants responded to the increasing aridity, the extinction of Ice Age megafauna, and the localization of resources by exploiting a far more diverse food base. In particular, they relied much more heavily on processed seeds, a shift reflected by the appearance of milling stones and other processing artifacts in the

Side-Notched Projectile Points

Desert Series (post-AD 1300). Desert Side-notched forms dating to after AD 1300 are small, triangular points with notches high on the sides. Large Side-notched forms may be older than the Desert form, but remain undated. This series subsumes many earlier point terms in the literature.

Unshouldered Projectile Points

The earliest unshouldered points are the Triple T Concave Base form, represented by a few specimens at Gatecliff Shelter and dated between about 3400 and 3200 BC. These have concave bases and rounded basal projections.

Humboldt Series (*c.* 3000 BC to AD 700). Unnotched, lanceolate points with concave bases of variable size. There are numerous varieties of Humboldt Series point.

Cottonwood Leaf-shaped and Triangular (post-AD 1300). Round-based and small, unnotched triangular points. Cottonwood points are widespread through the Great Basin after AD 1300.

The above is a simple summary of a complex typological problem. For full details and distinguishing criteria, see Thomas, 1981.

archaeological record. As the climate continued to warm up and many lakes and marshes dried up, Basin groups adopted far more complex settlement patterns that had them making use of semi-permanent winter base camps with basic storage facilities. In the northern and eastern Basin, much data for Archaic occupation comes from lake-margin dry cave sites around the Great Salt Lake in Utah (Aikens, 1982; Madsen, 1982). Perhaps these represent a skewed view of Archaic life in the region, but wide-ranging surveys suggest that, in fact, much human settlement was concentrated near this and other large lakes (Aikens and Madsen, 1986).

Many of these caves have remained completely dry for thousands of years. Three of them – Danger Cave near Windover, Utah, on the Nevada border (Jennings, 1957), Hogup Cave 75 miles (120 km) northwest of Salt Lake City (Aikens, 1970), and Sudden Shelter in central Utah (Jennings and others, 1980) – provide an exceptional record of Archaic life.

These and other less well-known locations contain deep deposits of rock spalls from their ceilings, windblown dust, droppings and other leavings from bats, packrats, wild sheep, and other animals – and debris from repeated human occupation. The deposits accumulated over thousands of years, reaching depths of 11 ft (3.3 m) at Danger Cave, and up to 14 ft (4.2 m) at Hogup. The human accumulations include not only stone and bone artifacts and food remains, but objects made of hide, fur, feathers, horn, sinew, grass, wood, and bark. Desiccated human feces survive by the hundred, documenting actual meals eaten thousands of years ago. The inhabitants carried grass, twigs, seeds, and bulrushes into the caves, which appear in layers stratified one above the other, as if the sites were occupied intermittently over immensely long periods of time. Danger, Hogup, and Sudden Shelter provide such a complete picture of early occupation in the eastern Great Basin that they have been used to divide the local late Paleo-Indian and Archaic into three technological and chronological periods.

Bonneville Period (9000 to 7500 BC) takes its name from the great Ice Age lake of that name, now a dry basin that forms much of the eastern Great Basin. Human occupation was sparse at best, but a few people camped in Danger Cave, lighting fires on the clean, sandy floor and leaving a scatter of stone flakes and milling stones there about 9000 BC (Jennings, 1957).

The Bonneville period occupation may be contemporary with, or later than, the scattered Paleo-Indian settlement of the Basin. Many fluted and stemmed points have been found around the margins of Early Holocene lakes throughout the Great Basin, but the relationships between them are still confused. Aikens and Madsen point out (1986) that the Bonneville period dates to a time of considerable environmental change. It may have been a time of transition between Paleo-Indian big-game hunting and the long-lived Desert Archaic tradition that followed.

Windover Period (7500 to 4000 BC). The Windover is an Early Archaic cultural tradition named after the town of that name on the Utah/Nevada border. Unlike earlier Bonneville occupation, Windover sites are found at many different altitudes and in a wide variety of environmental settings. Everything points to a mobile lifeway, in which settlement sites, often at familiar locations, were occupied at different times of the year. People hunted and foraged year-round, but the balance between these activities varied considerably at different seasons, with plant collecting assuming major importance at harvest time.

The lower levels of Danger and Hogup Caves testify to the great importance of plants in Windover diet. The inhabitants relied heavily on pickleweed (*Allenrolfea occidentalis*), a low-growing succulent that flourishes on the edge of salt pans and dried-up lake beds. Large stands of pickleweed were a staple, but the people also collected cattails, bulrush, and other marsh plants, as well as many other species. They gathered the harvest in coiled and twined baskets, then dried or parched the gathered seeds in tightly woven basketry trays, tossing them with some hot embers. Then they hulled and ground the seeds with hand stones and milling slabs, perhaps making them into cakes or gruel (Aikens and Madsen, 1986).

The Windover people who visited Hogup Cave hunted deer, pronghorn antelope, wild sheep, and bison. The cave deposits included 32 species of small animals and 34 of birds, many of which must have been taken and consumed by humans. Spearthrowers, stone-tipped and wooden spears, sometimes used with foreshafts, sufficed to dispatch many larger animals. The snaring and netting of rabbits, hares, and other rodents, also birds, was very important at Hogup during these millennia (Aikens, 1970). Judging from the fragments of nets and cordage in the deposits, the hunters used the same basic trapping methods that were employed in historic times. They would stretch long nets across narrow defiles, then drive dozens of rabbits into the broad traps with mass drives. Some simple loop snares came from Hogup, too, designed to catch the foot of a walking bird or of the many rodents that lived in the cave.

The hunters processed their quarry with stone-tipped knives and scrapers, not only consuming the meat but using animal by-products to make leather containers, and the bones as awls and needles for sewing and basketry, also netmaking. The people wore simple clothing, such as blankets fashioned from rabbit fur and transverse strands of plant fiber. These multi-purpose garments could serve for both clothing and sleeping. Woven fiber sandals protected the feet.

Black Rock Period (4000 BC to AD 500). After 4000 BC, population densities rose, and many more human settlements flourished near the Great Salt Lake, also at higher elevations and in areas that were hitherto apparently unsettled. The Black Rock period saw a continued trend toward greater aridity, with shrinking lakes, and perhaps a decrease in the availability of food resources close to the water. Human populations may have responded by adopting an even more mobile lifeway and by making greater use of upland piñon-juniper resources as well as mountain sheep, deer, and rabbits taken at higher elevations. Much of this hunting may have been the work of small family groups ranging far away from more permanent lake-side settlements (Madsen, 1982).

The Black Rock period is named after the cave of that name close to the southern end of the Great Salt Lake at the foot of the Oquirrh Mountains (Madsen, 1983). In strictly technological terms, the changeover is marked by the appearance of new and highly characteristic Elko and Gypsum projectile-point forms that replace earlier designs. Artifacts of this period abound not only at Danger and Hogup Caves, but at many new settlements.

Later in the period, about 2000 BC, the annual rainfall increased to effectively several times more than the Holocene average, with a resulting increase in local resource productivity. At the same time, lake levels rose significantly, sometimes flooding prized springs and marshes. At Hogup Cave, for example, the people were forced to change their subsistence activities significantly. Waterfowl and shore birds practically vanished from the deposits by about 1000 BC, for the marshy lake bed nearby had disappeared. The site was occupied more intermittently, seed utilization declined, and rabbits were less commonly taken (Harper and Alder, 1970).

Similar adjustments to subsistence activities may have occurred at Danger Cave and other settlements, but were by no means universal. The Desert Archaic lifeway persisted with local adjustments that reflected local environmental change. The people still relied heavily on a wide variety of plants and animals and used the same basic technology as their predecessors. About the most significant innovation came late in the Black Rock period, when the bow and stone-tipped arrow replaced the spear and atlatl. Projectile points became much smaller, even if they retained the same basic stem and corner-notched designs as their predecessors.

About AD 400 to 500, small amounts of pottery and occasional domesticated maize cobs appear in Black Rock sites, innovations that came to the eastern Great Basin and northern Colorado from sedentary horticultural societies in the Southwest. The new traits did not lead to any dramatic changes in Archaic life, for hunting and gathering still produced the subsistence staples, as they had for millennia. But piñon nuts became a major element in eastern Basin diet at about this time (Madsen, 1985). By AD 800, settled "Fremont" horticultural people had settled in many parts of the northern Colorado plateau and in the eastern Great Basin (Marwitt, 1986), and a new economy had taken hold in these long-settled areas (see below).

Desert Archaic in the Western Great Basin and Interior California
c. 5000 BC to European contact

The Desert Archaic traditions of this vast area were as diverse as those of contemporary groups to the east (Thomas, 1982; Elston, 1982, 1986). As in the east, the drying trend of the Early and Middle Holocene dried up many of the surface lakes, with temperatures reaching their maximum between about 3100 and 2200 BC.

Lovelock Cave, Nevada. (Right) General view. (Far right) Bird decoys and their wrappings after removal from the cave in 1924.

Early Archaic (c. 5000 BC to 2000 BC). The Early Archaic is poorly documented in the central and western Basin and may have begun sometime between 5000 and 4000 BC, somewhat later than in the north and east (Elston, 1986). Good archaeological data for characteristic Gatecliff series points come from only the latter part of this period, between 3300 and 1300 BC (Thomas, 1981). There is a possibility that the central and western Basin were unoccupied during the very Early Archaic. Big-game hunting may still have been important, but many finds of grinding equipment testify to the importance of seeds and plants in the diet.

The best evidence for Early Archaic occupation comes from the Carson and Humboldt Sinks of the Lahontan Basin. Human occupation of the Lahontan Basin intensified after 3000 BC, with intermittent use of the famous Lovelock Cave overlooking the Humboldt Sink starting as early as 2580 BC (Heizer and Napton, 1970).

Lovelock and other large caves were used predominantly as storage places or for burials by people living in residential base camps near lakes and sinks. Most such settlements are now marked by little more than small scatters of stone artifacts. The Cocanour locality on the Humboldt Sink has yielded two shallow, circular house depressions between 7.8 and 11.1 ft (2.4 to 3.4 m) across. The houses were surrounded with projectile points, scrapers, and other waste as well as *manos* and *metates*. Early Archaic peoples in the Lahontan Basin apparently subsisted on a diet of fish, birds, cattails, and piñon nuts (Thomas, 1970). Pacific marine shells and obsidian from both western Nevada and California document barter networks reaching far over the coastal mountains to the west.

Middle Archaic (c. 2000 BC to AD 500). The climate was now cooler and moister, with a resulting appearance of shallow lakes and marshes in areas where they had hitherto never existed (Janetski and Madsen, 1990). There were no great technological or subsistence changes, but local populations increased, with more diverse exploitation of food resources, and a trend

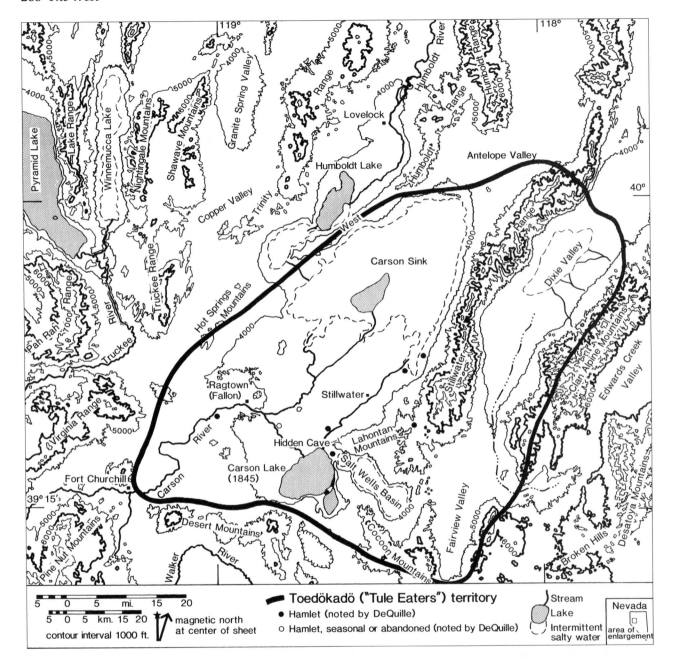

General map of the Carson Sink area showing the location of Lovelock and Hidden Caves. The heavy line delimits the territory of the historic Toedökadö people.

toward repeated reoccupation of winter base camps and seasonal settlements. Trade in marine shells, obsidian from volcanic rocks north of the Owens Valley, and in other exotics became ever more important.

While mountain sheep hunting was important in the Central subregion, and both big-game hunting and seed collecting were the focus on the Sierra Nevada slopes, the best-documented Middle Archaic settlements come from the Lahontan Basin, where lakeshore and marsh environments were exploited intensively. In some areas, village-like settlements served as base camps for the exploitation of lake resources. Lovelock Cave has yielded a bounty of finds that testify to the diverse lifeway along the Humboldt Sink. The people caught fish of every size from minnows upward, especially Lahontan chub, with nets, traps, and bone fish hooks (Butler, 1996). They used life-like duck decoys made of tule reed, some even covered with fully feathered skins removed from real birds. Sometimes the hunters would swim close to waterfowl using stuffed necks and heads of water birds for the purpose. The dry cave deposits yielded feathers from pelicans, herons, ducks, and geese, also the nets sometimes used for taking them.

We know a great deal about Middle Archaic diet at Lovelock from human coprolites. Over 90 percent of the foods in the cave came from the Humboldt-Carson sink nearby. The plants included bulrush and cattail, also wetland grasses like *Elymus* and *Panicum* that were staples. The Tui chub, ducks, and mudhens were favorite foods. The abundance and diversity of food resources apparently made it possible for the inhabitants to live in the same area for most of the year. Many of the plant foods found at Lovelock were harvested in fall and stored for winter use. The cold season was a good time for hunting waterfowl and collecting rhizomes of water plants.

The interpretation of Great Basin lake-side adaptations as revealed in sites like Lovelock has led to competing hypotheses. One long-held "limnosedentary" view argues that the inhabitants of desert lake environments enjoyed such predictable and diverse resources that they rarely had to move from their bases, indeed enjoyed a virtually sedentary residence pattern (Heizer and Napton, 1970). Heizer, Napton, and others based their arguments on the coprolite analyses from Lovelock Cave, which revealed a local diet of which 90 percent came from the lacustrine resources of the Carson Sink (see also Madsen and Lindsay, 1977). A contrasting "limnomobile" hypothesis argues that statements about sedentary settlement are based on single sites, not on a series of locations that reflect subsistence activities throughout the year. Limnosedentary living could have been a feature of local life for only a few weeks, Lovelock being but a snapshot of a small portion of a regular seasonal round, critics argue. Furthermore, the excessive costs of obtaining, processing, and storing marsh resources like cattail seeds, waterfowl, and fish may have made them less satisfactory staples than foods like piñon nuts. Thus, the inhabitants of desert lake environments were as mobile as bands living away from the water.

David Hurst Thomas (1985) excavated the Archaic deposits of Hidden Cave immediately south of Lovelock Cave and the Carson Sink to test these competing hypotheses. This was a comprehensive regional investigation that involved not only reexcavating the cave itself, but modeling lacustrine resource and possible subsistence strategies through use of ethnographic and historical records. Thomas found that the historic Toedökadö combined both foraging and collecting, strategies forced upon them by distances between resources and competing seasons for gathering different foods. During the winters they maintained relatively stable home bases either near marshes or in the nearby uplands, depending on stored food supplies and the condition of the marshlands. In spring

Excavations in progress at Hidden Cave, Nevada, in 1979.

and summer, families moved out to forage for food at many scattered locations, coming together in fall at the time of the piñon harvests. The excavations in Hidden Cave itself were combined with a regional survey. The grasses, seeds, fish bones, and piñon nut remains from the deposits revealed a location where people visited in spring and summer, months when they also consumed some stored foods and fish carried over some distance, the remains of which were identified in coprolites. Hidden Cave was also a place where visitors stored artifacts such as projectile points and worked wood in carefully prepared caches. People also stored what can loosely be called "low-ranked" foods and spare foods in the cave, a reflection of a constant concern with possible famine. Some of these low-ranked foods may have been consumed on the march, to sustain energy along the trail. The cave contained few artifacts used for exploiting marsh-side resources – birds or fish – artifacts that were commonplace at Lovelock. Perhaps, argues Thomas, Hidden Cave was a spring/summer location, while Lovelock was occupied during the winter.

Thomas believes that both the limnosedentary and limnomobile hypotheses are too extreme to be viable interpretations of desert lake adaptations. Rather, he believes that Hidden Cave, and many other such locations, were visited for centuries, serving at times as a kind of warehouse, at times as a place where the dead were buried, and often as a summer camp where one could escape the oppressive heat. The visitors to this and other caves were both foragers and collectors, hunter-gatherers adapted to an environment where resources were widely separated, relatively predictable and sometimes storable, even if their yield fluctuated wildly. Under these circumstances, sedentary settlement was impossible, but long stays at some locations during the winter months were possible.

Late Archaic (AD 500 to European contact and beyond). The climate of the western Great Basin became warmer and drier about the time of Christ. As over much of the west, the centuries of the Medieval Warm Period after AD 900 brought intense drought cycles and significant disruption over much of the Great Basin. Significant technological changes occurred. The bow and arrow replaced the spear and atlatl, with accompanying smaller and lighter Rose Spring and Eastgate projectile points, while pottery appeared after AD 1000. At the same time, people began to use much more elaborate plant-processing equipment, a reflection, perhaps, of new subsistence strategies that involved exploiting a more diverse resource base and different ecological zones. Plant foods and small game like rabbits assumed great importance, all possible signs of demographic stress caused in part by drought (Chapter 11).

Some authorities believe the appearance of these new technological artifices may reflect the expansion of Numic-speakers into the Great Basin from southern California within the past 1000 years (Lamb, 1958). A case can also be made for an indigenous, long-term development of Numic tongues in the Great Basin itself. However, as Bettinger and Baumhoff have argued (1982), the more intensive subsistence strategies now in use slightly resemble those found to the west, in California, in historic times. These new strategies were higher in cost, sustained higher population densities, and made more use of hard-to-process small seeds and less of large animals. They believe that the competitive advantages of these new high-cost strategies may have facilitated the spread of Numic-speakers into the Basin, a development that may have coincided with populations caused in part by the Medieval Warm Period (Jones and others, 1999; for essays on Numic controversies, see Madsen and Rhode, 1994).

The least-known area of the Great Basin is the extreme southwest, the vast area of the Mojave Desert. Dry, low-lying, and intensely hot in the summer, the desert offered meager fare for its ancient inhabitants, with only mesquites and agave providing dependable, nutritious staples. Human occupation spans at least 10,000 years, with two discernible trends: an increasing use of hill and mountain resources and a low reliance on processed seeds until surprisingly late, about 2000 years ago. In contrast, milling stones, the indicators of seed processing, appear as early as 10,000 years ago in the northern Great Basin and about 8000 years ago in California.

The Late Archaic throughout the western Basin is marked by the rising importance of plant gathering and processing, and by the exploitation of very diverse food resources, a similar trend to that documented in California. In the central subregion, the Alta Toquima village on Mount Jefferson documents a high-altitude base camp with substantial circular rock-walled houses and storage areas (illus. p. 272). Between about 2000 and 1000 BC, Alta Toquima was a hunting camp, but the later occupants lived there longer, processing plants as well as hunting. Perhaps both men and women visited the settlement, living there longer than in earlier centuries (Thomas, 1982). Another series of high-altitude sites comes from high in the White Mountains of eastern California. In the Grass Valley area of central Nevada, piñons were a staple, so abundant that many groups lived in comparatively sedentary villages, precursors of large Western Shoshone villages in historic times. The Owens Valley saw a decrease in upland

The high-altitude Alta Toquima site under investigation.

hunting in favor of low-altitude settlement, a shift that coincides with historic Paiute culture, a culture that made use of irrigation to water wild plant stands. This adaptation required permanent settlement in the lowlands.

Throughout the western Great Basin, the Archaic adaptation involved gathering large surpluses of seasonal foods and storing them for winter use. This meant that the people often built substantial base camps with ample storage facilities, fanning out into special camps at different times of the year (Bettinger and Eerkens, 1999).

The Desert Archaic in all its diversity was an adaptation that was based on opportunism and flexibility, so much so that the same basic lifeway persisted for thousands of years. Lakes would dry up during severe drought cycles. The people would adapt by moving away from the dried up basin and exploiting higher altitudes with apparently little effort or social change. When rainfall increased and lakes appeared, they would congregate along the marshy shores, adopting a new annual round that took advantage of the new diversity of food resources.

The Great Basin was never a stable environment, but a highly diverse one that changed constantly. Populations increased gradually over the millennia, exploiting new resources as they appeared, such as the piñon-juniper woodland that expanded over parts of the Basin after the Middle Holocene. As Robert Elston remarks (1986), the Archaic peoples of the western Great Basin resisted "change through change" with subtle technological innovations and intensive exploitation of a wide range of food resources. Had not European expansion disrupted and overwhelmed the ancient Archaic lifeway, it would have continued indefinitely.

The Fremont Culture and Great Basin Horticulture
AD 400 to 1300

About four centuries after Christ, more-or-less sedentary horticultural communities appeared in eastern Nevada, western Colorado, and southern Idaho, as well as much of Utah. These "Fremont" people lived in scattered farmsteads and small villages, their culture displaying some Southwestern Pueblo traits (Marwitt, 1986). After nine centuries, these people disappeared and Archaic societies continued to flourish in the Great Basin until the arrival of European settlers. Ever since the days when the Great Basin was considered a periphery of the Southwest, the Fremont culture has generated controversy.

Origins. The "Fremont culture" was named by archaeologist Noel Morss after the river of that name in south-central Utah, a drainage where he located many farming sites (Morss, 1931). Morss and others recognized many Southwestern traits in Fremont culture, including pithouses, stone architecture, pottery, and maize cultivation. He believed that the local Archaic people adopted farming from Southwestern contacts, perhaps as a result of a population movement from the south. His ideas left many questions unanswered. Did the Fremont culture emerge from a Desert Archaic base, with an infusion of culture traits from the Anasazi region of the Southwest (Jennings, 1957)? Or did people actually migrate from the Southwest for a while, then return to their ancestral homeland centuries later? Or were they Great Plains people who moved into the Great Basin, then withdrew in the face of Numic-speakers expanding from the west (Aikens, 1967)? The controversy remains unresolved (for discussion, see Madsen, 1989).

It is difficult to develop a viable hypothesis about Fremont origins, for Fremont occupation appears at different times in different places. Melvin Aikens (1970) found a clear transition from Archaic to Fremont at Hogup Cave after AD 400. The people simply added pottery, maize, and other Fremont artifacts to their traditional Archaic culture without any apparent disruption of their lifeway. Elsewhere, Fremont occupation dates to as late as AD 800 to 900. So far, no one has been able to pin down the beginning date with any greater accuracy. This may be because different regional populations had different ethnic origins – in the Great Basin itself, on the Great Plains (for northern Fremont sites show strong Plains influence (Aikens, 1966)), or in the Southwest. David Madsen believes (1979) that there were two or maybe three groups in the Fremont area that shared little more than some common artifacts, perhaps acquired through trade, and some common religious beliefs expressed in rock art, or by anthropomorphic clay figurines. This theory is difficult to support with hard evidence, but it

Fremont Culture: clay figurines, from the Old Woman site. Height of tallest c. 11.5 cm.

has the advantage of accounting for a wide range of beginning dates and for the great variation in Fremont culture.

Whatever the ultimate origins of the Fremont, there can be little doubt that there was a strong indigenous tradition in this farming culture, one that stemmed from the great environmental diversity of the Great Basin, and from the specialized nature of many of the Archaic adaptations in it.

Regional Variation. Fremont culture displays so much variation that some authorities question whether the term has any practical use at all. However, Fremont persists, if only as a convenient label that subsumes a multiplicity of local cultural names. This local variation is characteristic of Fremont from its first appearance, presumably reflecting the great diversity of Basin environments and the Archaic cultures that flourished in them. John Marwitt (1970, 1986) has identified five major, but provisional, geographical variants of Fremont culture, variants distinguished by characteristic artifacts, subsistence patterns, and settlement patterns. Each has links to the others, but they are each a distinctive adaptation to local conditions (see Table 12.2).

The End of the Fremont Culture (c. AD 1250 to 1350). By the mid-14th century AD, most Fremont people had abandoned the Great Basin and the

(Right) Fremont ceramic vessels from, left to right, Caldwell Village, Evans Mound, Snake Rock, and Evans Mound. Height of tallest c. 27 cm.

(Below) Fremont bowl from Grantsville Mound (Ivie Creek Black on White); diameter 26 cm.

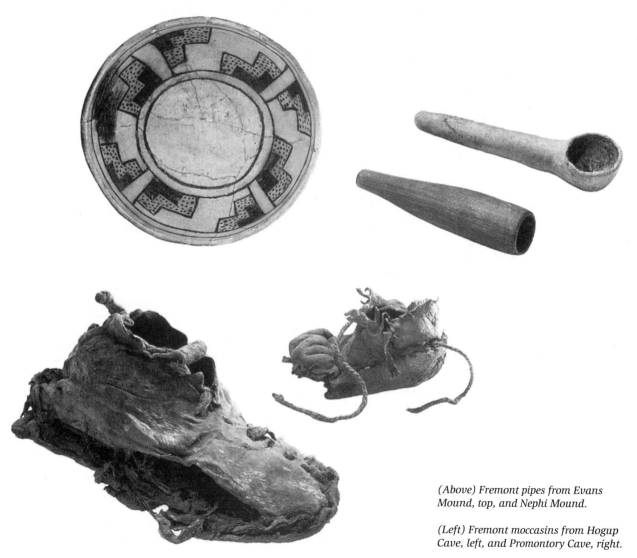

(Above) Fremont pipes from Evans Mound, top, and Nephi Mound.

(Left) Fremont moccasins from Hogup Cave, left, and Promontory Cave, right.

TABLE 12.2

Regional Variations of Fremont Culture

All variants are distinguished by pottery styles, projectile points, and settlement types (after Marwitt, 1986).

Variants Confined to the Great Basin Itself (sometimes combined under the label "Sevier" (Madsen and Lindsay, 1977):

Parowan Fremont (before AD 900 to 1250). Maize farmers, also hunter-gatherers, centered in southwestern Utah, with a culture that shows strong Anasazi influence. Many large settlements of pithouses.

Sevier Fremont (*c.* AD 870 to 1250). Central-western Utah and eastern Nevada. Smaller communities than Parowan, many temporary settlements, many close to permanent water supplies and marshes. Maize agriculture and plant foraging both important.

Great Salt Lake Fremont (AD 400 to 1350). Hunting and plant gathering were more important than agriculture, for lakeside soils were too saline for farming. Few permanent settlements. The distinctive side-notched projectile points, pottery forms and bone artifacts of this variant are found around the Great Salt Lake, also as far away as the foothills of the Rocky Mountains in south-central Idaho.

Other Variants:

Unita Bay Fremont (AD 650 to 950). Occurs in the high altitude Unita Basin of northeastern Utah. Small pithouse hamlets, with deer hunting and plant gathering important in an area with short growing season.

San Raphael Fremont (AD 700 to 1250). Small settlements based on the Watsatch Plateau of eastern Utah and extreme western Colorado, where maize agriculture was very important. Sedentary settlement in an area where marshes were rare, in contrast to other regions where marshes allowed such settlement.

Colorado Plateau, except, perhaps in the north. The same droughts of the Medieval Warm Period that affected the entire globe in the early 2nd millennium and decimated Anasazi societies south and east on the Colorado Plateau seem to have eliminated maize cultivation as a viable subsistence strategy throughout the Fremont area (Janetski, 1999; Jones and others, 1999). The kinds of intensive forager adaptations that marked much of the Great Basin at a time of severe drought gave hunter-gatherers an advantage over farmers and small numbers of such people endured in the region.

Was population replacement also involved? Some scholars argue that there is no evidence for cultural continuity between Fremont peoples and

Fremont rock paintings from the Great Gallery, Barrier Canyon, Utah.

historic, Numic-speaking groups like the Shoshone. They believe that Numic-speakers expanded into the Great Basin somewhere between AD 1250 and 1450, perhaps replacing farmers (Aikens, 1994). To have been ancestral Shoshone and Paiute as well as Fremont peoples, the Numic migration would have had to have taken place four to five centuries earlier – and there is no evidence that it did.

Given the great diversity of the Fremont culture, and the high degree of flexibility in Great Basin adaptations, it is most unlikely that all these many populations suffered a common fate. Each local group adapted to changing climatic conditions, to local environmental circumstances, to the arrival of new population groups. We know from Hogup Cave and other locations that Numic-speaking peoples replaced Fremont groups. At Hogup the newcomers made pottery and other artifacts that have clear links with historic Western Shoshone peoples. In other parts of the Great Basin, the same replacement pattern occurs. Initially, Fremont groups may have interacted with their successors, but in time earlier artifacts and cultural patterns vanished completely, for reasons that are still a mystery (Marwitt, 1986).

By the time of European contact, only a few groups cultivated maize on a limited scale, among them some Southern Paiute (Fowler, C., 1982), and some bands in the Mojave Desert. What Steadman Upham (1994) calls "an adaptive mosaic" of hunter-gatherers, part-time cultivators, and village farmers flourished in the western interior after AD 700. There were even some local groups irrigating, but not cultivating, native plants in the Owens Valley (Lawton and others, 1976). Hunting and gathering traditions honed over millennia of ancient times survived generations of sporadic contact with whites. The harsh desert and rough topography inhibited European settlement and immigration. For instance, the Western

Shoshone, who lived in the area between Death Valley, highland central Nevada, and into northwestern Utah, dwelt in one of the last areas of the United States to be settled by Anglo-European settlers. Many groups throughout the Basin were unable to survive the spurts of European development that disrupted their fragile ecology. But others had the time to develop responses to white settlement, to adapt to the radically different circumstances of a new era. Their material culture and subsistence patterns changed dramatically and rapidly, but many elements of traditional social organization and religious life survived into the 20th century.

Further Reading

D'Azevado, W. (ed.). 1986. *Handbook of North American Indians, vol. 11: The Great Basin*. Smithsonian Institution Press, Washington DC.
  A fundamental source on the indigenous populations of the Great Basin and their ancient antecedents.
Grayson, Donald K. 1993. *A Natural History of the Great Basin*. Smithsonian Institution Press, Washington DC.
  A well-written account of changing Great Basin environments, aimed as much at the general reader as the scientist. Strongly recommended.
Madsen, David, and O'Connell, James (eds.). 1986. *Man and Environment in the Great Basin*. Society for American Archaeology, Washington DC.
  An edited volume of articles that summarize theoretical, environmental, and cultural issues in the Great Basin. Very high-quality papers.
Thomas, David Hurst. 1981. "How to Classify the Projectile Points from Monitor Valley, Nevada," *Journal of California and Great Basin Anthropology* 3,1:7-43.
  Every classifier of projectile points should read this paper, which is of seminal importance to Great Basin archaeology.
——1983. *The Archaeology of Monitor Valley: 1: Epistemology*.
  American Museum of Natural History, Anthropological Papers 58,1. New York.
  An important statement about theoretical issues in Great Basin archaeology.
——1985. *The Archaeology of Hidden Cave, Nevada*. American.
  Museum of Natural History, Anthropological Papers 61,1. New York.
  A monograph describing excavations and a reinterpretation of desert lake sites in the Great Basin. Useful for its close theoretical reasoning.

CHAPTER 13

THE ARCHAIC OF THE SOUTHWEST AND LOWER PECOS

The area known as the "Southwest" is often defined as extending from Las Vegas, Nevada, in the west to Las Vegas, New Mexico in the east, and from Durango, Mexico, in the south to Durango, Colorado, in the north (Cordell, 1997; Hunter-Anderson, 1987). The Southwest is a region of dramatic environmental contrasts, between deserts and forested mountain ranges, areas of low and moderate rainfall. This environmental variation was important throughout the Southwestern past. What distinguishes the Southwest from neighboring areas of North America in archaeological terms is agriculture. Hunter-gatherer peoples flourished in the Great Basin to the north and in California to the west. Nomadic Plains bison-hunting groups frequented the Plains in the east, while to the southeast the Lower Pecos Valley and the Rio Grande supported hunting-and-gathering societies long after agriculture came to the Southwest. This chapter introduces the varied environments of the Southwest and discusses the Archaic societies not only of the Southwest itself, but of the semi-arid regions of the Lower Pecos Valley and Texas coast, where descendants of Archaic peoples continued to flourish into historic times. The Lower Pecos was a frontier between the Southwest and other semi-arid environments, and between more hilly country and the Southern Plains. Its archaeological record reflects such a frontier.

As Linda Cordell points out (1997), the Southwest itself can be defined culturally in two ways:

— By agriculture, a variety of farming artifacts and characteristic pottery styles, and also by multi-room villages with some public architecture. The diverse peoples of the Southwest came to adopt radically different subsistence strategies, cultivating maize, beans, and squashes, using all manner of ingenious techniques to combat temperature extremes and constant water shortages. They were also responsible for some of the most spectacular architecture in ancient North America, adobe and stone buildings erected in caves or as multi-story pueblos, often occupied over many generations.

— By the *absence* of formal social stratification, large cities, writing, and major, monumental architecture on the scale of such great Mesoamerican urban centers as Teotihuacán or Tikal.

Not that Southwestern peoples lived in isolation from their neighbors. They interacted with many groups near and far over long periods of time, through long-distance exchange networks that extended south to the Sea of

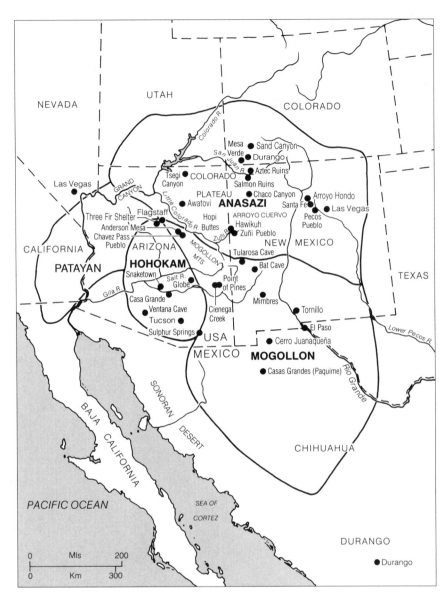

Sites and major cultural divisions of the Southwest.

Cortez and into Mexico, west to the Pacific coast where sea shells were to be obtained, and far north and east onto the Plains and north and west into the Great Basin. They acquired their basic crops, perhaps the art of pot making, and possibly some irrigation techniques from Mesoamerica, but adapted the techniques and ideas they received to the varied environmental realities of the Southwest. (Some authorities believe both ceramics and irrigation were indigenous developments.) This was always a land of hot and dry landscapes where risk was a way of life, an adaptive reality where unexpected droughts could last for years on end. The secret to survival was flexibility, so Southwestern societies were in a constant state of cultural change. This was especially true in later times, when there were centuries

Woman of the O'odham tribe, San Xavier Reservation, Arizona.

when large areas of the Southwest appear to have formed widespread economic and social systems. These larger units never lasted long in the face of variable rainfall and endemic drought. The people abandoned large centers and returned to dispersed villages again.

Southwestern Peoples

Despite generations of contact with Europeans, many descendants of the ancient population still flourish in their homelands, retaining their languages, important religious customs, and their value systems. There are four major cultural traditions, whose roots we shall trace in the next three chapters:

(1)   Yuman-speaking peoples of the Colorado River Valley, the nearby uplands, and also of Baja California, living to the west. These groups practiced floodplain agriculture where possible, but relied heavily on hunting and gathering. The Yuma in particular were skilled warriors and active traders, maintaining exchange networks with the Pima in southern Arizona and with the Pacific coast.

(2)   O'odham and other peoples living in southern Arizona, Sonora, and parts of northern Mexico. These are Uto-Aztecan speakers, who live in a vast territory that encompasses not only inhospitable deserts and rugged uplands, but some relatively lush river valleys. All these people live in what are commonly called *rancherias*, small hamlets housing several nuclear or extended families in separate dwellings.

(3)   The Pueblo Indians of Arizona and New Mexico, who speak diverse languages but share much common culture. The Hopi live on and around mesas (tablelands) at the southern rim of Black Mesa, Arizona. The Zuñi, now living in one village, occupied six villages near the Zuñi River in New Mexico at European contact in the 16th century. East of Zuñi dwell the Acoma, Laguna, and various other Keresan and Tanoan-speaking groups.

The compact settlement of Zuñi pueblo.

The various languages spoken by the Pueblo have roots in neighboring areas, Tanoan, for example, with the Kiowa-Tanoan language family that has relationships with Great Plains dialects (for details, see Cordell, 1997).

Pueblo groups tended to live in compact settlements rather than in *rancherias*, relying not only on various agricultural techniques, but heavily on hunting and gathering, too. Their villages were built of stone and adobe, often houses with interconnecting rooms for living and storage, some of multi-story design. All pueblos have special ceremonial rooms known as *kivas*. (*Kiva* is a Hopi word meaning "ceremonial room.")

There are important social, political, and religious differences between Pueblo groups. Among the Western Pueblo such as the Hopi, social organization above the level of the household is dominated by matrilineal, exogamous clans. In contrast, the Eastern Pueblo are organized around bilateral extended families and non-exogamous moieties. The moiety leaders coordinate tribal activities, as do ceremonial associations that cut across moiety lines. These broad generalizations disguise a great deal of cultural diversity within the Eastern and Western Pueblo, which can be ignored for the sake of this discussion.

(4) Apache and Navajo peoples, Athabaskan-speaking peoples with an ancestral homeland far to the north in Canada. The ancestors of the Apache and Navajo probably entered the Southwest during the early 16th century AD, perhaps as early as AD 1450.

The Southwestern Environment

View looking north from the top of Hunts Mesa into Tse Biyi, Monument Valley, Arizona. Merrick Butte is near the center of the picture.

The Southwest straddles several major physiological zones, with rugged, parallel mountain ranges to the south and west, ranges separated by large basins, the lowest no more than 100 ft (30.5 m) above sea level. The central and north-central parts of the Southwest lie at high elevations on the

Colorado Plateau, most of the land lying over 5000 ft (1524 m) above sea level. There are extensive tablelands (mesas), steep-sided canyons, and vast gorges, also volcanic deposits that were important obsidian sources in ancient times. To the east, the Southwest spills over into the southern Rocky Mountains, the ranges in this area providing a significant watershed for much of the region. Some farmers settled on the edges of the Great Plains, in major drainages like the Cimarron and Pecos rivers.

This highly diverse region has always enjoyed an arid to semi-arid climate, but a climate that is highly localized, making it hard to make any broad generalizations about Holocene climatic change. In the west, from Sonora, Mexico, through eastern California, Arizona, and north, rainfall comes twice a year. Winter storms from the Pacific bring soaking rain or snow to higher elevations between December and March, moisture that greens spring grazing areas. Most rainfall comes in July and August, short and intense local thunderstorms. To the east, from Chihuahua, Mexico through New Mexico, western Texas, and Colorado, July and August bring most of the year's rainfall in the form of Gulf thunderstorms. The position of the jet stream can have dramatic effects on the amount and distribution of annual rainfall, leading to unpredictable cycles of exceptional rainfall and drought.

In general, the desert areas in the south receive an average of less than 8 in (20 cm) of rain a year, while the uplands enjoy nearly 20 in (50 cm). But these are mere averages, which mask extraordinary variations in annual rainfall. Over much of the Colorado Plateau, farmers relied on springs and natural seeps, many of them emerging from natural contact lines between soft sandstones and impenetrable lower strata. The Rio Grande to the south and east was another matter. Irrigation was important along its banks, despite periodic floods that wiped out crops and entire settlements. The southern deserts support creosote brush and bursage, giving way in much of Arizona and New Mexico to higher ground that

Desert vegetation, Maricopa County, Arizona.

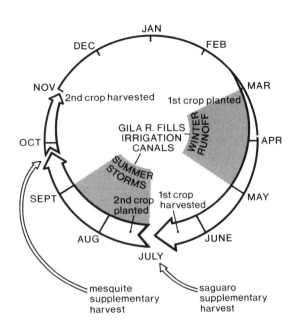

(Above) Paiute women in Arizona wearing basketry caps and carrying burden baskets for foraging.

(Above right) Successful agriculture in the Southwest depends on careful use of scarce water resources. The diagram shows how the O'odham Indians of southern Arizona, possible descendants of Hohokam people (see p. 286), schedule their plantings and harvests around rainfall seasons. The varying thickness of the arrows indicates seasonal variations in abundance of food.

supports mixed grasses, shrubs, and open pine, piñon and juniper forest over about 7000 ft (2133 m). The Colorado Plateau supports arid grasslands at low altitudes, with widespread sage brush and open piñon-juniper woodland. The diverse vegetation of the Southwest includes many edible plants, among them agave, whose leaves and centers were roasted and stored. Sotol, yucca, cactus fruits, mesquite, and cholla are important in desert regions. Wild onions and potatoes can be roasted and boiled. Many seasonal fruit such as hackberry and juniper assumed importance. Nuts and seeds are important supplemental foods, ground down and mixed with corn meal.

Southwestern weather patterns are so erratic that many plant species remain dormant much of the time, making it hard to predict harvests and to collect adequate yields from one stand, forcing people to wander over large areas in search of edible plants. The animals that feed on the natural vegetation tend to be omnivorous feeders, including the ubiquitous mule deer, big-horn sheep in rugged terrain, and pronghorn antelope. Ancient hunters took many species of small animals, including jack rabbits, cottontails, gophers, prairie dogs, and voles. Birds were an important food source, as well as providing feathers for religious paraphernalia. Rivers, marshes, and small lakes, perhaps even humanly flooded agricultural land, are important habitats for migrating waterfowl. Some groups domesticated the turkey, everyone possessed dogs. But the staple for most Southwest peoples of the past 2000 years was maize agriculture.

Altitude, summer temperature, humidity, surface evaporation rates, and the length of the frost-free season all limited agriculture in the Southwest. This is an arid region, so maize requires longer to reach maturity, and hence a longer growing season. The hottest temperatures occur in the southern desert areas. There, the growing season is sufficient for maize cultivation, provided there is enough moisture. Temperatures decrease as one moves northward and onto higher ground. Agriculture is much riskier in mountain and high-altitude mesa areas, where the growing season is often too short, and varies dramatically one year to the next. Local factors can be of vital importance for successful agriculture. For example, farmers can receive quite different crop yields and enjoy different growing seasons from one end or side of a deep canyon to another, simply because one flank may receive more direct sun than the other. Successful agriculture in the Southwest depended on careful use of scarce water sources and on minimizing risk of crop failure through careful placement of gardens.

The Lower Pecos Valley and extreme southwestern Texas comprises semi-arid to sub-humid brushland dominated by thorny brush, with coastal marshes along those parts of the Gulf coast protected by barrier islands. Pollen data tell us the Lower Pecos saw an Early Holocene piñon and juniper woodland cover give way to drier grassland and cactus vegetation between about 6500 and 4000 BC. This climatic shift forced long-established human populations to adapt to much drier conditions. There were short intervals of warmer and more humid conditions, which may have had important short-term effects on hunter-gatherer groups. Some of the most dramatic environmental changes may have resulted from European settlement, which saw the replacement of widespread grasslands by thorny brushland. This change may have resulted from severe drought cycles, overgrazing by cattle, and, most important of all, the cessation of natural (and sometimes humanly-set) range fires, which controlled brush and increased grass species density (for discussion see Black, 1989). We discuss the historic hunter-gatherer populations of the area below.

The Basic Framework for Southwestern Archaeology

In Chapter 2, we saw how North American archaeology literally came of age in the Southwest, culminating in the brilliant stratigraphic researches of Alfred Kidder at Pecos pueblo, New Mexico. When he started work in 1915, it was with the avowed ambition of tying together cultural developments in different areas. Pecos was an ideal site for the purpose, with the longest documented history of occupation of any pueblo on the Rio Grande. It was in use before the first Spanish visit in 1540, and was only abandoned in 1838 (Kidder, 1924; 1931). The so-called Pecos classification resulted from this work and Kidder's consultations with his colleagues, a developmental framework for the Southwest that has remained in use, albeit in modified form, ever since (Kidder, 1927).

The Pecos classification was based on architecture, pottery styles, tools, and to some extent on skeletal characteristics. It was developed at a time when tree-ring chronology was still in its infancy, for A.E. Douglass did not succeed in linking ancient and historic ring sequences until 1929. The scheme as originally proposed consisted of eight culture stages:

Basketmaker I was a pre-agricultural stage, a term no longer used, as this comes under the Archaic;

Basketmaker II (sometimes called Basketmaker), where people were farming and using spearthrowers;

Basketmaker III (sometimes called Post-Basketmaker): pottery came into use, people lived in pit or slab houses;
Five Pueblo stages, I to V, which subdivided the rise of Pueblo culture right into historic times.

Kidder proposed this as a developmental, not a chronological scheme. Inevitably, it was modified by later research. For instance, the Basketmaker-Pueblo sequence was found to be characteristic of the northern Southwest, so Kidder proposed the term Anasazi to cover this northern tradition. The word "Anasazi" means "early ancestors" in Navajo, often translated as "old people." This is offensive to some Pueblo groups, so the term "Ancestral Pueblo" is sometimes used instead. (We have retained Anasazi here, as it is deeply embedded in the literature.) The Pecos classification has been much modified by ever more local researches in recent years, and suffers from being far too linear and ladder-like to reflect actual ancient reality, nor does it mirror the great diversity of ancient settlement now known to have existed throughout the Southwest. Furthermore, it is based on pottery styles often assumed to have been made at individual villages, and rarely traded from one area to another. In fact, there is mounting evidence that pottery was a commodity of often restricted production that was widely traded over large areas (Plog, S. 1980).

Today, we can think of the Southwestern past within a broad, culture-historical framework that begins with a Paleo-Indian tradition, subsuming human settlement before about 5500 BC. This is followed by the Southwestern Archaic, dating to between about 5500 BC and AD 200, then "later" times, the time when the so-called Pueblo cultures flourished, when considerable regional variation is found in the archaeological record. The later past is now divided into four major cultural traditions that are in turn subdivided into chronological phases. The four traditions are:

Anasazi (?AD 1 to modern times). The Anasazi tradition flourished in the northern Southwest and subsumes the old Basketmaker-Pueblo developmental scheme. Such major developments as Chaco Canyon and Mesa Verde with their magnificent pueblo architecture lie within the Anasazi tradition.

Hohokam (c. AD 400 to 1500). The O'odham word "Hohokam" means "those who have gone." The Hohokam tradition differs from Anasazi in its rectangular, single-unit dwellings, low platform mounds, ball courts, cremations, and reliance on extensive irrigation systems, as well as in its paddle-and-anvil decorated pottery. This tradition flourished in the southern desert regions of the Southwest, and has been subdivided into as many as six periods at various times. Hohokam experienced considerable elaboration during its later history, maintaining trading connections with Mexico to the south. Irrigation canals, ball courts, platform mounds, and elaborate pottery, stone, and shell work are characteristic of Hohokam at the height of its development.

Mogollon (?250 BC to c. AD 1450). This tradition, centered on the mountains of that name in southeastern Arizona and southwestern New Mexico, is named after an early Spanish Colonial governor of New Mexico. The

Part of Cliff Palace, Mesa Verde, among the finest of all Anasazi pueblo architecture. See p. 335 for a view of the whole site.

distinctive plain and corrugated brown or red Mogollon ceramics are found over a large area from the Little Colorado River in the north well into Mexico in the south, and from Globe, Arizona, to El Paso, Texas, in the east. The Mogollon displays great variation, and has been divided into several stages on the basis of changing pithouse designs and ceramic styles.

Patayan (AD *875 to modern times).* The name Patayan comes from the Yuman, "old people," used to describe ancient cultures that once flourished west of the Hohokam region and north to the vicinity of the Grand Canyon. Patayan is a still inadequately defined entity. Various alternative terms have been proposed, together with several much discussed cultural stages (see Cordell, 1997).

This very broad-brushed, general developmental scheme masks a great deal of cultural variation, and is inadequate to describe such variation accurately, or to plot or evaluate the complex paths of culture change throughout the ancient Southwest. It was put together long before the advent of radiocarbon dating, and much of it developed while dendrochronology was still in its infancy. Nevertheless, the scheme is useful as a basic frame of reference. Generations of scholars have developed local chronological and cultural sequences under its umbrella. Tree-ring and radiocarbon chronologies and these frameworks have provided the basis for the much more sophisticated ecological, regional, and settlement studies that have been characteristic of Southwestern archaeology in recent years. A combination of all these approaches forms the portrait of the Southwestern past that follows.

Paleo-Indian Tradition
before 10,500 to c. 7500 BC

There is well-documented Clovis and Folsom occupation in the Southwest, associated with the bones of extinct big-game species (see Chapter 5). This includes several mammoth and bison kill sites, also the important Blackwater Draw locations (Wendorf and Hester, 1975; Haynes, 1975). Throughout Paleo-Indian times, the human population of the Southwest was small and very scattered, probably enjoying a generalized hunting and gathering adaptation. By the end of Paleo-Indian times, the hunter-gatherer populations of the region were pursuing very diverse subsistence strategies. In the east, bison were of importance, while San Dieguito peoples in the west may have relied more heavily on plant remains. In both areas, population growth was slow, but the long-term consequences of adopting quite different food-getting strategies were to prove significantly different, especially as far as sedentary settlement and population growth rates were concerned.

Southwestern Archaic
before 6500 BC to AD 200

As the Middle Holocene climate warmed up, vegetation patterns began to approach their present distributions, Southwestern people diversified their subsistence strategies even more, coming to rely more heavily on smaller animal species and especially on plant foods. The beginning of the Archaic coincided with drier weather in some areas of the Southwest, in part with the so-called Altithermal. Both pollens and packrat middens document more arid conditions, with Early Holocene forest cover giving way to desert scrub and more grassland around 6000 BC. This was a rapid, general change that saw woodlands retreat from the warm desert areas of the Southwest (Van Devender and Spaulding, 1979; Huckell, 1996). But the Altithermal was not a prolonged, very dry period as Ernst Antevs originally thought (1948). Rather, it was a period of constant change with generally drier conditions. After about 2500 BC, there may have been occasional cycles of higher rainfall, reflected in fluctuations in lake levels and local increases in forest cover. Whether these rainfall increases were widespread enough to call them a wet phase is uncertain.

The Southwestern Archaic is still a rather sparse entity, for the scattered archaeological remains of these millennia are overshadowed by the much more spectacular sites and material culture of the past 2000 years (Huckell, 1996). Except in highly favored locations, too, Archaic bands exploited generally arid environments, where food resources were widely dispersed and where constant mobility was adaptive. Many Archaic encampments were highly transitory settlements, occupied for a few days or weeks at a time. Thus, the archaeological record is highly incomplete, except for occasional caves and rockshelters where dry conditions have preserved a wider range of artifacts, including such perishable items as basketry, fiber sandals, and fur blankets. However, the Archaic was a vital formative period in the Southwestern past, for it was during the later centuries of the period that some local groups adopted the deliberate cultivation of domesticated plants, among them maize (Matson, 1991; Wills, 1989).

The human responses to the drier conditions of the Early and Middle Archaic were highly varied, as is only natural in an environment of great contrasts. Settlement studies are slowly revealing some of these responses. In the southern and southwestern Southwest, Early and Middle Archaic groups living at higher elevations made but little use of low-lying river valleys. But, as moister conditions developed after 2000 BC, people moved into the formerly dry valleys of the south, excavating wells for water and, eventually, planting crops on the fertile alluvium (Huckell, 1996). The San Juan Basin and Black Mesa also saw but sporadic human settlement, probably summer visits by people living on surrounding higher ground. But, once again, the Late Archaic saw many more sites, extensive use of storage pits, and, eventually maize farming (Huckell, 1995; Mabry and others, 1997). For thousands of years, the Archaic groups of the Southwest shifted their mobile lifeways to make use of food resources wherever they were available, with well-digging playing an important role in their ability to adapt to drier environments.

In some respects, the study of the Southwestern Archaic has paralleled that of the Great Basin. As we saw in Chapter 12, the concept of a "Desert Culture," a long-lasting Archaic tradition, sparked a new generation of research into Holocene climate change and human responses to changing conditions. Eventually, the Desert Culture concept was abandoned and replaced with more sophisticated formulations. In the southern Southwest, the term Cochise Culture was coined to cover a similar long Archaic occupation, and then elaborated into three general phases: Sulphur Spring, Chiricahua, and San Pedro (Berry and Berry, 1986; Sayles and Antevs, 1941; Sayles, 1983). As is inevitable, especially when archaeologists think in linear terms, there was a proliferation of new traditions, phases, and local variants. These reflected an increasingly complex and puzzling archaeological record.

These "gradualist" models assume that Southwestern Archaic hunter-gatherer traditions developed relatively stable adaptations to generally arid conditions and very varied local environments over as long as 5000 years. In subsistence and adaptive terms, the Southwestern Archaic was seen as forming part of a much wider desert adaptation that flourished over much of the interior west, marked by a "specialized, successful way of life geared to the rigor and apparent biotic parsimony of the Desert West" (Jennings, 1964). Throughout the Southwest a scattered Archaic population subsisted off small game and wild plant foods for a long period of time under relatively stable climatic conditions, conditions far more stable than those of Paleo-Indian times. This may have led to a gradual population increase over the millennia, but with densities always remaining low throughout the area.

Clearly, there is a strong element of cultural continuity through the Southwestern Archaic, but the gradualist model is based on relatively unsophisticated views of desertic environments. A new generation of

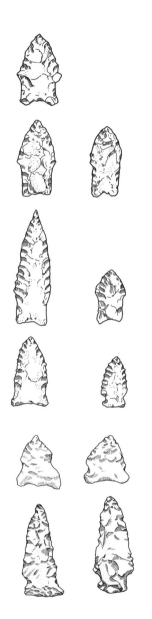

Southwestern Archaic projectile points. (Top) Pinto Basin point. (Second, third, and fourth rows) Bajada, San Jose, and Armijo points respectively. (Fifth row) Chiricahua Cochise points. (Bottom row) San Pedro Cochise points. Length of Pinto Basin point 3.7 cm.

multidisciplinary research, using not only archaeological finds, but sophisticated climatic data, has shown that the Southwest and adjacent areas were settled by a very complex, multidimensional mosaic of Archaic hunter-gatherer societies. These many groups maintained the same general technological traditions for many thousands of years over wide areas, but there was great local, and often short-term, variation. This reality means adopting a very different approach to Archaic studies, one that focuses on reconstructing jigsaws of local adaptations using data from both archaeological and climatic sources, then fitting these many local adaptations together into a wider, much more complex, picture (Berry and Berry, 1986; Huckell, 1996). Such researches are still in relative infancy, but promise a much more complex picture of the Southwestern Archaic for the future. We must, however, summarize a general version of the gradualist sequence first, for it is still widely used in the literature and in the field.

Cynthia Irwin-Williams (1968; 1979) argued for two levels of Archaic analysis. The first level was an integrative one. It identified traits that were common to many local cultures. For example, small *manos* and grinding stones occurred on Archaic sites throughout the Southwest. They were clear evidence for seed processing, an activity that was almost universal in the desert west. Most of the characteristics of the Southwestern Archaic fell into this integrative category. They were general traits defining a general stage.

Irwin-Williams then moved on to what she called an "isolative" level of analysis. This was a far more detailed comparison, where one tried to isolate specific traits such as characteristic projectile points that served to distinguish local cultures one from another, and to set up local culture-historical sequences through time. This was difficult with the Southwestern Archaic, for there were few truly distinctive, local artifacts to work with. As is the case in other parts of North America, investigators have tended to emphasize projectile-point forms for this purpose (Beck, 1995).

Projectile points have long been a primary way of distinguishing between different Paleo-Indian and Archaic groups throughout North America. There are, of course, numerous theoretical objections to this practice, for such variables as sharpening can modify point design, as more than one observer has pointed out. Robert Musil (1988) takes another approach, where he points out that there were three major hafting traditions in ancient North America. Fluted and lanceolate points are common in Paleo-Indian cultures, while contracting, stemmed forms come into use somewhat later, which signal the first use of a socketed haft. In some parts of the west, notched points come into fashion at the beginning of the Archaic and become predominant in later times, probably because they provide not only more secure hafting, but also the practical advantage that, when they broke, it was usually across the notches. Thus, the user could simply make new notches higher up on the point and rehaft it in a short time, without the trouble of making an entirely new head. If Musil is correct, then projectile points are an indicator of the adoption of more efficient hafting methods that made earlier designs and projectile-point forms obsolete.

The use of projectile points to distinguish different Archaic groups is especially difficult in the Southwest, where securely dated sites are few and far between. However, we can say that, just as they did in other parts of North America, projectile-point styles extend over enormous areas during Paleo-Indian and early Archaic times. This standardization gives way to a significant proliferation of point styles used over smaller areas during later centuries, at a time when each group made increasing use of purely local sources of tool-making stone rather than the more limited exotic sources of earlier times. This may reflect higher population densities, less mobility, and more restricted territories where plant remains were used more intensively. At the same time, long-distance exchange networks became less important as everyone relied more heavily on local contacts.

Despite these many theoretical and methodological problems, Irwin-Williams (1968) developed a descriptive framework for the Southwestern Archaic, which is still widely used in the literature. She identified four interacting Southwestern Archaic traditions – Cochise, Oshara, Pinto, and Southeastern.[1]

Southwestern Archaic Traditions

San-Dieguito-Pinto (Western) Tradition (c. 6500 BC to c. AD 200 or later) is the westernmost Archaic manifestation, extending from southern California in the west deep into southern Arizona. It is found within the Great Basin as far north as southern Nevada. Pinto apparently evolved from Paleo-Indian San Dieguito roots (Chapter 5) and is identified by "Pinto Basin" points with straight stems and concave bases, especially in the eastern Great Basin (*c.* 6300 to 4300 BC).

Oshara (Northern) Tradition (c. 5500 BC to c. AD 600) is centered in north-central New Mexico, the San Juan Basin, the Rio Grande Valley, southern Colorado and southeastern Utah (Irwin-Williams, 1979). The Oshara may have ancestral roots in earlier Paleo-Indian traditions, but these postulated roots are much disputed and the debate is unresolved (Cordell, 1997). Irwin-Williams dates the beginnings of Oshara to about 5500 BC and has developed a sequence of Archaic culture for Oshara in the Arroyo Cuervo area of north-central New Mexico. This sequence defines no fewer than six phases of occupation, each identified by projectile-point forms and other less well-defined artifacts. Jay, Bajada, San Jose, Armijo, En Medio, and Trujillo – the successive phases, of importance only to specialists, chronicle local Archaic culture from its earliest manifestations right up until AD 600, by which time Anasazi culture is flourishing in the area. The Arroyo Cuervo researches are thought by Irwin-Williams (1979) to define a long-term cultural development of the local Archaic into Pueblo-Anasazi culture.

The Cochise (Southern) Tradition (?before 5000 to c. 200 BC) lasted for a very long time, with its earliest manifestations, known as Sulphur Spring, perhaps before 5000 BC. Its two later phases, the Chiricahua and San Pedro, are much better known.

---

[1] Irwin-Williams coined the term "Picosa" as a generic label for these four groups, an acronym developed from three of the four Southwestern traditions: Pi from Pinto Basin, co from Cochise, and sa from San Jose. This label is not widely used today, but appears in even recent literature.

San Pedro Phase oval pithouse.

Chiricahua Cochise tools include a variety of projectile points and many seed-processing artifacts. The phase has been dated to between about 3500 and 1500 BC, but the chronology is open to doubt and the beginnings may be much earlier (Whalen, N., 1975; Berry and Berry, 1986), and has been formulated on the basis of occupations in Ventana Cave, near Sells, Arizona, and from other locations in the state, as well as in western New Mexico (Haury, 1950).

San Pedro follows the Chiricahua in the southern Southwest, characterized by large projectile points with corner or side notches and straight or convex bases. Provisional radiocarbon dates have San Pedro flourishing from about 1500 to 200 BC (Whalen, N., 1975). By this time, the Archaic population of the Southwest appears to have grown, with groups exploiting a wider range of environmental zones and sometimes living in larger, perhaps more permanent, settlements. Some San Pedro sites contain oval pithouses excavated about 1.6 ft (0.5 m) below ground level, dwellings requiring sufficient effort to build that they must have been occupied for some time. Without question, some San Pedro communities were cultivating maize and other crops.

San Pedro occupations have been chronicled at many locations, among them Bat and Tularosa Caves in New Mexico, as well as Cienega Creek, sufficient to show that the later Mogollon tradition developed from the earlier San Pedro Cochise (Huckell, 1995; Martin, 1979). Emil Haury excavated the Cienega Creek site, where he found San Pedro Cochise artifacts that he felt documented cultural continuity not only to Mogollon, but to another later tradition, the Hohokam (Haury, 1950). As we shall see in Chapter 15, he has subsequently changed his mind, and believes that the Hohokam were people who migrated north from Mexico and were not descended from the Cochise (Haury, 1976). The question is still much debated (see Berry and Berry, 1986).

The tripartite subdivision of the Cochise is still ill-defined, to the point that there is a real question whether it, in fact, represents a continuous, unitary tradition of Archaic culture at all. The three stages probably represent an interrupted, rather than a continuous, sequence. In some places, they may have actually been contemporaneous (Berry and Berry, 1986).

Chihuahua (Southeastern) Tradition (?6000 BC to c. AD 250) of south-central New Mexico and Chihuahua, Mexico, is still poorly defined and probably includes several local adaptations that evolved over long periods of time (Beckett and MacNeish, 1994; Cordell, 1997).

Irwin-Williams' hypothesis of four interacting Southwestern Archaic traditions, which differ from other traditions such as the Plains Archaic is still, at best, provisional, for we still do not have the information even to subdivide the phenomenon into two, three, or more time periods (Huckell, 1996).

A Population Movement and Climate Model

Claudia and Michael Berry (1986) point out that the complicated mosaic of Archaic settlement throughout North America cannot be understood on purely a local basis alone. This is especially true in the Southwest, where many projectile-point forms used to subdivide different cultural stages were also in widespread use elsewhere. The Berrys used 288 radiocarbon dates from 119 Southwestern sites to show that there were numerous gaps in Archaic occupation both on the northern Plateau and in the southern Basin and Range areas. These gaps should not be there, if the gradualist model is correct. There are peaks with many dates, as if there were bursts of cultural activity. If these gaps and peaks reflect actual reality, then the development of Southwestern Archaic culture was much more complex than hitherto suspected. New surveys since 1986 confirm this complex picture.

The Berrys have developed a model of population movement and climatic change that compares what is known of Holocene climatic change with this new, discontinuous Archaic chronology. They believe there was no one-to-one correlation between climatic variation and the intensity of ancient occupation in any given local area, that one cannot think purely in terms of drier conditions equalling lower population densities, and higher rainfall associated with higher numbers of people.

The model is subdivided into three periods, which are purely arbitrary formulations, mere organizational devices, which do not imply continuous occupation.

Period I (8000 to 3000 BC). Almost nothing is known of the human populations of the Southwest during this long period of fluctuating warm-wet and cool-dry climate, for radiocarbon-dated sites are rare. The Colorado Plateau, for example, may have been utilized on a transitory basis. The sparse population was probably concentrated around clusters of food resources, but even then occupation was probably intermittent. A number of distinctive projectile-point forms are associated with this period, among them Pinto – generally agreed to be the earliest Archaic point in the eastern

Great Basin and Colorado Plateau – Elko, Humboldt, and Northern side-notched (see Table 12.1).

Period II (3000 to 1000 BC). With the onset of a period of greater rainfall about 3000 BC, both the Plateau and the Basin Range were occupied more intensively, with a "peak" of cultural activity. There is a proliferation of new projectile-point forms, including the Gypsum point with its contracting stem, which occurs as early as 2500 BC. Contracting-stem points are found at Ventana and in the Trans-Pecos region of Texas, and are part of an Archaic culture there that has strong similarities to earlier Archaic assemblages from the Tehuacán Valley and elsewhere in Mexico. The Berrys believe that these similarities are the result of population movements from the Mexican highlands, where climatic conditions were deteriorating at the same time as they were improving in northern Mexico and the Southwest.

Period III (1000 BC to AD 500). Rainfall patterns changed fairly drastically about 1000 BC, as conditions became drier throughout the Southwest. It was during these protracted drought conditions that maize cultivation took hold among Archaic groups, during the so-called San Pedro stage of the Cochise culture. It is interesting to find another peak of radiocarbon-dated sites just before 500 BC, as many Archaic groups became sedentary cultivators, centuries after the first introduction of maize to the Southwest (Chapter 14).

This model is a far more sophisticated formulation than the gradualist interpretation, based as it is on an emerging array of paleoclimatic data and hunter-gatherer theory. It is founded on notions that some areas were more productive than others, with productivity varying dramatically through time from one locale to another. In some areas like the eastern Great Basin, for example, long-term, successful adaptations were based on exploitation of lacustrine resources during dry spells, on upland plant foods during drought cycles. On the Plateau and in the southern Basin and Range of New Mexico and Arizona, it was not possible to develop such complementary strategies to accommodate climatic cycles, so these areas with their broadly similar food resources remained sparsely occupied until the higher-rainfall conditions of Period II.

The Berry model also espouses not gradual change (although, obviously, this was a factor), but population movements. The process of Archaic population movements was an extension of the annual mobility characteristic of most hunter-gatherer groups. These expansions, contractions, and shifts in Archaic settlement were not conscious migrations. Rather, they followed the constantly changing annual availabilities of food resources, so their movements were short-term reactions to abrupt changes in resource availability. At times, they encountered new foods and developed new technologies to exploit them. But throughout the Southwest, and indeed the Great Basin, desert Archaic societies adopted conservative strategies that allowed them to feed themselves within local environments, adjusting to short-term minor changes within these, even when the Holocene climate in the longer term changed in major ways.

The key to understanding the Southwestern Archaic will be new generations of research that evaluate changes in Archaic land-use patterns that explain gaps in the archaeological record in terms of local climate change and availabilities of food resources (Huckell, 1996).

Foragers to the South and East
c. 11,000 BC to modern times

The Lower Pecos Canyonlands. The semi-arid Lower Pecos Canyonlands lie around the confluences of the Pecos and Devils rivers with the Rio Grande in extreme southwestern Texas (Bement, 1989; Shafer, 1986). More mountainous country lies to the west, and the Edwards Plateau to the north, with the mesquite savanna of south Texas to the east. The Canyonlands are famous for their dry caves and pictographs, which have been the subject of archaeological investigations for more than 80 years. Bonfire Shelter lies within the area, the southernmost, and earliest known bison jump in the Americas. Stampeding bison would tumble over a 125-ft (37-m) high cliff, where they were slaughtered and butchered. At least three Paleo-Indian hunts of about 40 *Bison antiquus* apiece between 10,000 and 8000 BC have been recorded. Nearly 8000 years later, Late Archaic hunters stampeded three herds over the cliff, a total of about 800 beasts (Dibble and Lorrain, 1968).

The dry caves of the Lower Pecos provide an unusual portrait of the more perishable material culture of local Archaic groups. Like their contemporaries in the Southwest and Great Basin, the Lower Pecos people made extensive use of plant fibers especially from desert succulents, to make twined, plaited, and coiled baskets, also sandals, mats, and bags. They wove cane partitions to separate living quarters in the caves. Bags, blankets, and pouches from bison, deer, and rabbit hide come from many sites, as do fragments of rabbit-fur robes ingeniously made from long strips twisted to bring fur upward on both sides of the garment. Archaic groups used wooden digging sticks and curved boomerang-like sticks for clubbing rabbits. Atlatls were fashioned from straight sticks, with the hook carved at one end. Freshwater shells served as spoons and scoops, while bone and antler pins and weaving tools abounded.

The excellent preservation conditions along the Lower Pecos have enabled the development of a long culture-historical sequence, which begins with possible human occupation at Bonfire Shelter as early as 11,000 BC, then continues with a very early Archaic "Bonfire" phase between 10,000 and 7000 BC. The Pecos Archaic sequence, divided into Early, Middle, and Late periods, persists from about 7000 BC until the threshold of historic times, further subdivided into seven phases, culminating in the Late Archaic "Cibola" phase, famous for its bison jumps at Bonfire Shelter (Bement, 1989). The Archaic sequence is documented at Baker Cave, a dry site high in a canyon above a tributary of the Devils River (illus. p. 296). Baker Cave was occupied as early as 7000 BC, when the climate was wetter than today (Chadderdon, 1983). A thick Early Archaic occupation dates to between 6000 and 3500 BC, by which time conditions were much like today. Middle and Late Archaic deposits at the site have yielded plant remains and perishable artifacts like sandals, including evidence of specific activity areas for cooking and sleeping that were used again and again until as late as AD 1400 (Hester, 1989; Shafer, 1988).

White shaman in Val Verde County, Texas. An example of Lower Pecos rock art images.

Baker Cave, Val Verde County, Texas. This site yielded evidence of occupation during the Early, Middle and Late Archaic periods.

The Lower Pecos region is best known for its rock art, both pictographs and petroglyphs (Bement, 1989; Newcomb, 1967; Shafer, 1986; 1989; Boyd and Dering, 1996). The earliest, so-called Pecos River Style includes abstract representations of humanoid figures in various mineral colors, some animal and human forms painted almost life-size. Deer, fish, zoomorphs, and shamans' paraphernalia, also shaman figures, accompany the large polychrome figures. Most experts believe the Pecos River Style, with its depictions of atlatls and darts, belongs to the Middle Archaic San Filepe Phase, radiocarbon-dated to about 2000 BC. Other Pecos River Style artists depicted miniature human figures in red engaged in group activities, including deer roundups and processions in which headdresses depict individuals with special status. Bison and deer are sometimes shown being driven into netlike barriers or into jump areas. Late ancient art styles depict bows and arrows, while historic paintings show crosses, men on horseback, and cattle, also active hostility to Spaniards (for an intriguing new interpretation of Lower Pecos rock art, see Boyd and Dering, 1996).

In general terms, the Lower Pecos region is part of a much larger hunter-gatherer adaptation to the arid lands of southern North America, which began as desert conditions and became established during the earlier Holocene, as early as 7000 BC. These same adaptations persisted into historic times.

Other well-documented examples of long-lived Archaic lifestyles come from the Edwards Plateau of central Texas and the coastal plain of south Texas. At the Wilson-Leonard site west of Austin, a long chronology has been documented from Clovis times through later times (Collins, M., 1998). A sequence of shifting dart-point styles through the Archaic is accompanied by specialized cooking features, including earth ovens. By the Middle Archaic, earth ovens were in such regular use for plant cooking that thousands of burned rock middens were formed, the most common site type in central Texas (Black and others, 1997).

South Texas hunter-gatherers are harder to chronicle, as they preferred unstemmed triangular projectile points through much of the Archaic. However, they developed specialized toolkits that included chipped-stone adzes, known as Clear Fork tools, that reflect their extensive wood-working activities, long missing from their open occupation sites (Hudler, 1997). There is, however, evidence of increasing social complexity and territoriality in the Middle and Late Archaic, reflected in large cemetery sites with extensive grave goods, some obtained from long-distance trade (Ernest Witte site: Hall, G., 1981; Lorna Sandia site: Taylor and Highley, 1995). At the mouth of the Rio Grande, the Brownsville complex peoples traded mass-produced marine-shell ornaments with the Late Postclassic Huastecan culture of the Mexican Gulf coast, as reflected in the exchange of Huastec pottery, obsidian (chemically sourced to Mexican outcrops), and jadeite artifacts (Hester, 1995).

Historic Peoples

Coastal Archaic societies of the south Texas coast exploited both maritime resources and game or plant foods inland. The earliest sites date to around 4000 BC, but it seems certain much earlier societies dating back to Early Archaic and Paleo-Indian times lie under the waters of the Gulf of Mexico. Again, on the coast, one has a strong impression of cultural continuity far back into the remote past, disrupted by historic period population movements (for Texas archaeology, see Hester, 1980; Nunley, 1989; Turner and Hester, 1993).

At European contact, the descendants of 11,000 years of a continuous hunter-gatherer tradition lived in central and south Texas (Newcomb, 1961). Ethnohistoric studies of historic groups suggest their ancestors ranged over large territories (Hester, 1989). They were displaced by Spaniards, with their mission system, moving in from the south, and by native American bison-hunting groups such as the Lipan Apache and Comanche, who moved into Texas from the north and west after AD 1700. Dozens, perhaps hundreds, of small hunter-gatherer groups shared similar lifeways, divisible linguistically into at least seven larger groups. They are mostly known from a tidbit of Spanish description about their location, some information on their lifestyle and customs, and recent ethnohistorical researches, like those of Martin Salinas (1990) in the Rio Grande Delta. Tom Hester (1989) describes the Coahuilteco-speakers as living in small groups, each with a distinct name, living a semi-nomadic existence, and ranging over seasonal territories which overlapped with those of their neighbors. They lived in bands averaging about 45 people, hunted antelope, deer, small game and reptiles, fished, but obtained most of their diet from plant foods. The prickly pear was vitally important in summer, acorn and pecan crops in fall. Everyone dwelt in small, round brush or mat-covered huts and wore blankets or capes fabricated from deer and rabbit skins. Hester believes this generalized description applies to most, if not all, other central and southern Texas hunter-gatherer groups at European contact. The first Spaniard to cross Texas was Alvar Nuñez Cabeza de Vaca, who was shipwrecked near present-day Galveston in 1528. He and his companions made their way to Mexico, suffering great hardships along the way. Coronado and his conquistadors crossed the Texas Plains in search of gold and silver in 1540, but there was no permanent settlement in western Texas until the 18th century, by which time native American populations had been decimated by smallpox.

Further Reading

Cordell, Linda S. 1997. *Archaeology of the Southwest.* 2nd ed. Academic Press, New York.
   This important synthesis focuses on both cultural process and culture history. A definitive account.
Huckell, Bruce B. 1996. "The Archaic Prehistory of the North American Southwest." *Journal of World Prehistory* 10(3): 305-374.
   A summary of the Southwestern Archaic at a technical level. Includes valuable ecological information.
Lekson, Stephen. 1999. *The Chaco Meridian: Centers of Political Power in the Ancient Southwest.* Altamira Press, Walnut Creek, CA.
   Lekson's provocative synthesis is a refreshing perspective on the Southwest. Not available for the writing of this edition.
Plog, Stephen. 1997. *Ancient Peoples of the American Southwest.* Thames & Hudson, London and New York.
   A beautifully illustrated summary of Southwestern archaeology for the general reader.
Reid, Jefferson, and Whittlesey, Stephanie. 1997. *The Archaeology of Ancient Arizona.* University of Arizona Press, Tucson.
   A nice general account of Arizona's ancient cultures.
Shafer, Harry (ed.) 1986. *Ancient Texans: Rock Art and Lifeways along the Lower Pecos.* Witte Museum of the San Antonio Museum Association, San Antonio, Texas.
   A beautifully illustrated popular account of archaeological research and rock art along the Lower Pecos. A superb introduction to the region, alas now out of print.

CHAPTER 14

THE ORIGINS OF SOUTHWESTERN AGRICULTURE AND VILLAGE LIFE

Agriculture, the deliberate planting and harvesting of domesticated plants, seems, on the face of it, like a startlingly revolutionary invention. But, as the great English anthropologist Edward Tylor pointed out as long ago as 1883, "agriculture is not to be looked on as a difficult or out-of-the-way invention, for the rudest savage, skilled as he is in the habits of the food-plants he gathers, must know well enough that if seeds or roots are put in a proper place in the ground they will grow." We can be sure that Archaic peoples knew millennia before they felt any necessity to do so that deliberately planted seeds would germinate.

In the final analysis, plant production involves the deliberate manipulation of plants, intervening in their life cycle to make sure that some useful parts are available for eating or for some other use. There was no one single moment when ancient North Americans domesticated plants. Rather, plant domestication was part of a long continuum of human interaction with the natural vegetation that started with first settlement (Ford, 1985).

Tending, Cultivation, and Plant Domestication

Foraging and Unintentional Tending. For thousands of years, Paleo-Indian and Archaic peoples foraged for wild vegetable foods in season, gathering nut harvests, harvesting wild grasses in river valleys, digging for tubers and roots. The very act of gathering vegetable foods can lead to unintentional tending of plants – accidental seed dispersal and trampling can benefit the wild resource. Intensive gathering of, say, larger seeds at the expense of smaller ones can also have unexpected genetic consequences, selecting against less desirable traits. These changes can be maintained over time, even if intensive human exploitation ceases. For instance, such accidental genetic changes may have caused the condensing of the lateral branches and tiny cobs of teosinte, the indigenous wild grass that is thought to have been the ancestor of domesticated maize.

In many parts of North America, hunter-gatherers used fire to encourage the regeneration of grasses and edible plants. The California Indians used fire to eliminate plant competitors under edible acorn oak trees, also to encourage growth of *Corylus* sprouts, much prized for basket manufacture. Deliberately set fires will select for certain species, but such techniques can hardly be called deliberate plant production.

Cultivation. Richard Ford argues that food production begins with "deliberate care afforded the propagation of a species" (1985), an activity he calls "cultivation." Such cultivation does not imply full domestication. But it does mean that people have disrupted the life cycle of a plant, usually to collect larger quantities of food or to enable them to obtain its products with greater ease.

Cultivation proceeds in several ways. Weeding, pruning, and otherwise tending plants is a commonplace practice in many parts of the world. Tending is a casual activity, usually removing competing vegetation around root plants or weeding the soil near important medicinal species, as is done in the Southwest. Usually, a higher yield results. Such techniques are, of course, impossible to identify from archaeological remains, but there is no reason not to assume that tending of wild plants was commonplace in Archaic times.

Tilling the soil with digging sticks (illus. p. 255) or simple hoes tends to encourage the germination of naturally dispersed seeds. Grubbing the earth with a simple digging stick or hoe can increase moisture retention or aerate the ground. Many foragers use a digging stick to obtain tubers, removing lateral roots or bulbets at an early stage in growth. This very process could encourage further growth and tuber production. Again, such activities are impossible to identify from archaeological finds.

Transplanting takes the process of manipulation a stage further, the deliberate process of digging up plants and replanting them at a new location. Much transplanting is really a form of thinning out to enhance yields, but if a plant is moved to a new habitat, then the transplanter will have to care for it over its entire growth cycle. Such long-term care may lead to selection for new genetic characteristics and to hybridization with closely related plants. Historic American Indian groups regularly transplanted small herbs or shrubs, many of them ceremonial or medicinal plants. The transplantation was sometimes casual, sometimes to a space deliberately reserved for nurturing a variety of plants.

Sowing seed can be seen as a form of transplanting. It can be as casual as the deliberate dispersal of harvested seed to foster future growth. There are many more complex forms of sowing, like, for example, storing the dormant seed and then planting it in small plots cleared in advance, or sowing in completely different habitats. Procedures such as this can result in selection for useful traits, such as winnowing for large seeds, or planting all the seeds at once so they germinate simultaneously and are all harvested at the same time.

Cultivation of wild plants and potential domesticates that are undergoing genetic change does not necessarily produce stable crops. In all probability, early cultivation efforts were aimed at producing seasonal supplements to broad-based vegetable diets. The additional plant yields were a form of guarantee that the harvest would be at least partially bountiful, perhaps, also, eliminating the need for wide-ranging searches for additional foods.

All these forms of plant manipulation were in use for thousands of years, until people created new food plants through deliberate selection. At that point, humanly created plant communities became the dominant component in ancient diet.

Plant Domestication. Plant domestication is the final stage in the process of food production, the point at which cultural selection for useful traits

"Waffle garden" at Zuñi pueblo, New Mexico. Gardens such as these were an ingenious way of conserving moisture in the soil for growing domesticated plants.

results in new plants that depend on human beings for their existence. Such plants cannot survive without human assistance, and may initially be a dietary supplement. However, as time goes on, they often become ever more important and more and more land is allocated to food production. The most important characteristic of domesticated plants is that one can increase their production by clearing a natural habitat and creating an environment favorable for growing a chosen domesticated plant. The result is what Ford calls "field agriculture," based on land where only a few species are grown in carefully chosen combinations that supplement each other, like maize with beans and squash.

Theories of the Origins of Agriculture

Few topics have generated so much theoretical speculation as the origins of agriculture. We now know that agriculture and animal domestication began in many parts of the world at about the same time, and that the changeover from hunting and gathering to food production was a long process involving a complicated set of interacting variables (Flannery, 1973b). The most recent attempts to understand these processes have invoked such factors as population pressure and environmental stress (Cowan and Watson, 1992). These hypotheses usually involve placing newly domesticated plants in their ecological and cultural context, in a theoretical environment that involves thinking of human cultures as cultural systems that interact not only with the natural environment, but as being made up of many different components that interact with one another (Redman, 1978).

The world's earliest farming societies emerged in Mediterranean and tropical environments. In contrast, North America is a continent of often dramatic winter and summer extremes, presenting difficult challenges to subsistence farmers in both the Southwest and Eastern Woodlands (Ford, 1985). In the east, for example, plant growth was dormant for many months of the year. The nut harvests and productivity of wild-grass stands varied dramatically from year to year, so predicting food supplies was very hard. In the Southwest, irregular rainfall, many months of intense heat, and sometimes harsh winters, played havoc with wild vegetable foods.

In the Southwest, Archaic hunter-gatherer groups could overcome food-shortage stress by covering large distances, by possessing knowledge of potential food sources over wide areas. They also concentrated on less-preferred food plants, and sometimes exploited food sources like acorns that required a great deal of effort to prepare, and a greater energy expenditure by everyone involved. Another option was to respond to changed conditions by deliberately cultivating native plants, as happened in the Eastern Woodlands long before maize spread east (Chapter 18).

The Origins of Southwestern Agriculture

Maize (corn), squash, and beans were domesticated somewhere in Mesomerica sometime before 5000 BC, centuries before they appeared in North America. Richard MacNeish's classic excavations in the Tehuacán Valley of central Mexico and in the Sierra de Tamaulipas in the northeast of the country have documented a changeover from hunting, gathering, and sporadic cultivation to a heavy dependence on farming that took many generations to complete (Smith, B., 1994).

Richard Ford (1985) has grouped the earliest Southwestern crops – maize, beans, and squash – into what he calls the Upper Sonoran Agricultural Complex. He points out that the crops within this complex had a long and complicated history before they reached the Southwest. They were cultivated in northern Mexico for some time before being introduced further north. Maize farming is an economic activity that may require sedentary living for much of the year, but we can assume that there were at least some sporadic contacts with nomadic hunter-gatherers living in desert regions to the north. Thus, it would have been easy for knowledge of plants, even gifts of seeds or seedlings, to pass from south to north. Such is the archaeological record that we shall probably never know what specific mechanisms diffused farming to the Southwest. The important point is that the opportunity for adopting the crops was probably present long before anyone thought it worth doing so. And domesticated plants had one major advantage: they might not be highly productive, but they were predictable. Cultivators of the new crops could control their location, and their availability at different seasons through storage. Under this argument, conditions favoring adoption of cultigens by Archaic groups could include both uncertainties about the productivity of the environment and changes in population densities (Huckell, 1995; Matson, 1991; Wills, 1989).

The Southwestern climate was relatively stable during the Archaic, with a possible period of wetter conditions from about 2500 BC to about 100 BC. It was an environment where hunting and gathering were high-risk subsistence strategies, mainly because of highly variable rainfall distributions. Despite generally low population densities, local populations may have occasionally reached saturation point, resulting in food shortages. Wills (1989) argues that many Archaic populations grew rapidly as the distribution of piñons, desert succulents, and other valuable supplementary foods expanded during the arid Middle Holocene. The scattered hunter-gatherer population was mainly based on stream drainages, but as contrasts between vegetational zones became more pronounced when the climate became more arid, many groups developed a seasonal pattern of exploiting lowland resources during the winter and early summer, then moving to the cooler uplands to exploit piñons and other foods during mid-summer and fall. There was often repetitive use of the same, favored locations. Wills documents a northward shift of more numerous later Archaic settlements that paralleled a northward shift in piñon-juniper woodlands and savannas.

Wills also examined the distributions of projectile-point forms through the Archaic in the central Southwest, and found that there was considerable emphasis on stylistic variation during the later part of the mid-Archaic, with less concentration on such features in favor of technological efficiency in the later Archaic. He notes that there are modern ethnographic analogies for the use of projectile-point styles to convey social information, perhaps to reflect perceived, if not physical, territorial boundaries. Conceivably, then, the changing emphases on style may reflect decreasing success at foraging, reflected in a great need for information about one's neighbors, and for defining one's relationship with them in terms of control of resources. During the later centuries of the Archaic, groups were controlling resources in more formal terms, with specific territorial boundaries. Under these circumstances, more predictable food supplies would be an invaluable addition to Archaic diet.

Linda Cordell (1997) believes that Southwestern groups adopted agriculture when what she calls a "situation of regional imbalance" developed between local populations and local resources. Such situations could result from either environmental degradation or population increases. She believes that climatic changes during the Archaic were not sufficient to cause local degradation. Thus, rising population densities may have been a factor (see also Matson, 1991).

There are several possible ways in which rising population densities may have caused environmental degradation and the adoption of agriculture. Michael Glassow (1980) argued that sedentary agriculturalists in northern Mexico moved over into the Southwest, placing pressure on indigenous hunter-gatherer groups. There were contemporary sedentary populations on the California coast, also, populations who may also have spilled over into the interior, again creating pressure on Archaic peoples in the Southwest.

Another hypothesis points to the western Plains, where a dramatic increase in bison hunting during the Late Archaic may have led to the establishment of large, seasonal camps along the western margins of the flat country (Frison, 1992). The presence of these camps may have led to local resource shortages and resulted in some hunter-gatherer groups in the eastern Southwest planting crops to supplement reduced natural plant yields.

One could argue that foragers accept crops in order to become more effective foragers, not because they want to become farmers. Thus, one can argue that there were increasing environmental differences during the Archaic that saw the lowland and desert areas producing fewer resources for foragers, while the upland and northern regions were ever more seasonal in their food supplies. Wills (1989) suggests that lowland groups may have accepted crops to offset seasonal shortages in spring, for they could store the resulting grain. Upland groups might have accepted crops to allow them greater effective control over upland areas. If this view is correct, then lowland sites may one day yield cultigens slightly before they appear at higher elevations.

Whatever the precise cause, the origins of horticulture in the Southwest appear to have resulted from an imbalance between population and available natural resources. In a sense, Archaic culture in the Southwest, as elsewhere in North America, with its elaborate seed-processing equipment, *manos* and grinders, was pre-adapted to agriculture. Had Southwestern peoples wanted to adopt agriculture as an opportunistic venture perceived to be of advantage, they would have done so much earlier, cultivating maize soon after it appeared far to the south. Ultimately, they adopted a low-yielding form of maize during the late 2nd or 1st millennium BC some time after it came into use in Mexico. The addition of farming to the economy, even as a part-time activity, placed immediate boundaries on seasonal movement, for people had to return to the locations where they had planted crops, both to weed and harvest them. Perhaps, too, as Stephen Plog (1997) argues, farming may have increased the division of labor in Archaic society, with some segments of the population, including older people, remaining close to growing crops, while others foraged elsewhere.

Maize Agriculture

Maize (*Zea mays*), sometimes called Indian corn, was the staff of life in the Americas at European contact, all the way from Argentina to southern Canada, and from sea level high into the Andes (Galinat, 1985). Over the millennia, hundreds of races of maize evolved, each a special adaptation to every environment imaginable, from swamplands to intensely hot deserts. The crop was first domesticated somewhere in Mesoamerica, or perhaps even further south, from a common wild grass, teosinte. The transition from wild grass to the maize cob probably took a very short time, perhaps a century or so, a shorter time span than that required to develop highly productive maize forms. Richard MacNeish traced the gradual emergence of maize agriculture in the Tehuacán Valley, Mexico, and observed how the earliest maize cobs were of very small size. His excavations at Coxcatlán Cave and other nearby sites show that it took many generations for the farmers to create larger, more productive cobs that were capable of producing crop yields to support large agricultural populations (Smith, B., 1994).

Maize, the staff of life in the ancient Americas. (Above left) Some 5000 years of the evolution of maize from the tiny corn cob on the left to an example on the right dating to about AD 1500. Modern corn is much larger and more productive than the earlier forms, which were developed from a wild grass, teosinte, that still grows in Mexico. (Above right) Hopi woman shelling corn, Arizona.

Maize is a demanding crop, not a cereal that one can rely on to provide all one's food if one plants it casually, and simply return to harvest the resulting stand later, as one can many native plants like goosefoot. Maize also lacks two of the vital amino acids needed to make protein, lysine and tryptophan (high in squash), and is only an effective staple when grown in combination with other crops like beans (lysine-rich) or squash (tryptophan-rich) that provide the necessary protein ingredients for a maize-based diet. Since most Southwestern groups continued to enjoy a highly mobile lifeway for at least a millennium after maize first appeared north of the Rio Grande, there is good reason to believe that it first served as a casual supplement to wild plant resources, especially in favorable areas where corn could be planted and then left largely untended, the process of cultivating it not being allowed to interfere with other subsistence activities.

Zea mays is a tropical cultigen, one that is always at risk in such northern latitudes as the Southwest (Matson, 1991). The hardy, low-yielding maize that first entered the Southwest was the so-called Chapalote form of *Zea mays*, a small-cob popcorn of great genetic diversity. Everyone agrees that Chapalote was the primeval Southwestern maize, but there is great uncertainty about the date of introduction (for discussion, see Upham and others, 1987). One scenario has Chapalote arriving in the Southwest early in the 2nd millennium BC, with AMS dates for maize cobs at Three Fir Shelter near Flagstaff in northern Arizona dating to the 1750 to 1650 BC range. Despite these early dates, the archaeological evidence for the first appearance of Southwestern corn is still very scattered and comes mainly from caves and rockshelters (Wills, 1989). However, isolated cobs and AMS dates from highlands and lowlands definitely place the introduction of maize agriculture during a period of higher rainfall in the central and eastern Southwest in the 1st millennium BC.

Shortly after its arrival, continues the same scenario, Chapalote was introgressed with the indigenous wild grass teosinte, creating a highly varied hybrid maize that appears at such well-known Southwestern Archaic sites as Bat Cave. The maize forms that resulted from this process of introgression often displayed more rows of kernels and large cob sizes, more productive forms that spread rapidly throughout the Southwest.

It was not Chapalote but radically different maize, Maiz de Ocho, which is thought to have been the key development in Southwestern life (Wills, 1989). Maiz de Ocho is adapted to dry conditions and yields large, more productive, flowery kernels that are easily milled. Until recently, it was commonly agreed that Maiz de Ocho had spread into the Southwest from northern Mexico even as late as AD 700, and then diffused from there to the Eastern Woodlands in about AD 1100. This was before Steadman Upham and Richard MacNeish excavated Roller Skate and Tornillo rockshelters in southern New Mexico. The latter yielded an AMS date of 1225 ± 240 BC, obtained from eight maize samples, including two complete cobs of an early form of Maiz de Ocho. All the maize fragments came from a single natural layer in the shelter. Two later levels at the same site contain Maiz de Ocho and date to 1029 ± 130 BC and 652 ± 60 BC respectively. Obsidian-hydration dates from both Tornillo and Roller Skate tend to confirm these dates (Upham and others, 1987). It may be, then, that maize agriculture took hold at lower elevations earlier than in the uplands, but it is only fair to say that the dating of these sites still needs further testing (Smith, B., 1994; Wills, 1989).

The spread of maize across the Southwest was not a linear process, with sedentary villages flourishing in the south during the 1st millennium BC. By about 500 BC, if not earlier, large pithouse villages, like the Santa Cruz Bend site, flourished in the river valley of that name near Tucson, Arizona (Mabry and others, 1997). Floodplain maize agriculture was a staple of this settlement. Across the border in northwestern Mexico, Robert Hard and John Roney (1998) have excavated the Cerro Juanaqueña farming village with 5 miles (7 km) of stone house terraces, where maize cobs have been dated to about 1150 BC. This was also a substantial farming settlement, equivalent to about a 135-room pithouse village, where native grasses may also have been processed. The northern parts of the Southwest did not use maize on a large scale until about the time of Christ.

These new dates raise the possibility that Maiz de Ocho evolved in or near the Southwest from earlier, highly variable Chapalote maize, including forms with a thick rachis (hinge) that held the kernel to the stalk. Maiz de Ocho may have resulted from a selection for a large kerneled corn, which was easier to grind, also for earlier flowering. Such an attribute was vital in the hot and arid Southwest, where growing seasons are often restricted by irregular timing and distribution of rainfall, leaving little time for large kernels to fill out. These characteristics of Maiz de Ocho were highly adaptive in North America, with its short growing seasons and very diverse temperate environments.

Eight-rowed Maiz de Ocho dates to the 12th century AD in southeastern Colorado and spread rapidly into the Eastern Woodlands at about that time. It was apparently preceded across the southern Plains into the Southeast by

Hoeing around a maize plant.

a small-cob 12- and 14-rowed race of hard flint corn, known as "Northern American pop" (Smith, B., 1994). Eight-row maize dominated eastern agriculture after AD 1100. At European contact, Maiz de Ocho, often called "New England flint corn" grew from the Dakotas across to New England and up to the northern limits in southern Canada, places like the Gaspe Peninsula.

Southwestern farmers experimented with the genetically variable maize grown at higher elevations for many centuries. *Zea mays* is at the northern limits of its range in the Southwest, intolerant of too short growing seasons, weak soil conditions, and such hazards as crop disease and strong winds. The most important factors of all were soil moisture and water supplies. By careful seed selection, the farmers developed higher-elevation varieties with elongated corn cobs and distinctive root structures, whose seeds could be planted at considerable depth, to be nourished by retained ground moisture. They became experts at selecting the right soils for cultivation, those with good moisture-retaining properties on north- and east-facing slopes that receive somewhat less direct sunlight. The farmers favored floodplains and arroyo mouths where the soil was naturally irrigated. They would divert water from streams, springs, or rainfall runoff to irrigate their crops. As with hunting and foraging, risk management was vital. So the cultivators dispersed their gardens widely from one another to minimize dangers of local drought or flood. They learned how to shorten the growing season from the 130 to 140 days needed in such a hot, arid environment closer to 120 days by planting on shaded slopes, planting in different areas, and at varying elevations. Over the centuries, a great diversity of highly effective dry-climate agricultural techniques developed throughout the Southwest.

Squashes and beans also form part of Ford's Upper Sonoran Agricultural Complex. Squashes (*Cucurbita pepo*) appear in Southwestern sites after 1000 BC, and were all of the same variety until about AD 900, when other forms were grown. This versatile plant was used for containers and harvested for its seeds and fruit.

Common beans probably appeared in the Southwest by 500 BC, and became a widespread staple throughout the region. Beans were a very important crop in the Southwest and elsewhere in North America, especially when grown with maize, for the two complement each other. Beans as we have seen contain a high level of lysine, which aids in the effective digestion of the protein found in corn. Not only that, but beans, being legumes, can return vital nitrogen to the ground, nitrogen that is depleted by maize. Thus, by growing maize and beans in the same garden, Southwestern farmers could maintain the fertility of the soil for longer periods of time. The late arrival of beans was probably one reason why some time elapsed between the first appearance of maize and significant dependence on agriculture.

The factors that governed the acceptance of domesticated plants in the Southwest were very different from those in the Eastern Woodlands (see Chapter 18). There, basically sedentary cultures adopted maize, beans, and squash at different times. In the Southwest, these three crops arrived at different times, adopted by small, mobile social groups, among whom crop cultivation required a major adjustment in settlement patterns and hunting-foraging activities (Wills, 1989). The point is that the dispersal of domesticated plants into the Southwest was not just a matter of them being available for cultivation. Their adoption involved a conscious decision by

Bean plants, Hotevilla pueblo, Hopi, Arizona, c. 1919.

individual, scattered, mobile Archaic hunter-gatherer groups to utilize these more predictable foods. This decision probably involved deliberate efforts by groups living at low elevations to enhance winter and springtime food supplies. Later, Wills speculates, maize and other crops were planted in the uplands, but as part of a different strategy – one that allowed people to monitor wild-plant food resources at high altitudes while living off stored agricultural products. To argue that food production spread uniformly and immediately all over the Southwest is a gross simplification of very complicated processes.

The Lower Sonoran Agricultural Complex
AD 300 to 500

Another set of crops came to the Southwest from Mexico considerably later, between AD 300 and 500. These new crops, all plants that are tolerant of high desert temperatures, tended to require irrigation. This Lower Sonoran Agricultural Complex (Ford, R., 1981) includes sieve beans (somewhat similar to the familiar lima) and other bean varieties, cushaw squashes, pigweed, and cotton. Apparently, these crops were introduced to the Hohokam, who were already practicing irrigation agriculture in parts of the lower Sonoran desert. Their use was confined almost entirely to the hot regions of the south.

The Consequences of Southwestern Agriculture

The appearance of corn did not trigger a dramatic revolution in Southwestern life in the short term. The early corn was not very productive, and could be planted fairly casually without the careful tending needed to produce bountiful crops – at altitudes above 656 ft (200 m). Under these conditions it was probably about as high yielding as a stand of wild seeds. As Linda Cordell points out (1997), a plot of corn tended and harvested in a small garden would require less caloric energy to grow than wild seeds scattered in isolated locales over a wide area. This is not a problem when people hunt and forage over large territories. If mobility is restricted, however, then the advantage of stands of even low-yielding corn is considerable. Corn does not have as much food value as some wild foods, especially piñons and walnuts. But, as we have seen, piñon harvests in particular are subject to great cyclical variations, making them a less reliable food source than the newly cultivated crops.

The maizes grown in the Southwest were adapted to a wide variety of environmental conditions and were drought-resistant strains. Eventually, they became of staple importance to many Southwestern peoples, who became expert at growing maize using simple irrigation techniques or natural springs or seeps to water their crops and amplify sporadic rainfall.

The expansion of food production resulted from a long-term process of successfully manipulating crops. Serious maize agriculture in an arid region like the Southwest requires a great investment of time and energy, strong incentives for adopting more sedentary lifeways. As people settled down near their maize fields, they still relied on wild plant foods exploited in far smaller territories, territories restricted in size by their sedentary lifeway. The shortage of these wild foods in turn tended to encourage not only more cultivation, but the founding of new agricultural communities in neighboring areas where farming could be safely practiced.

The adoption of agriculture was not an inevitable process. The archaeological record of more than 2000 years of Southwestern farming shows cycles of expansion and contraction, of growing population densities within limited areas that suddenly dispersed over the landscape. At others, the expansion succeeded and stable farming populations survived over many centuries. Sometimes, the experiment failed and the land was abandoned. But once agriculture took hold in the Southwest, exclusive reliance on hunting and gathering was no longer a viable adaptation. And the farmers adapted to a high-risk agricultural environment with ingenuity and remarkable technological skill, skills that survived until European contact and beyond.

The Beginnings of Village Life in the Southwest
AD 200 to 900

By the end of the Archaic in about 200 BC, Southwestern groups had become less mobile as they adopted at least part-time cultivation as part of their economies. However, it was not until AD 600 to 800 that permanent villages appear in any numbers. This sedentary way of life developed over many centuries, partly because agriculture was a high-risk activity in contrasting environments where rainfall varied constantly from year to year. Thus, food supplies may have varied more dramatically than was the case with wild plants and game, while people were more restricted in their movements. Everyone now relied more heavily on efficient storage and large storage pits, to guard against shortages. At the same time, people built more substantial dwellings and permanent settlements.

The new, fixed communities varied greatly in size, but were made up of individual oval to circular houses that were occupied over some length of time. In other parts of North America like the Midwestern river bottoms, sedentary settlements appear to have developed long before agriculture took hold. In the Southwest, agriculture was an essential prerequisite for abandoning a more mobile lifeway.

The term "sedentary settlement" conjures up images of quite large villages clustered near a patchwork of cultivated gardens, with much the same size of settlement being commonplace over considerable areas. In fact, Southwestern villages varied greatly in size, partly because of the highly diverse environment with its highly localized natural resources, and also because opportunities for cultivation varied greatly from one location to the next. Nowhere did the villagers subsist off agriculture alone. Wild plant foods were always of significant importance.

These early village communities, sometimes still grouped under the loose term "Basketmaker" over much of the northern Southwest (Chapter 2), owed much to their Archaic predecessors. At first, the people used simple, small *manos* and basin-like *metates* to grind both wild and domesticated seeds. In time they developed more elaborate grinders – large slabs or troughs worked with *manos* needing two hands to operate, presumably for grinding larger amounts of maize more efficiently. Stone technology remained much the same as in earlier millennia, except for the introduction of the bow and arrow, the latter tipped with small side-notched and stemmed stone projectile points. The appearance of the bow and arrow may have coincided with the rising importance of agriculture. It was a means of acquiring more game protein, for the bow and arrow enabled hunters to ambush a wide variety of game, shoot it from a greater distance, and to hunt in more wooded country.

One important innovation appears in the Southwest in about AD 200 – pottery. Clay containers were an important technological innovation that made sedentism and significant dependence on agriculture possible, because they enabled households to boil stored maize and beans, a process that maximized their nutritional value. They were also useful for storage, were strong and easily manufactured, and lasted for a long time.

In the north and in the mountains, the earliest villagers lived in pithouses, dwellings where part of the walls are formed from the sides of an

Hopi woman making pottery in Oraibi village. She is using a coiling technique to build up the walls of the vessel.

excavated pit. According to Robin Farwell (1981), pithouses are thermally efficient, for the heat loss from underground structures is less than for above room pueblos. Farwell's calculations show that a pithouse required less manpower or fuel to heat in winter, a feature that would make them adaptive at higher altitudes.

Most pithouses were round or oval, up to 16.4 ft (5 m) across, their floors dug to varying depths, often about 1.6 ft (0.5 m) below ground surface. They often contained storage pits or fire pits. As far as is known, the

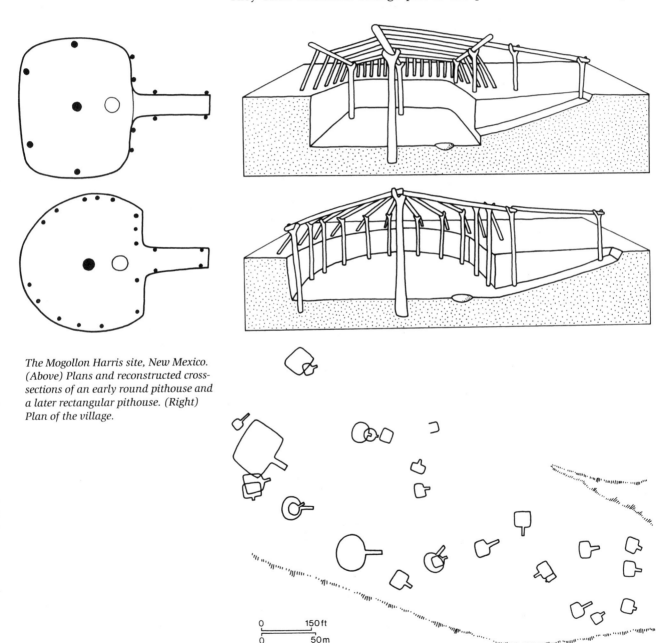

The Mogollon Harris site, New Mexico. (Above) Plans and reconstructed cross-sections of an early round pithouse and a later rectangular pithouse. (Right) Plan of the village.

0   150 ft

0   50 m

superstructures were usually a mud-covered framework of vertical poles set round the pit, the roof supported on strong post supports, or with a single cross-beam. Pithouse forms evolved into more-or-less standardized designs as the generations passed. Houses in the Mogollon region varied from round to rectangular, with fire pits set into the floor in front of the sloping entryway. Anasazi area pithouses boasted of adobe walls that subdivided them into kitchens and living areas. Ventilators, air deflectors, and raised sleeping platforms were common features, as were roof hatches accessible with a wooden ladder.

Lower Sonoran desert houses were quite different, not pithouses as such, but rectangular or square houses built in pits. The floor was excavated up to 8 in (21 cm) below the ground, the roof and walls being formed of poles, reeds, grass, and mud. Small hearths lay just inside the entrances.

Early villages in the north varied greatly in size, from hamlets of merely two or three pithouses to large settlements that contained as many as 25 to 35 houses, perhaps sometimes many more. Everywhere, the houses were arranged without apparent order, associated with storage pits and cooking ovens. Settlements in the Hohokam area of the Sonoran desert were made up of loose clusters of houses covering much larger areas. At all but the smallest villages, one or more structures appear to have had special functions. These are usually pithouses, but ones that display unusual

Reconstruction of a Mogollon pithouse village from the Pine Lawn phase by the Chicago Natural History Museum.

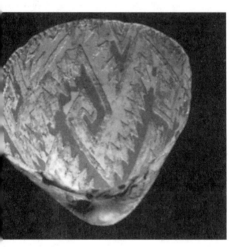

*Long-distance trade in luxuries.
(Top) Copper bells found at Mimbres
sites were imported from Mexico.
(Above) Hohokam etched shell.*

architectural features or greater dimensions than residential structures. The Sabik'eschee village in Chaco Canyon, New Mexico, comprised at least 60 pithouses and 45 well-built storage bins. One structure stood out, a pithouse with a difference – a low bench that encircled the interior and a floor area more than five times the size of the average dwelling in the settlement. The excavators believe the structure was only partially roofed. Many experts believe this is one of the earliest examples of a "Great Kiva," a ceremonial building commonplace in later centuries (Wills and Windes, 1989).

By AD 700 to 900, such kiva-like structures were a regular feature of Southwestern villages, which, by now, placed great importance on rituals that commemorated the endless cycle of passing seasons, reinforced the close kin ties that were central to farming in a high-risk environment, and provided a context for redistribution of food supplies, as well as reducing the potential for conflict.

There were considerable differences in the size of early farming villages throughout the Southwest, also in the range of trade objects in various settlements, as well as in house size and storage capacity. Clearly, these differences have important implications for understanding early social and political organization. Were these villages independent entities, or were some of them linked by alliances or other political ties? Do early farming settlements large and small, and a great diversity of pottery styles and material culture from village to village represent differences in social organization? Despite occasional large centers, most settlements were little more than simply family households, the so-called *rancheria*.

Not that these were completely self-sufficient settlements. Anyone farming in the Southwestern highlands had to maintain constant contacts with the lowlands, which were often only a short distance away, as was the case with historic Mormon populations living in the area (Plog, F., 1983). To argue that early Southwestern farming villages were autonomous, egalitarian, and completely self-sufficient appears to go against the environmental realities of the area. Any form of long-distance exchange of essentials and luxuries by farming cultures usually results in some form of ranked society. Modern Pueblo groups are far less egalitarian than often thought, a phenomenon that can also be observed in early Spanish records (Upham, 1982). Whether earlier Archaic, or even Paleo-Indian, societies were ranked is a matter of on-going debate.

Trade relationships probably played an important role in village social organization. Many essential commodities like obsidian, chert, and other raw materials were exchanged over considerable distances, sometimes even hundreds of miles. Utilitarian artifacts like pots passed through many hands. Luxuries like turquoise, copper bells, and sea shells were exchanged over enormous distances (Ericson and Baugh, 1993). The trade was apparently highly organized and conducted by local leaders (Upham, 1982). Some kivas may have served as centers for exchange systems.

Judging from historical records of intercommunity exchange in the Southwest, it involved a complex series of economic and social processes. It was conditioned by the great environmental diversity and the differences in productivity from one area to the next. With unpredictable rainfall, food shortages can result from poor piñon harvests or crop failure. Survival depended on gift exchanges between trading partners and friends, and on the social ties between them. So exchange equalized resources and also allowed the acquisition of valuable surpluses of luxury goods that might be traded later for food and other necessities. Every Southwestern group was dependent on others for ritual paraphernalia, items such as buffalo hides, red ocher, macaw feathers, sea shells, even coiled baskets used in naming ceremonies. The exchange could be between neighboring communities, along long, well-established trails that were in use for thousands of years, between friends or complete strangers, whose language one did not understand.

At first, exchange may have resulted from regular informal contacts, but in time these became more formalized. One set of rules and conventions applied to fellow villagers, normally based on notions of continuous sharing and mutual assistance, seasonal gambling, ceremonial redistribution, and trading parties. Everyone had access to local commodities and goods from afar. Exchange between neighboring communities often involved trading with relatives, or with non-strangers, with visitors bringing gifts in the expectation that they would be reciprocated in the future. Inter-community trading was constant, and sometimes took the form of informal markets, often on ceremonial occasions.

In recent times, southern desert villages would engage in inter-village entertainments where food and gifts were exchanged. These would distribute grain to needy communities, and also create trading friendships that could last for many generations. Long-distance trade was normally in the hands of men and conducted along a myriad trails, some possibly marked by petroglyphs and shrines. One ancient trail brought Pacific sea shells from near Los Angeles across the desert to Needles, along the Gila River, and then along various branches to many villages and pueblos. A complex trail network linked the Plains, Great Basin, Sonora, the Southwest and California at European contact, most of them maintained not by parties of traders, but by chains of exchange and gift friendship that handled different commodities like sea shells, buffalo robes, and turquoise ornaments over enormous distances (Doyel, 1991). Somewhat similar trail networks extended all over the Southeast after about 2000 BC. Exchange was an integral part of social relations, one that corrected economic differences, forged alliances and served as a basis for resolving disputes before warfare erupted.

Extensive cultural resource management surveys in many areas of the Southwest have changed earlier perceptions of ancient social organization. Prior to about AD 1100 most Southwestern sites averaged about three rooms. After 1100, the number increased to around 10. In both cases up to half the rooms were used for storage alone, with, perhaps, about 10 to 15 people living at each location. Most of these small communities were engaged in basic subsistence activities. They did not exist in isolation, for the inhabitants of each *rancheria* may have interacted with one another all the time, as well, perhaps, as maintaining ties with a common kiva, as is known to have happened in some areas of Arizona, or with one larger, central site. There were reciprocal ties between different communities that enabled individual households to acquire foodstuffs by exchange when shortages developed.

Occasionally, however, people lived in communities that formed more structured "alliances" (Upham, 1982), which shared some general characteristics:

— One or more central sites, even a central "zone" of clustered sites;
— Basically uniform architecture;
— Relatively homogeneous ceramic styles;
— Some signs of specialized craftsmanship;
— Regular trade and exchange;
— Some degree of social ranking or stratification.

On the Colorado Plateau, Fred Plog (1983) paints a picture of thousands of small farming communities that flourished for many generations. Occasionally, however, broader regional ties developed that connected multiple local exchange networks. These can be identified in the archaeological record by very homogeneous architecture and ceramic styles. These broad networks involved some trade relations, but more often were simply the product of a shared, more uniform ritual framework and world view. Society became more complex, but never to the higher degree of stratification that developed to the south in highland and lowland Mexico. These alliances waxed and waned, but wherever they developed, they were associated with dramatic population increases.

The Plog hypothesis, with its emphasis on spatial rainfall variations and food scarcities, contrasts with other theories that argue for alliances developed in environmentally favorable areas. Its main weakness is the great difficulty of reconstructing how alliances were structured. Were expert traders and entrepreneurs or powerful kin leaders, "Big Men" in common anthropological parlance, responsible for political leadership? Or did some other social mechanism allow development of more formal ties between scattered communities? At the moment, we do not know. Whatever these mechanisms, however, the closing centuries of pre-Columbian times saw a dramatic efflorescence and elaboration of Southwestern culture as population densities increased rapidly in the central and northern Southwest during the 11th century AD.

Further Reading

In addition to the references for Chapter 13:
Gumerman, George. 1984. *A View from Black Mesa*. University of Arizona Press, Tucson.
  A popular account of the Black Mesa area, scene of a major CRM research project in the Southwest.
Plog, Fred. 1974. *The Study of Ancient Culture Change*. Academic Press, New York.
  Plog examines the pithouse-pueblo transition in this much-quoted monograph.
Vivian, R. Gwinn. 1974. "Conservation and Diversion: water-control systems in the Anasazi Southwest," *in* Theodore Downing and McGuire Gibson, *Irrigation's Impact on Society*. University of Arizona Press, Tucson, Anthropological Papers 25, pp.95-112.
  Base-line article on water control and agriculture in the Southwest.
Wills, S.H.1989. *Early Prehistoric Agriculture in the American Southwest*. School of American Research Press, Santa Fé, NM.
  Closely argued and impressive statement on the origins of Southwestern agriculture based on up-to-date evidence.

CHAPTER 15

VILLAGES AND PUEBLOS

If there is one broad theme in Southwestern archaeology, it is that of cultural continuity that extends back deep into Archaic times and persists right up through the eventful centuries of Pueblo culture that immediately preceded European contact in the 16th century AD. We must now examine some of the complex cultural processes that took hold in the Southwest after the emergence of village life early in the Christian era (summaries in Cordell, 1997; Plog, S. 1997).

Pithouses remained in general use throughout the northern Southwest and the mountains until about AD 700. The next three centuries saw a change from pithouse villages to settlements made up of multi-room buildings constructed from adobe clay or masonry. In some areas, like Mesa Verde, Colorado, the change was a gradual one, with the first rooms being storage areas built behind pithouses. Later people moved into surface rooms, turning their old pithouses into kivas or ceremonial rooms. In other areas, the shift was a rapid one. The rate of changeover is so varied that no general cause like climatic change can be invoked (Cordell, 1997). Rather, an increased dependence on agriculture and more sedentary settlement followed from population growth (for discussion, see Plog, S., 1990). Large grain stocks were now husbanded from one harvest to the next, both as seed for the next season and as food surplus for the lean months. Domestic activities now took up much more space than hitherto. Semi-subterranean houses were too small for the purpose, and it is hard to build interconnecting underground rooms without walls collapsing. So instead of constructing further below-surface rooms, the farmers erected above-ground structures for milling, storage, and other activities (illus. p. 318). Such rooms were not so well insulated as semi-subterranean dwellings. In time the farmers built series of rooms abutting on one another, forming pueblos, a thermally relatively efficient way of living above ground in a climate with hot summers and cold winters. Such arrangements may have been more adaptive, but they were by no means universal. In many parts of the northern Southwest, people lived in dispersed or one- or two-room dwellings. Whether these differences are the result of using a variety of agricultural technologies or field systems is unknown.

The process may have been more complicated. Fred Plog (1974) used survey and excavation data from the upper Little Colorado River Valley and chronicled a population increase between Basketmaker and Pueblo times. He found that the people engaged in more and more diverse activities, and

Sites mentioned in Chapter 15.

Interior of a Pueblo room: Hopi women grinding corn, 1895. The transition from pithouse to pueblo involved increasingly specialized use of space.

were more sedentary, after about AD 200. Three hundred years later, the pithouse villages were much larger, then progressively abandoned as people dispersed into smaller villages. This dispersal did not, apparently, coincide with a major climatic change, so Plog believes that the villages were too large and the social organization too simple to handle the complex environmental and social problems that developed over many generations. The concentration of people into larger communities may have resulted in more complex exchange networks, increased food sharing, and cooperation in hunting and foraging. These broke down when the population scattered, so individual communities turned to more dependence on agriculture as a more productive way of feeding smaller population densities. The Plog study shows how complicated the change from Basketmaker to Pueblo was, a change involving not only population growth, but new subsistence strategies and ways of integrating society into larger social units (for womens' roles, see Mobley-Tanaka, 1997).

Between AD 750 and 900, village settlement expanded greatly throughout the northern Southwest, and especially on the Colorado Plateau. There was a great diversity of settlement, everything from large sites to tiny *rancherias*, representing a great heterogeneity of social organization and political life. Some of the largest settlements of the period in southwestern Colorado and northwest New Mexico were home to as many as 100 to 120 households (Wilshusen and Blinman, 1992).

The Chaco Phenomenon
AD 900 to 1150

Chaco Canyon is a dramatic place, set in a stark landscape. The huge cliffs of the canyon glow yellow-gold in the sun, contrasting with the softer tones of desert sand, sage, and occasional cottonwood trees. Great shadows fall across the canyon as the sun sets, the grandiose landscape dwarfing the walls of the great pueblos that are camouflaged naturally against the high cliffs. A thousand years ago, flickering fires, barking dogs, and the echoing murmur of human voices would have greeted the evening visitor (Cordell, 1997; Noble, D. 1984). Today, the ancient human settlements of the Anasazi are silent, an integral part of a spectacular desert landscape (Crown and Judge, 1991).

Beginnings. The Chaco sites document a dramatic increase in population density and cultural complexity that began in the 860s and lasted two and a half centuries (Windes and Ford, 1996). During this time, the distinctive so-called "Chaco Phenomenon" expanded from its canyon homeland to encompass an area of more than 25,000 sq. miles (64,750 sq. km) of the San Juan Basin and adjacent uplands. (Recent estimates more than double this area, and research continues (Lekson and others, 1988).) The people constructed large, well-planned towns, extensive road and water-control systems, and outlying sites that were linked to the canyon by roads and visual communication systems. Many farmers still lived in small, dispersed villages. Many luxury items are found in Chaco sites of this period, items traded from afar: turquoise, the bones of exotic macaws, and copper bells, to mention only a few.

Many intriguing questions surround the Chaco Phenomenon. How did such an elaborate efflorescence of Anasazi culture arise so suddenly, and collapse with such rapidity? What were the cultural processes that led to the sudden emergence of regional integration in this area of the Southwest (Adler, 1996; Adler, Pool, and Leonard, 1996)? The Chaco area is a desert environment, with long winters, short growing seasons, and marginal rainfall. How could the Anasazi have developed such an elaborate culture in a high-risk environment, where the most one might expect were communities of widely dispersed farming villages? The number of residential rooms suggests a far larger population than could be supported by the available arable land. What activities in the Canyon prompted a much higher use and breakage of clay vessels than usual and the construction of many miles of long, wide roads through a sparsely vegetated desert where such constructions appear unnecessary?

Nineteenth-century artist's reconstruction of Pueblo Bonito, Chaco Canyon, New Mexico.

More than 2400 archaeological sites tell the story of this place. Paleo-Indian and Archaic people hunted and foraged in Chaco Canyon. During the 1st millennium BC, semi-sedentary hunter-gatherers began to cultivate squash and corn in the Canyon. About AD 490, locally developed strains of corn and perhaps an increase in annual rainfall led to the appearance of the first sedentary villages in the south of the Canyon, as small groups of farmers took advantage of locally developed corn strains and more plentiful rainfall. Among them was Shabik'eschee, a village farming (Basketmaker III) settlement of shallow, earth-walled pithouses with wood and mud roofs (see Chapter 14) (Wills and Windes, 1989). Each pithouse had a stone storage hut behind it to store corn, squash, beans, and other foods. The largest village in the Canyon boasted as many as 20 pithouses clustered close to one another. How permanent settlement was here has been questioned, as scarcities of piñon nuts may have caused people to disperse at intervals.

During village (Basketmaker) times, the Chaco Canyon population was still small. Then, between AD 700 and 900, the Anasazi Pueblo Indians largely abandoned pithouses and now lived in surface, masonry dwellings. Originally, they were enlarged versions of the Basketmaker storerooms, often facing the southeast to take advantage of the winter sun for warmth. The clusters of rooms, known as pueblos, were shaped into small arcs, a layout that made each room equidistant from the circular pithouses in the center. These gradually became kivas, the focal points of ceremonial life. Despite these changes, the Canyon population was still very small, perhaps between 1000 and 1500 people.

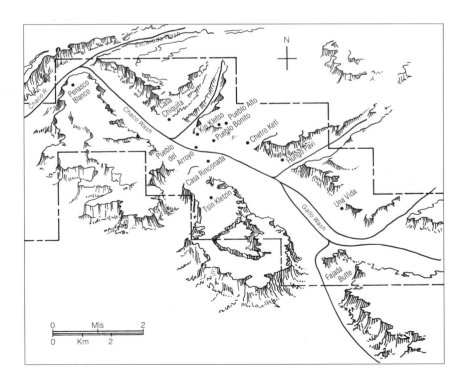

The main sites in Chaco Canyon, New Mexico. The dashed line indicates the extent of the National Monument.

The Great Houses. During the 9th and 10th centuries, summer rainfall was highly variable. Instead of dispersing, the Chaco Anasazi built three "great houses" – Penasco Blanco, Pueblo Bonito, and Una Vida – large pueblos located at the junctions of major drainages. The largest of these, Pueblo Bonito near the northeast wall of the Canyon, stood five stories high along its rear wall and remained in use for more than two centuries. The first pueblo structure rose on the site of a pithouse village and expanded rapidly. Construction of the semi-circular town began in the 850s and accelerated between 1030 and 1079, when the builders added the two great kivas. In its 11th-century heyday, Pueblo Bonito had at least 600 rooms in use and could house about 1000 people.

Chaco architecture was based on rectangular rooms, built in contiguous blocks and round chambers (Lekson, 1984). Some of the latter were subterranean, located in the plaza areas in front of room blocks. Many others were elevated into room blocks and built into rectangular rooms, usually enclosures built exclusively for this purpose. Construction was simple. Once the site had been leveled and the foundations laid, a room block typically began as a series of continuous, long parallel walls. Cross walls were added later, as the long sides rose higher. Once one story was complete, the rooms were roofed individually and then used as the foundation for the next story. Chacoan walls were built of local Cliff House sandstone in both harder and softer forms from different cliff strata. The harder rock could easily be split at right angles, making it easier to shape for wall building. The builders used a variety of methods to shape the exposed stone faces, among them grinding and pecking. Clay-sand from Canyon alluvial deposits mixed with water served as mortar. The main load on the walls at Pueblo Bonito was the upper stories, so the masons built the walls wide and stable, reducing the width with each story for stability. The ceilings are high, rooms well constructed with cored masonry covered on both sides with carefully selected ashlar, sometimes arranged in alternating courses of large and small stones to form patterns. These decorative veneers were covered with adobe plaster or matting. The great kivas were built with care, roofed over with carefully dressed pine beams, many of them carried in from considerable distances away. This extravagance may reflect the religious importance of the major towns (Marshall and Doyel, 1981).

No one knows why the Chaco people congregated in "great houses." It may have been to avoid building on valuable agricultural land and a way of concentrating food resources. Interestingly, by no means everyone lived in the great houses, which lie on the north side of the canyon. The opposite wall sheltered smaller settlements, many of them little more than a few households, located in areas where farming land was more spread out.

Archaeologists disagree as to whether Pueblo Bonito and the other great houses were built according to a master plan. The towns were really agglomerations of households, organized along kin lines, each of which built its own rooms inside the semi-circular outer wall, which was erected by communal effort. The outer walls were battered to support the massive weight of five stories of rooms, which were terraced to allow access without an interior system of ladders. Each kin group used its smaller kivas in the heart of the room blocks as workshops and as places for educating children,

Cylindrical Anasazi vase with painted, polychrome decoration from Pueblo Bonito, c. AD 1200, height 20 cm.

storytelling, and family ceremonies. The great kivas stood on either side of a line of rooms that divided the pueblo into two areas that probably reflected the duality of social organization in Anasazi pueblos, like the Winter and Summer people of modern pueblos. Here the people gathered for more formal ceremonies and to make decisions about the governing of the community as a whole.

The nine larger settlements within Chaco Canyon all have at least one great kiva. The most famous example at Casa Rinconada is about 63 ft (19.2 m) across, and others are almost as large. The amount of labor involved in digging these subterranean chambers and constructing the walls, roofs, and antechambers must have been considerable, for some kiva walls were at least 11 ft (3.4 m) high. They are entered by a ladder or through recessed stone staircases, often through an antechamber beyond the stairs. Common kiva features include wall niches where offerings of beads and pendants were sometimes placed, encircling benches around the walls, pairs of masonry lined vaults, and a raised firebox in the center (Morgan, W., 1994).

By AD 1050, five great pueblos dominated Chaco Canyon. We do not know how many people lived within its cliffs and in the immediate vicinity. Estimates range from 2000 to as high as 20,000. Gwinn Vivian (1990) has calculated the potential carrying capacity of the Canyon soils. He believes no more than about 5500 people ever lived in the Canyon: the landscape could support no more. Vivian is probably right, for Chaco was no Garden of Eden. The nearby mesa is the boldest topographic feature for many miles and a rich source of wild plant foods. Some of those who disagree with him theorize that the great houses were constructed to accommodate far larger

(Right, and opposite) Pueblo Bonito, Chaco Canyon: a photograph taken earlier this century, and a plan. One entered the pueblo by climbing ladders over the protective wall. The lower rooms were probably used mainly for storage.

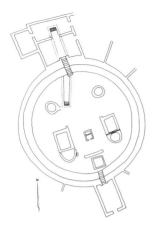

(Above) Plan of the great kiva at Casa Rinconada, Chaco Canyon, showing the subfloor passage, fire box, fire screen, parallel vaults or foot drums, seating pits for the roof-support columns, and the north antechamber rooms.

influxes of people, who came to the Canyon occasionally, perhaps for regular religious observances. The controversy is still unresolved (Crown and Judge, 1991).

Trade and Leadership. Despite diverse food resources, the Chaco people were trapped inside the narrow confines of their canyon. Unable to disperse easily over a wider territory, they took advantage of long-standing kin and trade links with communities living elsewhere on the Colorado Plateau and made themselves the hub of a much wider world. No one knows who held authority in a society that would be classified as a mid-level complex society where prominent individuals lacked the authoritarian power that enabled them to achieve complete dominance. Rather, Chaco and other Anasazi pueblos were probably riddled with intense competition and factionalism between different individuals and kin groups (Upham, 1991). Violence may have played an important role (see p. 343).

During the 10th century, Chaco Canyon assumed a dominant role in the processing of turquoise into finished ornaments (Toll, 1991). Turquoise does not occur in the area, but the Chaco people had access to, and may even have controlled, sources near Santa Fé, New Mexico, about 100 miles (161 km) to the east and elsewhere. Many small Chaco villages contained turquoise workshops, and ritual ornaments in all stages of manufacture have been found among the more than 60,000 turquoise fragments found in the Canyon. Other ritual objects associated with Chaco towns include cylindrical vases, human effigy vessels, pottery incense burners, copper bells, sea-shell trumpets, painted tablets and wooden effigies, also macaw skeletons, and elaborate inlaid decoration in selenite, mica, and turquoise

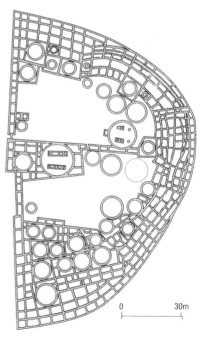

0   30m

on shell, wood, or basketry. Chaco itself may also have assumed an important role as ritual center in its own right. Whatever the religious role of the Canyon, it seems certain that the turquoise trade was of importance to its inhabitants.

By about AD 1050, the Chaco Phenomenon was in full swing, a number of dispersed communities that interacted constantly with one another, linked by regular exchanges of essential foods and other commodities. Tree-rings show that the next 80 years were ones of generally good rainfall, a weather cycle that may have kept the system going longer than it might otherwise have done. Chaco Canyon's central role in the Phenomenon is not disputed, but exactly what this role was remains somewhat of a mystery.

The Chaco pueblos are remarkable for the small number of burials found within their precincts, probably of important leaders. These burial clusters are associated with very large numbers of cylinder vessels, wooden staffs, and other artifacts associated with important individuals. The people buried in these clusters were also taller, suggesting a better diet (Akins, 1986). Pueblo Bonito (illus. pp. 322–323) as we have seen has more than 600 rooms, yet only between 50 and 60 burials can be associated with the town during its 150-year life (Hayes and others, 1981). Neil Judd once estimated that the settlement should have experienced between 4700 and 5400 deaths during the same period. The frequency of burials in Chaco Canyon generally is far smaller than elsewhere in the Southwest. Perhaps few people were buried within the confines of the Canyon.

Beyond the general indications of farming, hunting, and foraging, we know little about the activities that took place in larger Chaco settlements. But there are some curious features in the archaeological record, especially from the Pueblo Alto site, which lies above the Canyon, not on its floor. This large settlement was built between 1020 and 1060, but only 5 of the 85 rooms were actually inhabited. The remainder were large suites without interconnecting doors that may have had some social or political importance, or small, connected storerooms that opened not into the settlement with its plaza, but onto the adjacent road. These were inaccessible from within the pueblo. It is as if the residents had but limited control over these storehouses. Pueblo Alto's trash middens yielded over 150,000 potsherds, a breakage rate quite out of proportion to the tiny population of the pueblo. Many of the vessels were made of clay imported from the Chuska area, some 45 miles (72.4 km) to the west. Unusually large quantities of animal bones and imported Washington Pass chert, also from the Chuska area, came from the same trash middens. The trash in the Pueblo Alto middens is layered, as if it was deposited intermittently, perhaps when people converged on Chaco for regular seasonal gatherings (Lekson and others, 1988).

Outliers. By AD 1115, at least 70 communities dispersed over more than 25,000 sq. miles (64,750 sq. km) of northwest New Mexico and parts of southern Colorado were linked through the socioeconomic and ritual networks centered on Chaco Canyon. Judging from other such networks, the trade and ritual activities of the Chaco Phenomenon were probably controlled by a small number of people. But whether these individuals formed a social elite with special privileges reserved to them, and them alone, or were simply members of an important kin group, is still uncertain (Sebastian, 1991).

Outlying sites display considerable cultural variation, but they share architectural features such as great or tower kivas with Pueblo Bonito and other large Canyon centers, and contain much Chaco pottery. In most places, the people used Pueblo Bonito-style architecture, often choosing dramatic settings such as cliffs or canyon walls for their pueblo.

The center of the Chaco regional system shifted northward in the early 1100s, as the architectural styles in the Canyon changed from D- and E-shaped houses to more block-like styles (known as the McElmo-style) (Lekson, 1984). The Salmon Ruin near Bloomfield, New Mexico, is a 290-room pueblo with a Great Kiva and tower kiva. It was constructed in three planned stages between AD 1088 and 1106. The distribution of local and Chaco vessels through the pueblo suggest that Salmon was founded by both local San Juan people and migrants from Chaco itself. Chaco pottery was associated with the tower kiva and associated rooms, as if there was a strong ideological component to the organization of what appears to have been an egalitarian community. It was, however, a site whose inhabitants had a "high degree of technical knowledge and specialization, and a centralized authority structure, tight social control, and membership in a central network economically and physically linked to the Chaco" (Irwin-Williams,1980).

In a sense, outlying communities like Salmon were not colonies, but rather descendant communities, places that were often established in somewhat marginal agricultural areas as a result of population growth or factionalism within older communities. Some were formed to exploit nearby natural resources. The Pueblo Bonito-style architecture used to build them often made dramatic use of the natural landscape, the buildings extending mesa cliffs, forming parts of canyon walls. Some pueblos stand in complete isolation in the harsh desert, what has been called a "human monument in the void of the desert plain." "It is as if the environment is personified with attributes of mythological character, and the placement of structures was dictated by Chacoan cosmography and sacred geography, balanced by certain economic considerations" (Marshall and Doyel, 1981).

Chaco's "Roads". The Chaco Phenomenon is famous for its "road system." Chacoan "roads" were first identified in the 1890s and again in the 1920s. In the 1930s, early aerial photographs revealed faint traces of what appeared to be canals emanating from the Canyon. During the 1970s and 1980s, a new generation of investigators used aerial photographs and side-scan radar to place the Canyon at the center of a vast ancient landscape. Perhaps as many as 400 miles (650 km) of unpaved ancient trackways link Chaco in an intricate web with over 30 outlying settlements. The "roads" are up to 40 ft (12 m) wide and were cut a few inches into the soil, or marked by low banks or stone walls. Sometimes, the road makers simply cleared the vegetation and loose soil or stones from the pathway, lining some segments with boulders. The roads run straight for long distances, in one instance as long as 60 miles (95 km). They do not follow contours, but change direction in abrupt turns, with stairways and ramps to surmount steep obstacles. These may be little more than toe holds, or elaborate stairways with wide steps cut out of bedrock or formed from masonry blocks. Each approaches the Canyon, then descends via stonecut steps down the cliffs to the valley floor. There they merge in the narrow

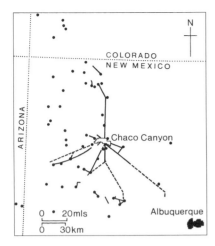

The Chacoan road system. (Right) Jackson Stairway, Chaco Canyon. (Above) Map of the road system, and outlying sites of the Chaco Phenomenon (black dots). Solid lines indicate roads documented by ground surveys, dashed lines segments known from aerial surveys.

defiles and split, each leading to a different great house. At three locations where they merge, there is a groove in the center of the road, which clearly demarcates one side from the other.

By using aerial photographs, fieldworkers have been able to trace roads extending from Chaco almost to the Colorado/New Mexico border and Aztec Ruins, some 50 miles (80 km) away. Other roads connect Chaco to natural resource source areas in modern-day Zuñi country and elsewhere. More than 250 miles (402 km) of roads have been detected on air photographs so far, but the system may have extended as far north as the San Juan Range in the Rocky Mountains to the north, the Mogollon Mountains to the south, and from the turquoise mines near Santa Fé in the east to the Little Colorado River in the west. Current thinking suspects that the Chaco Phenomenon was the center of a vast regional system that extended far beyond the San Juan Basin (Crown and Judge, 1991).

Chaco road construction must have involved the deployment of large numbers of people and considerable group organization. Unlike the trail systems that connected hundreds of ancient communities in the far west and in the Eastern Woodlands, these were wide, straight highways, whose significance still eludes us. Were they highways for transporting valuable natural resources to major pueblos? Or were they, as James Judge argues, pilgrim roads? Or did they have some much more profound spiritual importance?

One prevalent hypothesis argues that without draft animals or wheeled carts, the Chaco people had no use for formal roads for their everyday business. Originally, perhaps, people traveled from outlying communities to Chaco to acquire turquoise objects, to trade food for ritual paraphernalia. In time, this trade became institutionalized in regular ceremonies and festivals, where people gathered from many miles around for seasonal rituals, for exchange of food and other commodities, and where leaders from widely dispersed communities gathered to cement political and economic alliances. Each member of the network would have complex obligations to fulfill, among them, presumably, the supplying of people to construct and maintain the road system, to transport wooden beams for building large pueblos in Chaco (more than 200,000 were needed to build them), and for many communal tasks. In other words, the Chaco system was a mechanism for integrating a large number of communities scattered widely in a harsh and unpredictable environment. By regulating and maintaining a large and far-flung exchange system, the leaders who controlled this intricate system were able to support far more people than the area would normally have carried, using a very simple agricultural technology to do so. Every leader must have been a player in a complex, and ever-shifting political environment, where the periphery was as important as the center (Kantner, 1996).

This ingenious theory stumbles on two points. First, the focus of Anasazi life was the household and ties of kin, which were the means by which people fed themselves and passed on accumulated expertise about making a living from one generation to the next. Second, many of the Chaco roads go nowhere, although they are linked to a Great House or kiva. We Westerners tend to think of roads as traveling from A to B, which means that we have tended to join incomplete segments of Chacoan roads with straight dotted lines. The roads may not have actually been joined. While major north and south tracks radiated from Chaco, only about 155 miles (250 km) of the roads have been verified on the ground.

A more likely explanation lies in Pueblo cosmology. The so-called "Great North Road" travels 40 miles (63 km) north from Chaco before it disappears abruptly in Kutz Canyon. North is the primary direction among Keresan-speaking Pueblo peoples, who may have ancestry among the Chaco people. North led to the origin, the place where the spirits of the dead traveled. Perhaps the Great North Road was an umbilical cord to the underworld and a conduit of spiritual power. The Keresan also believe in a Middle Place, a point where the four cardinal directions converged. Pueblo Bonito is laid out according to these directions and may have served as Chaco's Middle Place.

Thus, Chaco and its trackways may have formed a sacred landscape which gave order to the world and linked outlying communities with a powerful Middle Place through spiritual ties that remained even as many households moved away from the Canyon. Think of a giant ideological spider's web with a lattice of obligations among its component parts, and you probably have a credible model for Chaco's role in the 11th-century Anasazi world. The great houses of the Canyon lay at the center of the web, connected to communities many miles away by kin ties and regular exchanges of food and other commodities. Gwinn Vivian believes the landscape was a powerful statement, which he calls "We the Chaco" (discussion in Vivian, Gwinn, 1997).

Frank Cushing and other early anthropologists commented on the elaborate ceremonial life among more sedentary Pueblo peoples like the Zuñi. Many of these ceremonies made use of astronomical observations, sometimes a place-specific horizon calendar (Williamson, 1981). By standing in a particular place and observing the sun's cycles throughout the year, priests were able to correlate their agricultural and ceremonial calendars to sunrise and sunset points on the surrounding horizon. Cushing watched a Zuñi sun priest at his astronomical observations. "He slowly approached a square open tower and seated himself just inside on a rude, ancient stone chair, and before a pillar sculptured with the face of the sun, the sacred hand, the morning star, and the new moon. There he awaited with prayer and sacred song the rising of the sun," he wrote. "Nor may the Sun Priest err in his watch of Time's flight; for many are the houses in Zuñi with cores on their walls or ancient plates imbedded therein, whole opposite, a convenient window or small port-hole lets in the light of the rising sun, which shines but two mornings in the three hundred and sixty-five on the same place" (Cushing, 1882-83). Horizon calendars are still used by Hopi and other Pueblo Indians (McCluskey, 1977).

There can be little doubt that similar calendars and other astronomical observations were in use during Anasazi times. The Hovenweep pueblo structures in Colorado were erected by a group of Anasazi related to the Mesa Verde people in the late 12th and mid-13th centuries. They include round, square, or D-shaped towers that were originally two or three stories high. At least one of these towers, Hovenweep Castle, has a room with special sun-sighting ports aligned with the summer and winter solstices. Nearby Holly House contains petroglyph panels with symbols that may represent the sun and other heavenly bodies. There is also possible evidence for astronomical observation in Chaco Canyon, at Casa Rinconada and Pueblo Bonito. As far as can be determined, Southwestern ancient astronomy was entirely solar, with considerable emphasis on the solstices (Williamson, 1981; 1984).

The Chaco Collapse. Between 1050 and 1100, the rains were plentiful. Building activity engulfed the Canyon as the Great Houses expanded. Chaco's web of interconnections prospered, perhaps longer than it might otherwise have done. The Chaco population rose steadily, which was not a serious problem as long as winter rainfall fertilized the fields. Then, in AD 1130, tree-rings tell us that 50 years of intense drought settled over the Colorado Plateau. "We the Chaco" became a meaningless fiction in the face of crop failure and famine. Soon the outlying communities ceased to trade and share food with the great houses, which forced the Canyon towns to rely on their own already overstressed environment. The strategy they had adopted centuries earlier fell apart and trapped them in their home under more desperate conditions than ever before. Dry year followed dry year, causing crop failures and reducing wild plant and animal resources in an area that was relatively marginal for agriculture at the best of times. By 1130, the Chaco system had probably been expanded to its effective limits by growing population densities. There was a population decline after 1130 until the next century.

The only recourse was deeply ingrained in Anasazi philosophy – movement (see Naranjo, 1995). Within a few generations, the great pueblos stood empty, as well over half Chaco's population dispersed into villages, hamlets, and pueblos far from the great arroyo. Those who remained settled in small communities even the parched land could support. But they were gone by the early 1200s. We have, of course, no means of knowing how many people perished when the 50-year drought desiccated the land. It was but a short-term episode on a much larger climatic canvas that brought long-term fluctuations in rainfall patterns, water tables, and river flows at about 500-year intervals. The emptying of big houses like Pueblo Bonito and Chetro Ketl seems like an epochal event at a distance of 900 years, but it was merely part of the constant ebb and flow of Anasazi existence.

The Chaco system collapsed, but the collapse appears to have been a natural one, in the sense that the people either moved to other, more productive areas where they maintained long-term alliances, formed independent, highly scattered communities, or simply remained in environmentally favorable areas. Some may even have reverted to the largely mobile hunter-gatherer lifeway of their Archaic predecessors.

Some communities still continued to flourish in the Canyon, and at outlying pueblos like Aztec and Salmon to the north, but they now show strong influence from Mesa Verde, both in kiva architecture and ceramics, among other features. Whether these changes were the result of migration from the Mesa Verde area (Vivian, G. and Mathews, 1965) or simply the diffusion of ideas is a matter of discussion (Toll and others, 1980). Mesa Verde was the last remaining large population center in the general area at the time (see below), so the transfer of some culture traits is hardly surprising. Throughout the area once integrated by the Chaco system, the reorganized society that emerged from the prolonged drought cycle probably bore some resemblance to Pueblo Indian society in the area immediately before European contact.

The Chaco Phenomenon was by no means the only centralized political and social system flourishing in the Southwest about 900 years ago, for there were other complex societies living in sharply contrasting ecological zones.

Hohokam
AD 300 to 1500

The Hohokam (O'odham: "those who have gone") tradition of the southern desert regions of the Southwest represents a second great tradition of ancient Pueblo society. Until quite recently, the celebrated Snaketown site on the Gila River dominated any discussion of the Hohokam (Haury, 1976). But a new generation of researches with a regional focus has given us very different perspectives on a long-lived and unique desert adaptation (Crown and Judge,1991; Gumerman, 1990).

The earliest sedentary agricultural settlements in southeastern Arizona date to between 1000 and 500 BC (Huckell, 1995). They lack ceramics, which first appear before AD 300. The origins of the subsequent Hohokam culture are still controversial, with one school of thought favoring a movement of outsiders into the Hohokam area from northern Mexico,

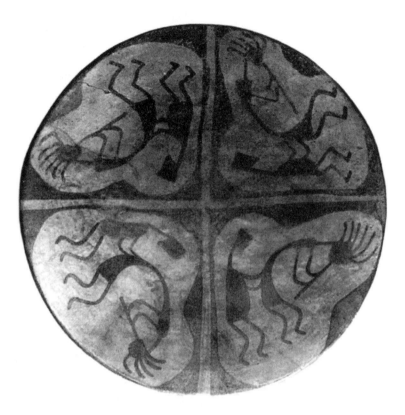

The Hohokam site of Snaketown, Arizona. (Right) Pottery bowl with flute players, diameter c. 27 cm. (Below) The Snaketown ball court.

while others consider it an indigenous development (Crown, 1991). Most, if not all, the elements which made up subsequent Hohokam culture were present in indigenous farming communities by the beginning of the so-called Pioneer Period, which dates from about AD 300 to 775.

The Snaketown site (so called after the O'odham name Skoaquik, "place of snakes") lies on the upper terrace of the Gila River. Wide expanses of undulating mounds distinguish the site from the surrounding countryside, mounds that have attracted archaeological attention since the late 19th century. Emil Haury (1976) conducted the most extensive excavations at Snaketown, investigating 167 houses out of the hundreds at the site. He also dug into Mound 29, where he identified seven phases of Hohokam settlement, subsequently modified by others (Wilcox, McGuire, and Sternberg, 1981). Even in its earliest stages, the Snaketown houses surrounded a central plaza, three large ones facing north, west, and south. At this period, the Snaketown farmers were probably dry-farming maize, for there are no signs of major irrigation works (for a discussion of phases, see Crown, 1991). But by late in the Pioneer Period, the farmers were using irrigation canals, while macaw and parrot bones, also shells and turquoise, provide evidence for long-distance trade. By AD 700, characteristic red-on-buff Hohokam potsherds occur over a broad area far beyond the confines of the Gila-Salt and Tucson basins of southern Arizona.

The Colonial Period (AD 775 to 975) saw the appearance of house clusters, with three or four structures opening on a common courtyard. By this time, Snaketown was a large village, with a ball court and several capped storage pits (discussed below). Most Hohokam sites were smaller than Snaketown, some little more than farmsteads, others hamlets of two or three house clusters. Farming activity picked up, as canal systems along major rivers became more extensive, people experimented with new crops such as tobacco and agave, and expanded dry fields.

Snaketown reached its greatest extent during the Sedentary Period (AD 975 to 1150), when three new mounds were built around the central plaza and a second ball court constructed (Wilcox and Sternberg, 1983). Many of Snaketown's mounds were trash heaps, which provided Haury and other excavators with an invaluable record of human occupation over many centuries. One of the new mounds built around the central plaza was somewhat different, being made of material dug from the surrounding area mixed with a little trash, then capped with a hard clay mixture and enclosed within a pole palisade. Hohokam farmers continued to expand their irrigation canals, and added amaranth to their crop repertoire. The Hohokam regional system now reached its greatest extent, revealed by a wide distribution of ball courts and red-on-buff pottery over a large area from near the Mexican border to far up the Verde River.

The Classic Period (AD 1150 to 1350) shows change from earlier times. Snaketown itself was abandoned suddenly, if the evidence for many burned houses is to be believed. The area around the site was never really occupied again, though the basic farming pattern was continued along the Gila and Salt Rivers. Hohokam occupation of the Salt-Gila Basin intensified, but disappeared in more outlying areas, for reasons which are not understood. The larger ceremonial sites now boasted contiguous-walled, pueblo-like structures of coursed adobe, the most famous being the Great House at Casa Grande, where the courses rise four stories high (Wilcox

Snaketown stone pigment mortar in the shape of a toad, length 12 cm.

and Shenk, 1977). The Hohokam regional system shrank drastically, for the platform mounds which now measure its extent are confined to the Salt-Gila Basin and a loop southward into the desert (Wilcox and Sternberg, 1983; McGuire and Howard, 1977).

Hohokam settlement systems developed around self-sufficiency, where each community, and each hierarchy of communities, tended to look inward, within its own drainage area. Despite the wide distribution of ball courts, there was no formal Hohokam regional settlement system, nor was there close economic interdependency on a regional scale, or the political relationships that might accompany such a development (Gregory, 1991). There was never anything like the Chaco road system or any other form of connecting hub in Hohokam country, where local environmental variables were of vital importance to people dependent on river flows and skilled irrigation works. Nevertheless, relationships between different settlements were both more complex and varied than the archaeological record suggests at first glance. As Bruce Masse has pointed out in a synthesis of Hohokam subsistence (1991), the Hohokam never mastered the desert. "The desert was the master, and the Hohokam were never quite able to throw off the shackles of their environmental bondage," despite their expertise at irrigation and long-distance contacts. Local environmental conditions were all-important.

Hohokam trade and exchange have generated controversy, for Snaketown and other communities are known to have traded shell, stone, and other commodities over an enormous area, most of it within the confines of southern Arizona's Sonoran desert, but also much further afield (Doyel, 1991). The Hohokam exchanged foodstuffs and utilitarian raw materials, ceremonial objects and ornaments like macaw feathers and shells, prestige items, as well as information. The controversy surrounds the relationship between the Hohokam and cultural groups on the other side of the Mexican border. Many archaeologists believe capped platform mounds, clay figurines, certain forms of polished and painted vessels, and ball courts show the Hohokam were immigrants from Mexico. Others argue that Mexican imports were confined to a limited range of ceremonial artifacts and that the Hohokam were of indigenous origin. Copper bells, mosaic mirrors, and tropical birds from Casas Grandes (see below), while relatively rare, are often cited as imports. The Hohokam were middlemen in the sea-shell trade from the Gulf of California and the southern California coast (where some Hohokam sherds have been found). Between AD 800 and 1100, the Hohokam traded through a network of ball-court communities between the Little Colorado in the north and the Mexican border in the south. The extent of this network has been traced through distinctive artifacts and materials and through sourcing studies of tool-making stone and other commodities. About 1150, the Gila Bend area ceased to supply sea shells, long-distance trade contracted, and many of the Hohokam's most famous products were no longer made. The exchange system worked by people traveling direct to the sources of, say, tool-making stone or shells, or through the use of middlemen. Communities probably received items from the Colorado Plateau by what is often called "down-the-line trade," where desirable commodities or artifacts are passed from hand-to-hand over long distances, with progressively fewer being available the further one lives from the source. There are also a few instances of isolated Hohokam dwellings in remote locations, for example the pithouse in a small village in the upper Verde Valley close to an important source of argillite stone (Fish and Fish, 1977), as if people were traveling to exploit key resources.

Hohokam communities lay at the hub of the trade routes which extended from the Great Plains all the way to the California coast and into Mexico. They were strategically placed to handle salt and shell, two key commodities in Southwestern life, with major river valleys draining through the Phoenix Basin providing natural corridors between the Plains and the Pacific coast. Within Hohokam country, trade fairs and markets at sites with ball courts and plazas allowed the exchange not only of utilitarian commodities, but of prestige objects like carved stone and tropical bird feathers. One function of the more than 225 ball courts of the Sedentary Period may have been to facilitate the exchange of people and goods. The Terrace Garden site in the New River Drainage contains a ball court which was used from AD 800 to 1050. A large ground-stone tool manufacturing area was associated with the court, the entire complex being surrounded by stone and potsherd scatters which seem to be evidence of temporary occupations. David Doyel and Mark Elson (1985) believe the court was associated with the manufacture and trading of ground-stone tools.

The Hohokam tradition flourished for more than 1000 years. What began as a web of interconnected villages became increasingly more complex as the centuries passed and cultural and social boundaries formed. Large-scale irrigation led to the formation of corporate kin groups, themselves cross-cut by sodalities, which were integrated over a large region by a ceremonial exchange system centered around ball courts (Wilcox, 1991). This system disintegrated in about AD 1100, giving way to much smaller, local systems, as patterns of both subsistence and settlement changed considerably. Between about AD 1350 and 1450, some of the largest irrigation systems and sites in the Salt-Gila Basin were abandoned, perhaps as a result of flooding from unusually high river flows, which swept away long-established canal systems, putting the clusters of Hohokam population along their banks at considerable risk (Gregory, 1991). Fortified sites appear, as if fighting erupted, as the villagers intensified their efforts at irrigation. About 40 families, who lived on platform mounds in the Phoenix Basin, appear to have assumed responsibility for administering canals and other irrigation works. By the 14th century, the authority of these families was in decline, and a century later the Hohokam vanished from history. The relationships between the surviving Hohokam populations and the people found living in the area by Spanish explorers are not yet clearly understood. But many archaeologists believe the present-day O'odham inhabitants are descended from the Hohokam.

Mesa Verde and Mimbres
AD 500 to 1300

Between AD 900 and 1150, most of the Southwest was not part of the Chaco or Hohokam regional systems. There were many local cultural developments, where population densities were higher than usual, where soil and water conservation were practiced, and where some quite large settlements flourished. These were the areas between the regional systems, localized developments without the regional settlement hierarchies so characteristic of Chaco, and Hohokam, and, later, Casas Grandes.

Mesa Verde (AD 500 to 1300). Mesa Verde covers an area north and northwest of the San Juan Basin (Noble, D., 1985; Rohn, 1977; 1989). This is a lusher environment that is wetter than much of the Southwest, with a natural juniper and piñon vegetational cover and many natural springs and seeps. As early as AD 950, there were significant differences between the Anasazi communities at Mesa Verde and Chaco, differences reflected in kiva architecture, burial practices, and perhaps ceramics. The Mesa Verde people used a different building technique, employing single – or double-coursed masonry for their kivas and pueblos.

Human occupation was probably sparse in the Mesa Verde area before about AD 575, but always greater than at Chaco. By AD 600, Basketmaker peoples were farming in the area. These Anasazi communities typically sheltered an extended family, villages of six to ten pithouses. Between 750 and 1150, the Anasazi Pueblo groups constructed surface villages made up of lines of post-and-mud rooms and associated subterranean pithouses. By the 9th century, these structures had become fully fledged pueblo complexes, that is to say, blocks of living and storage rooms, many of them as much as twice the size of earlier Basketmaker communities.

During the 12th century, hundreds of Anasazi households moved from dispersed communities into large towns, situated by the banks of rivers, in sheltered valleys, and built into natural rockshelters in the walls of deep canyons. The population of the northern San Juan region was concentrated in the Montezuma Valley some distance from Mesa Verde, perhaps numbering some 30,000 people, mostly concentrated in villages of 1000 people or more. Sand Canyon and other open-country pueblos in the Moctezuma Valley area achieved considerable size, but outlying populations lived in deep canyons, about 2500 of them in the remote Mesa Verde area. They became expert at conserving local water supplies. At the Mummy II location on Chapin Mesa, there are some 36 separate sites with 200 to 400 people situated near an artificial water supply (Rohn, 1971). This consisted

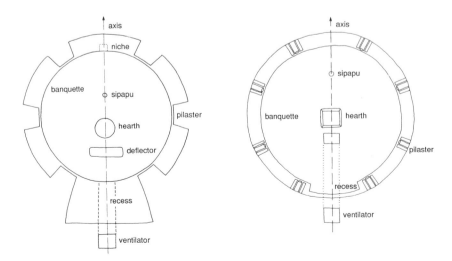

Differences in kiva architecture. (Right) Mesa Verde-style kivas in the northern San Juan Basin had a banquette-level recess on the south side which resulted in a distinctive keyhole-shaped outline to the structure. (Far right) The Chacoan kiva had stone-and-log pilasters that rested on the banquette and supported the roof.

(Opposite) The Cliff Palace, Mesa Verde, Colorado.

of a stone-lined depression about 88.5 ft (27 m) across with high, artificial banks on two sides. A series of ditches brought water from a nearby catchment area through a feeder ditch 2637 ft (804 m) long. This impressive water-control system supplied the domestic needs of hundreds of villagers.

Between AD 1200 and 1300, the focus of settlement moved south from the area around Mummy Lake to Cliff and Fewkes canyons (Rohn, 1977). By late Pueblo III times, Fewkes Canyon supported at least 33 habitation sites with between 530 and 545 rooms and 60 kivas, housing for 600 to 800 people. None are as famous or as spectacular as the Cliff House in Mesa Verde. The celebrated cattle rancher and pueblo explorer Richard Wetherill was the first Westerner to visit the Cliff House, in 1888. Three years later, Swedish scientist Gustav Nordenskiöld (1973) rode through monotonous piñon forest for hours until he suddenly emerged on the edge of a precipitous canyon. Across the valley, he saw the Cliff House, "framed in the massive vault of rock above and in a bed of sunlit cedar and piñon trees below ... With its round towers and high walls rising out of the heaps of stones deep in the mysterious twilight of the cavern and defying in their sheltered site the ravages of time, it resembled at a distance an enchanted castle."

Cliff House, with its 220 masonry rooms and 23 kivas, has a spectacular setting but actually differs little from large pueblos elsewhere. Perhaps half the population of nearby Chapin Mesa occupied the site. People had moved from living in open locations to shelters and ledges in canyon walls, perhaps a defensive measure. Only a few precipitous trails led from the canyon to the plateau farmlands above.

Many Mesa Verde pueblos now boast of what appear to be defensive artifices, including walls that restrict access to ledges, large towers, and loopholes in walls flanking entries. However, there are no signs of warfare in the archaeological record.

Not that Mesa Verde was the main focus of settlement. The nearby Montezuma Valley supported eight pueblos larger than the Cliff/Fewkes Canyon villages. One of them, Yellow Jacket, contains about 1800 rooms and probably housed some 2500 people, more than the whole of Mesa Verde. Another large settlement, Sand Canyon Pueblo in extreme southwestern Colorado, boasted about 700 inhabitants (Lipe, 1992). Sand Canyon surrounded a large spring, as did other large towns in the area. Around 1250, the residents-to-be erected a huge enclosure wall, which may have taken 30 to 40 people two months to build. Over the next 30 years, they added over 20 separate room blocks, which incorporated at least 90 kivas and about 420 rooms. However, every household maintained its own identity, with a cluster of structures – a living space, storage room, place to eat, and a kiva, just as they had in their original dispersed settlements. At the same time, multiple households dwelt within a single architectural complex, as if the wider ties of the family had become more important than in earlier times. The Four Corners settlements form a rough line running from northwest to southeast; other clusters of Pueblo population occur elsewhere in the Montezuma Valley and in southeast Utah.

Both in Mesa Verde itself and in the surrounding country, large villages, almost towns, were homes for between 1000 and 2500 people, living in room clusters associated with kivas and other ceremonial buildings, also managed water supplies. The same communities were the focus of ceremonial life and exchange activities.

Map of the Mesa Verde area.

Although much of the population was apparently concentrated in the larger sites, there are few indications of social stratification. Cliff Palace appears to have been a focus of the Mesa Verde community, and there were some purely ceremonial sites, among them Fire Temple and Sun Temple. Fire Temple has been described as a modified great kiva, a rectangular structure at the foot of a cliff with antechambers, paired vaults, a bench, and raised firebox (Cassidy, 1965). In contrast, Sun Temple is D-shaped, with two massive stone walls enclosing two kiva-like structures ventilated by subsurface ventilators similar to those used at Chaco Canyon (Rohn, 1971; Cordell, 1997).

Many of the Mesa Verde sites were excavated long before modern archaeological methods came to the Southwest, so information on the social organization of the Mesa Verde people is sadly lacking. Arthur Rohn's excavations at the Mug House, a 13th-century 94-room cliff dwelling in Wetherill Mesa, provide some useful insights. He was able to show that the earliest inhabitants of the site built a series of rooms and a kiva associated with a trash heap and a single courtyard. Later on, the site grew to four house clusters, two within the Mug House Cave itself, two situated close by. Towards the end of the occupation, these four household clusters came together into a single pueblo that may have been divided into two parts separated by a wall (Rohn, 1977). The Mug House community was not marked by any pronounced social differentiation, and, as Rohn argues, may have consisted of the inhabitants not only of this larger pueblo but of people living at nearby small settlements as well.

Mesa Verde's pueblos were constrained by the caves and rock overhangs under which they sheltered. Nevertheless, some communities reached considerable size. Judging from the numerous kivas, some of them multiple structures, there was considerable ritual activity, and there were numerous occasions when the inhabitants of different communities organized large labor parties to carry out sophisticated water-control works and other communal projects. Everywhere in Mesa Verde, the emphasis appears to have been on individual communities, not on the kind of larger-scale regional integration so characteristic of Chaco, and the Hohokam area.

The Anasazi Abandonment (AD 1300). The 12th and 13th centuries saw the culmination of four centuries of rapid social and political development in the Mesa Verde region. About AD 1300, the entire San Juan drainage, including Mesa Verde, was abandoned by Puebloan peoples.

A team of scientists has studied agricultural productivity in the Sand Canyon region, relying both on modern-day environmental and agricultural data and on tree-ring readings that provide a measure of ancient conditions (Lipe, 1992). Environmental scientist Carla Van West has reconstructed the severity of droughts for the month of June between AD 900 and 1300 for soils at five different elevations (Van West, 1996). She also calibrated variations in moisture levels with potential agricultural productivity, using data from crop fields between 1931 and 1960. Van West put all her data into a vast Geographical Information System that allowed her to create environmental models, display contour maps, then overlay them with areas of potential agricultural productivity for a specific year. She ended up with a graph of potential maize production in the study area over the period when the Anasazi occupied and then abandoned the Sand Canyon area. Using modern land-carrying-capacity data, Van West estimated that the area could have produced enough maize to support an average local population of about 31,360 people at a density of 21 people per sq. km over a 400-year period. Her figures showed that the 12th-century drought which caused the Anasazi dispersal at Chaco had little effect in regions like Sand Canyon where there was still enough land to support the dispersed farming population. In other words, the people had enough room for the movement that was central to their survival.

Van West was also able to show that potential agricultural productivity varied considerably from place to place and from year to year. The farmers tended to locate near consistently productive soils. They could survive the harshest of drought cycles *if* there were no restrictions on mobility or on access to the best soils, and *if* they could acquire food from neighbors when crops failed. However, their ability to move was severely restricted once population densities approached the carrying capacity of the land and the people had cultivated effectively all the most productive soils. At that point, surviving extreme short-term climatic change was much harder, especially when longer-term climatic cycles happened to coincide with a serious drought cycle, as happened during the major drought of AD 1276 to 1299.

As the drought cycle hit, pueblo construction suddenly slowed and ceased altogether by the 1290s (Lipe, 1995). Some sections of Sand Canyon were abandoned and used as midden dumps, but the final abandonment occurred in a hurry. Large numbers of clay pots and stone tools still lie where they were left by their owners. Some kivas contain traces of abandonment rituals, as if their owners made a deliberate decision to move elsewhere. In some cases, the departing Anasazi left large, hard-to-carry utilitarian objects behind them because they were going on a long journey.

By 1300, the great Anasazi pueblos of the Four Corners were silent. The people dispersed widely and joined distant communities elsewhere. For 200 years, the Colorado Plateau saw tremendous cultural upheaval. The Anasazi largely abandoned the San Juan drainage as they dispersed into less-affected regions. They moved south and southeastward into the lands of the historic Hopi, Zuñi, and Rio Grande pueblos, where they retained the same basic community organization, with villages, perhaps better called towns, that never exceeded about 2500 inhabitants. There were larger pueblos elsewhere in the 14th century. Their descendants developed sophisticated irrigation agriculture, refined their dry farming, and dwelt in a great variety of settlements of all kinds. They developed new social and religious ideas over many generations of cultural uncertainty, until stability returned with improved environmental conditions after AD 1450.

Mimbres (AD 1000 to 1130). Mimbres sites lie along the river of that name in southwestern New Mexico. Between AD 1000 and 1130, Mimbres potters created magnificent painted ceremonial bowls adorned with geometric and pictorial designs (LeBlanc, 1983; 1989). These superb examples of ancient artistry are usually found in Mimbres burials, usually inverted over the head of the deceased, ceremonially "broken" by a small hole in the base. Unfortunately, these fine vessels have become a highly prized item on the illegal antiquities market and many Mimbres burials have been violated by looters.

The Mimbres people lived in settlements of up to 150 rooms that consisted of single-story, contiguous and rectangular rooms built of river pebbles and adobe. The pueblos grew gradually into groups of room clusters loosely arranged around an open plaza. At the well-known NAN Ranch and Galaz sites, the pueblo room clusters grew according to household needs, rooms sometimes being subdivided and remodeled (Shafer, 1995). Ceremonial structures included large, rectangular and semi-subterranean kivas somewhat like those of earlier Mogollon people, sometimes with entry ramps and ceremonial offerings under the floors. Smaller, quadrilateral kivas entered through the roof may have been used by small kin groups rather than the community as a whole.

The elaborate domestic pottery fabricated by Mimbres women gives the impression that the people enjoyed an elaborate ceremonial life. For all this apparent elaboration and craft skill, there are few signs of the long-distance trading contacts found at Chaco Canyon or Snaketown. Most ceremonial activities appear to have taken place at the community and household level, reflecting a relatively isolated, egalitarian pueblo society.

Both Mesa Verde and Mimbres boast large settlements that give an impression of a much more nucleated society than was, in fact the case. Both cultural traditions display distinctive architectural and pottery styles that were widely used within relatively small areas. In fact, neither Mesa Verde

Mimbres ceramics. (Above left) Bowl painted with enigmatic human figures, possibly representing the contrast between life and death, or male and female. The hole through the base "killed" the object, helping release the vessel's spirit into the next world. Diameter c. 30 cm. (Above right) Bowl showing the Guardians of the Four Directions. Diameter c. 30 cm.

nor Mimbres are typical of the very dispersed settlement patterns that were characteristic of much of the Southwest between AD 900 and 1150. For example, the Rio Grande Valley from about Albuquerque northward was relatively sparsely inhabited during these centuries, mostly by people living in small, pithouse villages, some of them perhaps seasonal settlements (Blevins and Joiner, 1977). These appear to have been isolated communities, with no contacts with the Chaco system.

Between AD 900 and 1150, Southwestern agricultural peoples displayed great cultural variation. Some of them lived in more nucleated settlements. They enjoyed standardized agriculture, craft specialization, and participated in widespread trading networks. These more hierarchical systems are quite different from the more egalitarian patterns found elsewhere. The Mesa Verde and Mimbres people often dwelt in larger pueblos that consisted of conglomerations of formerly more dispersed settlements. These were still relatively egalitarian societies, while many Southwestern groups continued to live in dispersed pithouse villages, many of them seasonal bases for people who still relied on hunting and gathering as well as farming for their subsistence. In the centuries that followed, it was the aggregated and more dispersed cultural systems that survived, while the nucleated systems at Chaco and elsewhere collapsed, for reasons that are still little understood.

Climate Change and Risk

The complex aggregations and abandonments of Anasazi history have been the subject of much debate over the past century. Early theories for the collapse, for example, focused on raiding Athabaskans, on intercommunity warfare, and many other simplistic factors such as major environmental change, epidemics, and disruption of Mexican trading contacts (summary, Cordell, 1997). In recent years, as in California and the Great Basin, researchers have made increasing use of evolutionary ecology and fine-grained evidence for short-term climatic change, as a way of explaining both aggregration and collapse (Larson and others, 1996). Thanks to tree-ring research, we now know that the Southwestern climate between AD 400 and 1425 was highly varied, with long cycles of above-average rainfall and severe drought. The Laboratory of Tree-Ring Research at the University of Arizona has undertaken a massive dendroclimatic study that has yielded a reconstruction of relative climatic variability in the Southwest from AD 680 to 1970 (Dean, 1988; 1996). By using a spatial grid of 27 long tree-ring sequences from throughout the Southwest, Dean and his colleagues have compiled maps which plot the different station values and their fluctuations like contour maps, one for each decade. This enables them to study such phenomena as the progress of what Dean sometimes calls the "Great Drought" of AD 1276 to 1299 from northwest to southeast across the region. In 1276, the beginnings of the drought appear as negative standard deviations from average rainfall in the northwest, while the remainder of the region enjoys above-average rainfall. During the next ten years, very dry conditions expand over the entire Southwest before improved rainfall arrives after 1299. This form of mapping allows close correlation of vacated large and small pueblos with short-term climatic fluctuations.

When the research team looked at the period AD 966 to 1988, they found that the tree-ring stations in the northwestern region accounted for no less

Archaeological sites in the Southwest. The map also shows areas of rainfall in the region. The shaded line marks the frontier between the winter and summer rainfall patterns of the northwestern region and the more predictable summer rainfall of the southeastern area.

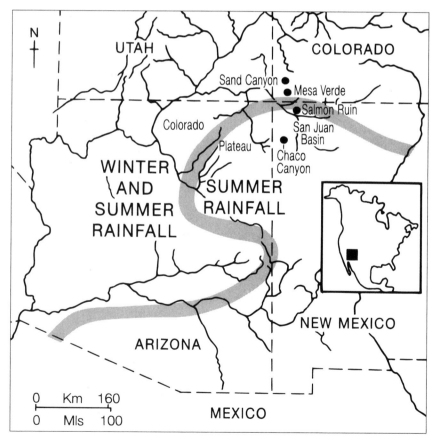

than 60 percent of the rainfall variance. In contrast, stations in the southeastern part of the Southwest accounted for only 10 percent. This general configuration, which persisted for centuries, coincides with the modern distribution of seasonal rainfall in the Southwest: predictable summer rainfall dominates the southeastern areas, while the northwest receives both winter and summer precipitation. Winter rains are much more uncertain. When the scientists examined this general rainfall pattern at 100-year intervals from 539 to 1988, they observed that it persisted most of the time, even though the boundary between the two zones moved backward and forward slightly.

But this long-term pattern broke down completely from AD 1250 to 1450, when a totally aberrant pattern prevailed in the northwest. The southeast remained stable, but there was major disruption elsewhere. For nearly two centuries, the relatively simple long-term pattern of summer and winter rains gave way to complex, unpredictable precipitation and severe droughts, especially on the Colorado Plateau. The change to an unstable pattern would have had a severe impact on Anasazi farmers, especially as it coincided with the Great Drought of AD 1276 to 1299.

Shorter-term, high-frequency changes were risks that were readily apparent to every Anasazi: year-to-year rainfall shifts, decade-long drought cycles, seasonal changes, and so on. Drought cycles and other high-frequency changes required temporary and flexible adjustments, such as farming more land, relying more heavily on wild plant foods, and, above all, movement across the terrain. Such risk-reduction strategies worked well for centuries, as long as the Anasazi farmed their land at well below its carrying capacity. When the population increased to near-carrying capacity, however, as it did at Chaco Canyon in the 12th century, and in the Four Corners region a century later, people became increasingly vulnerable to drought cycles, which could stretch the capacity of a local environment within months, even weeks. In evolutionary terms, they adapted to an unpredictable environment with specialized farming, elaborate storage systems, and widespread exchange of basic commodities which buffered them against local shortages (evolutionary arguments in Larson and others, 1996; Leonard, 1989; Leonard and Jones, 1987). Their vulnerability was even more extreme when long-term changes – such as a half-century or more of much drier conditions – descended on farming land already pushed to its carrying limits. Under these circumstances, a year-long drought or torrential rains could quickly destroy a local population's ability to support itself. Anasazi households in this situation had few options left to them but to disperse.

When the political and social apparatus behind the system collapsed, some dispersal of population was inevitable, for the labor-intensive investment that fed them in marginal areas had vanished. Those who remained still continued to hunt, forage, and farm, but within local contexts. There may be an appearance of population decline in the archaeological record, but it may in fact have been one of decentralization, reduced coordination of labor, and major changes in village layout away from the large, formal pueblos of earlier centuries into smaller communities less visible in the archaeological record. There was, then, considerable continuity in Southwestern life, despite major population dispersals and shifts in subsistence strategies.

Violence in Ancient Pueblo Life

Inevitably, warfare has surfaced as an explanation for the Anasazi dispersal, after years of widespread agreement that the Anasazi were peace-loving people, who lived in harmony with their environment. This belief stemmed from an assumption that the world has not always been as war-ridden as in the 20th century. Steven Le Blanc has recently published a study of warfare in the ancient Southwest (1999), which comprises an examination of artifacts, settlement patterns, burnt rooms, and evidence of butchered bones. He argues for three periods of warfare that span the entire length of Pueblo life in the Southwest. Small-scale warfare was commonplace, indeed endemic, from AD 200 to 900. From AD 900 to 1200, the period of the Chaco Phenomenon, warfare was much diminished. There was still violence, but Le Blanc believes, on the basis of mutilated bodies cast into kivas, that some classes of Chaco society were treated badly and sometimes even killed, something very different from warfare. From AD 1250 to 1500 and later, warfare exploded throughout the Southwest as many people, especially in the Colorado Plateau and White Mountain regions, congregated in well-defended, compact, and large settlements. Le Blanc argues that warfare was a fact of life in the ancient Southwest, a socially sanctioned form of violence with close ties to changing economic and political fortunes.

While Le Blanc makes a useful point about the presence of warfare as a catalyst for Pueblo cultural change, biological anthropologists Christy and Jacqueline Turner have gone much further (1999). They examined large numbers of human remains from 76 Southwestern sites and others in Mexico. After exhaustive analyses, they recorded numerous instances of burning, butchering, and cooking of human bones, especially at Penasco Blanco, one of Chaco Canyon's Great Houses. Like Le Blanc, the Turners concluded violence was common throughout Pueblo times, but they argued further that terror was an instrument of social control at Chaco Canyon, with cannibalism and human sacrifice as ways of controlling village communities. Who were these violent "death squads?" The Turners claim they were Toltecs, a sociopathic cannibal warrior cult from Mexico, who entered the Chaco region around AD 900 and forced the indigenous farming population to adopt their religious beliefs and political system. The Turner hypothesis is, to put it mildly, a historical sketch and has little credibility with most Southwestern archaeologists, as well as being offensive to Native Americans. Both the Turner research and Le Blanc's important monograph are certain to spark lively debate and a new focus on aspects of ancient Pueblo life that have been neglected until now.

Kachinas and Warriors
AD 1300 to European contact

The abandonments of the late 13th and early 14th centuries changed the social landscape of the Southwest. Many once densely populated areas were virtually empty as the gravity of human settlement moved south and east to areas of greater summer rains – to the Phoenix Basin, the Rio Grande Valley, the Zuñi region of west-central New Mexico, and the Casas Grandes area of northern Mexico (Plog, S., 1997). At the same time, more people moved from villages into bigger communities, some of them much larger than the greatest pueblos of earlier times. These aggregations of population posed fresh challenges and created new political equations, as well as a need for more substantial food surpluses and efficient, well-organized leadership.

Not that these aggregations were permanent, for, as in earlier centuries, local populations ebbed and flowed and pueblos rose into prominence, then were abandoned or became a shadow of their former selves. The pueblos of the Rio Grande Valley, one of the few perennial rivers in the Southwest, epitomize this constant change. Until the 12th and 13th centuries, relatively few people lived in the valley. Then the population swelled rapidly, both as a result of local growth and from migration into the valley from the north and northwest. Several pueblo sites, notably Arroyo Hondo just south of modern-day Santa Fé, reflect not continual growth but the characteristic ebb-and-flow in and out of Rio Grande settlements. A single room block rose at Arroyo Hondo by AD 1315. Within 15 years, about 1200 two-story rooms arranged over 24 blocks centered around 13 plazas. Just as quickly, the huge pueblo emptied, until it was almost deserted by the mid-1330s.

Aerial view of Arroyo Hondo pueblo, New Mexico.

A second cycle of growth followed in the 1370s and 1380s with the building of 200 rooms, destroyed by a fire in 1410.

The checkered history of Arroyo Hondo reflects a remarkable social fluidity, marked by repeated movements of entire groups, some of whom moved over distances of several hundred miles from the Mesa Verde region and elsewhere. One reason for this fluidity lay in the larger size of these growing settlements in an unpredictable environment where maize cultivation was at best chancy. At Arroyo Hondo, for example, even the best agricultural land could feed no more than 400 to 600 people in an average year, making it hard to accumulate adequate food reserves against drought years. The discovery of famine foods such as cattails and grass seeds at Arroyo Hondo hints strongly at periods of hunger (Plog, S., 1997). The farmers tried to minimize famine by irrigating river lands and also planting better-watered fields at higher elevations, but the burials at Arroyo Hondo and elsewhere display signs of endemic malnutrition and high infant- and child-mortality rates.

Population growth in the Rio Grande coincided with declines elsewhere, even as people still congregated in larger pueblos, as did the ancestors of the Zuñi in west-central New Mexico and the Hopi of northeastern Arizona. The Hopi pueblos in particular defied the pattern of ebb and flow and were occupied for many centuries. Awatovi pueblo was occupied by between 500 and 1000 people until as late as the early 18th century, while the Hopi pueblo at Oraibi still flourishes today, the longest continually occupied settlement in the United States. No one knows why some communities flourished, then declined, but others endured for many centuries, despite drought cycles and regular food shortages. But both archaeology and oral tradition suggests that warfare and other forms of violence played an important role in Pueblo life (Haas and Creamer, 1992).

Late 13th- and early 14th-century pueblos show a major concern for defense (Wilcox and Haas, 1994). The builders of Arroyo Hondo and other towns erected room blocks at right angles to one another, forming enclosed plazas and restricting access to the settlement. Only narrow passages opened into the plazas, while ground-floor rooms were accessible only by ladder from the roof. When possible, protected wells were dug into the plaza floor. A visitor was confronted by blank masonry walls. Even if an invader penetrated the central square, he would need a ladder to gain access to the rooms. A well-designed pueblo was an effective fortress, as the Spaniards discovered when they attacked the Zuñi pueblo at Hawikuh in 1540. The inhabitants attacked the conquistadors with large stones hurled from the rooftops. In many cases, a pueblo was built in a strategic location that was difficult of access, like the 750-room Zuñi pueblo at Atsinna atop Inscription Rock in El Morro National Monument. Sometimes, groups of settlements clustered together for protection, as they did in the Hopi and Cibola regions, with long distances between them. Skeletal remains from several sites show ample evidence of war injuries, scalping, and even butchering (White, 1992).

The changing times of the 13th and 14th centuries also witnessed major changes in Pueblo ritual, marked by new styles of kiva murals, pervasive decorative styles on ceramics, and much larger plazas. For the first time, the plazas became important settings for public ceremonies, especially kachina dances. Kachinas play a prominent role in modern-day western

Hopi artisans carve wooden Kachina dolls to teach their children about the many kachinas that are important in Pueblo ritual.

Pueblo belief and ritual. They are ancestral spirits that serve as intermediaries between the living and the deities of the supernatural world as well as bringing rain in clouds that they summon to the pueblos (Adams, 1991). Kachinas are present on earth from the winter to summer solstice. For the other half of the year they live in the underworld, to which they return through the *sipapu*, the entrance to the lower regions. Kachina dancers wear costumes and masks that impersonate the ancestral spirits during their stay on earth, male impersonators who assume the sacred powers of the spirit.

We can chronicle the increasing importance of kachina rituals not only through architecture, but in distinctive mural patterns found on kivas of the period, sometimes painted again and again in annual replasterings of the walls. The murals, quite unlike earlier geometric designs, show anthropomorphic figures with features just like those of historic kachinas, also plants, animals, and depictions of wooden altars used in kiva rituals (Smith, W., 1952). Ceramics also share common features over wide areas – yellow, orange, and red Salado vessels with black-and-red designs, with not only geometric motifs, but also birds and human figures. Fanged serpents are especially common, perhaps a representation of horned serpents, believed to control flooding and rain. Patricia Crown (1994) believes this and other symbols are reflections of the cosmology that lay behind the ritual life of the pueblos.

Stephen Plog (1997) and others believe that the elaboration of kachina rituals was a way of binding together the inhabitants of much larger, more densely populated pueblos. Everyone in the community was a member of a kachina society, whose membership cut across potentially divisive kin and lineage lines, while ensuring that public ceremonies were conducted properly. Cooperative behavior was vital for survival and kachina rituals, with their emphasis on rainmaking (as well as warfare) provided important social guidelines and validation for the community as a whole.

Associated with the development of kachina ritual was the increasing appearance of red, orange, or yellow vessels with black, white, and red designs.

Casas Grandes
14th century AD

Long-distance trade flourished throughout the Southwest, even in troubled times, as commodities such as turquoise, tropical bird feathers, cotton, tool-making stone, and buffalo hides passed along ancient trade routes. We can gain a unique portrait of this trade from the Cases Grandes site in northern Mexico.

The Casas Grandes area of Chihuahua in northern Mexico lies in relatively high-altitude basin and range country, centered on a wide, fertile

Casas Grandes, Chihuahua, northern Mexico. (Right) Aerial view showing a ball court, lower right, and excavation of room blocks, lower left corner. (Below) Effigy bowl from the site, height 22 cm.

valley long inhabited by an indigenous, Mogollon-like population (Di Peso and others, 1974). Between AD 1130 and 1300, the beginning of what Charles Di Peso calls the Medio period, the inhabitants of this valley began to congregate in a large settlement known as Paquime (or Casas Grandes). Originally, Charles Di Peso argued for a date between the 11th and 14th centuries for Casas Grandes. This chronology has been replaced by more recent tree-ring dates that assign the heyday of Casas Grandes to the 14th century (Dean and Ravesloot, 1989).

Initially, Paquime consisted of 20 or more house clusters, each with a plaza and enclosing wall (Ravesloot, 1988). The people lived in single-story adobe houses, with a single water system for the entire settlement. One compound contained rows of rectangular boxes apparently used for breeding macaws for their colorful feathers – pollen analyses have yielded traces of the nesting material, even eggshell fragments, skeletons, and traces of wooden perches were found. Paquime may have been one of the sources of macaws for Anasazi communities located far to the north. Macaw feathers were widely used in Pueblo rituals and were attached to ceremonial regalia and prayer sticks. They served as conduits to the supernatural (Minnis and others, 1993).

During the 14th century, the entire community was rebuilt. Paquime-phase multi-storied adobe apartment complexes, built of a form of marley concrete that is like clay, now formed the central core of the settlement and housed as many as 2240 people. I-shaped ball courts, stone-faced platform and effigy mounds, a market area, and elaborate water-storage systems lay in the public and ceremonial core of the site outside the residential areas in the center. This was a thriving town where many specialist craft activities took place, among them the large-scale production of copper bells, ornaments, and ceremonial axe heads made by the "lost-wax" process, a far from simple procedure. Marine mollusks were turned into trumpets, beads, and engraved or inlaid ornaments. (For ball courts, see Whalen, M. and Minnis, 1996.)

At the height of its power, Casas Grandes lay at the center of a small region, its influence perhaps extending about 18 miles (30 km) from the town. It was a mid-level complex society, probably marked by intense factionalism and competition (Whalan, M., and Minnis, 1996). Like the earlier Chaco Phenomenon, Casas Grandes did not flourish for long. "Two and one-half generations sat idly by and watched the magnificent city of Paquime fall into disrepair. The artisan-citizens continued to produce an abundance of marketable goods, but civil construction and public maintenance all ceased." Thus does Di Peso describe the decline of Paquime during the Diablo phase. The population of the town apparently increased, but public works were neglected. Some families moved into ceremonial areas and turned them into dwellings. The entire Casas Grandes system fell apart, but it was not until the early 15th century that Paquime was finally abandoned. As far as is known, Casas Grandes was not affiliated with any Mesoamerican state.

No one knows who ruled over Casas Grandes, but there is good reason to believe that a small number of privileged families competed with one another and controlled long-distance trade and presided over the rituals that unfolded in the ceremonial precincts of the pueblo. Later Pueblo societies appear to have been basically egalitarian, simply because drought cycles and other variables made it hard for any individual or small group of people to accumulate unusual wealth (Plog, S., 1997; for a theoretical discussion, see McGuire and Saitta, 1996). But some scholars believe that those who controlled the most fertile lands, monopolized local cotton production or trade routes may have become special office holders with authority to make important decisions over land allocation and other matters. It may have been, too, that social distinctions based on supernatural power of knowledge of ritual procedure may have weighed heavily in creating social inequality. Such distinctions based on power leave few traces in the archaeological record, except, perhaps, for the imposing tower-like "big houses" built at late Hohokam pueblos like Casa Grande near modern-day Phoenix. Here, the builders erected a four-story tower atop an adobe platform to serve as a residence for important individuals. It may also have served as an astronomical observatory, with holes in the walls to observe solstices, equinoxes, and the movements of the heavenly bodies. The ritual calendar that governed planting and harvest, the cycle of life that lay at the heart of pueblo life depended on these observations.

Aerial view of Pecos pueblo in the Rio Grande area of New Mexico. The Spanish Mission of the 1620s stands at left. Spanish missionaries often erected their churches and missions on the sites of important pueblos that, like Pecos, had been occupied for many centuries and were important centers of political and social activity. Native Americans built the original pueblo here c. 1450, a multi-storied quadrangle around a central plaza with 660 living and storage rooms and at least 22 kivas.

During the 14th century, Casas Grandes was burned and the large towns of the southern desert were abandoned, as simpler social institutions prevailed in another cycle of abandonment and downsizing. Only the Zuñi and Hopi pueblos endured, together with those of Acoma and the Rio Grande Valley (illus. p. 349), to witness the arrival of Spanish conquistadors in the 16th century.

Further Reading

The following references amplify the general accounts cited in earlier chapters:

Cordell, Linda S., and Gumerman, George J. (eds.) 1989. *Dynamics of Southwest Prehistory.* Smithsonian Institution Press, Washington DC.
A series of essays summarizing research in different areas of the Southwest. A good starting point after reading the Southwestern chapters in *Ancient North America.*

Creamer, Winifred. 1993. *The Architecture of Arroyo Hondo Pueblo, New Mexico.* School of American Research Press, Santa Fe.
A fascinating monograph on a pueblo that flourished, was abandoned, then flourished again.

Crown, Patricia L., and Judge, W. James (eds.). 1991. *Chaco and Hohokam.* School of American Research Press, Santa Fe, NM.
Authoritative essays resulting from a professional seminar which compared Chaco and Hohokam. Southwestern archaeology at its best. Informative and analytical, of use even to the general reader.

Haury, Emil. 1976. *The Hohokam, desert farmers and craftsmen: Excavations at Snaketown, 1964-1965.* University of Arizona Press, Tucson.
Haury's monograph summarizes this important site.

Larson, Daniel O., and others. 1996. "Risk, Climatic Variability, and the Study of Southwestern Prehistory," *American Antiquity* 61(2): 217-242.
An important paper that epitomizes recent multidisciplinary research in evolutionary theory, climate change and archaeology in the Southwest. Comprehensive bibliography.

LeBlanc, Steven A. 1983. *The Mimbres People: ancient pueblo potters of the American Southwest.* Thames and Hudson, London and New York.
A lavishly illustrated introduction to some of North America's finest ceramics and the people who made them.

Noble, David G. (ed.). 1984. *New Light on Chaco Canyon.* School of American Research, Santa Fé, New Mexico.
A fine volume of popular essays on Chaco Canyon. Ideal for the general reader.

Rohn, Arthur. 1971. *Mug House, Mesa Verde National Park, Colorado.* National Park Service, Washington DC.
Rohn's monograph contains much valuable information on Mesa Verde as a whole.

White, Tim. 1992. *Prehistoric Cannibalism at Mancos 5MTUMR-2346.* Princeton University Press, Princeton.
An elegant piece of scientific research into the butchery of human bone in an Anasazi pueblo.

PART SIX

THE EASTERN WOODLANDS

"Outside, some distance from the lodge, was a meadow of dry grass … the woman said, 'when the sun goes down, you must take me by my hair and drag me across the field. After that you may eat.' … when evening came he did as he had been told. The woman disappeared, but wherever he had dragged her, a tall and graceful plant arose. On it were golden clusters of grain … It was corn, the friend of all humankind…"

Algonquian Legend

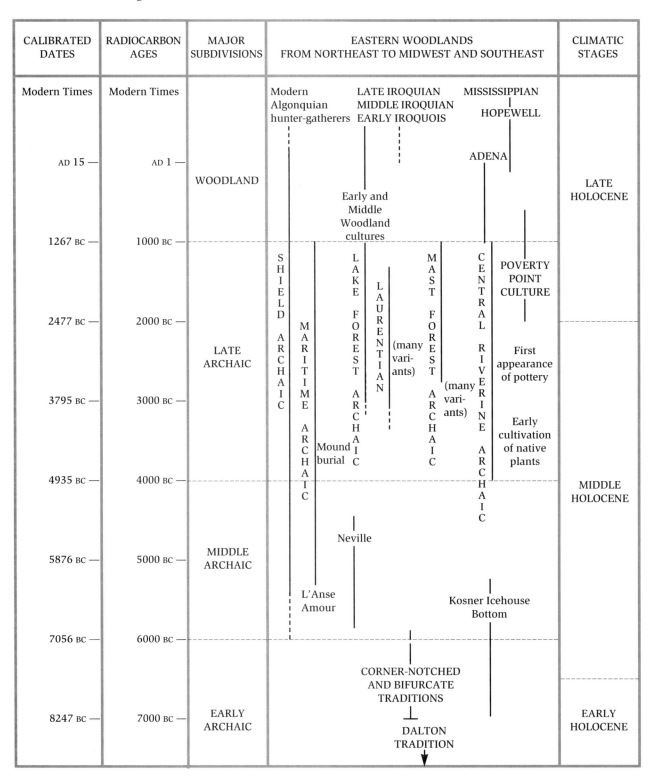

CALIBRATED DATES	RADIOCARBON AGES	MAJOR SUBDIVISIONS	EASTERN WOODLANDS FROM NORTHEAST TO MIDWEST AND SOUTHEAST					CLIMATIC STAGES
Modern Times	Modern Times		Modern Algonquian hunter-gatherers	LATE IROQUIAN MIDDLE IROQUIAN EARLY IROQUOIS		MISSISSIPPIAN HOPEWELL		
AD 15 —	AD 1 —	WOODLAND		Early and Middle Woodland cultures		ADENA		LATE HOLOCENE
1267 BC —	1000 BC —		SHIELD ARCHAIC	LAKE FOREST ARCHAIC	LAURENTIAN (many variants)	MAST FOREST ARCHAIC (many variants)	CENTRAL RIVERINE ARCHAIC	POVERTY POINT CULTURE
2477 BC —	2000 BC —	LATE ARCHAIC						First appearance of pottery
3795 BC —	3000 BC —		MARITIME ARCHAIC					Early cultivation of native plants
4935 BC —	4000 BC —			Mound burial				MIDDLE HOLOCENE
5876 BC —	5000 BC —	MIDDLE ARCHAIC		Neville				
7056 BC —	6000 BC —		L'Anse Amour			Kosner Icehouse Bottom		
8247 BC —	7000 BC —	EARLY ARCHAIC		CORNER-NOTCHED AND BIFURCATE TRADITIONS				EARLY HOLOCENE
				DALTON TRADITION				

CHAPTER 16

EARLY AND MIDDLE ARCHAIC CULTURES IN THE EASTERN WOODLANDS

Large hunting territories, long days of tracking bison, caribou, mastodon, and smaller game, seasonal foraging of plant foods – these were the characteristics of free-wandering Paleo-Indian life in the Eastern Woodlands before 10,000 BC, until the Ice Age megafauna vanished. The hunter-gatherers of eastern North America now adapted to progressively warmer and more diverse Eastern Woodlands environments. They turned from big-game to the exploitation of forest mammals like the white-tailed deer, also, increasingly, to nuts and plant foods. We must now examine this important adaptive shift, part of a trend that was to continue for thousands of years in the east. This development was to culminate after 1000 BC in more sedentary lifeways, restricted hunting and foraging territories, and in extensive trading and elaborate mortuary customs. People adapted in many ways, with more-or-less equal efficiency, to different circumstances (Sassaman and Anderson, 1996).

This appealing scenario of a gradual shift from big-game exploitation to more generalized hunting and gathering is nothing more than a hypothesis. Preservation conditions at all but a handful of locations militate against the survival of food remains of any kind. Where organic remains do survive, they are in small numbers, barely enough to compile short lists of some of the plant foods that were exploited by the inhabitants. Cumulatively, however, these lists from excavated sites in the 10,500 to 6000 BC range hint that the early inhabitants of the Eastern Woodlands were exploiting a broad variety of foods – both forest resources like grey squirrels and nuts, and foods from more grassy environments like white-tailed deer and pioneering seed-bearing grasses. It seems certain that small game, fish, mollusks, and vegetable foods assumed greater importance in eastern diet in late Paleo-Indian and Early Archaic societies.

Back in 1958, Illinois archaeologist Joseph Caldwell noted: "If there is any overriding pattern to be seen in the history of the East before the establishment of food production as an economic basis, it is in the evidence for increasing efficiency and success in exploiting the resources of the forest." He coined the term "Primary Forest Efficiency" to characterize "a degree of settled life ... a more efficient accommodation to life in the forest" that came into being during the long millennia of the Archaic. Caldwell's theory endured in the literature for a generation. However, recent research has shown that plant exploitation was a vital part of eastern foraging cultures even in Paleo-Indian times. There were changes in the plants most

intensively exploited, but grasses, nuts, and other wild vegetable foods were never unimportant. Even the earliest groups knew their plant foods well. The productivity of their exploitation may have increased over the millennia, but the basic lifeway stayed much the same throughout much of the Holocene. There were no large-scale migrations from other areas that brought new populations into the Eastern Woodlands. The basic toolkits used by Archaic people changed but little for thousands of years, except for minor stylistic alterations in ubiquitous stone projectile points.

Projectile Points and the Early Archaic
c. 10,500 [cal] to 6000 BC

After about 8500 BC, Clovis-like points gave way to new projectile points throughout the Eastern Woodlands, points derived from earlier fluted designs (Smith, B. 1986). We do not know what these stylistic changes mean in cultural terms, but dozens of changing projectile-point forms chronicle the Paleo-Indian and Archaic societies of the region.

 This bewildering array of points from the Eastern Woodlands has fascinated archaeologists for generations. "Were we to note all the varieties which suggest themselves, we would be led into a multiplicity of illustrations ... [of] the individual skill and fancies of the respective workmen, the various casualties to which these implements have been subjected ... and the modifications of form consequent thereupon," wrote a frustrated collector, Charles Jones, in his *Antiquities of the Southern Indians* as long ago as 1873. The classificatory confusion lasted until the 1950s, when excavations at a few stratified sites such as Hardaway, North Carolina (Coe, 1964; Daniel, 1996), and St Albans, West Virginia, yielded the first chronological sequences for these projectile-point styles. The deep deposits of the St Albans site yielded no fewer than 41 stratigraphic levels with each type of projectile-point form confined to one or two zones.

 In the 1950s, Joffre Coe (1952; 1964) excavated a series of sites in the North Carolina Piedmont. He discovered at once that stratified sites had survived on the alluvial floodplains of the Piedmont. Not only that, but the stratigraphy was sensitive enough that short-term occupations could be identified, something that was well-nigh impossible on the jumbled open sites found on nearby ridges and eroded terraces. Then, he wrote, "the usual hodgepodge of projectile-point types are not found – only variations of a specific theme [within an individual occupation layer]." In other words, changes in the features of projectile points were a potential chronological marker over centuries, if not millennia, of human occupation.

 Coe excavated four sites – Doerschuk, Gaston, Hardaway, and Lowder's Ferry – and analyzed nearly 66,000 stone fragments from them. In 1964, he used his stratigraphic observations and analyses to identify a sequence of changing projectile-point forms that began with the "Hardaway Complex," named after a construction company that had used the site where Hardaway points were stratified. Palmer, Kirk, Stanly, Morrow Mountain, Guilford – Coe traced minute projectile-point changes over thousands of years, but unfortunately he obtained no radiocarbon samples from his excavations.

 A decade later, Canadian archaeologist James Tuck expanded Coe's work with radiocarbon-dated information from many more sites. He proposed

(Opposite) Sites and regions of the Eastern Woodlands referred to in Chapters 16–21.

(1974) three Early Archaic horizons in the Eastern Woodlands for the period 8500 to 6000 BC – Dalton (Hardaway), Big Sandy, and Kirk, horizons that could be identified over large areas of the Eastern Woodlands. As Tuck and others pointed out, there was apparently a remarkable uniformity of hunting and gathering culture all the way from Labrador in the north to the Carolinas far to the south, with regional differences reflected in part by minor stylistic variations in projectile points. Even as Tuck was writing, Jefferson Chapman (1975; 1994) was excavating a series of floodplain sites in Eastern Tennessee that added a fourth and later "Bifurcate" horizon to the Dalton-Big Sandy-Kirk tripartite sequence. He also confirmed the basic validity of Tuck's scheme.

There is now general agreement that the 7000 years of the Eastern Woodlands Archaic, from about 8000 to 700 BC, are marked by widespread changes in projectile styles, even if there was considerable local variation (Sassaman and Anderson, 1996). This sequence, which may reflect more efficient hafting designs, begins with highly varied Early Archaic *side-notched* points that developed from the widespread, Paleo-Indian Dalton form. Next come *corner-notched* designs, such as the Kirk point, then *bifurcate-base* points, and lastly several *stemmed* forms. The rest of the stone artifact toolkit remained much the same as in Paleo-Indian times, except for the appearance of more varied scraper forms.

The Dalton Tradition
c. 8500 to 7900 BC

Dalton points appeared over much of the Southeast in about 8500 BC (Morse and Morse, 1983; Morse, 1997 (for regional surveys, see Sassaman and Anderson, 1996)). They are distinctive artifacts with concave bases with "ears" that sometimes flare outward. These were highly versatile artifacts that served not only as points, but as saws and serrated knives. Archaeologist James Mitchie has used replicas to butcher white-tailed deer and saw up their bones with the tough, saw-like edges. Sometimes the hunters recycled and sharpened the points again and again, turning them progressively into knives, then chisels or scrapers. The Dalton point of the Southeast is ubiquitous except in Florida and known from the South and Midwest and as far north as New England. The contemporary Hardaway point in North Carolina is a variant on the Dalton, but has a more triangular shape, with side notches and flaring ears. Both Dalton and Hardaway forms remained in fashion until about 7900 BC, when they gave way to new designs. Dalton groups also made use of a distinctive chipped-stone adze for wood-working and canoe building.

This millennium near the close of the Early Holocene saw oak-dominated deciduous forest gradually expanding northward as the ice sheets retreated, replacing spruce and jack pine forests in the Northeast. This northward expansion may have coincided with a gradual adaptive shift toward more intensive exploitation of nuts and other vegetable foods, also use of rock-shelters for longer-term camps (Walthall, 1998). Thanks to excavations in the Little Tennessee Valley and northeast Arkansas, we know something of the Early Archaic adaptation in the river valleys of the Southeast, an

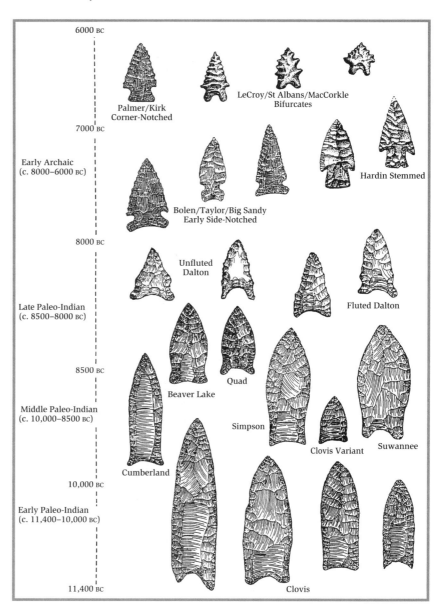

Paleo-Indian and Early Archaic chronology and diagnostic projectile points.

adaptation that may have flourished in many different minor variations over much of the region where these points are found.

Brand, Lace, and Sloan. Dan Morse and his Arkansas colleagues (Morse and Morse, 1983) have excavated three important sites that reflect different aspects of Dalton life.

The now-destroyed Lace site lay on a small knoll near the L'Anguille River, in the center of a cluster of smaller Dalton locations. The elevated location was once bordered by sloughs and shallow lakes, an ideal place for a base camp. The main portion of the settlement covered about 1.2 acres

Aerial view of the Lace site, Arkansas (above), and excavations in progress at the nearby Brand site (right).

(0.5 ha), with some midden accumulation to a depth of as much as 3 ft (1 m), site dimensions that argue strongly for it once having been a base camp.

The Brand site nearby lies on a natural knoll about 2.6 ft (0.8 m) high and 0.25 acre (0.1 ha) in area. Morse excavated five oval Dalton artifact clusters averaging about 125.9 sq. ft (11.7 sq. m). Each contained an average of 83 tools, all of them hunting or butchering artifacts like points, knives, choppers, and hammerstones. Each cluster was probably left by a single hunter group butchering its share of a kill (Goodyear, 1974). Each is oriented slightly north of east–west, as if the hunter's back faced the sun or a meat-drying rack straddled the cluster. However, the diversity of tools suggests that the site was occupied by families engaged in a wide range of domestic activities.

The Sloan site is believed to have been a cemetery (Morse, 1997). Some 488 Dalton artifacts, 144 of them points, came from a sand dune along the edge of the Cache River floodplain near the northern Mississippi River delta. The artifacts were found in distinctive 6.6-ft (2-m) clusters parallel to the dune's long axis. Groups of associated artifacts within the patterns may have been buried in containers. In one case, four Dalton points appeared to have been rolled into a bundle, as hefted points on foreshafts or handles.

Some of the Sloan points were made from cherts from as far away as St Louis, nearly 200 miles (321 km) distant. Unfortunately, only a few bone fragments survived in the dune, but soil tests reveal abnormally high calcium levels, as if skeletons were once present. Morse estimates that between 12 and 25 graves once lay in the sand dune. If his interpretation is correct, Sloan is the earliest known cemetery in the Americas dating to before 7000 BC.

Icehouse Bottom and Early Archaic Subsistence

After 8000 BC, Jefferson Chapman tells us (1980; 1994), rains and floods resulting from erosion and runoff from once-frozen slopes of the Smoky Mountains in Tennessee deposited sands and silts down the Little Tennessee River, sediments that formed sand bars, islands, and new bottomlands. The local people soon took advantage of these locations, camping on shallow sand bars that were periodically flooded. The inundations brought down fresh layers of silt and sand that covered abandoned camp sites. The hunters would return to the same location again and again, creating a kind of archaeological layer-cake of Early Archaic and later occupation at such well-known sites as Icehouse Bottom and Rose Island (Chapman, 1973; 1975).

Chapman believes that the people whose occupation is represented by the lowest levels of Icehouse Bottom in about 7500 BC, also other base camps, lived in a series of small hunter-gatherer bands who dwelt not only in the Little Tennessee Valley, but moved from there into the Upper Tennessee River drainage and into the southern Ridge and Valley Province of Virginia as well. They were constantly on the move, each band having a base camp or series of such repeatedly used settlements. Icehouse Bottom provided not only comfort and security, but was close to diverse food resources like game and wild vegetable foods (Chapman, 1994). The base camp was near rock outcrops that yielded fine-grained chert. The people picked up or dug out nodules from the hillside, brought them back home and fashioned them into adzes, points, knives, drills, and other tools used for wood-working, preparing hides, and many other purposes. The camp itself was used by several households, living separately, probably in skin, bark, or matting shelters scattered along several hundred feet of a riverside terrace. Each household had its own hearth, fashioned from red clay brought in from a hillside close by. Twenty-nine of the early Icehouse Bottom hearths bore traces of basketry and netting preserved as clear impressions in the fire-hardened clay.

Although preservation conditions at Icehouse Bottom are poor, Chapman believes that hunting and foraging habits changed but little from Early Archaic right into the historic period. The Icehouse Bottom people and their neighbors probably subsisted off white-tailed deer, a meat diet supplemented with black bear and other mammals like elk, fox, opossum, raccoon, squirrel, and rabbit. They hunted turkeys and passenger pigeons,

Excavations at Icehouse Bottom, Little Tennessee River Valley.

collected box turtles each spring, and also fished. They took suckers as they spawned in the shallow waters of spring, also catfish and drumfish. Freshwater mussels and gastropods were occasionally eaten as supplemental foods.

Wild vegetable foods were as important as game in Icehouse Bottom diet. Hickory nuts were a vital crop each fall, for they yielded crucial fats and protein without any special processing to make them edible. Chapman (1994) quotes the great 18th-century botanist William Bartram, who observed Southeastern Indians harvesting hickory nuts. "I have seen above an hundred bushels of these nuts belonging to one family," he wrote. "They pound them to pieces, and then cast them into boiling water, which, after passing through fine strainers, preserves the most oily part of the liquid: this they call by a name which signifies hiccory milk; it is as sweet and rich as fresh cream, and is an important ingredient in most of their cookery, especially hominy and corn cakes." The Indians would skim off the oil, then the meat, which was mashed, dried, and kept for use in lean months. The cook simply soaked cakes of nut meat in warm water before cooking them. Even the shells were used as fuel – carbonized hickory shells are commonplace in many Eastern Woodlands sites.

The Icehouse Bottom people also gathered acorns, but made less use of them than did their successors. Acorns provide only one-third the calories of hickory, but are rich in fats and carbohydrates that make them a valuable supplement to hickory. However, they have a bitter taste that has to be eliminated by leaching out the tannic acid (Petruso and Wickens, 1984). Many later Indian groups did this by immersing the acorns in boiling water or by passing water through the powdered meat in a basket. The acorn meal was often used to make a form of pastry bread. Walnuts, hazelnuts, and chestnuts were also collected upon occasion, but the most important wild vegetable foods were acorns and hickory nuts (Talalay, Keller, and Munson, 1984).

Plant foods of many species were abundant near Icehouse Bottom from late spring to late fall, not only nuts but young shoots of green vegetables like pokeweed, fruit such as wild blackberries, strawberries, raspberries, and plums. Occasional roots served as starchy vegetables. Wild vegetable foods were not only eaten fresh but carefully dried for winter use.

The key to the successful exploitation of river valleys such as the Little Tennessee may have revolved around successful alliance formation (Sassaman, 1996). Close ties of kin and the reciprocal obligations that came with them were strong guarantees of long-term economic security that were far more powerful than any number of technological innovations. As Sassaman argues, the production of elaborate and labor-intensive bannerstones (atlatl weights) and stone vessels makes little sense at a local level, but when produced as objects used in broad exchange networks tied to cooperative alliances, such artifacts have considerable value. He believes that many of the important technological innovations of the Archaic resulted from just such successful alliances which made life more secure in an unpredictable environment of patchy food resources.

The diversity of predictable seasonal food resources, animal and vegetable as well as aquatic, made deliberate scheduling of hunting and foraging a highly adaptive subsistence strategy. Each fall saw the upland forest floors covered with a rich mast, a carpet, as it were, of falling oil-rich nuts and other foods that was a magnet for white-tailed deer and other animals. The same trees yielded bountiful and easily harvested hickories and acorns. Winter and early spring floods often inundated favorite seasonal camps near the rivers. In high flood years, people would move to higher ground, where game was to be found. As the water level fell, they would shift back onto the floodplain and spear fish in shallow pools left by the falling waters. As long as population densities remained relatively small, there was little incentive to exploit anything but a fairly narrow spectrum of animal, plant, and aquatic foods in favored locations.

David Anderson and Glen Hanson (1988) developed a hypothetical model of Early Archaic settlement within the Savannah River basin, on the South Atlantic Slope. Their model was based on optimal foraging theory, on the assumption that where food resources are homogeneously distributed, foragers will be dispersed, whereas if they are patchy, the optimal distribution for gatherers is to cluster in larger aggregations. They hypothesized that Early Archaic bands living in this area used well-provisioned base camps on the warmer coastal plain during the winter. These were sited within river drainages, close to raw material sources, and placed according to the availability of food resources, including deer, which tended to move in larger groups during winter. In early spring, the deer dispersed and edible plant resources appeared over much of the landscape, first at the coast, then

David Anderson and Glen Hanson's model of Early Archaic settlement on the South Atlantic Slope. A macroband of some 500 to 1500 people occupied the region. The macroband comprised 8 bands, each exploiting a contiguous northwest to southeast drainage area in a pattern of seasonally shifting camps. Other macrobands occupied adjoining regions.

further inland. The people moved out into small, regularly spaced camps, their distribution reflecting the fairly even distribution of food resources. To some extent, the bands were "tethered" to raw material sources, which were irregularly distributed over the landscape. They foraged over the Upper Coastal Plain and the Piedmont during summer. Come fall, the people moved downstream, probably choosing base-camp locations that were different from the year before, for resources at those locations were still depleted. Anderson and Hanson believed that between 50 and 150 people lived in each neighboring drainage at the beginning of the Early Archaic, a figure that rose over the centuries, resulting in decreases in annual range as bands fissioned into new groups.

The distribution of Early Archaic bands over the South Atlantic Slope reflected the northwest to southeast flow of most major drainages, from the Appalachians to the sea. Anderson and Hanson believed that, to maintain a viable equilibrium population, bands from three to five drainages had to be in regular contact. The people maintained what one might call mating networks both through the movements of individuals and through regular gatherings, probably in fall, reflected by major sites located midway between winter and summer foraging grounds. Anderson and Hanson hypothesized that there was a South Atlantic Macroband of between 500 to 1500 people, perhaps made up of as many as 8 separate groups living in contiguous drainages. Other such macrobands may have lived on all three sides of the region, those to the south and west separated from the South Atlantic Slope by natural geographical barriers. These Early Archaic adaptations were conditioned not only by the local environment, but by biological interaction, population spacing, and restraints of information exchange between neighboring groups.

The Anderson and Hanson model has now undergone a decade of testing in different environments throughout the Southeast and has triggered extensive research, which has suggested, among other things, a greater degree of winter mobility and group ranges determined by the availability of tool-making stone. But the general model has survived the test of time to the point that it provides a more generalized model for the settlement not just of a few valleys, but of much of the region. Their model of colonization does not require massive population growth after first settlement, but a natural movement out of fertile river-valley staging areas resulting from social fissioning and relocation that reduced tensions between bands, families, and larger groups. The overall population, even in fertile areas, was sparse, with the impression of overcrowding coming from cultural perceptions rather than actual pressure on resources. And as the movements continued, so different groups, near and far, developed their own specific adaptations to local areas, which come down to us in the archaeological record in the form of minor variations in projectile points and other surviving material remains (Anderson, D.G., 1996).

Corner-Notched and Bifurcate Traditions
c. 7000 to 6000 BC

The change from side-notched to corner-notched projectile points may reflect a change in hunting weapons from thrusting spears to lighter weapons propelled by the atlatl, the throwing stick (Chapman, 1994). Corner-notched projectile points form a well-defined Archaic tradition all over the Eastern Woodlands and have been classified into many different local forms, including the well-known Kirk form found over much of the Southeast and further afield (Smith, B. 1986).

Icehouse Bottom, Bacon Farm, Calloway Island, and Rose Island in the Little Tennessee Valley all document Early Archaic occupation in the Southeast for a millennium after the end of the Dalton tradition. Jefferson Chapman's meticulous excavations in the 1970s chronicle more than 9000 years of human occupation, beginning in the Early Archaic (Chapman, 1973; 1975; 1978; 1979). The food remains reveal that Icehouse Bottom and the other sites were summer-fall-early winter base camps used regularly for the next 1500 years, perhaps visited as part of a regular seasonal migration pattern. Through the centuries, the way of life changed little, an adaptation very similar to that recorded in earlier times.

(Right) Archaic hunter throwing a spear with an atlatl. (Below) Artist's reconstruction of a camp at Icehouse Bottom c. 6500 BC. The hut designs are conjectural.

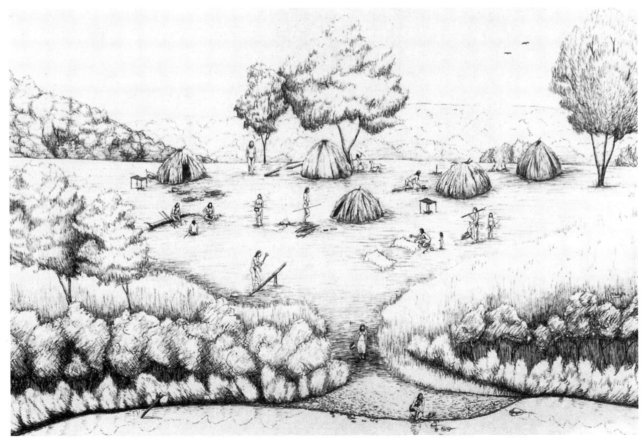

Such cultural changes that did occur are reflected in only one category of artifact – stone projectile points/knives. The Early Archaic saw a decline in, and then the abandonment of, highly curated toolkits made of fine quality stone, but point variability proliferated. In the lower Tennessee and elsewhere in the east, corner-notched points gave way to bifurcate forms after 7000 BC (Bense, 1994). These projectile heads have distinctive, bifurcated bases, perhaps a device to increase the lateral strength of the hafted point when cutting and scraping.

The making of bifurcate points in the east continued for about 500 to 700 years. They occur throughout the Eastern Woodlands as scattered finds and in many varieties, named after the sites where they were originally found. The distribution of bifurcate points extends as far east as the Atlantic seaboard, and south into the oak-hickory-pine forest zone of the South. They are found in the oak-hickory forests of southern Michigan, far into the Northeast and southern Canada, with a western boundary along the eastern edge of the Mississippi River Valley. Chapman (1994) observes that this distribution coincides with the extent of eastern deciduous forests. Perhaps the bifurcated head was an adaptation to hunting certain species of forest game.

Bettye Broyles (1971) subdivided the bifurcate points found in her excavations at St Albans, West Virginia, into various distinctive forms, or groups as Chapman calls them. The Rose Island excavations allowed Chapman (1975) not only to place the different groups into stratigraphic order, but also to study the stylistic development of the bifurcate point

Stratigraphic profile and radiocarbon chronology at the Icehouse Bottom site. The projectile-point styles contained in each of the levels are shown at left: (a) Morrow Mountain I Stemmed; (b) Stanly Stemmed Cluster; (c) Kanawha Stemmed; (d) LeCroy Bifurcated Stem; (e) St Albans Side-Notched; (f) Kirk Corner-Notched; (g) Kirk Corner-Notched.

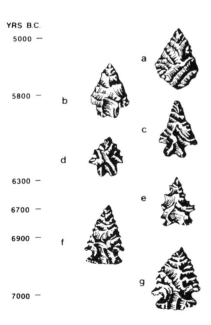

through the centuries. Four groups of points are stratified within the Bifurcate Point horizon at Rose Island, one of the few sites in the east where many bifurcate specimens are found. The MacCorkle, St Albans, LeCroy, and Kanawha phases are each named after the sites where the point forms were first identified. Chapman believes there was widespread homogeneity in projectile-point forms during the Early Archaic, and implies that his Bifurcated phases can be used as chronological markers over the entire distribution of bifurcated points in the east.

The Meaning of Projectile-Point Sequences

Stemmed points and other projectile forms provide useful chronological markers across the Southeast, and probably further afield. For example, notched forms date from about 8200 to 7500 BC, and corner-notched forms like Kirk and Palmer from *c.* 9500 to 8500 BC. The same general sequence appears in most stratified sites across the Southeast, but efforts to delineate early subregional variants are still in their infancy.

The horizon style sequence has validity in the Southeast, and can also be used in the Northeast, where sites with artifacts dating between 11,000 and 6000 BC are rare. There are dozens of isolated, surface projectile-point finds, hinting at the presence of a complex of lanceolate points in this general region. In addition to some Folsom-like specimens, unfluted points resembling Plano forms from the west are found north of Ohio and into the Great Lakes region, as well as on the Plenge site in New Jersey and in western New York. These points are known to date to at least 10,000 BC in the west. Kirk stemmed, serrated, and corner-notched points in the Northeast are contemporary with equivalent Southeastern artifact forms. Projectile points in all their variety do provide at least a crude way of identifying cultural change over large areas (Musil, 1988).

Furthermore, the broad geographic similarities between projectile points do not necessarily reflect a homogeneous adaptation to the great environmental diversity of the Eastern Woodlands, nor can they be taken to represent the frontiers of actual social groups. Dean Snow, a Northeastern specialist, has argued (1980) that widely distributed projectile-point styles may in fact result from the exchange of finished points between individuals who were maintaining social connections with their kin through reciprocal gifts. So the uniformity of projectile heads may reflect widespread exchange networks, an important way in which far-flung hunter-gatherer bands maintained contact with one another (for another perspective, see Braun in Carr, 1995).

Between 8000 and 6000 BC, most Easterners lived in small family bands, probably inhabiting well-defined territories that were more constrained than those used by their big-game hunting predecessors. The megafauna had vanished, so people exploited a wider range of food resources, wandering within more restricted areas where, perhaps, seasonal foods assumed greater importance. Group territories may have been arenas where neighboring bands came into frequent contact, where every group could understand everyone else's speech. Beyond these familiar frontiers stretched unknown country where other bands lived, people with a multiplicity of basically similar dialects that grew steadily more unintelligible the further one moved from home.

What language did these Early Archaic people speak? Linguists have established that the modern Algonquian and Gulf languages are related in such a way that the relationships must have developed a very long time ago. Gordon Willey (1966) has hypothesized that Early Archaic peoples spoke related Algonquian-Gulf languages throughout the Eastern Woodlands. This would provide a suitable medium for projectile points to be diffused over a very wide area indeed.

Then there is the issue of individual use of projectile points. A hunter might employ different point types against specific prey, or even use one form as a knife, another as a spearhead. One man could make, use, and exchange several projectile points, each of them designed for a special purpose, but each still having the same overall function, that of serving as a point or knife. Since stone-tipped spears were employed for specific subsistence activities, the use of a particular form over a period of time implies that the artifact was well adapted to a well-defined purpose. Thus, it is quite possible that more than one projectile-point type was in use in a particular area at one time, each having a different purpose. This would also explain why the distributions of many projectile-point forms are discontinuous, sometimes appearing in widely separated locations.

Although, then, there are some broad chronological horizons for Early Archaic projectile-point forms, the real problem is to identify the adaptive and cultural significance of each type, a task that has barely begun.

Restricted Mobility: Early and Middle Archaic Koster
6500 to 3600 BC

By the beginning of the Middle Holocene in about 6000 BC, the scattered Eastern Woodlands population was relying more and more heavily on the hunting of small mammals, fishing and the harvesting of seasonal plant foods such as pecan and hickory nuts wherever they were plentiful (Smith, B., 1986). The overall population was still very low, with the greatest concentrations of hunter-gatherer bands in areas that offered the greatest diversity of local resources. Now that big-game species had vanished and people were relying on food sources closer to seasonal base camps, the carrying capacities of many less-favored locations may have been reached. This may have left slowly growing hunter-gatherer populations with little option but to lead more circumscribed lifeways, with the greatest occupation densities in resource-rich river valleys where a wide diversity of animal and plant foods were concentrated.

In the South Atlantic area, for example, Middle Archaic groups made almost exclusive use of local raw materials, as if rising population densities had restricted their annual ranges (Blanton and Sassaman, 1988). Sassaman describes the South Atlantic Middle Archaic Morrow Mountain adaptation as one of "adaptive flexibility," with mobile groups occupying fairly small territories and using what he calls an "expedient" technology. Morrow groups contrast sharply with more logistically organized Middle Archaic populations in the Mid-South, who were deeply engaged in long-distance exchange, warfare, and mound-midden construction between about 6000 and 4000 BC (for architecture, see Sassaman and Ledbetter, 1996).

The famous Koster site in the Illinois River Valley, with its 14 stratified occupation levels, provides an extraordinary chronicle of human exploitation of a bountiful Midwestern environment from about 8500 BC until AD 1200 (Struever and Holton, 1979). The first people to camp at Koster were transitory Paleo-Indian visitors. Early Archaic settlement radiocarbon-dated to about 6500 BC came from Horizon 11, a seasonal camp with temporary dwellings that covered about 0.75 acre (0.3 ha). Distinctive St Albans points serve to link Koster 11 technologically to the stratified Archaic site of St Albans itself in West Virginia, while notched specimens are similar to such points found at Graham Cave near the Prairie Peninsula in Missouri. An extended family group of about 25 people returned to the same location repeatedly over the centuries, perhaps to exploit the rich fall nut harvests in the valley. They hunted white-tailed deer and small mammals, caught fish, ate freshwater mussels, and collected hickory and pecans by the tens of thousands, a vital source of high-energy fat. Broken nuts, grinders, and hand stones for preparing vegetable foods lay close to several hearths. Four adults and three infants lay tightly contracted in oval graves, some covered with logs or limestone slabs. The inhabitants also buried three dogs in shallow pits. (The exact date of dog domestication in North America is unknown.)

The seasonal Early Archaic camp at Koster contrasts dramatically with a substantial Middle Archaic settlement in Horizon 8, radiocarbon-dated to between about 5600 and 5000 BC. Computer-generated analyses of the archaeological remains break down Horizon 8 into at least four occupations, each of them the remains of substantial settlements covering 1.75 acres (0.7 ha) or so, occupied on several occasions for a century or more. The houses measured 20–35 by 12–15 ft (6–7.5 by 3.5–4.5 m), their long walls formed by wooden posts up to 10 in (25 cm) in diameter set in

Excavations at the Koster site in the Illinois River Valley, where fourteen occupation levels have been identified stretching from c. 7500 BC to AD 1200.

Analysis of the habitats within a 5-km (3.1-mile) radius of Koster. The site was strategically located to exploit a wide range of environments, from upland forest to bottomland prairie and aquatic habitats (the thick black line running north to south on the left of the diagram is the Illinois River).

⊞ BOTTOMLAND FOREST

⊛ UPLAND FOREST

○ BOTTOMLAND PRAIRIE

○ UPLAND PRAIRIE

● AQUATIC HABITAT

trenches about 8–10 ft (2.4–3.0 m) apart. Branches and clay filled the gaps between them. Apparently, there were no end walls. Perhaps they were covered with hides or mats.

The Horizon 8 dwellings were intended for long-term use, perhaps for all, if not most, of the year. The growth patterns of fish scales recovered from the deposits hint that people lived at Koster from late spring through the summer. In the fall, they gathered freshwater mussels and harvested hickory nuts. Perhaps they abandoned the site during the winter, relying on stored nuts and deer from the uplands for much of their diet. What is striking is that the Middle Archaic inhabitants practiced what many theorists might call optimal foraging strategy. They concentrated on a relatively narrow spectrum of readily exploitable foods, using only small quantities of edible grasses, and virtually ignoring such staples as acorns, black walnuts, hickory, and pecans. It is interesting to note that walnuts and hickory, while highly nutritious, are much harder to harvest, for the shells have to be broken open by hand. Not only that, but walnut tree roots contain a hormone that inhibits growth of other such trees nearby. So walnuts are scattered through the forest, while the easily harvested hickory occurs in dense groves. As long as the Middle Archaic population remained relatively stable, the Koster people could find most of the narrow range of food resources they depended upon within 3 miles (4.8 km) of their settlement.

A similar shift from a generalized hunter-gatherer economy to a narrower range of foods can be seen at other Midwestern sites, too. The Modoc rockshelter near the Mississippi in Randolph County, Illinois, lies in a hickory-rich riverine environment about 90 miles (149 km) southeast of Koster (Ahler, 1993; Fowler, M. 1959; Styles and others, 1983). Some 27 ft (8.2 m) of midden accumulation spans human occupations dating from between about 8000 and 2000 BC. The first occupants were general hunter-gatherers, without any particular dietary focus. Early Archaic levels at Modoc show little use of aquatic resources before about 5600 BC, when fish, mussels, and freshwater crayfish assume more importance, just as they did at Koster and other contemporary Midwestern sites like the Rodgers Shelter in central Missouri. The Modoc people exploited many small mammals, including cottontail rabbits, muskrats, and squirrels, but few larger animals. The same emphasis is found at both the Rodgers Shelter and the Graham Cave in central Missouri, but at all locations white-tailed deer become a major food source later in the Middle Archaic, before about 1600 BC (Smith, B. 1986).

At first Modoc was used as a short-term camp. But during the Middle Archaic, selective use of food sources like hickory nuts increased and people used Modoc for longer periods of time. As fish and other bottomland foods came into greater use, Modoc probably became a base camp, used for much of the year. Later it was a place used for more specialized activities, visited when people hunted deer on the nearby uplands and waterfowl in the shallow creeks and ponds nearby.

These changes in Modoc's role may reflect more restricted mobility in many areas during the Middle Archaic, restrictions that may have been the result of climatic change. But, in general, as sites like Koster, Modoc, and Rose Island in Tennessee show, the Middle Archaic saw conservative, seasonal exploitation of the Eastern Woodlands environment – even if we still know little of winter, spring, and summer activities. This seasonal exploitation required at least a degree of careful scheduling to maximize the potential of nut harvests, and to capitalize on the game that fed on the forest mast each fall. (For uplands, see Stafford, 1994.)

Riverine Adaptations in the Southeast

In the Southeast, the Middle Archaic witnessed a host of local adjustments to changes in local resource distributions, the catchment areas, if you will, of each band's hunting and gathering territory (Bense, 1994; Dye, 1996). There was, however, one universal exception to the local rule: a dramatic increase in the use of riverine aquatic species, which eventually became a major component in the diet of Southeastern river-valley populations. The evidence is striking: hundreds of different shallow-water mollusk species are to be found in shell middens along parts of the St Johns, Savannah, Tennessee, and Cumberland Green rivers (Claasen, 1996). By about 2500 BC, sea levels in the Southeast were close to those of today. It can be no coincidence that extensive shell middens appear close to Gulf estuaries, marshes, and brackish water sounds between 2200 and 1800 BC. Shell resources were probably exploited even earlier, but the resulting shell middens are under modern sea levels.

Rises in ocean sea levels lowered the gradients of interior rivers and streams, making them more sluggish and perhaps more suitable environments for mussels and bottom fish to flourish. This may have led to a new focus on freshwater aquatic resources in the interior. Such intensification is documented at several well-excavated sites from southern Illinois to northern Mississippi, north of 34°N and west of the Appalachians. Unfortunately, the archaeological evidence for the beginnings of this remarkable phenomenon is obscured by natural disturbance in the lower levels of many valley midden deposits. But there is no doubt that the intensification coincides with the warm Hypsithermal climatic episode (the equivalent of the Altithermal in the west). Between about 4500 and 4000 BC, many Midwestern and Southeastern rivers stabilized and accumulated silt in their floodplains. Backwater swamps and oxbow lakes formed. Shallow-water and shoal habitats as well as active streams provided abundant, easily accessible aquatic resources, including fish and mollusks. Thus, aquatic habitats were enhanced. They increased the level of aquatic biomass available for exploitation along long sections of river floodplains.

There is also reason to suspect that changing forest compositions on the uplands tended to impoverish the resource base available on higher ground. Many people have theorized that population growth exploded as a result of the increased exploitation of aquatic food sources, but there is little solid evidence for such an explosion. Bruce Smith (1986) summarizes the situation best when he views the increasing exploitation of river backwaters and shoal areas as "an opportunistic response to the advantageous emergence of a localized, seasonally abundant, dependable, and easily collected resource." This response led to the gradual adoption of sedentary lifeways in many parts of the Eastern Woodlands. Others disagree, and argue that increased population densities forced people to turn to alternative food resources.

Icehouse Bottom in the Little Tennessee Valley and other locations elsewhere in the Southeast document the first 1000 years of the Middle Archaic in this region (Chapman, 1994). Judging from the wide range of projectile-point forms, people still relied on hunting for much of their diet, hunting activity that must have concentrated on such solitary animals as the white-tailed deer. But they were probably now exploiting wild vegetable foods, on a more intensive scale than their predecessors. The Icehouse Bottom site has yielded charred nuts as well as nutting stones, also grinding and pounding stones used for processing wild vegetable foods. The inhabitants were fishing, too. Jefferson Chapman found large numbers of water-smoothed river cobbles notched on both sides for securing a line to them. These may have served as net sinkers or line weights, part of large stone traps laid on the shoals of rivers, and became much more common during the subsequent Late Archaic. He had excellent historical analogies. Englishman James Adair spent 40 years in the 18th century living among, and trading with, Indians in the Southeast: "The Indians have the art of catching fish in long crails, made with cranes and hiccory splinters, tapering to a point. They lay these at a fall of water, where stones are placed in two sloping lines from each bank, till they meet together in the middle of the rapid stream, where the intangled fish are drowned. Above such a place, I have known them to fasten a wreath of long grape vines together, to reach across the river, with stones fastened at proper distances to rake the bottom; they will swim a mile with it whooping and plunging all the way, driving the fish into the large cane pots" (Williams, 1930). This fishing method was so effective that early white settlers were still using similar stone traps along the Little Tennessee River well into the 19th century.

By 4000 BC, pollen studies document a slight increase in mean annual temperature and a decrease in rainfall. This may have led to lowered water levels in streams, lakes, and rivers in much of the South, perhaps reducing the carrying capacity of the land, for Chapman records fewer sites dating to between 5000 and 3000 BC than are known from earlier millennia of the Archaic. There was still considerable reliance on hunting. The inhabitants of the Eva site in western Tennessee not only took aquatic and vegetable foods, they also ate bear, raccoon, opossum, and turkey. But between about 5200 and 3500 BC, white-tailed deer taken with stone-tipped spears and spearthrowers represented about 90 percent of all the bone from the middens, a similar hunting preference to that in the Midwest (Lewis and Lewis, 1961).

The Windover Site
c. 6000 to 5000 BC

The Windover site near Titusville, Florida, gives us a tantalizing look at the organic components of Early Archaic culture. Windover was an Early Archaic burial area, a place where human remains and artifacts were deposited in a pond (Doran and Dickel, 1988; Purdy, 1992). The remains of at least 160 individuals, ranging from newborns to people in their 60s and 70s have come from the waterlogged archaeological levels, covered with 3 to 6 ft (1 to 2 m) of water. The dead were submerged within 48 hours of death in peat and water deposits with neutral chemistry, resulting in superb preservation. Brain tissue survived in at least 90 cases, allowing analysis of DNA and cell structure (Doran and others, 1986; Lawlor and others, 1991). The excellent preservation conditions also allowed the archaeologists to recover at least seven different textile weaves used for clothing made of the Sabal palm and/or saw palmetto. The Windover weavers produced not only garments with weaves as fine as 10 strands per 0.3 in (1 cm), but also bags, matting, and possibly some forms of blanket or poncho. Composite artifacts such as atlatls, consisting of wooden shaft, bone hook, and stone weight, came from the excavations, as did numerous bone artifacts, including awls and projectile points.

The Windover people subsisted over a broad range, which may have extended from the St John's River to the Atlantic Coast. They hunted white-tailed deer, made use of a wide variety of edible plants, and used bottle gourds (*Lagenaria siceraria*), the earliest such vegetable container yet discovered in North America (Doran and others, 1990).

The Issue of Sedentism

Studying the settlement patterns of Early and Middle, let alone better-documented Late, Archaic cultures requires a great deal more archaeological data than is currently available from any part of the Eastern Woodlands. But there are now clear signs from Middle Archaic sites like Koster and Carrier Mills in Illinois that some favored locations were in use for most of,

Handwoven fabrics were found with many burials at the Windover site in Florida.

if not all, the year (Smith, B., 1986). At least 60 mound groups, some of considerable size, in the Southeast from Arkansas to Florida are known to be Archaic earthworks (Russo, 1994; 1996). The most spectacular is Wilson's Brake in northeastern Louisiana, built as early as 3900 BC [cal] (Saunders and others, 1997). Eleven mounds and an oval enclosure cover 11 acres (4.45 ha) near the once swampy, lush Ouachita River Valley. For at least nine centuries, forager groups spent spring and early summer here, taking many fish and collecting rich stands of native plants. Wilson's Brake's earthworks are 1900 years earlier than those at Poverty Point (Chapter 17).

Some floodplain midden sites in the Midwest and Southeast have been claimed as probable year-round settlements. The descriptions are loosely cast, for more often they in fact mean permanent to semi-permanent summer to fall, low-water seasonal base camps where many activities took place. Many were located on lower terraces or in low-lying areas that were liable to flooding in late winter and early spring. At that season, goes the argument, everyone moved onto higher ground, to the edge of the valley or onto the uplands. In other words, there was a change from "free wandering" with no particular base camp to "centrally based wandering," a seasonally mobile lifeway that involved returning to the same base location year after year.

This change to centrally based wandering after 4500 BC was not a dramatic shift from earlier habits, but rather involved a slight increase in the length of time spent at summer base camps when water levels were low. During the Early Holocene and early Middle Holocene, the bands ranged up and down regular segments of river valleys with a fairly even distribution of resources. The best way to exploit food sources was to move one's base camp regularly. But when backwaters and oxbows formed after 4500 BC, the biomass level of aquatic resources increased in some well-defined areas to the point where it paid to stay in one place for much longer periods of time, long enough for thick middens to form.

Identifying Sedentary Settlement

In archaeological terms, this change is documented by a change in major site phenomena. Before 4500 BC, Archaic peoples tended to occupy brief, transitory camps widely scattered along floodplain levees and terraces. Their successors often favored the same places year after year, so that midden deposits are now found stacked up on convenient hills or slight rises close to significant backwaters, shellfish beds, or fish spawning grounds. This change does not necessarily mean that the people exploited smaller territories or never visited the uplands. It implies, however, that sedentism, more permanent settlement, was now important.

Identifying sedentism from the archaeological record is far from easy. Many criteria have been used – a greater variety of artifacts in an occupation deposit, the presence of seasonal foods, dense scatters of tools and food remains, an increase in heavy artifacts, even evidence for storage pits. But each of them suffer from major disadvantages, largely because they are so difficult to document in convincing terms.

Two criteria are thought to hint at more sedentary settlement at a number of locations – more substantial dwellings like those at Koster, and cemeteries. Few sites other than Koster have yielded relatively permanent houses. Specially prepared clay house floors occur in Middle Archaic midden sites along the Upper Tombigbee River Valley in Mississippi. These floors were being built before 4300 BC and were apparently swept clean of occupation debris at regular intervals (Smith, B., 1986). They were probably reoccupied annually by kin groups during summer and early fall, sheltered with temporary or more permanent brush and timber or hide structures. Unfortunately, there is no means of knowing how long the floors were occupied in terms of weeks, months, or years. But there is evidence of flooding, so the sites must have been abandoned regularly. Sites like Rose Island and Icehouse Bottom in Tennessee offer proof that the same locations were used repeatedly over many years.

Human burials are also a potential measure of sedentary occupation. Early Archaic settlements sometimes yield the bodies of individuals buried within the confines of the camp. But Middle Archaic peoples in the central Mississippi drainage tended to bury the dead quite differently, in formal cemeteries. Their cemeteries usually consist of large, shallow pits that contain burials of up to 40 or more people laid in graves with no particular spacing. Sometimes the pits were dug into natural knolls or bluffs overlooking the valley where people lived. In other cases, the people may even have raised a low, artificial mound above the graves to enhance the visibility of the cemetery. The artifacts or caches of offerings deposited in these cemeteries are usually associated with the grave site as a whole rather than with specific individuals. Perhaps these represent the identity of the kin group that maintained the cemetery. Some such offerings are found with juvenile burials in the cemeteries, as if they were to identify the family and kin group to which the uninitiated young person belonged. Everything points to egalitarian societies in which individual status was unimportant where leadership and authority were reflected more in age and experience or skill as a hunter, than in material possessions.

By no means all Middle Archaic burial grounds were formal cemeteries in the sense that they were maintained purely for the use of members of a specific corporate kin group. Dozens of burials come from sites in the Southeast and Florida, in middens and other occupation or subsistence deposits that may not have been formal cemeteries. The Eva site in western Tennessee, where 118 burials date to between 5000 and 3000 BC, and the well-preserved skeletons from Little Salt Spring in Florida are two examples (Lewis and Lewis, 1961).

The Black Earth site at Carrier Mills in southern Illinois is a rich Middle Archaic midden accumulated over a thousand-year period after about 4000 BC (Jefferies, 1987). The site is remarkable not only for its abundant food remains and many pits for storing, processing, and cooking foods, but for its 154 burials. Since only part of the site was excavated, Richard Jefferies estimates as many as 400 to 500 Middle Archaic people may have been buried at this location over the centuries.

The Carrier Mills burials were mostly individual interments, but as many as four people were sometimes deposited in the same pit. Only 27 percent of the graves contained any form of artifact. There was little to differentiate male or female, and no grave goods that denoted social ranking within Carrier Mills society. Eight individuals, mainly males, had been buried in clay-capped grave pits, as if they were especially important. One 43-year-old

The Black Earth site at Carrier Mills, southern Illinois: excavations in the Area A midden.

man had been buried with a bag or bundle of eagle talons, sections of bear's paw bones, projectile points, a miniature grooved axe, and other objects. Jefferies thinks he may have been a shaman, a man celebrated for his curing skills and ability at communicating with the ancestors.

Burials and the Lands of the Ancestors

The sudden appearance of cemeteries and artificial burial mounds near resource-rich river valleys may mark a dramatic change in Archaic life. Douglas Charles and Jane Buikstra (1983) have studied Archaic burial sites in the central Mississippi drainage. They drew on modern studies of sedentary populations to make a basic assumption – that when people start passing vital resources from one generation to the next through lineages and other kin organizations, they will tend to bury their dead in cemeteries. Under this argument, rights of kin groups to use and control vital food resources will be legitimized by popular religion and rituals that reaffirm the kin groups and their rights. One form of this ritualization of inheritance is to reserve a permanent burial area for members of the kin group, a cemetery located on the land the group controls, the land once owned by their ancestors.

Charles and Buikstra used assumptions that had been developed from observations of sedentary farmers. They argued that mobile Midwestern hunter-gatherers like Early Archaic bands did not use cemeteries. However, as early as 4000 BC, their Middle Archaic successors lived in base camps and even year-round settlements that flourished because of the diverse and relatively abundant food resources nearby. Cemeteries on bluffs now appear, overlooking several major Middle Archaic sites in the central Mississippi drainage. Corporate behavior in human societies is actually a form of territorial behavior, a near universal among animals. The relationship between sedentism, resources inherited through kin organizations, and cemeteries hinges on one reality – that the resources involved are fixed in space, predictable, and sufficiently abundant and diverse that a group can focus its activities around them. If a group wishes to claim rights of ownership and inheritance to these resources, one logical way to do so is through maintaining a corporate cemetery, the ritual home of one's ancestors, the primeval owners of the land. This relationship between cemeteries and the "resource catchment areas" of major archaeological sites has been demonstrated in general terms for Anglo-Saxon cemeteries in England. Similar relationships have been shown to exist for later settlements in the central and lower Illinois Valley. Thus, there are good grounds for arguing that sedentism and the appearance of Middle Archaic cemeteries go together as early as 4000 BC in some resource-rich areas.

The argument can be taken even further. With the emergence of fixed territories, perhaps during a warmer and drier period that tended to restrict denser human populations to river valleys, there may have been competition for resources and territories with fixed boundaries for the first time. This competition may have been reflected in sporadic tribal warfare, so far undocumented. But it may also be reflected in a distinctive form of territorial marking: bluff-top cemeteries under low mounds. "Perhaps the most distinctive way to indicate a relationship between a particular group and its inherited rights of access to a particular resource locale is ... to place its ancestors in burial mounds or knolls atop the prairie covered ridges at the edge of the bluff, where they would be clearly visible from the valley floor" (Charles and Buikstra, 1983). They point out that this type of bluff-top location was chosen, and remained in use, for more than 5000 years, until maize agriculture took hold throughout the Midwest. The prominent, bluff-top cemeteries of the Middle Archaic may be seen, then, as monumental structures that served as indicators of hereditary rights to important local resources. Formal cemeteries, and the burial mounds, earthworks, or natural hills associated with them, were to remain a vital element in Eastern Woodlands life for thousands of years, right into historic times in some areas.

It would be a mistake to speak of sedentism in this context in the same breath as that of permanent farming villages, for example. There were many variations in the degree and nature of sedentism. A few sites, like Carrier Mills' Black Earth location, may indeed have been fully sedentary settlements, occupied at least by some people for every month of the year.

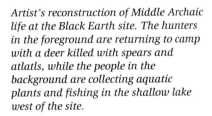

Artist's reconstruction of Middle Archaic life at the Black Earth site. The hunters in the foreground are returning to camp with a deer killed with spears and atlatls, while the people in the background are collecting aquatic plants and fishing in the shallow lake west of the site.

They were situated at prized locations, at a time when the warmer and drier climate of the Hypsithermal concentrated many river-valley populations near productive wet environments where there was perennial water and a rich diversity of animal, aquatic, and plant foods. There may have been other groups who divided their time between two base camps, one on the edge of a productive river valley, near upland hunting grounds, the other on the floodplain itself, used when rivers were low. Two processes were under way – increased utilization of floodplain aquatic species, and a long-term trend toward increasingly permanent settlement and carefully delineated group territories, sometimes reflected symbolically in conspicuous cemeteries used over many generations. These were the homes of the ancestors, the true owners of the land.

The Northeast: L'Anse Amour and Neville
c. 6000 BC and later

Everywhere in the Eastern Woodlands, the Middle Archaic was marked by major, but gradual, changes in hunter-gatherer lifeways. There was more deliberate scheduling of hunting and foraging nutritious, easily acquired "first-line" foods, followed by a slow broadening of the resource base with a wider range of seed and other vegetable foods, and an increasing use of aquatic resources wherever they occurred. The same long-term trends are to be found in the Northeast, although they are still only dimly discerned, owing to a lack of stratified, thoroughly excavated sites. But, for the most part, there was remarkable uniformity of Middle Archaic hunting and gathering culture all the way from Labrador in the north to the Carolinas far to the south, with regional differences reflected in part by minor stylistic variations in projectile points.

With the general amelioration of the climate during the Middle Holocene, it would be logical to expect Northeastern Archaic peoples to be exploiting sea mammals and coastal fisheries. But Atlantic sea levels were still about 30 ft (9 m) lower than today in 6000 BC, so many fishing camps dating to earlier than 3000 BC are now under water and beyond archaeological reach.

L'Anse Amour, Labrador. Far to the north in Labrador, the land rose as an adjustment to the retreat of massive ice sheets. So some early sites have survived above modern sea levels. At L'Anse Amour, James Tuck found the burial of a 12-year-old child deposited face-down in a 3-ft (0.9-m) deep pit and radiocarbon-dated to about 5600 BC (McGhee and Tuck, 1977). The skeleton was associated with an antler toggle harpoon head (Chapter 9) and line holder, a walrus tusk, three quartzite knives, a caribou antler pestle, a bone whistle, some stemmed and socketed bone points and six stone projectile points, and various other artifacts. The grave was covered with a mound of earth and stones, apparently the earliest artificial burial tumulus in North America. Judging from the grave furniture, the L'Anse Amour people probably followed the breeding and migrating patterns of sea mammals and caribou, moving between the coast and interior at different seasons of the year.

Coastal exploitation further south is well documented by dozens of clam- and oyster-shell middens dating to later than 3000 BC. But some shellfish

TABLE 16.1

Holocene Climate Change in Eastern North America

Much of temperate eastern North America, known to archaeologists as the "Eastern Woodlands", was largely deciduous forest at European settlement. a region of great botanical and environmental diversity. Like the west, Holocene times are conventionally, and arbitrarily, subdivided into three stages (Delcourt and others, 1985).

Early Holocene (*c.* 14,700 years ago to 6500 BC). About 14,700 years ago, the first signs of warming appeared. As the Laurentide ice sheet retreated rapidly, cool–temperate tree species spread northward, dominating vegetational cover throughout the mid-latitudes of the Eastern Woodlands. A surge of glacial meltwater coursed down the Mississippi, diluting the salinity of the Gulf of Mexico. The tundra retreated northward with the ice. Spruce forest, a transitional zone between tundra and boreal forest, expanded across the newly deglaciated landscape. The 1100 years of the Younger Dryas interrupted warming with a return to near-glacial conditions in about 10,950 BC. By 9000 BC, the Laurentide ice sheet had retreated from the Great Lakes region. There was still tundra along the St Lawrence River and in New England, with open spruce forest in Canada's Maritime Provinces, in New England, and Manitoba. Spruce-jack pine forest extended from Wisconsin to New York. Mixed-conifer northern hardwood forest expanded northward over much of the Midwest, with oak-hickory and mixed hardwood forests to the south and east. These vegetational changes were important to human settlement, because boreal spruce and pine forests offer few wild vegetable foods and even sparser game populations. In contrast, oak and hickory forests yield bountiful harvests of nuts and more diverse game resources.

Middle Holocene (*c.* 6500 to 2000 BC). The Middle Holocene was marked by warming and increasing aridity, perhaps the result of stronger prevailing warm, dry, westerly air flows that may have led to greater incidences of summer drought. Prairie, oak savannah, and oak-hickory forests shifted eastward as the mixed hardwood forest was reduced in extent. The boundary between forest and prairie reached its easternmost limit about 5000 BC. Sea levels reached their modern levels by 3000 BC, by which time basically modern vegetation patterns were established throughout the Eastern Woodlands. This was a period of rising population densities and increasingly diverse Archaic adaptations.

Late Holocene (*c.* 2000 BC to the present). The climate and vegetation of the Late Holocene were essentially similar to that of the present time. There have been minor fluctuations in temperature and precipitation in climatically sensitive areas, and along boundaries between ecological zones, but the overall resources available in the Eastern Woodlands did not change dramatically. For example, the southern frontier of the boreal forest moved southward because of increased rainfall and a cooling trend. The prairie peninsula retreated westward, too (Delcourt and others, 1986).

collectors of 5000 BC camped on steep bluffs well above the waters of the lower Hudson River Valley, so their sites are preserved (Snow, 1980). Unfortunately, there are apparent discrepancies between radiocarbon dates from some of these sites and the projectile points found in them, which are thought to have been in use some 2000 years later, so the dating of at least some of these early middens is in doubt. The base of the Dogan Point shell mound has been radiocarbon-dated to about 5000 BC, while layers containing giant oyster shells give readings of between 4500 and 1500 BC. It is likely, however, that more intensive exploitation of coastal shellfish and other marine resources was a later phenomenon.

Neville, New Hampshire. Some of the L'Anse Amour stone projectile points resemble those of the Neville site, close to the Amoskeag Falls on the east bank of the Merrimack River, New Hampshire (Dincauze, 1976). Foragers visited the riverside settlement intermittently for more than 8000 years.

The first inhabitants lived in a mixed pine-oak forest environment close to a river that must have swarmed with anadromous fish such as salmon that could be harvested with ease in late spring. This fishery would have been the major attraction of the terrace location, but preservation conditions did not allow the survival of fish bones. However, chemical tests of the occupation layers revealed unusually high mercury concentrations, a clear sign of intensive fishing – mercury compounds existed in ocean fish even before modern industrial pollutants became a factor.

Dena Dincauze has named the first occupation the Neville Complex. The people made characteristic "Neville" stemmed points, bifacial projectile points with carefully shaped tips and symmetrical bodies, clearly intended for piercing. Neville points are found as far north as central Maine, through Connecticut to perhaps as far south as Staten Island in New York. They bear a strong resemblance to the contemporary Stanly stemmed points of the Southeast, and may be considered a variant of this well-known type. Neville points were made between about 5800 and 5000 BC. The remainder of the toolkit included scrapers, perforators, and knives, and rough choppers. At first the inhabitants used local quartz, a technically unattractive raw material, but they eventually became aware of the buff-colored volcanic rhyolite from the Lake Winnipesaukee area of eastern New Hampshire. Dincauze argues that hunting and plant processing were not important activities at Neville – artifacts associated with such work are absent. The location was an important base camp for spring fishing and domestic activities.

Some time before 5000 BC, new projectile-point forms appear. The basic toolkit remains much the same, with some minor changes in scraper forms that may reflect a greater range of activities at the camps. By this time, the bands who fished at Amoskeag may have spent most of the year in the same region. In about 3900 BC, they ceased to visit the falls area, for reasons that are still a mystery. Perhaps some minor climatic fluctuation impoverished the fishery.

The Neville site shows that the Middle Archaic people of the Northeast had significant cultural relationships with similar cultures along the Atlantic seaboard and on the Carolina Piedmont far to the south. The stemmed projectile points and flake tools from Neville are directly related to even older Archaic complexes in the Southeast. Dena Dincauze believes

Middle Archaic Neville stemmed points from New England, length of one at left 6 cm.

that these ancient complexes expanded northward as mixed-oak forests spread into more northern areas during the Early and Middle Holocene.

The Middle Archaic is still so shadowy in the Northeast that we can do little more than speculate about the cultural systems of the period. Neville and other sites may have been base camps where anadromous fish could be taken in large numbers. During the summer and fall, the people may have moved to the shores of freshwater lakes and river valleys where nuts and other plant foods were available, retiring to winter camp sites in the interior, where deer and other game could be taken (for discussion, see Nicholas, 1988). Shellfish were a useful food in scarce months. All the evidence points to an ever-broader series of adaptations to local environments, to the emergence of group territories centered around important base camps – a "centrally-based wandering" pattern that may reflect more restricted mobility, as it did in many parts of the Midwest and Southeast. Just as in the central Mississippi drainage, the Middle Archaic may have seen more conscious scheduling of seasonal activities and increasing reliance on aquatic resources. And the relative lack of exotic cherts and other materials from distant sources suggests that territories were more restricted and circumscribed by those of others. It was only later that Northeastern cultures broke down this pattern of apparent isolation and developed kin and trade contacts over wide areas.

The Middle Archaic was of crucial importance in setting the stage for the brilliant efflorescence of human cultures that was to follow throughout the Eastern Woodlands.

Further Reading

Anderson, David G., and Sassaman, Kenneth E. (eds.) 1996. *The Paleoindian and Early Archaic Southeast*. University of Alabama Press, Tuscaloosa.
General essays and regional surveys that summarize the latest information on these periods in the Southeast. A superb resource.
Bense, Judith. 1994. *Archaeology of the Southeastern United States*. Academic Press, San Diego.
A basic summary of regional archaeology for general readers and students.
Chapman, Jefferson. 1994. *Tellico Archaeology*. 2nd ed. University of Tennessee Press, Knoxville.
Chapman's clearly written summary gives an excellent portrait of Archaic life in the Southeast. Strongly recommended for the general reader.
Griffin, James. 1967. "Eastern North American Archaeology: A Summary," *Science* 156:175-91.
A useful basic survey, dated, but an excellent overview of the fundamentals.
Sassaman, Kenneth E. and Anderson, David G. (eds.). 1996. *Archaeology of the Mid-Holocene Southeast*. University Press of Florida, Gainesville.
An up-to-date and authoritative synthesis of Archaic culture in the Southeast. Strongly recommended and another first-rate resource.
Snow, Dean. 1980. *The Archaeology of New England*. Academic Press, New York.
Snow summarizes the archaeology of the Northeast in a somewhat dated, but provocative, synthesis. Much basic data, somewhat outdated, but still the best summary.
Finally, a Web site, which records all fluted-point finds:
http://www.adp.fsu.edu/paleoind.html
Constantly updated, this is an invaluable resource.

CHAPTER 17

LATE ARCHAIC CULTURES IN THE EASTERN WOODLANDS

"All too frequently, the Archaic peoples, who were greatly diversified culturally through space and time, are treated as if they were a homogeneous array of hunters and gatherers, as though they were *idiots savants* capable only of changing styles of artifacts, producing an occasional nicely ground piece of stone, continuously foraging for a precarious and uncertain subsistence, and in general doing little more than surviving as noble and unspoiled primitives." Howard Winters wrote these words in 1968, rebelling against the simplistic view of Archaic society perpetuated by myopic culture historians. Today, what we know about the complex technology, sophisticated adaptations, and long-distance trade, and emerging mortuary customs of the Eastern Woodlands of 5000 BC belies the long-held stereotypes of earlier archaeologists. These trends toward greater complexity and sophistication accelerated between 4000 and 1000 BC, and afterwards, during a period when the human population of the Eastern Woodlands rose sharply.

The Issue of Population Growth

Population growth after 4000 BC coincided with the closing stages of the Middle Holocene that witnessed the final wastage of the Laurentide ice sheet (Delcourt and Delcourt, 1981; Delcourt, H.R. and others, 1985). This environmental development opened up vast areas of eastern Canada to caribou and human colonization. Rising sea levels and warming water temperatures along the Atlantic seaboard allowed a steady northward expansion of fish and shellfish habitats. River estuaries were flooded, too, creating far more favorable conditions for anadromous fish migrations in spring or fall. Water levels in the Great Lakes rose also, reducing stream gradients and improving fishing conditions in the now warmer water. Higher sea levels brought more sluggish waters to the Mississippi and other Midwestern and Southeastern rivers, too. Their swampy backwaters, low-lying levees, and lush floodplains became rich and diverse habitats for hunters and foragers. Rising water tables on the Gulf coastal plain established swamps and marshes over wide areas of Florida, while coastal resources were much richer than they had been for thousands of years. Deciduous trees spread north into parts of the once boreal forest-covered Great Lakes region and the Northeast, especially nut-bearing trees like oak, hickory, beech, and chestnut. This increased the amount of plant food available for human consumption in these areas. These changes coincided with a marked increase in human populations throughout the Eastern Woodlands after 4000 BC.

As we pointed out in Chapter 16, successful alliance building appears to have been a vital factor in Archaic life. Such links, which could often extend over many generations, came from kin ties and reciprocal obligation, also exchange networks (Sassaman, 1996). Such alliances could foster larger settlements and more sedentary living as populations rose during the Middle Archaic (Amick and Carr, 1996).

Population Growth and Sedentism

We have seen how a trend toward more sedentary settlement began during the Middle Holocene, a move that may have coincided with greater aridity and with restrictions on mobility in many areas (Johnson, J., 1994). More sedentary living may have had a significant impact on many aspects of Archaic life. More permanent base camps allow one to store nuts and other winter foods on a much larger scale than is possible if one is constantly on the move. This creates larger food surpluses, the ability to support more people year-round, and opportunities for kin groups and individuals to play important roles in controlling labor and the redistribution of food and luxury goods.

The technology of storage, using baskets, subterranean pits, perhaps special structures, was greatly enhanced by a major technological innovation – the development of waterproof, clay containers in the Southeast (Sassaman, 1993). These earliest North American ceramics appear along the South Carolina coastal plain as early as 2500 BC. They were unimpressive, shallow clay vessels tempered with plant fibers, modeled on wooden and fiber bowls and trays that had been manufactured for thousands of years.[1] At first, pottery-making was an apparently insignificant innovation, for the technology was rudimentary at best. Ken Sassaman (1993) theorizes that the slow spread of pottery technology was the result of gender resistance. He argues that men resisted the innovation because it would reduce the need for their exchange networks that handled steatite cooking slabs and bowls. In time ceramics were a major technological advance that provided a highly effective way of storing not only grain and other foods, but also water and valuables. Clay pots and bowls could also hold boiling water, enabling people to process foods like acorns much more readily than they could with fire-heated stones and other simple devices. Whether Sassaman is correct or not will probably never be established. Nevertheless, pottery-making was a success and spread to the lower Mississippi Valley, perhaps as a result of an extensive steatite trade in the Southeast, a raw material much used for making weights, ornaments, and large containers.

As we noted in Chapter 14, clay vessels are fragile and often heavy, and far from easy to carry from one camp to the next. Large-scale ceramics production could only flourish in more sedentary settlements, such as

[1] Temper is the ingredient added to clay to help it dry uniformly. All kinds of material are used, everything from fine sand to ground shell or plant fiber. Shell temper sometimes acts as a flux that can harden the clay.

began fully to develop in the Late Archaic. It should be noted that the invention of pottery-making is not nearly as revolutionary as is sometimes claimed. Any hunter-gatherer who uses open hearths knows that soft earth and clay are baked hard by hot flames and ashes. However, it is hardly advantageous to make clay containers when they are heavier than baskets or skins, and are likely to be broken in transit from one camp to the next.

Archaic territories contained a diversity of food resources and raw materials, but there was always something that was lacking – perhaps flint for making projectile points, red ocher for ornamentation, shells, stone for making ground-edged wood-working adzes used in dugout canoe building. This was where ties of kin and reciprocity came in, forging and maintaining alliances and trade networks. Archaic exchange was probably intermittent, often based on family and household, and probably of limited economic significance.

In archaeological terms, Late Archaic population increases are reflected in much higher site densities. Unfortunately, this cultural diversity is reflected inadequately in the poorly preserved archaeological record. At least five distinctive regional variants of Late Archaic culture have been identified on the basis of projectile-point styles and other artifacts. We now summarize these, but it should be stressed that they are but generalized archaeological abstractions, which mask a multitude of ancient cultures and local adaptations over at least 3000 years.

The Shield Late Archaic
c. 5000 BC to modern times

As early as 5000 to 4000 BC, the descendants of Paleo-Indian hunters were moving into newly deglaciated lands north of the Great Lakes, into the vast wilderness of the Canadian Shield (Wright, J., 1972). They settled over an enormous area from the north shores of the lakes all the way to the headwaters of rivers flowing into James Bay and Hudson Bay, and far eastward into Quebec and the Maritime Provinces of Canada. There they developed the distinctive Shield Archaic tradition, an adaptation to a country of lakes, rivers, and boreal forest with but sparse game and vegetable resources. The people lived in small bands, mostly near lakes and rivers and close to regular caribou migration routes. They subsisted off caribou and fish, taking other seasonal game such as bear, beaver, moose, and muskrat. The boreal environment provided minimal spring and summer plant foods.

The Shield Archaic was a profoundly conservative adaptation, one that changed but little over many millennia. The earliest projectile-point styles are somewhat reminiscent of Plano-like forms from further south, with fairly broad-bladed, notched, corner-removed, or stemmed points appearing later. Heavy duty end and side scrapers, flaked knives and other implements manufactured from exotic flints occur at many sites. For thousands of years, in places right up until European times, Shield Archaic bands flourished in almost complete isolation from the more temperate world to the south. Some Late Archaic copper artifacts like fish hooks and knives occur on Shield sites closer to the Great Lakes, but most of the later boreal forest hunters relied on basically the same Early Archaic technology as their remote ancestors. The sheer vastness and isolation of their harsh, forested wilderness shut off most possibilities of cultural transmission from more sophisticated societies to the south. The Shield Archaic people were probably the ancestors of the Algonquian-speaking hunter-gatherers of the Canadian Shield at European contact.

The Maritime Tradition of the Northeast
c. 6000 to c. 1000 BC

Three overlapping, and generalized, Late Archaic traditions – Maritime, Lake Forest, and Mast Forest – have been identified over much of the temperate Northeast and east. The oldest identifiable language phylum in this area is Algonquian, a language widely spoken in the Eastern Woodlands at the time of European contact, and thought by some experts to have been in use by at least 8000 to 6000 BC. Linguists have reconstructed proto-Algonquian words for important animals and plants, especially the tamarisk and beech trees. Since both species were identified in proto-Algonquian, the experts theorize that their distribution coincides broadly with their ancient distribution. Thus, they pinpoint the ultimate homeland of the language as lying in the general area occupied by the Maritime, Lake Forest, and Mast Forest adaptations. Like the Shield Archaic, these three diverse Late Archaic adaptations were the ancestors of historic peoples encountered by Europeans thousands of years later.

The Maritime Archaic, at best a general label, has associations with the "Red Paint People," one of the pervasive myths of North American archaeology, a myth as persistent as that of the Moundbuilders. The Red Paint folk first appeared in archaeological literature in 1912, identified in some red ocher-smothered graves from Maine, a cemetery that seemed quite unlike any known ancient Indian find. Fifteen years later, amateur archaeologist Walter Smith published *The Lost Red Paint People of Maine*. He claimed the Red Paint People tribe were drowned when great tidal waves inundated thousands of square miles of a once much larger Maine. It happened that canoe loads of later Indians were paddling around offshore. To their astonishment, they were suddenly deposited on the vacant land. "It would have been the fastest and cleanest population replacement in the history of the world," remarks Dean Snow (1980). A surge of professional research since the 1960s has banished the Red Paint People to the legendary world where they belong. The cemeteries attributed to them belong within the Maritime Archaic tradition.

James Tuck introduced the term Maritime Archaic after excavating an important cemetery at Port aux Choix, Newfoundland, radiocarbon-dated to about 2350 BC (McGhee and Tuck, 1975; Tuck, 1976; 1982). Ninety-nine individuals had been buried in graves sealed with layers of limestone rocks and sandy soil mixed with crushed shell. The dead divided almost equally between males and females, with large numbers of infants and newborns. Everyone had been sprinkled with powdered red ocher, with offerings of tools and weapons accompanying most people, young or adult. The Port aux Choix people were buried with slender, bayonet-like spearheads and ground points. They used bone and antler harpoons and bone daggers that were sometimes mounted in antler hefts. Not only the slate bayonets but

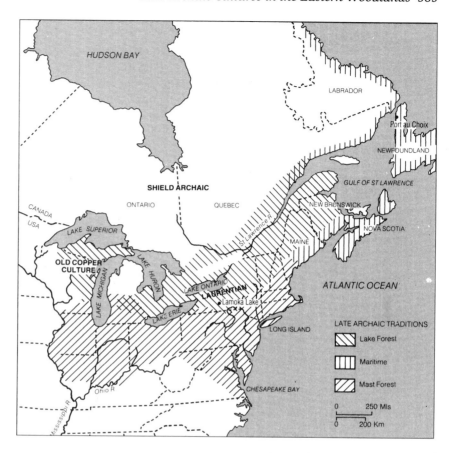

Late Archaic traditions of the Northeast.

similar heavy wood-working tools – axes, adzes, and gouges – are also found to the south in Maine. Tuck recovered ground beaver incisors that were once mounted in antler handles and used as knives, bone needles, bone combs, pendants, also carved bird and whale effigies from the cemetery. He believes the Port aux Choix people were caribou hunters, who also took sea mammals with their harpoons. They also exploited salmon runs and hunted sea birds, including the now extinct great auk.

The distinctive maritime flavor of the Port aux Choix site is repeated at other Archaic locations along the coasts and rivers of New Brunswick and

Port aux Choix, Newfoundland. (Above) Bone comb in the shape of a waterbird. (Below) Bayonet-like dagger.

Maine, through the Maritime Provinces of Canada and along the coasts of Quebec, Labrador, and Nova Scotia that border the Gulf of St Lawrence, which is why Tuck developed the notion of a widely distributed Maritime Archaic tradition based on caribou and seal hunting. Inland Maritime tradition sites tend to be located at strategic points on large rivers or on the lower reaches of major tributaries. Caribou flourish on heavy lichen growth, such as grew in the region's pine, hemlock, and spruce forests between about 5000 and 2300 BC, easily killed with heavy spears when trapped in water or deep snow. Their hunting methods may have resembled those of historic caribou hunters of Canada's Barren Grounds. They located their camps near established seasonal migration routes and would drive large numbers of animals between converging lines of stone cairns toward lurking hunters, or into water covered with thin ice, where waiting canoes dispatched the trapped beasts.

Archaic sites south of the St Lawrence reveal considerable local cultural diversity within a generalized Maritime tradition based on fishing, hunting, and foraging. For example, Bruce Bourque (1995) excavated the Turner Farm site on North Haven Island in Penobscot Bay, Maine, a shell midden on a terrace facing a gravel beach. The site's complex stratigraphic sequence covers nearly five millennia and extends into the early historic period. Bourque has identified Late Archaic occupation between about 2500 and 1800 BC, which he calls the Moorehead I phase, an independent Late Archaic culture from the Maritime Archaic tradition based on deep-sea fishing, including swordfish, at a time of warmer ocean temperatures in the Gulf of Maine. He believes these people, with their elaborate technology and mortuary ceremonialism associated with Red Paint cemeteries, developed out of earlier local Archaic cultures, maintaining close links by boat with Late Archaic groups living on the other side of the St Lawrence River (for discussion, see Bourque, 1995). The Moorehead phase ended with rapid ocean cooling, which may have favored cod fishing, but decimated warm-loving swordfish populations.

The various Late Archaic cultures along the Atlantic coast enjoyed sophisticated coastal adaptations, based not only on the exploitation of inshore fish and harbor seal hunting, and on the scavenging of beached whales, porpoise, and black fish, but also on offshore fishing of cod and swordfish. Swordfish almost never drift ashore, for they are a deep-water fish. But they often sun themselves near the surface off the Maine coast during the summer months. The only way Maritime people could take them was by stalking them in large dugout canoes and spearing their prey with harpoons.

Everything points to a regular seasonal round. During the summer months, the coastal people would live at waterside locations hunting and fishing inshore and offshore in large dugout canoes. Come fall, they would take advantage of bountiful fish runs, hunting caribou inland through the winter until the spring salmon runs began. This was a centrally based wandering system, with, perhaps, somewhat larger band sizes than occurred in earlier times, for the relatively predictable food resources of coast and interior permitted a somewhat higher population density than before. These were skilled ocean hunters with a well-developed religious tradition reflected in careful disposal of the dead. But the graves from Port aux Choix and an Archaic site at Hathaway, North Carolina, show no signs of social ranking.

Almost certainly, the Maritime Archaic evolved from local Middle Archaic cultures in the region, perhaps drawing some of the maritime elements in its culture from the Sub-Arctic to the northeast, where sea-mammal hunting and fishing were long established.

Lake Forest Late Archaic
c. 3200 to c. 1000 BC

The Lake Forest Archaic covers a broad cultural continuum of Late Archaic culture associated with the pine and hardwood forests that extend from the Great Lakes into New York State and the St Lawrence Valley (Mason, R., 1981; Snow, 1980). Lake Forest people who lived to the northeast in the St Lawrence drainage had access to both heavy fish runs in spring and fall, and also to harbor seals who flourished in Lake Ontario and Lake Champlain. Their adaptation may have resembled that of the Maritime tradition. The Lake Forest Archaic was predominantly an inland adaptation, a lifeway that was varied, highly flexible, and based on a multitude of primary and secondary, overlapping food sources. Deer and other mammals medium-sized and small, fish, shellfish, reptiles, waterfowl, ground-running and tree-roosting birds, and all manner of plant foods – all were part of Lake Forest subsistence. Population densities were generally low, except in the most food-rich and resource-diverse areas. The people probably lived in small bands within well-defined territories where they used a regular base camp returned to year after year, but with much seasonal mobility.

The great diversity of the Lake Forest tradition is confusing, even to specialists, partly because of terminological confusion, and also on account of the proximity of its southern boundaries to the dense Late Archaic populations of the Midwest and Southeast. For our broad, descriptive purposes, there are two widely recognized variants which merit more extended discussion: Laurentian, and the Old Copper culture.

Laurentian (3200 to 1400 BC). If there is one phrase that can be used to describe the Laurentian, it is Ronald Mason's (1981) telling "unity within diversity." The term was originally used to describe the Late Archaic cultures of northern New York, southern Ontario, and both banks of the St Lawrence into southern Quebec and Vermont, now known to date to between 3200 and 2000 BC (Ritchie, 1969; for history, see Funk, 1988). But the definition was soon found to apply to Late Archaic sites far from this core area, in New England, the Upper Great Lakes, and south into Pennsylvania and New Jersey. So the term "Laurentian" covers a multitude of local variants and adaptations known to specialists under a multiplicity of archaeological labels that may, or may not, bear resemblance to ancient cultural reality. In general, however, the Laurentian was a diverse woodland adaptation, based on a wide variety of mammals, wild vegetable foods, and fish. Laurentide subsistence patterns varied with the season and the location, with marked seasonal exploitation of nuts, waterfowl, and other locally plentiful resources.

In archaeological terms, the Laurentian is identified by some characteristic artifact forms, especially the broad-bladed and side-notched Otter Creek

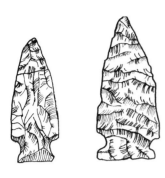

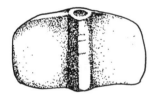

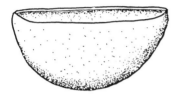

Laurentian artifacts from New York State. Top to bottom: two side-notched Otter Creek points, a ground-slate ulu, and two perforated bannerstones. Length of longest point c. 12.5 cm.

point from the Lake Champlain drainage. Related point designs have come from contemporary sites in New England, and far south and west into the Mississippi Valley and Midwest. In all probability, the Otter Creek point developed from earlier Middle Archaic forms used over much of the Eastern Woodlands. Laurentian artisans also made polished "bannerstone" atlatl weights, chipped-stone gouges and adzes for wood-working, and a wide variety of antler and bone points, ornaments, and small tools.

While many artifact forms like scrapers, whistles, and awls are virtually universal, others, such as projectile-point styles, ground-slate tools, and copper objects, appear to have more discrete distributions. In general, ground-slate artifacts and other "northern" tools tend to be more common in eastern Laurentian sites: knives, projectile points, and characteristic semi-circular *ulu* knives, artifacts used by ancient and historic Inuit to skin fish and treat sea-mammal hides. This technological component of Laurentian culture may have stemmed from the rich Maritime Archaic of the St Lawrence Valley. Artifacts made of native hammered copper from the Great Lakes region are much more common in Laurentian sites to the west, evidence of widespread trade in this metal over a wide area. The Laurentian tradition is made up of diverse technological strands, derived not only from the Maritime provinces of the Northeast, but also from much further afield in the Midwest and south as well.

In New York, Vermont, southern Ontario, and Quebec, the Laurentian is subdivided into three regional phases that overlap in space and time: Brewerton, Vosburg, and Vergennes. The Vergennes phase emerged around 3200 to 3000 BC. Vergennes sites are centered in northeast New York State and in nearby Maine, Vermont, and southern Ontario. This is the "classic" Laurentian, with a full range of characteristic artifacts, including Otter Creek points. There are some signs of a formative version of the Vergennes dating to earlier centuries. The Brewerton phase of central New York and the Lake Ontario region and the ill-defined Vosburg of the Mohawk and Hudson drainage are broadly contemporary. Neither contain the full range of Laurentian artifacts. They are distinguished by different projectile-point forms (for full discussion, see Funk, 1988).

These local variations, and many others, are hardly surprising, for the Lake Forest tradition was a highly adaptable culture that absorbed artifacts and other culture traits from neighbors on every side.

Old Copper Culture (c. 3000 to 2500 BC). In a few parts of the world, ancient peoples used abundant native copper outcrops as a source of "stone" for making artifacts of all kinds without actually smelting the metal. The Lake Superior Basin was one of those regions. Vast outcrops of very pure copper occur on or near the surface along the Brule River in northwest Wisconsin, on Lake Superior's Keweenaw Peninsula, on Isle Royale on the Canadian shore, and on the northern shore of the lake (Halsey, 1996). The Indians picked the ore off the surface, or could dig it out with the simplest of tools. For thousands of years, ancient peoples made use of this convenient raw material to make artifacts of all kinds, shiny tools and ornaments that were passed from hand to hand over thousands of miles of eastern North America.

No one knows when Archaic people first exploited Wisconsin's copper outcrops, but tens of thousands of Late Archaic metal artifacts have turned up in the eastern part of the state, with outlying finds far into northeast

Two spearheads cold hammered from Lake Superior copper. Location unknown.

Canada and all over the Great Lakes drainage, also in the east and Midwest. These finds have given rise to a loosely defined western variant of the Lake Forest Tradition – the Old Copper culture, identified by a wide variety of copper implements that bear striking resemblances to Laurentian and Maritime Archaic slate tools. Its type sites are three poorly understood Wisconsin cemeteries – Oconto, Osceola, and Reigh, all disturbed by collectors and industrial activity before investigation. Ronald Mason (1981) dates Old Copper to between about 3000 and 2500 BC. It would be a mistake, however, to think of the Old Copper culture as a rigidly delineated cultural entity. Most likely, it covers a large number of small, diverse hunter-gatherer societies that shared a common copper technology, just as slate artifacts were made in similar ways, and in basically equivalent forms, over much of the Northeast.

Copper projectile points often substituted for stone-tipped weapons. Men hammered out axe and adze blades, gouges, *ulus*, wood splitting wedges, and awls of many forms. Fish hooks and gorges, even gaffs for landing the catch (some dredged from the lake bed in modern fishermen's nets) were fashioned in the shiny metal. The artisans made simple ornaments – tubular and barrel-shaped beads, bracelets, and headdress pieces.

The Lake Superior copper industry had a long and varied history. A large number of western Lake Forest societies exploited the metal and enjoyed its many advantages. In time, word of the shiny metal spread far and wide. Copper artifacts and ornaments passed from hand to hand between close and more distant kin. The further away from the outcrops copper objects passed, the greater the perceived value and prestige associated with them. Over the centuries, extensive trade in copper developed from the Upper Great Lakes far into the east, Midwest, and Southeast. Most of the native copper circulated within the Great Lakes and Laurentian areas, within a radius of about 350 miles (563 km) from the sources. The people living this close to the outcrops employed copper for utilitarian objects such as spearheads and adze blades that were used in life and deposited with the dead. Even when used for day-to-day artifacts, copper was a highly esteemed commodity, a shiny material that made "ordinary" artifacts of wood, bone and stone look prosaic. In time, this prized metal became a symbol of social identification both for the living and the dead, who carried their cherished artifacts with them to the world of the ancestors. Outside the 350-mile (563-km) radius, copper assumed a vastly enhanced prestige value, as something rare and highly prized. The metal was fashioned into ornaments that appear in graves, a clear sign of social prominence carried with one into the afterlife. Lustrous copper artifacts and ornaments were a staple of complex long-distance trading networks that developed all over the Eastern Woodlands between 4000 and 1000 BC. They were also an important element in evolving mortuary traditions, in which grave ornamentation, social ranking, and kin identity played important parts.

Mast Forest Late Archaic
c. 2700 to 1200 BC

Coastal, Piedmont, Mast Forest. . . names for this somewhat ill-defined Late Archaic tradition have proliferated over the years, into what Dean Snow (1980) has called "a thicket of competing abstractions." Whatever the

Susquehanna point, length 6.9 cm.

appropriate label, this regional expression extends from the Merrimack drainage of southern New England through coastal drainages as far south as North Carolina and west across the basins of Ohio River tributaries to the southern shores of Lake Erie and into southern Michigan (Funk, 1988; 1994). Since it largely coincides with forests with a higher oak tree component, the term Mast Forest is perhaps most appropriate.

As always in the Eastern Woodlands, projectile-point forms have played an important role in distinguishing not only between different Mast Forest complexes, but also between Lake Forest and Mast Forest sites. What are potentially more striking, however, are the adaptive contrasts between the two traditions. Mast Forest sites tend to contain more pestles, grinders, and other artifacts for preparing wild vegetable foods, implying that their makers made greater use of nuts, especially acorns. Deer were the major game animal throughout the mast forest, but simple fishing with spears and harpoons was important in rivers and lakes.

Two Late Archaic traditions occur in southern New England under the general rubric of the Mast Forest (Dincauze, 1971, 1976; Ritchie, 1969). The Narrow Point tradition, characterized by points of that style, extended from southeastern New York into southern New England between about 2650 and just after 2000 BC. The better known Susquehanna tradition formed a single cultural province from eastern Pennsylvania to Maine and out onto the now-submerged continental shelf where points have been dredged up. It replaced the Narrow Point over part of this area and lasted from about 1800 to 1200 BC. The relationships between these traditions and others to the south and west are still little understood, but they are associated with signs of more elaborate burial ceremonies involving cremations and possible multiple burials involving the digging of large pits.

The Mast Forest Archaic includes the famous Lamoka site on the lake of that name, first identified by New York archaeologist William Ritchie in 1932 as part of his Archaic stage of North American prehistory (Ritchie, 1969). Lamoka and related sites lie in the undulating country of west-central New York State, where small bands of hunter-gatherers lived mainly along the tributaries of Lake Ontario around 2500 BC. The Lamoka Lake site itself was probably a base camp used for months on end. It consisted of about 27 houses, a community of perhaps about 150 to 200 people, covered about 0.9 acre (0.4 ha), and formed a midden up to 4.9 ft (1.5 m) deep. The inhabitants lived in rectangular dwellings with up to 215 sq. ft (20 sq. m) of floor space, frames of poles or saplings screwed into the ground and covered with bark, skins, or mats. Acorn-roasting beds up to 49 ft (15 m) long, hearths, and storage pits, also fish- and meat-drying racks, abounded in the settlement.

Most other known Lamoka-related settlements were much smaller and more transitory, reflecting a centrally based wandering system that dispersed the population for much of the year. The hunters used atlatls and spears to take deer, turkey, and passenger pigeons, as well as small mammals of all kinds, staple game animals over much of the Eastern Woodlands at this time. They were also expert fishermen, both with fish spears and with hooks and gorges, as well as nets. Ritchie and others have found enormous numbers of stone fish-net weights, also bone net-making artifacts. The Lamoka people also exploited wild vegetable foods in spring, summer, and fall, especially annual harvests of hickory and acorns.

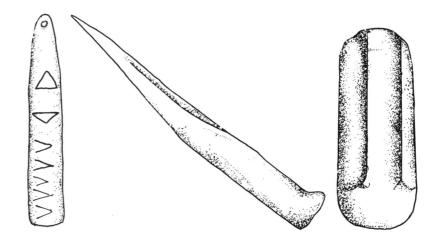

Lamoka artifacts: (right; left to right) antler pendant with geometric design; bone dagger; beveled adze; and (above) one side-notched and two stemmed points. Length of adze c. 13.5 cm.

Lamoka toolkits are remarkable for their heavy wood-working tools – hatchets and the characteristic beveled Lamoka adze, perhaps used in canoe building. The people manufactured a wide range of small, narrow-stemmed stone projectile points, small bone tools, and pestles and mortars used for preparing vegetable foods. Many polished-bone or turtle-shell pendants come from Lamoka sites, usually perforated and scored lightly on the edges. Simple geometric designs appear on some of these pendants, similar to artifacts that also occur in Kentucky. Perhaps the Lamoka people maintained some tenuous connections with groups far to the south.

Like the Maritime Archaic people, the Lamoka hunter-gatherers buried their dead with sedulous care, curled up in a flexed position, although not in cemeteries but in village middens. Occasionally, the bones of the deceased are bundled up, as if they had been collected and buried after decomposition. Their skeletons reveal they were long-headed people, men standing about 5 ft 6 in (1.68 m) high, the women slightly shorter. Most graves had red ocher and a few personal possessions like adzes.

Lamoka society was by no means peaceful. Several individuals had been killed by Lamoka-style projectile points still embedded in their skeletons. A few were mutilated after death, then buried without heads, hands, or feet. Perhaps these people were victims of territorial disputes or of the kind of constant, low-level blood feuding that still smolders on for generations in egalitarian societies throughout the world to this day. Perhaps the Lamoka people practiced sporadic ritual cannibalism, too, for fragments of split and burnt human bone come from some settlements.

The highest Mast Forest population densities may have been near the Atlantic coast. About 2500 BC, a group of Mast Forest people built a stake fish weir on the site of what is now Boylston Street, Boston, on a river bed that is now about 16 ft (5 m) below modern sea level (Conger and others, 1949). Coastal bands like this one probably spent the summer months close to shore, moving inland to hunting camps in the cold season. Shellfish were also an important resource in southeastern New England and along the Atlantic coast. As early as 3900 BC, large oysters were harvested in the Lower Hudson estuary, while the quahog and soft-shelled clam were important New England resources.

Most Mast Forest communities were probably of small size, with occasional larger base camps, like the Bent site on the Mohawk River which covers about 5 acres (2 ha) (Snow, 1980). Six circular post-framed dwellings 30 to 45 ft (9 to 14 m) across, together with a larger, perhaps ceremonial structure, once stood at the Wapanucket 6 site in southeastern Massachusetts. The dwellings had winding, shaped entrances, perhaps for security or to keep out the cold, so the doorways were formed by overlapping walls. They were large enough to house a nuclear family or slightly larger group.

The Mast Forest Archaic shows great regional diversity, with little apparent exchange of exotic raw materials between neighbors. (For a discussion of the Terminal Archaic of the Northeast, see Chapter 21, where these cultures are discussed as background to later prehistory.)

Central Riverine Archaic
c. 4000 to 1000 BC

Lamoka Lake and other Mast Forest sites show how higher population densities could develop in areas where plentiful, diverse, and predictable food resources were to be found. The same situation pertained in the major river valleys of the Midwest and Southeast. The Central Riverine Archaic was the most elaborate and well developed of all eastern Late Archaic traditions, for it was centered in and near Midwestern and Southeastern river valleys. Here, both rich deciduous forests and bountiful floodplains provided a superabundance of aquatic, game, and plant foods – also unlimited potential for human interaction, an important factor in fostering more complex societies. The Central Riverine is found in or near the Mississippi, Ohio, Cumberland, and Tennessee valleys, a tradition that developed over thousands of years as rivers stabilized during the Middle Holocene. As we saw in the previous chapter, Early and Middle Archaic occupations at sites like Carrier Mills, Eva, and Koster document the trend toward more sedentary lifeways and ever more efficient exploitation of aquatic and vegetable resources (Brose, 1994; Johnson, J., 1994; Smith, B., 1986).

Koster (3900 to 2800 BC). Horizon 6 at Koster dates to between 3900 and 2800 BC, a time when people lived there year-round (Phillips and Brown, 1983; Struever and Holton, 1979). The village, part of what is called the "Helton" phase, covered about 5 acres (2 ha), perhaps housing 100 to 150 people. Stuart Struever and his colleagues found six houses, built on sunken earthen floors that were cut like shallow terraces about 18 in (45 cm) into a hill slope. The builders erected rows of stout posts along the long walls, then filled in the gaps between them with woven brush and clay. Apparently they covered the ends with skins, mats, or more brush. Each dwelling covered between 96 and 140 sq. ft (12 to 15 sq. m), sufficient space for a nuclear family.

The food remains from this settlement reveal striking contrasts with earlier Archaic diet in the Illinois Valley. Earlier fishermen had concentrated mainly on fish species that preferred faster-moving river water. Their Horizon 6 successors exploited the shallow backwater lakes and swamps that now abounded near Koster. They speared and netted vast numbers of sluggish,

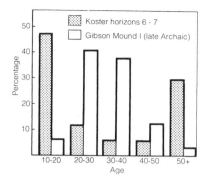

Histogram comparing the preponderance of adolescent and elderly burials in the Koster Horizons 6–7 cemetery with contemporary burials under Gibson Mound, where a much higher proportion were those aged between 18 and 40.

shallow-water fish like bass, buffalo fish, and catfish, species that can be eaten fresh or dried or smoked for consumption during the winter. Dozens of fish could also be taken by poisoning the water with the chemicals in powdered hickory nut husks, or by driving fish into oxygen-starved pools where they could be scooped up with baskets. One Illinois fisheries biologist has estimated that the Helton occupants of Koster could have taken between 300 and 600 lbs (136–272 kg) of fish flesh per acre every year from backwater lakes that covered hundreds of acres. The same shallow lakes also contained rich mollusk beds that could be used as supplementary food.

Like their predecessors, the Helton people relied on the fall hickory and acorn harvests, as well as black walnuts, pecans, and hazelnuts. But they now exploited many more seed plants, including marsh elder (sumpweed), a swampside grass, grinding the seeds with stone pestles and mortars. The hunters took deer and other small mammals, but they now had a new seasonal food – waterfowl that paused to feed and rest on the shallow lakes of the Illinois Valley during spring and fall migrations. The Illinois is on the Mississippi flyway, the narrow migration route used by millions of waterfowl flying north and south to and from their Canadian breeding grounds each year. The Helton people could take hundreds of ducks, geese, and other migrants with bows, or by trapping them with light, weighted nets cast over sleeping birds, or by using silently paddled canoes to drive them into waiting cages during stealthy dawn raids.

Everything in Koster Horizon 6 points to the exploitation of a much broader spectrum of animal, aquatic, and vegetable foods. This implies larger food surpluses, surpluses used to feed more people. Enhanced food-procurement abilities coincide with more commonplace sedentary occupation, perhaps resulting in part from even more restricted territorial mobility than in the Middle Archaic. But, with more mouths to feed, there may have been food shortages. It cannot be a coincidence that Late Archaic people were now harvesting not only nuts but seed plants, a much broader range of vegetable foods, and also taking opportunistic advantage of migratory birds and other seasonal phenomena.

A small cemetery of eight burials smothered in red ocher came from the edge of the Horizon 6 settlement, most of them men older than 40 years old, who had been crippled by arthritis or serious injury. There were adolescent burials, too, young and old both buried with grinding stones, points, drills, and other day-to-day artifacts. Another cemetery of the same age lay under the later Gibson Mound across the river from Koster. This offered a dramatic contrast – not the infirm, but the skeletons of healthy men and women between 18 and 40 years old, associated with more elaborate grave goods. Stuart Struever has argued that these able-bodied villagers may have enjoyed a higher social status than the adolescent and unproductive sick and older people laid to rest at the edge of the settlement.

Koster was abandoned in about 2800 BC, then occupied again about 800 years later by deer-hunting people of the so-called "Titterington" phase from the St Louis area, people who buried prominent members of society with beautiful shell ornaments from the Gulf of Mexico.

Green River Culture *(3000 to 2000 BC)*. To the east, the Green River joins the Ohio River at Evansville, Indiana, part of a floodplain area that offered rich food resources for Late Archaic hunters and foragers. Between about

3000 and 2000 BC, large, stable Indian communities flourished in this part of the Ohio drainage. They remained at, or near, the same locations for centuries, accumulating huge shell middens that were a magnet for early archaeologists, so much so that the term "Shell Midden" Archaic was once coined to describe them (Webb, 1974). The famous Indian Knoll site in southwestern Kentucky is the best-known location. Excavated by William Webb during the Great Depression, it alone has yielded more than 1000 burials. Collectively, the Green River sites are a mine of information on Late Archaic riverine societies of 2500 BC, and on the people who lived there.

Thousands of freshwater shells come from Indian Knoll, Carlston Annis, and other Green River settlements, but they were probably little more than a supplemental food in this resource-rich environment. The dietary staples were both animal (deer and many small mammals) and vegetable. The hunters took game with spears and atlatls. At least 70 Indian Knoll graves contained handles, weights, and atlatl hooks, still lying in place with the wooden shaft decayed away. Shallow-water fish were commonly eaten, but the rich range of vegetable foods is especially striking. Easily stored hickory nuts were the overwhelming favorites, but acorns were also exploited. Less cyclical in their harvest abundance, acorns may have assumed greater and greater importance during the Late Archaic, partly because they were a more consistent crop than the hickory. Some domesticated squashes appear in the Green River sites, evidence that people were now turning to small-scale horticulture to amplify natural food supplies, also growing gourds as containers.

The Indian Knoll people show a close physical resemblance to those from other Midwestern Archaic cemeteries. Life expectancy was short, only about 18.6 years, compared with the 32.8-year figure from Carrier Mills in southern Illinois, which is even better than that for early 19th-century Americans (Jefferies, 1987). A surprising number of people died violently. Nearly 11 percent of the Indian Knoll skeletons had suffered fractured bones, and at least 23 were associated with stone or antler projectile points that may have been the cause of death. Perhaps these casualties reflect sporadic blood feuding, or even, as some authorities have argued, competition for prized resources. Indian Knoll and other large Green River sites lie in highly favored locations. Perhaps the inhabitants had to defend themselves regularly against those who did not have similar access to such abundant food supplies.

Judging from the Indian Knoll graves, the Green River people lived in a fairly egalitarian society, where everyone owned much the same material possessions. Men were buried with axes, wood-working tools, fish hooks, awls, and stone-working punches. Women wore bone beads and owned nutcracking stones. One curious funerary anomaly finds male weapons like

Atlatl parts from Indian Knoll, Kentucky: handle (left), weight (center), and hook (right).

atlatls occurring with female and child burials. Perhaps, as Nan Rothschild has argued, this phenomenon may mark the beginnings of some form of rank distinction in Late Archaic society, privileges that were inherited and symbolized by prestigious artifacts. Some men and women carried their turtle-shell rattles, bone flutes, and shamans' bones with them at death (Rothschild, 1979).

About 4 percent of the Indian Knoll burials yielded exotic objects from afar. Five burials included metal ornaments of Lake Superior copper. Conch shells and shell ornaments such as beads and gorgets, also cups, accompanied 42 skeletons, the *Marginella* and *Olivella* species from the Gulf of Mexico and the southern Atlantic seaboard hundreds of miles away. Both adult men and women owned valuable copper and conch objects, as did infants and children. Some 18,378 disk-shell beads of imported shell came from 143 Indian Knoll graves. Rothschild believes that young people were buried with imported goods because of their kin ties to privileged adults of high status and wealth. Whether such privileges were inherited or acquired by adults during their lifetimes remains unknown.

There is some debate as to how complex these shell-mound Archaic societies were. Cheryl Classen has argued (1986) that some shell middens were used as formal, ceremonial burial areas. In contrast, Milner and Jefferies (1998) theorize that people were just buried in the middens as a normal course of affairs.

The Riverton Culture (1500 to 1000 BC). The Green River culture was, of course, a local society, centered in an area like the Lower Illinois Valley where a great diversity of food resources supported higher-than-average population densities. There were other such rich areas, too, local culture areas with their own distinctive societies. The Riverton culture of eastern Illinois' central Wabash River Valley flourished between about 1500 and 1000 BC. It was based on a linear territory along about a 40-mile (64-km) length of the central Wabash River in eastern Illinois, with about 10 miles (16 km) between major base camps.

Howard Winters (1968) excavated three large Riverton shell middens in the valley, between 1 and 3 acres (0.4 and 1.2 ha) in area. Judging from the food remains, including migratory birds, each of the sites was occupied at a different season of the year as the people exploited upland and floodplain resources. Riverton itself was a base camp occupied from mid-May to late September. Then the people moved to Swan Island, a temporary autumn camp where foraging was important. During the winter months, until late March, they settled at Robeson Hills, a cold weather settlement on a promontory overlooking the floodplain. There they hunted deer and other mammals, as well as exploiting valley resources. In spring, the hunters returned to Swan Island.

Riverton has sufficiently distinctive artifacts for it to be distinguished from contemporary Late Archaic adaptations elsewhere in the Central Riverine area, from cultures like that centered on Indian Knoll and the Titterington culture of the St Louis region. Where food resources were diverse and abundant, Central Riverine Late Archaic cultures, with their well-demarcated territories, restricted mobility, and relatively sedentary lifeways, were very local phenomena. Important riverine cultures also flourished in the Tennessee Valley (Chapman, 1994).

Exchange and Interaction

The emergence of social ranking among Late Archaic societies in the east was the culmination of economic and social trends that began at least 3000 years earlier. By 4000 BC, the diverse hunter-gatherer populations of the Eastern Woodlands were living under very different social conditions from those enjoyed by their remote ancestors. Each group lived in its own territory, under much more "closed" social conditions, where territorial boundaries and relations with neighbors were more rigidly defined than they had been in Paleo-Indian times. This greater degree of closure is reflected in much greater regional variation in artifacts and stylistic traditions, especially after about 2000 BC. Under these new economic and social circumstances, relationships with neighbors assumed much greater importance. Such relationships would take many forms – informal bartering of fine-grained rocks, occasional communal hunts and ceremonies, more formal gift exchanges, and ever-shifting political and social alliances based on obligations of kin and reciprocity between individuals. As time went on, the manipulation of social alliances, and the barter and exchange that went with them, led to enhanced concerns with prestige and social distinction, to more complex social orders (Baugh and Ericson, 1994).

Prized materials were exchanged over vast distances in the Eastern Woodlands. Marine shells, one such material, are seen here in use as receptacles for a luxury drink at a council meeting of Florida Indians in this engraving by Theodore de Bry (1591).

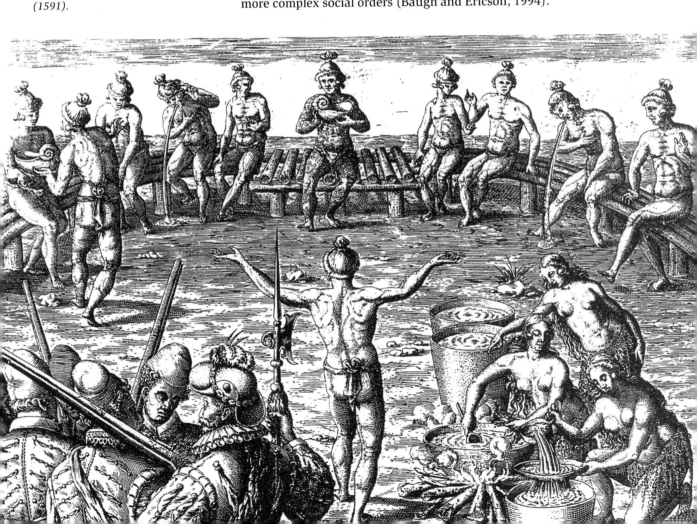

Not that social change was rapid, for the archaeological record reflects a profound, inherent conservatism reflected not only in artifacts and choice of base camps, but in burial customs, subsistence patterns, and inter-community relationships as well. Few eastern societies of 1000 BC were much larger than a few hundred souls, and even those that were, were still predominantly egalitarian in their social organization.

As we have seen, long-distance exchange of prized materials such as marine shells and copper appeared for the first time in the middle South between about 5000 and 4000 BC and escalated gradually over the next 3000 years. Exotic materials of all kinds passed from band to band, occasionally over enormous distances – Lake Superior native copper and hematite, Atlantic and Gulf Coast sea shells, galena from the Appalachians, Ozarks, and the Upper Mississippi Valley, jasper from eastern Pennsylvania, chalcedony and black slate from Canada, cherts, hornstones, and other fine-grained rocks for ornaments and tool-making from all over the Midwest and east (Johnson, J., 1994). All these materials were exchanged between individuals and groups, passed "down the line" from settlement to settlement, valley to valley through informal exchange networks that evolved and maintained an essential continuity over thousands of years. The range of exotic materials is astounding. The Koster people, at the time a small group, were receiving copper, galena, sea shells, Arkansas bauxite, fluorspar from southern Illinois, and chert from many regions of the Midwest well before 2000 BC (Struever and Holton, 1979).

These precious materials circulated in raw and finished form. As the distribution of copper objects from the western Great Lakes shows, trade objects in any form appear to have assumed a greater prestige value the further away from the source they were exchanged. *Busycon* shells from Florida were made into axe blades and gouges by those who collected them or who lived close inland. But the groups far in the interior who received precious shells placed a quite different value on the same material. Shell

Late Archaic bannerstones (atlatl weights).

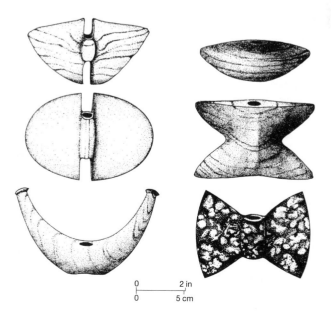

0   2 in
0   5 cm

ornaments and necklaces had prestige value and a highly specific social context; a social context which, as yet, is still dimly understood (Goad, 1980).

From the Mid Archaic onward, people invested more labor in fashioning socially valued artifacts and ornaments like finely ground "bannerstones" (atlatl weights) (illus. p. 397), delicate slate ornaments and weapons, and steatite gorgets and bowls. As Sassaman (1996) has argued, these objects, expensive to manufacture, may have played an important role in alliance building. Finely incised bone points are found widely along the eastern seaboard and in Midwestern valleys. There are signs, too, that access to some precious materials was carefully controlled. Huge caches of fine chert preforms are found in Maritime Archaic and Laurentian graves, as if the value of these trade goods was deliberately manipulated.

Some groups living in areas where different trade networks intersected may well have exploited their strategic locations and become middlemen in long-distance trade. It is possible, for example, that the Green River people exploited the opportunities of both the copper trade from the northwest and the shell exchange from the south and southeast.

Within this context of regular social gatherings and exchanges, a modest degree of social differentiation based on reciprocity may have emerged in Late Archaic society. This may have been nothing more than a degree of ranking between younger and older members of society, or perhaps the emergence of one kin group as the "ranking" lineage, the one from whom social and ritual leaders traditionally came. Judging from increasingly elaborate mortuary customs, both kin-based and individual social ranking took place within a context of increasing ritual elaboration, in which exotic objects and fine ornaments played a major part. Cemeteries themselves assumed a special significance, often placed, as we have seen, on elevated ground, sometimes beneath low, artificial mounds.

By 1000 BC, social differentiation is well documented by the grave goods found in Central Riverine Archaic graves at Indian Knoll, in Riverton and Titterington sites, and other cemeteries (Smith, B., 1986). This differentiation was nothing dramatic, for it was still firmly based in kin ties and reciprocity.

Anthropologists have long recognized the importance of reciprocity in hunter-gatherer societies, obligations between individuals that place the common good ahead of personal interest. Such reciprocity must have been characteristic of all early North American societies, however unsophisticated: their survival depended upon it. But, under conditions of more sedentary settlement, higher population densities, and regular contacts between neighboring groups, some form of emerging social ranking based on reciprocity is almost inevitable.

We can only speculate as to how this occurred. One possible scenario might go something like this – some individuals, perhaps respected shamans or elders, leaders of a particular lineage, might assume roles as ritual and social mediators in newly sedentary societies. They were the people who arbitrated disputes and controlled relations with neighboring, and sometimes perhaps competing, groups. It was they who gave gifts to influential neighbors and participated in formal gift exchanges, who became traders, people with reciprocal obligations that extended to other individuals and kin leaders living near and far. It was they, too, who were responsible for internal reciprocity, for redistributing food, essential raw materials, and luxury goods through the community. Some of these people were better at trading, at dealing with allies and enemies, at attracting the loyalty of kinspeople and followers. They had the quality of being able to persuade people to work for them, hunting, fishing, and gathering, perhaps digging out chert and blocking it into preforms. Social and ritual arbitrators, skilled diplomats and acquisitors, these individuals became the leaders of the ever more complex human societies of the Eastern Woodlands after 1000 BC.

The Poverty Point Culture
2200 to 700 BC

These slow, incremental culture changes did not affect every region of the Eastern Woodlands in the same ways. Many groups continued to live much as they had in earlier millennia, even if they exploited nut harvests more intensively and stored small, starchy seed crops for later use. In some areas, they deliberately cultivated sunflowers, marsh elder, knotweed, and other indigenous wild plants in small gardens. The yields from some native plants may have rivaled those of maize in later times, resulting in important changes in foraging societies. Maize, and, later, bean cultivation, did not become widespread in the Eastern Woodlands until the late 1st millennium AD.

The Poverty Point culture of the Lower Mississippi Valley and adjacent Gulf coast offers a dramatic contrast (Gibson, 1996). More than 100 Poverty Point sites form ten regional discrete clusters within natural geographical boundaries, each apparently grouped around a regional center that belongs within the Poverty Point culture. The earliest Poverty Point sites date to about 2200 BC, forming the earliest component in a cultural sequence that lasted for 1500 years.

The Poverty Point site, the largest of these centers, lies on the Macon Ridge overlooking the Mississippi floodplain, near the confluences of six rivers. This was a strategic point to trade up and downstream, to receive exotic materials, not only along the Mississippi, but the Arkansas, Red, Ohio, and Tennessee rivers as well. Poverty Point's great horseshoe earthworks are a remarkable contrast to the humble base camps typical of the Eastern Woodlands at the time, although foreshadowed in Wilson's Brake (c. 3500 BC) and other enormous Archaic mounds. Six concentric semi-circular earthen ridges divided into segments average about 82 ft (25 m) wide and 9.8 ft (3 m) high. They are set about 131 ft (40 m) apart, each capped with midden and fill deposits in places over 3.2 ft (1 m) deep. Perhaps they were designed to elevate houses above the surrounding, lowlying terrain. To the west lies an artificial mound more than 66 ft (20 m) high and more than 660 ft (200 m) long. A person standing on this mound can sight the vernal and autumnal equinoxes directly across the center of the earthworks to the east. This is the point where the sun rises on the first days of spring and fall, but whether this had ritual significance to the inhabitants is a mystery.

The Poverty Point habitation area covers about 494 acres (200 ha). Built between about 1000 and 700 BC, Poverty Point took more than 1,236,007 cu. ft (35,000 cu. m) of basket-loaded soil to complete, an organized building effort that would not be undertaken again in North America for another millennium. One authority has calculated that 1350 adults laboring 70 days a year would have taken three years to erect the earthworks, but the actual permanent population of the site remains unknown.

The great center was a natural location for exchanging raw materials and finished products, artifacts made of a remarkable variety of exotic materials – argilite, slate, copper, galena, jasper, quartz, and steatite were only a few of the tool-making materials at the site, some of them from as far as 620 miles (1000 km) away. Poverty Point exchange peaked between 1400 and 1100 BC and brought enormous quantities of exotic rocks and minerals from more than ten sources in the Midwest and Southeast into the local culture area (Gibson, 1994). For a short period, the Poverty Point site and its associated lesser centers were the nexus of a vast exchange network that helped foster an unprecedented level of cultural complexity. But this brief flowering endured little more than two to three centuries before the exchange system and the political forces that drove it collapsed. Although no burials of such people have been found, this may have been the kind of social environment in which individual leaders first came into prominence. These Poverty Point chieftains exported and imported a wide range of goods and materials.

The Poverty Point people enjoyed the same general adaptation as other Central Riverine societies, exploiting wild vegetable foods and fishing in nearby oxbow lakes, as well as cultivating bottle gourds and squashes. The major centers appear to have been sited near natural escarpments, close to unusually bountiful floodplain swamps and oxbow lakes, and to upland hunting grounds. But we still know nothing about the internal organization of the sites, or about the relationship between those who lived at the larger settlements and the dozens of smaller communities and the regional centers associated with them.

Over 2000 years later, the Natchez Indians of the lower Mississippi lived in ranked societies that distinguished between privileged nobles and chiefs and common people. They were dual societies, that is to say they were organized into moieties, halves associated with two cardinal directions. Individuals of one moiety married partners of the other moiety. J.L. Gibson analyzed 19,000 artifacts from Poverty Point, and found different artifact groups on the northern and southern sides of the site. This, he claims, is evidence for similar social organization two millennia earlier. Perhaps, too, the Poverty Point leaders followed another Natchez rule: nobles not only married commoners, but commoners from the other moiety. Gibson believes that the limited distributions of stone pipe bowls, red jasper beads, and zoomorphic pendants in the Poverty Point earthworks are evidence of social differentiation, ornaments associated with prominent people and no one else, but this hypothesis is at best an intelligent guess, based on historical analogy.

Many questions about Poverty Point remain unanswered. Did people from throughout Poverty Point territory contribute labor to the great earthworks, or were they merely the work of the actual inhabitants? What were the social and political relationships within the Poverty Point culture? Who were the leaders who organized the vast communal efforts

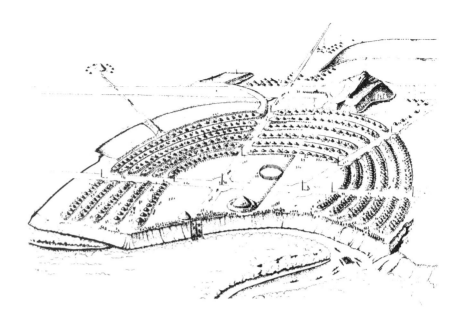

*Poverty Point, Louisiana.
(Right) Artist's reconstruction. The
artificial earthworks cover 1 sq. mile.
(Below) Aerial view of Poverty Point
toward the northwest.*

needed to build earthworks, organize trade, and control the local exchange of goods throughout the Poverty Point area? How did they control the loyalties of the hundreds, if not thousands, of people who erected and used the great earthworks? Excavations at the greater center, and outlying sites have barely begun. At present, Poverty Point stands as an isolated and enigmatic phenomenon, but as a prophetic symbol of cultural developments that were to emerge in the remaining millennia of eastern prehistory that lay ahead.

Further Reading

In addition to the references for Chapter 16:

Jefferies, Ron. 1987. *Carrier Mills*. Center for Archaeological Investigations, Carbondale, Illinois.
    This important monograph describes major Middle and Late Archaic settlements. Strongly recommended.

Mason, Ronald J. 1981. *Great Lakes Archaeology*. Academic Press, New York.
    Mason's synthesis is a regional survey of the northern parts of the Eastern Woodlands. Somewhat outdated.

Muller, Jon. 1986. *Archaeology of the Lower Ohio Valley*. Academic Press, New York.
    Analysis of a major culture area in the Midwest, with a focus on cultural process and basic data.

Neusius, Sarah W. (ed.). 1986. *Foraging, Collecting, and Harvesting: Archaic Period Subsistence and Settlement in the Eastern Woodlands*. Center for Archaeological Investigations, Carbondale, Illinois.
    Essays that focus on subsistence issues, and amplify the general account given here.

Struever, Stuart, and Holton, Felicia. 1979. *Koster: Americans in Search of their Prehistoric Past*. Anchor Press, New York.
    Popular account of a major Midwestern site. Vivid reconstructions of prehistoric life, and rich in provocative interpretation. Strongly recommended for the beginning reader.

CHAPTER 18

EARLY WOODLAND AND THE ADENA COMPLEX

After 1000 BC, Eastern Woodlands societies embarked on a complex, multi-faceted trajectory of cultural change and elaboration, culminating in the brilliant efflorescence of the Mississippian cultural tradition in the closing centuries of ancient times. But these two-and-a-half millennia, the so-called "Woodland" period, saw no dramatic wars of conquest or major economic revolutions. The Adena, Hopewell, Mississippian cultural traditions, and their equivalents in other regions of the east, stemmed not from military campaigns or major population movements, but from the culmination of long-term adaptive and cultural trends that had emerged during the Archaic, some of them before 4000 BC (Seeman, 1992). These trends are simply enumerated – more intensive exploitation of diverse food sources in highly localized environments, a move toward more sedentary living and better-established territorial boundaries, more intensive exchange of scarce materials, and the emergence of more complex social orders.

At the very beginning of the Woodland, three important innovations took hold in many eastern societies – pottery manufacture, deliberate cultivation of native plants, and interment under funerary mounds. Each was to have an important impact on human life (Bense, 1994).

Pottery and the "Container Revolution"

As we saw in Chapter 17, crude, fiber-tempered clay vessels appeared along the South Carolina coastal plain by 2000 BC. Similarly tempered clay vessels appeared in the Lower Mississippi Valley by about 1300 BC (Sassaman, 1993).

Thick, grit-tempered pottery spread, or was being made, all over the Eastern Woodlands between 2000 and 500 BC, from the Mississippi to New England, and from the Ohio to the St Lawrence Valley. Everywhere, the potters used simple methods, building up vessel walls with coils of clay, then thinning them out and welding the coils by paddling the sides with an anvil held inside the pot. Most ceramic containers had wide mouths and flat to rounded bases. The paddle anvil was often wrapped with cords, creating cord-markings on both inside and outside of the vessel. Many Early Woodland pots have been described as crude flower-pots, heavy and clumsy containers that took some time to make and were difficult to carry around.

Bruce Smith (1986) has described the introduction of pottery, and an apparently widespread trade in gourds, as a "container revolution" in the Eastern Woodlands. As eastern societies became more sedentary, he argues, their new lifeway enabled them to manufacture and use vessels that were too easily broken by societies on the move. Pots must have played an important part in more intensive exploitation of wild seed crops. For instance, experiments have shown that pottery did allow more efficient processing of hickory nuts, and probably other species, where crushing and boiling increases the amount of nutmeats processed in one hour at least tenfold (Talalay, Keller, and Munson, 1984). The earliest eastern pottery is thick-walled and easily broken when heated. Judging from the lack of sooting on the exteriors, heated soapstone slabs, baked-clay objects, and heated rocks were used to boil water in them (Sassaman, 1993). It was only later that thinner-walled vessels came into use, pots that were more break resistant when heated. The greater demand for waterproof containers may be associated with a major, and in the long term revolutionary, development in the Eastern Woodlands after 2000 BC – the development of highly efficient seed collection systems and the deliberate manipulation of native plants, a process that led to full domestication of several indigenous plant species.

So Bruce Smith's "container revolution" is part of a much broader set of cultural developments in the east that began during the Archaic and continued to unfold right up to European contact and beyond.

Cultivation of Native Plants

By 1500 BC, every human population in the Eastern Woodlands relied heavily on wild vegetable foods, and usually on a relatively small constellation of plants for most of its vegetable diet. When these plants were in short supply, the people turned to a wide range of secondary food sources (Smith, B., 1992).

This strategy works well in areas where there is plenty of territory to exploit – people can forage alternative patches of staple foods. The hunter-gatherers probably overcame food shortage stress by covering large distances, by possessing knowledge of potential food sources over wide areas. But what happened if population growth or social conflict, or just inadequate food supplies, restricted peoples' ability to feed themselves by exploiting large territories? They could forage for less-preferred food plants, increase the energy expended collecting food and processing it and exploit alternative food sources like, say, acorns, that required a great deal more effort to prepare – or they could cultivate certain native annuals that flourished in disturbed habitats, *provided* the disturbed habitat was maintained by deliberate human intervention.

In the Eastern Woodlands, these three strategies were adopted by many Late Archaic groups faced with restricted territory owing to population growth and other factors. Richard Ford (1985) believes that food production began as a result of deliberate cultural responses to changing conditions. First, people faced with inadequate food supplies turned to intensive harvesting of small, starchy nuts. Although these are lower in calories and require much more work to prepare, they can fulfill nutritional requirements and allow people to remain within restricted territories (Petruso and Wickens, 1984; Talalay, Keller, and Munson, 1984). Ford believes this may have been the first step toward effective food production.

This scenario can be developed further. As populations increased, territories became smaller, alternative collecting areas became inaccessible. Many homelands were inadequate to supply basic nutritional requirements even of a stable population. Inevitably, the people turned to new food-getting strategies. They could rely on generations-old kin ties, reciprocal ties that ensured everyone shared food supplies. They could trade for basic food-stuffs with more fortunate neighbors or take up residence with relatives to obtain food in times of need. They could also use technological solutions, developing more effective food storage systems to tide them over lean months. Some groups also used their food-gathering technology to clear natural vegetation, to create space within their territories where they could cultivate several food species.

These Late Archaic strategies were effective for many centuries, being progressively adopted by many groups throughout the east after about 2000 BC. The strategy of small-scale cultivation worked well for centuries. It was much later, after about AD 800 in the American Bottomlands near St Louis, and some two centuries later in the mid-South, that the cultivators intensified their efforts, modifying the landscape on a large scale to maximize the environmental requirements of a single plant species – maize. This was true farming, clearing large tracts of forest to eliminate competing vegetation and to increase sunlight, sometimes building earthen or stone terraces to conserve precious soil. At this point, domesticated maize, and later beans, both non-natives, largely replaced crop yields from native plant communities, even cultivated ones (Chapter 14).

To what extent stress actually played a role in early cultivation in the Eastern Woodlands is unknown. Most current thinking focuses on the relationship between human groups and the plants and plant communities associated with them (Smith, B., 1994). Under these "Weedy Floodplain" arguments, stress was not a primary cause of plant domestication. Human groups created and sustained a disturbed habitat that transported seeds of a wide variety of plants from their natural floodplain and upland niches into their local, and disturbed, habitat. These were casual and unintentional activities, with plant and animal populations, including Archaic groups, tied together in a series of opportunistic adaptations to changes in the structure and composition of floodplain ecosystems. A whole set of variables, among them the establishment of human base camps, produced a significant change in floodplain ecosystems. These ecosystem changes allowed some of the floodplain plant species to occupy, and evolve within, newly disturbed habitats. A number of on-going selective pressures acted on these plants within these disturbed habitats that were clearly related to human activities. These were unintentional activities, not the result of deliberate human actions. Some of these pressures may have increased seed production in sumpweed, gourds, and other plants, also have reduced dormancy periods and also enhanced the ability of species to occupy disturbed ground. All of these pressures would have set plant evolution in a direction that increased their economic potential and their attractiveness as human food sources. All humans would have done to achieve this was to sustain a disturbed habitat and to tolerate species with economic value. Recent research has found many domesticated plants in more upland sites, so there are grounds for challenging the "Woody Floodplain" hypothesis.

At some point, humans would have begun to categorize some of these plants as useful, others as mere weeds. They may have started to discourage the weeds to encourage the spread of economically useful plants, thereby managing natural stands of the latter. This simple process of encouraging, intervening, and deliberately planting harvested seeds, even on a small scale, marked the beginnings of deliberate cultivation – if sustained in the longer term. At this point, automatic selection within the affected plant population begins, with minimal effort by human beings. Their casual efforts at encouragement result in an ever more dependable and abundant, easily monitored local food resource. Thus, human land clearance and genetic changes in plants may have been a major factor in the emergence of horticulture in eastern North America independently of elsewhere, the so-called Eastern Agricultural Complex (for full discussion, see Smith, B., 1992).

This plausible scenario is supported by rapidly accumulating archaeological evidence from Late Archaic and Woodland sites throughout the Eastern Woodlands. Late Archaic groups in the Eastern Woodlands cultivated a variety of plants, among them sunflowers, sumpweed, and goosefoot, but also gourds and squashes, at least 2000 years before they turned to maize agriculture.

Gourds and Squashes. The North American progenitor of the domesticated gourd was *Cucurbita pepo* ssp. *ovifera* var. *ozarkana*, which was recently identified in the Ozarks (Smith, B., 1994). The gourd was domesticated by

The white-flowered bottle gourd, Lagenaria siceraria *(right) with immature fruit (far right).*

2300 BC. Another gourd from Texas, *Cucurbita texana*, may be a surviving wild North American variety of *C. pepo* that was once widely distributed elsewhere in the north, but has now vanished. Perhaps, botanist Charles Heiser theorizes (1985), it once flourished in the very habitats that humans chose for their settlements. They eliminated it by excessive harvesting and hybridization with domestic forms.

C. pepo was probably first domesticated for its seeds rather than its bitter flesh and thin rind that is of little use for containers (Smith, B., 1994). In contrast, the bottle gourd (*Lagenaria siceraria*) is ideal for containers in its domesticated form. Originally an African native, it appears to have floated across to the Americas, perhaps to Brazil, thousands of years ago, long before it was domesticated. Bottle gourds are known from Mexico at least as early as 7000 BC, and perhaps spread into North America as a weed following moving human populations. Whether they arrived in domesticated form or were tamed in the east quite independently is still a completely open botanical question (Heiser, 1985). The earliest record in the Eastern Woodlands comes from the Windover site in Florida in 5000 BC, but it is not known if this is a domesticated specimen (Anderson and Sassaman, 1996).

Sunflowers and Indigenous Plants. A number of indisputably native plants were domesticated in North America in Archaic times (Smith, B., 1992). The wild sunflower (*Helianthus annuus*) was widespread in the west and became a favorite food source. It was introduced into central and eastern regions in ancient times and was apparently domesticated there, as early as 2265 BC, both for its seeds and its dye and oil (Crites, 1993). The Jerusalem artichoke (*Helianthus tuberosus*) is widely distributed in eastern North America, and may have been domesticated – the evidence is uncertain.

Perhaps the most common domesticated native plant is sumpweed or marsh elder (*Iva annua*), a lake- and river-side oily-seeded plant that flourished in eastern river valley bottoms. David and Nancy Asch studied this little-known native, documenting it from flotation samples taken at the Koster site and other locations in the Midwest's Illinois River Valley (Asch and Asch, 1978; 1985). As early as 3800 BC, in Koster's Horizon 6, sumpweed comprises 40 percent of seed samples. This may be the result of harvesting wild growth, for none of the achenes (hard seeds) show signs of selection for domesticated forms. The Aschs have measured achenes from dozens of Archaic sites and believe that domestication was well under way by 2000 BC. Thereafter, cultivation may have been sporadic in Illinois, but sumpweed was an important component in horticultural activities in Kentucky during the 1st millennium BC (Yarnell, 1978; Smith, B., 1992).

Goosefoot (*Chenopodium berlandieri*) was one of a series of small, starchy seeds that were an important component in Illinois Early, Middle and Late Woodland subsistence (Asch and Asch, 1985; Smith, B., 1994). The other species were knotweed (*Polygonum erectum*), maygrass (*Phalanx caroliniana*), and little barley (*Hordeum pusillum*). Goosefoot was probably a minor food in west-central Illinois during most of the Archaic, recorded from Koster by at least 6500 BC. It was extensively exploited and probably domesticated by Late Archaic Titterington people

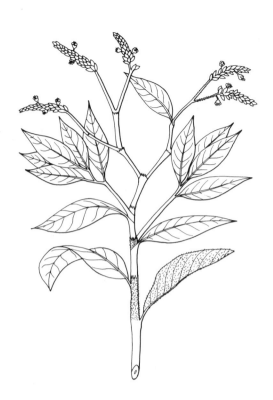

(Above) Goosefoot (Chenopodium berlandieri). *(Above right) Knotweed* (Polygonum erectum).

in the Midwest in about 2000 BC (Asch and Asch, 1985). Goosefoot was definitely cultivated in Illinois by Early Woodland times (Smith, B., 1994), and was a major food in Kentucky after 1500 BC.

Knotweed was economically important in the Upper Mississippi and Illinois Valleys, but was apparently little exploited before Middle and Late Woodland times. Maygrass is a southern wild species that assumed much greater economic importance after 2000 BC. Apparently it was intentionally propagated, with seeds being planted in fall or late spring. A cold-resistant species, maygrass was grown considerably north of its natural range. Two or three weeks later, in the early summer, and at a time when no other cultivated foods were available, people could harvest little barley. However, the grain was hard to separate from the stalks and how the people did this is unknown (Asch and Asch, 1985).

Lastly, tobacco (*Nicotiana* sp.) seeds have been recovered from a Middle Woodland context at the Smiling Dan site in Illinois, dating to about AD 250. Tobacco is not a native North American plant. It is thought to have been introduced from Mexico and was widely cultivated throughout the east at European contact (Yarnell, 1978). Many pipes occur in eastern sites, but they do not necessarily document tobacco smoking. People smoked hemp and many other substances as well.

Thanks to the development of the highly effective flotation method for collecting seed samples from archaeological sites thousands of years old, we can now be certain that some Late Archaic and many Early Woodland people were cultivating several highly productive native plants by 2000 BC and had started farming quite independently of their distant neighbors in Mexico. However, the domestication of these indigenous species did not lead to a total dependence on agriculture, or to anything even remotely like it. Until about AD 800, agriculture was a way of producing valuable supplemental foods, of amplifying food supplies by enhancing wild crop yields, of helping feed locally dense hunter-gatherer populations. It was only with the introduction of maize in the 1st millennium AD that agriculture became the major means of subsistence in the Eastern Woodlands (Watson, 1985).

Early Woodland: Burial Mounds and the Adena Complex
before 1000 BC to AD 100

Many Archaic burials and cemeteries testify to the great symbolic importance of death and funerary rituals in eastern life. These mortuary rites assumed increasing complexity and importance during the Late Archaic, when the first small burial mounds came into use. Many communities buried their dead in low, natural ridges overlooking river valleys and at other strategic locations. As we have seen, some groups used low, artificial mounds, perhaps as territorial markers, kin-based burial grounds that were respected by neighbors.

A similar special concern for the dead appears in other parts of the Eastern Woodlands well before 1500 BC. Mound burials commemorated the Maritime Archaic dead in Labrador as early as 5600 BC, while Glacial Kame Late Archaic groups living between southern Ontario and Indiana around 1500 to 1000 BC interred the departed in the summits of low hills of glacial gravel. Tools and exotic ornaments of copper and sea shell lay with the dead in these natural tumuli. From using natural ridges and hills, it was but a short step to erect small artificial mounds in strategic places, which served the same symbolic purposes – perhaps to mark territory and commemorate kin affiliations.

The idea of building earthworks was nothing new, witness mounds recently discovered in the South, which date to at least 4000 BC and the great earthen banks at Poverty Point in Louisiana, but it did involve the cooperative labors of many families over considerable periods of time, people to dig and pile up basketfuls of earth by the thousand, not only individual families but entire villages, perhaps gatherings of close kin or several neighboring communities. Judging from what we know of Late Archaic and Early Woodland subsistence, hunting, foraging, and cultivation were family activities, but activities that sometimes involved exchange of vital raw materials between neighbors near and far. These same exchange

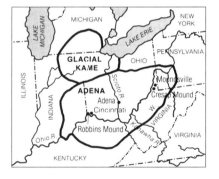

(Above) Adena and Glacial Kame culture areas.

(Right) A typical artifact of the Glacial Kame culture was the sandal-sole gorget, such as this example with an animal cut in relief. Length 18 cm.

networks may have helped foster elaborate communal burial cults involving the interment of kin group members and perhaps the commemoration of lineages and ancestors.

During Early Woodland times, and especially after 500 BC, burial mounds were an important part of mortuary ceremonialism from the western Appalachians to the Mississippi Valley, and north into Wisconsin and Michigan. But the most marked ceremonialism is found in the so-called Adena complex of the central Ohio Valley.

Adena is not so much a culture as a ceremonial complex, perhaps best described as the climax of the Early Woodland (Muller, 1986). Adena has been identified from Indiana's Whitewater River Valley in the west to Pittsburgh in the Upper Ohio Valley in the east, and from the Blue Grass region of the Licking and Big Sandy and Kanawha Rivers in the south and east, to the upper reaches of the Scioto and Muskingum of Ohio in the north. Adena mounds also occur in the Canadian Maritimes (Turnbull, 1976).

Most Adena sites are burial mounds, perhaps once numbering 300 to 500 in the heartland (Webb, W. and Snow, 1945; Webb, W. and Baby, 1957; Dragoo, 1963, 1976). During Early and Middle Adena, in the last centuries before Christ, burial mounds and funerary customs were still simple. The people started with a small mound that covered the burial of a single person in a shallow, elliptical pit lined and covered with bark. Sometimes the burial lay in a house, at other times in an open area within the village. As more and more burials were added to the tumulus, it grew in size. Sometimes the dead were cremated, sometimes entire bodies were deposited in the mound. Occasionally the mourners simply deposited a bundle of bones, as if the body had been exposed on an open platform until the flesh decayed – or perhaps the dead person died away from home and the bones were brought back for burial. In some cases, only a few parts of the body were buried in the mound, as if the corpse had been dissected before burial.

Early and Middle Adena burials were often sprinkled with powdered red ocher, sometimes with yellow ocher, graphite, or manganese dioxide in small amounts. Apparently, grieving relatives painted the corpse with red ocher paint as well. They prepared the paint on crude stone tablets, convenient thin slabs of limestone, sandstone, and other rocks. Some of the tablets are deeply grooved by the rubbing of pieces of hematite. There are few signs of any social distinction between individuals, as if society was still basically egalitarian.

At first Adena mourners buried the dead with mostly utilitarian objects, artifacts such as flint blades, drills, scrapers, stone axes and adzes, also simple bone tools. These appear to have been the personal possessions of the deceased. The dead wore strings of small copper beads, shells, including some large marine gastropods, and occasionally bone. Some people owned quadrilateral slate or copper gorgets with concave sides (ornaments named after a French term for neck armor). The most distinctive grave artifacts were tubular pipes, fabricated from clay-stone or very fine-grained silicate in straight or cigar-shaped tubes with a blocked end. Such pipes are common in the Upper Ohio Valley.

Late Adena, dating to about 2000 years ago, saw sweeping changes in burial customs, reflected in far more elaborate mound interments. The Robbins Mound in Kentucky was one of many Late Adena sites where simple graves gave way to large burial chambers or enclosures that

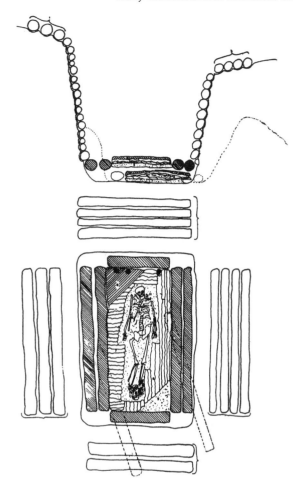

Cross-section and plan of an Adena burial from the Wright Mound, Kentucky.

Cutaway reconstruction of a restored Adena structure that may have had a mortuary function. Postmold plan at the left.

contained one or more bodies. These structures lay on, or beneath, house floors, often circular houses with thatched walls and wood post frames that were burned down before the mound was built. Perhaps the structures were used to expose the dead for long periods of time. This form of charnel house burial contrasts dramatically with later mortuary customs where people were buried in mounds that accumulated gradually over several generations.

Many Adena bodies were painted with bright pigments, attended with offerings of food and valuable artifacts. Sometimes people erected a canopy over the grave and surrounded it with a log platform. Occasionally, the mourners applied paint to the bones, as if the bodies were exposed long enough for the flesh to decay completely. Subsequently, the grave was buried under a large earthen mound. Some mounds were used again and again, with more log tombs being added to an existing tumulus, until it reached vast dimensions. Some of the largest and most elaborate are found in the central Ohio Valley, like the famous Grave Creek mound at Moundsville, West Virginia, which was originally over 67 ft (20 m) high, with a volume of nearly 2.47 million cu. ft (70,000 cu. m).

The Late Adenans sometimes built circular earthen enclosures near their burial mounds. These "sacred circles" may have been the meeting places for the kin group using the associated tumulus (Webb, W. and Snow, 1945). Perhaps the individuals buried in log tombs in the mounds were important kin leaders. Sometimes, the sacred enclosures occur in groups of two to eight, as if the people were divided into formal social units such as clans.

As treasure hunters discovered generations ago, Late Adena burials carried a rich variety of grave goods with them, especially the individuals interred in log tombs. Some important burials were interred with a long-defleshed skull often laid on the lap. One such find at the Cresap Mound in West Virginia bore a slight polish, as if it had been treasured and handled regularly for some time. Mark Seeman (1988) has shown beyond reasonable doubt that these were "trophy skulls," perhaps the heads of enemies or revered ancestors.

Although fine flint blades, awls, and other utilitarian objects like drills were still deposited with the dead, there were many more distinctive ornaments in the graves. These included copper bracelets and finger rings. There were crescents and sheets fabricated from North Carolina mica, some marine shells, adzes, and other items from Lake Superior copper. There

(Below) Adena stone effigy pipe in the shape of a human, from the Adena Mound, Ross County, Ohio. Height 20 cm. (Below right) Adena platform effigy pipe in the image of a dog, from Newark, Ohio.

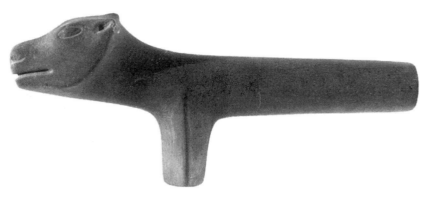

Two engraved stone Adena tablets.
About half-size.

were many forms of gorgets and distinctive atlatl weights. Pipe designs were far more elaborate than earlier Adena forms, with carved animal effigies coming into fashion for the first time. Tubular Ohio pipestone pipes were exchanged as far away as Ontario, New England, and Maryland. The stone tablets used for preparing ocher were now much more carefully prepared, sometimes adorned with zoomorphic or animal designs, including carrion crows (Webb, W. and Baby, 1957). Some other characteristic grave goods include large, leaf-shaped spearheads and knives, often made of bluish grey hornstone from Indiana or Illinois, artifacts sometimes found in caches. Perhaps such point collections were exchanged as gifts. Small triangular points made of local materials are often found in Early Woodland cemeteries, artifacts often made of chert and apparently exchanged over long distances. They occur from Wisconsin and Illinois all the way to New England. Carved bird effigies known as "birdstones," and "boatstones" replace the bannerstones of the Late Archaic. Finely made three-quarter grooved axes and adzes were widely used for wood-working.

Several Late Adena mounds have yielded wolf palates, each carefully trimmed, with the upper and lower incisors removed, so that they could be worn in a man's mouth. William Webb and Raymond Baby (1957) made an ingenious reconstruction of this form of mask, with the skin of the wolf head fitting over the head. The great 19th-century painter George Catlin depicted similar masks being worn by western Indians. Puma and other animal masks may also have been used. Some of these artifacts may have

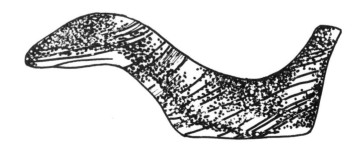

Birdstones, such as this example from Milwaukee, may have served as atlatl weights.

been shamans' masks, or they may have been used in rituals that depicted the symbolic relationships between familiar animals and different clans.

"Adena" is a convenient archaeological term that covers dozens of local Early Woodland cultures in the Eastern Woodlands, cultures that were contemporary, often close neighbors, and interacting with one another continuously. The label is probably not specific enough to chronicle many local sequences, nor did Adena necessarily develop into Hopewell in all areas (Greber, 1991). After 500 BC, many local cultures flourished in the Midwest and Southeast, cultures remarkable for their diverse artifacts, widespread trading contacts, and burial ceremonialism. They are distinguished one from another by pottery styles and other artifacts and the details need not concern us here (see Farnsworth and Emerson, 1986).

Most Early Woodland settlements were small, perhaps consisting of no more than a dozen or so houses (Muller, 1986). People lived in relatively cramped dwellings, but the villagers occasionally built larger structures, capable of holding as many as 40 people.

Everyone now agrees that the distinctive, elaborate, and varied Adena burial traditions developed from Late Archaic roots, perhaps in the Ohio Valley. The Early Woodland was a time of accelerating culture contacts over wide areas that brought Ohio pipestone from the lower Scioto Valley to Lake Huron and the upper St Lawrence Valley, copper from Lake Superior deep into the Ohio Valley, and sea shells from the Gulf coast far inland in the Midwest. In some areas, local population densities rose. There were Adena sites along every major tributary stream of the Ohio River from southeastern Indiana to central Pennsylvania by 2000 years ago, with great concentrations of burial mounds in some well-defined areas – the Scioto Valley of south-central Ohio, the Kanawha River in West Virginia, and around Cincinnati, Ohio, to mention only three. Perhaps these reflect a tendency toward concentration within tribal territories.

Inter-regional Exchange

As population densities rose and group territories became more and more defined and circumscribed, styles of projectile points and other artifacts appear to display more local variation, as if they became stylistic boundary markers (Brose, 1994). There are some precedents from studies of modern societies in New Guinea and elsewhere to show that such "markers" develop within single cultural and ecological zones where several groups are in partial competition for the same resources. Ethnic boundaries develop as a result, as ways of reducing the dangers of unwanted confrontation by clearly delineating rights of access to different resources (Barth, 1975). Thus, considerable variability in projectile-point styles in northern parts of the Eastern Woodlands after 1000 BC may reflect a trend toward better-defined local territories, and toward more formal exchange mechanisms that structured the bartering of essentials and prestigious luxuries from area to area in a web of reciprocal obligations and formal gift-giving. It is noticeable that a similar elaboration of projectile-point traditions is not found further south, where seasonal contrasts are much less marked, and there are not such highly localized and short-lived abundances of food resources.

At about the same time, too, the first signs of more elaborate traditions appear in the northern woodlands – overlapping sets of burial traditions, ways of treating corpses, of depositing them, constructing graves. These Early Woodland complexes were highly localized – Adena was one, Red Paint in the Northeast another. They flourished alongside dozens of Late Archaic communities that still lived as they had done for centuries.

As territorial boundaries became more marked and interaction between neighbors increased, so membership in social groups assumed much greater importance, for it was these lineages and clans that controlled access to food and other resources. It is probably no coincidence that the Early Woodland sees a continuing trend toward at least semi-sedentary settlement, with people living at one base location for many months on end. This may have helped foster a growing sense of corporate identity, reinforced by regular burial ceremonies at earthworks where important clan leaders and others were buried for many generations. And in areas like the northern woodlands, where the Late Archaic adaptation was often precarious, different groups were probably careful to maintain rights of access to resources located outside their own territories, as a form of "insurance" in lean years when frosts or other natural phenomena decimated local foods. In other words, people used social processes to maintain exchange networks to handle not only food, but to maintain access to resources of restricted distribution at a distance.

Judging from living societies, the main participants in such exchange systems would have been lineage leaders, individuals honored at death with special artifacts, funeral ceremonies, and adorned with the ceremonial items that recognized their social role and importance and that were their right. Thus, burial rites assumed great importance in Early Woodland life. They validated not only group identity on a regular basis, but commemorated the status of prominent kin leaders. These individuals were those who organized community work efforts by clan members when needed – to erect burial mounds, construct earthworks, and to carry out other projects that were to the collective benefit. Everyone who participated received gifts of redistributed food and other goods. And the highly prized status goods such as mica sheets, copper ornaments, and carved pipes buried with clan leaders not only proclaimed their social standing, but maintained their high prestige by vanishing below the ground when their owner died.

This is a convincing model for Early Woodland subsistence, exchange, and burial ceremony, one that contains mechanisms for both fostering inter-group relationships and for ameliorating food shortages. As David Brose argues (Brose and Greber, 1979), such mechanisms provided increasing social and economic stability, reinforced trends toward sedentary living and specialized exploitation of local resources, and probably led to population increases.

In a sense, these developments merely accentuated the pressures they evolved to reduce, for their very success permitted higher levels of population growth, growth that in turn triggered additional responses – more ranked and well-integrated social systems that replaced the more flexible ones of earlier times. David Brose believes that there was what he calls a "trajectory" of long-term cultural change. These changes first developed in areas where there was maximal pressure or very low potential carrying capacity. The more closely integrated social systems emphasized rank within individual lineages, rank validated by exotic objects of great prestige from afar and by seasonal ceremonies when all the members of lineages, from near and far, came together to reinforce their social identity and common goals. About the time of Christ, this trajectory of cultural change led to far more elaborate social institutions and ceremonial life during the Middle Woodland.

Further Reading

In addition to the references for the previous chapter:

Smith, Bruce. (ed.) 1992. *Rivers of Change: Essays on Early Agriculture in Eastern North America*. Smithsonian Institution Press, Washington DC.
Essays which describe native agriculture. Invaluable at the more advanced level.

Webb, William S. and Baby, R.S. 1957. *The Adena People no. 2*. Ohio Historical Society, Columbus.

Webb, William S. and Snow, C.E. 1945. *The Adena People*. University of Tennessee Press, Knoxville.
Still authoritative accounts of the Adena Complex. Most recent literature is in scientific journals.

See also the references for Chapter 19.

MIDDLE WOODLAND AND THE HOPEWELL

The term "Middle Woodland" is sometimes used to refer to the period between about 200 BC and AD 400 when the Hopewell culture extended over much of eastern North America. The name "Hopewell" comes from a farm in Ross County, Ohio. The Southeast was home to a great variety of sophisticated hunter-gatherer societies during these same centuries, societies that regularly cultivated native plants (Bense, 1994; Seeman, 1992).

The Hopewell Culture
c. 200 BC to AD 400

Hopewell stands out as a remarkable cultural phenomenon in many ways, both for its flamboyant burial customs and for its complex exchange networks that traded both raw materials and finished artifacts over vast areas of North America (Brose and Greber, 1979). Hopewell earthworks in Ohio assumed enormous proportions, sometimes clusters of mounds and enclosures that covered many acres. These were the "forts" and "tumuli" of the lost civilizations described by Moundbuilder cultists in the 19th century (Silverberg, 1968).

The Hopewell culture flourished over much of the Midwest, but achieved its greatest elaboration in the Ohio Valley. The Scioto Valley near Chillicothe is the center of Hopewell development in Ohio. Elaborate mounds and spectacular geometric earthworks enclose from 10 to hundreds of acres (4 to many hectares). There are other centers of Hopewell earthworks near Marietta and in southwestern Ohio. These clusters of Ohio Hopewell were clearly the foci of important religious, political, and economic activities. Hopewell influence extended far from its Midwestern homelands. Many contemporary societies from eastern North America are known to have shared mortuary customs, ritual and religious beliefs, and artifact styles with the Ohio Hopewell. Hopewell artifacts and beliefs spread widely through the Southeast, where mortuary rituals assumed great complexity.

Origins

There can be little doubt that much of the Ohio Hopewell originated in the Adena tradition. Olaf Prufer once went as far as to remark (1964) that "one might say that Ohio Hopewell minus the elaborate ceremonial and artifactual

Aerial view of the Ohio Mound City complex.

A Hopewell man wearing earspools and pendants of beaten native copper, and pearl beads of freshwater shellfish. Reconstruction in the Field Museum of Natural History, Chicago.

trappings would not be much different from Adena." In general, he is probably right, for Adena has a long history in the Ohio Valley, as well as respectable antecedents in the Late Archaic of the Midwest and Northeast. But we know that Adena did not develop into the flamboyant Hopewell tradition everywhere, for the Adena-rich Hocking Valley in Ohio does not yield Hopewell sites (Greber, 1991). Prufer believed that the explosion of Hopewell ceremonial and trading activity resulted from the older Adena tradition merging with some newly introduced ideas, perhaps even being the consequence of population movements. He hypothesized that these new beliefs, or people, arrived in Ohio from southern Indiana and the Midwest.

At about the same time as Hopewell traits emerge in the Ohio Valley, they also appear in southern Illinois. Since some of these features may be slightly earlier in the west, one could argue that Hopewell originated in Illinois and spread or diffused into Ohio – but this is little more than speculation. More likely, some groups, within a relatively restricted geographical area, greatly elaborated upon, and changed, what had once been widespread, common ritual and ceremonial themes to form the Hopewell.

Whatever the ultimate origins of the Hopewell, anyone who reviews its complex archaeological manifestations has to synthesize a number of regional variations on the Hopewell tradition, each of them with their own pottery styles and local environmental adaptations. All these regional expressions have in common a number of highly characteristic artifact styles and exotic raw materials. The latter include copper, marine shells, mica, and obsidian, also such items as shark and alligator teeth, meteoric

Hopewell artifacts. (Above left) Clay figurine depicting a man, possibly a shaman, with a topknot hair style. From an unknown location in Ohio. (Top right) Raven or crow cut from native sheet copper, with a freshwater pearl for an eye. From an unknown location in Ohio, length 38 cm. (Above) Sheet mica depiction of the claws of a bird of prey. From an unknown location in Ohio, length 28 cm. (Far left, and left) Four clay bird-effigy smoking pipes. Locations unknown, height of tallest 6 cm.

iron, and many other materials. The finished objects common to each area include cymbal-like copper ear spools, copper breast plates, obsidian artifacts, marine shells used as containers, and mica sheets cut into geometric and representational forms. There are plain and effigy platform pipes, clay human figurines, and special pottery vessels, especially small jars, known in both Illinois and Ohio as "Hopewell Series." All of these materials and artifacts were obtained through complex exchange networks, sometimes called the "Hopewell Interaction Sphere." This exchange zone flourished from as early as 100 BC to about AD 300 to 500.

As long ago as 1958, Joseph Caldwell identified a number of regional traditions throughout the Eastern Woodlands in Early Woodland times and later. These he distinguished on the basis of pottery forms and decoration, each of them also remarkable for distinct ecological adaptations as well. These regional traditions formed an important part of Caldwell's basic thesis – that both Archaic and Woodland peoples achieved greater efficiency in the exploitation of forests, and in so doing became more and more diverse and specialized in their adaptations (Caldwell, 1958). The Hopewell traits found in these traditions are all found in restricted locales, but with varying degrees of participation in the interaction sphere.

Hopewell Exchange Systems

The Hopewell exchange zone, and local imitations of it, cover most of the Eastern Woodlands, from the Southeast into southeastern Canada (Seeman, 1979a). Within this vast area, local societies participated in exchange to a highly variable degree, with the greatest activity along major waterways (Brose and Greber, 1979). Judging from Ohio burials, the amount of non-local raw material acquired by some Hopewell trading parties reached impressive proportions (Griffin, 1967). They obtained native copper from the Lake Superior region, silver from the same place, and also from deposits near Cobalt, Ontario. Mica, quartz crystal, and chlorite came from the southern Appalachians. The exchange networks handled large marine shells from the Florida east and west coast, and smaller maritime shell species from the Southeast and Florida Gulf Coast. Galena cubes came from northwestern Illinois or Missouri, nodular flint from Illinois and Indiana. Neutron activation studies on Hopewell obsidian reveal sources as far away as the Yellowstone Park area of the Rocky Mountains, while flint came from the Knife River area of North Dakota (Hatch and others, 1990).

Most of these exotic materials were obtained by people living in major trading and manufacturing areas. They then converted them into finished artifacts or ornaments that were often exported through local and regional exchange networks. For example, copper artifacts may have been exported from Ohio as far afield as Tennessee and the Deep South, and from New York to Iowa and Missouri. Characteristic Hopewell platform pipes fabricated from Ohio pipestone are found from New York State west to Wisconsin and Iowa, and as far southwest as Hardin County, Illinois. There are also Hopewell-like burial mounds in Ontario, Canada (Johnston, 1968).

Two "core areas" are marked by high concentrations of Hopewell-style finished goods – the Mississippi and Illinois river valleys in Illinois, and the Scioto and Miami valleys in southern Ohio (Braun, 1986). Each of these

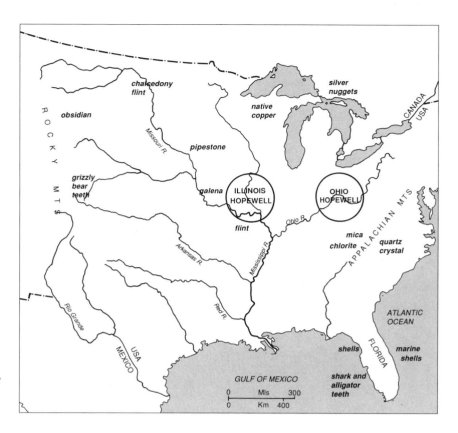

Hopewell exchange zone. Indicated here are the far-flung sources of materials that were exchanged.

two areas, the one to the east, the other to the west, stands at the center of a large, inter-regional exchange network. In time, they overlapped with one another, but they never lost their own identities (Struever and Houart, 1972).

Hopewell exchange outside the Ohio/Illinois area is sharply reduced, but Hopewell artifacts and beliefs entered the southeast from the Midwest and Great Lakes through mound centers in the Tennessee Valley and north-western Georgia. A complex ceremonialism based on mound burial appeared in this region about 2000 years ago. Mound building had actually begun much earlier, during the Archaic, and accelerated with the flourishing of the Poverty Point culture. But by 2000 years ago the ceremonialism began to include burial offerings and graveside rituals that involved the use of exotic objects brought in from Hopewell sites in the Midwest. These imported artifacts were small in number, were probably passed between important individuals in a form of ceremonial exchange. The barter that brought these prestigious artifacts was not a matter of formal long-distance trade, but a form of overlapping, intercommunity exchange that passed not only objects but ritual information into areas like the lower Mississippi Valley, to people who may never have known of the existence of Hopewell groups far to the north. The exchange was not at the same level as routine bartering of foodstuffs, tool-making stone, and other essentials along major waterways. Rather, the contacts were between important leaders living at some distance from one another, often far from rivers, a trade conducted along winding village paths (Gibson, 1994). What prompted this Hopewell exchange remains a mystery, but the motives must have been political and religious rather than economic, involving just a few people, who, presumably, were major political and religious players. The ceremonial artifacts handed from individual to individual became power symbols so important they were buried with their owners at death.

The widespread distribution of Hopewell objects, mound building and burial customs throughout the Southeast hints at a close similarity in religious beliefs over a wide area. Well over a thousand Hopewell mounds are known from the region, but less than 50 formed discrete groupings of earthworks. The Pinson mound center in southwestern Tennessee, used between 50 BC and AD 450, was the largest of all Hopewellian centers in the Southeast, covering 400 acres (160 ha), with a series of conical and platform mounds centered around a 75-ft (23-m) flat-topped mound in the center (Mainfort, 1996; Mainfort and Sullivan, 1998).

The Marksville culture, named after the Louisiana town of that name in the Lower Mississippi Valley, is the most important of a series of Hopewellian groups identified through the Southeast and dating to the early 1st millennium AD (summary in Bense, 1994). At Marksville, three earthen enclosures stand on a low bluff overlooking a now-dried-out channel of the river. The largest is a C-shaped embankment enclosing an area about 1500 ft (460 m) across, where three conical and two rectangular platform mounds stand. Another smaller, circular enclosure about 300 ft (90 m) across stands just to the south. A series of small conical mounds also form part of the site. One of these mounds, excavated in the 1930s, began as a rectangular hard clay platform 5 ft (1.5 m) high and at least 25 ft (7.6 m) long. A structure for cremating corpses may have stood on the platform, where numerous cremations were deposited. A burial vault with timber log roof was dug into the platform, which contained several burials, separated by layers of clay and cane mats. Later, a mound 25 ft (7.6 m) high and 100 ft (30 m) across rose above the platform, where more burials were laid to rest. Another major Marksville culture center is at Helena, 225 miles (360 km) upstream, near modern-day Memphis, Tennessee. The tombs under the Helena mounds yielded finely made copper ornaments, buried with the bodies of important individuals, who were laid to rest in their finest clothing.

Regional exchange systems had been functioning in one form or another since at least 4000 BC. Not that they flourished uninterrupted. There is good reason to believe that the networks went through constant cycles of expansion, then dissolution, with ever-changing geographic ranges. What did happen, however, was that the *scale* of the networks grew, with a broad trend toward more complex exchange systems as time went on. The diversity and number of distinctive, but similarly styled, artifacts handled along the networks increased over the centuries, as did the complexity of the social hierarchy that controlled the circulation. Thus, the Hopewell may have developed as a result of common evolutionary processes over much of the Eastern Woodlands in the centuries immediately before the Christian era.

Dispersed Homesteads and "Big Men"

Hopewell burial customs and earthworks are so spectacular that generations of archaeologists have concentrated their efforts on excavating mounds and other conspicuous monuments, at the expense of humbler settlements. So we still know little of Hopewell subsistence, settlement patterns, or daily life (Dancey and Pacheco, 1997a). In 1964, Olaf Prufer hypothesized that Ohio Hopewell communities lived in dispersed households clustered around, but not in, areas where burial mounds and ceremonial earthworks occurred. Prufer thought that Hopewell ceremonial precincts were largely empty, just as his contemporaries working on the Maya civilization believed that ceremonial centers like Tikal were empty, with the population living in the hinterland. This "Dispersed Agricultural Hamlet" model has been discredited as far as the Maya are concerned, but no one has yet produced evidence from Hopewell country that contradicts Prufer's theory of many years ago.

William Dancey and Paul Pacheco (1997b) have drawn on a generation of new field data to formalize Prufer's original idea into a "Dispersed Sedentary Community" model. They believe that Hopewell communities were made up of single- or multiple family households scattered across the landscape, but concentrated around centrally located burial mounds and ceremonial precincts. These households were stable, long-term settlements, occupied by people who not only foraged, but cultivated indigenous domesticated plants (Wymer, 1996). A dispersed settlement pattern was necessary to accommodate the often conflicting demands of cultivation and intensive foraging activity. Many local communities lie in areas defined by local drainage systems, with household sites, specialized camps, and ritual precincts, normally close to the center of the community and the focus of local life. While individual households were stable units, the constant hiving off of new generations made for a dynamic settlement pattern, where different settlements were occupied for shorter or longer periods of time, with the number of settlement clusters increasing through time. Ceremonial precincts also changed continually through time, with the building of new burial mounds, fresh earthworks, and other features.

At a larger scale, neighboring communities may have formed what one might call "peer polities," anchored by centrally located earthworks and burial mounds (Braun, 1986). Hopewell, Newark, and other earthwork groups may represent examples of such larger polities, each strategically located at the intersections of different physiographic provinces. This may reflect a basic self-sufficiency in foodstuffs during good years, but the need for intercommunity exchange to balance out shortages during cycles of drought cycles and other scarce times caused by short-term climatic shifts. These exchange links also extended to outlying areas where contemporary societies still retained strong Adena ties and did not adopt Hopewell beliefs (Greber, 1991).

This model of interacting polities, which were still basically egalitarian, is the most commonly accepted blueprint for Hopewell settlement, but new data may change the picture in future years. (For evaluations of alternative hypotheses, see Dancey and Pacheco, 1997b.)

No question, intercommunity exchange was vital to Middle Woodland groups, among them the Hopewell. The overall expansion of trading activity may reflect a contemporary rise in local population densities, decreased mobility, and increasing complexity in subsistence activities. A major element was reciprocity, social obligations outside the narrow compass of household and community that led to the reciprocal exchange of food and other goods over large areas, the exchange serving as a form of "savings account" against lean years (Ford, R., 1974). At the center of these transactions were local kin leaders, the individuals who negotiated exchanges and maintained contacts with neighboring communities. In some areas, like Ohio's Scioto Valley, people may have moved into concentrations of settlements where more coordinated decision-making was possible. These may have been the places where more aggressive leaders, people some anthropologists call "Big Men," acquired political and economic power and prestige through their expertise at gift exchange, through acquiring loyal followers among their fellow kin (Smith, B., 1986).

The notion of trade, reciprocity, and "Big Men" is associated with the researches of two anthropologists. The first is Bronislaw Malinowski, who studied the celebrated *kula* ring trade of the Trobriand Islands of the southwestern Pacific. The other is Marshall Sahlins, who studied isolated island communities in the same general area. He found these islands were linked by the ties formed by entrepreneurs, who exchanged symbolic gifts and acted as political and economic brokers in egalitarian, autonomous societies. They were, as Sahlins picturesquely writes, "a shunting station for goods flowing reciprocally between their own and other like groups of society" (Sahlins, 1972).

Bruce Smith believes that the "Big Men" model is appropriate in the river valleys of the Southeast, places where communities were interdependent, yet isolated. The gift-giving and social transactions reinforced friendly feelings between neighboring communities and enhanced the prestige of each "Big Man." They, in turn, redistributed goods to their followers. As time went on, these leaders would compete with one another in competitive displays of wealth and prestige, both in life and death, taking their symbols of individual power with them to the grave. "Big Men" were opportunists, people who took advantage of ever-changing circumstances, whose status was highly individual, never inherited, and always volatile, vanishing the moment they were interred. Their grieving followers would continue to live as they always had until another kinsman emerged as a new leader, a new "Big Man." The separation of occasional, more richly decorated burials in Southeastern mounds may, then, reflect the commemoration of "Big Men" in death with the symbols of prestige and wealth they had accumulated while living. But it is only fair to state that the evidence for social differentiation is poor and there is one big difference between ethnographic cases of "Big Men" and Hopewell individuals. The former gave away items in life, the Hopewell "Big Man" were commemorated with exotic objects in death. The debate over this model continues.

The inter-community ties fostered by such individuals can never have been permanent, never particularly strong. The archaeological record for the Hopewellian culture and for contemporary Middle Woodland societies seems to mirror such ever-changing small-scale chiefdoms. The tangible signs of successful "Big-Man-ship" only survive in rare richly decorated burials and distinctive mortuary customs.

Hopewell was never a widely distributed, uniform culture, in the sense that Maya civilization extended over a vast area of Mesoamerica. Rather, it was a local phenomenon, with greatly differing degrees of flamboyance and elaboration in Illinois, Ohio, and other areas – and the Hopewell style, characterized by elaborate burial customs and distinctive artifact and art styles, was diffused over a vast area of eastern North America through a maze of local and regional exchange networks. Along these routes, too, may have flowed distinctive religious beliefs that served to give scattered kin groups a sense of common identity.

Hopewell Exchange and Artifact Standardization

Hopewell exchange networks covered such a large area that many archaeologists have thought of this trade as a relatively unified system of transactions, carried out over enormous distances (Prufer, 1964; Struever and Houart, 1972). They argue that many pipes, small clay jars, copper ear spools, and other artifacts display remarkable stylistic similarity, as if they were traded as part of a well-organized exchange system that also handled raw materials over large distances.

These theories tend to pre-date detailed analyses of the distribution of different exotic artifacts and raw materials. In fact, each style of finished artifact and each raw material has a distinct and unique distribution (Griffin, 1965). Furthermore, these new studies have shown that many exotic raw materials tended to move directionally, in what Braun (1986) calls a "preferential" way. Perhaps they were collected by small parties of people from Hopewell core areas, who journeyed many miles to collect a stock of raw material for local manufacture back home. In contrast, the exchange of finished artifacts appears to have been a more local phenomenon presumably on a reciprocal basis.

How are we to account for the standardization of artifact style over enormous distances? It is not enough to invoke such explanations as a small number of specialists who created prestigious artifacts, or to argue for a broadly unifying symbolism of individual authority – in any case close analysis of the exchange networks does not bear such theories out. Rather we should think in terms of networks of cooperation and interaction between close and more distant neighbors that developed out of local pressures. In time, these exchange relations developed their own language, as it were, a set of exchange tokens with easily recognized designs and style that evoked similar meanings between scattered groups of people who shared at least some broad, philosophical ideas about the world.

It is difficult to prove the validity of this hypothesis, but there are some telling clues, especially from a distinctive form of Hopewell ceremonial ware found in many burial mounds. This pottery comes in the form of small, squat jars that are quite distinct from local pottery forms. Wherever it is found, the ceremonial ware has a thickened, vertical rim and is adorned with bands of cross-hatched lines, punctuations, and body decoration in curvilinear, geometric, or bird-motifs, depicting raptorial or spoon-billed species.

Hopewell ceremonial vessel from the Marksville site. Roulette motif outlines the design incised into the clay. Height c. 11.4 cm.

These distinctive vessels appear in the lower Mississippi, in the central Missouri, and the lower Illinois valleys. The same avian motifs are found on stone, bone, copper, and shell in western Illinois and southern Ohio, also in the southern Appalachians. Perhaps, believes David Braun (1986), the same symbols were used in several regions at the same time. They indicated not necessarily the exchange of actual artifacts, but a decorative imagery that communicated a broadly similar ritual message in many different, widely separated areas.

We tend to think of Hopewell exchange in terms of exotic, prestigious artifacts and materials, but in fact both the exchange mechanisms and the reasons for trading assumed many forms (Goad, 1979). Local exchange would have involved such prosaic items as foodstuffs, day-to-day raw materials, transactions that evened out local shortages between neighbors. Long-distance trade may have had nothing to do with feeding households and scattered villages (Griffin, 1965). It was an increasing need for exotic goods such as copper objects or marine shells that differentiated social status that led to regional and longer-distance exchange.

Sharon Goad (1979) examined historic Indian trails and trade routes in the Southeast and believes that Middle Woodland exchange moved along similar kinds of trails, the mechanism of exchange being a form of reciprocity. In the Southeast, for example, Goad believes copper, galena, and other Midwest and Great Lakes items entered the region through northern centers such as Wright and Roden in Alabama, and Tunacunnhee in northwestern Georgia. Exotic objects from the north are rare in the Southeast, as if these northern centers were obtaining some exotics from the north and not passing them far into the Southeast. Most Middle Woodland trade in the Southeast appears to have been regional, with regional networks overlapping with their neighbors and sometimes transporting artifacts and especially raw materials over longer distances.

Hopewell exchange is best seen as an intricate patchwork of regional exchange systems, each of which developed to satisfy local needs and obligations, using long-established trails and trade routes that changed constantly over the centuries. Over these myriad trails traveled symbolic exotica and fine artifacts with intense ritual and social meaning, items that linked widely distributed Hopewell centers with a broad semblance of ritual and cosmological unity that was but superficial, hiding a bewildering diversity of Middle Woodland cultural traditions.

Hopewell Mortuary Customs

We know more about Hopewell burial customs than about any other aspect of the Middle Woodland, largely because most excavators have concentrated on spectacular mounds and earthworks, and on the multiplicity of decorated Hopewell graves found in them (Brose and Greber, 1979; Mainfort and Sullivan, 1998). Unfortunately, many of these excavations took place before the advent of rigorous scientific methods, and still more remain unpublished, the artifacts scattered in museums throughout the Midwest.

The most spectacular burial mounds come from the Ohio Valley. At Hopewell itself, a mound complex near Chillicothe, 38 mounds lie within a rectangular enclosure covering 110 acres (45 ha) (Greber and Ruhl, 1989). Other mound groups are as impressive. The Seip Mound is 30 ft (9 m) high, 250 ft (76 m) long, and 150 ft (46 m) across, after Hopewell itself the largest tumulus of all. The average size of Ohio mounds is about 30 ft (9 m) high and some 100 ft (30 m) across, with a volume of about 500,000 cu. ft (14,000 cu. m). Each represents over 200,000 hours of earthmoving using the simplest of stone-bladed tools and baskets.

Like their Adena predecessors, Hopewell monuments were erected inside sacred earthworks, but earthworks on a much more imposing scale. At

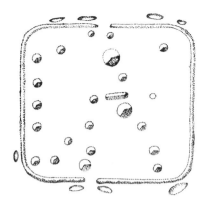

(Above) The Ohio Mound City complex consists of several mounds within an enclosure.

Mound City, Ohio, for example, 24 mounds lie within an enclosure covering 13 acres (5.2 ha). A vast complex of circles, a square, and an octagon linked by avenues encircles the burial mounds at Newark, Ohio, the entire mortuary landscape covering more than 4 sq. miles (10.4 sq. km).

Hundreds of burials have been excavated from these and other Hopewell earthworks by both treasure hunters and archaeologists. More than 1150 individuals have come from the major Ohio mound groups alone, buried in many different ways. More than three-quarters of scientifically studied burials were cremated, with, apparently, only the elite being deposited intact into the ground. Hopewell mourners used both burial crypts and charnel houses. The former were large boxes constructed for the storage of the dead and their grave goods. They were simple structures sunk into the ground and covered with heavy roofs, often built on isolated high-spots clear of the settlement. Crypts were maintenance free, and apparently served as corporate facilities for a single community (Brown, 1979).

Charnel houses were designed both to shelter the dead and the burial activities associated with them. The bodies of the deceased were subjected to considerable preparation, preparation that may have reflected the status of the dead. These structures and the rituals associated with them required much more effort by the communities associated with them. Both cremated

Cross-section and perspective view of the Hopewell WH6 burial mound, with multiple burials.

individuals and entire corpses were placed in large charnel houses with thatched roofs and substantial post frames. Once the charnel houses had fulfilled their role, they were burnt to the ground and an earthen mound erected over them (for a detailed discussion of crypts and charnel houses and their possible significance, see Brown, 1979).

The elite in Hopewell society were buried in log-lined tombs within the charnel houses, accompanied by far richer grave ornaments than anything found in Adena burials. A young man and woman buried together in the main mound at Hopewell wore copper ear spools, copper breast plates, and necklaces of grizzly-bear teeth. The woman went to her grave wearing thousands of freshwater pearl beads, and copper-covered wooden and stone buttons. Both had artificial copper noses. A log tomb within the Seip mound yielded four adults and two children deposited with thousands of freshwater pearls, copper tools, and ornaments of mica, silver, and tortoise shell. Some of the men in the mounds may have been expert artisans, like an individual from Hopewell buried with 3000 mica sheets and 198 lbs (90 kg) of galena. Another was an expert obsidian worker, buried with hundreds of stone fragments.

Hopewell mounds contained not only richly decorated burials but caches of exotic objects, many of them obtained from long distances away. The mourners deposited copper axes, cut-out silhouettes of birds, fish, claws, and human heads or hands in copper or mica, flint and chlorite disks, finely polished stone atlatl weights and beautiful effigy pipes. There were engraved human bones, painted fabrics, occasional clay figurines depicting bare-breasted women in belted skirts, men in loincloths.

We know almost nothing about Hopewell funerary rituals, for archaeological traces of such activities have not been preserved, except for frequent scatters of broken animal bones associated with the charnel houses, perhaps the remains of meals consumed nearby. Our only analogies are far-removed at best, and come from Southeastern societies of centuries later.

Charnel houses were in widespread use in the Southeast at European contact, some of them restricted in use to the elite. Those of the Choctaw, however, were accessible to all members of society. Choctaw chiefs were often buried in a special house, but there were others for everyone else, probably controlled by different kin groups (Swanton, 1931). Among the Choctaw, the dead were placed on covered platforms in the open with special food offerings. When the flesh had decomposed some months later, the deceased's relatives called in fellow clan members, priestly specialists who defleshed the bones and placed them in a chest. A communal feast followed, a ceremony when the bones were deposited in the charnel house. The burial remained in the charnel house for some time, commemorated at regular ceremonies and feasts. Eventually, sometimes when the charnel house was full, the bones were ceremonially removed and interred. The regular feasts associated with mortuary ceremonies and charnel houses may have served a practical role in Choctaw society, to ensure redistribution of game meat and other foods throughout society, to compensate for periods of scarcity, perhaps to stimulate production.

Superficially, Choctaw burial customs seem to parallel those found under Hopewell mounds quite closely (Seeman, 1979b). Both sets of customs involved a sequence of exposure, defleshing, sometimes cremation, redepositing of the dead in charnel houses, and reinterment in burial mounds. If the animal bones found under many Hopewell mounds are the remains of meals, then mortuary customs may also have provided a context for redistribution of food supplies. But there are significant differences as well. Hopewell people relied more heavily on cremation, placed great importance on exotic artifacts and materials in burial furniture, and destroyed their charnel houses when they were full. (The Iroquois Feast of the Dead, described in Chapter 21, may have Middle Woodland roots.)

To suggest that Hopewell and Choctaw burial customs were identical, that one can use historic custom in a straightforward manner to interpret mortuary remains from much earlier times, is the height of folly. Rather, as Mark Seeman argues (1979b), Hopewell charnel houses may have served as a catalyst for prominent kin leaders to manage food resources, not only the increasing yield from native plant gardens, but also game meat, food that flowed into the charnel house as offerings and was redistributed at feasts and other ceremonies. Perhaps, too, local Hopewell leaders were reinforced in their political and ritual authority, for, as is well known from societies all over the world, chiefdoms obtain their political power from their spiritual authority, perhaps, in this case, an authority intimately associated with game animals, the wild creatures depicted so frequently in Hopewell art and commemorated with dance masks and other artifacts.

Two stages in Hopewell mound building. First the people cremate a body and bury it within a sacred enclosure. Funerary offerings are placed on altars at right front and upper right. Then the mourners heap up basketloads of earth over the burial to form a mound. From an exhibit in the Field Museum of Natural History, Chicago.

MOUND OF EARTH BUILT OVER SACRED ENCLOSURE

CREMATION AND BURIAL IN A SACRED ENCLOSURE LATER COVERED BY A MOUND OF EARTH

It should be stressed, however, that Hopewell is a set of beliefs and ritual phenomena rather than a widespread culture with finite boundaries. There may have been ritual and exchange links between neighboring population concentrations in Ohio, Illinois, and further afield. The underlying culture was always local, displaying a variety of adaptations and local variations, many of them in communities that had never seen a Hopewell earthwork or given support to a "Big Man."

Interpreting Hopewell Earthworks

Circles and squares, octagons and causeways – the earthworks built by the Hopewell people bewilder the eye, especially when seen from the air. Some mound complexes, like that at Mound City, Ohio, covered areas equivalent to several New York City blocks, with a greater surface area than the base of the Old Kingdom Pyramid of Khufu in Egypt.

In about AD 250, the Hopewell people living near the modern city of Newark, Ohio, embarked on a major earthwork construction project (Lepper, 1996). Over several generations (the duration of construction is uncertain), they laid out an intricate maze of mounds, circles, an octagon, and a square over 4 sq. miles (10.4 sq. km) of countryside. From the air, the Newark earthworks seem like a jumble of enclosures and earthen mounds, which defy ready explanation, especially since much of the site now lies under the city streets and a golf course. Fortunately for science, Victorian archaeologists Ephraim Squier and Edwin Davis surveyed the earthworks in the 1830s and 40s, when they were still largely intact. Physicist Ray Hively and philosopher Robert Horn (1982) have examined the now much-disturbed monument using 19th-century surveys. They were surprised to find that the enclosures and mounds display an astonishing precision, with exact corners and precise astronomical orientation. For example, the Newark octagon covers 44 acres (18 ha), with openings at each corner, built with the aid of the diameter of the nearby circle. A perfect 1054-ft (321.3-m) diameter "Observatory Circle" is attached to the octagon. Hively and Horn studied the diameters of the circles, the sides of the octagons, and diagonals, in addition to the sides of the earthen squares and calculated that the builders used an exact unit of measurement of unknown length to lay out the earthworks.

The Hively and Horn survey provided clear evidence that the Newark earthworks were aligned with the moon. Using astronomical tables, the two scholars calculated the azimuths for the rising and setting of the sun and moon in AD 250, the estimated building date. They compared these azimuths with earthwork features such as linear embankments, axes of symmetry, and special points like the centers of central earthworks, and found no evidence for solar alignments. However, the Newark octagon fits the northern and southern extremes of the rising point of the moon along the horizon, which oscillate between two fixed azimuth points every 18.61 years. The long 5-ft 6-inch (1.7-m) high walls of the octagon would have allowed an observer to define precise azimuths within a quarter degree. Hively and Horn developed tables which show that the axis of the avenue between the Newark octagon and a nearby circular earthwork marked 5 of the 8 extreme lunar points with an accuracy of a

The circular and octagonal Hopewell earthworks near Newark, Ohio.

half degree, the observation points for these alignments being at 4 vertices of the octagon.

The Newark lunar alignments were probably accurate enough to allow the prediction of years when lunar eclipses would occur near the winter or summer solstices. They also permitted the Hopewell inhabitants to monitor the monthly and 18.6-year lunar cycles. The precision of the Newark earthworks suggests they provided a means of observing cyclical, lunar time. Some experts believe the Newark octagon and circle reflect a Hopewell concern not only with the burial of revered ancestors in mounds within the earthwork complex, but with seasonal rituals governed by astronomical phenomena, as if the Hopewell people arranged their earthly environment to mirror the heavens.

Symbolic Geography

Ancient Hopewell religious beliefs and the symbolic landscapes associated with them lie far in the past. The last burial mounds were erected in about AD 400, more than a millennium before European contact. This chronological gap of over ten centuries makes conventional ethnographic analogy from historic peoples impossible except in the most general of terms.

Archaeologist Warren DeBoer (1997) has used a combination of archaeology, ethnographic observation in Ecuador, and data from historical peoples to attempt a provocative interpretation of Hopewell symbolic geography.

DeBoer lived among the Chachi Indians of northern coastal Ecuador's Cayapas Basin in the late 1980s. He spent some time at Punta Venado, a Chachi ceremonial center laid out in a flattened U, which flanks a plaza with the church in the center. DeBoer believes Punta Venado is a map of Chachi country, a symbolic "Big House", with a settlement plan that reflected the cosmos itself. He points out that a broadly similar way of thinking and general settlement layout occurs among many eastern North American groups. DeBoer believes that this kind of notion was widespread in ancient native American societies, and that it offers a way of interpreting Hopewell earthworks.

Another method of interpretation is based on persistent notions of duality in human existence. The Cherokee, Creek, and other Eastern Woodlands peoples used a continuous form of seasonal duality in their domestic architecture. They built both circular winter ("hot") houses and adjacent or nearby rectangular summer dwellings. The same duality occurs in pre-Columbian Mississippian villages, and even in much earlier settlements, where rectangular and circular dwellings occur within the same site.

Major earthworks of the Scioto Basin. The earthworks are shown at a magnified scale.

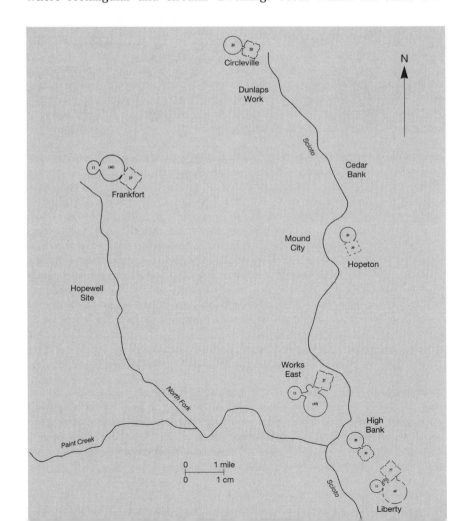

Among historic groups, a rich geometric symbolic duality is associated with the placement of houses, which goes far beyond the seasons. Winter is to summer as circle is to rectangle. DeBoer extends this further to local and foreign, peace and war, upperworld and underworld. He says (1997): "There is a historically deep-seated repertoire of polarities – a given structural field of play, if you will – that provides a lexicon for interpreting the form and meaning of both traditional and iconoclastic action performed by very real human actors." We know the basic duality has historical roots, but is it also a part of the Hopewell earthworks?

Hopewell people laid out their geometrically precise earthworks over a course of about five centuries. We theorize that they carried out mortuary rituals and other major ceremonies, as well as celebrated feasts, and organized causeway-directed foot races at these locations. Hopewell enclosures follow striking patterns of circles and squares, with the occasional octagon, but defy accurate chronological ordering. DeBoer's approximate seriation begins with Adena sacred circles, the square enclosure being added early in Hopewell times. At first the circles and squares are symmetrical, as if reflecting an orderly duality. Some time later, the earthworks become more irregular: shapes are blurred and fluctuate in size, and the squares always have openings. DeBoer speculates that these changes reflect the occurrence of a social crisis. For example, at Newark the largest square covering 49 acres (20 ha) may reflect a local leader aspiring to prestige and power, as earthworks elsewhere shrank in response to power shifts. In time, the more standardized pattern, of a big circle of about 39 acres (16 ha) in size and a smaller square about 27 acres (11 ha) in size aligned obliquely and separated by a circular insert, again became predominant. It is as if powerful, and ancient, domestic orthodoxy reasserted itself in the face of new, reactionary ideas. Perhaps earthwork architecture served as a symbolic barometer of changing social conditions.

In addition to the duality of circles and squares, many Hopewell sites occur in pairs, sometimes on either bank of a river, or some kilometers distant from one another. In the most extreme example of this pairing, archaeologist Brad Lepper believes two centers, High Bank and Newark, 70 miles (113 km) northeast, were linked by a causeway he calls the "Great Hopewell Road," parts of which appear on aerial photographs.

All of this would be pure speculation from ethnography, historical records, and earthwork survey, but for some telling clues in the archaeological record itself. For example, Henry Shetrone unearthed northern and southern altars under Mound 17 at the Hopewell mound complex itself. White-colored mica and domestic artifacts lay nearby. The northern altar area yielded red-colored copper and stone projectile points. The artifact distributions hint at a powerful opposition. Two mounds at the Turner site reveal a striking polarity. Mound 4 to the northeast yielded offerings of white mica, and images of "horned serpents." The southwestern Mound 3 contained most of the copper offerings and projectile points, as well as depictions of birds of prey. DeBoer theorizes that this duality reflects the upper- and underworld of the cosmos. However, the cappings of the mounds seem to reverse the duality. The summit of Mound 4 is covered with white mica sheets, while the mourners sprinkled black-colored cannel (a coal-like substance) over Mound 3. DeBoer points to living societies where members of a clan opposite to that of the dead are major players in burial rites. He reads binary contrasts into the archaeological evidence: cannel as a foreign commodity, traded from afar long before Hopewell times; mica as new goods, an exotic material intimately, and distinctively, associated with the Hopewell exchange networks.

Stone platform pipes carved into animal effigies also provide some clues. Ephraim Squier and Edwin Davis recovered a cache of more than 200 smashed pipes from Mound City in the Scioto Valley alone. The nearby Tremper Mound contained another 136 pipes. Almost all the animal motifs occurred in both mounds, and combined herons eating fish (sky-water), and otter with a fish in its mouth (land-water), and so on, as if "a triangular superstructure with sky, earth, and water pieces would appear to scaffold the choice of animal representations." When DeBoer arranged the pipes on a sky-earth-water triangle, he found the earth-water axis to be the most prominent and otters to be the most common. He says: "The skyward wafting smoke from Hopewell pipes thus intimated a ternary cosmos mapped and wrapped in zoomorphic imagery."

Warren DeBoer's research draws on data from anthropology, archaeology, and ethnohistory, and unashamedly uses analogy to bridge many centuries. Some archaeologists feel he has thrown caution to the wind, others that he has not gone far enough! Archaeologically, he relies on data collected over many years, and is concerned with general structures of Hopewell cosmology and earthwork layout. At no point does he claim that he has deciphered the meaning of the earthworks, but his analysis of duality gives a provocative insight into the ancient dualities of native American culture. He has shown convincingly that a polarity existed in Hopewell society, which was reflected in large earthworks. The full meaning of Hopewell earthworks can, however, never be deciphered, for the interpretation of any monument made to last begins as soon as it is built, and is in the hands of all of us: builder, user, scientist, and visitor alike. One thing is certain: the building of the earthworks required the labors of many people and the organization that implies.

Woodland Adaptations in the Southeast
c. 500 BC to AD 400

There were significant differences between mainstream Hopewell culture and contemporary societies to the south and east, despite regular trading contacts between the Midwest and Southeast. The great diversity of Southeastern society after about 500 BC is reflected in a proliferation of new pottery styles and in many local adaptations. Potters experimented with decorative motifs, new vessel forms, and many different clay tempers. These included grit, limestone, and sand, as opposed to the vegetable fibers used in earlier times. Southeastern archaeologists have used these many variations to chronicle different local cultures across the Southeast. Unfortunately, however, many of their ceramic samples for the four centuries after 500 BC come from shallow sites with a high prevalence of mixed occupation levels (Muller, 1986; Smith, B., 1986).

Coastal Adaptations. The long, low-lying coastal strip along the south Atlantic coast from North Carolina to Florida's St John River was exploited by numerous hunter-gatherer bands, who camped on higher ground close to salt swamps, marshes, freshwater estuaries, and lakes. These people are known to us mainly from shell middens, which give the impression that they subsisted almost entirely off oysters and clams. In fact, closer examination reveals a much broader-based economy, one that took advantage of the remarkable diversity of the marshes and coasts. The people subsisted off deer and other terrestrial animals, also fish, shellfish, and a wide variety of nuts, seeds, and other plants (Byrd, 1976; Milanich, 1993). In all probability, too, these coastal peoples cultivated some native plants, including gourds and squashes (Smith, B., 1986).

All the hunter-gatherers did was to graft the planting and harvesting of some native plants onto a long-standing marsh and coastal adaptation. (There are isolated occurrences of maize from the Southeast as early as AD 200, but these do not represent widespread corn agriculture (Smith, B., 1994).) By AD 1, many coastal communities were small, semi-permanent villages linked to seasonally occupied camps along the shore and close inland.

Along the northeast Gulf of Mexico coast and in the interior, the so-called Deptford people lived in small villages of about 5 to 10 families, spaced about every 10 miles (16 km) along the coast and in large communities in the interior river valleys of the Atlantic coast. During the winters, the 60 or so people in each village appear to have dwelt in oval-shaped houses with internal hearths about 22.9 by 32 ft (7 by 10 m) across, occupying smaller, open oval structures during the summer months (Milanich, 1993). This was by no means a uniform settlement pattern, for there were many smaller, often short-term coastal and inland camps.

River Valley Adaptations. Much interior settlement in the Southeast concentrated along the banks of large and small rivers. Many communities consisted of small- or medium-sized villages that were occupied for much, if not all, of the year. Some covered as much as 1.5 acres (0.6 ha). As on the coast, many groups used both summer and winter dwellings, often within the confines of the same settlement (Milanich, 1973a, b).

These interior populations show clear cultural links to earlier Archaic traditions. Dramatic changes in subsistence were, however, under way by 500 BC. By this time, people living north of the evergreen forest zone were exploiting annual nut crops more intensively, especially acorns, less heavily used in earlier times. Perhaps this increased reliance on nuts and acorns was the result of improved processing technology that enabled people to process large numbers of acorns – well-made ceramic vessels that permitted large-scale boiling of the harvest to leach out toxic tannic acids. The process itself was nothing new, for Archaic peoples had boiled nuts in laboriously manufactured steatite vessels. In fact, such containers may have been more effective, but clay pots were easier to manufacture, and with reasonably careful use were very durable (Smith, B., 1986).

Many interior sites of this period reflect another important technological advance – much better storage facilities. Many communities now used deep, circular storage pits, perhaps lined with woven fiber or bark to store their surplus gathered and cultivated foods. These resources they consumed during the scarce winter months, while dwelling in more permanent winter villages. Improved storage may have selected for more sedentary settlement and an investment in the extra labor needed to erect more substantial, permanent dwellings that were used for years on end.

Just as in Archaic times, the river valley populations traded a wide variety of exotic and more prosaic materials up and down local rivers. The Hopewell exchange systems extended into the Southeast, indeed some of the societies that were originally part of these systems continued to flourish after more northerly centers in Illinois and Ohio went into decline. Fine-grained chert, copper, marine shells, mica, and steatite were handled through these exchange networks, with a few artifacts such as tubular pipes from northeastern Tennessee. These may testify to occasional fleeting contacts with populations living north of the Ohio River.

Mounds and "Big Men" in the Southeast
AD 1 to 450

Between AD 1 and about 450, two important cultural developments emerged in the Southeast. First, despite thousands of years of mound building, mortuary customs became far more elaborate. Second, there are now signs that some individuals achieved greater social and political importance among what had been egalitarian societies. There was still basic cultural continuity from earlier centuries, a continuity reflected in great variations in settlement size and the persistence of ancient lifeways from Archaic and Early Woodland times.

These four-and-a-half centuries saw the construction of hundreds of low, oval or circular earthen burial mounds throughout much of the Southeast, a practice that continued in some areas up to European contact. Superficially, all these tumuli looked much the same, but their interiors reflect considerable diversity of burial custom. Many mounds contain no fewer than two dozen burials, perhaps a way of commemorating the common social affiliation of the kin buried in them. Others yielded but a few interments.

When excavating burial mounds, it is not enough just to examine the core of the earthwork and the central burials. One has to excavate the surrounding areas, the original land surface, too, to search for information on the funerary activities and rituals that took place before the mound itself was built. Only a few Southeastern excavations have probed more than mound cores, but it seems that many communities laid out their dead in charnel houses. When sufficient corpses had accumulated, or after a specified period, the people gathered for public funeral ceremonies. Judging from the great variety of interments found in the mounds, the initial treatment of the dead varied considerably. Some corpses were defleshed and merely the bones buried. Others were deposited in tightly flexed postures.

The Crooks Mound in eastern Louisiana witnessed at least six episodes of burial activity, with the dead being deposited in almost equal proportions as flexed interments and disarticulated skulls or bone bundles. It is as if a nearby charnel house was emptied periodically (Brown, 1979). Sometimes, a few individuals were given special treatment, occasionally deposited in rock- or log-lined tombs, or on special platforms under the mound. Some burials in special pits or even wooden dugout canoes were separated from other interments, as if they were individuals of special importance. Often, one or two people were given preferential treatment by being buried in special graves, accompanied by many more grave goods, prestigious items like copper pan pipes, ear spools, or breast plates.

The Hopewell Decline
after AD 400

The intricate Hopewell exchange systems endured in the Midwest until about AD 400. Then the networks collapsed, inter-regional art styles broke down, and moundbuilding by entire communities was interrupted. One has an impression of overall disruption, but a disruption that is still little understood, partly because chronological information is imprecise.

Two main long-term theories hold the stage, theories that complement one another (Braun, 1986). The first argues that horticulture became so successful that the ecological incentives for long-distance exchange, for reciprocal gift-giving, were removed – there was much less variation in resource availability between local areas, so ample food was available closer to hand. By the same token, local leadership by talented individuals became less important.

The second hypothesis argues that any form of agriculture may increase the carrying capacity of the land, but it carries serious risks with it owing to variations in rainfall and other natural phenomena from one year to the next. The best strategies for minimizing such risks are those of developing food storage systems, diversifying the crops planted and growing them in different considerably separated fields, and by developing reciprocal ties with kin living outside the immediate local area. Much of Hopewell exchange may have been based initially on competition, on individuals vying for prestige and success, rather than on the need to provide for mutual assistance in scarce times. Thus, goes the argument, long-distance exchange networks and personal prestige became less important as maize cultivation became more important, more intensive and more successful.

William Dancey (1996) has turned to an evolutionary, ecological scenario (for discussion of this approach, see Chapter 11) which argues that specialized food production became common among dispersed, stable groups, of which Hopewell was one, during the 1st millennium BC. Such strategies developed around plants cultivated as part of the Eastern Agricultural Complex (Smith, B., 1989). More fixed territories resulted, which contained such permanent features as earthworks. Population growth resulting from the higher production rates of more specialized production sparked competition for good arable land. This may have been the period when Hopewell ceremonialism flowered, with enormous expenditure of energy, perhaps meant, even, as a device to control growing population. During the early Late Woodland, significant aggregation of human settlements occurred, as larger settlements dominated the landscape. By this time, Hopewell ceremonialism had vanished, for densely settled communities no longer needed to come together for religious observances at central places, as their more dispersed Hopewell predecessors had done.

It is very difficult to marshal archaeological evidence in support of any these theories, because of a lack of data. We still know little of the causes of the Hopewell demise.

The centuries between AD 800 and 1200 were those when maize agriculture spread from the Central Mississippi Valley through the Southeast and the Eastern Woodlands (Potter, 1993). There are clear signs of gradual population growth, continued inter-community exchange, and increasing cultivation of native plants by sedentary peoples in river valleys and along sea coasts. The Late Woodland was a period of still little-understood, and highly varied, cultural change, which culminated in a series of remarkable riverine cultures after AD 800, in the great Mississippian tradition of the South and southern Midwest. We examine the Late Woodland antecedents of the Mississippian and the Mississippian itself in the next chapter.

Further Reading

In addition to earlier references:

Brose, Davis S. and Greber, N'omi. (eds.). 1979. *Hopewell Archaeology*. Kent State University Press, Kent, Ohio.
    The proceedings of a Hopewell conference, the papers in this volume cover the entire spectrum of the subject. Comprehensive bibliography.

Dancey, W.S. and Pacheco, Paul J. (eds.) 1997. *Ohio Hopewell Community Organization*. Kent State University Press, Kent, OH.
    An edited volume with excellent articles on Hopewell settlement patterns, a hitherto little known subject. Important evaluations of different models and a mass of basic data.

DeBoer, Warren. 1997. "Ceremonial Centers from the Cayapas (Esmeraldas, Ecuador) to Chillicothe (Ohio, USA)," *Cambridge Archaeological Journal* 7(1): 1–15.
    A wonderfully provocative interpretation of Hopewell earthworks and centers using ethnographic analogy and archaeology.

Mainfort, R.C. and Sullivan, Lynne P. (eds.) 1998. *Ancient Earthen Enclosures of the Eastern Woodlands*. University Press of Florida, Gainesville.
    An edited volume on the latest generation of earthwork research.

Pacheco, Paul. J. (ed.) 1996. *A View from the Core: A Synthesis of Hopewell Archaeology*. Ohio Archaeological Council, Columbus.
    Useful articles on all aspects of Hopewell for a specialist audience. Excellent bibliographies and much new data.

CHAPTER 20

MISSISSIPPIAN CLIMAX

Over 6000 years of continuous, gradual cultural evolution in the Midwest and Southeast culminated in one of North America's most brilliant achievements – the Mississippian tradition. With its great centers and myriad smaller communities, this complex patchwork of chiefdoms large and small flourished for about six centuries, up to European contact and beyond. The Mississippian's ultimate cultural and social roots lie in much earlier Archaic and Woodland cultures that flourished long before maize agriculture became widespread in the great river valleys of the Eastern Woodlands (Bense, 1994; Smith, B., 1986; Steponaitis, 1986).

The Weeden Island Culture
AD 200 to c. 1000

Perhaps the best known of the many cultures that flourished in the Late Woodland Southeast is the Weeden Island culture, which arose among the ancient peoples who lived among deciduous and mixed pine forests, near lakes, rivers, and wet prairies on the Gulf coastal plain between Florida, Alabama, and Georgia about two centuries after Christ (Milanich and others, 1997).

Characteristic Weeden Island pottery appears at about AD 200, and may have developed out of earlier Swift Creek ceramic traditions in the Apalachicola-Chattahoochee valleys on the Alabama-Georgia border. Weeden sites extend into western parts of northern Florida and as far west as the Tombigbee River in Alabama along the Gulf coast and into the interior. An early Weeden Island I period lasted from about AD 200 to 700, Weeden Island II from 700 to between 900 and 1000, each distinguished by characteristic pottery styles (Bense, 1994). About AD 900 to 1000, Weeden II developed *in situ* into local forms of Mississippian culture at many locales, to the point that it might legitimately be called "proto-Mississippian" (Milanich and others, 1997). Some Weeden II communities may have survived in parts of northern Florida into the 15th century. The Weeden people were surrounded by other Late Woodland cultures, among them the Troyville and Coles Creek developments of the low-lying Mississippi and Louisiana coast, and the St Johns culture to the southeast that developed continuously from Middle Archaic times right into the historic eastern Timucuan groups encountered by both Spanish and French explorers in the 16th century.

Weeden Island is part of a long evolutionary continuum that started right back in Paleo-Indian times, continued through the Archaic and Woodland, and culminated in the Mississippian. As populations increased during Late Archaic and Early Woodland times, the inhabitants of the Southeast developed more complex settlements and more elaborate forms of social organization. Jerald Milanich and his colleagues argue that by AD 200, lineages and other forms of social status were well established among all Southeastern peoples. At times, too, even more complex forms of social organization may have appeared for brief periods – witness Poverty Point (Chapter 17). All these economic, social, and ideological changes culminated during the three centuries after AD 700, among Weeden II and related cultures.

Weeden Island has developed as an archaeological construct over more than a century and is a far more complex culture than might superficially appear. William Sears (1956) excavated the Kolomoki site in Georgia, which led him to draw parallels between the social organization and ceremonial life of the Kolomoki Weeden Island peoples and the Natchez and other historic peoples in the Southeast. He pointed out that there was a sharp dichotomy between the sacred and the secular in these societies. In the case of the Hopewell and Mississippian, there was great uniformity in ceremonial paraphernalia, mound construction, and even in settlement hierarchies throughout much of the Southeast and Midwest. Yet there were numerous local variations in secular life, in economic conditions, technology, and other traits – to the point that the Weeden Island culture can be interpreted in several ways. On the one hand it is an ever-changing, secular pottery complex that occurs at most village sites through Weeden Island territory. On the other, it is a sacred, ceremonial complex, that may have developed from earlier Hopewell-like belief systems and religious usages. This complex may have revolved around elaborate mortuary rituals centered on low platform mounds used as bases for charnel houses, the residences of important individuals, and for preparing bones for burial. The nature of this complex was illustrated dramatically at the McKeithen site in northern Florida (Milanich and others, 1997).

The McKeithen site is a village with three low platform mounds, none more than 6 ft (2 m) high (for platform mounds, see below). It was a horse-shoe-shaped settlement encompassing three mounds with a central plaza, the village and its extensive middens being open to the west-northwest. Excavations showed the site was occupied between AD 200 and 700 during Weeden Island I. The three low platform mounds had been constructed at about the same time, between AD 350 and 475, during the period of densest occupation and highest population – radiocarbon dates cannot tie down the date for the tumuli more accurately. About AD 475, the structures on the mound platforms were burnt and removed, and the mounds capped. The village was still occupied after that date, but its importance as a center declined.

The exact position of the McKeithen mounds was planned to allow the rising sun at the summer solstice to be observed from the summit of one of the mounds, the three earthworks forming an isosceles triangle. Each mound began as a low platform, then structures with walls supported by vertical posts were erected on top of two of them. One was probably a residence or temple, inhabited by an individual, probably a religious specialist, who was later buried in it. This was a female in her mid- to late

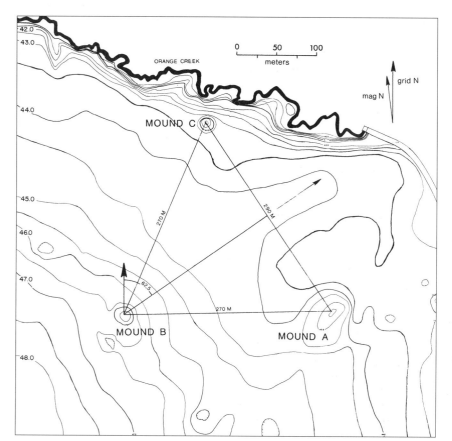

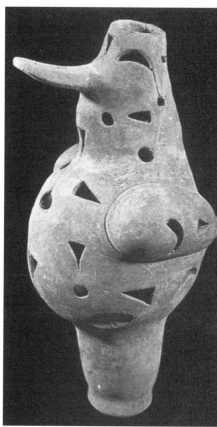

Weeden Island culture. (Above) Plan of the McKeithen mounds. The three mounds form an isosceles triangle. The perpendicular, formed by a line from mound B to the triangle base, points toward the position of the rising sun at the summer solstice. (Above right) Weeden Island Red pedestaled duck effigy from Kolomoki Mound D. Height 34 cm.

Weeden Island Punctated bowl, from Carter Mound 1.

thirties, and buried with a small, triangular stone projectile point in her hip (this does not seem to have been the cause of death). The body had been exposed for some days, then buried in an extended position, perhaps wearing a headdress of animal and human bone. A ceramic turkey vulture's head from an effigy pot lay less than 3 ft (1 m) from the head. The building on the mound was burnt down over the grave.

The structure on the second mound was probably a charnel house. The third platform mound was topped with a pine-post screen, and the area behind it was used to inter and exhume burials. This may have been where the bones of the dead were cleaned before being taken over to the charnel house. There they were stored until buried under the cap of the completed mound. Together, the mounds formed part of a complex mortuary process, presumably supervised by the man buried in the temple or residence. He may also have kept track of the yearly calendar, of the summer solstice. Mortuary activities may have ceased with the death of this important individual. The structures were burnt down, the mound platforms capped with clean sand.

Platform mounds of the general type found at Kolomoki and McKeithen are found in Florida, Georgia, Tennessee, Alabama, and Mississippi. Most date from AD 150 to 400, a few as late as AD 750. Their design was probably related to the burial ceremonies conducted on them. Occasionally, the people added additional burials as the mound was being built, some complete interments, others in the form of bone bundles or even single skulls. Some scholars believe these were the burials of slaves and retainers sacrificed at the death of the important personage under the mound. Sometimes the mourners deposited caches of elaborate clay vessels in the mounds, many of them ceremonial pots in the shape of humans, birds, or animals. They were punctured with holes through the base, some of them before they were even fired. (For a fascinating discussion of the process of moundbuilding and its significance, see Schnell and others, 1981.)

Each Weeden Island village or lineage had a religious practitioner, an individual who provided a link to the supernatural (Milanich and others, 1997). This person probably had special social status, was a true "Big Man" for the time when he was active, and was supported by members of his lineage, who were buried in the communal burial mound. Burial in such a tumulus was an affirmation of lineage membership, and ensured that ritual obligations occurred at central locations. The individuals who carried out these rituals had an exalted status in society, positions that enabled them to develop outside contacts, to manipulate long-distance trade, to acquire some political power. Individual villages like McKeithen could assume great importance in inter-lineage activities for a short period of time, while their "Big Man" was at the height of his powers.

The social organization characteristic of McKeithen and other Weeden Island sites appears to have lain somewhere between the basically egalitarian structure of Archaic hunter-gatherers and the chiefdoms characteristic of later Mississippian society. Between AD 700 and 1000, village centers like McKeithen and their religious specialists assumed ever-greater importance as maize agriculture and harvest rituals became more central features of Southeastern life. Over these centuries, the social, political, and ideological institutions of later Weeden Island agricultural communities and their contemporaries evolved into those associated with the Mississippian.

The Great Serpent Mound in Ohio is a celebrated example of an earthwork built during the Fort Ancient culture, a tradition contemporary with the Mississippian. It is perhaps a symbolic representation of an important lineage buried within its confines. With its tightly curved tail, the earthen serpent wriggles with convoluted folds for 1254 ft (382 m) along a low ridge, its open jaws enclosing an oval burial mound.

The underlying catalysts for the brilliant flowering of Mississippian culture after AD 1000 were, firstly, widespread political and religious changes that saw the appearance of important chieftains, secondly, the widespread adoption of maize cultivation throughout the Eastern Woodlands after AD 800, and last, the efflorescence of sacred ceremonial complexes that led to the emergence of numerous powerful chiefdoms throughout the Southeast.

Major political changes began before widespread maize cultivation, with important thresholds that saw the abrupt appearance of complex chiefdoms at Cahokia, and later at Lake George, Moundville, and elsewhere. Lesser chiefs must have emulated their more powerful peers in the regions between the major centers, but the sheer size and power of Cahokia and later large centers may have stunted the full historical potential of neighboring areas (Anderson, D.G., 1997). But what were the remarkable political and religious institutions that distinguished the Mississippian from its predecessors?

Defining the Mississippian

The term "Mississippian" defies precise definition. Bruce Smith (1978) used the term to define ancient populations living in the Eastern Woodlands from AD 1000 to 1500/1600 "that had a ranked form of social organization, and had developed a specific complex adaptation to linear, environmentally circumscribed floodplain habitat zones." Smith's definition is flexible, and allows for great differences in social organization. Another archaeologist, James Knight (1986), believes that distinctive social and religious institutions set the Mississippian apart from other cultural traditions. He argues convincingly that the religious institutions of Mississippian societies were highly distinctive, "a prevalent variety of socio-religious organization crosscutting other cultural and ecological boundaries, recognizable by virtue of shared classes of *sacra* [sacred artifacts]."

Chiefly Warfare Cult (The so-called "Southern Cult"). Knight envisages a pluralistic Mississippian institutionalized religion, with a chiefly cult of elite nobles based on warfare, which can be identified by exotic motifs and symbols and by costly raw materials such as sea shell or imported copper. Such objects occur in elite burials, together with war axes, maces, and other weapons. These warrior symbols occur alongside other artifacts which bear exotic cosmic imagery, depicting animals, humans, and mythic beasts. This symbolic imagery bound together warfare, cosmology, and nobility into a coherent whole. Some of these categories of artifacts were used as markers of chiefly office, which varied from one location to another.

Dozens of Mississippian cemeteries and mound centers contain finely made pottery and other artifacts associated with this chiefly cult, bearing elaborate decoration and distinctive artistic motifs. They include axes with head and shaft carved from a single piece of stone, copper pendants adorned with circles or weeping eyes, shell disks or gorgets showing woodpeckers, rattlesnakes, elaborately decorated clay pots and effigy vessels, copper plates, and engraved shell cups adorned with male figures in ceremonial dress (Brain and Phillips, 1995; Phillips, P. and Brown, 1978).

The themes and motifs have many features in common over a vast area, not only from classic Mississippian centers like Etowah, Georgia, and Moundville, Alabama, but also from Spiro mound in Oklahoma, part of the related Caddoan moundbuilding culture (Bell, 1984). They even occur as glyphs on the walls of Tennessee caves (Faulkner, 1988). Generations of archaeologists have grouped these artifact styles and art themes into a distinctive "Southern Cult," which appeared to link sites hundreds of miles apart, which originated in earlier centuries. The oldest art objects of any complexity found in the Eastern Woodlands are found in Early and Middle Woodland sites. These can be shown to have general connections with the basic themes of "Southern Cult" art. Such themes include widespread use of bird symbolism, "weeping eyes," and circles and crosses. They appear to have been common to all eastern societies, themes that were used, refined, and developed as new traditions and beliefs arose.

The term "Southern Cult" is probably somewhat outdated, for it reflects a complex, highly variable set of religious mechanisms that supported the authority of local chieftains, which defy precise definition (for discussion of the Cult, see Muller, 1989).

Earth/Fertility. A second Mississippian cult, set against a communal earth/fertility cult, was associated with the earthen platform mounds, which may seem like unlikely religious artifacts. However, the act of rebuilding them, of adding additional layers of earth over burials, served as a symbol of renewal, which renewed the earthwork as much as human life. The earthen platform served as the earth, a symbolism which endured into historic times. There are historically documented connections between additions to platform mounds and the communal "green corn" ceremony, which celebrated the new harvest and the fertility of the earth. The quadrilateral, flat-topped design of many platform mounds may represent the Southeastern Indian belief that the earth was a flat surface oriented toward four quarters of the world.

Ancestor Worship. Still a third cult may have mediated between the two dominant ones, one represented by well-preserved temple statuary representing both men and women kneeling in deathlike poses. Such figures occur in many Mississippian centers, among them Moundville and Spiro, as well as dozens of smaller sites. Knight believes that ethnohistorical data link such statues to ancestor cults, which were organized by temple priests, but archaeological finds add little to the ethnohistorical sources.

This triad of Mississippian cult institutions had distinctive features. The warfare cult was exclusive, confined to certain kin groups and gave privileged rights to chiefly posts within these groups, while, in its cosmological aspects, serving to underpin and sanctify political power by means of chiefly rituals. In contrast, the platform-mound cults were communal rituals, which involved entire kin groups and communities, who labored in their construction as part of ceremonies that drew on deeply felt religious beliefs common to all society, such as survived among Southeastern Indians until historic times. Ancestor cults were supervised by priests who were responsible for maintaining temples, burial houses, sacred fires, and mortuary rituals. These ancestor rituals, supervised by individuals with special supernatural powers, must have intermeshed with both chiefly and communal cults, to the point that they may have mediated between different interests within society.

James Knight theorizes that the sudden expansion of the Mississippian tradition unfolded within the context of developing political and religious institutions. Newly emerging cults, which, themselves, developed from much earlier and simpler institutions, provided a framework of changing social forms, where co-existing cult institutions struggled constantly to assimilate ever-expanding spheres of influence by manipulating supernatural beliefs.

If Knight is correct, then the development of the Mississippian tradition was a complex process driven more by political and social changes than by economic considerations. The powerful Mississippian cults which defined both chiefly and communal society cut across the South and Southeast and all their different local cultural and ecological boundaries. They created a dynamic, constantly changing, and highly factionalized society. The archaeological record documents the tremendous variation in social complexity in the Mississippian culture area, with major centers like Cahokia in the so-called American Bottom near the modern city of St Louis at one end of the spectrum, and hundreds of small, local centers and minor chiefdoms at the other. (For a minor Early Mississippian center, see Schnell and others, 1981.)

Subsistence

With the exception of maize, and later bean, agriculture, there was nothing dramatically new in the way Eastern Woodlands people lived in the late 1st millennium AD. It was just that the diversity and intensive scale of river floodplain cultures reached new heights.

Woman grinding maize: a stone effigy pipe from Spiro Mound, Oklahoma. Height 25 cm.

The Mississippian coalesced over much of the Southeast during the 11th and 12th centuries, with an early efflorescence in the Cahokia region in about AD 1050 (Pauketat and Emerson, 1997). It developed in river valleys large and small, often expanding up small tributaries of major waterways. This restriction of Mississippian populations to floodplains was not only because of easily cultivable alluvial soils. For thousands of years, river valley peoples had adapted to low-lying environments where locally concentrated aquatic, game, and vegetable resources were abundant. Fertile agricultural soils formed bands within these same valleys, providing additional diversity of food resources in traditional homelands.

A constant supply of water-borne nutrients helped these floodplain areas sustain a rich biomass of animals and plants, and resulting high human population densities. The Mississippians who lived in these environments developed complex, yet very flexible, subsistence patterns, which involved exploiting fish, migratory waterfowl, terrestrial game (deer, raccoon, and turkey), nuts, fruits, and berries, and seed-bearing native plants. They selectively exploited these optimum energy sources within the floodplain ecosystem and deliberately destroyed the natural vegetation on preferred soils to grow maize, beans, squash, and some native plants.

Just as important, local topography, the amount of spring flooding and summer drain off, and location relative to migratory waterfowl flyways, were of critical importance for people maximizing their floodplain habitats. As a result, fish and waterfowl together may have contributed at least half of the total protein intake of Mississippian populations living along the bottomlands of the great river, in places where oxbow lakes and abandoned channel meanders were plentiful. Add to this effective cultivation of nutrient-rich soils fertilized by regular floods, and it is safe to claim that the Mississippians enjoyed a unique subsistence opportunity in the Eastern Woodlands (Nassaney, 1987; Smith, B., 1978).

As we saw in Chapter 14, maize cultivation began in the Southwest before the 1st millennium BC. The maize pool in that region was highly diverse (Smith, B., 1994), and a small-cob 12- and 14-rowed race of hard flint maize, sometimes called "North American pop," was probably the first to spread across the southern Plains into the Southeast 2000 years ago. Maize has been AMS-dated to between 170 BC and AD 60 at the Holding site on the American Bottom in the Mississippi Valley near East St Louis (Riley and others, 1994). Eight-rowed, hardy Maiz de Ocho later became a staple over much of the Midwest and Eastern Woodlands. Flotation samples from eastern sites document a transition from sporadic occurrences of maize to intensive cultivation after about AD 700 to 750. For example, a Late Woodland occupation at Koster East in west-central Illinois dating to about AD 620 contains but one occurrence of maize, whereas a later one of about AD 830 contains 24 percent maize (Asch and Asch, 1985).

Beans (*Phaseolus vulgaris*) were introduced into the Eastern Woodlands in about AD 1000 (Smith, B., 1994), and were not in common use until Late Mississippian times, after AD 1200. Beans provided an important protein source for Eastern Woodlands peoples, as they did elsewhere in the Americas (Chapter 14).

Begun initially to create more supplemental foods, the new agriculture transformed the landscape in such ways that hunting and foraging provided much less food for energy expended than maize cultivation.

Within a short time, an entirely new economic pattern came into being. It is difficult to know how important hunting was in Mississippian life. Apart from waterfowl and fish in favored areas, the game species from many sites include such familiar species as deer, but many of them were animals that would prey regularly on growing maize fields.

Wild plant foods were of vital importance to Mississippian communities, especially the rich nut harvests of fall. In bountiful years, nuts would provide enough food to feed a much higher population density than actually lived even in the most favored locations. By the same token, and judging by modern experience, good agricultural years could yield far more than the 19th-century average for the United States of about 22 bushels an acre (1320 kg/ha), a figure close to current worldwide production counts (figures quoted from Muller, 1987). In the so-called Black Bottom area of the Lower Ohio Valley in which the well-known Kincaid site lies, there were an estimated 1482 acres (600 ha) of occupied agricultural land in Mississippian times (Cole, 1951). With yields like this, an average maize year could support some 2000 people, about double the maximum population estimated for the region.

Short-term climatic change, especially serious droughts, played a hitherto unsuspected role in political and economic change. Intensive researches into the Mississippian chiefdoms of the Savannah River Basin have combined archaeology and tree-ring chronologies in an attempt to develop quantitative reconstructions of Mississippian food storage capabilities from AD 1005 to 1600 (Anderson and others, 1995; Anderson, 1994). The combination of simple storage models and tree-ring data suggests that there were long periods of plentiful food supplies and of serious shortages, which had a profound effect on the rise and fall of individual chiefdoms. David Anderson and his colleagues estimate that maintaining a year's food reserves would have given local populations enough time to switch to other foods and minimize the impact of poor rains and lower-than-average harvests. But a prolonged drought would have caused major stress and economic and political disruption, bringing small chiefdoms into contact with much more powerful neighbors as they competed for scarce food resources. Anderson, however, cautions that political factors as well as environmental change played an important role in the constant ebb and flow of chiefdoms in this region and elsewhere.

Bountiful yields in good years meant good living, but yields from both fields and nut trees varied dramatically from year to year. The bottomlands of the Mississippi and Ohio rivers flood regularly in the spring, and can be subject to inundation as late as July. These floods are irregular, but not infrequent, making farming on such lands a high-risk proposition even today. It was no coincidence that many Mississippian communities and their gardens were concentrated on fertile, well-drained ridges, or on nearby terrace soils that were never flooded, even if the risk of drought was higher. Almost certainly most villages maintained fields both in high-risk flood areas and on higher ground. Here other factors came into play – crop diseases spreading through closely placed gardens and build-up of weeds and pests resulting from repeated cropping of the same land.

This meant that most Mississippian communities lived with the constant threat of food shortages. The people dwelt in permanent settlements, so they could not adopt the age-old strategy of shifting base when local resources were in short supply. In some locations, there may have been occasional episodes of extreme stress. A series of complex studies of some Mississippian burials reveal stress lines on limb bones (known as Harris lines) and other clear signs of cyclical stress, some of which were probably caused by dietary factors, confirming the Anderson team's findings (Buikstra and others, 1986).

What strategies, then, could prevent starvation in lean years? Most of the time, the household was a self-sufficient entity. But at least once or twice a decade the yields of gardens and trees were probably insufficient, creating a real need for vital, supplemental resources – and for social mechanisms to minimize the risk of famine.

Each household may have cultivated a mosaic of several gardens, situated in separate environmental zones. People short of food could rely on kins-people living in other areas for seed and rations, knowing that one day they might have to reciprocate in kind. Or a community or kin group could stockpile surplus food from one year for use in lean times. Several of these strategies required some form of coordination, either through kin leaders or on a larger scale (Muller, 1987).

Some groups may have even gone so far as to maintain communal granaries under the control of a local chieftain, like those observed among the historic Muskogean Indians of the Southeast by the 18th-century botanist William Bartram:

"There is a large crib, or granary, erected in the plantation, which is called the king's crib; and to this each of the family carries and deposits a certain quantity, according to his ability or inclination ..." This, wrote Bartram, was a "public treasury" "to which every citizen has the right of free and equal access, when his own private stores are consumed; to serve as a surplus to fly to for succor; to assist neighboring towns, whose crops may have failed ..." The chief, Bartram tells us, had the task of distributing "comfort and blessings to the necessitous" (Bartram, 1853).

This account treats of a people who were under strong European influence. But Jon Muller (1987) believes that the emergence of an elite within Mississippian society may have been a way of mitigating risks for households and entire villages. These leaders were the people who oversaw the stock-piling of food supplies, who ensured that cultivated lands were maintained in different environmental zones, so that chances of crop failure were much reduced. Some of these strategies could be operated through ties of kin and reciprocity, but only up to a certain point of scale. At times, food shortages may have been such that entire regions had to cooperate with one another, cooperation requiring organized leadership and coordination in a more formal way. At the center of these mechanisms of reciprocity and cooperation lay complex local and long-distance exchange systems, developed in various forms over many centuries. But new settlement evidence from the American Bottom near Cahokia and elsewhere contradicts this hypothesis and suggests that a process of "top-down" political consolidation that turned minor chiefdoms into much larger and more powerful entities with greater authority played a major role (Pauketat, 1993; Emerson, 1997a).

Chiefdoms

Most Mississippian exchange took place at the household level, the domestic unit that organized and scheduled food gathering and production. Apparently, however, Mississippian communities were grouped into larger political and social units, headed by local kin leaders, individuals who probably rose to prominence, just as their predecessors had done for centuries. These leaders, whose survival depended on their ritual and political skills in societies riven by factionalism, perhaps functioned as a way of balancing the distribution of vital foods and raw materials.

Many exotic objects are found in Mississippian burials, with the result that archaeologists have tended to describe all such interments as those of "high-status" individuals. This is a dangerous assumption, for most burial excavations have concentrated on centrally located, "high-status" cemeteries, often places where a much greater variety of artifacts occurs anyhow. Were, then, such exotic objects as shell cups, engraved shells, and other fine artifacts badges of rank, or merely trade objects that were widely distributed in societies that showed little social or material distinction between commoner and elite?

Mississippian exchange networks linked hundreds of communities large and small, mainly with local transactions. Production of artifacts of every kind was a dispersed activity throughout Mississippian territory. For instance, sea shells were exchanged over vast areas of the Southeast. The complete shells were turned into ornaments and often engraved with distinctive designs by specialists. The motifs executed by different individuals can be recognized in many cases (Phillips, P. and Brown, 1978).

Sea shells were traded over vast areas of the Southeast in Mississippian times. (Below) Conch shell engraved with an abstract face from Arkansas. (Below right) Conch shell engraved with a flying shaman, from Oklahoma.

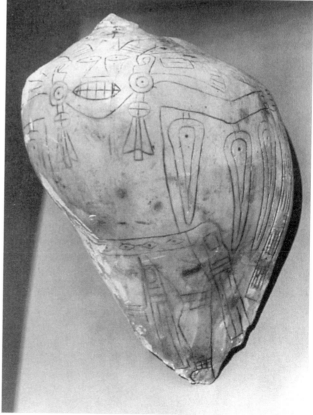

Chert from the famous Union County quarries in Illinois may have been quarried by local, part-time specialists. Much of it was turned into stone hoes, exchanged and used throughout the northern Lower Mississippi Valley. Salt production assumed much greater importance as maize cultivation took hold in the Southeast, for farmers have to supplement their diet artificially with salt. Cake salt was manufactured at a limited number of places. According to 18th-century French explorer Le Page du Pratz, people would come from long distances to make salt at locations like Great Salt Spring near the Saline River in southeast Illinois (Le Page du Pratz, 1758). There may have been some centers of local production, but at best this was probably a part-time activity, involving work parties from communities at a distance.

As far as we can tell, person-to-person bartering or gift-giving and formal redistribution were the only means of exchange of goods and commodities in Mississippian society. This means that highly diverse Mississippian communities were not organized along very formal, rigid social class lines, even if local politics played a vital role in day-to-day existence. The modes of production were little more complex than those found in earlier Woodland societies, although the elite certainly supported men and women who produced prestige goods and ritual objects when needed (Pauketat, 1993).

Mississippian communities were highly politicized, exchanging and producing goods and commodities through ties of kin and reciprocal obligation. Judging from historic accounts, the more elite members of society may have been involved in the storage and redistribution of grain. Apparently these stockpiles could reach impressive proportions. We know this because in later centuries early European explorers like Spaniard Hernando de Soto and his conquistadors were able to loot considerable quantities of stored grain from Southeastern villages on occasion.

Much grain redistribution activity may have taken place at formal ceremonies. As late as the 17th century, Southeastern communities from many miles around would congregate for feasts and dances, at which people would barter goods, share food, and reaffirm ties with other villages and individuals. Native American groups still congregate for ceremonial gatherings in this region today.

Mississippian Polities: Cahokia and Moundville

The ancient societies that are loosely classified under the label "Mississippian" flourished over a wide area of the Midwest and South, enjoying complex cultures that varied widely from one location to the next. Most Mississippian communities were small, many of them grouped into a multiplicity of chiefdoms that were probably in a constant state of political flux as the followings of important individuals waxed and waned, chiefs died, alliances were forged and fell apart, and new people came into prominence (Rogers and Smith, 1995). But there are some Mississippian centers that appear to have nurtured more complex social and political structures. The most famous of these are Cahokia in the American Bottom on the Mississippi River opposite St Louis, and Moundville in Alabama. These centers raise important questions about the complexity of Mississippian society, about the political organization of the most elaborate of all ancient North American cultures.

Map showing the main Mississippian groups and locations of some key sites.

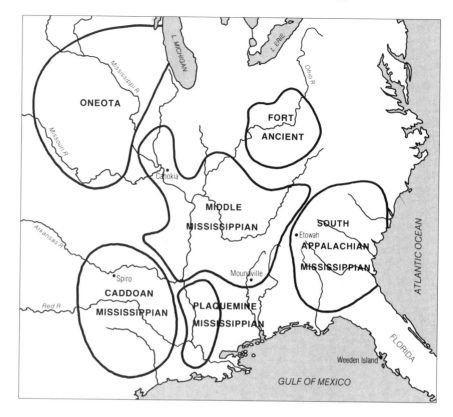

(Below) Cahokia and surrounding sites located in part of the Mississippi floodplain known as the American Bottom.

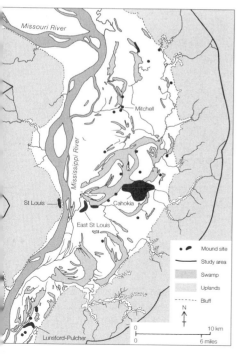

Cahokia. The American Bottom is a pocket of low-lying river floodplain along the Mississippi from the confluence with the Illinois River near Alton, Illinois, past Dupo, as far south as Chester, Illinois. The Bottom is only about 25 miles (40.2 km) from north to south and 11 miles (17.7 km) wide at its greatest extent. It was formed by the meanderings of the Mississippi and Missouri river channels over the flatlands, forming swamps and oxbow lakes in its abandoned channels. The result was an environment of exceptional diversity, rich in aquatic resources, game, and vegetable foods, a floodplain with fertile soils lying on the borders of several ecological zones. It was here that Cahokia flourished, with probably the highest ancient population density north of Mexico (Milner, 1990).

Sedentary villages existed at or near the Cahokia site after AD 600, but the huge mound-and-plaza complex we see today was built between the 11th and 13th centuries. For these three centuries, a hitherto dispersed rural population was suddenly transformed into a much more tightly integrated society, partly by manipulating communal religious symbolism (Pauketat, 1998). Yet, Cahokia only held close sway over a small area of the American Bottom, a vortex, as Tim Pauketat calls it, of a close-knit regional phenomenon. Pauketat calls this "Greater Cahokia," an area in Illinois and Missouri that encompassed an area some 60 to 90 miles (100 to 150 km) from its core in the Bottom, although Cahokia-like artifacts and ideas spread much further afield, far north in the Midwest.

Cahokia mounds, c. AD 1150.
The 100-ft (30.4-m) high Monk's
Mound dominated the site, with many
smaller mounds and houses
surrounding it. Trading and major
public ceremonies took place in the
central plaza. A log stockade protected
the central precincts, with a solar
calendar at the far left. Maize gardens
surrounded Cahokia, and water
supplies came from Cahokia Creek and
small lakes that formed in borrow pits
dug to quarry clay for moundbuilding.

Thanks to enormous bodies of new data, we now have a much more accurate chronology for Cahokia than even a few years ago. As a result, we now know that the great center emerged as a regional capital with dramatic suddenness, not as a result of external trade, or gradual cultural evolution, but through a complicated and still little understood process of political and social negotiation which melded new political realities with the everyday lives of communities and households (Pauketat, 1998). A new generation of excavations and foot surveys, and more precise local chronologies have documented abrupt changes in household refuse and craft production, also in regional settlement patterns during the two or three decades around AD 1050. Instead of early Mississippian villages, hamlets, and farmsteads, a new three-tiered settlement hierarchy suddenly appears – a great capital at Cahokia, several smaller political and administrative centers, and rural homesteads in the northern part of the floodplain, a diverse and highly organized settlement pattern (Emerson, 1997a). Cahokia's population suddenly rose five-fold a few decades after AD 1050. Hundreds of people were resettled in small and large villages, even at some distance from Cahokia. This complex process involved political negotiations, the use of force, and of carefully orchestrated integrative strategies that fostered a common interest between the center and the periphery, between chief and villager. Imposing public structures and shrines, sweat houses, common art traditions and the promotion of carefully chosen community traditions – all may have been symbols that linked elite and commoner in displays of common cultural meanings and values that helped create a regional chiefdom that combined Cahokia's authority with ancient community interests. The result was a short-lived, imposing polity that lasted a century and a half, where competing factions and periodic inabilities to mobilize community labor fashioned an inherently unstable chiefdom that appeared and dissipated with bewildering speed. After AD 1100, Cahokia's population gradually tapered off over the next century and a half, as people migrated outward from the American Bottom and a more dispersed settlement pattern again prevailed.

By this time, Cahokia was virtually deserted. But it had once been a magnificent capital. At the height of its power, between AD 1050 and 1250, Cahokia extended over an area of more than 5 sq. miles (13 sq. km) (Fowler, M., 1997; Milner, 1998; Pauketat, 1998). Some 2000 acres (800 ha) of this vast area were covered with dwellings, housing at Cahokia's peak perhaps as many as 16,000 people (Pauketat and Lopinot, 1997), although others argue for much smaller numbers. The inhabitants lived in pole-and-thatch houses clustered along a central east–west ridge. Several residences per acre was the rule, the same building site being used again and again over the generations. The dwellings vary greatly in size, perhaps a reflection of different social status. They may have been grouped in clusters, each associated with mound and plaza complexes, subdivisions of the community.

The Cahokia people erected more than 100 earthen mounds over the centuries, mounds of various sizes, shapes, and functions in an apparently carefully planned layout. Most of them cluster along the central ridge of the

Cahokia. (Right) Aerial view of Monk's Mound, the largest ancient earthwork in North America. It was built in stages from AD 1050 to 1200.

site, the driest higher ground in the vicinity. They are grouped around a series of what must have been open plazas (Holley and others, 1993). The most extensive grouping lies around Monk's Mound, the largest earthwork built by the ancient North Americans.

Monk's Mound was built on four level stages starting before AD 1000 and ending some three centuries later. The mound is 100 ft (30.4 m) high, measures 1037 by 790 ft (316 by 240 m), and covers 16 acres (6.4 ha). The builders, probably teams of villagers supervised by expert mound builders, heaped up more than 21,700,000 cu. ft (614,478 cu. m) of earth in baskets to erect this vast tumulus. The entire earthwork would have taken a theoretical 370,000 work days to complete, with additional days for contouring and finishing the mound.

The mound builders were concerned to prevent slumping and erosion from heavy rainfall. Recent excavations on the second stage following a slump caused by heavy rains show that this platform was built between about AD 1000 and 1100. An occupation surface of sandy loam covered the stage when it was in use. The underlying strata comprised basketloads of earth taken from other parts of Cahokia, much of it from occupation middens. However, the builders used sophisticated engineering methods to stabilize the growing mound, placing thousands of basketloads in a

(Below) Artist's impression of the central Cahokia mound complex in its heyday, looking across the Grand Plaza to Monk's Mound.

structural "dome" that supported the loamy covering. The architects also alternated bands of sand and clay to prevent the deposits from becoming unduly waterlogged. Excavators James Collins and Michael Chalfont (1993) believe a small group of elite mound builders with specialist expertise constructed the mound.

The third and fourth levels rose after AD 1200 on the northeast quadrant of the earthwork. Excavations in 1971 revealed a large building measuring 100 by 40 ft (30 by 12 m) on the summit of the highest terrace, with a large wooden post in front of it. This may be the remains of a thatched temple that stood on the summit of Monk's Mound. Equivalent structures may have stood on lower stages, but the archaeological evidence is inconclusive. Monk's Mound is more than twice the size of any other Cahokia earthwork, so the large building that once stood on its summit in its final stages was probably the focus of the entire ceremonial complex. A stairway once led from ground level up the south side to the first stage, and perhaps higher.

Some of the largest Cahokia mounds lie in two rows on either side of Monk's Mound with a central 47-acre (19-ha) plaza area immediately to the south. Most of these were platform mounds, flat-topped earthworks where important public buildings or elite residences of pole and thatch lay. Excavators believe that charnel houses once stood on some of the Cahokia mounds, where the dead were exposed while their flesh decayed and before their bones were interred. A large log palisade with watchtowers and gates surrounded the entire 200 acres (80.9 ha) of the central area, perhaps to isolate Monk's Mound and other ceremonial structures and high-status individuals from commoners. The defensive wall was rebuilt at least four times in a similar style to those found at other centers – the result of serious factional conflict in the region.

We do not know if the whole of Cahokia was occupied all at the same time, but it was a large, complex site during the so-called Lohmann phase (AD 1050 to 1100), when the population reached its zenith at an estimated 16,000 people after a rapid climb from a mere 1000 to 3000 people. Population dropped rapidly during the subsequent Stirling (AD 1100–1200) (7000 to 5000 people) and Moorehead (AD 1200–1275) (4500 to 3000 people) phases. Cahokia was long abandoned by the 17th century, when Europeans first penetrated the St Louis area.

During Cahokia's heyday, some individuals enjoyed higher social status, living in larger houses and being buried in great splendor. There is striking evidence for elaborate burial customs in Mound 72 at Cahokia. Melvin Fowler (1997) records a male burial laid out on a platform of 20,000 shell beads. This was an important man, for he was accompanied by three high-status men and women buried nearby. About 800 arrowheads, copper and mica sheets, and 15 polished stone disks used in a spear-throwing game lay with these skeletons, perhaps those of close relatives sacrificed at the funeral. Nearby were the bodies of four decapitated men with their heads and hands cut off. More than 50 young women aged between 18 and 23 were buried in a pit close by. Fowler suspects they were strangled to death.

Much of Cahokia's power came not only from compelling ideologies, but also from a highly centralized economy, where foodstuffs, like communal labor, were appropriated by the elite. Most of the prestigious objects manufactured at the site were made from local materials for domestic use. Few of them were exported to distant locations. Cahokia's leaders achieved dominance by appropriating everything to themselves, including ideology in what can be described as a "centrifugal process" (Earle, 1991; discussion in Pauketat, 1998). During the 13th century, this centrally controlled chiefdom fell apart. Cahokia's demise is still little understood, but was probably as much political as economic. The site is unique in offering us the beginnings of an understanding of the mechanisms of ancient political and social changes. As Tim Pauketat remarks (1998): "More than an archaeological site, Cahokia is a linch-pin in the archaeology of eastern North America." He is right.

Moundville. Cahokia was by far the largest Mississippian community, but its power declined after AD 1250 when other large towns achieved prominence. Moundville lies by the Black Warrior River in west-central Alabama and flourished between AD 1250 and 1500. The site with its 29 or more earthen mounds covers more than 185 acres (75 ha) (Steponaitis, 1983; Knight and Steponaitis, 1998a). The larger mounds delineate a

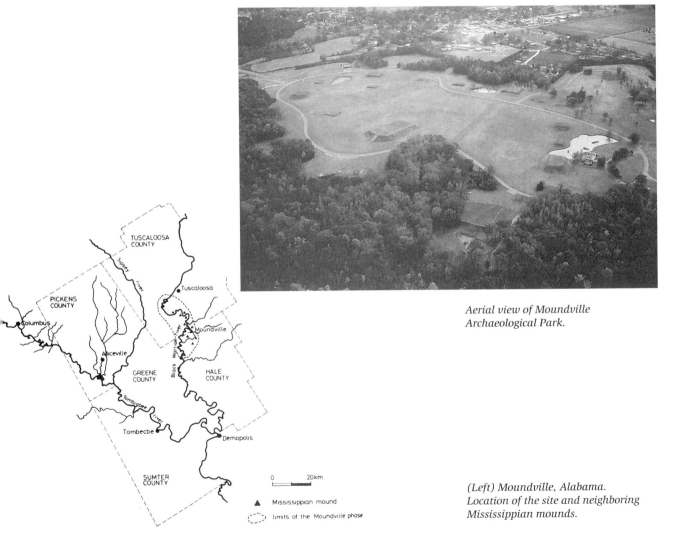

Aerial view of Moundville Archaeological Park.

(Left) Moundville, Alabama. Location of the site and neighboring Mississippian mounds.

quadrilateral plaza of about 79 acres (32 ha), some supporting public buildings or residences for important individuals, a few associated with skull caches, with a sweat house and charnel structure lying just outside the southern side of the plaza, which is oriented on the cardinal directions. Mound B is the highest, with an altitude of about 56 ft (17 m). Higher-status people lived, and were buried, east of the mounds on the eastern side of the plaza. The three sides of the site away from the river were protected by a bastioned and much rebuilt palisade during some of Moundville's history. As at Cahokia, hundreds of people lived within the general site area, perhaps as many as 1000 souls. Altogether 3051 burials have been excavated at Moundville, with the leaders being discovered in the mounds. People of lesser status were buried in the major village areas along the northern boundary of the site (Knight and Steponaitis, 1998a; Peebles, 1979).

In AD 900, a relatively small number of Woodland people lived in the Moundville area at a time of considerable political and economic unrest and increasingly circumscribed territory (Knight and Steponaitis, 1998b). This West Jefferson phase saw the local people relying on nut harvests and other wild foods, until maize production intensified between AD 950 and 1000 (Welch, 1991). They dwelt in relatively small settlements, which seem to have grown in size as a response to higher agricultural production, increased production of freshwater shell beads, and warfare. We do not know if Moundville itself was occupied during this period, but it seems unlikely.

Between AD 1050 and 1250, the Moundville I phase saw the first platform mounds and distinctive Mississippian architecture and pottery appear at the site. This was a time when maize and bean agriculture assumed increasing importance, providing as much as 40 percent of the diet. The Black Warrior Valley became an important maize farming area, as the population dispersed into smaller agricultural communities, some little more than farmsteads, some probably much larger. By Moundville I, the site had become an important ceremonial center, with at least two mounds, the only two in the valley.

In about 1250, the beginning of Moundville II, the site changed completely in character from a dispersed settlement to a compact, highly formalized and fortified town. The inhabitants laid out a quadrilateral plaza with accompanying earthworks arranged in their proper order. They imposed a symbolic landscape on the natural one. Moundville now had an east–west symmetry, a pairing of residential mounds with mortuary temple mounds, and a well-defined ranking of social spaces within the site. The palisade first rose in about 1200 and remained in use for about a century as people moved in to live inside it. By now, about 1000 people lived in compact groupings of square pole-and-mud houses, each with a floor area of about 205 sq. ft (19 sq. m). At the same time, Moundville assumed an importance beyond its own boundaries, as several second-level mound centers rose in the Black Warrior Valley. Knight and Steponaitis (1998b) call these secondary administrative centers inhabited by lesser members of the elite, who presided over both local ritual activity and tribute collection from surrounding farmsteads. By 1250, such tribute gathering was an integral part of the political economy centered on Moundville, whose leaders formed a privileged nobility, dining off special

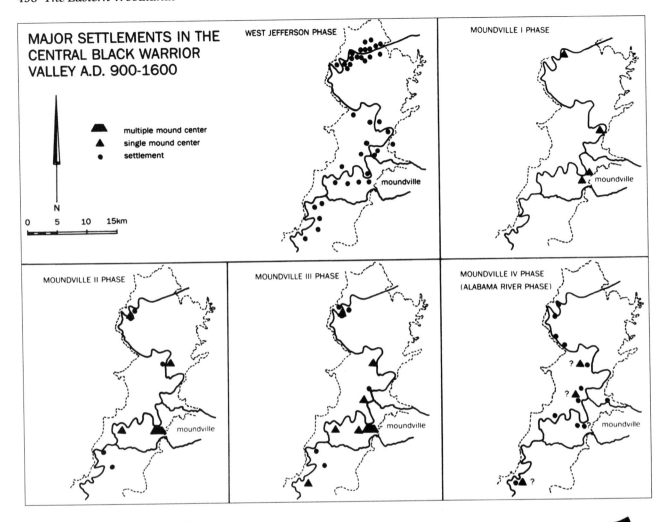

MAJOR SETTLEMENTS IN THE CENTRAL BLACK WARRIOR VALLEY A.D. 900-1600

- ▲ multiple mound center
- ▲ single mound center
- • settlement

N
0 5 10 15km

WEST JEFFERSON PHASE
moundville

MOUNDVILLE I PHASE
moundville

MOUNDVILLE II PHASE
moundville

MOUNDVILLE III PHASE
moundville

MOUNDVILLE IV PHASE
(ALABAMA RIVER PHASE)
moundville

Changing settlement patterns in the Moundville area. Moundville itself rose to dominance in Phases II and III (AD 1250–1500), before disappearing as a significant center in Phase IV (after 1550). (Right) The site at its peak, with 20 mounds built around a central plaza on the south bank of the Black Warrior River.

MOUNDVILLE III PHASE

- • burial/gravelot - moundville III
- ○ burial/gravelot - moundville III or alabama river
- ☐ mound - definite

escarpment

0 125 250 m

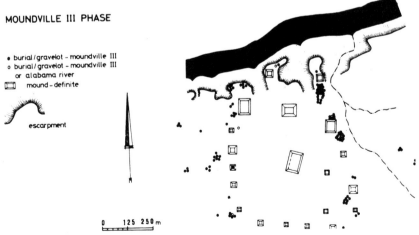

burnished pottery. Moundville had expanded from an important ceremonial center to the capital of a single kingdom ruled by a paramount chief supported by tribute and engaged in long-distance exchange. The formal layout of public architecture in the heart of the site probably reflected the status relationships of different kin groups set in the context of a sacred landscape. And the paramount chief derived his power both from his supernatural authority and the power conferred on him by the sacred landscape.

For a century and a half after 1300, Moundville was ruled by a firmly entrenched chiefly dynasty, reflected in a series of lavishly adorned burials in its burial mounds. The dynasty's increasing power isolated them both symbolically and practically from their subjects, as the population moved out of the hitherto compact town into the surrounding countryside. Only the elite and their retainers seem to have remained at the now unprotected site. No one knows why the people dispersed. It may have been as a result of administrative decision, an adjustment to soil exhaustion, or simply lessened danger of attack. Whatever the cause, Moundville now became a sparsely inhabited ceremonial center and a necropolis, with cemeteries occupying former residential areas. Many of the burials within them came from outlying communities. The elite burials, mostly in the northern part of the site, were richly adorned, despite an apparent decline in long-distance exchange, with clay vessels and other objects bearing images associated with chiefly cults (described below), many of them depicting trophy heads, weapons, scalps, and other symbols of warfare. Political power was highly centralized, drawing on tribute and labor from centers as far as nearly 45 miles (72 km) away. Steponaitis assumes that those minor centers closest to Moundville paid more tribute, simply because transport costs were lower. He calculated that a distance of about 9 miles (14.5 km) was about the maximum for large-scale tribute gathering on a regular basis without serious difficulties in transporting supplies and enforcing assessments.

(Below) Slate palette from Moundville incised with a hand-and-eye motif within two entwined horned rattlesnakes. Diameter 32 cm.

During this period (Moundville II and early Moundville III), the elite seem to have distanced themselves from the rest of the 10,000 or more people who lived under their tribute network. At the same time, the wide distribution of distinctive cult motifs on clay vessels seems to suggest that more people than ever had access to the religious symbolism of chieftain-ship. Between 1300 and 1450, the ruling elite consolidated their power at the northern end of the town, while lower-ranked social groups, allocated space at the southern side, seem to have abandoned their mounds and shrines as their rivals expanded theirs, a clear sign of dissension and trouble to come.

Moundville went into decline after 1450 (late Moundville III). The great center became a shadow of its former self. Elite burial ceased, although a nominal chief may have presided over the site. Perhaps chronic factionalism and resistance to authority among lesser leaders led to the collapse of the once rigid Mississippian hierarchical system, resulting in a patchwork of local chiefdoms, who may have shown some allegiance to a hereditary paramount still living among the mounds of his ancestors. Some people still lived at Moundville when Spanish conquistador Hernando de Soto passed through the area in 1540, but we do not know whether a still shadowy chiefdom still existed or whether it had become entirely decentralized.

At the height of their powers, Cahokia, Moundville, Etowah, Georgia (Larsen, 1971), Lake George, Winterville (Williams and Brain, 1983), and Spiro, Oklahoma (Brown, 1971), were large, complex communities, ruled by high-status individuals of great political, social, and religious influence. Steponaitis (1978) has called them "Complex Chiefdoms."

Complex Chiefdoms

The simplest chiefdoms are single-level societies, where the chief is but a part-time administrator, who still farms the land. The chief is self-sufficient. He does not live off tribute and other foodstuffs supplied by his followers. He is expected to be a generous kinsman, who redistributes most goods back to other members of society. Under these circumstances, there is a balanced flow of goods between different levels of the community, with reciprocity playing an important part in society (Steponaitis, 1978).

More complex chiefdoms have two or even three tiers of political hierarchy. Nobles are clearly distinct from commoners and do not usually engage in any form of agricultural production. Thus, the higher-status members of society consume most of the goods that are passed up the hierarchy as tribute. Reciprocal obligations are fulfilled by the nobles carrying out ritual or secular services that only they can perform. They may also make token, symbolic redistributions of food and other goods.

In two- or three-tiered chiefdoms, higher-ranking chiefs have control over a number of lesser-ranking individuals, each of whom control specific territory or a social unit. Political control rests on the chief's ability to maintain access to a sufficiently large body of tribute, passed up the line by lesser chiefs. They in turn collect from those below them, from communities close to their own center. At the apex sits the most powerful chieftain of all (Barker and Pauketat, 1992).

What were the dynamics of such polities? The debate about the evolution of chiefdoms has raged unabated for decades, with a chiefdom being defined somewhat loosely as "a centralized polity that organizes a regional population in the thousands" (Earle, 1989). Some degree of inherited social ranking and economic stratification appears to go with such chiefdoms.

The formation of any complex political organization like a chiefdom requires that a leader create ties of loyalty to his person, by controlling peoples' labor in ways that cause them not to move away. Thus social and technological changes are needed to organize large numbers of people at close quarters. So the leader has been thought of as a "manager." Thus, he was an entrepreneur who succeeded in making his position hereditary under circumstances where a variety of factors, including population growth and economic change, were creating conditions favorable to such political consolidation.

More recent research is focusing on the political processes that lead both to the creation and maintenance of chiefdoms. There are many ways of doing so. Chiefs can use naked force, make people indebted to them through feasting or by improving the distribution and availability of food supplies. They can encourage circumscription, forge external ties with neighbors, and seize control of all production and distribution of wealth.

(Right) Symbol of a hierarchical society? A warrior decapitates a victim on this Mississippian stone effigy pipe from Spiro Mound, Oklahoma. Height 25 cm. (Far right) Religion and ceremonial may have been an important means by which Mississippian chiefs asserted their authority. This cedarwood mask, perhaps worn by a shaman, has shell inlay and antlers carved in imitation of those of a deer. From Spiro Mound, Oklahoma. Height 29 cm.

They can control long-distance trade, or become masters of the forces of the supernatural (Steponaitis, quoted by Earle, 1989).

All of these strategies for seizing control depend, of course, on the willingness of the population at large to accept them. In the case of the Mississippian, increasing control of long-distance exchange, especially in exotic, prestigious goods, and the use of this wealth to control local labor may have been important catalysts for political change. There is every indication that Mississippian chiefs used the exotic, and highly valuable, objects they received from outside as symbols of their legitimacy, of their special relationship to supernatural powers that were theirs alone to control. This form of ideological governance is vulnerable to the uncontrollable forces of long-distance exchange, so stability was achieved by linking the exotic objects used in major ceremonies with ceremonial architecture, and with land ownership. Thus, the great earthworks of Cahokia, Moundville, and other centers were an albeit inherently unstable way of fostering bonds between the people and the elite, between one community and another.

There are no signs that Mississippian chiefs exercised strict economic control over commoners. It is as if local populations were "drawn into sociopolitical systems in part by 'smoke and mirrors'" (Earle, 1989). This was a religious ideology, with its distinctive cult items reflected in ceremonial objects, that was based on notions of centrality, a centrality symbolized by large ceremonial structures and by exchanges of exotic objects of great symbolic value.

Under these circumstances, Mississippian chiefdoms were fragile institutions, the end-products of a constant process of balancing economic interdependence, ideology, and force. These chiefdoms were in a constant state of flux, as centers of power changed, some chiefdoms collapsed, and others nearby rose in their place. Local and regional conditions changed frequently, fueled by the competitive political dynamics that are so characteristic of chiefdoms everywhere – societies with few high-status positions. In the long-term we face a formidable task explaining the rise of complex chiefdoms in Mississippian society. We will have to understand not only local political conditions, but the shifts in long-distance exchange networks, and ideologies over much larger areas as well.

The Mississippian was no political and social monolith, with important rulers maintaining absolute authority over vast areas of the Midwest and South. Rather, hundreds of local societies fall under the general category "Mississippian." They enjoyed an infinite variety of local subsistence patterns, which exploited a very diverse resource base, and varied greatly in their dependence on maize-and-bean agriculture. Long-distance exchange networks brought a degree of cultural continuity to the entire vast area, and there was some common religious tradition among many of them, reflected in widely used art styles and abiding ritual symbolism. The people lived under dozens of chiefdoms, many of them virtually egalitarian, others, like Cahokia, highly complex, powerful political and social units. But these complex chiefdoms still depended heavily on kin ties and notions of reciprocity to function properly. With their regular feasts and elaborate ceremonies, Mississippian chiefs validated their authority in vivid, symbolic ways, well aware that their power depended on a fine line between coercion and reciprocity and on the balance of the powerful cults that underpinned human existence over wide areas.

Mississippian Cosmos: Fertility and Duality

Thanks to the growing body of information from Cahokia, we can begin to piece together the ancient cosmology and religious beliefs behind the site. This involved combining archaeology in the American Bottom with ethnohistory derived from historic southeastern Indian groups (Emerson, 1997a; Hall, R., 1997; Pauketat and Emerson, 1997).

The layout of Cahokia and other major centers reflects a traditional southeastern cosmos with four opposed sides, reflected in the layout of their platform mounds, great mounds, and imposing plazas. By AD 1050, the rectangular plaza surrounded by mounds reenacted the ancient quadripartite pattern of the cosmos, seen in much earlier settlements along the Mississippi. As we have seen, four-sided Mississippian platform mounds may portray the cosmos as "earth-islands," just as historic Muskogean Indians of the Southeast thought of the world as flat-topped and four-sided. Archaeologist John Douglas (quoted in Pauketat and Emerson, 1997) used ethnographic and archaeological data to argue that the four-sided cosmos had a primary axis that ran northwest to southeast, with an opposite axis dividing the world into four diamond-shaped quarters. Cahokia is oriented along a slightly different north–south axis, but it certainly perpetuates the notion of spiritual links between opposites and a cosmos divided into quarters. Researchers believe that the orientation reflects observations of the sun rather than the moon and that Cahokia's rulers used the sun to schedule the annual rituals that commemorated the cycles of the agricultural year.

As we saw with the Hopewell, Southeastern cosmology revolved around dualities. In the case of Cahokia, these included the upper- and underworld, and a powerful and pervasive fertility cult linked to commoners and a warrior cult associated with the nobility (Emerson, 1997a and b). These dualities were carried through to the smallest ritual centers. Changing settlement layouts imply that, at first, local communities and kin groups controlled fertility rituals in villages divided into symbolic quarters, with ceremonial structures facing a central square. Later centers displayed more formal layouts, with central plazas, elaborate sacred buildings, and storage and ritual pits filled with pots and other ritual offerings made during fertility and world-renewal ceremonies. By this time, Emerson and others believe, power was passing from local kin leaders to a powerful elite based at Cahokia, a shift reflected in increasingly elaborate ceremonial architecture, residences for local nobles at local centers, and mortuary complexes controlled by full-time priests.

During the heyday of Cahokia, after AD 1050, some centers possessed temple structures, sacred fire enclosures, ceremonial courtyards, and grave houses and burial areas where the bodies of the dead from select lineage

The belief systems of the later peoples of the Southeast were closely tied to local political and social organization. The people depicted complex symbols on clay vessels, stone, copper, and shell objects. The meanings of many of these symbols elude us, but they include "weeping eyes," birds, serpents, skulls, and hands, motifs that may be associated with ancestor rituals. As in many agricultural societies around the world, these ancestral ties reaffirmed social status. Serpents were also associated with the fertility of crops and the soil. (Below) Shell head with weeping eye and other facial decoration, height 6 cm. (Right) Weeping eyes appear on this pottery human effigy vessel.

groups were processed. Thomas Emerson (1997a) believes that such centers had close links with local kin groups, as well as political and religious leaders related to nobility at Cahokia itself. Their carefully laid out centers brought two central ritual themes together: the spiritual realm of fertility and life, and the validation of living rulers, who were intermediaries with the supernatural realm.

Mississippian religious beliefs are still elusive, but distinctive artifacts yield a few clues. Emerson (1997a) investigated a small rural shrine at the so-called BBB Motor site near the great center, and carried out additional excavations at a larger rural ceremonial complex called the Sponemann site nearby. Both shrine excavations produced Cahokia ritual artifacts and paraphernalia, especially a series of Cahokia-style figurines fabricated from soft red stone, found in an undisturbed archaeological context. One figure shows a woman kneeling or squatting on a circular base, with a square pack on her back. Her head rests on the head of a feline-headed serpent and her right hand holds a hoe that is stroking or tilling the serpent's back. The serpent's back bifurcates on the woman's left side and changes into gourds growing on vines, which entangle the woman's body.

A second figure also depicts a woman with sloping forehead kneeling on a rectangular base formed of corn ears or reed bundles woven into a mat. She wears a skirt, her long hair hanging down her back. A rectangular basket lies in front of her. A now-broken maize stalk emerges from the base and passes through the woman's hand, sweeping back to an attachment above her ear. Emerson and others believe that the woman is an Earth Mother figure, historically depicted wearing a short skirt, and associated with the serpent monster and with the giving of plants to humankind. On her back she carries a sacred bundle, another gift to humanity. Ethnographic sources hint that the Earth Mother assumed many forms: goddess of death, and an Old Woman, to mention only two.

The feline-headed serpent motif occurs widely on Mississippian and later artifacts. In fact, the serpent monster theme was widespread in historic Southeastern rituals, and has considerable antiquity. Serpents appear in temples and other public structures, as tattoos, and in dance themes. They possessed the attributes of several animals, and symbolized water monsters and other mythical beasts. Serpents were underworld creatures, associated with lightning, thunder, rain, water, and power over plants and other animals. The underworld was the source of water, fertility, and power against evil.

If this perspective is correct, then Cahokia and other Mississippian centers reflect an ancient cosmology in a symbolic language intelligible to noble and commoner alike. Sacred artifacts, structures, and rural centers linked outlying villages and the rural population to Cahokia, thereby integrating society with pervasive concepts and rituals of fertility and cosmos reflected in harvest and other ceremonies. Pauketat and Emerson (1997) call these rituals "rites of intensification"; they played a vital role in linking commoner and elite.

The religious beliefs behind Mississippian society had their ancestry in far earlier tradition and ritual intimately connected with the symbolic world of millennia of earlier human experience.

(Above) The "weeping-eye" motif appears on this embossed Mississippian copper face. (Top right) Shell disk with symbolic crested woodpeckers, from Sumner County, Tennessee. Diameter 8.5 cm. (Bottom right) Shell gorget depicting a flying shaman with a death's head in one hand and a ceremonial mace in the other. Diameter 10 cm.

The ideas and ideologies known generically as "Mississippian" diffused over an enormous area of the South, Midwest and eastern Plains. Caddoan-speaking peoples at Spiro, Oklahoma, formed one major center of Mississippian culture, trading with groups living up the Missouri River and out onto the Plains. Mississippian artifacts and ideas had spread far upstream into the Upper Mississippi Valley by at least AD 1100.

Mississippian ceramics. Late Mississippian goose effigy bowl (right) and human head effigy jar (below) found at Shawnee Village site, Arkansas. (Below right) 'Big Boy' pipe from Spiro site, Oklahoma.

Here local Late Woodland societies, celebrated for their Effigy Mounds, which depicted animals and other symbols, melded their own cultural traditions with new Mississippian traits to form the Oneota Complex, distributed over a wide area from northern Illinois and Wisconsin into southwestern Minnesota and Iowa, then across to the middle Missouri Valley (Henning, 1998). Oneota sites vary greatly in size, from a few wigwam-like dwellings to large fortified villages of sub-rectangular or oval houses. Like other Midwestern groups of the day, Oneota communities interacted not only with their neighbors, but with much more distant locations. Clay vessels with obvious Oneota associations come from sites as far away as Michigan and the central Mississippian Valley, also in Middle Missouri villages. The Oneota Complex can be associated with the ancestors of several historic groups, among them the Chiwere-speaking Sioux and the Winnebago of Wisconsin.

Natchez, Coosa, and the 16th Century

By the time European traders and explorers reached the Mississippi Valley, Cahokia was long past its apogee. The great center had reached the zenith of its political and economic power by AD 1250. New construction ceased in the 14th century and the site was abandoned by 1500. Moundville was also past its apogee, but still an important center. Nevertheless, numerous chiefdoms existed in the Mid-South and Southeast right up to European contact, and beyond. Some of them, like Moundville and Natchez, are quite well known through archaeological investigations (Hudson and others, 1985). Etowah, an important center in Georgia, was the hub of an important chiefdom before the 16th century (Larsen, 1971). Still others, like the little-known chiefdom of Coosa, are being reconstructed by combining archaeological data and early historical records.

Natchez. The Natchez chiefdom on the Lower Mississippi is especially well known, both from archaeological investigations and from observations by French explorers. The Natchez may have descended from an ancient cultural tradition known as the Plaquemine that brought elements of Cahokia culture into the local Coles Creek culture in about AD 1150 (Fiedel, 1993). They were still building earthen mounds in the 17th century, when French explorers first visited them. Decimated by European diseases, they numbered some 3500 people in 1700. They lived in at least six districts (earlier nine), each controlled by local chiefs. The entire tribe was ruled by the Great Sun, a paramount chief, and his younger brother, Tattooed Serpent, who was war chief. The Great Sun and Tattooed Serpent lived in the political capital, the "Grand Village" as the French rather grandiloquently called it, a scatter of about nine houses and a temple built on the summit of an earthen mound. Most Natchez families lived in small hamlets dispersed over the countryside (Swanton, 1911).

Every month, the Great Sun received tribute from his own people and local chiefs at regular feasts. "These feasts are normally undertaken when the great chief has a need of some provisions ... which they place at the door of his cabin in a heap the last day of the feast," wrote a French observer. Another remarked that the feasts were to thank the chief "for the benefits he has sent men."

In the year 1720, French explorer Le Page du Pratz (1758) spent some time living among the Natchez. He found himself in a rigidly stratified society, headed by a chieftain also known as the Great Sun. His relatives were known as Suns, and served as important officials. Under them were Nobles (Honored Men) and commoners, known to the elite as "Stinkards." The Great Sun was a despot with absolute power. Only a few chosen priests and the Great Sun could enter the temple where a sacred fire burned day and night. But the Great Sun and all members of the elite had to marry commoners. The only other way a Stinkard could achieve Honored rank was through prowess in warfare. When the Great Sun died, his wives, relatives, and servants accompanied him in death. Natchez society was apparently a complex, tiered chiefdom.

Coosa. Hernando de Soto and his conquistadors traversed the Southeast in 1539-41, and recorded sketchy impressions of the chiefdoms they encountered. They were impressed with the wealth of Cofitachequi, but

The French explorer Le Page du Pratz witnessed the funerary rites of the Natchez Chief Tattooed Serpent in 1720, a rare firsthand account of Mississippian ritual. The dead man was carried on a litter to his temple, high on an earthen mound. There he was buried with his wife and retainers, who had been strangled beforehand.

Mort et Convoi du Serpent piqué

Temple.

found more food in Coosa, a powerful chiefdom based on what is now known as the Little Egypt site near Carters, Georgia (Hudson, C., and others, 1985; Milanich and Milbrath, 1989). Little Egypt boasts three mounds and was occupied from *c.*1400 to 1600. Its deposits contained pottery types associated with the Lamar culture, and with the Mississippian Dallas and Mouse Creek phases. Historical accounts describe Coosa not as a town but as a series of communities separated by fertile gardens. After leaving Coosa, de Soto and his men marched for two days in the rain, to another large settlement named Itaba, thought to be the Etowah site. There is a Lamar component at Etowah and European artifacts have been found there. By careful correlation of historical records and archaeological sites, Charles Hudson and his colleagues have been able to establish the broad outlines of Coosa, and have associated the three subdivisions of the chiefdom with different archaeological phases identified by pottery styles and other artifacts.

There is clearly a considerable potential for identifying specific, archaeologically identified cultures and chiefdoms with documented polities in early Spanish records. It should also be possible to trace connections between ancient chiefdoms and their much-altered 18th- and 19th-century descendants. We will return to Coosa and other 16th-century chiefdoms when we examine the impact of European contact on the interior Southeast in Chapter 22.

Further Reading

In addition to earlier references:

Emerson, Thomas. 1997a. *Cahokia and the Ideology of Power*. University of Alabama Press, Tuscaloosa.
A fascinating book on Cahokia and its political and religious institutions.

Hall, Robert L. 1997. *An Archaeology of Soul: North American Indian Belief and Ritual*. University of Illinois Press, Urbana.
An excellent summary for general readers.

Knight, Vernon James, and Vincas P. Steponaitis (eds.) 1998a. *Archaeology of the Moundville Chiefdom*. Smithsonian Institution Press, Washington DC.
Essays on various aspects of Moundville and its hinterland.

Milner, George R. 1998. *The Cahokia Chiefdom*. Smithsonian Institution Press.
Milner has written an excellent introduction to this all-important Mississippian center.

Milanich, Jerald, Cordell, Ann S., Knight, Vernon J., Kohler, Timothy A. and Sigler-Lavelle, Brenda J. 1997. *Archaeology of Northern Florida, A.D. 200–900: The McKeithen Weeden Island Culture*. University Press of Florida, Gainesville.
A comprehensive analysis of the Weeden Island culture, which is fundamental to understanding Mississippian origins.

Pauketat, Thomas R. and Emerson, Thomas E. (eds.) 1997. *Cahokia: Domination and Ideology in the Mississippian World* . Nebraska: University of Nebraska Press, Lincoln.
Provocative essays on the meaning of Cahokia, which represent state-of-the-art research in the area.

Schnell, Frank T., Knight, Vernon J. Jr, and Schnell, Gail S. 1981. *Chemochobee: Archaeology of a Mississippian Ceremonial Center on the Chattahoochee River*. University Press of Florida, Gainesville.
This site report is remarkable for its description of a Mississippian ceremonial center and accompanying moundbuilding.

Steponaitis, Vincas P. 1983. *Ceramics, Chronology, and Community Patterns*. Academic Press, New York.
A study of Moundville ceramics that ranges widely over the development of this important site.

CHAPTER 21

ALGONQUIANS AND IROQUOIANS

"Their food is whatever they can get from the chase and from fishing; for they do not till the soil at all ... In the month of February and until the middle of March, is the great hunt for beavers, otters, moose, bears ... and for the caribou, an animal half ass and half deer. If the weather then is favorable, they live in great abundance, and are as haughty as Princes and Kings; but if it is against them, they are greatly to be pitied, and often die of starvation ..." (Pierre Biard, 1616, quoted by Snow, 1980).

"When we went further inland we saw their houses, which are circular in shape, about fourteen to fifteen paces across, made of bent saplings ..." (Giovanni da Verrazzano, 1524, quoted by Snow, 1980).

"Their food is generally boiled maize, or Indian corn, mixed with kidney-beans, or sometimes without. Also they frequently boil in this potage fish and flesh of all sorts, either new taken or dried, as shads, eels, alewives or a kind of herring, or any other sort of fish. Also they mix with the said potage several sorts of roots ... also several sets of nuts or masts ..." (Daniel Gookin, 1674, quoted by Snow, 1980).

Seventeenth-century sailors' accounts of coastal Indians of the Northeast are a palimpsest of impressions, accurate and inaccurate, tantalizing and confusing. By this time, coastal peoples in the Northeast had been in contact with Europeans for some time, sporadically trading beaver furs with occasional coasting ships – to the point that the Pilgrims were greeted at Plimoth Rock by an Indian named Samoset, who said, "Welcome Englishmen!" (For a detailed account of Northeastern societies at contact, see Snow, 1980.) The annual round of summer fishing and foraging in the Northeast, of winter caribou and moose hunting and forest trapping, still flourished as it had for thousands of years, ever since Archaic times. We must now unravel the complicated ancestry of these Northeastern societies, deep in the past. To do so, we must retrace our steps back into the Late Archaic and examine the primeval cultures of the region.

Algonquians and Iroquoians

People living in coastal drainages between Nova Scotia and North Carolina were Algonquian speakers. They are grouped into the Eastern Algonquian language group, isolated from their western and northern relatives by an intrusive block of Iroquoian and other languages in the interior.

The ultimate origins of Algonquian are still a mystery, but a form of this language probably goes back far into the past, to a time when ancient cultures in the Eastern Woodlands were more widespread and generalized than they were in later times. Both Algonquian and Gulf languages from the Southeast may, perhaps, be descended from a common group of related dialects once spoken throughout the Eastern Woodlands before 4000 to 3000 BC.

The Northern Iroquoian languages form the most important barrier between the coastal Algonquian speakers and those to the west. They form an insulating block between coast and far interior all the way from central Pennsylvania through New York State and down the St Lawrence Valley to the Gulf of St Lawrence in Canada. Every linguistic expert agrees that the Iroquoian language distribution represents an ancient intrusion of a different linguistic group into the Northeast, a group later associated with the powerful Iroquois confederacies that dominated a vast region between the St Lawrence and into New York at European contact. How, then, did Iroquoian-speaking peoples come to be living in the lower Great Lakes region with Algonquians around them, in territory that was once Algonquian? Fierce warriors, shrewd traders, and very sophisticated negotiators, the Iroquois were to play a dominant role in the Northeast to the very end of the Colonial period and beyond.

A central question in Northeastern archaeology is to establish when Iroquoian speakers first spread into their present homelands, and to identify them in the archaeological record (Snow, 1995). To do this requires examining Late Archaic cultures in the Northeast, for the roots of Iroquois culture probably lie deep in the past.

Terminal Archaic
1650 to 700 BC

Throughout the Eastern Woodlands, rivers large and small were arteries that flowed through the centers of Archaic territories. They provided not only aquatic resources and sustenance for the animal and plant populations on their banks, but vital communication arteries between widely scattered hunter-gatherer populations. The higher ground between the river valleys served as boundary land, sometimes remote, sometimes traversed by narrow trails, often serving as little more than a place where neighbors might hunt and collect wild vegetable foods. In the Archaic Northeast, one can think of these higher lands as buffers between different population concentrations. And these population concentrations were controlled in large part by the carrying capacity of the land during the leanest months of the year.

For thousands of years, ancient populations in the Northeast were nearly stable, at levels below the carrying capacity of the land. Population growth was slow. Dean Snow (1980) has estimated that no more than 25,000 people lived in New England before 8000 BC, and only between 158,000 and 191,000 in AD 1600. He calculates an average growth rate of 0.02 percent over these 9600 years, with occasional periods of rapid increase and sometimes catastrophic decline. In contrast the world population increase rate has been as high as 1.8 percent in recent years. This primeval population spacing lasted for thousands of years, only beginning to break down during the last six centuries before European colonization. By this time, the introduction of new storage technologies and of horticulture had allowed higher population densities in many parts of the Northeast.

After 1650 BC, the Archaic communities of the Northeast enjoyed a diverse, and carefully scheduled, hunting-and-gathering lifeway. This "Terminal Archaic" spanned 10 centuries, until about 700 BC, a period marked by long-distance trading of chert, soapstone, and other stone materials, and by the widespread use of carved soapstone bowls, also broad and narrow "fishtail" stone projectile points (Turnbaugh, 1975a). Many local cultural traditions flourished during this period (for full discussion, see Snow, 1980).

Orient fish-tailed point, length c. 11 cm.

Susquehanna and Orient Traditions. The so-called Susquehanna tradition of New York, Pennsylvania, and neighboring areas flourished during the earlier centuries of the Terminal Archaic (*c.* 1650–1320 BC), a widespread tradition marked by a variety of broad projectile points that may also have doubled as knives. The Susquehanna is more of a tradition of point manufacture than an actual cultural complex.

The Orient tradition replaced the Susquehanna in the New York region and is characterized by long, narrow points with fishtail-shaped bases that persisted in use during later Woodland cultures as well. Oval and rectangular soapstone bowls with flat bottoms and lug handles that appear to have been copies of wooden prototypes came into widespread use, especially in larger base camps, artifacts also used by Susquehanna people. These heavy cooking vessels were apparently highly prized, traded widely, and enjoyed long lives. The use of these stone vessels foreshadowed pottery manufacture after 700 BC.

Susquehanna and Orient flourished alongside Mast Forest and Lake Forest Archaic societies in many areas, with much human settlement concentrated near rivers and coasts. The millennia-old traditions of cremation continued. There were some population movements from New York and southern New England into more northern areas. These population movements and the population growth that may have attended them are still little understood. William Turnbaugh among others (1975b) has invoked a general warming trend and the stabilization of sea levels as possible factors favoring the expansion of Terminal Archaic cultures.

There is strong evidence for general cultural continuity in economic and social life over much of the Northeast from early in Archaic times, if not earlier (Trigger, 1985). Until after AD 800, we have insufficient evidence to argue that there was continuity in native populations as well.

Woodland Societies in the Northeast
c. 700 BC to AD 1000

Dean Snow has coined the term "Early Horticultural" to cover the 1700 years of the past immediately following the Terminal Archaic in the Northeast. He argues for the use of this term on the grounds that Early and Middle Woodland are very hard to define. We use it here both for simplicity's sake and also because it highlights the most important cultural innovation during this period – horticulture.

Pottery-making appeared in many Northeastern horticultural societies in the late 1st millennium BC, but the moment of appearance varied greatly. The overall population of the Northeast may have increased, as well as the number of small bands scattered in territories of widely differing size in river drainages, near lakes, and along sea coasts. The increasing use of pottery may signal a trend toward more sedentary lifestyles over the centuries. Small cooking pots with pointed bases, decorated with stamped and cord-marked patterns and manufactured with simple coiling techniques, were in common use throughout the Great Lakes region by about 500 BC. Further south, in New York State, the Meadowood phase provides strong hints of cultural influences from both earlier and contemporary cultural traditions.

Meadowood Phase (?c. 700 BC to ?300 BC). Meadowood sites occur throughout west and central New York State and into the Mohawk drainage to the east. The many Meadowood communities were probably anchored by larger base camps, some of them, perhaps, semi-permanent settlements close to places where native grasses were abundant. The resulting seed caches helped tide the people over the lean months.

There are strong indications that the Adena, and later, Hopewell trade networks extended into parts of the Northeast and into Meadowood country. The Meadowood people fabricated their characteristic points and blade blanks from Western Onondaga chert, also clay imitations of Adena tubular stone pipes. Copper ornaments, slate gorgets, birdstones, and boatstones from Ohio – these and many other grave goods hint at Adena cultural influence that went far beyond simple trade and exchange.

Meadowood cemeteries often cluster on low, natural hills, just like Glacial Kame burials in earlier centuries. The graves were closely packed together, the bodies usually cremated, but not always immediately after death. The mourners lined the burial pits with bark, laying out the cremated remains in red ocher-sprinkled shrouds. Projectile points and luxury items were usually buried with the dead, some of them obtained through trade networks that extended far into the Midwest.

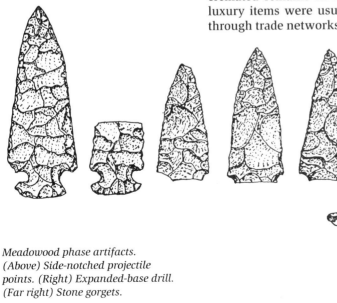

Meadowood phase artifacts. (Above) Side-notched projectile points. (Right) Expanded-base drill. (Far right) Stone gorgets.

In time, these exchange activities brought Adena mortuary practices from their Ohio homeland to the Northeast, reflected in later burial mounds containing Adena-style log-lined graves and characteristic artifacts such as tubular pipes, birdstones, and boatstones. Such tumuli are scattered across southern Ontario, in New Brunswick, New York, and parts of southern and western New England, also in the Delaware drainage. Gary Wright has argued that a widely adopted ideological system sustained later Hopewell exchange networks in the Midwest and far afield. The same may also be true of the Adena mortuary complex, which lasted in parts of the Northeast from the mid-1st millennium BC for seven centuries (Snow, 1980).

By AD 600, a great variety of early horticultural societies developed throughout the Northeast (Snow, 1980). Many of these societies were contemporary with the Hopewell tradition of the Midwest, but Hopewell exchange networks never penetrated far into New England.

In southern New England, the basic adaptation had primeval roots in the Mast Forest Late Archaic of earlier millennia, but there is increasing regional variation after 700 BC. In some areas, winter hunting camps lay close to small streams and ponds in the back country. Shellfish collecting was important near the coast. During the Terminal Archaic, ocean temperatures were warmer than today, so the people exploited bay scallops, oysters, and quahogs, shellfish that are sensitive to cold water. In contrast, early horticultural societies lived by colder seas and relied more heavily on the soft clam (*Mya arenaria*) in some areas.

Maine and northern New England societies were using pottery some time before the Christian era, considerably later than peoples to the south. They never became cultivators, remaining hunters, foragers, and shellfish collectors. Some of the coastal populations lived in substantial, semi-subterranean pit dwellings. These oval-shaped houses were between 11.4 and 13.1 ft (3.5 to 4 m) long, with a sunken hearth near the entrance and elevated sleeping benches along the walls. Apparently, they were conical wigwam or tipi-like structures excavated partially below ground level for additional warmth and insulation (Sanger, 1979). Judging from animal bones, many coastal aboriginal peoples dwelt in pithouse communities for fall, winter, and spring, perhaps moving inland during the summer to take salmon, alewife, shad, and eels from streams and lakes.

The same basic lifeway persisted among a great diversity of Northeast coastal populations in the coastal Northeast up to and beyond European contact in the 16th and 17th centuries AD.

Northern Iroquoian Origins

The origins of the northern Iroquoians ranks as one of the major controversies of North American archaeology. We can but summarize the major hypotheses here (summary in Snow, 1995).

Migration and in-situ development. Early anthropologists first became interested in the origins of the Iroquois speakers of the St Lawrence lowlands. There were no archaeological data on the early Iroquois, so they relied on oral traditions and linguistic connections for tracing their origins (for a history of research, see Trigger, 1985). Originally, they believed the

St Lawrence Valley was the homeland of all Iroquoian-speaking people, but these and related theories were abandoned about three-quarters-of-a-century ago, with the discovery of archaeological sites quite different from those of historical Iroquois groups.

At the same time, linguists found close ties between Iroquoian and Cherokee, the language spoken in the southern Appalachian region of the southeastern United States. This led to an influential theory that had the Iroquois arriving in their northern homeland from the south (Parker, 1916). This hypothesis persisted for generations, despite the discovery of early Iroquois societies with strong Algonquian features, partly because scholars of the day assumed native American cultures were static and immutable. Any changes in local society were modifications resulting from contact between invading Iroquois and indigenous Algonquian cultures. Today, the intellectual pendulum has swung far in the opposite direction, with an assumption of constant change in the past, so much so that many researchers are reluctant to use such historical terms as "Mohawk" or "Seneca" to describe local groups in the region as late as AD 1500.

In the late 1930s archaeologists began to speculate that Iroquoian culture might have developed among a population already living in the Northeast, for no ancestral version of Iroquois culture was known from the Southeast, nor were there any signs of their northward migration in the Ohio Valley. Richard MacNeish formally rejected the migration theory in a classic monograph published in 1952. He examined historical Iroquois pottery and traced its origins far back into ancient times, to the local Middle Woodland societies that archaeologists had hitherto assumed to be those of Algonquian speakers. MacNeish stressed local lines of development, an approach that has led to complex studies of evolving Iroquois settlement patterns, changing subsistence strategies, and burial practices (Trigger, 1985).

Almost total excavations of the Draper and Nodwell Iroquois settlements in Ontario have documented the remarkable diversity of Iroquois culture, changing subsistence patterns, and social organization (Wright, J., 1974; Finlayson, 1985; Warrick, 1984). For a generation or more, most Northeastern archaeologists have assumed that Iroquois-speaking cultures have local roots deep in ancient times – the problem is to identify them in the archaeological record.

Language. Linguistic research has come a long way since the pioneer days of the late 19th century. In recent years, both Cherokee and Iroquoian languages have been subjected to intense scrutiny, and are assumed to have separated from one another between 2000 and 1500 BC, during the Archaic (Lounsbury, 1978). The same authority believes that Iroquoian speakers lived for a long time in central New York, north-central Pennsylvania, and perhaps northeastern Ohio. Then some groups spread south, and others to the immediate north and west. However, the research of recent years places serious doubt on linkages between archaeological cultures and language groups in even the relatively recent past (Fiedel, 1987).

Complex lexical studies of Iroquoian have isolated a whole series of clues that place these languages in an environmental setting very similar to that of the northeastern Eastern Woodlands today, while skeletons from as early as Middle Woodland times are said to display anatomical features very similar to those of historic populations (Molto, 1983). Earlier migration theories thought of the Iroquois as relative latecomers, possessing a very different, horticultural culture quite unlike that of the indigenous Algonquian hunter-gatherers (Parker, 1916).

Culture History
1000 BC to AD 1100

Thanks to MacNeish's pioneer work, most archaeologists assume that Iroquoian-speaking people have lived around the lower Great Lakes for a long time. James Tuck (1977), James Wright (1984), and others believe the Iroquoians go back to Archaic times, and had their ultimate origins among societies which flourished before 2000 BC. Others argue that the arrival of the Iroquoians coincides with the earliest appearance of the Late Archaic Lamoka culture in New York State, in at least 2500 BC, a culture, which, as we have seen, has ties in common with Archaic cultures in the Southeast (Haviland and Power, 1981) (Chapter 17).

One popular candidate for primordial Iroquoian ancestry is the Point Peninsula culture of southern Ontario and New York.

Point Peninsula. At least three broadly contemporary Early/Middle Woodland cultures flourished in the St Lawrence lowlands during the 1st millennium AD, defined by differing artifact and pottery styles (summary in Snow, 1995). Each of these cultures was the work of several neighboring bands. They interacted with one another, but it is not clear just how ethnically distinct they were. The Laurel culture flourished in northern Ontario, parts of Manitoba, Michigan, and Minnesota (Wright, J., 1967), the Saugeen in southwestern Ontario (Ellis and Ferris, 1990). The best known is the Point Peninsula culture of central and eastern southern Ontario, with variants in southern Quebec and upper New York State, which dates from at least AD 600–700. All are variations on the same adaptive theme.

There was a general continuity in subsistence and social life in the St Lawrence lowlands from as early as Paleo-Indian times right up to the historic era. Point Peninsula and other Early/Middle Woodland cultures reflect this continuity, with a small, and widely scattered, indigenous population living in small bands, each with their own territory. The people were exploiting game, aquatic, and plant resources ever more efficiently, and some groups may even have been cultivating native plants. (The earliest record of maize is in about the 7th century AD (Crawford and others, 1997a).

During spring and summer, these small groups would congregate into larger concentrations of between 100 and 300 people at river- and lake-side fishing stations. These were the times when important burial ceremonies took place in cemeteries close to the fishing camps, when marriages were held, ceremonies enjoyed, exotic artifacts and raw materials exchanged. At Rice Lake in southern Ontario, important leaders were buried under earthen mounds with Hopewellian artifacts, probably obtained from Hopewell exchange networks for silver nuggets brought to the lake from northern Ontario (Spence, 1982).

This annual pattern of establishing friendly ties with neighbors was adaptive, in that it ensured that hunting, fishing, and foraging were not disrupted by warfare. It also made it possible for people to shift from one band to another as populations rose and fell, but it is uncertain whether men or women remained with their home bands upon marriage (Trigger, 1985). The climate was so harsh that there was never a sufficiency of food resources in one area to allow year-round, sedentary settlement. So the congregated bands had to scatter into small family groups during the long winter months to hunt forest game.

In the historical period Algonquians of central Ontario also enjoyed such an annual coming together. There were chiefs among them, often hereditary leaders from certain families, who were without formal political power, yet able to resolve conflicts during the summer months when tiny bands became a concentrated population of more than 100 people (Cleland, 1982). Perhaps the Middle Woodland peoples of southern Ontario had similar chiefs, the antecedents of the peace chiefs who were to emerge among later Iroquois groups (Trigger, 1985).

If Point Peninsula is the ancestor of later Iroquoian traditions, then it developed into at least four later cultures: Princess Point, Glen Meyer, and Pickering in Ontario, and Oswaco in New York.

Ontario: Princess Point and Glen Meyer. Canadian archaeologist James Wright (1966) established a sequence for later cultures in southern Ontario, dividing the Ontario Iroquoian tradition into three periods. His Early Iroquoian spans AD 900 to 1275, the Middle AD 1275 to 1400, with the Late Iroquoian (AD 1400 to 1650) covering the emergence and dispersal of historically known Iroquoian nations in Ontario (Snow, 1995).

Wright's Early Iroquoian includes the Princess Point and a pair of later cultures: Glen Meyer and Pickering (Stothers, 1977; Williamson, R.F., 1990). The dating of these three cultures is still uncertain, but some Princess Point sites date to some time after AD 650, Glen Meyer and Pickering appearing by AD 900 and flourishing contemporaneously.

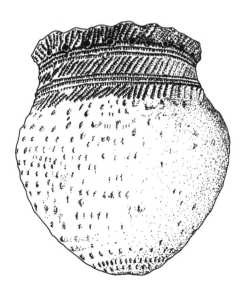

Typical Princess Point cord-decorated pot.

Many Princess Point settlements were located on river flats, by sheltered inlets or tributary streams. We still know little of Princess Point settlements, but they were relatively large and compact, similar in some ways to later Northern Iroquoian villages without the longhouses. Excavations at the Grand Banks and Lone Pine sites southwest of Lake Ontario have yielded maize fragments AMS-dated to between about AD 650 and 1000 [cal] (Crawford and others, 1997a). Initially, the new crop may have served as a valuable supplemental food to wild plants or dried fish, for the stored grain could help reduce the risk of starvation during the harsh winter months. Furthermore, maize could be planted in areas near summer fishing camps where nut trees did not grow, and wild rice never flourished. Thus, it added a new, reliable dimension to northern diet.

Princess Point is often assumed to be the ancestor of both Glen Meyer and Pickering, which are well established as branches of the early Ontario Iroquois tradition (Wright, J. and Fecteau, 1987).

New York: Owasco. To the south, in the Mohawk drainage and Finger Lakes region of upper New York State, the Late Woodland Owasco tradition emerged from earlier local cultures at about AD 900 or earlier, a very similar culture of small, loosely related communities of Northern Iroquois people. But already there were signs of considerable cultural diversification and of more nucleated settlements. For example, the Maxon-Derby site near

Maxon-Derby site, New York State: eastern end of House C, with wooden markers indicating outlines of the structure.

Syracuse, NY, lies on the terrace of a large stream and covers about 2.4 acres (1 ha) (Ritchie and Funk, 1973). Seven houses were excavated, one of them almost square, others more elongated, one an oblong dwelling measuring 26 by 59 ft (8 by 18 m). House design was far from standardized, but evolving toward the well-known Iroquois longhouse design that was used everywhere in later centuries.

Early Owasco summer settlements were used for many months, but by AD 1200 earthworks and palisades protect some villages, such as the Sackett site near Canandaigua. There the ditch and palisade enclose an elliptical area 203 by 242 ft (62 by 74 m) (Ritchie and Funk, 1973). By 1250 most major villages were palisaded, and maize, beans, and squash cultivation had assumed major importance in the subsistence economy. It is interesting to find a much higher incidence of tooth decay among Owasco populations at about this time, perhaps as a result of a higher carbohydrate content in the diet.

The fortified villages and increasing importance of overland trails coincide with the emergence of warfare as an important element in Iroquois life. Owasco cemeteries have yielded skeletons riddled with arrow points, while scattered human bones have come from village middens. No longer were the dead buried under mounds. Most people were deposited in cemeteries, fully clothed with few, if any, grave goods, for a trend toward less elaborate burial ceremonies had begun centuries earlier.

As Snow points out (1995), there are striking differences between the distribution of Owasco settlements and those of the earlier Point Peninsula culture.

In-Situ or From Outside? While admitting that prevailing opinion favors an in-situ development, Dean Snow (1995) casts doubt on this long-held belief, calling it "an almost universally controlling model." He argues that Northern Iroquoian groups migrated into their homeland, replacing not only Point Peninsula, but Princess Point societies. A relatively small, homogeneous group of Proto-Northern Iroquoian speakers occupied a homeland in central Pennsylvania, then spread northward at a time of warmer temperatures during the Medieval Warm Period, about AD 900. (This is, however, almost impossible to detect in pollen records (Crawford and others, 1997b).) Snow associates this small group with the Clemson's Island culture of central Pennsylvania that flourished after about AD 775 (see also Hart and Sidell, 1996). The newcomers displaced Algonquian-speaking groups in New York State and south-central Ontario, as separate Northern Iroquoian languages began to develop. Snow points out that the Iroquoians were matrilocal, with descent passing down the female line. These features, marked by distinctive longhouses, agriculture, and palisaded villages, appeared suddenly after about AD 1000. He cites arguments that matrilocal societies develop from patrilocal ones only under conditions of aggressive and hostile expansion. Under this scenario, earlier cultures like Princess Point would have been small, patrilineal, non-village societies. In archaeological terms, Snow argues for a sharp contrast between Point Peninsula and later pottery styles and technology, and in the different settlement patterns between the widely scattered Point Peninsula and the much more compact later cultures. He argues that the Northern Iroquoians derived from a culture in Pennsylvania that was also ancestral to the maize-farming Owasco culture, with its compact villages associated with burial mounds.

Snow's migration hypothesis has been undermined by the discovery of well-dated maize in Princess Point sites, already described, well before the date of his hypothetical migration. In a discussion of the migration theory, Crawford and Smith (1996) also observe that there appears to be continuity in settlement patterns between Princess Point and Glen Meyer. They also challenge Snow's claim of differences in pottery technology as well. They argue that his ancestral Pennsylvania group was but one of many societies, like Princess Point, undergoing major cultural change at the time. In a response to Crawford and Smith, Snow (1996a) now proposes that the frontier between Iroquoian and pre-Iroquoian was the Point Peninsula culture, thereby moving back the date of the supposed migration 300 years. The controversy is unresolved and awaits new research.

Middle Iroquoian
AD 1300 to 1350 or later

Throughout the Early Iroquoian period, most communities still only numbered a few hundred souls at the most favorable times of the year, just as they had done in Middle Woodland times. Some of the people, especially the elderly, may have lived in the same settlements year-round, but society was still organized in bands in the form of localized matrilineal clans. Each band had its own leader, was exogamous, and identified with a group of totemic animals. Intermarriage was an important way of cementing good relations with neighbors, but by the same token, there appears to have been little long-distance exchange of ceremonial goods, perhaps a reflection of less flamboyant burial customs (Trigger, 1985). Biologically, the southern Ontario Iroquois population was very homogeneous before AD 1350, as if there was considerable movement between one group and another. Since there is considerable pottery diversity over this area during these centuries and women are the potters, each community may have been matrilineal, with the men taking up residence with their wives and their kin after marriage.

Although we still know little about the rate of cultural change in Early Iroquoian times, there is good reason to believe that maize agriculture assumed increasing importance in Iroquois culture as time went on and population densities rose. The introduction of the common bean in about AD 1300 made a big difference (Crawford, 1999). Maize and bean agriculture may have been one of the factors behind the dramatic changes in Iroquoian life throughout the St Lawrence lowlands and in the Mohawk drainage during the 14th century.

The Middle Iroquois period may have lasted only a half-century or so, between AD 1300 and 1350, although some believe it lasted longer (see above). Apparently, it began first in southwestern Ontario, the cultural transitions spreading rapidly eastward to Iroquois groups to the east. This half-century or more saw the Iroquois living in much larger communities and becoming heavily dependent on maize farming. For example, two or three Glen Meyer communities near London, Ontario, now joined into a single, large settlement along a creek. Here they were much further away from productive acorn forests, but close to heavier soils that were hard to cultivate but less vulnerable to drought conditions.

Some of the largest Middle Iroquois settlements now covered more than 4.9 acres (2 ha). More families lived in the same dwelling, longer houses that were built closer together and sometimes parallel to one another in groups. Perhaps these groupings coincided with related matrilineages or individual clans. Placing longhouses closer together may have been a labor-saving device to reduce the amount of palisading needed to protect larger villages. By 1400, some of the largest Iroquois settlements regularly housed as many as 1500 people, with far more elaborate village plans, large work areas, and even garbage disposal zones (Warrick, 1984).

But larger settlements brought new pressures to Iroquois society. A community of 1500 people consumed enormous quantities of firewood, to say nothing of construction timber. Agricultural land was soon cleared and

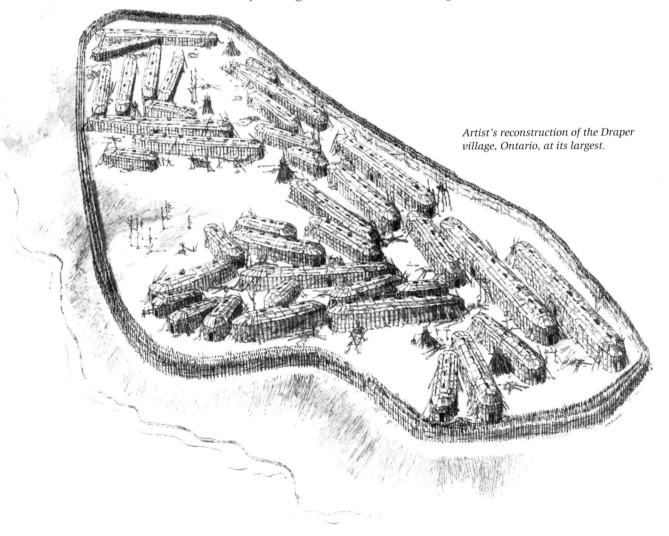

Artist's reconstruction of the Draper village, Ontario, at its largest.

exhausted, so these large settlements had to shift location more frequently than smaller ones. The men spent more and more time clearing land or in communal construction work. Nevertheless, a few Iroquois settlements achieved populations of more than 2000 people, about six clan groups. But factionalism may have strained dispute-resolving mechanisms to the limit and prevented large villages from lasting long. The largest known settlement is the Draper site in Ontario, which covered 19.76 acres (8 ha) and housed between 2000 and 3000 people for a few decades in the 15th century (Trigger, 1985).

Changes in the Social Order. These larger villages may have resulted from clusters of scattered communities coming together, perhaps for mutual protection. As these settlements developed, hitherto dispersed clans came into much closer proximity, with a much greater potential for serious disputes, factional quarrels, and other disruptions. Bruce Trigger (1985) believes the Iroquois now instituted more formal village councils made up of representatives from each clan. Among the historic Iroquois, these offices were hereditary among individual families in each clan. Just as among historic tribes in the Southeast, there may have been separate chiefs (*sachems*) for war and peace.

Peace chiefs kept a pulse on public opinion, settled domestic disputes, organized community works, rituals and ceremonies, and negotiated with others. War chiefs had more limited powers. They organized and led war parties, dealt with prisoners, and killed suspected witches. Both offices were sources of prestige rather than power, for no chief had the authority to do anything more than act as a spokesman. His family had to work hard to provide the additional food that enabled him to extend hospitality to other people in the village and to strangers. Since there was no fixed law of primogeniture, relatives would compete with one another for the succession, vying to prove their prowess as generous hosts, brave warriors, and expert hunters (Trigger, 1969). Among Iroquois groups living north of Lake Ontario, the solidarity of each community was now celebrated with the elaborate Feast of the Dead, a ceremonial reburial of those who had died while a village was inhabited, carried out before the settlement was moved to a new location.

Warfare and Cannibalism. Warfare became an important factor in Iroquois life during the 14th century. Many communities were now elaborately fortified, but others were still undefended, close to navigable waters, not away from them as became the rule in later, more turbulent, centuries. But cannibalism appears for the first time – in the form of split, cut, and cooked human bones found in Iroquoian sites throughout southern Ontario (Wright, J., 1966).

The consumption of human flesh was not a matter of obtaining extra protein, but an intensely symbolic act. Among the Aztecs and other Mexican civilizations, prisoners of war were sacrificed in elaborate public ceremonies, on altars located on high places. The victim was stretched across the altar, his heart ripped out in view of the sun, the body tumbled down the pyramid, dismembered, and parts consumed in private rituals. This symbolic act, the ritual of human sacrifice and the consumption of human flesh, may have diffused north from Mexico, just as maize and other crops did (Trigger, 1969). In time, the idea of this kind of ceremony reached the northern Iroquois. They waged war, at least in theory, to avenge the killing of kinsfolk by outsiders. The warriors would capture someone from the group who did the killing as a replacement for the victim. Or they would kill him, bringing his head or scalp home as a trophy. Male prisoners were often slain in elaborate sacrifices to the sun, women and children usually permitted to live.

Why did warfare suddenly assume such importance after 1300? Some theories argue that cooler and drier climatic conditions now led to more frequent droughts and food shortages, so that Iroquois groups living on the sand plains of southwestern Ontario and on New York's cool Allegheny Plateau may have moved away from their homelands in search of moister, more fertile soils. The result may have been more competition for prime farming land and other strategic resources (Warrick, 1984). However, population densities among the Iroquois were still low and there was more agricultural land available than people to occupy and cultivate it. Neighboring groups could have fought over hunting rights, but why go to war over deer, when the game population may have, in fact, increased with so much cleared agricultural land to graze on?

Perhaps warfare was closely connected with the quest for personal prestige (Trigger, 1985). As time went on, the basic tasks of hunting, fishing, and forest clearance, once great tests of a man's ability to support his family through the winter, became more collective tasks carried out by larger groups. Individual resource and prestige had once come from skill in the chase, but now this activity was no longer a way of acquiring individual prestige. Women, as the farmers, were now accounting for more food and were the dominant social lineages. Thus, men had to prove themselves and their worth. John Witthoft (1959) believes that warfare replaced successful food getting as the avenue to male prestige. Disputes between neighboring groups may have proliferated as the young men sought every excuse to wage war – perhaps to the point that every community had some enemies. Constant warfare, with its risk of premature death, especially for adults, may have caused hardship by disrupting critical subsistence activities (Milner and others, 1991).

Bruce Trigger develops the Witthoft theory still further. Perhaps, he argues, this led to a situation where some neighboring villages combined for self defence, resulting in much larger settlements. Fortified Middle Iroquois communities may have first developed in western Iroquois country, where the people had long fought with the Central Algonquians, then come into use over the entire region, resulting in major changes in local society. For generations, the Iroquois had maintained close ties between scattered communities by men or women marrying into neighboring villages. With larger settlements, the need for such marriage customs was reduced, so the ties were severed, ties that helped reduce conflict between neighbors. About the only alternative was to settle disputes by force.

Horticulture, especially maize agriculture, assumed ever greater importance in ancient Iroquois life. Much agriculture is women's work, and larger communities depended heavily on their crops. Perhaps the men felt threatened, and turned to warfare as a means, not only of acquiring prestige, but also captives, who were sacrificed to the sun, the symbol of fertility and life.

Thus, argues Trigger, the men assumed a prestigious role in a society that was becoming more and more sedentary and agricultural.

The Emergence of Tribes. After 1400, differences in pottery styles, burial practices, and house types chronicle major divisions between Iroquois groups living north of Lakes Ontario and Erie, while other archaeological "cultures" now define groups ancestral to historic tribes to the south. For example, between 1450 and 1475, a small and a much larger village near Syracuse, New York, deliberately settled within a few miles of one another to form the Onondaga nation. James Tuck was able to show that the larger village had itself been formed by the amalgamation of two smaller ones (Tuck, 1971). Similar fusions took place all over Iroquois country, with relatively dense local populations clustering in specific areas, separated from one another by largely uninhabited country. Periodic population movements and regroupings were much more frequent in Ontario to the north, perhaps because the people lived in environments close to the northern limits of large-scale maize cultivation and sedentary settlement was much harder.

These new tribal groupings resulted in greater social complexity in Iroquois life. Tribal councils emerged as an extension of village ones, designed to regulate life on a larger scale. Complex clan ties cut across village and tribal boundaries, clans identified by their totemic animals (Fenton, 1978). Among the historic Iroquois, some of these clans grouped themselves into associations, phratries, that organized much of ceremonial life, including funerals. There were medicine societies, too, societies that cured the sick and carried out curing rituals. All these complex mechanisms helped maintain links between expanding, and increasingly complex, Iroquois societies.

Why did large Iroquois settlements and tribes form? Some large communities may have controlled important resources and exchange networks. But warfare may have been the major factor in forging large communities and political alliances. And when a village reached its maximum practicable size, the inhabitants expanded into new communities, forming confederacies, tribes, and other associations. These settlement clusters depleted natural food resources more rapidly, making the people more dependent on horticulture. The constant political maneuvering and warfare led to more elaborate fortifications in the 16th century, villages with multiple palisades, earthworks, and massive tree-trunk ramparts.

Late Iroquoian
AD 1400 to European contact and later

Sometime before the end of the 16th century, neighboring Iroquois tribes in both Ontario and New York came together in loosely knit, larger associations, confederacies aimed at reducing blood feuding and warfare between close neighbors. The common link between them was an agreement to settle grievances by means other than bloodshed. A confederacy council of headmen from member tribes gathered occasionally for ceremonial feasts, conferences, and to adjudicate disputes and set reparation payments if called for. At European contact, the major Iroquois tribes were the Huron,

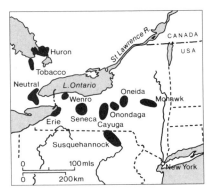

Map showing Iroquois groups in historical times.

Iroquois 18th-century wampum belt. Location unknown.

Erie, Tobacco, and Neutral in the north and, to the south, the famous League of the Iroquois, made up of the Five Nations: Seneca, Cayuga, Onondaga, Oneida, and Mohawk. The Susquehannocks were another Iroquois group living in the Susquehanna Valley (Snow, 1996b).

When did the Iroquois League and other confederacies come into being? Some scholars believe that they were the result of external pressures caused by the arrival of Europeans, that they were the way in which the Iroquois resisted the foreigners and traded effectively with them (Tooker, 1964). These confederacies were then further strengthened by the fur trade.

In fact, they probably formed many generations earlier. The Iroquois confederacies were made up of people who enjoyed similar culture and language, and used the same political institutions. Under such circumstances, confederacies may well have been adaptive, unlike historically known alliances between quite different groups with no cultural ties that sometimes formed to resist European encroachment in other areas, only to fall apart shortly afterward. Bruce Trigger (1976) believes that the Iroquois confederacies were a logical extension of complex, long-term forces that had much earlier replaced small hunting bands with larger groups, then with tribes. The confederacy was adaptive in that it allowed groups to legislate against unnecessary blood feuding, while still maintaining individual cultural and political identity in their dealings with others. The arrival of Europeans and their fur traders created a new, highly volatile political situation, in which it was clearly an advantage for neighbors to be linked in close alliances. Since the Iroquois already enjoyed confederacies, it would have been an easy matter to strengthen them in response to new circumstances.

For generations after the Iroquois League was formed, the Five Nations were greatly feared by the Huron and the Algonquian. The Iroquois themselves symbolized their League as a vast longhouse that stretched from west to east. The Seneca were the "Keepers of the Western Door," the Mohawk the "Keepers of the Eastern Door." The Onondaga were in the center, the "Keepers of the Council Fire." They were also "Keepers of the Wampum Belts."

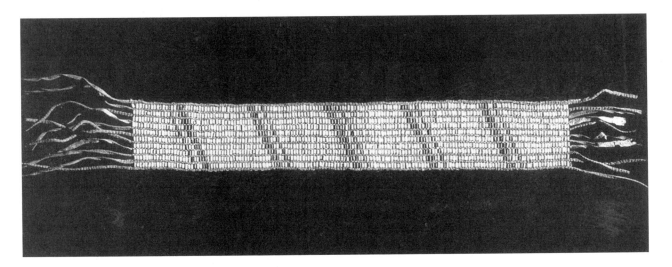

Both the Iroquois and the Algonquians of the Northeast strung white and purple or black shells into strands and complex belts named after the Algonquian word "wampum." The woven dark and white designs on these belts symbolized all manner of transactions – major events, treaties, and agreements. One Onondaga chief kept the treaty wampum for the Five Nations. It was he who knew the patterns and what they meant. Eventually wampum became a form of currency when Europeans arrived, but the beads were hard to manufacture even with iron drills and were soon replaced with cheap glass trade beads from overseas.

At European contact, all Iroquois-speaking peoples depended heavily on horticulture, with fishing also a vital part of the subsistence economy. Among the Huron of the north and the Seneca, horticulture – corn, beans, squash, and sunflowers – may have provided up to 80 percent of the diet. The northern Iroquois lived in fortified villages, in elm tree bark-covered longhouses shared by many families. They dwelt on either side of the central hearths. Unlike the Algonquians, the Iroquois were matrilineal, with the children living with their mother's clan. Each longhouse group was a subdivision of the matrilineal clan, for sisters with their husbands

Smoking a native tobacco in a zoomorphic pipe. Reconstruction of Iroquois life at the Keffer site, Ontario.

and children shared a common dwelling. The men, who cleared the land, hunted, fished, traded, and built houses and fortifications, were warriors, and moved into the longhouses of their wives at marriage. The women grew, weeded, and harvested crops, and tended the children.

With its confederacies and tribes, Iroquois society was governed highly effectively. Their political organizations seem precarious, based as they were on decisions made by a network of tribal and community councils, in situations where consent was needed on the part of all concerned. But, in fact, they were highly effective in suppressing blood feuds among populations numbering as many as 20,000 souls, and at coordinating at least a degree of diplomatic policy toward outsiders.

The northern Iroquois were unified by many common religious beliefs and ceremonial practices. But above all they were remarkable not for their material culture, but for the sophistication and finesse of social relationships. The Iroquois respected individual dignity and self-reliance. They looked down on public displays of emotion or open quarrelling, considered politeness and hospitality toward one another and toward strangers fundamental to correct social behavior. As later events were to show, these warlike and astute people were more than a match for the European fur traders and missionaries who settled among them.

In the year 1534, French master mariner Jacques Cartier sailed past Newfoundland and up the great St Lawrence River. Bad weather had his ships taking shelter in Gaspe Bay at the mouth of the river, where he encountered about 300 men, women, and children (Trigger, 1976). They wore only skins and loin cloths, fisherfolk with few possessions. The men shaved their heads except for a topknot tied into a knot with leather thongs. Cartier was unimpressed with what he called the "sorriest people in the world," people who had no furs to trade. But the French took the trouble to compile a word list, the earliest record of Iroquois language ever made. From this moment on, the Iroquois were destined to undergo catastrophic cultural change, as a result of economic factors operating far over the eastern horizons of the Atlantic, in distant Europe.

Further Reading

Snow, Dean. 1980. *The Archaeology of New England*. Academic Press, New York.
  This comprehensive survey is now somewhat dated, but still laden with good data and original ideas.
——1996b. *The Iroquois*. Blackwell, Oxford.
  A general account of the Iroquois ancient and modern. An excellent starting place.
Trigger, Bruce. 1972. *The Children of Aataentsic: A History of the Huron People to 1660*. 2 vols. McGill-Queen's University Press, Kingston and Montreal.
——1985. *Natives and Newcomers*. McGill-Queen's University Press, Kingston and Montreal.
  Bruce Trigger's elegant and thorough studies are definitive accounts of Iroquoian archaeology and history. The serious reader need look no further for authoritative analysis.
Tuck, J.A. 1971. *Onondaga Iroquois Prehistory*. Syracuse University Press, Syracuse, NY.
  A thorough study of changing settlement patterns in the late Northeastern past.

PART SEVEN

AFTER COLUMBUS

"It is terribly important that the 'small things forgotten' be remembered. For in the seemingly little and insignificant things that accumulate to create a lifetime, the essence of our existence is captured."

JAMES DEETZ
In Small Things Forgotten (1977)

CHAPTER 22

THE ARCHAEOLOGY OF EUROPEAN CONTACT

(Opposite) Excavations in progress at the Santa Catalina de Guale mission church, St Catherine's Island, Georgia. This project, directed by David Hurst Thomas of the American Museum of Natural History, has been one of the major recent field projects in post-contact North American archaeology. See pp. 505–507.

For more than 13,000 years the native Americans occupied the vast tracts of North America undisturbed. During these long millennia, they developed a huge diversity of responses to a bewildering array of natural environments. The trajectory of cultural change through these millennia was usually gradual, sometimes dramatically rapid, as was the case, for example, when maize and bean cultivation took hold in the Southeast. But the momentum of continual change was never disrupted. Then, in the year 1492, Christopher Columbus landed in the Indies. Now began the last, and perhaps least understood, chapter of native American history – five centuries of catastrophic and disruptive cultural change in the face of an inexorable European presence.

Until recently, surprisingly few archaeologists had paid attention to this important period of native American history, a period that lies, for the most part, outside comprehensive documentary records. When such records are available, they are concerned almost entirely with European affairs, the indigenous people merely serving as a backdrop for events considered important in Western minds. It is only recently that the full potential of archaeology as a source of historical information during the contact period has come to the fore. This interest has been furthered by a growing realization that excavated evidence provides a unique window into the daily lives of everyday people, who are often as anonymous in the historical record as their predecessors are in remoter times (Bass, 1988; Beaudry, 1987; Deetz, 1977; Orser and Fagan, 1995). Historical archaeology also has an important role to play in the study of early capitalism (Leone and Potter, 1999).

Archaeology offers the best chance for students of the past to examine cultural change in all societies, whether simple or complex, over long periods of time. Of no period of the North American past is this more true than of the 15th to 18th centuries AD, when the full impact of European contact fell upon indigenous society. Any form of cultural contact, however fleeting, is a two-way process, with often lasting impacts on both cultures involved (for a useful discussion, see Trigger, 1985). The European perspective on the exploration and settlement of North America is relatively well documented, but the effects of these developments on native American societies of the day are still little understood. This subject is, of course, an enormous one, and we can but summarize some of the major issues here. They revolve around a set of interconnected, fundamental questions. First, what was the effect of exotic European infectious diseases introduced at

Sites of the eastern United States referred to in this chapter.

contact on the indigenous population? Second, what were the short- and long-term results of direct and indirect contacts between European and native American cultures, in material, social, and political terms?

Disease and Depopulation

No one knows exactly when a European infected with smallpox or another exotic disease first landed in North America. Some very early explorers may have carried the disease and infected some local, isolated populations, but the epidemics may have died out without infecting wide areas. Whenever infectious diseases did arrive, the effects on the native American population were devastating.

Why were there no New World counterparts for European diseases? Perhaps the parasites were killed off by arctic temperatures as tiny founder populations migrated into the New World thousands of years ago. More likely, primeval population densities were too low. The survival of acute diseases depends on sustained contact between infected individuals, such as occurs in densely populated, sedentary settlements. North America, and even to some extent Mesoamerica, lacked the densely packed, urban settlements of the Old World. It was there that bacterial and viral diseases became fixed in urban populations (Crosby, 1986).

In epidemiological terms the turning point was 1519, when a Spanish conquistador infected with smallpox landed at Vera Cruz, Mexico. The conquistadors had some immunity to the disease, but the Indians did not. In months, smallpox spread like wildfire from the coast to the highlands. The first pandemic hit the Aztec capital in 1520. Indians died by the thousand. Other unfamiliar diseases, including influenza, measles, and typhus, ravaged the Mexican population during the next century. The population of Mexico has been estimated at 11 million in 1519. A mere 20 years later, it was under 6.5 million, by 1607 less than a fifth of that of a century earlier. Similar massive demographic catastrophes occurred throughout the Americas. For example, more than 310,000 Indians lived in California at the time of Spanish colonization in 1769. Coastal populations fell from about 72,000 to 18,000 by 1830. By 1900, the total number of California Indians was 20,000, less than 7 percent of the pre-contact population (Cook, 1978).

The nature and timing of Indian population declines has sparked great controversy among historians, anthropologists, and prehistorians, a debate that focuses on three fundamental issues. First, how large was the human population of North America at contact, and how great was the subsequent decline? Second, when exactly did the decline take place relative to the first census counts? Third, what role did infectious diseases play in the decline?

The great Berkeley anthropologist Alfred Kroeber and others argued that exotic diseases played a relatively minor role in the early decades after contact. But they agreed that aboriginal populations declined after sustained European contact. Under this rubric, the earliest historical census counts do not represent decimated populations. Thus, North American Indian populations were relatively small at contact, Kroeber (1939) estimating a figure of about 0.9 million people. This was a static view of such cultures at contact, the so-called "Ethnographic Present."

In contrast anthropologist Henry Dobyns (1983) assumes that infectious diseases attacked even isolated populations decades, if not centuries, *before* actual physical contact between Europeans and Indians and before historical records began. Thus, even the earliest post-contact census counts reflect populations reduced by as much as 95 percent from pre-contact highs. Dobyns proposed North American population figures as high as 18 million, a dramatic contrast to the conservative Kroeber figure.

Archaeologist Ann Ramenofsky (1987) evaluated these two contrasting approaches using archaeological evidence. Ramenofsky points out that both new multi-disciplinary researches and a much more complete archaeological record than that at Kroeber's disposal show beyond all reasonable doubt that there was constant cultural change not only throughout ancient times, but over the critical centuries of European contact as well. Thus, she argues, patterns of archaeological change in populations can be evaluated independently of ethnographic or historical records. This is important, for such attempts as have been made to develop population estimates have been based invariably on modern analogues, so that conservative figures based on some form of "ethnographic present" come into play. It is hardly surprising, then, that population estimates have been conservative.

Ramenofsky has measured population change by using comprehensive settlement data, data that is completely independent of ethnographic and historical records. She examined a single, testable archaeological hypothesis: "Did native Americans experience a population collapse immediately following contact with Europeans, but predating written records and sustained colonization?" Her study is based on three regions: the lower Mississippi Valley, central New York, and the middle Missouri Valley. Although she had to contend with sampling biases, a lack of quantitative data on house or settlement size, and gaps in regional coverage, she was able to discern some general patterns of considerable significance. In the lower Mississippi Valley, both historical and independent archaeological data identified an unambiguous and precipitous decline of aboriginal populations in the 16th century – after the De Soto expedition and before the French colonized the valley in the late 17th century.

The New York data came from the Finger Lakes region, the area inhabited by the Five Nations of the Iroquois at the beginning of the historic period. Had Iroquois populations and cultural systems remained constant right up to the American Revolution or had epidemics radically altered Iroquois society in the 16th or 17th centuries? Ramenofsky's calculations of settlement area and house roof area suggest that the Indian population was considerably reduced by the 17th century, but the exact date of the decline is in doubt. Historical descriptions of Iroquois society support and extend the archaeological record of collapse in these centuries with their chronicles of drastically reorganized settlements and the final breakdown of multi-family dwellings and fortified settlements. Historical descriptions of the Five Nations are those of populations developing new adaptive strategies, partly as a result of diminishing numbers.

The middle Missouri Valley sample was from the Northern Plains area, where European contact began in 1540 and colonization in the 18th century. Did exotic diseases cause catastrophic depopulation with colonization or during the two preceding centuries? Again, the archaeological data, mostly from large river basin surveys, was sufficient to reject the 18th-century hypothesis. Ramenofsky's settlement calculations suggest a decline at least a century earlier, perhaps coinciding with the appearance of European trade goods in the region. But again, the data are ambiguous as to the exact timing of the population loss, which may have occurred as early as the 16th century, before any significant numbers of trade goods appeared in the area.

In all three areas, archaeological data tend to confirm Dobyns' theory, derived from other sources, that demographic catastrophe preceded the major influx of Europeans by decades, perhaps in some areas by centuries. Ramenofsky estimates the pre-contact native American population of North America at about 12 million, a more conservative figure than Dobyns, but much higher than that espoused by Kroeber and his contemporaries.

Any study of cultural change among American Indian societies after European contact must be undertaken against a background of massive population decline that persisted in some areas until the 19th century. From the anthropological and archaeological point of view, these declines are important in that they confirm that the so-called "ethnographic present," the carefully compiled record of native American society after contact, is not necessarily a close mirror of pre-contact society. All of these societies, whether or not they had sustained physical contact with Europeans, had already undergone major change and readjustment long before they were studied by modern scientists. These changes are only now being studied closely by archaeologists.

The Onondaga of the Five Nations: Continuous Redefinition of Culture

In 1535, Jacques Cartier wintered on the banks of the St Lawrence River, and sustained contact between European and American Indians began in the Northeast for the first time. This contact was fueled in large part by the profits to be derived from the international fur trade. A century later, this relationship emerges into the full light of history, by which time both local European and Indian society had changed considerably (Trigger, 1976; 1985). The overall thrust of events is well known, but many details of the changes undergone by Iroquoian society are a mystery. James Bradley (1987) has studied the Onondaga, the group who emerged as the core of the Five Nations confederacy in the 17th century. For a start, the degree of influence was not necessarily even. For instance, at first the cultural patterns of the French colonists were shaped more strongly by their Iroquois neighbors than the other way round. The Onondaga's response to the French was that of a society that was perfectly capable of coming to terms with European culture.

The Onondaga's first response to Europeans was within the context of their existing cultural beliefs and values. They craved iron axes, for example, but viewed them from their own cultural perspectives. The people were selective in their response to European culture. They chose exotic artifacts for both ideological and utilitarian reasons. For at least 3500 years, they had acquired a series of indigenous, rarely occurring substances such as sea shell, native copper, and other raw materials, associated with life-enhancing, life-restorative "power" (Bradley, 1987). Initially, the Onondaga may have thought of Europeans as alien beings, as the traditional keepers of these powerful substances. The French often bartered mirrors, metal objects, and glass beads and other baubles, artifacts that tended to reinforce the perception of them as people from another world. The few European artifacts found on proto-historic Onondaga sites are restricted to a few categories – copper sheet, iron objects, and glass beads. These substitutes for earlier exotica appear to have become the substances of "power" during the 16th century.

During the late 16th and early 17th centuries, the ideological basis for Onondaga selection waned, as utilitarian preferences came to the fore. This may have been due to greater availability of European artifacts, to the point that they lost value and prestige. Ideological considerations were still important, for there is reason to believe that the categories of artifact with "power" associations were expanded to include new categories such as glazed ceramics and glassware. After the founding of a Jesuit mission in 1655, Christian symbols such as rings, medals, rosary beads, and other artifacts entered the spiritual arena.

By the late 16th century the Onondaga were using European copper and iron for many more utilitarian artifacts, using and re-using them until they were completely worn out. Iroquois sites of the 16th and 17th centuries contain both copper kettles and iron axes, artifacts sought not necessarily as objects, but also as sources of raw materials. Onondaga metalworkers then used these materials to fashion traditional Onondaga artifacts. Thus, the initial impact of European goods was conservative, not revolutionary, for the way in which they were used promoted traditional cultural patterns, not their change. European materials were accepted, not because they were superior, but because they made sense in an opportunistic, flexible culture both in spiritual and utilitarian terms (Fenton, 1978).

The Onondaga's response to their first century of exposure to European culture was one of continuity as much as change, the change being gradual

The recycling of a copper kettle by the Onondaga: (a) the iron handle is removed and ground into an awl; (b) heavier gauge material from the lug is scored and cut into triangular projectile points. At the same time, sheet metal from the body of the kettle is turned into (c) a knife blade; (d) a tubular bead; (e, f) a conical bangle or pipe bowl liner; and (g) a pendant.

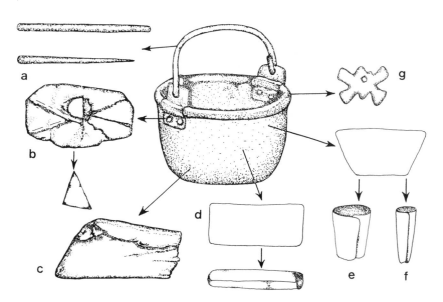

rather than catastrophic in nature. In the case of the Onondaga, and many other societies, Bradley believes that the first evidence of cross-cultural change will be in areas of a culture where it is most useful and least threatening to the existing cultural order.

Despite smallpox epidemics and other disruptions, the Onondaga still retained their basic cultural values and beliefs in the mid-17th century, living in a culture where European artifacts and materials had been grafted onto traditional society. After 1655, circumstances changed profoundly, for European contacts increased dramatically. Jesuit missionaries were in residence, a French settlement was nearby, and the Onondaga's European neighbors were increasingly aggressive. The archaeological record now shows more hybrid artifact forms, more blending of European and native culture. This increased blending is reflected in wampum, one of the major mediums of exchange between native and newcomer.

Wampum had been important in pre-contact days, but it assumed much greater significance to the Iroquois as a whole in the early 17th century. Wampum beads strung into belts became common, since they were now a commodity of major importance both to Europeans and Iroquois. To the former, the wampum belt was a valuable medium of exchange for use in the fur trade. The Dutch in particular were quick to seize on the possibilities of wampum, for they had long experience of shell as a trade item when buying slaves in faraway Africa. The same company was incorporated for fur trading in North America, turned to the same currency, and soon realized the potential of wampum. It was probably they who developed the notion of belts as a widespread, informal currency in a medium that had important cultural significance not only to the Five Nations. To the Iroquois, shell was a source of power, wampum life-enhancing and restoring, an important element in rituals that served to console close relatives of a deceased and to raise up another person to fill the void. The Onondaga were the keepers of wampum for the Five Nations, so it was of great importance to them as an emblem of diplomacy not only between Indians, but with Europeans as well.

The Iroquois confederacy of Five Nations had been formed as a means of redressing grievances among its members. Not that this prevented constant bickering among them, many of the tensions resulting from the differing trading opportunities that were available to different tribes. These quarrels, constant warfare, and devastating epidemics, so weakened the Iroquois that they were almost destroyed. But in the late 1660s the Onondaga used their diplomatic talents to restructure the Confederacy, redefining its workings so that the organization would act as the diplomatic front for all the Five Nations. The Five Nations now presented a more united front. This led to a series of treaties and alliances in 1677, agreements that stabilized and balanced the competing interests of the English colonies, which had supplanted French settlers to the southeast, the Five Nations, and other tribal groups. To the English this Covenant was a legal document, and to the Iroquois a set of social and political obligations that bound participants together to minimize differences between them. The Covenant with its diplomatic expertise, with its treaties expressed in terms of wampum belts and intricate rituals, was a product of long-drawn-out acculturative processes that saw Onondaga culture transformed not only in material ways, but in response to new external

Joseph Latifau's depiction of Iroquois leaders gathered to recite the laws of the Five Nations (1724). At the base is an enlarged view of the wampum belt, from which they "read" these laws.

realities, which, ultimately, they were sometimes able to exploit to their advantage.

The initial impact of European contact fell hardest, of course, on American Indian societies living near coasts or major waterways such as the St Lawrence or the Lower Mississippi. As European settlement spread, some coastal groups were conquered and employed as agricultural laborers. Others, in California, were forcibly resettled under deliberate "reduction" policies that brought them into the Spanish mission system, where the friars could more easily control both the process of conversion, and the economic life associated with it (Spicer, 1962). For several centuries, however, aboriginal groups living in the more distant interior largely avoided sustained contact with explorers, colonists, or missionaries, even if their economic, political, and social systems underwent drastic modification as a result of devastating epidemics.

The entire process of culture change as a result of European contact is still little understood. For the purposes of the remainder of this chapter, we focus on the Southeast, where systematic research into the interactions between Spaniard and American Indian has been most intense.

The Archaeology of De Soto

Hernando de Soto's foray through the Southeast in 1539–1543 is a terrible baseline in North American history, famous not only for its brutality, but for its legacy of smallpox and other diseases that decimated Indian populations, triggered long-term massive political and social change, and undoubtedly had profound psychological effects on Southeastern society. But what of the material remains of this extraordinary incursion? Until about 15 years ago, it seemed that De Soto and his force had passed through the Southeast without leaving an archaeological signature behind them. Part of the problem was that no one knew what to look for – 16th-century artifacts were largely a closed book even to historical archaeologists. However, the collaboration of archaeologists, anthropologists, and historians has produced significant results, and there are three possible locations where traces of De Soto, or at least very early Spanish contact, survive (Milanich and Milbrath, 1989; Milanich and Hudson, 1993).

Excavations at Tatham burial mound in Citrus County, Florida, have yielded large numbers of Spanish artifacts, including metal, glass beads, and armor fragments. More than 70 Indians had been buried in a mass grave in the tumulus, perhaps victims of an epidemic. Some bodies exhibit wounds from sword cuts (Mitchem and Hutchinson, 1987). Tatham dates to before 1550.

Even more dramatic discoveries come from the Coosa River in northwestern Georgia, from the King site that was once a frontier village of the Coosa chiefdom, visited by the Spaniards in the 16th century (Hudson, C. and others, 1985). King was a fortified settlement, whose dwellings surrounded a central plaza. Several Spanish artifacts came from the excavations, including a 16th-century basket-hilt sword manufactured in either Germany or northern Italy. Even more important, one of every five of the burials from the excavations exhibited fatal slashing wounds on legs

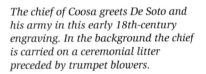

The chief of Coosa greets De Soto and his army in this early 18th-century engraving. In the background the chief is carried on a ceremonial litter preceded by trumpet blowers.

Artist's illustration of Spanish chain mail from the Martin site, Tallahassee, Florida, the Anhaica village where the De Soto expedition spent the winter of 1539–40.

and head that could only have been inflicted by long-bladed European swords, as opposed to Indian weapons – arrows and spears that would make puncture wounds. The victims were young women, also middle-aged males and females. No children or men of the warrior class were among the dead. Since Southeastern Indians usually killed warriors and captured women, the case for Spanish killing is even more compelling.

Of the three Spanish expeditions that penetrated Coosa in the 16th century, only De Soto's could have reached the King site. Wherever he went, De Soto took slaves, women for sexual purposes and others as carriers – the very segment of the King population that lay in these graves. Perhaps these people mounted a desperate resistance against enslavement, or violence stemmed from a Spanish attempt to extort or steal food from the village when the warriors were absent. The bones bear puncture and gnaw marks from opossums and rats, as if they lay in the open for a while before being interred by the survivors. The village may never have recovered from De Soto. It was abandoned by 1575 (Blakely and Matthews, 1990).

From October 1539 to March 1540, Hernando de Soto and his 600 conquistadors set up winter camp at the major Apalachee town of Anhaica, which lies today under downtown Tallahassee, Florida (Ewen, 1989). Anhaica was a sizeable settlement with 250 dwellings and other structures. The Apalachee abandoned their town to their unwelcome visitors, but harassed the Spaniards constantly. Calvin Jones, and later Charles Ewen, have excavated a small portion of the encampment, attempting to establish the dimensions of the camp and uncovering two circular wattle-and-daub Indian dwellings. The site has yielded five early 16th-century Spanish and Portuguese coins, Apalachee artifacts, and considerable numbers of Spanish artifacts and ceramics. This is hardly surprising, since we know that De Soto was resupplied from his ships in Tampa Bay. There were a fragment of a crossbow bolt, numerous European glass beads, and pieces of Spanish chain mail, also datable 16th-century imported majolica pottery. The chain mail fragments are of particular interest, for it was at Anhaica that the conquistadors discovered that chain mail was no protection against Indian arrows and turned to quilted cloth coats instead.

The search for further traces of De Soto's expedition continues, and the debate about his exact route still rages. These controversies are of more than academic interest, but the real issues surround not the events of the expedition itself, but the long-term consequences of his passage. And these consequences, still archaeologically little known, were to be momentous (Dye and Cox, 1990).

Culture Change in the Southeastern Interior

Marvin Smith (1987) has studied a portion of the interior Southeast centered on the Georgia and Alabama piedmont, in an attempt to measure the extent of early post-contact cultural change. European contact began in this region with the De Soto expedition of 1540. Both exotic diseases and foreign trade goods percolated into the area during the following century, this early period of indirect contact ending with the arrival of English settlers from Virginia and South Carolina in the 1670s. Smith points out that the situation in this region was very different from that, say, of the Five

Nations of the Iroquois, where the people were in sustained, direct contact with Europeans for generations. Here the contact was indirect. Acculturation of the type found among the Onondaga, for example, did not take place, yet there were major changes in population density and settlement patterns, to say nothing of political and social institutions.

The 16th-century Southeast was a land of flourishing and often complex chiefdoms with high levels of military organization. These presided over dense populations often housed in substantial settlements. The people were ruled by an elite, their lives governed by complex religious beliefs and elaborate rituals (Hudson, C., 1976). Like most chiefdoms of this complexity, there were several layers of hierarchy. In Smith's research area, the chiefdom of Ocute consisted of a capital with five mounds (the Shoulderbone mound group), two other multiple mound sites, two single mound centers, and many villages and smaller settlements. This densely inhabited "province" was surrounded by a large buffer zone of unoccupied land (Smith, M. and Kowalewski, 1980). By analyzing the routes taken by De Soto and other early Spanish explorers, Smith and his colleagues have been able to identify many 16th-century polities and actual named settlements, identifications that are the baseline for examining population decline and political restructuring during the century that followed.

Throughout much of the late 16th and early 17th centuries, the Southeastern interior remained unknown territory, although plenty was happening around the periphery. The Spanish mission system spread along the Georgia coast, through northern Florida, increasing both knowledge of foreigners and indirect contacts through the years. When English visitors first reached Cofitachiqui in South Carolina, a settlement visited by De Soto in 1540, it was still an important place. Its inhabitants were well aware of the Spanish, of a land to the west with bells and friars, and of people who rode on great deer (horses). The Cherokee of the Tennessee Valley were well equipped with firearms, brass pots, and kettles by 1673. French explorers entering the lower Mississippi from the Great Lakes region reported encounters with Indians armed with muskets, who also possessed glass bottles, iron axes, and other European goods, obtained from a coast said to be 10 days away. Peaches, chickens, and watermelons had spread widely from village to village (Sauer, 1980). These material changes were symptoms of much more profound alterations in Indian life.

Marvin Smith approached the problem of measuring cultural change from several archaeological angles. First, he established chronologies based on stylistic changes in categories of easily dated European trade goods that were exchanged with native peoples all over the world. This methodology, employed successfully in the Northeast, and often called the "Iroquois Methodology," works well where there is continual, sustained contact, as there was in the fur trading areas (Wray and Schoff, 1953). But in the Southeast the contacts were more complicated and less constant, the flow of European goods resulting not only from occasional direct trade, but from such diverse sources as slave trading, looting of shipwrecks, and through native middlemen. Intricate exchange routes had criss-crossed the Southeast since Archaic times: they were still in use and many exotica undoubtedly traveled along them.

In the Southeast, many of the earliest trade goods were quickly consumed as prestigious grave goods. Smith's seriations of European goods found in archaeological sites chronicle long-term changes. From 1525 to 1565 aboriginal culture was little affected by exotic influences, although European goods were buried with the elite, who controlled the supply. Native copper associated with the Southern Cult was still in use. Between 1565 and 1600, native copperworking was in decline, but other traditional crafts with important ritual associations such as shellwork were still common and important. After 1600, the pattern changed, as imports became more common and were no longer restricted to elite burials. Perhaps this reflects the breakdown of powerful chiefdoms. At any rate, more common artifacts, like iron axes, became more utilitarian possessions – just as they had in the Northeast. Only native ceramics remained unchanged. Between 1640 and 1670, firearms were in use, and English artifacts appeared more common, as if trade networks now extended to the Northeast.

These material changes took place against a background of massive depopulation resulting from epidemics. The chroniclers of the De Soto expedition make it clear that diseases introduced by earlier coastal visitors preceded the conquistadors into the interior. At the village of Talomeco in South Carolina, hundreds of bodies were stacked up in four of the houses. Evidence of epidemics from later decades is abundant. Sir Francis Drake's men contracted a highly contagious form of fever, perhaps typhus, in the Cape Verde Islands, and carried it ashore when they attacked the Spanish settlement at St Augustine, Florida, in 1586. Hundreds of Indians living nearby soon died of the same disease. And Thomas Hariot noted that the English settlers at Roanoke, in the colony of what was then called Virginia (now North Carolina), soon infected the local people. "Within a few days after our departure from everies such townes, people began to die very fast, and many in short space" (Crosby, 1972).

Without question these later coastal epidemics entered the interior, resulting in massive depopulation, perhaps killing as many as 90 percent of some village populations (Smith, M., 1987). Not only that, but the survivors probably suffered severely from starvation, especially if epidemics struck during periods of planting or harvest. The processes of depopulation may have been so rapid and devastating that ancestral traditions and much of indigenous culture may have been swept away in a few short months. The loss, in particular, of religious and genealogical lore is especially devastating to a traditional society, for such elements are an important element in helping people adjust to a new culture (Smith, M., 1987; Trigger, 1976). In the Southeastern interior, such a loss may have led to the fragmentation of hitherto powerful chiefdoms into much smaller, less centralized societies, and to population movements.

In archaeological terms, Smith believes that the epidemics and general social disruption may be reflected in a rapid increase in multiple burials during the 16th century, as is documented in sites of the Mouse Creek culture of eastern Tennessee and in the King site of northwestern Georgia, with graves dating to the period between 1525 and 1565. A visitor to the Arkansas people in 1698 remarked that "not a month had elapsed since they had rid themselves of smallpox, which had carried off most of them. In the village are now nothing but graves, in which they were buried two together, and we estimated that not a hundred men were left" (Phillips and others, 1951). Settlement sizes shrank, too, witness the Toqua site in

Tennessee. This fortified mound center was occupied from about 1215 to 1620. The earliest village covered some 420,000 sq. ft (39,018 sq. m) with dispersed houses. Later, between 1350 and the early 16th century, the occupied zone shrank to 210,000 sq. ft (19,509 sq. m). Around 1580-1600, the fortified area shrank to as little as 180,000 sq. ft (16,727 sq. m), a much smaller settlement in which three multiple burials were found (Smith, M., 1987).

The strongest evidence is for political breakdown, for there is ample historical documentation that the large and powerful chiefdoms encountered by De Soto had been reduced to dozens of small-scale societies that were to band together to form the Creek Confederacy in the early 18th century. These small societies were ruled by *mikos*, little more than village headmen. The fall of the chiefdoms was closely linked not only to epidemics, but to the severe loss of the manpower that peopled the hierarchical provinces of the Southeast. Archaeologically, the decline can be documented by a virtual cessation of mound building, known to have been a chiefly activity. In Smith's research area, no new mounds were built after about 1600. Some mound centers were abandoned, and there was a widespread trend during the 18th century toward more dispersed village settlements.

The hierarchical settlement patterns of larger centers and a well-defined ranking of lesser settlements were apparently abandoned during the 16th century, a loss well documented in the Wallace Reservoir area and Oconee drainage area of Georgia (Smith, M. and Kowalewski, 1980). By the early 17th century, the copper axes and spatulate axes, as well as other sumptuary goods symbolic of chiefly power, were no longer in use, as if such powers had eroded dramatically. Decimated, without the support of their traditional beliefs, the societies of the interior were left in a state of cultural impoverishment. By virtue of their remoteness from the coast, they had not been exposed directly to Spanish, French, and English culture and Christianity, as they were after 1673. Ultimately, the drastic cultural changes of the previous 130 years put the Indians in a position to accept more easily elements of European culture in the years that followed, when acculturation truly began. It was not until the 18th century that the peoples of the Southeast came together in the Creek Confederacy, a response to armed invasions by northern Indian groups, and to raids by European slave traders.

Text-aided Research: The Archaeology of La Florida

Historical archaeology, sometimes called text-aided archaeology, has been defined as "the archaeology of the spread of European culture throughout the world since the 15th century and its impact on indigenous peoples" (Deetz, 1977). The peoples it studies do not necessarily have to be literate, indeed only a minority of, say, early Spanish settlers or English colonists could write. But this minority wrote about the others and kept at least sketchy records of them. They sent reports to the homeland, recorded births, marriages, and deaths, kept tax rolls, laid out and administered tiny settlements according to regulations promulgated by distant monarchs. These records complement the archaeological record – the artifacts of literate and non-literate people living often simple lives, of different classes or ethnic groups with often quite distinctive artifacts, of Europeans interacting with native Americans. The material remains of their diverse existences chronicle the historical realities of recent centuries of North American history in ways that no official living at the time would consider worth recording. Historical archaeology provides fascinating perspectives not only on the European settlement of North America, but on the cultures of various major immigrant groups, and on every economic class of emerging American society, including the native Americans confronted by the newcomers.

Historical archaeology has assumed significant proportions in North America, both because of culture resource management and ardent historic preservation activities, and because most North Americans can identify more closely with historic sites from the recent past than they can with the ancient achievements of native American societies. In its early days, historical archaeology was restricted to selected, important sites such as forts, major missions, and the residences of major historical figures. Much excavation was conducted at the behest of architectural historians. In the past quarter-century, however, perspectives have changed. Both archaeologists, and to a lesser extent historians, have realized that archaeology gives access to a very broad range of human behavior, not only spoken, but preserved in the form of material remains (Deetz, 1977; Nöel Hume, 1969; Orser and Fagan, 1995). Much recent work, especially that concerned with the so-called Spanish Borderlands, has what can only be described as an anthropological orientation. This focus concentrates not only on material remains, but on the processes of interaction between different population groups.

What have been called the Spanish Borderlands were, in fact, an ever-shifting frontier on the margins of the vast Spanish Empire in the Americas. This northern boundary of New Spain was never fixed, and always changing, a part of New Spain where there was constant interaction between settlers and native Americans, between long-established indigenous societies and aggressive newcomers. Ultimately, the borderlands stretched from St Augustine, Florida, in the east to San Francisco, California, in the west. The processes of interaction and cultural change associated with them began with European contact, with the Ponce de Leon expedition in the east, with Fray Marcos de Niza in the Southwest, and with Juan Cabrillo's voyage up the California coast in 1542. They ended with the Mexican Revolution of 1821.

The complicated history of this vast area has long been studied by historians, but only recently by archaeologists. Inevitably, the historical picture has been burdened with offensive stereotypes and simplistic interpretations, some due to the intellectual and social climate of the times in which they were written, others the result of the limitations of documentary evidence. As David Hurst Thomas has pointed out, the objective perspective of text-aided archaeology is adding a new balance, new insights to the historical record. Nowhere are these perspectives more exciting than in La Florida, the Hispanic Southeast (Thomas, 1989).

Shortly after Columbus landed in the Indies, Spanish explorers extended their king's domains through the Caribbean, into Mexico, and into South America. They also explored much of the Gulf and Atlantic coasts of North America, the lands named La Florida by Ponce de Leon in 1513 (Chapter 1).

La Florida was far from wealthy and attracted few Spanish settlers until 1565, when Pedro Menéndez de Aviles overran a French colony near present-day Jacksonville, Florida, and founded two settlements – St Augustine and Santa Elena, the latter on Parris Island, South Carolina (South and others, 1988). The local Indians exercised such pressure against Santa Elena and its forts that it was abandoned by 1587, two years after Sir Walter Raleigh's colony was established in Virginia to the north.

St Augustine enjoyed a strategic position, located as it was close to the point where Spanish treasure fleets turned offshore with the north-flowing Gulf Stream that brought them up from the Indies. No less than 21 percent of the royal defense budget was spent in La Florida between 1564 and 1577, with resulting heavy ship traffic in and out of St Augustine, ships that brought provisions and other necessities as well as military reinforcements, missionaries, and settlers.

Sixteenth-century St Augustine was a tiny settlement, a small mission and presidio. By the end of the century, about 425 people living in 120 households dwelt in the town (Deagan, 1980; 1983). Only about 30 percent of them included women, and only half of those were Spanish. The rest were Indian wives or concubines. The garrison was plagued with flood, fire, and hurricanes, plundered by Sir Francis Drake in 1586. A member of his crew drew a map of the town, showing nine blocks of single-story, thatched structures with board walls (Manucy, 1985). Many earlier dwellings were made of wattle and daub. St Augustine survived and served as the capital of La Florida until 1702, when the British besieged its Castillo de San Marcos for six weeks. Eventually the defenders fled, after burning the wooden buildings of the town to the ground. This time, the colonists replaced them with masonry buildings, as the town expanded in the first half of the 18th century.

Kathleen Deagan and a team of archaeologists have investigated 18th-century and earlier St Augustine on a systematic basis since 1977 (Deagan, 1983), combining historic preservation with archaeological excavation. Excavating the 18th-century town has proved a difficult task, partly because the entire archaeological deposit for three centuries is only about 3 ft (1 m) deep at the most, and has been much disturbed. Nevertheless, the excavators have recovered dozens of barrel-lined trash pits, and the foundations of 18th-century houses built of tabby, a cement-like substance of oyster shells, lime, and sand. The builders laid foundations of oyster shell or tabby in footing trenches that were the shape of the intended house. Then the walls were added. The tabby floor soon wore out, so another layer of earth was added and a new floor poured on top.

The St Augustine excavations were highly informative, and showed that the layout of both St Augustine and Santa Elena was highly structured, rigidly organized, and very conservative. This is hardly surprising, since it was established by 16th-century government ordinances. Households and their barrel-lined wells were laid out at 50-ft (15.2-m) intervals, the streets on a grid pattern. Exactly the same rigid and conservative layout persisted into the 18th century. Only building materials changed. Every time the town grew, the expansion followed the original blueprint. Archaeology confirms what one might suspect from historical documents. The colonists maintained their "Spanishness," which was based on standards set elsewhere, partly as an adaptive strategy to survive within the Spanish

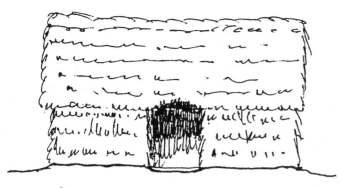

a. SOUTH ELEVATION

b. END ELEVATION

Sketch plan and elevations of a 16th-century thatched structure for a common settler in St Augustine, Florida.

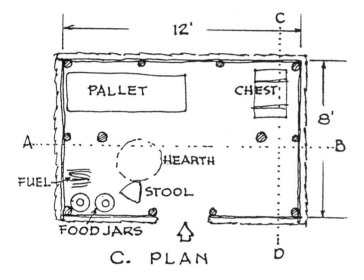

12'

C

PALLET

CHEST

8'

A .... B

HEARTH

FUEL →

STOOL

FOOD JARS

D

C. PLAN

(Right) Spanish 16th-century majolica ware recovered by Kathleen Deagan in her St Augustine excavations.

The stereotyped image of the Spanish colonists. Throwing Indians to the dogs, by G. Benzoni 1594.

colonial system. Local environmental and social factors led to some modification of the Spanish pattern, especially at the domestic level, where intermarriage may have introduced new foods and domestic artifacts into many households (Reitz and Scarry, 1986).

For generations, a pervasive attitude and mythology characterized the Spanish colonists as cruel, bloodthirsty, lustful, and responsible for the decimation of native American populations (Maltby, 1971). This stereotypical "Black Legend" has long been discredited, but it is interesting to note that the objective eye of historical archaeology has documented considerable differences in the ways in which Hispanic-American and Anglo-American cultures developed in North America (Thomas, 1989). Spanish colonial sites contain many more imported and native American ceramics than British settlements of the same period. The vigorous Spanish ceramic tradition resulted from many factors, not only a flourishing export trade but from the custom of subjugating native populations through mechanisms that bound their labor to Spanish masters. Most Spanish settlers were males, and the incorporation of local women into their households brought native ceramics into their settlements. By the time St Augustine was founded, the Spanish had developed a means of interacting with the local population that was based on religious conversion, intermarriage, and tribute (which was later abandoned). The Spaniards integrated themselves physically with local populations, while still maintaining detailed, rigid, and highly legalistic classifications of people by race. In contrast, British colonists based their interactions with Southeastern populations on trade, warfare, slavery, and servitude. There was some intermarriage on the frontier, but there were more English women in English colonies.

Archaeology reveals far fewer native American artifacts and influence in such sites.

There are other differences, too. At St Augustine, the settlers buried their trash in abandoned wells. In a hot climate where food spoils rapidly and fish was commonly eaten, this is a sensible precaution. Many British settlers were far more casual, tossing their trash on the ground around their dwellings (for discussion, see Deagan, 1983; South, 1977). Judging from the St Augustine excavations, Spanish colonists lived in a structured and highly organized social environment, an environment reflected by a tightly patterned material record. The pattern was conservative, in contrast to that recorded by James Deetz (1977) in New England, where an English rural tradition was soon replaced by local adaptations developed by people living not within a structured empire, but in almost complete isolation.

Spanish Missions in the Southeast

Only four Franciscan friars served the spiritual needs of all of La Florida in 1584 (Milanich, 1999). They spent most of their time ministering to the needs of the Spanish colonists of St Augustine and Santa Elena, activities that left them with little time to missionize among the local Timucua Indians, let alone the Guale to the north. Three years later, hostile Guale forced the abandonment of Santa Elena, so Spanish headquarters were moved to St Catherine's Island off the Georgia coast. The island with its Mission Santa Catalina de Guale represented the northernmost extension of Spanish influence along the Atlantic coast for most of the 17th century. The Mission was to flourish until it was abandoned after a British attack in 1680.

Santa Catalina de Guale was part of a large mission system in the Southeast (Thomas, 1988). By the mid-17th century as many as 70 Franciscans served approximately 25,000 Indians in a chain of 38 missions throughout La Florida. This extensive mission network compares with the 50 or so stations that were operating in the Southwest under the direction of 26 friars, and the 650-mile (1046-km) long chain of 21 Franciscan missions in Alta California with their 60 friars that were serving as many as 18,000 Indians in 1830. The California and Southwestern missions are relatively well known. Many of them are still places of worship for substantial congregations. In contrast, those of Spanish Florida are largely forgotten, despite their numerical and strategic importance three centuries ago. Hispanicized native Americans disappeared from La Florida as it came under British rule in 1763. The missions themselves soon fell into disrepair. They were modest structures constructed of mud and sticks, sometimes of "flimsy board and thatch." They were easily set afire, sometimes blown over by hurricanes, or inundated by floods. Hardly any of 16th- or 17th-century La Florida's buildings survive, so mission archaeology assumes particular importance in the Southeast.

According to historical accounts, the 16th-century Mission Santa Catalina de Guale consisted of but a church and a friary. Its 17th-century successor, built after the original was burnt down in 1597, was a square, fortified compound with palisades 193 ft (59 m) on a side and a central, shell-covered plaza. The compound protected the church, friary, the kitchen and garrison. Construction was probably simple, the buildings being held up with tree-trunks, then covered with wattle and daub. David Hurst Thomas of the American Museum of Natural History used archaeological survey and excavation to amplify vague historical records, and to throw detailed light on mission and Indian life during the Spanish period (Thomas, 1988). Thomas employed a battery of sub-surface testing methods not only to locate the major features of the mission, but to develop a baseline library of geophysical signatures for such sites. This archaeological record is a growing archive of resistivity signatures, radar profiles and so on, characteristic of different buried features such as palisade walls and cemeteries that will guide future researches at this and other comparable sites. At Mission Santa Catalina, soil resistivity surveys defined the shape, orientation, and extent of unexcavated buildings such as the friary and a series of contemporary Indian buildings, while proton magnetometer surveys provided information on lengths of clay walls, located a well, also the well-preserved church and kitchen. Cross-cutting, ground-penetrating radar profiles helped define the layout of palisades and bastions surrounding the central mission plaza. This remote-sensing approach had several advantages. It was much cheaper than large-scale excavation, enabled sample trenches to be positioned accurately, and provided valuable information about unexcavated portions of the mission. Careful test excavations based on the remote-sensing program exposed specific structures, many of which have since been excavated in detail.

The church was constructed with a single nave, a rectangular building 65.5 ft (20 m) long and 36 ft (11 m) wide. The wattle-and-daub facade supported a pointed gable and a thatched roof. Pine planking and wattle formed the whitewashed side walls, which may have been adorned with ornate metal panels. The sanctuary was planked, and elevated slightly, with a sacristy on the left side facing the altar. Thomas even recovered some wheat grains from this room, perhaps part of the grain used to bake the flatbread used for the Eucharist. A plaza surfaced with white seashells about 50 ft (15 m) on each side lay in front of the church. It was once enclosed with a low wall. Aerial photographs even revealed a worn pathway across to the doorway.

About 400 to 450 Christianized Guale Indians were buried under the nave and sanctuary, their graves associated with religious paraphernalia, rare majolica vessels, glass trade beads, and other artifacts. After examination, they are being reburied in reconsecrated ground at the Mission.

The Friary complex lay across the main plaza from the church. The first such wattle-and-daub structure was about 52 ft (16 m) long and 23 ft (7 m) wide. This was burnt down by the Guale in 1697, and replaced with two structures, one for the friars, the other a separate kitchen. The friars lived in small, sparsely furnished rooms, built around two central enclosures.

Like St Augustine, Mission Santa Catalina was the product of a rigid and highly conservative society, built along strict architectural specifications. By the same token, too, the American Indians who lived at these missions lived regimented lives where everything, including space, was organized by alien blueprint.

St Catherine's Island, Santa Catalina de Guale mission church undergoing excavation, June 1982. The foundations of the single nave are visible as a dark outline.

Anglo–American Culture: Martin's Hundred and New England

To the north, the English had founded Jamestown in 1607, which soon became an important trading center with tentacles that stretched far into the Southeast and included regular forays for slaves. The *Mayflower* anchored off Plimoth in New England in 1620. Forty-four years later, English colonists took New York from the Dutch, ending over 50 years of Dutch influence over fur trading in the Northeast. Even further north, the French had settled along the St Lawrence, where they dominated the fur trading activity in that region. Their fur traders and explorers had spread throughout the Great Lakes during the 17th century, while Marquette and Joliet descended the Mississippi Valley in 1673. La Salle followed in their footsteps and even tried to colonize the Texas coast. By 1700, the peoples of the Eastern Woodlands were surrounded by what Marvin Smith (1987) calls an "ever-tightening noose of the European presence." Dutch, English, French, and Spanish – each group had different, competing interests that exerted severe pressure on Indian groups often hundreds of miles away from actual direct contact with the foreigners. The dynamics of these pressures, of Indian responses to the European presence, are still little understood. It is only recently, indeed, that historical archaeologists have begun to define the distinctive Anglo-American culture of the British colonists, in Virginia, New England, and elsewhere.

Martin's Hundred. Late in 1618, 220 settlers were shipped from England to settle 20,000 acres (8000 ha) of uncultivated land named Martin's Hundred, facing the James River in Virginia (Nöel Hume, 1982). The settlers built what proved to be a short-lived community that included a small, palisaded fort for protection against Spaniards and Indians and a fledgling settlement named Wolstenholme Towne. This was little more than a hamlet of timbered and thatched houses, a settlement of some 30 to 40 people. At first the local Indians were friendly, but on 22 March 1622 they attacked the James River settlements without warning. Half the Martin's Hundred population was massacred or taken hostage. The survivors eked out a precarious existence for a few more years, but virtual starvation and contagious diseases eventually wiped them out. Wolstenholme Towne was almost forgotten for 350 years.

In 1970, Ivor Nöel Hume, then resident archaeologist at Colonial Williamsburg, was searching for vanished outbuildings, belonging to a colonial plantation in process of restoration. To his surprise, he uncovered 17th-century postholes, pits, and graves – the remains of Wolstenholme Towne (Nöel Hume, 1982). The excavations that followed explored an area of 2 acres (0.81 ha), a jigsaw of post holes, old tree holes, pits, and other long-decayed timber structures. The wooden fort was found to have covered 10,000 sq. ft (929 sq. m). Excavated in its entirety, it was four-sided, of trapezoidal shape, about 83 by 130 ft (25.2 by 39.6 m), with a stout watchtower at the southeast corner and a bastion at the southwest. This once held a cannon, aimed toward possible Spanish ships in the James River. Nöel Hume estimated the palisade was about 7.7 ft (2.3 m) high, with a clay-filled platform behind.

The dwellings were built of wattle, daub, and thatch, some of them built over large cellars as much as 30 ft (9 m) in diameter. In a piece of brilliant archaeological and historical detective work, Ivor Nöel Hume used historical records to show how impecunious farmers would start by living in cellar-like underground houses that they lined with timber and bark, floored with planks, erecting a roof and eaves above ground. A fragment of twisted gold thread and an iron cannonball enabled him to track down the owner of one dwelling through census records and sumptuary laws. It was one William Harwood, once the headman of the tiny settlement.

Excavations like Martin's Hundred are complicated jigsaws of archaeological and historical clues, testimony to the enormous complexities of historical archaeology. The Martin's Hundred finds took Nöel Hume as far afield as

Iron helmet of 1622 from the Martin's Hundred excavations.

The wooden fort of Wolstenholme exposed during Ivor Nöel Hume's Martin's Hundred excavations.

Germany, Ireland, England, and Bermuda, in search of such esoteric information as the design of 17th-century coffin lids and the pathology of cleaver wounds on murder victims.

New England. "The personalities of prehistory will remain forever nameless and without faces. Dynamic and charismatic personae have peopled the stage of history ... But in our not knowing them on personal, individual terms lies a great asset, for the true story of a people depends less on such knowledge than on a broader and more general familiarity with what life was like for all people." Thus does James Deetz (1977) distill the essence of historical archaeology. Archaeologists are concerned with the broad sweep of cultural change, with basic human motivations and behavior. By studying the material remains of the past, it records not the deeds of a select, literate elite, but the lives of members of society as a whole – of minorities, merchants, native Americans, and, above all, of the humble folk and their settlements long forgotten.

The tiny ship that anchored in Plimoth harbor in December 1620 brought a small group of settlers to New England to an unfamiliar land. But they brought with them a clear image of the culture they were going to recreate in their new homeland. It was a culture identical to that in distant England, a form of rural society that had strong roots in the Middle Ages. The colonists were mainly simple artisans and farmers, plain folk who used a familiar cultural blueprint to hack out farms in the more extreme climate of New England. For more than 40 years, New England colonial culture was essentially a copy of that of simple, rural England. Deetz (1977) has pointed out that the earliest colonial houses in the Northeast show considerable resemblances to English rural architecture, and have no surviving counterparts. Some of the Plimoth colony dwellings were thatched longhouses, subdivided into several rooms, built on massive sills rather than foundations. There was considerable architectural diversity reflecting the many homelands of their builders. By 1660, large numbers of colonials had never been to England, and more distinctive, local architectural styles began to develop.

Deetz and others have used such artifacts as New England gravestones and earthenware to document Anglo-American culture in the 17th century (Dethlefsen and Deetz, 1966). The latter were of great importance when Deetz excavated the foundations of a large house 50 ft (15.2 m) long and 30 ft (9.1 m) wide on an island in Wellfleet Bay on outer Cape Cod. The numerous artifacts included imported pottery and glassware that dated the house to c.1670 to 1740. They included very large numbers of clay pipe fragments and eating and drinking utensils, while one cellar contained a whale vertebra and a harpoon. The tavern – it could be nothing else – lay on a remote, high bluff overlooking a place where shoals of small blackfish whales were often to be seen. The location was ideal for whalers to gather and wait for their prey.

We cannot possibly survey the full range of discoveries made by historical archaeologists in North America in the space available, but several recent projects will serve to highlight what this important facet of archaeology does best – documenting the lives of humble men and women going about their daily lives.

The Black Experience and Archaeology

Historical archaeology in America has, until recently, mainly been concerned with the study of the dominant, European culture. Once it dealt mainly with architecture, artifacts, and settlement patterns, often as part of the process of reconstructing elegant country houses and colonial settlements (Orser and Fagan, 1995). With a new emphasis on social history in the 1960s, some scholars became aware of the great potential of archaeology for documenting much of the unrecorded experience of plantation life and slavery. Early excavations focused on plantation sites in the coastal regions of Georgia and South Carolina (Singleton, 1985). Artifacts from such excavations reveal that from 1740 to 1790, the African heritage was still relatively strong in slave communities. This legacy was systematically devalued by slave-owners between 1790 and 1861, and perpetuated during the tenant farming period that followed emancipation. Excavations in Virginia, South Carolina, and Texas have turned up additional examples of artifacts like clay pipe bowls that bear motifs with uncanny resemblances to ideo- and cosmo-grams from West Africa (Kelso, 1984).

Leland Ferguson (1992) has documented African-American resistance to their masters and mistresses in South Carolina, where, in 1740, blacks outnumbered whites by almost two to one, and one-half of that majority was African-born. He assumed that African-American eating habits were quite similar to those of West Africa and radically different from those of European-Americans. By studying what he calls the "container environment" of South Carolina, he was able to trace African-American-made, earthenware "Colono" pots and bowls from slave quarters, plantations, and missions over a wide area of the Southeast. Such vessels were, he believes, a form of unconscious resistance to slavery and the plantation system.

This search for African heritage is but part of researches into African-American history. Excavations are in progress in black communities such as Fort Mose, Florida, just north of St Augustine, the earliest free black town in North America, a place where escaped slaves sought sanctuary under Spanish rule.

Thomas Jefferson's estate at Monticello, Virginia, employed as many as 200 slaves. Jefferson was not only a politician, a philosopher, and an archaeologist, but a major landowner as well. His estate is carefully preserved for the modern visitor as an embodiment of Jefferson's times, but it is easy to forget that it looked very different in his lifetime. Again, the objective eye of the archaeologist has yielded significant information about the anonymous slaves who toiled on his estate (Kelso, 1986).

Monticello, Virginia. Excavations in progress of the Storehouse and Smokehouse/Dairy.

Some of Jefferson's slaves lived along Mulberry Row, the access road to Monticello, a road lined with 19 artisans' and laborers' dwellings, workshops, and storage buildings. William Kelso excavated this area, a task materially assisted by Jefferson's meticulous records. A slave working at Monticello could expect to live in a variety of dwellings, perhaps something as small as a 12 by 14 ft (3.6 by 4.26 m) log cabin with a dirt floor with wooden chimney, or in a much larger stone house, 34 by 17 ft (10.3 by 5.18 m), complete with stone and brick fireplace neoclassical facade and elevated pediment. One visitor to Monticello observed with justification that "the outhouses of the slaves and workmen ... are all much better than I have seen on any other plantation ..."

The occupants of Mulberry Row were somewhat more privileged than many of their fellow slaves on the estate, and certainly than those elsewhere (Kelso, 1986). There was probably a social hierarchy among them, and some of the ceramics found in the dwellings were of quite fine quality. Many of the beef and pork bones were poorer cuts of meat, less meaty portions that were used to make stews. It is interesting to note that slave sites on coastal plantations in Florida and Georgia have yielded many more bowls than planters' or overseers' houses, as if stew was a staple diet. There are signs that domestic trash was brought in from the main house to be picked over. Numerous buttons came to light, thought to be from discarded clothes that were made into heavy quilts.

All these excavations are helping redefine the relationship between modern African-American communities and those of the past, offering accurate depictions of slave life to replace the often-trivial depictions of many modern restorations.

Ships and Shipwrecks

Lakes, rivers, and other waterways were the highways of early European America, highways where thousands of humble, illiterate Americans spent their lives in quiet anonymity. Occasionally, a well-preserved shipwreck offers insights into their lives, and into the ships they manned.

In 1976, a group of archaeologists recovered a small 18th-century cargo boat from shallow water at Brown's Ferry, South Carolina (Albright and Steffy, 1979; Steffy, 1988). Such boats were the short-haul freighters of North America two centuries ago – sailed, poled, and rowed from one obscure waterway to another. They carried people, animals, and cargo, abandoned by a river bank or lake shore to sink forgotten at the end of their useful lives. The brick-filled Brown's Ferry boat lay at a favorite river dumping ground, covered with all manner of rubbish, including the remains of a horse-drawn buggy. More than two-thirds of the hull survived. Once the bricks were removed, a few artifacts including a beer mug, glass bottles, and a quadrant recovered, the hull was lifted from the river bed in a specially designed iron frame. Ship historian and modelmaker J. Richard Steffy pieced together the design of the boat from the actual timbers, from archival research, and from intelligent conjecture. The coaster was 50 ft 6 in (15.4 m) long on deck, with a beam of about 14 ft (4.2 m), a heavy, flat-bottomed vessel that enabled her to operate in shallow water and load from river banks. She was rigged with two masts, perhaps with a simple spritsail

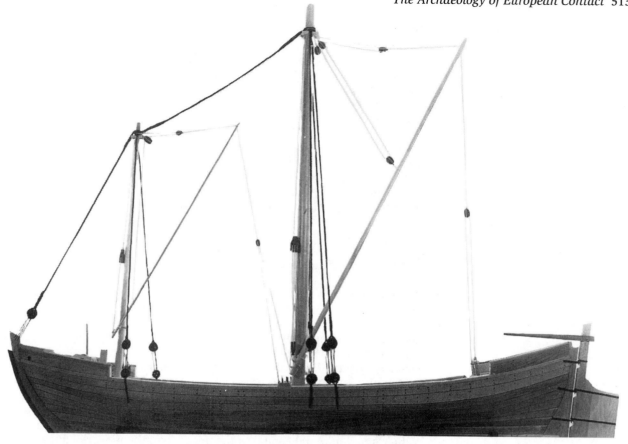

Model by J. Richard Steffy of the small 18th-century cargo vessel recovered at Brown's Ferry, South Carolina.

rig. The crew lived at both ends of the boat, with the galley stove forward of the foremast. The double-ended vessel had oak frames, pine planks, and was repaired and recaulked at least once. This humble craft, built by rural shipwrights and launched without ceremony, sank with a full load of bricks during her last voyage, a boat whose whole life depended on tides and currents. Her forgotten wreck gives the historian and archaeologist insight not only into ancient ship design and construction, but into the daily life of her crew more than two centuries ago.

The Brown's Ferry ship is only one of numerous historic wrecks now being revealed by underwater archaeology in North America. For example, the Ronson ship, unearthed in the heart of New York City, was an old vessel when she was condemned some time before 1750. She was filled with rubble and pressed into service as cribbage for a wharf along the local waterfront. This was another humble craft, this time an ocean carrier about 100 ft (30.5 m) long, used for long-hauling of all manner of cargoes (Steffy, 1988).

Special stern-wheelers with exceptional shallow draft plied the upper sections of such rivers as the Missouri and the Colorado during the 19th century. Many served as supply boats for military posts and mines, carrying not only people, but stores of every kind. The 161-ft (49-m) long *Bertrand* was one such vessel, wrecked on the Missouri River after striking an underwater obstruction on 1 April 1865. She was located under 26 ft (8 m) of water by treasure hunters, then investigated under the aegis of the National Park Service in 1968–69. The overlying silt was removed by dragline, high-pressure hose, and by hand. The lower portion of the hull up to the main deck was exposed, enabling the excavators to make detailed plans of the vessel. They also recovered almost 2,000,000 artifacts, among them foodstuffs, clothing, agricultural and mining supplies, medicines, liquor, and many types of domestic ware. There was ammunition for the Army's 12-pound (5.4-kg) mountain howitzers for their local garrisons, even crates of personal effects. This is the only large-scale excavation of a river steamboat of any kind, and the *Bertrand*'s contents tell us much about the mining and frontier economy of mid-19th-century North America. The local effects of this wreck were considerable, for her cargo was no less than 13 percent of the entire tonnage shipped to Fort Benson in 1865 (Simmons, 1988).

Mines and Miners

Western history is replete with images of rugged mining camps, peopled by individualists, small pockets of civilization surrounded by wilderness (Hardesty, 1988). The 19th-century Nevada mining frontier consisted of many such communities, islands of outsiders who brought their own social and cultural environment with them. These centers were controlled, financed, manned, and supplied from outside, from major business centers in America and Europe. As archaeologist Donald Hardesty points out, they were linked in a real sense to the world economic system of the day, through information networks that expanded fast with the completion of the transcontinental telegraph in 1860, bringing established Victorian values and additional capital to the mines. Supply networks linked to the world economic system transported supplies and mined ore, networks like the one that brought the *Bertrand* up the Missouri River in the upper Midwest. The same mines were linked into a complex migration network that brought miners from all over the United States, also from Asia and Europe, to remote Nevada communities.

Mining activity in Nevada is well documented through contemporary records, but archaeology adds valuable dimensions, by observing buildings, trash dumps, and ruined mines in a three-dimensional context of time and space – the same context used to study ancient sites. Archaeology and history collaborate best in the study of 19th-century mining technology, residential settlements, and individual households. Hardesty points out that only the archaeological record survives to document the layout of most smaller Nevada mining settlements. Most were little more than strips of houses along tracks, or clusters of buildings around mines and crushing mills.

The ethnically diverse Shoshone Wells mining camp in the Cortez Mining District was settled in 1863, reached a considerable size in the early 1880s, and was still occupied by Chinese and a few Italian immigrants as late as 1902. It provides a fascinating example of how text-aided archaeology can document ethnic neighborhoods. The existing archaeological site consists of 50 hut sites, most arranged into five clusters, each a distinctive neighborhood. One cluster of 22 adobe, dugout, and wood frame houses lay along a road on the valley floor. The artifacts associated with these houses are predominantly Anglo-European and Anglo-American or Chinese. Another cluster consists of four stone houses on the hillside above the other groups. These contain Italian artifacts such as Italian bitters bottles, and may have been the dwellings of Italian wood cutters mentioned in historical records.

Mine owner Simeon Wenban's house cluster contained Victorian artifacts such as fine French porcelain that reflected a much higher social status. Written records describe the mine owner's residence as a two-story redwood building standing in an irrigated lawn and garden. Wenban had trouble with his "turbulent and riotous" Cornish and Welsh miners, so he replaced them in the early 1870s with cheaper and less quarrelsome Chinese laborers. They lived along the road, and in the deep ravine below it. Their houses contain Chinese brownware, commonly used for food containers, opium tins and a pipe, gaming pieces, also European glassware bottles that once contained beer, champagne, and other drinks.

The importance of Shoshone Wells is that it gives an example of how a combination of archaeological and historical records can provide insights into the great variability among 19th-century mining communities. The archaeological study of mining provides a way of relating what Hardesty calls (1988) "the settlement," the archaeological record of houses and other structures, to "community," the actual people who lived in it. And such studies are invaluable when examining mining camps that were predominantly male, made up of people of very cosmopolitan origins living in a society where individualism and minding one's own business were the social norms.

The W.C. Hoff General Store, San Francisco. One link in the mining economic system was San Francisco. The California Gold Rush of 1849 brought a flood of humanity from all corners of the globe to the then obscure village that was San Francisco, a bayside settlement with less than 1000 permanent residents. Within three years it was a sprawling boomtown of hotels, bars, cheap rooming houses, and stores, many of them built on piles off the original shoreline. There were regular fires, culminating in the great waterfront fire of 3 May 1851 that virtually destroyed the town, including William Hoff's general hardware store. Hoff himself abandoned his collapsed store to the mud and set up shop elsewhere.

The remains of his once prosperous shop were covered with landfill and forgotten until 1986. Then excavations at the corner of Sacramento and Battery Streets probed 15 ft (4.5 m) below modern street level and recovered much of Hoff's stock buried in wet mud (Pastron, 1988). Hoff's Store was a remarkable snapshot of Gold Rush days, of clothing, furniture, medicines, firearms, construction tools and mining implements from the 1840s. It was a chronicle, not of the spectacular and the unusual, but of the humble and mundane, of kegs of nails, work boots, and Chinese porcelain. There were bottles of champagne and jars of imported olives alongside barrels of salt pork, dried beans, and cheap whisky. Army surplus goods including carbines, powder flasks, and lead shot accompanied many a miner into the interior. There were toilet sets and patent medicines. It is with sites like this that historical archaeology is often at its best, providing a wealth of information about daily life in North America as recently as the late 19th century.

San Francisco has yielded a rich archaeological record, including the remains of a Chinese fishing village located on Rincon Point, where both fishermen and shipwreckers working on abandoned Gold Rush ships dwelt. Excavations have revealed rice and opium bowls, medicines, and both Chinese and Euro-American artifacts. Judging from the large numbers of small ceramic crucibles, some of the inhabitants may have been in contact with mining claims in the Sierra Nevada. The Rincon Point finds reveal a community engaged in varied, and sometimes innovative, economic activities, spurred by the need to maintain the highest possible degree of economic self-reliance (Pastron, 1989). This quest for self-reliance is a reflection of the threatening and intolerant social climate of the day.

Eighteenth-Century Annapolis and the Archaeology of Gardens

Text-aided archaeology not only chronicles the lives of both rich and poor, of 19th-century urban black neighborhoods in eastern cities, of Southern slave plantations and Chinese fisherfolk in the Far West, it can throw light on prevailing social attitudes of past centuries (Orser and Fagan, 1995). For example, archaeologists from the University of Maryland have worked closely with historians on a citywide exploration of the Historic District of Annapolis (Leone and Potter, 1984; Shackel, 1994; Shackel and Little, 1994; Shackel and others, 1998). Annapolis enjoys a high level of historic preservation because the city escaped the Civil War and the Industrial Revolution and did not undergo any urban renewal until the 1950s. Many buildings and the archaeological record have been preserved, and archaeology has played an important part in the preservation process. Over the years, the excavators have investigated an 18th-century tavern, a printshop, several private residences, the site of a formal garden and three properties first occupied about 1690. Bottles, cups, and plates dating to that decade came from the bottom of the excavations of the Governor Calvert House (Yentsch, 1994), followed by intricate occupation layers, including a timber house of the early 1700s. Governor Calvert's brick house, whose first floor now forms part of a modern hotel, was subsequently built on the same site in the 1720s. Most of this structure was drastically rebuilt in the 19th century, but the original walls were preserved within the Victorian building. The excavations also revealed a brick heating system for channeling hot air to a greenhouse. This was partially torn up in the 1760s and filled with domestic refuse before being covered over by an addition to the 1720 house. The refuse proved a rich treasure trove of historical information, for it included animal bones, fish scales, pins, buttons, hair, pieces of paper, and cloth. The Calvert House enabled the archaeologists to recover complete layers of Annapolis history virtually intact.

The Annapolis research has far wider objectives than just historic preservation, however (Leone, 1984). Mark Leone and his colleagues work with broader anthropological concerns, which involve two basic premises. One is that space between buildings is as significant as the structures themselves. Managed landscapes can enhance the appearance of a house, more land may betoken greater wealth or social standing. The second is

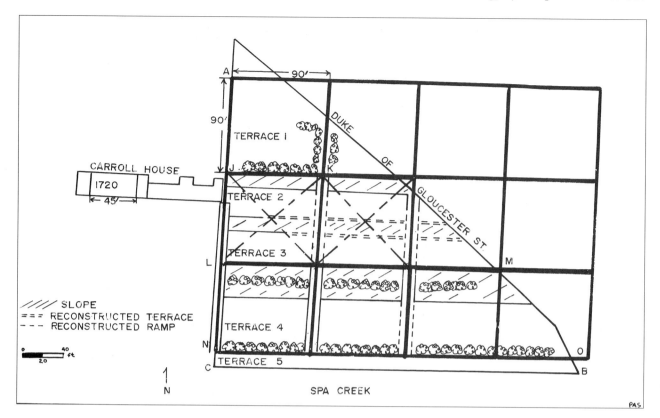

Annapolis. Plan produced by Mark Leone's research team showing how the Carroll House gardens were carefully terraced to enhance distant views and to bolster the civil and social authority of the owners.

that landscape helps to generate social life as well as reflecting it, research that has caused them to focus not only on houses, but on the gardens that surround them – on the premise that 18th-century gardens were important ways of creating social status and power (Leone and others, 1989). By using soil coring, topographical surveys, and family records and photographs, Leone's research team were able to reconstruct the gardens of the Charles Carroll residence, which covers 2 acres (0.8 ha). Their surveys showed that the garden had been designed with terraces that enhanced both the house and distant views, using optical illusions such as terraces, also path and flowerbed lines. The archaeologists' topographic map brought all the variations and hidden secrets of the Carroll garden together and showed how clever landscape design was used to bolster the civil and social authority of the owners, a central part of the 18th-century gentleman's self-definition in Annapolis.

The Annapolis excavations are but one example of the great potential of text-aided archaeology in achieving a more balanced, objective view of our remote and more recent past.

* * *

For more than 13,000 years, human beings have settled in North America, adapted to its many environments, and interacted with one another within its boundaries. It is well that all of us, members of one of the most ethnically diverse societies on earth, understand some of the processes that have created this diversity, and shaped the way in which we live. It is not enough merely to look at American history through European glasses, through ethnocentric spectacles based on historical documents and what can be myopic sources. As James Deetz urges (1977) "Don't read what we have written: look at what we have done." Our understanding of one another, and of ourselves, will be infinitely more perceptive as a result.

Further Reading

Bass, George (ed.). 1988. *Ships and Shipwrecks of the Americas*. Thames & Hudson, London and New York.
   Underwater archaeology in the Americas described by some of the leading authorities. A beautifully illustrated volume.
Deetz, James. 1977. *In Small Things Forgotten*. Anchor Books, New York.
   Deetz' charming essay on historical archaeology captures the essence of the subject.
Ferguson, Leland. 1992. *Uncommon Ground: Archaeology and Early African America, 1650-1800*. Smithsonian Institution Press, Washington DC.
   An exemplary study of African-American archaeology, which combines archaeology and historical records.
Leone, Mark P., and Potter, Parker B. (eds.). 1999. *Historical Archaeologies of Capitalism*. Kluwer Academic/Plenum Press, New York.
   Essays on archaeology and early capitalism, which range widely over the problems of historical archaeology. For the specialist reader.
Milanich, Jerald T. 1999. *Laboring in the Fields of the Lord: Spanish Missions and Southeastern Indians*. Smithsonian Institution Press, Washington DC.
   Mission archaeology in the Southeast for the general reader. An exceptional book.
Milanich, Jerald T. and Milbrath, Susan. 1989. *First Encounters*. University of Florida Press, Gainesville.
   A superb popular account of European-Indian contact in the Southeast.
Nöel Hume, Ivor. 1982. *Martin's Hundred*. Alfred Knopf, New York; Gollancz, London.
   One of the classics of historical archaeology. A beautifully written archaeological detective story.
Orser, C.E., and Fagan, B.M. 1995. *Historical Archaeology*. Harper Collins, New York.
   A short introduction to document-aided archaeology for students and general readers. International perspective.
Shackel, Paul. 1994. *Personal Discipline and Material Culture: An Archaeology of Annapolis, Maryland, 1695-1870*. University of Tennessee Press, Knoxville, TN.
   A useful summary of the historical archaeology of Annapolis, which relies on recent work.
Thomas, David Hurst.1988. *St Catherines: An Island in Time*. Georgia Endowment for the Humanities, Atlanta.
   A popular account of the Mission Santa Catalina de Guale researches, which is ideal for the beginning reader.

Bibliography

This Bibliography makes no pretence at being complete, and represents only a small proportion of the references used to research and write this book. The sources that follow, together with the Further Reading listings at the end of each chapter, will, however, enable the reader to delve more deeply into the diffuse literature of North American archaeology.

The World Wide Web has been an important source of information on North American archaeology in recent years and was used to research this edition. But Web sites appear and vanish with bewildering rapidity, making it virtually impossible to provide reliable information on addresses and sites. Readers are recommended to start with a permanent and much respected site, Arch.net, which is a Web Page dedicated to all aspects of archaeology, with links to every aspect of the subject imaginable: http://spirit.lib.uconn.edu/archaeology/html. In this way, you will always access up-to-date Web addresses.

Ackermann, Robert. 1982. "The Neolithic-Bronze Age cultures of Asia and the Norton Phase of Alaskan Prehistory," *Arctic Anthropology* 19(2):11–38.
———and others. 1985. *Archaeology of Heceta Island: a survey of 16 timber harvest units in the Tongass National Forest, Southeastern Alaska*. Center for Northwest Archaeology, Washington State University, Pullman.
Adair, Mary. 1993. *Prehistoric Agriculture in the Central Plains*. University of Kansas Publications in Anthropology, Lawrence, KS.
Adams, E. Charles. 1991. *The Origin and Development of the Pueblo Katchina Cult*. University of Arizona Press, Tucson.
Adler, Michael A. (ed.). 1996. *The Prehistoric Pueblo World, AD 1150–1350*. University of Arizona Press, Tucson.
———, Van Pool, Todd, and Leonard, Robert D. 1996. "Ancestral Pueblo Population Aggregation and Abandonment in the North American Southwest," *Journal of World Prehistory* 10(3):375–438.
Adovasio, James. 1980. "Yes, Virginia, it really is that old: A reply to Haynes and Mead," *American Antiquity* 45:588–595.
———1982. "Meadowcroft Rockshelter 1973–1977: A synopsis," in J.E. Ericson and others (eds.). *Peopling of the New World*. Ballena Press, Los Altos, California, pp.97–131.
———1984. "Meadowcroft Rockshelter and the Pleistocene/Holocene Transition in South-West Pennsylvania," in Hugh Genoways and Mary Dawson (eds.). *Contributions in Quaternary Vertebrate Paleontology of the Carnegie Museum of Natural History* 8.
———and Donahue, J. and Stuckenrath, R. 1990. "The Meadowcroft Rockshelter Radiocarbon Chronology 1975–1990," *American Antiquity* 55(2):348–354.
Ahler, S.R. 1993. "Stratigraphy and Radiocarbon Chronology of Modoc Rock Shelter, Illinois," *American Antiquity* 58(3):462–489.
———, Thiessen, T., and Trimble, M. 1991. *People of the Willows: The Prehistory and Early History of the Hidatsa Indians*. University of North Dakota Press, Grand Forks, ND.
Aigner, Jean. 1970. "The Unifacial, Core, and Blade Site on Anangula Island, Aleutians," *Arctic Anthropology* 7(2):59–88.
Aikens, C.M. 1966. *Fremont-Promontory-Plains Relationships*. University of Utah Anthropological Papers 82.
———1967. "Plains Relationships of the Fremont Culture: A Hypothesis," *American Antiquity* 32:198–209.
———1970. *Hogup Cave*. University of Utah Anthropological Papers 93.
———1978. "The Far West," in Jesse D. Jennings (ed.). *Ancient Native Americans*. W.H. Freeman, San Francisco, pp.131–182.
———1982. "Archaeology of the Northern Great Basin: an overview," in David Madsen and James O'Connell (eds.). *Man and Environment in the Great Basin*. Society for American Archaeology, Washington DC, pp.139–155.
———1983. "The Far West," in Jesse D. Jennings (ed.). *Ancient Native Americans*. W.H. Freeman, San Francisco, pp.149–201.
———1994. "Adaptive strategies and environmental change in the great Basin and its peripheries as determinants in the migrations of Numic-speaking peoples," in David B. Madsen and David Rhode (eds.). *Across the West: Human population movement and the expansion of the Numa*. University of Utah Press, Salt Lake City, pp.35–43.
———and Madsen, David. 1986. "Prehistory of the Eastern Area," in Warren D'Azevado (ed.). *Handbook of North American Indians. Vol.11: Great Basin*. Smithsonian Institution, Washington DC, pp.149–160.
Akins, Nancy J. 1986. *A Biocultural Approach to Human Burials from Chaco Canyon, New Mexico*. National Park Service, Albuquerque, NM.
Albright, A.B. and Steffy, J.R. 1979. "The Brown's Ferry Vessel, South Carolina," *International Journal of Nautical Archaeology* 8:121–142.
Ames, K.M. 1981. "The evolution of social rank on the Northwest Coast of North America," *American Antiquity* 46:789–805.
———1988. "Early Holocene mobility patterns ...," in J. Willig, C.M. Aikens, and John Fagan (eds.). *Paleo-Indian-Archaic interface in Western North America*. Nevada State Museum, Carson City. Paper 28.
———1991a. "The archaeology of the *longue durée*: temporal and spatial scale in the evolution of social complexity on the southern Northwest Coast," *Antiquity* 65:935–945.
———1991b. "Sedentism, a temporal shift or a transitional change in hunter-gatherer mobility strategies," in S. Gregg (ed.). *Between Bands and States: Sedentism, Subsistence, and Interaction in Small Scale Societies*. Southern Illinois University Press, Carbondale pp.103–33.
———1993. "Art and regional interaction among affluent foragers on the North Pacific Rim," in A.R. Blukis Anat (ed.). *Development of Hunting-Gathering-Fishing Maritime Societies on the Pacific*. Washington State University, Pullman, WA, pp.23–35.
———1994. "The Northwest Coast: Complex Hunter-Getherers, Ecology, and Social Evolution," *Annual Review of Anthropology* 23:209–229.
———and Maschner, Herbert D. 1999. *Peoples of the Northwest Coast: Their Archaeology and Prehistory*. Thames and Hudson, London and New York.
Amick, D.S. 1995. "Patterns of Technological Variation Among Folsom and Midland projectile Points in the American Southwest," *Plains Anthropologist* 40:23–38.
———and Philip J. Carr. (eds.). 1996. "Changing Strategies of Lithic Technological Organization," in Kenneth E. Sassaman and David G. Anderson. (eds.). *Archaeology of the Mid-Holocene Southeast*. University Presses of Florida, Gainesville, FL, pp.41–56.
Anderson, D.G. 1994. *The Savannah River Chiefdoms: Political Change in the Late Prehistoric Southeast*. University of Alabama Press, Tuscaloosa, AL.
———1996. "Models of Paleoindian and Early Archaic Settlement in the Lower Southeast," in David G. Anderson and Kenneth D. Sassaman (eds.). *The Paleoindian and Early Archaic Southeast*. University of Alabama Press, Tuscaloosa, AL, pp.29–57.
———1997. "The Role of Cahokia in the Evolution of Southeastern Mississippian Society," in Timothy R. Pauketat and Thomas E. Emerson (eds.). *Cahokia: Domination and Ideology in the Mississippian World*. University of Nebraska Press, Lincoln, NE, pp.248–268.
———and others. (eds.). 1982. *The Mattasee Lake Sites*. National Park Service, Atlanta, GA.
———and Hanson, Glen T. 1988. "Early Archaic Settlement in the Southeastern United States: A Case Study from the Savannah River Valley,"

American Antiquity 53:262–286.

———, David W. Stahle, and Cleaveland, Malcolm K. 1995. "Paleoclimate and the Potential Food Reserves of Mississippian Societies: A Case Study from the Savannah River Valley," *American Antiquity* 60(2):258–286.

——— and Sassaman, Kenneth E. (eds.). 1996. *The Paleoindian and Early Archaic Southeast*. University of Alabama Press, Tuscaloosa, AL.

Anderson, Douglas D. 1988. *Onion Portage: An Archaeological Site on the Kobuk River, Northwestern Alaska*. Anthropological Papers, University of Alaska, 20(1–2).

Antevs, Ernst. 1948. "Climatic Changes and Pre-White Man," in "The Great Basin with Emphasis on Glacial and Postglacial times "*University of Utah Bulletin* 38(20), Biological Series 10(7):168–191.

Arnold, Jeanne E. 1992. "Complex Hunter Gatherer-Fishers of Prehistoric California: Chiefs, Specialists, and Maritime Adaptations of the Channel Islands," *American Antiquity* 57(1):60–84.

———and Tissot, J.E. 1992. "Measurement of Significant Paleotemperature Variation Using Black Abalone Shells from Middens," *Quaternary Research* 39:390–394.

Asch, David, and Asch, Nancy. 1978. "The Economic Potential of *Iva annua* and its Prehistoric Importance in the Lower Illinois Valley," in Richard I. Ford (ed.). *The Nature and Status of Ethnobotany*, Museum of Anthropology, University of Michigan, Ann Arbor, MI, pp.300–341.

———1985. "Prehistoric Plant Cultivation in West-Central Illinois," in Richard I. Ford (ed.). *Prehistoric Food Production in North America*, Museum of Anthropology, University of Michigan, Ann Arbor, MI, pp.199–203.

Aten, L.E. 1983. *Indians of the Upper Texas Coast*. Academic Press, Orlando, FL.

Atwater, Caleb. 1820. "Description of the Antiquities Discovered in the State of Ohio and other Western States," *Transactions and Collections of the American Antiquarian Society* 1:105–267.

Bamforth, Douglas. 1988. *Ecology and Human Organization on the Great Plains*. Plenum Press, New York.

Bandelier, A.E. 1884. "Report on the Ruins of the Pueblo of Pecos," *Papers of the Archaeological Institute of America* 1:37–133.

Bandi, Hans-Georg. 1969. *Eskimo Prehistory*. University of Alaska Press, Fairbanks.

Bareis, C.J. and Porter, J.W. (eds.). 1984. *American Bottom Archaeology*. University of Illinois Press, Urbana, IL.

Barker, A.W., and Pauketat, T.R. (eds.). 1992. *Lords of the Southeast: Social Inequality and the Native Elites of Southeastern North America*. American Anthropological Association, Washington DC.

Barley, D. 1980. Marpole: *Anthropological Reconstructions of a Prehistoric Northwest Culture Type*. Occasional Paper 8, Department of Anthropology, Simon Fraser University, Burnaby, BC.

Barnett, H.G. 1955. *The Coast Salish of British Columbia*. University of Oregon, Eugene, OR.

Barreis, D.A., and Bryson, R.A. 1965. "Climatic Episodes and the dating of Mississippian Culture," *The Wisconsin Archeologist* 46(4):416.

Barth, Frederick. 1975. *Ritual and Knowledge among the Baktama of New Guinea*. Yale University Press, New Haven.

Bartram, William. 1853. "Observations on the Creek and Cherokee Indians (1789)," *American Ethnological Society Transactions* 3,1.

Basgall, M. 1987. 'Resource intensification among

hunter-gatherers: acorn economies in prehistoric California," *Research in Economic Anthropology* 9:21–52.

Bass, George. (ed.). 1988. *Ships and Shipwrecks of the Americas*. Thames and Hudson, London and New York.

Baugh, Timothy G. and Ericson, Jonathon E. (eds.). 1994. *Prehistoric Exchange Systems in North America*. Plenum Press, New York.

Baumhoff, M. 1963. "Ecological determinants of aboriginal California populations," *University of California Publications in Archaeology and Ethnology* 49(2):155–236.

———1978. "Environmental Background," in R.E. Heizer (ed.). *Handbook of North American Indians. Vol. 8: California*. Smithsonian Institution, Washington DC, pp.16–24.

Beaton, J.M. 1991. "Extensification and intensification in central California prehistory," *Antiquity* 65:946–952.

Beaudry, Mary C. (ed.). 1987. *Documentary Archaeology in the New World*. Cambridge University Press, Cambridge.

Beck, Charlotte. 1995. "Functional attributes and the differential persistence of Great Basin dart forms," *Journal of California and Great Basin Anthropology* 17(2):222–243.

———and Jones, George T. 1997. "The Terminal Pleistocene/Early Holocene Archaeology of the Great Basin," *Journal of World Prehistory* 11(2):161–236.

Beckett, Patrick H., and MacNeish, Richard S. 1994. "The Archaic Chihuahua Tradition of South-Central New Mexico and Chihuahua, Mexico," in Bradley J. Vierra, *Archaic Hunter-Gatherer Archaeology in the American Southwest*. Contributions in Anthropology 13(1):335–371. Eastern New Mexico University, Portales, NM.

Bell, R.E. (ed.). 1984. *Prehistory of Oklahoma*. Academic Press, Orlando, FL.

Bement, L.C. 1986. *Excavation of the Late Pleistocene Deposits of Bonfire Shelter, Val Verde County, Texas*. Texas Archaeological Survey, Austin, Archaeology Series 1.

———1989. "Lower Pecos Canyonlands," in T.R. Hester and others (eds.). *From the Gulf to the Rio Grande: Human Adaptation in Central, South, and Lower Pecos Texas*. Arkansas Archaeological Survey Research Series 33, pp.63–76.

Benn, David. (ed.). 1990. *Woodland Cultures on the Western Prairies*. Office of the State Archaeologist Report 10, Iowa City.

Benninghoff, W.S. 1968. "Biological Consequences of Quaternary glaciations in the Illinois region," in Robert E Bergstrom (ed.). *The Quaternary of Illinois*. University of Illinois Press, Urbana, Illinois, pp.70–77.

Bense, Judith. 1994. *Archaeology of the Southeastern United States*. Academic Press, San Diego.

Berry, C.E. and Berry, M.S. 1986. "Chronological and conceptual models of the Southwest Archaic," in Carol J. Condie and Don D. Fowler (eds.). *Anthropology of the Desert West: Essays in Honor of Jesse D. Jennings*. Department of Anthropology, University of Utah, pp.253–327.

Betancourt, J.L. and Van Devender, T.R. 1981. "Holocene vegetation in Chaco Canyon, New Mexico," *Science* 214:656–658.

Bettinger, R.L. 1991. *Hunter-gatherers: archaeological and evolutionary theory*. Plenum, New York.

———and Baumhoff, M.A. 1982. "The Numic Spread: Great Basin Cultures in competition," *American Antiquity* 47:485–503.

———and Baumhoff, M.A. 1983. "Return dates and intensity of resource use in Numic and PreNumic adaptive strategies," *American Antiquity* 48:830–834.

———and Jelmer Eerkens. 1999. "Point Typologies, Cultural Transmission, and the Spread of Bow-And-Arrow Technology in the Prehistoric Great Basin," *American Antiquity* 64(2): 231–242.

———, O'Connell, J.F., and Thomas, D.H. 1991. "Projectile Points as Time Machines in the Great Basin," *American Anthropologist* 93(1):166–173.

Bickel, R. McW. 1978. "Changing sea levels along the California coast: Anthropological Implications," *Journal of California Archaeology* 5:(1):6–20.

Bielawski, E. 1988. "Paleoeskimo Variability: The Early Arctic Small-Tool Tradition in the Central Canadian Arctic," *American Antiquity* 53(1):52–74.

Binford, L.R. 1978. *Nunamiut Ethnoarchaeology*. Academic Press, New York.

———1983. *In Pursuit of the Past*. Thames and Hudson, London and New York.

———and Chasko, W.J. Jr. 1976. "Numamiut demographic history: a provocative case," in Ezra Zubrow (ed.). *Demographic Anthropology: Quantitative Approaches*. University of New Mexico Press, Albuquerque, NM, pp.63–144.

Birket-Smith, Kaj. 1929. *The Caribou Eskimo*. Report of the Fifth Thule Expedition 1921–1924, 5. Glydenclalski Boghandel, Nordisk Forlag, Copenhagen.

Biswell, H.H. 1967. "The Use of Fire in Wildlife Management in California," in S.V. Ciriacy Wantrup and J.J. Parsons (eds.). *Natural Resources: Quality and Quantity*. University of California Press, Berkeley, pp.71–86.

Björk, S., and others. 1996. "Synchronized Terrestrial-Atmospheric Deglacial Records Around the North Atlantic," *Science* 274:1155–1160.

Black, S.L. 1989. "Environmental Setting," in T.R. Hester and others (eds.). *From the Gulf to the Rio Grande: Human Adaptation in Central, South, and Lower Pecos Texas*. Arkansas Archaeological Survey Research Series 33, pp.5–16.

———and others. 1997. *Hot Rock Cooking on the Greater Edwards Plateau: Four Burned Rock Midden Sites in West Central Texas*. Texas Archaeological Research Laboratory, Studies in Archaeology 22. University of Texas, Austin.

Blakely, R.L., and Mathews, D.S. 1990. "BioArchaeological Evidence for a Spanish-Native American Conflict in the Sixteenth-Century Southeast," *American Antiquity* 55(4):718–744.

Blakely, Robert. (ed.). 1988. *The King Site: Continuity and Contact in Sixteenth-Century Georgia*. University of Georgia Press, Athens, GA.

Blanton, D.B. and Sassaman, K.E. 1988. "Pattern and Process in the Middle Archaic of South Carolina," in A.C. Goodyear (ed.). *Papers in Honor of Robert L. Stapleton*. Institute of Archaeology and Anthropology, University of South Carolina, Columbia, SC.

Blevins, B.B. and Joiner, C. 1977. "The archaeological survey of Tijeras Canyon," in Linda S. Cordell (ed.). *The 1976 excavation of Tijeras Pueblo, Cibola National Forest, New Mexico*. US Department of Agriculture, Forest Service Southwest Region, Albuquerque, NM, pp.126–152.

Blitz, John H. 1988. "Adoption of the Bow in Prehistoric North America," *North American Archaeology* 9(2):123–145.

Boas, Franz. 1905–1909. "The Kwakiutl of Vancouver Island," *Memoirs of the American Museum of Natural History* 8:307–515.

Bobrowsky, P.T., and N.W. Rutter. 1990. "Geologic Evidence for an Ice-Free Corridor in Northeastern British Columbia, Canada," *Current Research in the Pleistocene* 7:133–35.

Borah, W. 1976. "The Historical Demography of Aboriginal and Colonial America: An Attempt at Perspective," in W.H. Denevan (ed.). *The Native Population of the Americas in 1492.* University of Wisconsin Press, Madison, pp.13–34.

Borden, C.A. 1975. *Origins and Development of Early Northwest Coast Culture to about 3000 BC.* Archaeological Survey of Canada, Mercury Series 45, Ottawa.

Bouey, P. 1987. "The intensification of hunter-gatherer economies in the southern North Coast Ranges of California," *Research in Economic Anthropology* 9:53–101.

Bourque, Bruce. 1995. *Diversity and Complexity in Prehistoric Maritime Societies.* Plenum Press, New York.

Boyd, Carolyn E. and Dering, J. Philip. 1996. "Medicinal and Hallucinogenic Plants Identified in the Sediments and Pictographs of the Lower Pecos, Texas Archaic," *Antiquity* 70(268):256–275.

Bradley, A.P. 1997. "The Bow and Arrow in the Eastern Woodlands. Evidence for an Archaic Origin," *North American Archaeologist* 18:207–23.

Bradley, James. 1987. *Evolution of the Onondaga Iroquois.* Syracuse University Press, Syracuse.

Brain, Jeffrey P., and Phillips, Philip. 1995. *Shell Gorgets: Styles of the Late Prehistoric and Protohistoric Southeast.* Peabody Museum, Harvard University.

Braun, David P. 1985. "Ceramic Decorative Diversity and Illinois Woodland Regional Integration," in Ben A. Nelson (ed.). *Decoding Prehistoric Ceramics,* Southern Illinois University, Carbondale, IL, pp.128–153.

———1986. "Midwestern Hopewellian Exchange and Supralocal Interaction," in Colin Renfrew and John Cherry (eds.). *Peer Polity Interaction and Sociopolitical Change.* Cambridge University Press, Cambridge, pp.117–126.

———1989. "Coevolution of Sedentism, Pottery Technology, and Horticulture in the Central Midwest, 200 BC–AD 600," in W.E. Keegan (ed.). *Emergent Horticultural Economies of the Eastern Woodlands,* Southern Illinois University Press, Carbondale, IL, pp.153–182.

Brink, Jack. 1989. *Final Report of the 1985 and 1986 Field Season at Head-Smashed-In Buffalo Jump, Alberta.* Edmonton: Archaeological Survey of Alberta, Manuscript Series no. 16.

Brose, David S. 1970. *The Summer Island Site: A Study of Prehistoric Cultural Ecology and Social Organization in the Northern Lake Michigan Area.* Case Western Reserve Studies in Anthropology 1.

———1994. "Trade and Exchange in the Midwestern United States," in Timothy G. Baugh and Jonathon E. Ericson, *Prehistoric Exchange Systems in North America.* Plenum Press, New York, pp.215–240.

———and Plog, Stephen. 1982. "Evolution of 'Tribal' social networks: theory and prehistoric North American evidence," *American Antiquity* 473:504–525.

———and Greber, N. (eds.). 1979. *Hopewellian Archaeology.* Kent University Press, Kent, OH.

Broughton, J.M. 1994a. "Late Holocene Resource Intensification in the Sacramento Valley, California," *Journal of Archaeological Science* 13:371–401.

———1994b. "Declines in Mammalian Foraging Efficiency during the Late Holocene, San Francisco Bay, California," *Journal of Anthropological Archaeology* 21:501–514.

———1997. "Widening Diet Breadth, Declining Foraging Efficiency, and Prehistoric Harvest Pressure: Ichthyofaunal Evidence from the Emeryville Shellmound, California," *Antiquity* 71:845–862.

———and O'Connell, James F. 1998. "On Evolutionary Ecology, Selectionist Archaeology, and Behavioral Archaeology," *American Antiquity* 64(1):153–165.

Brown, J.A. 1979. "Charnel Houses and Mortuary Crypts: Disposal of the Dead in the Middle Woodland Period," in David S. Brose and N'omi Greber (eds.). *Hopewellian Archaeology,* Kent University Press, Kent, OH, pp.211–219.

———1984. "Arkansas Valley Caddoan: The Spiro Phase," in R.E. Bell (ed.). *Prehistory of Oklahoma.* Academic Press, Orlando, FL, pp.241–264.

Broyles, B. 1971. *Second Preliminary Report: the St Albans site. Kanawka County.* West Virginia Geological and Economic Survey.

Bryan, A.L. (ed.). 1978. *Early Man in America from a Circum-Pacific Perspective.* Archaeological Research International, Edmonton, Alberta.

Bryant, Vaughn, and Holloway, Richard. (eds.). 1985. *Pollen Records of Late-Quaternary North American Sediments.* American Association of Stratigraphic Palynologists Foundation, Dallas, TX.

Buikstra, Jane E. and others. 1986. "Fertility and the Development of Agriculture in the Prehistoric Midwest," *American Antiquity* 51:528–546.

Burch, Ernest S. and Mishler, Craig W. 1995. "The Diaii Gwich'in: Mystery People of Northern Alaska," *Arctic Anthropology* 32(1):147–172.

Burns, James A. 1996. "Vertebrate Paleontology and the Alleged Ice-Free Corridor: The Meat of the Matter," *Quaternary International* 32:107–112.

Butler, Virginia L. 1996. "Tui Chub Taphonomy and the Importance of Marsh Resources in the Western Great Basin of North America," *American Antiquity* 61(4):699–717.

Byers, D. 1954. "Bull Brook–a fluted point site in Ipswich, Massachusetts," *American Antiquity* 19:343–351.

Byrd, K.M. 1976. "Tchefuncte Subsistence: information obtained from the excavation of the Morton Shell Mound, Iberia Parish, Louisiana," *Southeastern Archaeology Conference Bulletin,* 19.

Caldwell, Joseph R. 1958. *Trend and Tradition in the Prehistory of the Eastern United States.* Illinois State Museum, Springfield, Illinois.

Campbell, J.M. (ed.). 1962. *Prehistoric Cultural Relations between the Arctic and Temperate Zones of North America.* Arctic Institute of North America. Technical Paper 11, Montreal.

Campbell, Sarah K. (ed.). 1985. *Summary of Results: Chief Joseph Dam Cultural Resources Project, Washington.* Office of Public Archaeology, University of Washington, Seattle.

Cannon, Aubrey. 1991. *The Economic Prehistory of Namu.* Archaeology Press, Simon Fraser University, Burnaby, BC.

Carlson R. 1979. "The Early Period on the Central Coast of British Columbia," *Canadian Journal of Archaeology* 3:211–228.

———(ed.) 1983. *Indian Art Traditions of the Northwest Coast.* Archaeology Press, Simon Fraser University, Burnaby, BC.

———1994. "Trade and Exchange in Prehistoric British Columbia," in T.G. Baugh and J.E. Ericson (eds.). *Prehistoric Exchange Systems in North America.* Plenum Press, New York, pp.307–361.

Carr, C. 1995. *Style, Society, and Person.* Plenum Press, New York.

Cassidy, Francis. 1965. "Fire Temple, Mesa Verde National Park," in Gordon Vivian and Paul Reuter (eds.). *The Great Kivas of Chaco Canyon and their relationships.* School of American Research Monographs 22, pp.73–81.

Chadderdon, M.F. 1983. *Baker Cave Val Verde County, Texas: The 1976 Excavations.* Center for Archaeological Research, University of Texas at San Antonio Special Report 13.

Chapman, Jefferson 1973. *The Icehouse Bottom site 40MR23.* Department of Anthropology, University of Tennessee, Knoxville, TN.

———1975. *The Rose Island site.* Department of Anthropology, University of Tennessee, Knoxville, TN.

———1978. *The Bacon Farm site and a buried site reconnaissance.* Department of Anthropology, University of Tennessee, Knoxville,TN.

———1979. *The Howard and Calloway Island sites.* Department of Anthropology, University of Tennessee, Knoxville. TN.

———(ed.) 1980. *The 1979 Archaeological and Geological Investigations in the Tellico Reservoir, Eastern Tennessee.* Department of Anthropology, University of Tennessee, Knoxville. TN.

———1994. *Tellico Archaeology.* 2nd ed. University of Tennessee Press, Knoxville, TN.

Chard, C.S. 1974. *Northeast Asia in Prehistory.* University of Wisconsin Press, Madison, WI.

Charles, D.K. and Buikstra, J.E. 1983. "Archaic Mortuary Sites in the Central Mississippi Drainage: Distribution, Structure, and Implications," in James Phillips and James Brown (eds.). *Archaic Hunters and Gatherers in the Midwest.* Academic Press, New York, pp.117–145.

Chartkoff, J.L., and Chartkoff, K.K. 1984. *The Archaeology of California.* Stanford University Press, Stanford.

Chuing, Tang, and Pei, Gai. 1986. "Upper Palaeolithic Cultural Traditions in North China," *Advances in World Archaeology* 5:339–364.

Cinq-Mars, Jacques. 1978. "Bluefish Cave 1: a late Pleistocene eastern Beringian cave deposit in the northern Yukon," *Canadian Journal of Archaeology* 3:1–32.

Claasen, Cheryl. 1986. "Temporal Patterns in Marine Shellish Species Use Along the Atlantic Coast of the Southeastern United States," *Southeastern Archaeology* 5(2):120–137.

Clark, D.W. 1997. *The Early Kachemak Phase on Kodiak Island at Old Kiavak.* National Museum of Civilization, Mercury Series, Ottawa.

———1998. "Kodiak Island: The Later Cultures," *Arctic Anthropology* 35(1): 172–186.

Clark, J.G.D. 1954. *Star Carr.* Cambridge University Press, Cambridge.

Clausen, C.J. and others. 1979. "Little Salt Spring, Florida: A unique underwater site," *Science* 203:609–614.

Clay, R. Berle. 1998. "The Essential Features of Adena Ritual and Their Implications," *Southeastern Archaeology* 17(1):1–21.

Cleland, C.E. 1982. "The Inland Shore Fishery of the Northern Great Lakes: Its Development and Importance in Prehistory," *American Antiquity* 47:761–84.

Coe, Joffre. 1952. "The cultural sequence of the Carolina Piedmont," in James B. Griffin (ed.). *Archaeology of the Eastern United States.* University of Chicago Press, Chicago, pp.123–132.

———1964. "The formative cultures of the Carolina Piedmont," *Transactions of the American Philosophical Society,* 54,5.

Coe, M., Snow, D. and Benson, E. 1986. *Atlas of Ancient America.* Facts on File, New York and Oxford.

Cole, Fay-Cooper. 1951. *Kincaid.* University of Chicago Publications in Anthropology, Chicago.

Colinvaux, Paul. 1980. "Vegetation of the Bering Land Bridge revisited," *Quarterly Review of Archaeology* 1:18–36.

Collins, H.B. 1937. "Archaeology of St Lawrence Island, Alaska," *Smithsonian Miscellaneous*

Collections 96,1.
——1956. "Archaeological Investigations on Southampton and Coats Islands, Northwest Territories," *National Museum of Canada Bulletin* 142:82–113.

Collins, James M., and Chalfont, Michael L. 1993. "A second-terrace perspective on Monk's Mound," *American Antiquity* 58:319–32.

Collins, M.B. 1971. "A Review of Llano Escalado Archaeology and Ethnohistory," *Plains Anthropologist* 16:85–104.

——(ed.). 1998. *Wilson-Leonard, An 11,000-Year Archaeological Record of Hunter Gatherers in Central Texas.* 5 vols. Texas Archaeological Research Laboratory, Studies in Anthropology 31. University of Texas, Austin, TX.

Colten, R.S. and Arnold, J.E. 1998. "Prehistoric Marine Mammal Hunting on California's Northern Channel Islands," *American Antiquity* 63:679–701.

Condie, C. and Fowler, D.D. (eds.). 1985. *Archaeology of the Desert West: Essays in Honor of Jesse D. Jennings.* University of Utah Press, Salt Lake City.

Conger, P.S. and others. 1949. "The Boylston Street Fishweir II," *Papers of the Robert S. Peabody Foundation for Archaeology* 4,1.

Connelly, T.J. 1998. *Newberry Crater: A 10,000 Year Record of Human Occupation and Environmental Change in the Basin-Plateau Borderlands.* University of Utah Press, Salt Lake City.

Cook, S.F. 1976. *The Populations of the California Indians 1969–1970.* University of California Press, Berkeley.

——1978. "Historical Demography," in R.E. Heizer (ed.). *Handbook of North American Indians, Vol. 8: California.* Smithsonian Institution, Washington DC, pp.91–98.

Cordell, Linda S. 1997. *Archaeology of the Southwest.* 2nd ed. Academic Press, New York.

Coupland, G. 1988. "Prehistoric economic and social change in the Tsimshian area," in B.L. Isaac (ed.). *Research in Economic Anthropology. Supplement 3: Prehistoric Economies of the Pacific Northwest Coast.* JAI Press, Greenwich, CT, pp.211–214.

Cowan, C.W., and Watson, P.J. (eds.). 1992. *The Origins of Agriculture.* Smithsonian Institution Press, Washington DC.

Cox, S.L. 1986. "A re-analysis of the Shoop site," *Archaeology of Eastern North America* 14:101–170.

Crawford, Gary W. 1999. "Northeast Palaeoethnobotany: How are We Doing?" In John Hart (ed.). *Palaeoethnobotany in the Northeast.* New York State Museum, Albany, NY, pp. 227–236.

——and others. 1997a. "Dating the Entry of Corn (*Zea mays*) into the Lower Great Lakes Region," *American Antiquity* 62(1):112–119.

——and others. 1997b. "Floodplains and Agricultural origins: A Case Study in South-Central Ontario," *Journal of Field Archaeology.*

——and Smith, David G. 1996. "Migration in Prehistory: Princess Point and the Northern Iroquoian Case," *American Antiquity* 61(4):782–790.

Creamer, Winifred. 1991. *The Architecture of Arroyo Hondo, New Mexico.* School of American Research Press, Santa Fe.

Cressman, L.S. and others. 1960. "Cultural Sequences at The Dalles, Oregon: a contribution to Pacific Northwest prehistory," *Transactions of the American Philosophical Society* 50(10).

Crites, D. 1993. "Domesticated Sunflower in Fifth Millennium BP. Temporal Context: New Evidence from Middle Tennessee," *American Antiquity* 58(1):146–148.

Croes, Dale. 1989. "Prehistoric ethnicity on the Northwest Coast of North America: An evaluation of style in basketry and lithics," *Journal of Anthropological Archaeology* 8:101–130.

——1995. *The Hoko River Archaeological Complex: the Wet/Dry Site (45CA213), 3000–1700 BC.* Washington State University Press, Pullman, WA.

——and S. Hackenberger. 1988. "Hoko River Archaeological Complex: Modeling Prehistoric Northwest Coast Economic Evolution," *Research in Economic Anthropology* Supplement 3:19–85.

Crosby, A.W. 1972. *The Columbian Exchange.* Greenwood Press, Westport, CT.

——1986. *Ecological Imperialism: the Biological expansion of Europe, 900–1900.* Cambridge University Press, Cambridge.

Crowell, Aron L., and Mann, Daniel H. 1996. "Human Populations, Sea Level Change, and the Archaeological Record of the Northern Gulf of Alaska Coastline." *Arctic Anthropology* 33(2):16–37.

Crown, Patricia. 1991. "The Hohokam: Current Views of Prehistory and the Regional System," in Patricia Crown and W. James Judge (eds.). *Chaco and Hohokam: Prehistoric Regional Systems in the Southwest.* University of Washington Press, Seattle, WA, pp.135–158.

——1994. *Ceramics and Ideology: Salado Polychrome Pottery.* University of New Mexico Press, Albuquerque, NM.

——and Judge, W. James. (eds.). 1991. *Chaco and Hohokam: Prehistoric Regional Systems in the Southwest.* University of Washington Press, Seattle, WA.

Currey, D.R. and James, S.R. 1982. "Paleoenvironments of the Northeastern Great Basin and Northeastern Basin Rim Region: A Review of Geological and Biological Evidence," in David Madsen and James O'Connell (eds.). *Man and Environment in the Great Basin,* Society for American Archaeology, Washington DC, pp.27–52.

Cushing, Frank. 1882–3. *My Adventures in Zuñi.* American West, Palo Alto, CA (1970 edition).

Cybulski, J. 1990. "Human Biology," in Wayne Suttles (ed.). *Handbook of North American Indians. Vol. 7: Northwest Coast.* Smithsonian Institution Press, Washington DC, pp.52–59.

——1993. *A Greenville burial ground: Human Remains in British Columbia coast prehistory.* Ottawa: Archaeological Survey of Canada.

Damas, David. (ed.). 1984. *Handbook of North American Indians. Vol. 5: Arctic.* Smithsonian Institution, Washington DC.

Dancey, William S. 1996. "Putting an End to Ohio Hopewell," in Paul Pacheco (ed.). *A View from the Core: A Synthesis of Ohio Hopewell Archaeology.* Ohio Archaeological Council, Columbus, OH, pp.395–405.

——and Pacheco, Paul J. (eds.). 1997a. *Ohio Hopewell Community Organization.* Kent State University Press, Kent, OH.

——1997b. "A Community Model of Ohio Hopewell Settlement," in William S. Dancey and Paul Pacheco (eds.). *Ohio Hopewell Community Organization.* Kent State University Press, Kent, OH, pp.3–40.

Daniel, I. Randolph. 1996. *Hardaway Revisited.* University of Alabama Press, Tuscaloosa.

David, O.K. 1992. "Rapid Climate Change in Coastal Southern California Inferred from Pollen Analysis of San Joaquin Marsh," *Quaternary Research* 37(1):89–100.

D'Azevado, Warren (ed.). 1986. *Handbook of North American Indians. Vol. 11: Great Basin.* Smithsonian Institution, Washington DC.

Deagan, K. 1980. "Spanish St Augustine: America's first melting pot," *Archaeology* 33 (5):22–30.

——1983. *Spanish St Augustine.* Academic Press, New York.

Dean, Jeffrey S. 1988. "A Model of Anasazi behavioral adaptation," in George Gumerman (ed.), *The Anasazi in a Changing Environment.* Cambridge University Press, Cambridge, pp.25–44.

——1996. "Demography, Environment, and Subsistence Stress," in Joseph A. Tainter and Bonnie Bagley Tainter (eds.). *Evolving Complexity and Environmental Risk in the Prehistoric Southwest.* Addison Wesley, Reading, MA, pp.25–56.

——and Ravesloot, J.C. 1989. "The chronology of cultural interaction in the Gran Chichimeca," in Anne I. Woolsey and J.C. Ravesloot (eds.). *Culture and Contact: Charles C. Di Peso's Gran Chichimeca.* University of New Mexico Press, Albuquerque, NM.

DeBoer, Warren. 1997. "Ceremonial Centers from the Cayapas (Esmeraldas, Ecuador) to Chillicothe (Ohio, USA)," *Cambridge Archaeological Journal* 7(1):1–15.

Deetz, James. 1965. *The Dynamics of Stylistic Changes in Arikara Ceramics.* University of Illinois Press, Urbana, IL.

——1977. *In Small Things Forgotten.* Anchor Books, New York.

Delcourt, H.R. and others. 1985. "Quaternary palynology and vegetational history of the southeastern United States," in V.M. Bryant and R.G. Holloway (eds.). *Pollen Records of Late Quaternary North American Sediments,* American Association of Stratigraphic Palynologists Foundation, Washington DC, pp.1–37.

——1986. "Holocene Ethnobotanical and Paleoecological Record of Human Impact on Vegetation in the Little Tennessee River Valley, Tennessee," *Quaternary Research* 25:330–349.

Delcourt, P.A. and Delcourt, H.R. 1981. "Vegetation maps for eastern North America," *Geobotany* 11:123–165.

——1983. "Late Quaternary vegetational dynamics and community stability reconsidered," *Quaternary Research* 19:265–271.

Deloria, Vine Jr. 1992. "Indians, Archaeologists, and the Future," *American Antiquity* 57(4):595–598.

Dethlefsen, Edwin, and Deetz, James. 1966. "Death's Heads, Cherubs, and Willow Trees: Experimental Archaeology in Colonial Cemeteries," *American Antiquity* 31:502–510.

Deuel, Thorne. 1935. "Basic cultures of the Mississippi Valley," *American Anthropologist* 37:429–445.

Dewhirst, J. 1980. "The indigenous archaeology of Yoquot, a Nootkan Outside village," *National Historic Parks and Sites Branch, History and Archaeology* 39, Ottawa.

Dibble, D.S. and Lorrain, D. 1968. *Bonfire Shelter: A Stratified Bison Kill Site, Val Verde County, Texas.* Texas Memorial Museum, Miscellaneous Papers 1.

Dillehay, T.D. 1974. "Late Quaternary Bison Population Changes on the Southern Plains," *Plains Anthropologist* 19(64):180–196.

——1988. "How New is the New World?" *Antiquity* 62:94–97.

——1989. *Monte Verde: A Late Pleistocene Settlement in Chile, Vol. 1. Paleoenvironment and Site Context.* Smithsonian Institution Press, Washington DC.

——1997. *Monte Verde, Vol. 2.* Smithsonian Institution Press, Washington DC.

——2000. *First Settlement of the Americas.* Basic Books, New York.

——and Collins, M. 1988. "Early Cultural Evidence from Monte Verde, in Chile," *Nature* 332:150–152.

——and Meltzer, David. (eds.). 1991. *The First Americans: Search and Research.* CRC Press, Boca Raton, FL.

Dincauze, Dena. 1971. "An Archaic Sequence for southern New England," *American Antiquity* 36:194–198.

——1976. *The Neville Site: 8000 years at Amoskeag.* Peabody Museum, Harvard University, Cambridge, MA.

——1984. "An Archaeo-Logical Evaluation of the Case for Pre-Clovis Occupations," *Advances in World Archaeology* 3:275–323.

Di Peso, Charles C. and others. 1974. *Casas Grandes: a fallen trading center of the Gran Chichimeca.* Amerind Foundation, Dragoo, and Northland Press, Flagstaff, AZ.

Dobyns, Henry. 1983. *Their Numbers Became Thinned.* University of Tennessee Press, Knoxville, TN.

Dongoske, Kurt E., and others. 1997. "Archaeological Cultures and Cultural Affiliation: Hopi and Zuni Perspectives in the American Southwest," *American Antiquity* 62(4):600–608.

Doran, G.H., and others. 1986. "Anatomical, cellular, and molecular analysis of 8,000-year-old human brain tissue from the Wendover archaeological site," *Nature* 323 (6091):803–806.

——and Dickel, D.N. 1988. "Multidisciplinary Investigations at the Wendover Site," in Barbara A. Purdy (ed.). *Wet Site Archaeology.* Telford Press, Caldwell, NJ, pp.263–289.

——, Dickel, D.N., and Newsom, L.A. 1990. "A 7,290-year-old Bottle Gourd from the Wendover Site, Florida," *American Antiquity* 55(2):354–360.

Doyel, D.E. 1991. "Hohokam Exchange and Interaction," in Patricia Crown and W. James Judge (eds.). *Chaco and Hohokam: Prehistoric Regional Systems in the Southwest.* University of Washington Press, Seattle, WA, pp.225–252.

——and Elson, M.E. (eds.). 1985. *Hohokam settlement and economic systems in the central New River drainage, Arizona.* Soil Systems Publications in Archaeology 4, Phoenix, AZ.

Dragoo, D.W. 1963. "Mounds for the Dead: an analysis of the Adena Culture," *Annals of the Carnegie Museum* 37.

——1976. "Adena and the Eastern Burial Cult," *Archaeology of Eastern North America* 4:1–9.

Drass, Richard R. 1998. "The Southern Plains Villages," in W. Raymond Wood (ed.). *Archaeology on the Great Plains.* University Press of Kansas, Lawrence, KS, pp. 415–455.

Dumond, Don E. 1968. "On the Presumed Spread of Slate Grinding in Alaska," *Arctic Anthropology* 5(1):82–91.

——1971. "A Summary of Archaeology in the Katmai Region, Southeastern Alaska," *University of Oregon Archaeological Papers* 2.

——1982. "Trends and Traditions in Alaskan Prehistory: The Place of Norton Culture," *Arctic Anthropology* 19(2):39–52.

——1987. *The Eskimos and Aleuts.* 2nd ed. Thames and Hudson, London and New York.

Dunnell, R. 1980. "Evolutionary Theory and Archaeology," *Advances in Archaeological Method and Theory* 3:38–99.

——1982. "Science, Social Science, and Common Sense: the Agonizing Dilemma of Modern Archaeology," *Journal of Anthropological Research* 38(1):1–25.

Dye, D.H. 1996. "Riverine Adaptation in the Midsouth," in Kenneth C. Carstens and Patty Jo Watson (eds.). *Of Caves and Shell Mounds.* University of Alabama Press, Tuscaloosa, pp.140–158.

——and Cox, C.A. (eds.). 1990. *Towns and Temples along the Mississippi.* University of Alabama Press, Tuscaloosa, AL.

Earle, T.K. 1989. "The Evolution of Chiefdoms," *Current Anthropology* 30(1):84–88.

——(ed.). 1991. *Chiefdoms: Power, Economy, and Ideology.* Cambridge University Press, Cambridge.

Ellis, C.J., and Ferris, N. (eds.). 1990. *The Archaeology of Southern Ontario to AD 1650.* Ontario Archaeological Society, Toronto.

Elston, Robert G. 1982. "Good Times, Bad Times: Prehistoric Culture Change in the Western Great Basin," in David Madsen and James O'Connell (eds.). *Man and Environment in the Great Basin.* Society for American Archaeology, Washington DC, pp.186–206.

——1986. "Prehistory of the Western Area," in Warren D'Azevado (ed.). *Handbook of North American Indians. Vol. 11: Great Basin.* Smithsonian Institution, Washington DC, pp.135–148.

Emerson, T.E. 1997a. *Cahokia and the Ideology of Power.* University of Alabama Press, Tuscaloosa, AL.

——1997b. "Cahokian Elite Ideology and the Mississippian Cosmos," in Thomas R. Pauketat and Thomas E. Emerson (eds.). *Cahokia: Domination and Ideology in the Mississippian World.* University of Nebraska Press, Lincoln, NE, pp.190–228.

——and Lewis, R.B. 1991. *Cahokia and the Hinterlands: Middle Mississippian Cultures of the Midwest.* University of Illinois Press, Urbana, IL.

Epp, H., and Dyck, I. (eds.). 1983. *Tracking Ancient Hunters.* Saskatchewan Archaeological Society, Regina.

Ericson, J.E., and Baugh, T.G. (eds.). 1993. *The American Southwest and Mesoamerica: Systems for Prehistoric Exchange.* Plenum Press, New York.

Erlandson, J.M. 1994. *Early Hunter-Gatherers of the California Coast.* Plenum Press, New York.

——and Colten, R. (eds.). 1991. *Perspectives in California Archaeology 1: Hunter gatherers of Early Holocene Coastal California.* Institute of Archaeology, University of California, Los Angeles.

——and Glassow, Michael A. (eds.). 1995. *The Archaeology of the California Coast during the Middle Holocene.* Institute of Archaeology, UCLA.

Ewen, C.R. 1989. "Apalachee Winter," *Archaeology* 42(3):37–41.

Fagan, B.M. 1977. *Elusive Treasure.* Charles Scribners, New York.

——1987. *The Great Journey.* Thames and Hudson, London and New York.

——1990. *The Journey from Eden.* Thames and Hudson, London and New York.

——1997. *People of the Earth.* 9th ed. Addison Wesley Longman, New York.

——2000. *Ancient Lives.* Prentice Hall, New York.

Fages, P. 1972. *A historical, political, and natural description of California by Pedro Fages (1775), Soldier of Spain.* Ballena Press, Ramona, California.

Fagette, Paul. 1997. *Digging for Dollars: American Archaeology and the New Deal.* University of New Mexico Press, Albuquerque, NM.

Farnsworth. K. and Thomas Emerson. (eds.). 1986. *Early Woodland Archaeology.* Center for American Archaeology Press, Kampsville.

Farwell, R.E. 1981. "Pit houses: prehistoric energy conservation?" *El Palacio* 87(3):43–47.

Faulkner, C.H. 1988. "A Study of Seven Southeastern Glyph Caves," *North American Archaeologist* 9(3):223–246.

Fedje, Daryl W., and others. 1995. "Vermillion Lakes Site: Adaptations and Environments in the Canadian Rockies During the Latest Pleistocene

and Early Holocene," *American Antiquity* 60(1):81–108.

Fenton, W.N. 1978. "Northern Iroquoian cultural patterns," in Bruce G. Trigger (ed.). *Handbook of North American Indians. Vol. 15 Northeast.* Smithsonian Institution, Washington DC, pp.296–321.

Ferguson, Leland. 1992. *Uncommon Ground: Archaeology and Early African America, 1650–1800.* Smithsonian Institution Press, Washington DC.

Ferguson, W.M. and Rohn, A.H. 1987. *Anasazi Ruins of the Southwest in Color.* University of New Mexico Press, Albuquerque, NM.

Fiedel, Stuart J. 1987. "Algonquian Origins: A Problem in Archaeological-Linguistic Correlation," *Archaeology of Eastern North America* 15:1–11.

——1993. *Prehistory of the Americas.* 2nd ed. Cambridge University Press, Cambridge, Cambridge and New York.

——1999. "Older Than We Thought: Implications of Corrected Dates for Paleoindians," *American Antiquity* 64(1):95–115.

Finlayson, W.D. 1985. *The 1975 and 1978 Rescue Excavations at the Draper Site: Introduction and Settlement Patterns.* National Museum of Canada. Mercury Series 130.

Fish, P.R. and Fish, S.K. 1977. "Verde Valley Archaeology: Review and Perspective," *Museum of Northern Arizona Research Paper* 8.

Fish, S.K. and Fish, P.R. (eds.). 1984. *Prehistoric Agricultural Strategies in the Southwest.* Arizona State University, Tempe, AZ.

Fisher, Robin. 1977. *Contact and Conflict: Indian European Relations in British Columbia 1774–1890.* University of British Columbia Press, Vancouver, BC.

Fitzhugh, W.W. 1976. "Environmental factors in the end of the Dorset Culture: a marginal proposal for Hudson Bay," in Moreau Maxwell (ed.). *Eastern Arctic Prehistory: Paleoeskimo Problems.* Society for American Archaeology, Washington DC, pp.139–149.

——1978. "Maritime Archaic Cultures of the Central and Northern Labrador Coast," *Arctic Anthropology* 15(2):61–95.

——1980. "Preliminary Report on the Torngat Archaeological Project," *Arctic* 33:585–606.

——1984. "Residence Pattern Development in the Labrador Maritime Archaic: Longhouse Models and 1983 Surveys," in J.S. Thomsen and C. Thomsen (eds.). *Archaeology in Newfoundland and Labrador: 1983.* Historic Resources Division, Government of Newfoundland, Annual Report 4, St Johns.

——(ed.). 1988. *Crossroads of Continents.* Smithsonian Institution Press, Washington DC.

——and Crowell, Aron. (eds.). 1985. *Cultures in Contact: The European Impact on Native Cultural Institutions in Eastern North America, AD 1000–1800.* Anthropological Society of Washington Series, Smithsonian Institution, Washington DC.

Fladmark, Knud. E. 1983. "Times and Places in Environmental Correlates of Mid-to-Late Wisconsinian Human Population Expansions in North America," in Richard Shutler (ed.). *Early Man in the New World.* Sage Publications, Beverly Hills, California, pp.13–42.

——1986. *British Columbia Prehistory.* National Museums of Canada, Ottawa.

——1989. "Early Prehistory of the Queen Charlotte Islands," *Archaeology* 32(2):38–45.

Flannery, Kent V. 1973a. "Archaeology with a Capital A," in Charles Redman (ed.). *Research and Theory in Current Archaeology.* J. Wiley Interscience, New York, pp.337–354.

——1973b. "The Origins of Agriculture," *Annual Review of Anthropology* 2:271–310.

———and Joyce Marcus. 1993. "Cognitive Archaeology," *Cambridge Archaeological Journal* 3(2):260–267.

Ford, J.A. 1952. "Measurement of some Prehistoric Design Developments in the Southeastern States," *Anthropological Papers, American Museum of Natural History* 44(3).

———and Willey, G.R. 1941. "An Interpretation of the Prehistory of the Eastern United States," *American Anthropologist* 43(3):325–363.

Ford, Richard I. 1974. 'Northeastern archaeology: past and future developments," *Annual Review of Anthropology* 3:385–413.

———1981. "Gardening and Farming before AD 1000: patterns of prehistoric culture north of Mexico," *Journal of Ethnobiology* 1(1):6–7.

———(ed.). 1985. *Prehistoric Food Production in North America*. Museum of Anthropology, University of Michigan, Ann Arbor, MI.

Fowler, C.S. 1982. "Settlement Patterns and Subsistence Systems in the Great Basin: The Ethnographic Record," in David Madsen and James O'Connell (eds.). *Man and Environment in the Great Basin*. Society for American Archaeology, Washington DC, pp.121–138.

———1986. "Subsistence," in Warren D'Azevado (ed.). *Handbook of North American Indians. Vol. 11: Great Basin*. Smithsonian Institution, Washington DC, pp.64–97.

Fowler, D.D. and Jennings, J.D. 1982. "Great Basin Archaeology: A Historical Overview," in David Madsen and James O'Connell. *Man and Environment in the Great Basin*. Society for American Archaeology, Washington DC, pp.105–120.

Fowler, Melvin. 1959. *Summary Report of Modoc Rock Shelter*. Illinois State Museum Springfield, Illinois.

———1978. "Cahokia and the American Bottom: Settlement Archaeology," in Bruce D. Smith (ed.). *Mississippian Settlement Patterns*, Academic Press, New York, pp.455–478.

———1997. *The Cahokia Atlas: A Historical Atlas of Cahokia Archaeology*. Rev. ed. Illinois Transportation Archaeology Research Program, Urbana.

———and Hall, R.L. 1972. *Archaeological Phases at Cahokia*. Illinois State Museum, Springfield.

Fredrickson, D.A. 1973. "Early Cultures of the North Coast Ranges, California." University of California, Davis.

Frison, G.C. 1971. "The Buffalo Pound in Northwestern Plains Prehistory Site 48CA302," *American Antiquity* 36:77–91.

———1973. "The Wardell Buffalo Trap 48SU301: Communal Procurement in Post Altithermal Populations in the Northwestern Plains," *University of Michigan Anthropological Papers* 46:11–20.

———1974. *The Casper Site*. Academic Press, New York.

———1992. *Prehistoric Hunters of the High Plains*. 2nd ed. Academic Press, New York.

———1996. *The Mill Iron Site*. University of New Mexico Press, Albuquerque, NM.

———1998. "The Northwestern and Northern Plains Archaic," in W. Raymond Wood (ed.). *Archaeology on the Great Plains*. University Press of Kansas, Lawrence, KS, pp.140–172.

———and Bradley, B.A. 1981. *Folsom Tools and Technology at the Hanson Site, Wyoming*. University of New Mexico Press, Albuquerque, NM.

———and Stanford, D. (eds.). 1973. *The Agate Basin Site: a record of the Paleo-Indian occupation of the Northwestern High Plains*. Academic Press, New York.

———and Todd, L.C. (eds.). 1987. *The Horner Site*. Academic Press, New York.

———and Wilson, M. 1975. "An Introduction to Bighorn Basin archaeology," *Wyoming Geological Association 27th Annual Field Conference Guidebook*, pp.19–35.

Funk, R.E. 1988. "The Laurentian Concept: A Review," *Archaeology of Eastern North America* 16:1–42.

———1991. *Prehistoric Hunters of the High Plains*. 2nd ed. Academic Press, New York.

———1994. *Archaeological Investigations in the Upper Susquehanna Valley, New York State. Vol. 1*. Persimmon Press, New York.

Galinat, W.C. 1985. "Domestication and Diffusion of Maize," in Richard I. Ford (ed.). *Prehistoric Food Production in North America*. University Museum of Anthropology, University of Michigan, Ann Arbor, MI, pp.245–282.

Galm, J.R. 1984. "Arkansas Valley Caddoan Formative: The Wister and Fourche Maline Phases," in R.E. Bell (ed.). *Prehistory of Oklahoma*. Academic Press, Orlando, FL, pp.199–220.

Gardner, W.M. 1974. "The Flint Run Complex: Pattern and Process During the Paleo-Indian to Early Archaic," *Occasional Publications of the Catholic University of America, Washington DC*, pp.5–47.

———1977. "The Flint Run Paleo-Indian Complex and its implications for eastern North American prehistory," *Annals of the New York Academy of Sciences* 288:257–263.

Geist, Otto W. and Rainey, E.G. 1936. *Archaeological Excavations at Kukulik, St Lawrence Island, Alaska*. Miscellaneous Publications of the University of Alaska, Fairbanks, 2.

Geotcheus, V.G., Hopkins, D.M., Edwards, M.E., and Mann, D.H. 1994. "Window on the Bering Land Bridge: A 17,000-year-old Paleosurface on the Seward Peninsula, Alaska," *Current Research in the Pleistocene* 11:131–132.

Gerasimov, M.M. 1935. "Excavations of the Palaeolithic Site of Mal'ta," *Investia Gosudarstvennoy Akademii Istorii Material 'noy Kultury* 118:78–115.

Gero, Joan, and Conkey, Margaret. (eds.). 1991. *Engendering Archaeology*. Blackwell, Oxford.

Gerow, B.A. 1968. *An Analysis of the University Village Complex with a reappraisal of Central California Archaeology*. Stanford University Press, Palo Alto.

Gibson, J.L. 1994. "Empirical Characterization of Exchange Systems in Lower Mississippi Valley Prehistory," in Timothy G. Baugh and Jonathon E. Ericson. *Prehistoric Exchange Systems in North America*. Plenum Press, New York, pp.127–176.

———1996. "Poverty Point and Greater Southeastern Prehistory: The Culture That Did Not Fit," in Kenneth E. Sassaman and David G. Anderson. (eds.). *Archaeology of the Mid-Holocene Southeast*. University Presses of Florida, Gainesville, FL, pp. 177–199.

Giddings, J.L. 1960. *Ancient Men of the Arctic*. Alfred Knopf, New York.

———1964. *The Archaeology of Cape Denbigh*. Brown University Press, Providence, RI.

Gladwin, W. and Gladwin, H.S. 1931. "Some Southwestern Pottery Types, Series II," *Medallion Papers* 10, Globe, Arizona.

Glassow M.A. 1980. *Prehistoric agricultural development in the northern Southwest: a study in changing patterns of land use*. Ballena Press Anthropology Papers 16, Socorro, New Mexico.

———1996. *Purisimeño Chumash Prehistory*. Harcourt Brace, New York.

———, Wilcoxon, L. and Erlandson, J. 1987. "Cultural and Environmental Change during the Early Period of Santa Barbara Channel Prehistory," in Geoff Bailey and John Parton (eds.). *The Archaeology of Prehistoric Coastlines*, Cambridge University Press, Cambridge, pp.64–77.

Goad, S. 1979. "Middle Woodland Exchange in the prehistoric southeastern United States," in David Brose and N'omi Greber (eds.). *Hopewellian Archaeology*. Kent University Press, Kent, OH, pp.239–246.

———1980. "Patterns of Late Archaic Exchange," *Tennessee Archaeologist*, 5:1–16.

Goddard, I., and Campbell, L. 1994. "The History and Classification of American Indian Languages: What are the Implications for the Peopling of the Americas?" in R. Bonnichsen and D.G. Steele (eds.). *Method and Theory for Investigating the Peopling of the Americas*. Center for the Study of the First Americans. Corvallis, OR, pp. 189–208.

Goodyear, A.L. 1974.*The Brand Site: A Techno-Functional Study of a Dalton Site in Northeast Arkansas*. Research Series 7, Arkansas Archaeological Survey, Fayetteville, AR.

Goss, James A. 1977. "Linguistic Tools for the Great Basin Prehistorian," in Don D. Fowler (ed.). *Models and Great Basin Prehistory: A Symposium*. Desert Research Institute, University of Nevada, Reno, NV, 12.

Graham, R.W., and others. 1981. "Kimmswick: A Clovis-Mastodon Association in Eastern Missouri," *Science* 213:1115–1117.

Grant, Campbell. 1965. *Rock Paintings of the Chumash*. University of California Press, Berkeley.

Grayson, Donald. 1991. "Late Pleistocene mammalian extinctions in North America: taxonomy, chronology and explanations," *Journal of World Prehistory* 5:193–231.

———1993. *A Natural History of the Great Basin*. Smithsonian Institution Press, Washington DC.

Greber, N'omi B. 1991. "A Study of Continuity and Contrast Between Central Scioto Adena and Hopewell Sites," *West Virginia Archaeologist* 43(1&2):1–26.

———and Ruhl, Katharine C. 1989. *The Hopewell Site: A Contemporary Analysis Based on the Work of Charles C. Willoughby*. Westview Press, Boulder, CO.

Green, William, and Doersuk, John F. 1998. "Cultural Resource Management and American Archaeology," *Journal of Archaeological Research* 6(2):121–167.

Greenberg, J. 1987. *Language in the Americas*. Stanford University Press, Palo Alto.

———and others. 1986. "The Settlement of the Americas: A Comparison of the Linguistic, Dental, and Genetic Evidence," *Current Anthropology* 27:477–497

Gregory, D.A. 1991. "Form and Variation in Hohokam Settlement Patterns," in Pamela Crown and James W. Judge (eds.). *Chaco and Hohokam: Prehistoric Regional Systems in the Southwest*. University of Washington Press, Seattle, WA, pp.159–194.

Griffin, James B. 1946. "Culture Change and Continuity in the Eastern United States," in E. Johnson (ed.). *Man in Northeastern North America*. Robert S. Peabody Foundation for Archaeology. Andover, Massachusetts, pp.37–95.

———1961. "Some correlates of climatic and cultural change in eastern North American prehistory," *Annals of the New York Academy of Sciences* 95(1):710–717

———1965. "Hopewell and the dark black glass," in James Fitting (ed.). "Papers in Honor of Emerson F. Greenman," *Michigan Archaeologist* 11:115–155.

———1967. "Eastern North American Archaeology: A Summary," *Science* 156:175–191.

Grønnow, Bjarne. 1994. "Qeqertasussuk: the

Archaeology of a Frozen Saqqaq Site in Disko Bugt, West Greenland," in David Morrison and Jean-Luc Pilon (eds.). *Threads of Arctic Prehistory: Papers in Honor of William E. Taylor, Jr.* Canadian Museum of Civilization, Mercury Series 149, pp.197–238.

Grove, J.M. 1988. *The Little Ice Age.* Methuen, London.

Guidon, N. and Delibrias, J. 1986. "Carbon-14 Dates Point to Man in the Americas 33,000 years ago," *Nature* 321:769–771.

Gumerman, George 1984. *A View from Black Mesa.* University of Arizona Press, Tucson.

——1990. *Exploring the Hohokam.* University of New Mexico Press, Albuquerque, NM.

Gunnerson, James. 1969. "The Fremont Culture: a study in cultural dynamics on the northern Anasazi frontier," *Papers of the Peabody Museum of Archaeology and Ethnology* 59(2).

Guthrie, R.D. 1982. "Paleoecology of the large-mammal community in interior Alaska during the Pleistocene," *American Midland Naturalist* 79:346–363.

——1990. *Frozen Fauna of the Mammoth Steppe: The Story of Blue Boy.* University of Chicago Press, Chicago.

Haas, Jonathan, and Creamer, Winifred. 1992. *Stress and Warfare among the Kayenta Anasazi of the thirteenth century AD.* Fieldiana Anthropology, New Series, 21. Field Museum of Natural History, Chicago.

Hall, G.D. 1981. *Allens Creek: A Study in the Cultural Prehistory of the Lower Brazos Valley, Texas.* Texas Archaeological Research Laboratory, Research Report 61. University of Texas, Austin.

Hall, Robert L. 1997. *An Archaeology of the Soul: North American Indian Belief and Ritual.* University of Illinois Press, Urbana.

Halsey, John R. 1996. "Without Forge or Crucible: Aboriginal Native American Use of Metals and Metallic Ores in the Eastern Midwest," *The Michigan Archaeologist* 42(1):1–58.

Hanson, Jeffrey R. 1998. "The Late High Plains Hunters," in W. Raymond Wood (ed.). *Archaeology on the Great Plains.* University Press of Kansas, Lawrence, KS, pp. 456–480.

Hard, Robert J. and Roney, John R. 1998. "A Massive Terraced Village Complex in Chihuahua, Mexico, 3000 Years Before Present," *Science* 279:1661–1664.

Hardesty, D.L. 1988. *The Archaeology of Mining and Miners: A View from the Silver State.* Society for Historical Archaeology, Pleasant Hill, CA.

Harp, E.J. 1961. "The Archaeology of the Lower and Middle Thelon, Northwest Territories," *Arctic Institute of North America Technical Paper* 11.

——1962. "The culture history of the Central Barren Grounds," in J.M. Campbell (ed.). *Prehistoric Cultural Relations Between the Arctic and Temperate Zones of North America.* Arctic Institute of North America, pp.69–75.

——1976. "Dorset settlement patterns in Newfoundland and southeastern Hudson Bay," in Moreau S. Maxwell (ed.). *Eastern Arctic Prehistory: Paleoeskimo Problems.* Society for American Archaeology Washington DC, pp.119–138.

——and Hughes, D.R. 1968. "Five prehistoric burials from Port au Choix, Newfoundland," *Polar Notes* VIII:1–47.

——1983. "Pioneer Cultures of the SubArctic and the Arctic," in Jesse D. Jennings (ed.). *Ancient Native Americans.* W.H. Freeman, San Francisco, pp.95–129.

Harper, K.T. 1986. "Historical Environments," in Warren D'Azevedo (ed.). *Handbook of North American Indians. Vol. 11: Great Basin.*

Smithsonian Institution, Washington DC, pp.51–63.

——and Alder, G.M. 1970. "The Macroscopic Plant Remains of the Deposits of Hogup Cave, Utah, and their Paleoclimatic Implications," in C.M. Aikens, *Hogup Cave,* Anthropological Papers of the University of Utah 93:215–240.

Harrington, J.P. 1942. "Culture Element Distributions XIX: Central California coast," *University of California Anthropological Records* 7:1–146.

Hart, John P. and Sidell, Nancy Asch. 1996. "Prehistoric agricultural systems in the west branch of the Susquehanna River Basin, AD 800 to AD 1350."*Northeastern Anthropology* 52:1–30.

Hatch, J.W., and others. 1990. "Hopewell Obsidian Studies: Behavioral Implications of Recent Sourcing and Dating Research," *American Antiquity* 55(3):46–479.

Haury, E.W. 1950. *The Stratigraphy and Archaeology of Ventana Cave.* University of Arizona Press, Tucson.

——1957. "An alluvial site on the San Carlos Indian Reservation, Arizona," *American Antiquity* 23:2–27.

——1976. *The Hohokam, desert farmers and craftsmen: excavations at Snaketown 1964–1965.* University of Arizona Press, Tucson.

Haven, Samuel. 1856. *Archaeology of the United States.* Smithsonian Institution, Washington DC.

Haviland, W.A. and Power, M. 1981. *The Original Vermonters. Native inhabitants: Past and Present.* University Press of New England, Hanover, NH.

Hayden, Brian. 1982. "Interaction Parameters and the Demise of Paleo-Indian craftsmanship," *Plains Anthropologist* 27:109–123.

——and R. Schulting. 1997. "The Plateau Interaction Sphere and Late Prehistoric Cultural Complexity," *American Antiquity* 62(1):51–85.

Hayes, Alden C. and others. 1981. *Archaeological Surveys of Chaco Canyon.* University of New Mexico Press, Albuquerque, NM.

Haynes, Vance. 1966. "Elephant Hunting in North America," *Scientific American* 214(6):104–112.

——1975. "Pleistocene and recent stratigraphy" in F. Wendorf and J. Hester (eds.). *Late Pleistocene Environments of the Southern High Plains.* Fort Burgwin Research Center Publications 9:576–596.

——1980. "Paleo-Indian Charcoal from Meadowcroft Rockshelter: is contamination a problem?" *American Antiquity* 45:582–587.

——1982. "Were Clovis Progenitors in Beringia?" in David Hopkins and others (eds.). *The Paleoecology of Beringia,* Academic Press, New York, pp.383–398.

——1987 "Clovis Origins Update," *The Kiva* 52:83–93.

Heiser, Charles B. 1985. "Some Botanical Considerations of the Early Domesticated Plants North of Mexico," in R.I. Ford (ed.). *Early Food Production in North America.* University Museum of Anthropology University of Michigan, Ann Arbor, MI, pp.57–72.

Heizer, R.E. 1964. "The western coast of North America," in Jesse D. Jennings and Norbeck, Edward W. (eds.). *Prehistoric Man in the New World.* University of Chicago Press, Chicago, pp.117–148.

——and Elsasser, A.B. 1964. "Archaeology of Hum-67: the Gunther Island site in Humboldt Bay, California," *University of California Archaeological Survey Reports* 62:1–22.

——and Hester, T.R. 1978. *Great Basin Projectile Points: Forms and Chronology.* Ballena Press Publications in Archaeology, Ethnology, and History 10.

——and Napton, L.K. 1970. "Archaeology... as seen from Lovelock Cave, Nevada," *University of*

California Archaeological Research Facility Contributions 10(1).

——and Whipple, M.A. (eds.). 1971. *The California Indians: A Source Book.* University of California Press, Berkeley.

Henning, Dale R. 1998. "The Oneota Tradition," in Raymond Wood (ed.). *Archaeology on the Great Plains.* University Press of Kansas, Lawrence, KS, pp.345–414.

Hester, J.J. 1975. "Paleoarchaeology of the Llano Estacado," in E Wendorf and J. Hester (eds.). *Late Pleistocene Environments of the Southern Plains.* Fort Burgwin Research Center Publications, 9:247–256.

Hester, T.R. 1973. "Chronological Ordering of Great Basin Prehistory," *University of California Archaeological Research Facility Contributions* 17.

——1980. *Digging into South Texas Prehistory.* Corona, South Antonio, TX.

——1986. "Baker Cave, A Rich Archaeological Record," in H. Shafer (ed.). *Ancient Texans.* Texas Monthly Press, Austin, pp.84–87.

——1989. "Historic Native American Populations," in T.R. Hester and others (eds.). *From the Gulf to the Rio Grande: Human Adaptation in Central, South, and Lower Pecos Texas.* Arkansas Archaeological Survey Research Series 33, pp.77–84.

——1995. "The Prehistory of South Texas." *Bulletin, Texas Archaeological Society* 66:427–460.

——and others. 1989. *From the Gulf to the Rio Grande: Human Adaptation in Central, South, and Lower Pecos Texas.* Arkansas Archaeological Survey Research Series 33.

Hillebrandt, William R. and Jones, Terry L. 1992. "Evolution of Marine Mammal Hunting: A View from the California and Oregon Coasts," *Journal of Anthropological Archaeology* 11:360–401.

Hively, Ray, and Horn, Robert. 1982. "Geometry and Astronomy in Prehistoric Ohio," *Archaeoastronomy* 4: S1-20.

Hoffecker, J.F., Powers, W.R., and Goebel, T. 1993. "The Colonization of Beringia and the Peopling of the New World," *Science* 259:46–53.

Hoffman J.J. 1953. "Comments on the use and distribution of tipi rings in Montana, North Dakota, South Dakota, and Wyoming," *Montana State University Anthropological and Sociological Papers* 14.

Hofman, Jack L., and Graham, Russell W. 1998. "The Paleo-Indian Cultures of the Great Plains," in W. Raymond Wood (ed.). *Archaeology on the Great Plains.* University Press of Kansas, Lawrence, KS, pp.87–139.

Hofman, J., Amick, David, and Rose, R.O. 1990. "Shifting Sands: A Folsom-Midland Assemblage from a campsite in West Texas," *Plains Anthropologist* 35(129):221–254.

Holder, Preston. 1970. *The Hoe and the Horse on the Plains: A Study of Cultural Development among North American Indians.* University of Nebraska Press, Lincoln.

Holley, G.R., Dalan, R.A., and Smith, P.A. 1993. "Investigations in the Cahokia Site Grand Plaza," *American Antiquity* 58(2):306–319.

Holmes, C.E. 1996. "Broken Mammoth," in F.E.West (ed.). *American Beginnings: The Prehistory and Paleoecology of Beringia.* University of Chicago Press, Chicago, pp. 312–318.

——, R. VanderHoek, and T.E. Dilley. 1996. "Swan Point," in F.E.West (ed.). *American Beginnings: The Prehistory and Paleoecology of Beringia.* University of Chicago Press, Chicago. pp. 319–323.

Holmes, W.H. 1903. "Aboriginal Pottery of the Eastern United States," *Bureau of American Ethnology, 20th Annual Report,* Washington DC.

Holtved, E. 1954. "Archaeological investigations in the Thule District (Part 3): Nugdlit and Comer's Midden," *Medelelser om Greenland 146: CA Reitzels Forleg, Copenhagen.*

Hopkins, David O. and others (eds.). 1982. *Paleoecology of Beringia.* Academic Press, New York.

Huckell, Bruce B. 1995. *Of Marshes and Maize: Preceramic Agricultural Settlements in the Cienega Valley, Southeastern Arizona.* Anthropological Papers of the University of Arizona 59. University of Arizona Press, Tucson.

——1996. "The Archaic Prehistory of the North American Southwest," *Journal of World Prehistory* 10(3):305–374.

Hudler, D. 1997. *Determining Clear Fork Tool Function Through Use-Wear Analysis: A Discussion of Use-Wear Methods and Clear Fork Tools.* Texas Archaeological Research Laboratory, Studies in Anthropology 25. University of Texas, Austin.

Hudson, C. 1980. *The Southeastern Indians.* University of Tennessee Press, Knoxville.

——and others. 1985. "Coosa: A Chiefdom in the Sixteenth-Century Southeastern United States," *American Antiquity* 50:723–737.

Hudson T. and Blackburn, T. 1983. *The Material Culture of the Chumash Interaction Sphere.* Ballena Press, Socorro, New Mexico.

——and others (eds.). 1978. *Tomol: Chumash watercraft as described in the ethnographic notes of John P. Harrington.* Ballena Press, Socorro, NM.

——and others. 1979. "Solstice observations in Native California," *Journal of California and Great Basin Archaeology* 1(1):38–63.

——and Underhay, E. 1978. *Crystals in the Sky: An Intellectual Odyssey involving Chumash astronomy, cosmology, and rock art.* Ballena Press, Socorro, NM.

Huebner, J.A. 1991. "Late Prehistoric Bison Populations in Central and Southern Texas," *Plains Anthropologist* 36(137):343–358.

Hunter-Anderson, Rosalind. 1987. *Prehistoric Adaptation in the American South-West.* Cambridge University Press, Cambridge.

Husted, W.M. 1969. *Bighorn Canyon Archaeology.* Publications in Salvage Archaeology 12.

Hutchings, S.S. and Stewart, G. 1953. "Increasing Forage Yields and Sheep Production on Intermountane Winter Ranges," *US Department of Agriculture Circular 925, Washington DC.*

Ingstad, Anne. 1977. *The Discovery of a Norse Settlement in America.* Universitetsforlaget, Oslo.

——(ed.) 1985. *The Norse Discovery of America.* Norwegian University Press, Oslo.

Irwin, H.T. and Wormington, M. 1970. "Paleo-Indian tool types on the Great Plains," *American Antiquity* 325:24–34.

Irwin-Williams, C. 1968. *Archaic Culture History in the Southwestern United States.* Eastern New Mexico University Press, Portales.

——1973. "The Oshara Tradition: origins of Anasazi culture," *Eastern New Mexico University Contributions to Anthropology* 5,1.

——1979. "Post-Pleistocene archaeology 7000–2000 BC," in Alfonso Ortiz (ed.). *Handbook of North American Indians. Vol. 9: Southwest.* Smithsonian Institution, Washington DC, pp.31–42.

——1980. "Investigations at Salmon Ruin: Methodology and overview," in C. Irwin Williams and P.W. Shelley (eds.). *Investigations at the Salmon site: the structure of Chacoan Society in the northern Southwest.* Eastern New Mexico Press, Portales, NM, pp.107–170.

——and others. 1973. "Hell Gap: Paleo-Indian Occupation on the High Plains," *Plains Anthropologist* 19:40–53.

Janetski, J.C. 1999. "Fremont Hunting and Resource Intensification in the Eastern Great Basin." *Journal of Archaeological Science* 24.

——and Madsen, David (eds.). 1990. *Wetland Adaptations in the Great Basin.* Museum of Peoples and Cultures Occasional Papers 1. Brigham Young University, Provo, Utah.

Jefferies, R. 1987. *Carrier Mills.* Southern Illinois University Press, Carbondale, Illinois.

Jefferson, Thomas. 1797. *Notes on the State of Virginia.* J. Stockdale, London.

Jenkins, D.L., and Erlandson, J.M. 1997. "Olivella Grooved Rectangle Beads as Evidence of a Mid-Holocene Southern Channel Islands Interaction Sphere," *Pacific Coast Archaeological Society Quarterly* 29: 1–11.

Jennings, J.D. 1957. *Danger Cave,* University of Utah Anthropological Papers 27.

——1964. "The Desert West," in J.D. Jennings and Norbeck, E. (eds.). *Prehistoric Man in the New World.* University of Chicago Press, Chicago.

——1966. *Glen Canyon: A Summary.* Department of Anthropology, University of Utah.

——1978. *Prehistory of Utah and the Eastern Great Basin.* University of Utah Anthropological Papers 98.

——1986. "Introduction," in Warren D'Azevado (ed.). *Handbook of North American Indians. Vol. II: Great Basin.* Smithsonian Institution, Washington DC, pp.113–119.

——1987. *The Prehistory of North America.* 3rd ed. Mayfield, Palo Alto.

——and Norbeck, E. 1955. "Great Basin Prehistory: A Review," *American Antiquity* 21:1–11.

——and others. 1980. *Sudden Shelter.* University of Utah Anthropological Papers 103.

Johnson, A.E. 1992. "Early Woodland in the Trans-Missouri West," *Plains Anthropologist* 37(139):129–136.

Johnson, A. and Earle, T.K. 1987. *The Evolution of Human Societies.* Stanford University Press, Palo Alto.

Johnson, Craig. 1998. "The Coalescent Tradition," in W. Raymond Wood (ed.). *Archaeology on the Great Plains.* University of Kansas, Lawrence, KS, pp. 308–344.

Johnson, E. and Halliday, V.T. 1980. "A Plainview Kill-Butchering locale on the Llano Estacado: The Lubbock Lake Site," *Plains Anthropologist* 25:89–111.

Johnson, Jay. 1994. "Prehistoric Exchange in the Southeast," in Timothy G. Baugh and Jonathon E. Ericson (eds.). *Prehistoric Exchange Systems in North America.* Plenum Press, New York, pp. 99–126.

Johnson, Mary Ann and Johnson, Alfred E. 1998. "The Plains Woodland," in W. Raymond Wood (ed.). *Archaeology on the Great Plains.* University of Kansas, Lawrence, KS, pp. 201–234.

Johnston, R. 1968. *The Archaeology of the Serpent Mounds Site.* Royal Ontario Museum, Ottawa. Occasional Paper 10.

Jones, Terry L. 1996. "Mortars, Pestles, and Division of Labor in Prehistoric California: A View from Big Sur," *American Antiquity* 61:243–264.

——and others. 1999. "Environmental Imperatives Reconsidered: Evidence for Widespread Demographic Stress in Western North America during the Medieval Climatic Anomaly," *Current Anthropology.*

Judd, N.M. 1954. "The Material Culture of Pueblo Bonito," *Smithsonian Miscellaneous Collections* 124.

——1964. "The Architecture of Pueblo Bonito," *Smithsonian Miscellaneous Collections* 147(1).

——1967. *The Bureau of American Ethnology.*

University of Oklahoma Press, Norman.

Judge, W.T. 1984. "New light on Chaco Canyon," in David Noble (ed.). *New Light on Chaco Canyon.* School of American Research Press, Santa Fe, NM, pp.1–12.

Kantner, John. 1996. "Political Competition Among the Chaco Anasazi of the American Southwest," *Journal of Anthropological Archaeology* 15:41–105.

Kapjes, Mima. 1990. "The Spatial Dynamics of Ontario Iroquois Longhouses," *American Antiquity* 55(1):49–67.

Kay, Marvin. 1998a. "The Great Plains Setting," in W. Raymond Wood (ed.). *Archaeology on the Great Plains.* University Press of Kansas, Lawrence, KS, pp.16–47.

——1998b. "The Central and Southern Plains Archaic," in W. Raymond Wood (ed.). *Archaeology on the Great Plains.* University Press of Kansas, Lawrence, KS, pp.173–200.

Keegan, William E. (ed.). 1987. *Emergent Horticultural Economies of the Eastern Woodlands.* Center for Archaeological Investigations, Carbondale.

Kehoe, Alice. 1998. *The Land of Prehistory.* Routledge, London and New York.

Kehoe, T.F. 1960. "Stone tipi rings in north-central Montana and the adjacent portion of Alberta Canada. Their historical and archaeological aspects," *Bureau of American Ethnology Bulletin 173. Anthropological Papers* 62:421–473.

——1973. *The Gull Lake Site: A Prehistoric Bison Drive in Southwestern Saskatchewan.* Milwaukee Public Museum, Publications in Anthropology and History 1, Milwaukee, WI.

Kelly, Robert L.C. 1995. *The Foraging Spectrum: Diversity in Hunter-Gatherer Lifeways.* Smithsonian Institution Press, Washington DC.

—— and Todd, L.C. 1988. "Coming into the country: Early Paleo-Indian hunting and mobility," *American Antiquity* 53:231–244.

Kelso, W.M. 1984. *Kingsmill Plantation 1619–1800.* Academic Press, New York.

——1986. "Mulberry Row: Slave Life at Thomas Jefferson's Monticello," *Archaeology* 39(5):28–35.

Kidder, A.V. 1924. "A contribution to the study of Southwestern Archaeology with a preliminary account of the excavations at Pecos," *Papers of the Southwestern Expedition. Phillips Academy* 1. Yale University Press, New Haven.

——1927. "Southwestern archaeology conference," *Science* 68:489–491.

——1931. "The Pottery of Pecos (Vol. 1)," *Papers of the Southwestern Expedition. Phillips Academy* 5. Yale University Press, New Haven.

Kind, J.C.H., and Lidchi, Henrietta (eds.). 1998. *Imaging the Arctic.* University of British Columbia Press, Vancouver.

King, C.D. 1984. *The Evolution of Chumash Society: A Comparative Study of artifacts used in social system maintenance in the Santa Barbara Channel region.* University of California, Davis. Microform.

——1990. *Evolution of Chumash Society.* Garland, New York.

King, T.F. 1970. "Archaeological problems and research in the Coast Miwok area," *Treganza Anthropological Museum Papers* 6:32–81.

——1974. The evolution of status ascription around San Francisco Bay," in L.J. Bean and T.F. King (eds.). "? Antap: California Indian political and economic organization," *Ballena Press Anthropological Papers* 2:35–54.

——1998. *Cultural Resource Laws and Practice: An Introductory Guide.* Altamira Press, Walnut Creek, CA.

Kirk, Ruth. 1975. *Hunters of the Whale.* William Morrow, New York.

Kivett, M.F. 1953. "The Woodruff ossuary, a prehistoric burial site in Phillips County. Kansas," *Bureau of American Ethnology. River Basin Survey Bulletin* 154 (3):103–141.

——and Metcalf, George S. 1997. "The Prehistoric People of the Medicine Creek Reservoir, Frontier County, Nebraska: An Experiment in Mechanized Archaeology (1946–1948)," *Plains Anthropologist* 42(162). Memoir 3

Knecht, Heidi (ed.). 1997. *Projectile Technology.* Plenum Press, New York.

Knight, V.J. 1986. "The institutional organization of Mississippian Religion," *American Antiquity* 61:675–687.

——and Steponaitis, Vincas (eds.). 1998a. *Archaeology of the Moundville Chiefdom.* Smithsonian Institution Press, Washington DC.

——1998b. "A New History of Moundville," in Vernon James Knight and Vincas P. Steponaitis (eds.). *Archaeology of the Moundville Chiefdom.* Smithsonian Institution Press, Washington DC, pp.1–25.

Knudsen, R. 1983. "Organizational Variability in Late Paleo-Indian Assemblages," *Washington State University Laboratory of Anthropology. Report of Investigations* 60.

Knuth, Eigil. 1967. "Archaeology of the Musk Ox Way," *Contributions du Centre d'Etudes Arctiques et Finnoscandinaves* 5.

Kornfeld, M. and Todd, L.A. (eds.). 1989. *McKean/Middle Plains Archaic.* Occasional Papers on Wyoming Archaeology 4.

Krause, Richard A. 1972. "The Leavenworth Site: Archaeology of a Historic Arikara Community," *University of Kansas Publications in Anthropology* 3.

Kroeber, A.L. 1916. "Zuni Potsherds," *Anthropological Papers of the American Museum of Natural History* 18(1):7–37.

——1939. *Cultural and Natural Areas of Native North America.* University of California Publications on American Archaeology and Ethnology 38.

Kroeber, T. 1965. *Ishi in Two Worlds.* University of California Press, Berkeley.

Kunz, Michael, and Rainier, Richard E. 1995. "The Mesa Site: A PaleoIndian Lookout in Arctic Alaska," *Arctic Anthropologist* 32(1):5–30.

Lamb, S.M. 1958. "Linguistic Prehistory in the Great Basin," *International Journal of American Linguistics* 24(2):95–100.

Lambert, P.M. and Walker, P.L. 1991. "Physical anthropological evidence for the evolution of social complexity in coastal Southern California," *Antiquity* 65:963–973.

Landberg, L.C.W. 1965. *The Chumash Indians of Southern California.* Southwest Museum Papers 19.

Larson, D.O., Johnson, J.R., and Michaelson, J.C. 1994. "Missionization among the Coastal Chumash of Central California: A Study of Risk Management Strategies," *American Anthropologist* 96(2):263–299.

——and others. 1996. "Risk, Climatic Variability, and the Study of Southwestern Prehistory: An Evolutionary Perspective," *American Antiquity* 61(2): 217–242.

Larsen, Helge and Rainey, E. 1948. "Ipiutak and the Arctic Whale Hunting Culture," *Anthropological Papers of the American Museum of Natural History* 42.

Larsen, L.H. 1971. "Archaeological implications of social stratification at the Etowah site, Georgia," in J.A. Brown (ed.). *Approaches to the Social Dimensions of Mortuary Practices.* Society for American Archaeology Washington DC, pp.58–67.

Lawlor, D.A. and others. 1991. "Ancient HLA genes from 7,500-year-old archaeological remains,"

Nature 349:785–788.

Lawton, H.W. and others. 1976. "Agriculture among the Paiute of Owens Valley," *Journal of California Anthropology* 3(1):13–50.

LeBlanc, S.A. 1983. *The Mimbres People: ancient pueblo potters of the American Southwest.* Thames and Hudson, London and New York.

——1990. "Cultural Dynamics in the Southern Mogollon Area," in L.S. Cordell and G.J. Gumerman (eds.). *Dynamics of Southwest Prehistory.* Smithsonian Institution Press, Washington DC, pp.179–208.

——1999. *Prehistoric Warfare in the American Southwest.* University of Utah Press, Salt Lake City.

Lehmer, D.J. 1971. *Introduction to Middle Missouri Archaeology.* National Park Service, Anthropological Papers 1, Washington, DC.

——and Jones, D. 1968. *Arikara Archaeology: The Bad Phase.* Smithsonian Institution, Publications in Salvage Archaeology 7.

Lekson, S.H. 1984. *Great Pueblo Architecture of Chaco Canyon, New Mexico.* National Park Service, Albuquerque, NM.

——1999. *The Chaco Meridian: Centers of Political Power in the Ancient Southwest.* Altamira Press, Walnut Creek, CA.

——and others. 1988. "The Chaco Canyon Community," *Scientific American* 259(1):100–109.

Leonard, R.D. 1989. "Resource Specialization, Population Growth, and Agricultural Production in the American Southwest," *American Antiquity* 55: 227–249.

——and Jones, G.T. 1987. "Elements of an Inclusive Evolutionary Model in Archaeology," *Journal of Anthropological Archaeology* 6:199–219.

Leone, Mark. 1984. "Interpreting Ideology in Historical Archaeology: the William Paca Garden in Annapolis, Maryland," in D. Miller and C. Tilley (eds.). *Ideology, Power, and Prehistory.* Cambridge University Press, Cambridge, pp.25–35.

——1986. "Symbolic, Structural, and Critical Archaeology," in David Meltzer and others (eds.). *American Archaeology Past and Future.* Smithsonian Institution Press, Washington DC, pp.415–438.

——and Potter, P.B. 1984. *Archaeological Annapolis.* Historical Annapolis Inc, Annapolis, Maryland.

——and Potter, P.B. Jr. 1999. Historical Archaeologies of Capitalism. Kluwer/Plenum, New York.

——and others. 1989. "Power Gardens of Annapolis," *Archaeology* 42(2):34–40.

Le Page du Pratz, Antoine S. 1758. *Histoire de la Louisiane.* 3 vols. Paris.

Lepper, Bradley T. 1996. "The Newark Earthworks and the Geometric Enclosures of the Scioto Valley: Connections and Conjectures," in Paul J. Pacheco (ed.). *A View from the Core.* Ohio Archaeological Council, Columbus, OH, pp.224–241.

Lewis, T.M.N. and Lewis, M.K. 1961. *Eva: An Archaic Site.* University of Tennessee Press, Knoxville.

Lintz, C.R. 1984. "The Plains Villagers: Antelope Creek," in R.E. Bell (ed.). *Prehistory of Oklahoma.* Academic Press, Orlando, FL, pp.325–346.

Lipe, William D. (ed.). 1992. *The Sand Canyon Archaeological Project: A Progress Report.* Crow Canyon Archaeological Center, Cortez, Colorado.

——1995. "The Depopulation of the Northern San Juan: Conditions in the Turbulent 1200s," *Journal of Anthropological Archaeology* 14:143–169.

Lister, Robert H. and Lister, Florence C. 1981.

Chaco Canyon: Archaeology and Archaeologists. University of New Mexico Press, Albuquerque, NM.

Lobdell, John E. 1986. "The Kuparuk Pingo site: A northern Archaic hunting camp on the Arctic Coastal Plain, North Alaska," *Arctic* 39(1):47–51.

Lounsbury, E.G. 1978. "Iroquoian Languages," in Bruce Trigger (ed.). *Handbook of North American Indians. Vol. 15.* Smithsonian Institution, Washington DC, pp.334–343.

Lyman, R.L. and Dunnell, R.C. 1997. *The Rise and Fall of Culture History.* Plenum Press, New York.

——O'Brien, Michael, and Dunnell, Robert C. (eds.). 1997. *Americanist Culture History.* Plenum Press, New York.

Mabry, Jonathan B. and others. 1997. *Archaeological Investigations of Early Village Sites in the Middle Santa Cruz Valley.* Center for Desert Archaeology Anthropological Papers 18, Tucson.

MacDonald, G.E. 1968. "Debert: a Paleo-Indian site in central Nova Scotia," *Anthropology Papers* 16, National Museum of Canada, Ottawa.

——1983. "Prehistoric art of the northern Northwest Coast," in Roy Carlson (ed.). *Indian art traditions of the Northwest Coast.* Simon Fraser University, Burnaby, BC, pp.76–110.

——and Inglis, R.I. 1981. "An Overview of the North Coast Prehistory Project," *BC Studies* 48:37–63.

MacNeish, R.S. 1952. *Iroquois Pottery Types: A Technique for the Study of Iroquois Prehistory.* National Museum of Canada Bulletin 124, Anthropological Series 31, Ottawa.

Madsen, D.B. 1979. "The Fremont and the Sevier: Defining Prehistoric Agriculturalists North of the Anasazi," *American Antiquity* 44:711–722.

——1982. "Get it where the Gettin's Good: A Variable Model of Great Basin Subsistence and Settlement Based on Data from the Eastern Great Basin," in David Madsen and James O'Connell (eds.). *Man and Environment in the Great Basin.* Society for American Archaeology, Washington DC, pp.207–226.

——1983. "Black Rock Cave Revisited," *Utah Bureau of Land Management Cultural Resource Series* 14.

——1985. "Great Basin Nuts: A Short Treatise on the Distribution, Productivity, and Prehistoric Use of Pinyon," in C. Condie and D. Fowler (eds.). *Anthropology of the Desert West,* University of Utah Press, Salt Lake City, pp.110–125.

——1989. *Exploring the Fremont.* Utah Museum of Natural History, Salt Lake City.

——and Lindsay, L.W. 1977. "Backhoe Village," *Utah Division of State History Antiquities Section Selected Papers* 4(12).

——and O'Connell, James (eds.). 1982. *Man and Environment in the Great Basin.* Society for American Archaeology, Washington DC.

——and Rhode, David (eds.). 1994. *Across the West: Human population movement and the expansion of the Numa.* University of Utah Press, Salt Lake City.

Mainfort, R.C. 1996. "Pinson Mounds and the Middle Woodland Period in the Midsouth and Lower Mississippi Valley," in Paul J. Pacheco (ed.). *A View from the Core.* Ohio Archaeological Council, Columbus, OH, pp.370–392.

——and Sullivan, Lynne P. (eds.). 1998. *Ancient Earthen Enclosures of the Eastern Woodlands.* University Presses of Florida, Gainesville.

Malouf, C. and Conner, S. 1962. *Symposium on Buffalo Jumps.* Montana Archaeological Survey, Memoir 1.

Maltby, W.S. 1971. *The Black Legend in England: The Development of Anti-Spanish Sentiment.* Duke University Press, Durham, NC.

Mann, Daniel H., and others. 1998. "Holocene Geology and Climatic History around the Gulf of Alaska," *Arctic Anthropology* 35(1):112–132.

Manucy, A. 1985. "The Physical Setting of Sixteenth-century St Augustine," *The Florida Anthropologist* 38(1–2):34–53.

Marlowe, Greg. 1999. "Year One: Radiocarbon Dating and American Archaeology, 1947–1948," *American Antiquity* 64(1):9–32.

Marquardt, W. and Watson, P.J. 1983. "The Shell Mound Archaic of Western Kentucky," in J.L. Phillips and J.A. Brown (eds.). *Archaic hunters of the American Midwest*. Academic Press, New York, pp.323–332.

Marshall, M.P. and Doyel, D.E. 1981. *An Interim Report on Bi Sa'n ani Pueblo, with notes on the Chacoan Regional System.* Navajo Nation CRM Program, Window Rock, Arizona.

Martin, P.S. 1967. "Pleistocene Overkill," in P.S. Martin and H.E. Wright (eds.). *Pleistocene Extinctions: The Search for a Cause.* Yale University Press, New Haven, pp.53–68.

——1979. "Prehistory: Mogollon," in Alfonso Ortiz (ed.). *Handbook of North American Indians. Vol. 10: Southwest.* Smithsonian Institution, Washington DC, pp.61–74.

——and Klein, Richard (eds.). 1984. *A Pleistocene Revolution.* University of Arizona Press, Tucson.

——and Plog, E. 1973. *The Archaeology of Arizona.* Doubleday/Natural History Press, Garden City, NY.

Marwitt, J. 1970. *Median Village and Fremont Culture Regional Variation.* University of Utah Anthropological Papers 95.

——1986. "Fremont Cultures," in Warren D'Azevedo (ed.). *Handbook of North American Indians. Vol. 11: Great Basin.* Smithsonian Institution, Washington DC, pp.161–172.

Maschner, H.D.G. 1991. "The emergence of cultural complexity on the northern Northwest Coast," *Antiquity* 65:924–934.

Mason, Owen K. 1998. "The Contest between the Ipiutak, Old Bering Sea, and Birnik Polities and the Origin of Whaling during the First Millennium AD along Bering Strait," *Journal of Anthropological Archaeology* 17:240–325.

Mason, R. 1981. *Great Lakes Archaeology.* Academic Press, New York.

Masse, W.B. 1991. "The Quest for Subsistence Sufficiency and Civilization in the Sonoran Desert," in Patricia Crown and W. James Judge (eds.). *Chaco and Hohokam: Prehistoric Regional Systems in the Southwest.* University of Washington Press, Seattle, WA, pp.195–225.

Mathiassen, T. 1927. "Archaeology of the Central Eskimos, the Thule culture and its position within the Eskimo culture," in *Report of the Fifth Thule Expedition 1921–1924.* Glydenclalski Boghandel, Nordisk Forlag, Copenhagen.

Matson, R.G. 1989. "The Locarno Beach Phase and the Origins of the Northwest Coast Ethnographic Pattern," in A.B. Onat. *Development of Hunting-Fishing-Gathering Maritime Societies of the Pacific,* Vol. 3. Circum-Pacific Prehistory Conference Reprint Proceedings, Washington State University, Pullman, Washington, Part 2C.

——1991. *The Origins of Southwestern Agriculture.* University of New Mexico Press, Albuquerque, NM.

——and Coupland, G. 1995. *The Prehistory of the Northwest Coast.* Academic Press, Orlando.

Matthews, J.V. 1982. "East Beringia during Late Wisconsin Time: A Review of the Biotic Evidence," in David Hopkins and others (eds.). *Paleoecology of Beringia.* Academic Press, New York, pp.127–152.

Maxwell, M.S. 1960. "An archaeological analysis of eastern Grant Land, Ellesmere Island, Northwest Territories," *National Museums of Canada Bulletin* 180:20–25.

——1973. *Archaeology of the Lake Harbor District, Baffin Island.* Archaeological Survey of Canada, Mercury Series Paper 6, Ottawa.

——1976a. "Pre-Dorset and Dorset Artifacts: the view from Lake Harbor," in M.S. Maxwell (ed.). *Eastern Arctic Prehistory: Paleoeskimo Problems.* Society of American Archaeology, Washington DC, pp.58–78.

——(ed.). 1976b. *Eastern Arctic Prehistory: Paleoeskimo Problems.* Society for American Archaeology, Washington DC.

——1980. "Dorset site variation on the southeastern coast of Baffin Island," *Arctic* 33:505–516.

——1985. *Prehistory of the Eastern Arctic.* Academic Press, New York.

McCartney, A.P. 1977. *Thule Eskimo Prehistory Along Northwestern Hudson Bay.* Archaeological Survey of Canada, Mercury Series 70.

——1979a. "Archaeological Whale bone: a northern resource," *University of Arkansas Anthropology Papers* 1, Fayetteville.

——(ed.). 1979b. *Thule Eskimo Culture: An Anthropological Retrospective.* Mercury Series. Archaeological Survey of Canada Paper 88.

——1980. "The Nature of the Thule Eskimo Whale Bone," *Arctic* 33(3):517–541.

——1984a. "Prehistory of the Aleutian Region," in David Dames (ed.). *Handbook of North American Indians. Vol. 5 Arctic.* Smithsonian Institution, Washington DC, pp.119–135.

——1984b. "History of native whaling in the Arctic and Subarctic," in H.K. Jacob, and others (eds.). 1984. *Arctic Whaling,* Archaeological Center, Groningen, Netherlands, pp.79–112.

——1988. "The Cape York Meteorite as a Metal Source for Prehistoric Canadian Eskimos," *Meteorics* 23(3):288.

——1991. "Canadian Arctic Trade Metal: Reflections of Prehistoric to Historic Social Networks," *MASCA Research Papers in Science and Archaeology,* 8(11):2643.

——and Mack, D.J. 1973. "Iron Utilization by Thule Eskimo," *American Antiquity* 38:328–339.

——and Savelle, J.M. 1985. "Thule Eskimo Whaling in the Central Canadian Arctic," *Arctic Anthropology* 22(2):37–58.

——and others. 1998. "Northern Pacific and Bering Sea Maritime Peoples," *Arctic Anthropologist* 35(1).

McCluskey, S.C. 1977. "The Astronomy of the Hopi Indians," *Journal for the History of Astronomy* 8(2):174–195.

McDonald, J.N. 1981. *North American Bison.* University of California, Berkeley.

McGhee, R. 1970. "Speculations on climatic change and Thule culture development," *Folk* 11–12:172–184.

——1976. "Paleoeskimo occupations of Central and High Arctic Canada," in M.S. Maxwell (ed.). *Eastern Arctic Prehistory: Paleoeskimo Problems,* Society for American Archaeology, Washington DC, pp.15–39.

——1978. *Canadian Arctic Prehistory.* National Museums of Canada, Ottawa.

——1979. *The Paleoeskimo occupations at Port Refuge High Arctic Canada.* Archaeological Survey of Canada, Mercury Series 92, Ottawa.

——1982. "Norsemen and Eskimos in Arctic Canada," in E. Guralnick (ed.). *Vikings in the West.* Archaeological Institute of America, Chicago, Illinois, pp.38–52.

——1984a. "Contact Between Native North Americans and the Medieval Norse: A Review of Evidence," *American Antiquity* 49:4–26.

——1984b. "The Timing of the Thule Migration." *Polarforschung* 54(1): 1–7.

——1996. *Ancient People of the Arctic.* University of British Columbia Press, Vancouver, and the Canadian Museum of Civilization.

——and Tuck, James A. 1975. *An Archaic Sequence from the Strait of Belle Isle, Labrador.* Archaeological Survey of Canada, Mercury Series 34.

——1977 "An Archaic Indian burial mound in Labrador," *Scientific American* 235(5):122–129.

McGregor, J.C. 1941. *Southwestern Archaeology.* John Wiley, New York.

McGuire, R. 1992. "Archaeology and the First Americans," *American Anthropologist* 94(4):816–836.

——and Howard, A.V. 1977. "The structure and organization of Hohokam shell exchange," *The Kiva* 52(2):113–146.

——and Saitta, Dean J. 1996. "Although They have Petty Captains, They Obey Them Badly: The Dialectics of Prehispanic Western Pueblo Social Organization," *American Antiquity* 61(2):197–216.

McKern, W.C. 1939. "The Midwestern Taxonomic Method as an Aid to Archaeological Study," *American Antiquity* 4:301–313.

McKinnon, N., and Stuart, G.S.L. (eds.). 1987. *Man and the Mid-Holocene Climatic Optimum.* University of Calgary Archaeology Association, Calgary, Alberta.

McNett, C.A. (ed.). 1985. *Shawnee Minisink.* Academic Press, New York.

McNitt, Frank. 1957. *Robert Wetherill: Anasazi.* University of New Mexico Press, Albuquerque, NM.

Mehringer, P.J. 1986. "Prehistoric Environments," in Warren D'Azevedo (ed.). *Handbook of North American Indians. Vol. 11: Great Basin.* Smithsonian Institution, Washington DC, pp.31–50.

——and Foit, F.F. Jr. 1990. "Volcanic Ash Dating of the Clovis Cache at East Wenatchee, Washington," *National Geographic Research* 6(4):495–503.

Meighan, C. and Haynes, C.V. 1970. "The Borax Site revisited," *Science* 167:1213–1221.

Meldgaard, J. 1962. "On the Formative Period of the Dorset Culture," in J.M. Campbell (ed.). *Prehistoric Relations between the Arctic and Temperate Zones of North America.* Arctic Institute of North America, Technical Paper 11, Montreal, pp. 111–127.

Meltzer, David. 1983. "The Antiquity of Man and the Development of American Archaeology," *Advances in Archaeological Method and Theory* 6:1–51.

——1988. "Late Pleistocene Human Adaptations in Eastern North America," *Journal of World Prehistory* 2(1):1–52.

——1989. "Why Don't We Know When the First People came to North America?" *American Antiquity* 54:471–490.

——1991. "Altithermal Archaeology and Paleoecology at Mustang Springs, on the Southern High Plains of Texas," *American Antiquity* 56(2):236–267.

——and Collins, M.B. 1991. "Prehistoric Water Wells on the Southern High Plains: Clues to Altithermal Climates," *Journal of Field Archaeology* 14:9–28.

——1994. *Search For the First Americans.* Smithsonian Institution Press, Washington DC.

——and others (eds.). 1986. *American Archaeology Past and Future.* Smithsonian Institution Press, Washington DC.

——and others. 1994. "On a Pleistocene Human Occupation at Pedra Furada, Brazil," *Antiquity* 68 (261):695–714.

——and others. 1997. "On the Pleistocene Antiquity of Monte Verde, Southern Chile," *American Antiquity* 62(4): 659–664.

Merriwether, D.A., Rothhammer, F., and Ferrell, R.E. 1994. "Genetic Variation in the New World:

Ancient Teeth, Bone, and Tissue as Sources of DNA," *Experientia* 50:592–601.

Milanich, J.T. 1973a. *The Southeastern Deptford Culture: a preliminary definition*. Florida Department of State, Tallahassee, FL.

——1973b. "A Deptford Phase house structure, Cumberland Island, Georgia," *Florida Anthropologist* 26:105–118.

——1993. Hernando de Soto and the Indians of Florida. University of Florida Presses, Gainesville.

——1994. *Archaeology of PreColumbian Florida*. University Presses of Florida, Gainesville.

——1999. *Laboring in the Fields of the Lord: Spanish Missions and Southeastern Indians*. Smithsonian Institution Press, Washington DC.

——and Hudson, Charles. 1993. *Hernando de Soto and the Indians of Florida*. University Presses of Florida, Gainesville.

——and Milbrath, Susan (eds.). 1989. *First Encounters*. University of Florida Presses, Gainesville.

——and others. 1997. *Archaeology of Northern Florida, AD 200–900: The McKeithen Weeden Island Weeden Culture*. University Presses of Florida, Gainesville.

Milner, George R. 1990. "The Late Prehistoric Cahokia Cultural System of the Mississippi River Valley: Foundations, Florescence, and Fragmentation," *Journal of World Prehistory* 4(1):1–44.

——1998. *The Cahokia Chiefdom*. Smithsonian Institution Press, Washington DC.

——and Jefferies, R. 1998. "The Read Archaic Shell Mound in Kentucky," *Southeastern Archaeology* 17(2):119–132.

——and others. 1991. "Warfare in Late Prehistoric West Central Illinois," *American Antiquity* 56(4):581–603.

Minnis, Paul. 1989. "The Casas Grandes Polity in the International Four Corners," in S. Upham, K. Lightfoot, and R. Jewett (eds.). *The Sociopolitical Structure of Prehistoric Southwestern Societies*. Westview Press, Boulder, CO, pp.269–305.

——and others. 1993. "Prehistoric Macaw Breeding in the North American Southwest," *American Antiquity* 58(2):270–276.

Mitchell, Donald. 1988. "Archaeology of the Gulf of Georgia Area: A Natural Region and its Culture Types," *Syesis* 4.

Mitchem, J.M. and Hutchinson, D.L. 1987. *Interim Report on archaeological research at the Tatham Mound, Citrus County, Florida: Season III*. Miscellaneous Project Series. Florida State Museum, Gainesville.

Mobley-Tanaka, Jeanette L. 1997. "Gender and Ritual Space during the Pithouse to Pueblo Transition: Subterranean Mealing Rooms in the North American Southwest," *American Antiquity* 62(3):437–448.

Mochanov, Yuri A. 1977. *The Most Ancient Stages of the Human Settlement of Northeast Asia*. Science Press, Siberian Division, Novosibursk.

——and Svetlana A. Fedoseeva. 1996. "Aldansk: Aldan River Valley, Sakha Republic," in Frederick H. West (ed.). *American Beginnings*. University of Chicago Press, Chicago, 1996, pp.157–214.

Molto, J.E. 1983. *Biological Relationships of Southern Ontario Woodland Peoples: The Evidence of Discontinuous Cranial Morphology*. Archaeological Survey of Canada, Mercury Series 117, Ottawa.

Monks, G.C. 1987. "Prey as Bait: The Deep Bay Example, " *Canadian Journal of Archaeology* 11:119–142.

Moratto, M.J. 1984. *California Archaeology*. Academic Press, New York.

Morgan, Lewis H. 1877. *Ancient Society*. Henry Holt, New York.

Morgan, W.N. 1994. *Ancient Architecture of the Southwest*. University of Oklahoma Press, Norman.

Morison, Samuel Eliot, 1971. *The European Discovery of America. Vol. 1: The Northern Voyages*. Oxford University Press, New York.

Morlan, Richard. 1980. *Taphonomy and Archaeology in the Upper Pleistocene of the Northern Yukon Territory: A Glimpse into the Peopling of the New World*. National Museum of Man, Ottawa.

Morse, Dan F. 1997. *Sloan: A Paleoindian Dalton Cemetery in Arkansas*. Smithsonian Institution Press.

——and Morse, Phyllis. 1983. *Archaeology of the Central Mississippi Valley*. Academic Press, New York.

Morss, N.M. 1931. "The Ancient Culture of the Fremont Sevier in Utah," *Papers of the Peabody Museum of American Archaeology and Ethnology*, Cambridge 12(3).

Morton, Samuel. 1839. *Crania Americana*. J. Dobson, Philadelphia.

Moss, M.L. 1993. "Shellfish, Gender, and Status on the Northwest Coast," *American Antiquity* 95(3):631–652.

——and Erlandson, J.M. 1995. "Reflections on North American Pacific Coast Prehistory." *Journal of World Prehistory* 9(1):1–46.

——, Erlandson, J.M., and Stuckenrath, R. 1989. "The Antiquity of Tlingit Settlement on Admiralty Island, Southeast Alaska," *American Antiquity* 54(3):534–543.

——, Erlandson, J.M., and Stuckenrath, R. 1990. "Wood stake fish weirs and salmon fishing on the Northwest Coast: evidence from Southeast Alaska," *Canadian Journal of Archaeology* 14:143–158.

Muller, Jon. 1986. *Archaeology of the Lower Mississippi Ohio River Valley*. Academic Press New York.

——1987. "Salt, chert and shell: Mississippian Exchange and Economy," in E. Brumfiel and T.K. Earle (eds.). *Specialization and Exchange and Complex Societies*. Cambridge University Press, Cambridge, pp.10–21.

——1989. "The Southern Cult," in Patricia Galloway (ed.). *The Southeastern Ceremonial Complex: Artifacts and Analysis*. University of Nebraska Press, Lincoln, pp.11–26.

Muller, W.R. 1966. "Anthropological Linguistics in the Great Basin," in Warren D'Azevado and others (eds.). *The Current Status of Anthropological Research in the Great Basin*. Desert Research Institute, University of Nevada, Reno, Social Sciences Publications 1.

——and others. 1971. "A Lexicostatic study of Shoshoni Dialects," *Anthropological Linguistics* 13(4):142–164.

Müller-Beck, Hansjurgen. 1982. "Later Pleistocene Man in Northern Eurasia and the Mammoth Steppe Biome," in David Hopkins and others (eds.). *Palecology of Beringia*. Academic Press, New York, pp.329–352.

Musil, Robert R. 1988. "Functional Efficiency and Technological Change: A Hafting Tradition Model for Prehistoric North America," in J.A. Willig, C.M. Aikens, and J.L. Fagan (eds.). *Early Human Occupation in Far Western North America: The Clovis Archaic Interface*. Anthropological Papers 21, Nevada State Museum, Carsen, NV, pp.373–388.

Naranjo, Tessie. 1995. "Thoughts on Migration by Santa Clara Pueblo," *Journal of Anthropological Archaeology* 14:247–250.

Nassaney, Michael S. 1987. "On the Causes and Consequences of Subsistence Interactions in the Mississippi Alluvial Valley," in William Keegan (ed.). *Emergent Horticultural Economies of the Eastern Woodlands*. Center for Archaeological Investigations, Southern Illinois University, Carbondale, pp.129–151.

——and Cobb, C.R. (eds.). 1991. *Stability. Transformation, and Variation: The Late Woodland Southeast*. Plenum Press, New York.

——and Kendra Pyle. 1999. "The Adoption of the Bow and Arrow in Eastern North America: A View from Central Arkansas," *American Antiquitiy* 64(2): 243–263.

Nebraskaland Magazine. 1994. *The Cellars of Time*. Nebraska Game and Parks Commission, Lincoln, NE, 72(1).

Nelson, Nils C. 1916. "Chronology of the Tano Ruins, New Mexico," *American Anthropologist* 18(2):159–180.

Nelson, R.K. 1969. *Hunters of the Northern Ice*. University of Chicago, Chicago.

Nelson, Sarah M. 1997. *Gender in Archaeology*. Altamira Press, Walnut Creek, CA.

Neuman, Robert W. 1975. "The Sonota Complex and Associated Sites on the Northern Great Plains," *Nebraska State Historical Society, Publications in Anthropology* 6.

Newcomb, W.W. 1961. *The Indians of Texas*. University of Texas, Austin.

——1967. *Rock Art of Texas Indians*. University of Texas Press, Austin.

Nicholas, G.P. 1988. "Rethinking the Early Archaic," *Archaeology of Eastern North America* 15:99–124.

Noble, David. (ed.). 1984. *New Light on Chaco Canyon*. School of American Research Press, Santa Fe, NM.

——1985. *Mesa Verde National Park*. School of American Research Press, Santa Fe, NM.

Noble, W.C. 1971. "Archaeological Surveys and Sequences in Central District, Mackenzie, Northwest Territories," *Arctic Anthropology* 8(1):102–135.

Noël Hume, Ivor. 1969. *Historical Archaeology*. Alfred Knopf, New York.

——1982. *Martin's Hundred*. Alfred Knopf, New York.

Nordenskiöld, Gustav. 1973. *The Cliff Dwellers of the Mesa Verde, Southwestern Colorado*. AMS Press, New York (reprint).

Nunley, P. 1989. *A Field Guide to the Archaeological Sites of Texas*. Gulf Publishing, Houston, TX (formerly Texas Monthly Press, Austin).

O'Connell, James. 1967. "Elko Eared/Elko Corner-Notched Projectile Points as Time Markers in the Great Basin," *University of California Archaeological Survey Papers on the Great Basin Archaeology* 70. Berkeley.

——1975. "The Prehistory of Surprise Valley," *Ballena Press Anthropological Papers* 4, Ramona, California.

O'Connell, J.F. 1995. "Ethnoarchaeology Needs a General Theory of Behaviour," *Journal of Archaeological Research* 3:205–255.

——and others. 1982. "Some Thoughts on Prehistoric Archaeology in the Great Basin," in David Madsen and James O'Connell (eds.). *Man and Environment in the Great Basin*, Society for American Archaeology, Washington DC, pp.227–240.

O'Laughlin, Thomas C. 1980. "The Keystone Dam Site and other Archaic and Formative Sites in northwest El Paso, Texas," *Publications in Anthropology*. University of Texas. El Paso.

Orser, C.E., and Fagan, B.M. 1995. *Historical Archaeology*. Harper Collins, New York.

O'Shea, J.M. 1989. "Pawnee Archaeology." *Plains Archaeology* 1(1):49–107.

Osborn, A.J. 1983. "Ecological Aspects of Equestrian Adaptations in North America," *American Anthropologist* 85:563–591.

Pacheco, Paul. J. (ed.). 1996. *A View from the Core: A Synthesis of Hopewell Archaeology*. Ohio Archaeological Council, Columbus, OH.

Parker, A.C. 1916. "The Origin of the Iroquois as Suggested by their Archaeology," *American Anthropologist* 18:479–507.

Pastron, Allen G. 1988. "Bonanza from Old San Francisco," *Archaeology* 41(4):32–40.

——1989. "Golden Mountain," *Archaeology* 42(4):49–53.

Pauketat, Thomas R. 1993. *Temples for Cahokia Lords: Preston Holder's 1955–1956 Excavations of Kunnemann Mounds*. Museum of Anthropology, University of Michigan, Ann Arbor.

——1994. *The Ascent of Chiefs: Cahokia and Mississippian Politics in Native North America*. University of Alabama Press, Tuscaloosa.

——1998. "Refiguring the Archaeology of Greater Cahokia," *Journal of Archaeological Research* 6(1):45–89.

——and Emerson, Thomas E. (eds.). 1997. *Cahokia: Domination and Ideology in the Mississippian World*. Nebraska: University of Nebraska Press, Lincoln, NE.

——and Lopinot, N.H. 1997. "Cahokian Population Dynamics," in Thomas R. Pauketat and Thomas E. Emerson (eds). *Cahokia: Domination and Ideology in the Mississippian World*. University of Nebraska Press, Lincoln, NE, pp.103–123.

Peebles, C. 1979. *Excavations at Moundville 1905–1951*. Museum of Anthropology, University of Michigan, Ann Arbor.

Petruso, K.M. and Wickens, J.M. 1984. "The Acorn in Aboriginal Subsistence in Eastern North America," in P.J. Munson (ed.). *Experiments and Observations of Aboriginal Wild Plant Foods Utilized in Eastern North America*. Indiana Historical Society Indianapolis, pp.360–378.

Phillips, J.L. and Brown, J.A. (eds.). 1983. *Archaic Hunters and Gatherers in the American Midwest*. Academic Press, New York.

Phillips, P. 1970. "Archaeological Survey in the Lower Yazoo Basin, Mississippi 1945–1955," *Papers of the Peabody Museum of Archaeology and Ethnology* 60.

——and Brown, J. 1984. *Pre-Columbian Shell Engravings from the Craig Mound at Spiro, Oklahoma*. 2 vols. Peabody Museum of Archaeology and Ethnology, Harvard University.

——and others. 1951. "Archaeological survey in the Lower Mississippi alluvial valley, 1940–1947," *Peabody Museum Papers* 25.

Plog, Fred. 1974. *The Study of Prehistoric Culture Change*. Academic Press, New York.

——1983. "Political and economic alliances on the Colorado Plateau, AD 400–1450," *Advances in World Archaeology* 2:289–330.

Plog, S.E. 1980. *Stylistic variation in prehistoric ceramics: design analysis in the American Southwest*. Cambridge University Press, Cambridge and New York.

——1990. "Agriculture, sedentism, and environment in the evolution of political systems," in Steadman Upham (ed.). *The Evolution of Political Systems*. School of American Research Press, Santa Fe, NM, pp.177–199.

——1997. *Ancient Peoples of the American Southwest*. Thames and Hudson, London and New York.

Plumet, Patrick. 1985. "Archéologie de l'Ungana: le site de la Pointe aux Belougas (Qilalugarsiuvik) et les maisons longues dorsetiennes," *Collection Paléo-Québec* 18.

Potter, Stephen R. 1993. *Commoners, Tribute, and Chiefs: The Development of Algonquian Culture in the Potomac Valley*. University of Virginia Press, Charlotteville.

Powell, S. 1983. *Mobility and Adaptation: the Anasazi of Black Mesa, Arizona*. Southern Illinois University Press, Carbondale.

——and others, 1993. "Ethics and Ownership of the Past: The Reburial and Repatriation Controversy," *Archaeological Method and Theory* 3:124–149.

Powers, W.R. and Hamilton, T.D. 1978. "Dry Creek: A Late Pleistocene human occupation in central Alaska," in A.L. Bryan (ed.). *Early Man in America from a Circum-Pacific Perspective*. Archaeological Research International University of Alberta Edmonton, pp.71–77.

——and Hoffecker, John. 1989. "Late Pleistocene Settlement in the Nenana Valley, Central Alaska," *American Antiquity* 54(2):263–287.

Preucel, Robert W. and Hodder, Ian. (eds.). 1997. *Contemporary Archaeology in Theory*. Blackwell, Oxford.

Prufer, Olaf. 1964. "The Hopewell Complex of Ohio," in R. Caldwell and R.L. Hall (eds.). *Hopewellian Studies*, Illinois State Museum, Springfield, pp.35–84.

Purdy, Barbara. 1992. *The Art and Archaeology of Florida's Wetlands*. CRC Press, Boca Raton, FL.

Raab, L.M. 1995. "Debating Cultural Evolution: Regional Implications of Fishing Intensification at Eel Point, San Clemente Island." *Pacific Coast Archaeological Society Quarterly* 31:3–27.

——1996. "Debating Prehistory in Coastal Southern California: Political Economy vs Resource Intensification," *Journal of California and Great Basin Anthropology* 18:64–80.

——1997. "The Southern Channel Islands During the Middle Holocene: Trends in Maritime Cultural Evolution," in J.M. Erlandson and M.A. Glassow (eds.). *Archaeology of the California Coast during the Middle Holocene*. Institute of Archaeology, UCLA, Los Angeles, pp.23–24.

——and others. 1995. "Return to Little Harbor, Santa Catalina Island, California: A critique of the marine paleotemperature model," *American Antiquity* 60(2):287–308.

——, Bradford, K., and Yatsko, A. 1994. "Advances in Southern Channel Islands Archaeology: 1983 to 1993," *Journal of California and Great Basin Anthropology* 16(2):243–270.

——and Larson, Daniel O. 1997. "Medieval Climatic Anomaly and Punctuated Cultural Evolution in Coastal Southern California," *American Antiquity* 62(2):319–336.

——and Yatsko, A. 1992. "Ancient maritime adaptations of the California bight: A perspective from San Clemente Island, California," *Journal of Ethnobiology* 12(1):63–80.

Ragir, S.R. 1972. "The Early Horizon in Central California prehistory," *University of California Archaeological Research Facility Paper* 15.

Rainey, E.G. 1941. "Eskimo Prehistory: The Okvik Site on the Punuk Islands," *Anthropological Papers of the American Museum of Natural History* 37(4):443–569.

Rainier, Richard E. 1995. "The Antiquity of PaleoIndian Materials in Northern Alaska," *Arctic Anthropology* 32(1):31–50.

Ramenovsky, A. 1987. *Vectors of Death: The Archaeology of European Contact*. University of New Mexico Press, Albuquerque, NM.

Rasmussen, K. 1931. "The Netsilik Eskimos: social life and spiritual culture," *Report of the Fifth Thule Expedition 1921–1924*:8. Glyndendalske Boghandel Nordisk Forleg, Copenhagen.

Ravesloot, J.C. 1988. *Mortuary Practices and Social Differentiation at Casas Grandes, Chihuahua, Mexico*. University of Arizona Press, Tucson.

Redman, Charles L. 1978. *The Rise of Civilization*. W.H. Freeman, San Francisco.

Reeves, Brian O.K. 1973. "The Concept of an Altithermal Cultural hiatus in Northern Plains Prehistory," *American Anthropologist* 75(5):1221–1253.

——1978. "Head-Smashed-in: 5500 Years of Bison Jumping in the Alberta Plains," *Plains Anthropologist*, Memoir 14, 23(82), Part 2, pp.151–174.

Reher, C.A. 1974. "Population Study of the Casper site bison," in George Frison (ed.). *The Casper Site*. Academic Press, New York, pp.231–240.

——and Frison, G.E. 1980. "The Vere Site, 48CK302, a Stratified Buffalo Jump in the Wyoming Black Hills," *Plains Anthropological Memoirs* 16.

Reid, Jefferson, and Whittlesey, Stephanie. 1997. *The Archaeology of Ancient Arizona*. University of Arizona Press, Tucson.

Reitz, E.J. and Scarry, M.C. 1986. *Reconstructing Historic Subsistence with an Example from Sixteenth-Century Spanish Florida*. Society for Historical Archaeology, Glassborough, N.J, Special Publication Series 3.

Renfrew, C. and Bahn, P. 2000. *Archaeology: Theories, Methods, and Practice*. 3rd ed. Thames and Hudson, London and New York.

Ricklis, R.A. 1992. "The Spread of a Late Prehistoric Bison Hunting Complex: Evidence from the South-Central Coastal Prairie of Texas," *Plains Anthropologist* 37(140):621–274.

Riley, Thomas J. and others. 1994. "Accelerator Mass Spectrometry (AMS) Dates Confirm Early *Zea mays* in the Mississippi River Valley," *American Antiquity* 59(3):490–498.

Ritchie, W. 1969. *Archaeology of New York State*. Natural History Press, Garden City, New York.

Ritchie, W.A. and Funk, R.E. 1973. *Aboriginal Settlement Patterns in the Northeast*. New York State Museum and Science Service Memoir 20, Albany.

Rogers, J. Daniel, and Smith, Bruce D. (eds.). 1995. *Mississippian Communities and Households*. University of Alabama Press, Tuscaloosa.

Rohn, A.H. 1971. *Mug House, Mesa Verde National Park, Colorado*. National Park Service, Washington DC, Archaeological Research Series 7D.

——1977. *Cultural Change and Continuity on Chapin Mesa*. Regents Press of Kansas, Lawrence, KS.

——1989. "Northern San Juan Prehistory," in Linda Cordell and George Gumerman (eds.). *Dynamics of Southwestern Prehistory*. Smithsonian Institution Press, Washington DC, pp.149–178.

Roosa, William. 1977. "Great Lakes Paleo-Indian: the Parkhill Site, Ontario," in Walter Newman and Bert Salwen (eds.). "Amerinds and Their Paleoenvironments in Northeastern North America," *Annals of New York Academy of Sciences* 228:349–354.

Rothschild, N.A. 1979. "Mortuary behavior and social organization at Indian Knoll and Dickson Mounds," *American Antiquity* 44:658–675.

Rountree, H. 1989. *The Powhatan Indians of Virginia*. University of Oklahoma Press, Norman.

Rudenko, S.I. 1961. *The Ancient Culture of the Bering Sea and the Eskimo Problem*. Translated by Paul Tolstoy. Arctic Institute of North America, Toronto. Translations from Russian Sources 1.

Russo, Michael. 1994. "A Brief Introduction to the Study of Archaic Mounds in the Southeast." *Southeastern Archaeology* 13: 89–93.

——1996. "Southeastern Preceramic Archaic Ceremonial Mounds," in Kenneth E. Sassaman and David G. Anderson (eds.). *Archaeology of the Mid-Holocene Southeast*. University Presses of Florida, Gainesville, FL, pp. 259–287.

Sahlins, M. 1972. *Stone Age Economics*. Aldine, Chicago.

Salinas, Martin. 1990. *Indians of the Rio Grande Delta*. University of Texas Press, Austin.

Samuels, Stephen R. (ed.). 1991. *Ozette Archaeological Project Research Reports*. Department of Anthropology, Washington State University, Pullman, WA.

Sanger, D. 1979. "The Ceramic Period in Maine," in D. Sanger (ed.). *Discovering Maine's Archaeological Heritage*. Maine Historic Preservation Commission, Augusta, ME, pp.99–115.

Sassaman, K.E. 1993. *Early Pottery in the Southeast*. University of Alabama Press, Birmingham.

——1996. "Technological Innovations in Economic and Social Contexts," in Kenneth E. Sassaman and David G. Anderson (eds.). *Archaeology of the Mid-Holocene Southeast*. University Presses of Florida, Gainesville, FL, pp. 57–74.

——and Anderson, David G.(eds.). 1996. *Archaeology of the Mid-Holocene Southeast*. University Presses of Florida, Gainesville.

——and Ledbetter, R. Jerald. 1996. "Middle and Late Archaic Architecture," in Kenneth E. Sassaman and David G. Anderson (eds.). *Archaeology of the Mid-Holocene Southeast*. University Presses of Florida, Gainesville, FL, pp. 75–96.

Sauer, C.O. 1980. *Seventeenth Century North America*. Turtle Island, Berkeley.

Saunders, Joe W., and others. 1997. "A Mound Complex in Lousiana at 5400–5000 Years Before Present," *Science* 277:1796–1799.

Savelle, J.M. and McCartney, A.P. 1988. "Geographical and Temporal Variation in Thule Eskimo Subsistence Economies: a model," *Research in Economic Anthropology* 10:21–72.

Sayles, E.B. 1936. "Some Southwestern Pottery Types, Series V," *Medallion Papers*, Gila Pueblo, Globe, Arizona 21.

——1983. "The Cochise Culture Sequence in Southern Arizona," *Anthropological Papers of the University of Arizona* 42.

——and Antevs, E. 1941. "The Cochise Culture," *Medallion Papers* 25.

Scarry, C.M. (ed.). *Foraging and Farming in the Eastern Woodlands*. Southern Illinois University Press, Carbondale, IL.

Schell, D.M. 1983. "Carbon-13 and Carbon-14 abundances in Alaskan aquatic organisms: delayed production from peat in Alaskan food webs," *Science* 219:1068–1071.

Schledermann, P. 1979. "The "Baleen Period" of the Arctic whaling hunting tradition," in Alan McCartney (ed.). *Thule Eskimo culture: an anthropological retrospective*. National Museum of Man, Ottawa, Mercury Series 88:134–148.

——and McCulloh, K. 1980. "Western elements in the early Thule culture of the eastern High Arctic," *Arctic* 33:833–842.

——1990. *Crossroads to Greenland: 3000 Years of Prehistory in the Eastern High Arctic*. Arctic Institute of North America, Calgary.

——1996. *Voices in Stone*. Arctic Institute of North America, Calgary.

Schmidts, L.J. 1978. "The Williamson site and the Late Archaic El Dorado Phase in Eastern Kansas," *Plains Anthropologist* 32(116):153–174.

Schnell, E.T. and others. 1981. *Cemochechobee: Archaeology of a Mississippian Ceremonial Center on the Chattahoochee River*. University Presses of Florida, Gainesville.

Schulting, R.J. 1995. *Mortuary Variability and Status Differentiation on the Columbia-Fraser Plateau*. Archaeology Press, Simon Fraser University, Burnaby, BC.

Schweger, C.E. 1990. "The Full-Glacial Ecosystem of Beringia," *Prehistoric Mongoloid Dispersals* 7:35–52.

Sears, W. 1956. *Excavations at Kolomoki: final report*. University of Georgia Press, Athens.

——1973. "The sacred and the secular in prehistoric ceramics," in D. Lathrap and J. Douglas (eds.). *Variations in Anthropology: essays in honor of John McGregor*. Illinois Archaeological Survey, Urbana, pp.31–42.

Sebastian, Lynne. 1991. "Sociopolitical Complexity and the Chaco System," in Patricia Crown and W. James Judge (eds.). *Chaco and Hohokam: Prehistoric Regional Systems in the American Southwest*. School of American Research Press, Santa Fe, NM, pp.109–134.

Seeman, M.E. 1979a. *The Hopewell Interaction Sphere: the evidence for Interregional Trade and Structural Complexity*. Indiana Historical Society, Indianapolis.

——1979b. "Feasting of the Dead: Ohio Hopewell Charnel House Ritual as a Context for Redistribution," in David Brose and N'omi Greber (eds.). *Hopewellian Archaeology*. Kent University Press, Kent, OH, pp.39–46.

——1988. "Ohio Hopewell Trophy-Skull Artifacts as Evidence for Competition in Middle Woodland Societies circa 50 BC–AD 350," *American Antiquity* 53:565–577.

——1992. Woodland Traditions in the MidContinent: A Comparison of Three Regional Sequences," in Dale R. Croes, Rebecca A. Hawkins, and Barry L. Isaac, eds. *Long-Term Subsistence Change in Prehistoric North America*. JAI Press, Greenwich, CT, pp.3–46.

Shackel, P. 1994. *Personal Discipline and Material Culture: An Archaeology of Annapolis, Maryland, 1695–1870*. University of Tennessee Press, Knoxville, TN.

——and Little, Barbara. (eds.). 1994. *Historical Archaeology of the Chesapeake*. Smithsonian Institution Press, Washington DC.

——and others. (eds.). 1998. *Annapolis Pasts: Historical Archaeology in Annapolis, Maryland*. University of Tennessee Press, Knoxville, TN.

Shafer, H.J. (ed.). 1986. *Ancient Texans: Rock Art and Lifeways along the Lower Pecos*. Witte Museum of the San Antonio Museum Association, San Antonio, Texas.

——1988. "Prehistoric Legacy of the Lower Pecos Region of Texas," *Bulletin of the Texas Archaeological Society* 59:23–52.

——1995 "Architecture and Symbolism in Transitional Pueblo Development in Mimbres Valley, S.W. New Mexico," *Journal of Field Archaeology* 22(1):23–47.

Shaw, R.D. and Holmes, C.E. 1982. "The Norton Interaction Sphere: Selected Papers from a Symposium," *Arctic Anthropology* 19(2).

Shipley, W. 1978. "Native Languages of California," in R.E. Heizer (ed.). *Handbook of North American Indians. Vol. 8 :California*. Smithsonian Institution, Washington DC, pp.80–90.

Shott, M.J. 1990. "Stone Tools and Economics: Great Lakes Paleo-Indian examples," *Research in Economic Anthropology* Supplement 5:3–43.

Shutler, R. and others. 1974. "The Cherokee Sewer site (13CK405)," in Dale R. Henning (ed.). *A Preliminary Report of a stratified Paleo-Indian Archaic site in northwestern Iowa*. Journal of the Iowa Archaeological Society 21.

Silberman, N.A. 1989. "The Black Experience in America," *Archaeology* 42(5):62–72.

Silverberg, R. 1968. *Mound Builders of Ancient America: the archaeology of a myth*. New York Graphic Society, Greenwich, Connecticut.

Simmons, A.A. 1984. *Archaic Prehistory and Paleoenvironments: the San Juan Basin, New Mexico*. University of Kansas Museum of Anthropology, Lawrence, KS.

——1986. "New Evidence for the Early Use of Cultigens in the American Southwest," *American Antiquity* 51:73–88.

Simmons, J.J. III. 1988. "Steamboats on Inland Waterways: Prime Movers of Manifest Destiny," in George Bass (ed.). *Ships and Shipwrecks of the Americas*. Thames and Hudson, London and New York, pp. 189–206.

Singleton,T.A. 1985. *The Archaeology of Slavery and Plantation Life*. Academic Press, Orlando.

Smith, B.D. (ed.). 1978. *Mississippian Settlement Patterns*. Academic Press, New York.

——1984. "*Chenopodium* as a Prehistoric Domesticate in Eastern North America: Evidence from Russell Cave, Alabama," *Science* 226:165–167.

——1986. "The Archaeology of the Southeastern United States: From Dalton to de Soto, 10,500 to 500 BP," *Advances in World Archaeology* 5:1–92.

——1990. *The Mississippian Emergence*. Smithsonian Institution Press, Washington DC.

——(ed.). 1992. *Rivers of Change: Essays on Early Agriculture in Eastern North America*. Smithsonian Institution Press, Washington DC.

——1994. *The Emergence of Agriculture*. Scientific American Library, New York.

Smith, G. Hubert. 1972. *Like-a-Fishook Village and Fort Berthold, Garrison Reservoir, North Dakota*. US Department of the Interior, National Park Service Anthropological Papers 2.

Smith, Marvin T. 1987. *Archaeology of Aboriginal Culture Change in the Interior Southeast*. University of Florida Presses, Gainesville.

——and Kowalewski, S.A. 1980. "Tentative Identification of a prehistoric "province" in piedmont Georgia," *Early Georgia* 8:1–13.

Smith, S. 1977. *Method and Theory in Historical Archaeology*. Academic Press, New York.

——1980. *The Discovery of Santa Elena*. Institute of Archaeology, University of South Carolina, Columbia, SC.

Smith, Watson. 1952. *Kiva Mural Decorations at Awatavi and Kawaika-a with a Survey of Other Wall Paintings*. Papers of the Peabody Museum of Archaeology and Ethnology 37. Cambridge, MA.

Snow, Dean. 1980. *The Archaeology of New England*. Academic Press, New York.

——1994. "Paleoecology and the Prehistoric Incursion of Northern Iroquoians into the Lower Great Lakes Region," in B.G. Warner and R. MacDonald (eds.). *Great Lakes Archaeology and Paleoecology: Exploring Interdisciplinary Initiatives for the Nineties*. Quaternary Sciences Institute, University of Waterloo, Ontario, pp.283–293.

——1995. "Migrations in Prehistory: The Northern Iroquoian Case," *American Antiquity* 60(1):59–9.

——1996a. "More on Migration in Prehistory: Accommodating New Evidence in the Northern Iroquoian Case," *American Antiquity* 61(4):791–796.

——1996b. *The Iroquois*. Blackwell, Oxford.

Snow, Dean and Forman, W. 1976. *The Archaeology of North America*. Viking, New York (published in Britain as *The American Indians*. Thames and Hudson, London).

South, Stanley. 1977. *Research Strategies in Historical Archaeology*. Academic Press, New York.

——and others. 1988. *Spanish Artifacts from Santa Elena*. Institute of Archaeology, University of South Carolina, Columbia, SC.

Spaulding, A.C. 1953. "Statistical Techniques for the Discovery of Artifact Types," *American Antiquity* 18:305–313.

——1973. "Archaeology in the Active Voice: The New Anthropology," in Charles Redman (ed.).

Research and Theory in Current Archaeology.
John Wiley Interscience, New York, pp.337–354.

Spence, M.W. 1982. "The Social Context of Production and Exchange," in J. Ericson and T. Earle (eds.). *Contexts for Prehistoric Exchange.* Academic Press, New York, pp.173–197.

Speth, J.D. 1983. *Bison Kills and Bone Counts.* University of Chicago Press, Chicago.

Spicer, E.H. 1962. *Cycles of Conquest.* University of Arizona Press, Tucson.

Spielmann, K.A. (ed.). 1991. *Farmers, Hunters, and Colonists: Interaction Between the Southwest and the Southern Plains.* University of New Mexico Press, Albuquerque, NM.

Spier, L. 1917. "An Outline for a Chronology of Zuni Ruins," *Anthropological Papers of the American Museum of Natural History* 18,3.

Sproull-Thomson, J. 1979. "Recent Studies in Thule art: metaphysical and practical aspect," in A.R. McCartney (ed.). *Thule Eskimo prehistory: an anthropological perspective.* National Museum of Man, Ottawa, Mercury Series 88, pp.85–494.

Squier, E.G. and Davis, E.U. 1848. *Ancient Monuments of the Mississippi Valley.* Smithsonian Institution, Washington DC.

Stafford, C.R. 1994. "Structural Changes in Archaic Landscape Use in the Dissected Woodlands of Southwestern Indiana," *American Antiquity* 59(2):219–237.

Stanford, D. 1976. "The Walakpa Site, Alaska," *Smithsonian Contributions to Anthropology* 20.

———1978. "The Jones-Miller Site: An Example of Hell Gap Bison Procurement Strategy," in L. Davis and M. Wilson (eds.). *Bison Procurement and Utilization: A Symposium, Plains Anthropologist Memoir* 16:90–97

———and Day, J. (eds.). 1992. *Ice Age Hunters Of the Rockies.* University Press of Colorado, Niwot, CO.

Stark, B.L. 1986. "Origins of Food Production in the New World," in David Meltzer and others (eds.). *American Archaeology Past and Future.* Smithsonian Institute Press, Washington DC, pp.277–322.

Starna, W.A. and Funk, R.E. 1994. "The Place of the In Situ Hypothesis in Iroquoian Archaeology," *Northeast Anthropology* 47:45–54.

Steffy, J.R. 1988. "The Thirteen Colonies: English Settlers and Seafarers," in George Bass (ed.). *Ships and Shipwrecks of the Americas.* Thames and Hudson, London and New York, pp.107–128.

Steinacher, Terry L. and Carlson, Gayle F. 1998. "The Central Plains Tradition," in W. Raymond Wood (ed.). *Archaeology on the Great Plains.* University of Kansas, Lawrence, KS, pp.235–268.

Stenton, D.R. 1991. "Caribou Population Dynamics and Thule Culture," *Arctic Anthropology* 28(2):13–32.

Steponaitis, V. 1978. "Location theory and complex chiefdoms: a Mississippian example," in B.D. Smith (ed.). *Mississippian Settlement Patterns.* Academic Press, New York, pp.417–453.

———1983. *Ceramics, Chronology, and Community Patterns: An archaeological study at Moundville.* Academic Press, New York.

———1984. "Technological Studies of prehistoric pottery from Alabama: Physical properties and vessel function," in S.E. van der Leuw and A.C. Pritchard (eds.). *The Many Dimensions of Pottery.* Ven Giffen Institute, University of Amsterdam, pp.79–122.

———1986. "Prehistoric Archaeology in the Southeastern United States 1970–1985," *Annual Review of Anthropology* 15:363–404.

Steward, J. 1938. "Basin-Plateau Aboriginal Sociopolitical Groups," *Bureau of American Ethnology Bulletin* 120.

———1955. *A Theory of Culture Change.* University of Illinois Press, Urbana.

Stoltman, J. 1978. "Temporal Models in Prehistory: An Example from Eastern North America," *Current Anthropology* 19(4):703–746.

Stone, A.C., and Stoneking, M. 1998. "MtDNA Analysis of a Prehistoric Oneota Population: Implications for the Peopling of the New World." *American Journal of Human Genetics* 62:1153–1170.

Storck, PL. 1984. "Research into the Paleo-Indian occupations of Ontario: A Review," *Ontario Archaeology* 41:3–18.

———1997. *The Fisher Site: Archaeological, Geological, and Paleontological Studies at an Early Paleo-Indian Site in Southern Ontario.* Museum of Anthropology, University of Michigan, Ann Arbor.

Story, D. 1985. "Adaptive Strategies of Archaic Cultures of the Gulf Coastal Plain," in R.I. Ford (ed.). *Early Food Production in North America.* Museum of Anthropology, University of Michigan, Ann Arbor, pp.19–56.

Stothers, D.M. 1977. *The Princess Point Complex.* Archaeological Survey of Canada, Mercury Series 58, Ottawa.

Strong, W.D. 1935. "An Introduction to Nebraska Archaeology," *Smithsonian Miscellaneous Collections* 93,10.

———1940. "From History to Prehistory in the Northern Great Plains," *Smithsonian Miscellaneous Collections* 100:353–394.

Struever, S. and Holton, E. 1979. *Koster: Americans in Search of the Prehistoric Past.* Anchor Press, NY.

———and Houart, G. 1972. "An analysis of the Hopewell Interaction Sphere," in E. Wilmsen (ed.). *Social Exchange and Interaction.* University Museum of Anthropology, University of Michigan, Ann Arbor, pp.47–80.

Styles, B.W. 1981. *Faunal Exploitation and Resource Selection: Early Late Woodland Subsistence in the Lower Illinois Valley.* Northwestern University Archaeological Program Scientific Paper 3.

———and others. 1983. "Modoc Rock Shelter Revisited," in J.L. Phillips and J.A. Brown (eds.). *Archaic Hunter-Gatherers in the American Midwest.* Academic Press, New York, pp.261–297.

Suarez, B.K. and others. 1985. "Genetic Variation in North American Populations: The Geography of Gene Frequencies," *American Journal of Physical Anthropology* 67:217–232.

Swann, Brian K. (ed.). 1994. *Coming to Light.* W.W. Norton, New York.

Swanton, J.R. 1911. "Indian Tribes of the Lower Mississippi and adjacent coast of the Gulf of Mexico," *Bureau of American Ethnology Bulletin* 43.

———1931. "Source material for the social and ceremonial life of the Choctaw Indians," *Bureau of American Ethnology* 103.

Swidler, Nina, and others. 1997. *Native Americans and Archaeologists: Stepping Stones to Common Ground.* Altamira Press, Walnut Creek, CA.

Talalay, L. and others. 1984. "Hickory nuts, walnuts butternuts, and hazelnuts: Observations and experiments relevant to their aboriginal exploitation in Eastern North America," in P.J. Munson (ed.). *Experiments and Observations on Aboriginal Wild Plant Food Utilization in Eastern North America.* Indiana Historical Society Prehistoric Research Series 6(2):338–359.

Tankersley, K.B. 1994. "Was Clovis a Colonizing Population in Eastern North America?" in W.S. Dancey (ed.). *The First Discovery of America.* Ohio Archaeological Council, Columbus,

pp.95–116.

———1998. "Variation in the Early PaleoIndian Economies of Late Pleistocene Eastern North America." *American Antiquity* 63(1):7–20.

———and Isaac, B.L. (eds.). 1990. *Early Paleo-Indian Economies of Eastern North America.* JAI Press, Greenwich, CT.

Taylor, A.J. and Highley, C.L. 1995. *Archaeological Investigations at the Loma Sandia Site (41LK28), a Prehistoric Cemetery and Campsite in Live Oak County, Texas.* 2 vols. Texas Archaeological Research Laboratory, Studies in Anthropology 20. University of Texas, Austin.

Taylor, W.E. 1956. "A description of Sadlermiut houses excavated at Nature Point, Southampton Island, NWT. *National Museum of Canada Bulletin* 62:53–99.

———and Swinton, G. 1967 "Prehistoric Dorset Art," *The Beaver* 298:32–47.

Taylor, W.W. 1948. *A Study of Archaeology.* American Anthropological Association, Menasha, WI.

Thomas, David H. 1970. "Artiodactyls and man in the prehistoric Great Basin," *Center for Archaeological Research, Davis, Publication* 2:199–208.

———1981. "How to classify the projectile points from Monitor Valley, Nevada," *Journal of California and Great Basin Archaeology* 3(1):7–43.

———1982. "The 1981 Alta Toquima Village project: A Preliminary Report," *Desert Research Institute Social Sciences Technical Report Series* 27.

———1983. *The Archaeology of Monitor Valley 1. Epistemology, 2. Gatecliff Shelter.* Anthropological Papers of the American Museum of Natural History 58, Pt. 1 and 59, Pt. 1.

———1985. *The Archaeology of Hidden Cave, Nevada.* Anthropological Papers of the American Museum of Natural History 61, Pt. 1.

———1988. *Mission Santa Catalina de Guale.* Anthropological Papers of the American Museum of Natural History 63.

———1989. *Columbian Consequences. Vol. 1 The Spanish Borderlands.* Smithsonian Institution Press, Washington DC.

———and Bettinger, R.L. 1976. "Prehistoric piñon ecotone settlements of the Upper Reese River Valley, central Nevada," *American Museum of Natural History Anthropological Papers* 53(3):263–366.

Thurmond, J.P. 1990. "Late Paleo-Indian Utilization of the Dempsey Divide on the Southern Plains," *Plains Anthropological Memoir* 25, pp.35–131.

Todd, L.C., Hofman, J.L., and Schultz, C.B. 1992. "Faunal Analysis and Paleo-Indian Studies: A Re-examination of the Lipscomb Bison Bonebed," *Plains Anthropologist* 37(140):137–165.

Toll, H.W. 1991. "Material Distributions and Exchange in the Chaco System," in Patricia Crown and W. James Judge (eds.). *Chaco and Hohokam: Prehistoric Regional Systems in the American Southwest.* School of American Research Press, Santa Fe, NM, pp.77–108.

Toll, H. and others. 1980. "Late ceramic patterns in Chaco Canyon: the programmatics of modeling ceramic exchange," in R.E Fry (ed.). *Models and Methods in Regional Exchange.* Society for American Archaeology, Washington DC, pp. 95–118.

Tooker, Elizabeth. 1964. *An Ethnography of the Huron Indians, 1615–1649.* Bureau of American Ethnology, Bulletin 190, Washington.

Toom, Dennis L. 1992. "Early Village Formation in the Middle Missouri Subarea of the Plains," *Research in Economic Anthropology Supplement*

6: 131–191.

Toth, E.A. 1974. *Archaeology and Ceramics at the Marksville Site*. Museum of Anthropology Archaeological Papers 56, University of Michigan, Ann Arbor.

Trigger, Bruce G. 1969. *The Huron: Farmers of the North*. Holt, Rinehart, and Winston, New York.
——1976. *The Children of Aataentsic: A History of the Huron People to 1160*. 2 vols. McGill Queens University Press, Montreal.
——1985. *Natives and Newcomers*. McGill Queens University Press, Montreal.
——1989. *A History of Archaeological Interpretation*. Cambridge University Press, Cambridge.

Tuck, James A. 1970 "An Archaic Indian Cemetery in Newfoundland," *Scientific American* 222(6):112–121.
——1971. *Onondaga Iroquois Prehistory: A Study in Settlement Archaeology*. Syracuse University Press, Syracuse, NY.
——1974. "Early Archaic Horizons in eastern North America," *Archaeology of Eastern North America* 2(1):72–80.
——1975. "Prehistory of Saglek Bay Labrador: Archaic and Paleo-Indian occupations," *Archaeological Survey of Canada Publications* 34.
——1976. *Newfoundland and Labrador Prehistory*. National Museums of Canada, Ottawa.
——1977. "A Look at Laurentian," *Researches and Transactions of the New York State Archaeological Association* 17(1):31–40.
——1984. *Maritime Provinces Prehistory*. Archaeological Survey of Canada, Ottawa.

Turnbaugh, W.A. 1975a. *Man, Land, and Time: The Cultural Prehistory and Demographic Patterns of North-Central Pennsylvania*. Lycoming County Historical Society, Williamsport, PA.
——1975b. "Toward an Explanation of the Broadpoint Dispersal in Eastern North American Prehistory," *Journal of Anthropological Research* 31(1):51–68.

Turnbull, Christopher. 1976. "The Augustine Site: A Mound from the Maritimes," *Archaeology of Eastern North America* 4:50–62.

Turner, Christy. 1984. "Advances in the Dental Search for Native American Origins," *Acta Anthropogenetica* 8(1,2):23–78.
——1986. "The First Americans: The Dental Evidence," *National Geographic Research* 2:37–46.
——and Jacqueline A. Turner. 1999. *Man Corn*. University of Utah Press, Salt Lake City.

Turner, E.S., and Hester, T.R. 1993. *Stone Artifacts of Texas*. 2nd ed. Gulf Publishing, Houston, TX (formerly Texas Monthly Press, Austin).

Upham, Steadman. 1982. *Politics and Power: an economic and political history of the Western Pueblo*. Academic Press, New York.
——(ed.). 1991. *The Evolution of Political Systems: Sociopolitics in Small-scale Sedentary Societies*. School of American Research Press, Santa Fe.
——1994. "Nomads of the Desert West: A Shifting Continuum in Prehistory," *Journal of World Prehistory* 8(2):113–168.
——, Lightfoot, K.G., and Jewett, R.A. (eds.). 1989. *The Sociopolitical Structure of Prehistoric Southwestern Societies*. Westview Press Boulder, CO.
——and others. 1987. "Evidence concerning the origin of Maize de Ocho," *American Anthropologist* 89(3):410–419.

Van Devender, T.R. and Spaulding, W.R. 1979. "Development of vegetation and climate in the Southwestern United States," *Science*

204:701–710.

Van West, Carla. 1996. "Agricultural Potential and Carrying Capacity in Southwestern Colorado, AD 901 to 1300," in Michael A. Adler (ed.). *The Prehistoric Pueblo World, AD 1150–1350*. University of Arizona Press, Tucson, pp. 214–227.

Vega, Garcilaso de la. 1951. *The Florida of the Inca*. University of Texas Press, Austin.

Vehik, Susan. 1983. "Middle Woodland Mortuary Practices along the Northeastern Periphery of the Great Plains: A consideration of Hopewellian Interactions," *Midcontinental Journal of Archaeology* 8:211–256.
——1984. "The Woodland Occupations," in Robert E. Bell (ed.). *Prehistory of Oklahoma*. Academic Press, Orlando, FL, pp.175–198.
——1986. "Oñate's Expedition to the Southern Plains," *Plains Anthropologist* 31(111):13–33.

Veltre, Douglas W. 1998. "Prehistoric Maritime Adaptations in the Western and Central Aleutian Islands," *Arctic Anthropology* 35(1):223–233.

Vivian, Gordon. 1979. "The Hubbard site and other tri-wall structures in New Mexico and Colorado," *National Park Service Archaeological Research Series* 5, Washington DC.
——and Mathews, T.W. 1965. "Kin Kletso, A Pueblo III Community in Chaco Canyon, New Mexico," *Southwestern Monuments Association, Technical Series* 6, Globe, AZ.

Vivian, Gwinn R. 1974. "Conservation and Diversion: water-control systems in the Anasazi Southwest," in Theodore Downing and McGwire Gibson (eds.). *Irrigation's Impact on Society*. University of Arizona Anthropological Papers 25, pp.95–112.
——1988. "Kluckhohn Reappraised: the Chacoan System as an Egalitarian Enterprise," *Journal of Anthropological Research* 45(1):101–113.
——1990. *The Chacoan Prehistory of the San Juan Basin*. Academic Press, Orlando, Florida.
——1997. "Chacoan Roads: Morphology" and "Chaco Roads: Function," *The Kiva* 63(1): 7–34; 35–67.

Wahlgren, Erik. 1986. *The Vikings and America*. Thames and Hudson, London and New York.

Walker, P.L. 1986. "Porotic Hyperostosis in a Marine-Dependent California Indian Population," *American Journal of Physical Anthropology* 69(3):345–354.

Wallace, W.J. 1978. "Post Pleistocene Archaeology," in R.F. Heizer (ed.). *Handbook of North American Indians. Vol. 8: California*. Smithsonian Institution, Washington DC, pp.462–470.

Walthall, John A. 1998. "Rockshelters and Hunter-Gatherer Adaptation to the Pleistocene/Holocene Transition," *American Antiquity* 63(2):223–238.

Warren, C.N. 1967. "The San Dieguito Complex: A review and hypothesis," *American Antiquity* 32(2):168–185.
——and True, D.L. 1961. "The San Dieguito Complex and its place in California prehistory," *UCLA Archaeological Survey Annual Report 1960–1961*:246–338.

Warrick, Gary. 1984. *Reconstructing Ontario Iroquoian Village Organization*. Archaeological Survey of Canada, Mercury Series 124, pp.1–180.

Watson, P.J. 1985. "The Impact of Early Horticulture on the Upland Drainage of the Midwest and Midsouth," in R.I. Ford (ed.). *Early Food Production in North America*. University Museum of Anthropology, University of Michigan, Ann Arbor, pp.73–98.

Wauchope, R. 1972. *Lost Tribes and Sunken Continents*. University of Chicago Press, Chicago.

Webb, W.S. 1974. *Indian Knoll*. 2nd ed. University

of Tennessee Press, Knoxville.
——and Baby, R.S. 1957. *The Adena People no.2*. Ohio Historical Society, Columbus.
——and Snow, C.E. 1945. *The Adena People*. University of Tennessee Press, Knoxville, TN.

Wedel, Waldo. 1938. "The Direct-Historical Approach in Pawnee Archaeology," *Smithsonian Miscellaneous Collections* 97,7.
——1953. "Some aspects of human ecology in the central Plains," *American Anthropologist* 55(4):499–514.
——1959. *An Introduction to Kansas Archaeology*. Bureau of American Ethnology Bulletin 174.
——1961. *Prehistoric Man on the Great Plains*. University of Oklahoma Press, Norman.
——1983. "The Prehistoric Plains," in J.D. Jennings (ed.). *Ancient North Americans*. W.H. Freeman, San Francisco, pp.202–241.
——1986. *Central Plains Prehistory*. University of Nebraska Press, Lincoln, NE.

Welch, P.D. 1961. *Prehistoric Man on the Great Plains*. University of Oklahoma Press, Norman.
——1991. *Moundville's Economy*. University of Alabama Press, Tuscaloosa, AL.
——and others. 1968. "Mummy Cave: Prehistoric record for the Rocky Mountains of Wyoming," *Science* 160:184–186.

Wendorf, and Hester, J. (eds.). 1975. *Late Pleistocene environments on the Southern High Plains*. Fort Burgwin Research Center Publication 9.
——and Kreiger, A.D. 1959. "New Light on the Midland Discovery," *American Antiquity* 25:6678.

West, F.H. 1981. *The Archaeology of Beringia*. Columbia University Press, New York.
——(ed.). 1996. *American Beginnings*. University of Chicago Press, Chicago.

Wettlaufer, B.N. 1955. "The Mortlach Site in the Besant Valley of Central Saskatchewan," *Anthropological Series No 1, Department of Natural Resources, Regina*.

Whalen, M.E. 1994. "Moving out of the Archaic on the edge of the Southwest," *American Antiquity* 59:622–638.
——and Minnis, Paul. 1996. "Ball Courts and Political Centralization in the Casa Grandes Region," *American Antiquity* 61(4):732–746.

Whalen, N.M. 1975. "Cochise site distribution in the San Pedro River Valley," *The Kiva* 40(3):203–211.

Wheat, J.B. 1972. *The Olsen-Chubbock Site: A Paleo-Indian Bison Kill*. Society for American Archaeology, Washington DC.

White, Tim. 1992. *Prehistoric Cannibalism at Mancos 5MTUMR-2346*. Princeton University Press, Princeton.

Whitley, David S. (ed.). 1998. *Reader in Archaeological Theory: Post-Processual and Cognitive Approaches*. Routledge, London and New York.

Whittlesey, Stephanie M. and others. 1997. *Vanishing River: Landscapes and Lives of the Lower Verde Valley*. SRI Press, Tucson.

Wilcox, David R. 1985. "The Teipiman Connection: A model of Mesoamerican-Southwestern Interaction," in Randall H. McGuire and Francis Joan Mathier (eds.). *Ripples in the Chichimec Sea*. Southern Illinois University Press, Carbondale, IL, pp.86–94.
——1991. "Hohokam Social Complexity," in Patricia Crown and W. James Judge (eds.). *Chaco and Hohokam: Prehistoric Regional Systems in the Southwest*. University of Washington Press, Seattle, WA, pp.253–276.
——and Haas, J. 1994. "The scream of the butterfly: Competition and conflict in the prehistoric Southwest," in George Gumerman. (ed.). *Themes in Southwestern Prehistory*. School

of American Research Press, Santa Fe, NM, pp.211–238.
——, McGuire, T.R., and Sternberg, C. 1981. "Snaketown Revisited," *Arizona State Museum Archaeological Series* 155. University of Arizona, Tucson, AR.
——and Shenk, L.O. 1977. *The Architecture of the Casa Grande and its Interpretation.* Arizona State Museum Archaeological Series 115. University of Arizona, Tucson, AR.
——and Sternberg, C. 1983. *Hohokam Ballcourts and Their Interpretation.* Arizona State Museum Archaeological Series 160. University of Arizona, Tucson, AR.
Willey, G.R. 1953. "Prehistoric Settlement Patterns in the Virú Valley, Peru," *Bureau of American Ethnology Bulletin* 155.
——1966. *Introduction to American Archaeology.* Vol. 1: North America. Prentice Hall, Englewood Cliffs, NJ.
——and Phillips, R. 1958. *Method and Theory in American Archaeology.* University of Chicago Press, Chicago.
——and Sabloff, J.A. 1993. *A History of American Archaeology.* 3rd ed. W.H. Freeman, San Francisco.
Williams, S.C. (ed.). 1930. *Adair's History of the American Indians.* Watauga Press, Johnson City, TN.
Williams, S. and Brain, J.R. 1983. "Excavations at the Lake George Site, Yazoo City, Mississippi, 1958–1960," *Papers of the Peabody Museum of Archaeology and Ethnology* 68.
Williamson, R.A. 1981. 'North America: A Multiplicity of Astronomies," in Ray A. Williamson (ed.). *Archaeoastronomy in the Americas.* Ballena Press, Los Altos, California, pp.61–80.
Williamson, R.F. 1984. *Living the Sky.* University of New Mexico Press, Albuquerque, NM.
——1990. "The Early Iroquoian Period of Southern Ontario." In C.J. Ellis and N. Ferris (eds.). *The Archaeology of Southern Ontario to AD 1650.* Ontario Archaeological Society 5, Toronto, pp.291–320.
Wills, W.H. 1989. *Early Prehistoric Agriculture in the American Southwest.* School of American Research, Santa Fe, NM.
——and Windes, Thomas C. 1989. "Evidence for Aggregation and Dispersal During the Basketmaker III Period in Chaco Canyon, New Mexico," *American Antiquity* 54:347–69.
Wilmsen, E. and Roberts, E.H.H. 1978. "Lindenmeier 1934–1974. Concluding Report on Investigations," *Smithsonian Contributions in Anthropology* 24.
Wilshusen, R., and Blinman, E. 1992. "Pueblo I village formation: A Reevaluation of sites recorded by Earl Morris on Ute Mountain tribal lands," *The Kiva* 58(3):251–269.

Windes, Thomas C. and Ford, Dabney. 1996. "The Chaco Wood Project: The Chronometric Reappraisal of Pueblo Bonito," *American Antiquity* 61:295–310.
Winham, R. Peter and Calabrese, F.A. 1998. "The Middle Missouri Tradition," in W. Raymond Wood (ed.). *Archaeology on the Great Plains.* University of Kansas, Lawrence, KS, pp.269–307.
Winters, H. 1968. *The Riverton Culture: a 2nd Millennium occupation in the Central Wabash Valley.* Illinois State Museum, Springfield, IL.
——1974. "Introduction," in W. Webb, *Indian Knoll.* University of Tennessee Press, Knoxville, TN, pp.v–xxvii.
Witthoft, J. 1952. "A Paleo-Indian site in eastern Pennsylvania: An early hunting culture," *Proceedings of the American Philosophical Society* 96:464–495.
——1959. "The Ancestry of the Susquehannocks," in John Witthoft and W.E. Kinsey, III (eds.). *Susquehannock Miscellany.* Pennsylvania Historical and Museum Commission, Harrisburg, PA, pp.19–60.
Wobst, H.M. 1974. "Boundary Conditions for Paleolithic Social Systems: A Simulation Approach," *American Antiquity* 39:147–77.
Wood, W.R. 1967. *An Interpretation of Mandan Culture History.* Bureau of American Ethnology, Bulletin 198, River Basin Surveys Paper 39.
——(ed.). 1977. *Trends in Middle Missouri Prehistory: A Festschrift Honoring the Contributions of Donald J. Lehmer.* Plains Anthropologist Memoir 13, Lincoln, NE.
——1980. *G. Hubert Smith: The Explorations of the La Verendryes in the Northern Plains, 1738–43.* University of Nebraska Press, Lincoln, NE.
——(ed.). 1998. *Archaeology on the Great Plains.* University of Kansas Press, Lawrence, KS.
Workman, William B. 1998. "Archaeology of the Southern Kenai Peninsula," *Arctic Anthropology* 35(1):146–159.
Wray, Charles E. and Schoff, Harry L. 1953. "A Preliminary Report on the Seneca Sequence in Western New York," *Pennsylvania Archaeologist* 22:53–63.
Wright, H.E. (ed.). 1983. *Late-Quaternary Environments of the United States. Vol. 2: the Holocene.* University of Minnesota Press, Minneapolis.
Wright, J. 1966. *The Ontario Iroquois Tradition.* National Museum of Canada, Bulletin 210.
——1967. *The Laurel Tradition and the Middle Woodland Period.* National Museum of Canada, Bulletin 177.
——1972. *The Shield Archaic.* National Museum of Man, Ottawa.
——1981. *The Only Land They Knew.* Free Press, New York.

——1984. "The Cultural Continuity of the Northern Iroquoian-Speaking Peoples," in M.K. Foster and others (eds.). *Extending the Rafters: Interdisciplinary Approaches to Iroquoian Studies.* State University of New York Press, Albany, pp.283–299.
——1987. "Iroquoian Agricultural Settlement," in R.C. Harris (ed.). *Historical Atlas of Canada to AD 1650.* University of Toronto Press, Toronto, plate 12.
Wyckoff, D.G. 1984. "The Foragers: Eastern Oklahoma," in R.E. Bell (ed.). *Prehistory of Oklahoma.* Academic Press, Orlando, FL, pp.119–160.
Wylie, A. 1985. "The Reaction Against Analogy," *Advances in Archaeological Method and Theory* 8:63–111.
Wymer, Dee Anne. 1996. "The Ohio Hopewell Econiche: Human-Land Interaction in the Core Area," in Paul J. Pacheco (ed.). *A View from the Core.* Ohio Archaeological Council, Columbus, OH, pp.36–53.

Yamura, K. 1979. "On the origin of Thule culture as seen from the typological studies of toggle harpoon heads," in A.R. McCartney (ed.). *Thule Eskimo prehistory: an anthropological retrospective.* Archaeological Survey of Canada, Ottawa, Mercury Series 88, pp.474–484.
Yarnell, R.A. 1978. "Domestication of sunflower and sumpweed in eastern North America," in R.I. Ford (ed.). *Early Food Production in North America,* University Museum of Anthropology, University of Michigan, Ann Arbor, MI, pp.285–299.
Yentsch, Ann. 1994. *A Chesapeake Family and their slaves.* Cambridge University Press, Cambridge.
Yesner, David. 1987. "Life in the 'Garden of Eden': the causes and consequences of the adoption of marine diets by human societies," in M. Harris and E. Ross (eds.). *Food and Evolution.* Temple University Press, Philadelphia, pp.285–310.
——1998. "Origins and Development of Maritime Adaptations in the Northwest Pacific Region of North America: A Zooarchaeological Perspective." *Arctic Anthropology* 35(1):204–222.
Young, S.B. 1982. "The vegetation of Land-Bridge Beringia," in David Hopkins and others (eds.). *Paleoecology of Beringia.* Academic Press, New York, pp.179–194.

Zeder, Marilyn A. 1997. *The American Archaeologist: A Profile.* Altamira Press, Walnut Creek, CA.
Zimmerman, Larry. 1985. *Peoples of Prehistoric South Dakota.* University of Nebraska Press, Lincoln, NE.

Illustration Credits

Index and Glossary